RECONCEPTUALIZING LITERACY IN THE MEDIA AGE

ADVANCES IN READING/LANGUAGE RESEARCH
Peter B. Mosenthal
Research and Language Arts Center, Syracuse University
Series Editor
(formerly edited by Barbara A. Hutson,
Division of Curriculum and Instruction,
Virginia Polytechnic Institute and State)

RECONCEPTUALIZING LITERACY
IN THE MEDIA AGE

Edited by   ANN WATTS PAILLIOTET
Department of Education
Whitman College

PETER B. MOSENTHAL
Department of Reading and Language Arts
Syracuse University

 JAI PRESS INC.
Stamford, Connecticut

CONTENTS

**SECTION IV. RECONCEPTUALIZING FUTURE LITERACY
THEORIES AND DIRECTIONS**

PREFACE

Barry Duncan

Reconceptualizing Literacy in the Media Age is an ambitious collection of articles which describes and assesses new understandings about media, communication technology, and literacy. Central to this collection is the recognition of the necessity of adopting an expanded definition of both literacy and culture, the better to understand the new and evolving paradigms which enable us to conceptualize multiple literacies, including print, visual, media, computer, digital, and informational.

In spite of the abundance of books on coping with the age of information, there are very few which attempt to bring together the many dimensions of today's multiple literacies. Typically, academics and other cultural commentators suffer from cultural myopia because of the limitations of academic specialization and their own special-interest groups. It seems that there are few cyber gurus providing us with the larger picture, the meaningful context, and the interdisciplinary breakthrough. By the end of *Reconceptualizing Literacy in the Media Age*, the reader should be able to ponder some of the key insights about multiple literacies, raise important questions, and suggest new agendas for discussing new and converging technologies and multiliteracies.

There are many threads which run through this collection. Here are some of the main ones:

- The critical role of the new media in their relationship to the changing roles of our social communities.

- The critical relevance of media literacy, visual literacy, and "deep viewing" for deconstructing the signs and symbols of our culture and reading today's media texts, both new and traditional.
- The extensive use of discourse analysis as one of the most profitable methods of unpacking the meanings of our communicative practices.
- The importance of positioning readers and viewers, not as empty vessels and passive dupes of hegemonic media but as active participants in negotiating meaning. The emphasis here is less on what media does to people and more on what people do with media.
- Because much of this book is ultimately directed to educators, several of the writers address critical classroom practice, including teaching through and about the media. There are several examples in the collection of curriculum designed for high school and university classes which accommodate institutional constraints—for example, the expectations of state departments of education or the mission statements of university faculties.

With the advent of new communication technologies, there has been a constant struggle for reconceptualizing and a search for appropriate vocabulary. The notion of using the term "text" to encompass more than just examples from print is a good example. For anyone working in schools where teachers are trying to grasp new theories, the willingness to accept such an expanded definition is often a minor cultural victory. In their chapters, Roberta F. Hammett and Patricia Mulcahey-Ernt demonstrate how students may analyze and generate new media texts. The authors provide detailed descriptions and examples of how media literacy involves many texts and textual processes: artistic, electronic, print literature, visual representations, and even music. These essays make an eloquent case for defining a new literacy and encouraging the examination and generation of multiple texts.

Using the most common definition of media literacy in the United States and one that is used by media educator Renee Hobbs, "Media literacy is the ability to access, analyze, evaluate, and communicate messages in a variety of forms" (Hobbs, 1997, p. 1), T. A. Callister, Jr. provides us with a tough-minded critique by demonstrating its shortcomings in multimedia practices. Among other things, in "Media Literacy: On-ramp to the Literacy of the 21st Century or Cul-de-sac on the Information Superhighway?" he points out that media are more than just tools; they come with a great deal of cultural baggage. Callister draws attention to the processes used with online information and concludes that the idea of simple decoding is inadequate to describe the cognitive operations. Why? Well, today's multitasking kids like to fool around and explore multiple options. Thus, assessing only the final product can be misleading. He notes, "Having used new information technologies such as computers, Web browsers, and hypertextual databases, a new post-typographic notion of literacy [see Reinking, 1995] will also need to incorporate the skills to decode the process of getting to that information."

David Considine and Lyn Lacy are among the handful of visionary leaders in media education in the United States. Their scholarship and experience in teaching media education make their contributions especially valuable. Considine's "Media Literacy as Evolution and Revolution in the Culture, Climate, and Context of American Education" provides a useful survey of the state of the art: the failures, successes, and insights into the limitations of current models. Furthermore, he highlights his experience in developing exemplary media education models in his own home base of North Carolina. We should heed his most important admonishment: "It is ironic indeed, that those foisting technology on the nation's schools fail to perceive the most obvious fact that tools don't change schools; teachers do. To make those changes they need to be active partners in the transformation process."

Considine places the struggles of American media literacy against those of school reform, new curriculum expectations from educational authorities, and even the mental health movement. To give added credibility to his arguments, he offers numerous comparative references to media education developments in other countries such as Australia, Canada, and the United Kingdom. Considine concludes on a realistic note: "We have a long way to go before we can truly say that media literacy is both visible and viable. We will know that day has arrived when we talk simply about literacy, taking it as a given, that its meaning embraces what we now call media literacy."

American media educators who can see the big picture of their work know that there is regrettably very limited activity in elementary schools. In "Integrating Standards in K–5 Media Literacy," Lyn Lacy provides a narrative account of her implementation of the standards used in grades K–5 for Media Literacy in Minnesota. The standards attempt to measure both the knowledge of content and the demonstration of that knowledge through performance. In addition, there is a thematic unit plan which aims to achieve a balance among print, computer, and film/video instruction in the third grade. These assessment and planning tools will do much to forestall the criticism that doing media in schools is a trivial, unstructured subject, another time waster, and, above all, not subject to accountability.

Several other writers offer concrete examples of classroom practice of key media education concepts. Ladi Semali was concerned about the impact of media bias on his students and devised a curriculum that would do more than just deconstruct media texts; the class was asked to "read oppositional texts and employ the language of criticism. This allows students and teachers to move beyond 'commonsense' readings of daily life narratives." What was really empowering, however, was the culminating activity of "[creating] a newspaper, a Web site, a mural, or a dramatic presentation to convey their new understandings."

Perhaps the most controversial area for media educators is that of citizenship and civic responsibility. In the course proposed for a new general education program at Illinois State University, Arnold S. Wolfe states: "[A]s the forces that have formed the information society institutionalize, 'critical appreciation' of the role communication plays in democracy is what we need as much as, if not more than, ever. We need to have caring communities that are infused with democratic principles." Throughout Wolfe's well-conceived and provocative curriculum is the notion of a critical media literacy and the nurturing and reflective elements of an empowering critical pedagogy. In the last ten years, audience research, particularly that associated with reception theory, has been on the cutting edge of current understanding of how people make sense of the media. Loosely centered around ethnographic studies, this work is essential for anyone trying to navigate the murky waters of gender, race, multiculturalism, class, and age.

Ladi Semali's and Arnold Wolfe's use of the term "critical media literacy" exhorts teachers to examine the ideological import of all media texts including the role of the media industries. Too often American media educators have ignored these areas because they may be too controversial or too abstract. For English teachers who assume the media teacher role the most frequently, such topics may seem too remote from the familiar ground of literary forms, themes, and aesthetics. Semali and Wolfe offer concrete accounts and solutions.

The case is made by several contributors for "deep viewing" (Watts Pailliotet, 1998, 1999), a process of unpacking the wider meanings of media texts through a series of reflective stages. Lynn Craigue Briggs uses these techniques in the context of a writing center to further writing instruction and create a caring, people-centered community. In "Media Literacy and Sprituality: Tales from a University Writers' Center," Briggs uses a series of narratives to describe the transformative results of the technique for her staff and college community. She writes, "We began the process of deep viewing, a videotaped heuristic, as a way of listening to ourselves and each other more critically, but found it enabled us to listen more humanely." Ultimately, Briggs contends the process "contributed to our spiritual understanding of both writing and our work in the center."

Jackie K . Giles, Sherry L. Macaul, and Rita K. Rodenberg used deep viewing in a study entitled "Inquiry-Based Learning and the New Literacies: Media, Multimedia, and Hypermedia." After learning some basic media theory, their middle school students applied their insights to such areas as peer tutoring as well as critiquing material from NIE (Newspapers in Education).

Several of the contributors look at media and multiple literacies in the social context of the communities they serve. For example, Linn Bekins in "Theorizing the Internet for the Practice, Instruction, and Study of Disciplinary Writing" uses the concept of a "discourse community" to embrace disciplinary communities. Bekins conveys the variety of points of view that are part of literacy and computer networks that relate "clearly to the social contexts that affect and often define their use."

This notion of continual reflection in addressing the new literacies is apparent in "Preparing Teachers to Teach with Understanding" by Victoria Risko whose thesis is that it is essential when using multimedia to "engage prospective teachers in actions that are reflective rather than routine and a call for building reflective actions." The ability to answer the "why" questions is critical because there is a contested body of research from the techno-skeptics who assert that computers make little difference in improving learning or enhancing teaching.

In "Using Media Ethnographies to Study Response to Media as Activity," Richard Beach explores the way viewers make sense of popular television programs, surveys the role played by fan clubs such as those formed by Trekkies, critiques the fascinating zines created by marginalized communities, and makes the important case for creating alternative media. Discourse analysis has a key role here in illuminating how groups and individuals talk or write about their favorite media texts. The media ethnographies conducted by his class as their culminating activity should be inspirational to teachers who need to see a sound methodology and a variety of exemplary projects. Identity formation is central to their pursuit and the author concludes: "Through defining links between real-world and virtual-world activity, pupils may then reflect on their uses of tools/genres and their construction of identities across different worlds."

The text concludes with several innovative theories developed from varied disciplinary perspectives. Robert Maribe Branch, a professor of educational technology, lays out a new taxonomy for visual literacy and assessing elements in visual media. In "The Challenge of Multimedia Literacy," psychologist Richard E. Mayer analyzes techniques for learning to make sense of multimedia messages, outlines techniques for multimedia generation, and provides a future research agenda. Through numerous examples and diagrams, Peter B. Mosenthal lays out the types of knowledge needed for modern literacies.

There is a considerable degree of eclecticism in this collection: different disciplines and academic environments, different research methodologies, pedagogies, and technological paradigms. But in a domain with such mind-boggling diversity, in which change is the only constant, that is a strength—not a weakness.

REFERENCES

Hobbs, R. (1997). Literacy for the information age. In J. Flood, S. B. Heath, & D. Lapp (Eds.), *Handbook of research on teaching literacy through the communicative and visual arts* (pp. 7–14). New York: Simon & Schuster/Macmillan.

Reinking, D. (1995). Reading and writing with computers: Literacy research in a post-typographic world. In K. A. Hinchman, D. J. Leu, & C. K. Kinzer (Eds.), *Perspectives on literacy research and practice* (Vol. 44, pp. 17–33). Chicago: National Reading Conference.

Watts Pailliotet, A. (1998). Deep viewing: A critical look at texts. In S. Steinberg & J. Kincheloe (Eds.), *Unauthorized methods: Strategies for critical teaching* (pp. 124–136). London: Routledge.
Watts Pailliotet, A. (1999). Deep viewing: Intermediality in preservice teacher education. In L. Semali & A. Watts Pailliotet (Eds.), *Intermediality: The teachers' handbook of critical media literacy* (pp. 31–51). Boulder, CO: Westview.

FOREWORD:
EXPANDING LITERACY IN A SHRINKING WORLD

Kathleen Tyner

It is difficult to know if the growing use of digital media begs for a new concept of literacy, or simply a recombination of literacy practices from the past. *Reconceptualizing Literacy in the Media Age* explores this issue in all of its complexity and offers fresh insight into the uses of new media for teaching and learning.

One thing that the history of literacy reveals is that although new technologies may alter literacy practices, they do not automatically replace older forms of literacy. The printed word did not displace oral culture; video did not doom film to oblivion; radio still thrives in spite of television. Given this precedent, it is safe to say that digital publishing will not end the use of the printed word. Although communication technologies change, literacy practices and purposes remain surprisingly robust. Computers, books, cameras, and printing presses are a means to create records, but records are the end products—not the process of literacy.

As the McLuhanists note (McLuhan, 1951, 1964; McLuhan & Powers, 1989), each upstart medium launches its way into the public mind by selectively cannibalizing the conventions of the media that came before. These conventions go much further than "look and feel," e.g., the design and aesthetic of the screen. They also play out in social contexts in the real work through shared knowledge about genre, discourse, and applied information. In other words, the way that communication channels present information to audiences depends very much on audiences' prior knowledge about media and their readiness to accept the information. Thus, in order to attract readers, printed books from the 1400s were constructed to look very much like the more familiar illuminated manuscripts that came before. Even so, the technologies that made movable type possible were not automatically revolutionary. In fact, they were of little importance to existing social institutions of the time until significant numbers of the population developed a threshold of literacy sufficient to make use of print.

McLuhan also remarked that "the medium is the message" (McLuhan & Fiore, 1967). This begs the question of technical determinism, that is, how much form influences content. Again, media forms, or at least the codes and conventions of media discourses, show more evidence of convergence than divergence. New media mimic old to attract audiences with familiar forms and, in turn, audiences freshen the conventions of each new media as they use it. Nineteenth-century films draw from the aesthetic of photography. Depression radio sounds like vaudeville. Early television samples from theater and radio. Contemporary newspapers mimic television discourse and graphics. Web pages are reminiscent of billboards. Email uses many of the conventions of both Victorian letters and the telephone, and so on. Although "the medium is the message" is an interesting concept that deserves much closer scrutiny, it is far more satisfying to compare the conventions of specific records and their uses in specific contexts. Generalizations about the differences between technologies such as books or computers yield very little insight when isolated from their historical and cultural uses and contexts.

This does not curb the tendency to predict the effects of media and technology on society, predictions ranging from dire pessimism to buoyant optimism. In light of the hype surrounding digital technologies from both ends of the spectrum, the complex and ephemeral history of literacy is important to keep in mind. Although the superiority of print is often asserted, literacy scholars long ago debunked a hierarchy of literacy that elevates alphabetic literacy practices over those of oral forms as "false dichotomies." It would serve no purpose to further extend this divide to arbitrarily elevate the value of print over that of electronic media. A more useful question about the relative value of literacies might be "valuable for what purpose?" Besides, the conventions of alphabetic literacy have shown particular resiliency on the Internet. Book sales are robust at the turn of the 20th century and it could be argued that alphabetic literacy is in its prime.

Perhaps this is why new forms of media are forced to define themselves in reaction to alphabetic literacy. Thus, new definitions of literacy attempt to explain multimedia practices: computer literacy, visual literacy, media literacy, information literacy, and so on. These labels represent hybrids as electronic forms of literacy are superimposed over oral and alphabetic forms and can be called *multiliteracies*. Curiously, although electronic media are ubiquitous, a concept of literacy that goes beyond alphabetic texts to include analog and digital media has yet to gain casual acceptance. Predictions about literacy are risky, but it is surely only a matter of time before multiliteracy qualifiers—computer, visual, media, information—fade away as digital forms of media become widely used and accepted under the broad banner of literacy.

Until then, multiliteracies provide a way to explore the dimensions of electronic forms of literacy. Multiliteracies attempt to build on a broad understanding of the practices of alphabetic literacy and to expand the concept of literacy to include a random combination of digital practices used with video, audio, interactivity, still images, and so on. Although these practices are still crude and experimental, new media does seem to present the possibility that literates are interacting with texts in new and unexpected ways.

The most visible change brought about by digital media is the sheer volume of information available to the public, and availability is arguably what digital media currently does best. Certainly the amount and diversity of information is unprecedented in history. Digital archives change the way that information is researched, cited and processed. The boundaries between private and public discourse, categories and genre collapse in the haste to make texts available to the public.

The voluminous character of new media is not so much an explosion as an accelerated implosion of all the traditional print and electronic practices that came before. Not only are the codes and conventions of content merging, represented by specialized discourses for information, advertising, entertainment genre, the actual media forms of text, sound, and image are combining at the same time. This amalgamation of form, content, and context creates new practices and new possibilities for literacy. It also generates confusion about the relationship of literacy to social, economic, and political institutions such as schooling.

Another difference seems to be one of acceleration. Creators and audiences are asked to work harder and faster as they use complex new technologies to make sense of their worlds. The immediacy and nonlinear nature of linked narratives favors the readers who appreciate risk, challenge, and change. These readers seem to negotiate compressed information and multiple, nonlinear narratives with relative ease. Whether this is a case of style over substance remains to be seen. Certainly, all readers do not appreciate the interactive capability of digital media. There is still something pleasing—even nostalgic—about browsing bookshelves, handling, smelling, and perusing a book. An abiding love of books, or at least a love of the idea of books, seems to still define the concept of literacy and perhaps in the whole scheme of things, theoretical foundations for alphabetic literacy are still appropriate.

Changes in both volume and speed produce a certain degree of anxiety for readers, especially those who conceive of literacy as a fixed and obtainable commodity. Because of the power of literacy, such anxiety is not altogether unwarranted. History demonstrates that this power has been used for both controlling and liberating purposes and every individual hopes to be on the receiving end of literacy. Literacy scholar Karl Kaestle comments:

> The uses of literacy are various. As a technology, it gives its possessors potential power; as a stock of cultural knowledge within a given tradition, literacy can constrain or liberate, instruct or entertain, discipline or disaffect people. (Kaestle, 1991, p. 27)

As literacy practices shift from oral to alphabetic to electronic, communication technologies became a site of struggle between those who want to maintain the social status quo and those who are change agents for more marginalized populations. Literacy undoubtedly boosts the life chances of each individual by offering them access to a wider range of discourse and social involvement. At its most liberating, literacy can be used to amplify voices of resistance in response to oppression and inequity. But literacy has a darker side when it is used for purposes of domination and subjugation. In the past, conquering armies tried to control printing presses, literature, information, and languages. Now they seek out broadcast facilities and computer networks. But literacy is tethered tightly to the very ideas that resist control: the free flow of information, freedom of expression, investigation, and criticism. The study of its strategic uses over time, under specific conditions, provides insight into the future uses of literacy in contexts of new and emerging media.

The history of literacy is rife with evidence that social control can be accomplished through the use of gatekeepers who control the amount and kind of information that is allowed to flow to the populace. Socrates commented in the *Phaedrus*: "And once a thing is put in writing, the composition, whatever it may be drifts all over the place, getting into the hands not only of those who understand it, but equally of those who have no business with it; it doesn't know how to address the right people, and not address the wrong" (Hamilton & Cairns, 1989, p. 521, 275e).

For example, until Martin Luther encouraged individuals to read the Bible for themselves, priests were used to interpret the Bible for parishioners in a way that was favorable to the social dominance of the medieval church. The convention of gatekeeping continues throughout this history of literacy in the form of newspaper reporters, editors, television newscasters, and radio broadcasters. Anyone who doubts the ability to control both the processes and products of literacy can read a history of the life and times of William Randolph Hearst, Walter Winchell, Bill Gates, or Rupert Murdoch.

In addition to the acceleration and volume of available information, the Internet demonstrates a real shift in the practice of information gatekeeping. Not only are traditional gatekeepers bypassed, but increasingly smaller and smaller units of discourse have an opportunity to be broadcast to increasingly larger publics in a process that can be called *disintermediation* (Abate, 1998, p D1). The trend toward disintermediation favors communication by each individual and seems to signal a genuine departure from the literacy practices of the past. In addition to the vast quantity of information available to users, the ability of readers to customize their information and of authors to strategically target audiences is increasing. It also places a greater burden on the reader to access, selectively filter, and analyze information. Disintermediation raises questions about the nature of literacy in regard to authorship, ownership, genre, the authenticity of information, the difference between private and public discourse, and so on. The end result of such a practice resembles a very elegant form of personal expression between producers and consumers of media.

The question of whether or not the quality of information is degraded when disseminated without the benefit of gatekeepers remains to be answered. History demonstrates that although the free flow of information facilitates literacy practices, access alone will not guarantee the benefits of literacy. The mastery of the discourses of each new medium is just as important to literacy as access to information and technologies. Especially when the world is awash in information, the average literate person must be selective, discerning, analytical, and creative in order to accrue the maximum benefit from literacy. The reliability, amusement, or usefulness of media depends on the degree of literacy that is brought to bear in its use.

In the meantime, the debate in educational circles about how to introduce new forms of media into schooling continues to be preoccupied with questions of access. Thus, although access to technology and information is essential, access alone does not guarantee the benefits of literacy.

> Literacy is discriminatory with regard to both access and content. Problems of discrimination are not resolved just because access is achieved: there is a cultural price tag to literacy. Thus, whether literacy is liberating or constraining depends in part on whether it is used as an instrument of conformity or of creativity. (Kaestle, 1991, p. 30)

Current trends toward Internet portals and the consolidation of media ownership demonstrate that the tendency to control information and literacy is always at work. Debates about the direction of these trends in a digital environment attest to the vital nature of literacy, its capacity for change, and its importance to individuals. The authors in this volume take the discussion of literacy and its relationship to schooling to the next threshold, beyond access to content and context.

Educational researcher Karen Sheingold (1992) asks: "How do we help teachers to teach in ways they were not taught, to create classrooms unlike the ones they studied in, and to develop confidence that they are doing the right thing for their students?"

Reconceptualizing Literacy in the Media Age addresses this question as it explores the nature of literacy in action. It looks at the way that accelerated, changing forms of media can be best utilized for learning. As others far removed from the classroom attempt to set policies for the uses of technology for teaching and learning, the articles in this volume resonate from personal and practical experiences in the classroom. They are a fine example of the power of teachers as researchers and have broad implication for a wide range of scholarship and policy related to new literacy tools and new ecologies for teaching and learning.

REFERENCES

Abate, T. (1998, September 12). Internet cuts out the middleman. *San Francisco Chronicle*, p. D1.
Hamilton, E., & Cairns, H. (1989). *Plato: Collected dialogues*. Bollinger Series LXXI. Princeton, NJ: Princeton University Press.
Kaestle, K. (1991). Studying the history of literacy. In C. F. Kaestle, H. Damon-Moore, L. C. Stedman, K. Tinsley, & W. V. Trollinger, Jr. (Eds.), *Literacy in the United States: Readers and reading since 1880* (pp. 3–32). New Haven: Yale University Press.
McLuhan, M. (1951). *The mechanical bride: Folklore of industrial man*. New York: Vanguard Press.
McLuhan, M. (1964). *Understanding media*. New York: McGraw–Hill.
McLuhan, M., & Fiore, Q. (1967). *The medium is the massage*. New York: Penguin Books.
McLuhan, M., & Powers, B. R. (1989). The global village: Transformations in world life and media in the 21st century. New York: Oxford University Press.
Sheingold, K. (1992). Technology integration and teachers' professional development. In *Learning technologies essential for education change* (pp. 41–51). Washington, DC: Council for Chief State School Officers.

INTRODUCTION:
RECONCEPTUALIZING LITERACY IN THE MEDIA AGE

Ann Watts Pailliotet

McLUHAN WAS RIGHT: ENTERING THE MEDIA AGE

Decades ago, Marshall McLuhan announced, "the medium is the message" (McLuhan & Fiore, 1967). With the proliferation of mass media and electronic technologies, McLuhan envisioned an emerging "global village" where the natures of perception, communication, literacy, schooling, education, and social experience would be transformed (McLuhan, 1962, 1964; McLuhan & Fiore, 1968). In many ways, McLuhan was right.

Mass media and visual texts impact and interact with individuals, schools, and society in myriad ways, influencing literacy learning (Dyson, 1997; Flood, Heath, & Lapp, 1997), perceptions of teachers and schooling (Weber & Mitchell, 1995), and social behaviors and cultural norms (Giroux & Simon, 1989). Reinking (1995) asserts that the rise of electronic texts is creating a "post typographic world" that will lead to "fundamental changes in the way we communicate and disseminate information, the way we approach the task of reading and writing, and the way we think about helping people become literate" (p. 17). Eisner (1997) argues that multiple forms of representation inherent in mass media texts profoundly impact thinking processes, educational products, and the ways we represent and perceive the world. The language, images, and messages we receive ("read") and construct ("write") through popular culture and mass media are now interdependent components and essential elements of modern literacy (Barthes, 1971; Fox, 1994; Messaris, 1994; Neuman, 1991; Robinson, 1997; Watts Pailliotet, 1998).

Individuals' definitions shape their beliefs, agendas, and actions (Mosenthal, 1983, 1993). Therefore, as educators and citizens living in a media age, we must redefine our views of what constitutes literacy processes, texts, and instruction (Thoman, 1993). The rise of mass media and visual technologies have led researchers to call for new definitions of literacy theory, practice, study, and policy (Flood et al., 1997; Hobbs, 1997). For example, Flood and Lapp (1995) propose a "broader conceptualization in which literacy is defined as the ability to function competently in the 'communicative arts' which include the language arts as well as the visual arts of drama, art, film, video, and television" (p. 1). Tyner (1998) defines modern "multiliteracies" and details at length the many elements they involve. Leveranz and Tyner (1996) advocate fundamental rethinking of schools: "positioning media arts, instead of traditional language arts, at the heart of all disciplines in the curriculum" (p. 10).

But merely modifying our newfound intellectual understandings is not enough. We must translate our media theories into empirical research, practical pedagogy, and socially just actions. Recent works underscore the importance of further in depth, systematic study of media and visual literacy (Flood & Lapp, 1995; Flood et al., 1997). For example, Reinking (1995) believes we must "realign research" to focus on strategies needed to understand electronic and popular texts. Buckingham (1998) stresses the importance of conducting classroom based media education research, and Leu et al. (1998) assert new technologies must "accommodate the instructional needs of teachers for literacy and learning" (p. 203). In particular, Ducharme and Ducharme (1996) note that future inquiry about technology use in teacher preparation programs is essential if we are to prepare educators to instruct in relevant ways. New media literacy conceptions also require vastly expanded educational resources (Thoman, 1998), as well as accounts of new skills and strategies (Thoman, 1999). Additionally, a growing number of scholars argue that our definitions and understandings of media education must be critical or even radical ones, leading to praxis, reflection, transformation, and social justice in classrooms and society (e.g., Buckingham, 1993b; Giroux, 1988; Hall, 1996; McLaren, Hammer, Sholle, & Reilly, 1995; Semali & Watts Pailliotet, 1999b).

Furthermore, in recognition of changing educational and social communicational contexts, a growing number of jurisdictions and organizations across the United States and Canada have established new policies and standards for explicit media literacy instruction that involve reading, writing, speaking, listening, representing, and viewing (e.g., Atlantic Canada English Language Arts Curriculum, 1996; NCTE/IRA Standards for English Language Arts, 1996; Essential Learning Benchmarks in Washington State, 1996; The New Compact for Learning in New York,

1991). New media based educational standards and technologies require increased accountability and new assessment forms (Farr & Jongsma, 1997).

We have clearly entered the media age. Next, I outline important topics in media literacy scholarship and explain how our authors address them.

"THE TIMES, THEY ARE A CHANGING": RECONCEPTUALIZING LITERACY DEFINITIONS, PRACTICES, RESEARCH, POLICY, AND THEORY

Call it what you will—the new literacy (Foster, 1979); visual literacy (Messaris, 1994); media literacy (Considine & Haley, 1992; Fiske, 1989; Hobbs, 1997); information literacy (Lehtonen, 1988; Tyner, 1998); television literacy (Buckingham, 1993a ; Masterman, 1980); teleliteracy (Bianculli, 1992); technological, computer, or electronic literacy (Reinking, McKenna, Labbo, & Keiffer, 1998 ; Streibel, 1985); digital literacy (Edwards, 1991; Tyner, 1998); critical media pedagogy (McLaren et al., 1995); or critical media literacy (Semali & Watts Pailliotet, 1990a; Sholle & Denski, 1993). To paraphrase Bob Dylan, the times, they are *definitely* changing. Evolving technologies and modern communications environments pose important new problems for educators, offering exciting new possibilities and requiring new definitions. However, much media instruction, research, and policy remains rooted in assumptions and practices of the former print paradigm (Burton, 1990; Hobbs, 1997; Witkin, 1994).

Certain important topics about media education are either only beginning to emerge or are largely absent from current scholarship. These include issues and procedures for assessment of media or multimedia texts, practices, and policies; media-generated preservice and inservice teacher education or reflection; interdisciplinary curriculum; uses of multiple texts; use of mass media and technology to extend existing teaching methodologies; in-depth reviews of how media and visual literacy support, relate, and extend current print literacy theories and practices; explicit examples and results of research methodologies; new theories of literacy and examples of their applications; classroom research at diverse levels; or accounts of media literacy or multimedia instruction implementation procedures and policies in schools, classes, districts, states, and/or colleges.

In *Reconceptualizing Literacy in the Media Age*, we answer these calls for media scholarship and address these important topics. The various authors define literacy in broad, innovative, and sometimes provocative ways. Our text includes chapters written by diverse individuals, who detail advances in visual and media research, instruction, theory, and policies. In doing so, they discuss many media-related educational, methodological, cultural, and social issues. Because of its inclusive authorship and diverse topical focus, this book has a potentially wide interdisciplinary audience that includes theorists, researchers, and practitioners in fine and commercial arts, communications, sociology, cultural studies, textual criticism, and education. It may be of interest to mass media analysts, cultural and critical theorists; psychologists or sociologists; researchers working with mass media and visual texts; artists, authors, and illustrators; educational planners, policymakers, classroom teachers, preservice teachers, teacher educators, and media specialists.

I now describe how our book extends existing media literacy scholarship and explain its theoretical basis.

ABOUT THIS BOOK:
EXTENDING LITERACY DEFINITIONS, PRACTICES, RESEARCH, POLICY, AND THEORY

Although informative, many recent publications about media and visual literacy share some common limitations. First, as Barry Duncan notes in the Preface, most are written by individuals who share a single disciplinary background (e.g., cultural studies, reading, computers and technology, sociology, textual criticism) and are targeted at limited audiences in narrowly defined, academic discourse communities. Our book transcends these traditional boundaries. We examine varied topics across practical, policy, research, and theoretical levels. Our contributing authors come from diverse disciplines and backgrounds. Some are classroom teachers in schools; others are teacher educators in reading, English education, media literacy/media studies, curriculum and instruction, educational foundations, literature, or instructional technology. Others come from fields of rhetoric and composition, writing instruction, psychology, communications, or media literacy organizations.

Second, most media literacy texts are authored by individuals from a single country or geographic location, although advances in media education vary widely according to national and regional locales. Our text includes contributors from across the United States and Canada who offer diverse visions of media education through their discussions of important issues, uses of varied texts, and novel instructional or research processes.

Third, some media education texts are presented through print-dominated formats, containing few illustrations, graphics, figures, or examples of student-generated texts. This seems at odds with the visual nature of much of modern media. Here, many of our authors provide rich and varied visual information that will enable the reader to see, as well as understand, what we mean by media literacy.

Fourth, many works focus on a single medium like film, television, children's picture books, computers, or newspapers. Others merely replicate print-based literacy instruction, projecting existing teaching practice onto new media. Given the rapidly evolving and complex natures of modern media, these approaches seem somewhat limited. Other current publications tend to focus on one informational level. Some present theories, narratives, textual critiques, or social analyses with little connection to specific research methods or educational practices; others offer classroom materials and instruction with few in-depth explanations of how they relate to theories, research, or larger social contexts. However, writing about theory without practice and practice without theory is of little use to media educators (Buckingham, 1998). While most media literacy texts focus on either "how to" methods or theoretical discussions (critical/cultural analyses), the authors in this volume offer innovative syntheses of media literacy theories, texts, and processes.

Next, many media literacy publications seem to take limited or simplistic perspectives. Some serve up the "bad news": visions of technological doom, negative stances toward the media, or scathing critiques of current educational practices, texts, and social conditions. Others seem to offer only the "good news": decontextualized instructional prescriptions that seem somewhat facile and even disempowering to students and teachers. "Just do these two or four or six simple steps. . . . Use this text or method or reproducible handout," many seem to say, "and everything will be wonderful—you and your students will be instantly media literate." In contrast, the authors here recognize the complex nature of media literacy. In their narratives, drawn from real-life contexts, they discuss both their successes and failures, identify influences and outcomes, explore multiple pitfalls and promises, and offer richly detailed, complex accounts of media literacy experiences and issues.

Last, our authors share several guiding premises. They reject protectionist media stances, instead extending and reconceptualizing print-based paradigms, embracing new opportunities, and envisioning many exciting possibilities of the media age. All seek to create connections among people, theory and practice, texts, and contexts. All move beyond a receptive stance that assumes viewers and teachers to be passive consumers of media, and show many ways that individuals can generate new media forms. Finally, the authors provide examples of what it means to be reflective "transformative intellectuals" (Giroux, 1988) and critical, media-literate educators (Semali & Watts Pailliotet, 1999b) through their ideas, actions, and innovations.

THE FOUR "I'S" OF MEDIA LITERACY: IDENTITY, INTERMEDIALITY, ISSUES, AND INNOVATIONS

The authors' contributions suggested to me a new reconceptualization of literacy, as well as the organization for this book. I call this the "four 'I's' of media literacy": identity, intermediality, issues, and innovations. Below, I briefly explain each concept, and preview the contexts of this text.

Identity

Buckingham (1993a, 1998) asserts that considerations of identity are essential for relevant media education. Much research has been done about the impacts of media on identity and personal behaviors. Critics link media exposure to many aspects of identity formation: everything from increases in violent behaviors (Comstock & Paik, 1991); to eating disorders (Richins, 1991); decreases in literate behaviors (Postman, 1985; Shenkman, 1985); passivity and mental distancing from everyday experience (McKibben, 1992); perpetuation of social norms (Barnouw, 1975); conceptions of race, class, and gender (Dines & Humez, 1995); body image (Richins, 1991); and socialization into traditional gender roles (Pierce, 1990; Wolf, 1991). What much (but not all) of this scholarship shares, however, is an explicit or tacit protectionist, innoculationist stance that assumes media *act on* largely passive individuals in negative ways, rather than positing that individuals *actively resist or construct* media texts as ways to express and develop positive identities.

Buckingham offers some questions to guide media educators and students in their explorations of relations among media and identity. These include:

> To what extent can popular culture adequately be seen as 'belonging' to the students, or as an 'authentic' expression of their own investments and identities? To what extent can young people be seen as 'active' or 'passive' in their relationships with the media? . . . To what extent are they able to reflect upon those relationships? . . . What is the relationship between students' subjective investments and pleasures and the academic discourses and procedures of critical analysis? (Buckingham, 1998, pp. 9–10)

In Section One of *Reconceptualizing Literacy in the Media Age*, "Identity," the authors address many of Buckingham's queries. Richard Beach provides a lively account of how media ethnographies enabled his students to actively research and construct media texts, thus examining and giving voice to their personal identities within media cultures. Linn Bekins describes how through critical study of the Internet, her students were able to develop professional identities as writers, rather than being passively appropriated by existing disciplinary discourses. Last in this section, Lynn Briggs sets forth an entertaining and thought provoking narrative, describing how implementation of deep viewing (Watts Pailliotet, 1995, 1998), a process of reflective and critical media analysis, changed relations and power roles in a writing center. Briggs describes how media analysis may result in new social, academic, and spiritual identities.

Intermediality

The concept of "intermediality" grew out of conversations among literacy educators at the 1996 National Reading Conference. Subsequently, we developed its guiding premises more fully (Semali & Watts Pailliotet, 1999b). Intermediality assumes that many theories inform media literacy. It defines a "text" broadly, positing that texts are laden with shifting meanings and reflect cultural ideologies. Furthermore, it regards all texts as constructions involving active, varied transactions of meaning making. Intermedial processes involve "the ability to critically read and write with and across multiple symbol systems" (Semali & Watts Pailliotet, 1999b, p. 6)—reading is defined as active engagement; writing, as generating texts through multiple media forms. Furthermore, intermediality embraces the connectedness among texts, processes, and contexts, and views media literacy as the "linchpin. . . that connects learning contexts and curricula" (p. 7). Last, intermediality insists on theory into praxis, where students and teachers must transform their newfound critical understandings into agency, positive acts and effects in themselves and others" (p. 8).

The authors in Section Two provide classroom-based examples of intermedial concepts, processes, texts, and outcomes. Victoria J. Risko discusses how multimedia environments can transform teacher preparation programs from transmission pedagogies to ones that demonstrate the power of dynamic, generative, and collaborative learning. Roberta F. Hammett explores how hypermedia composing activities can facilitate and connect literacy learning and teaching advocated within reader response, critical, and constructivist approaches. Patricia I. Mulcahy-Ernt shares exciting examples of literature response, representing readers' interpretative stances through varied forms, including print, visual , and performing arts. Finally, Jackie K. Giles, Sherry L. Macaul, and Rita K. Rodenberg illustrate the positive outcomes that occur when teachers, teacher educators, and students collaborate in media literacy inquiry. They report the results of a study involving middle school children who engaged in structured and nonstructured deep viewing of various media, then represented what they learned through their inquiries by generating varied media and multimedia representations, and developed evaluation criteria.

Issues

Media literacy scholars assert that changing understandings and media literacy implementation are complex issues which must be examined and understood within varied social contexts (e.g., Fiske, 1989; Giroux, 1993; Kellner, 1995b; Tyner, 1998). These considerations must occur both at macro, societal levels and at micro, classroom levels. For instance, Reinking (1995) believes that social changes in the age of technology and media require us to rethink our basic assumptions about literacy. He goes on to write, "such fundamental changes in literacy may have social, political and cultural repercussions" (p. 17). Buckingham (1998) asserts, "To discuss pedagogy is to focus on the theories of teaching and learning which inform classroom practice—and more specifically, on the *social relationships* between students and teachers" (p. 3). In particular, there are key issues that contemporary media theorists and educators view as pressing. The first is media literacy assessment and standards (Buckingham, 1998; Farr & Jongsma, 1997). The second involves interdisciplinary applications of media literacy (Considine, 1987; Hobbs, 1998; Leveranz & Tyner, 1996). The third investigates the social (Kellner, 1995a) and institutional conditions of schools that foster or prevent change (Farber, Provenzo, & Holm, 1994; Giroux & Simon, 1989; Semali, 1994).

Section Three offers four views of these critical issues. Arnold S. Wolfe enters the conservative "belly of the beast" at a comprehensive state university to propose a new interdisciplinary critical media literacy course. In his account, Wolfe not only details pedagogical components and assessment of his course, but also shows how one may negotiate new theory and practice within existing educational objectives and contexts. Next, Lyn Lacy, an experienced elementary media educator, offers a sometimes humorous and always pragmatic narrative about how she implemented changing state standards for media literacy instruction across the curriculum in K–5 classrooms. Readers will enjoy Lacy's inclusion of varied teaching materials and examples. Third, Ladi Semali presents a case study of preservice teachers attempting to develop and implement media literacy curricula. In his accounts of student newspaper analysis, which involved critical viewing, reading, and authoring, Semali shows how these future teachers employed interdisciplinary curricula to detect and resist media representations and bias. Last, noted media author David M. Considine examines many issues involved with media literacy implementation in U.S. schools. He discusses historical trends; institutional contexts, organizational cultures, resistance, and power relations in schools and classrooms; evolving media literacy goals; teachers' purposes, principles, and pedagogy; and teacher preparation programs. Concluding that externally mandated change can never substitute for internally motivated change, Considine provides examples of several innovative teacher programs and a case study that enable readers to better address key media issues.

Innovations

Changing conditions of the media age require changing conceptions and innovations. In Section Four, our authors pose exciting new theories and outline directions for the future of media literacy. Through text, graphics, and numerous examples, Peter B. Mosenthal first offers a model for types of knowledge needed for modern literacy. Next, Richard E. Mayer, a psychologist, details aspects of multimedia literacy: definitions, situations, examples of learning, techniques for creation of messages, and a future research agenda. Robert Maribe Branch then describes a tentative, highly ambitious taxonomy of visual literacy. He also notes its many applications to instructional design of varied texts and outlines needed study. Last,

T. A. Callister, Jr. provides a provocative inquiry about existing media literacy definitions and metaphors. Through a series of anecdotes and critical questions, Callister both extends key media literacy concepts of accessing, analyzing, evaluating, and communicating (Hobbs, 1997) and encourages readers to reflect on the moral, ethical, pedagogical, and metaphoric implications of our existing media conceptions.

Afterword

Reconceptualizing Literacy in the Media Age ends with an extended media literacy resource chapter. Our annotated recommendations are organized according to the following categories: Media Education Texts for Elementary Students and for Secondary Students; Production Resources; Research and Reflection on Media Education; Periodicals; Electronic Resources about Media Literacy; Electronic Resources for Teachers; Bookmarks: Digital Resources; and Media Education Centers and Organizations.

It is our wish that readers use these resources to reconceptualize their own literacy theories, practices, research, and policies in the media age.

REFERENCES

Barnouw, E. (1975). *Tube of plenty: The evolution of American television*. New York: Oxford University Press.

Barthes, R. (1971). *Image, music, text* (S. Heath, Trans.). New York: Hill and Wang.

Bianculli, D. (1992). *Teleliteracy*. New York: Continuum.

Buckingham, D. (1993a). *Children talking television: The making of television literacy*. London: Falmer Press.

Buckingham, D. (1993b). Introduction: Young people and the media. In D. Buckingham (Ed.), *Reading audiences: Young people and the media* (pp. 1–23). Manchester, UK: Manchester University Press.

Buckingham, D. (1998). Introduction: Fantasies of empowerment? Radical pedagogy and popular culture. In D. Buckingham (Ed.), *Teaching popular culture: Beyond radical pedagogy* (pp. 1–17). London: UCL Press.

Burton, G. (1990). *More than meets the eye: An introduction to media studies*. London: Edward Arnold.

Comstock, G., & Paik, H. (1991). *Television and the American child*. San Diego: Academic Press.

Considine, D. M. (1987). Visual literacy and the curriculum: More to it than meets the eye. *Language Arts, 64*(6), 34–40.

Considine, D. M., & Haley, G. E. (1992). *Visual messages: Integrating imagery into instruction*. Englewood, CO: Teacher Ideas Press.

Dines, G., & Humez, J. M. (Eds.). (1995). *Gender, race and class in the media*. Thousand Oaks, CA: Sage.

Ducharme, E. R., & Ducharme, M. K. (1996). Needed research in teacher education. In J. Sikula (Ed.), *Handbook of research on teacher education* (2nd ed., pp. 1030–1046). New York: Simon & Schuster/Macmillan.

Dyson, A. H. (1997). *Writing superheroes: Contemporary childhood, popular culture and classroom literacy*. New York: Teachers College Press.

Edwards, B. L., Jr. (1991). How computers change things: Literacy and the digitalized word. *Writing Instructor, 10*(2), 68–76.

Eisner, E. W. (1997). Cognition and representation: A way to pursue the American dream? *Phi Delta Kappan, 78*(5), 349–353.

(1996). *English language arts curriculum*. Nova Scotia Department of Education and Culture.

Farber, P., Provenzo E. F., Jr., & Holm, G. (Eds.). (1994). *Schooling in the light of popular culture*. Albany: SUNY Press.

Farr, R., & Jongsma, E. (1997). Accountability through assessment and instruction. In J. Flood, S. B. Heath, & D. Lapp (Eds.), *Handbook of research on teaching literacy through the communicative and visual arts* (pp. 592–604). New York: Macmillan/Simon & Schuster.

Farstrup, A. E., & Myers, M. (Eds.). (1996). *Standards for the English language arts*. Urbana, IL and Newark, DE: National Council of Teachers of English and International Reading Association.

Fiske, J. (1989). *Understanding popular culture*. Boston: Unwin Hyman.

Flood, J., Heath, S. B., & Lapp, D. (Eds.). (1997). *Handbook of research on teaching the communicative and visual arts*. New York: Macmillan.

Flood, J., & Lapp, D. (1995). Broadening the lens: Toward and expanded conceptualization of literacy. In K. A. Hinchman, D. J. Leu, & C. K. Kinzer (Eds.), *Perspectives on literacy research and practice: Forty-fourth yearbook of the National Reading Conference* (pp. 1–16). Chicago: National Reading Conference.

Foster, H. M. (1979). *The new literacy: The language of film and television*. Urbana, IL: National Council of Teachers of English.

Fox, R. F. (Ed.). (1994). *Images in language, media and mind*. Urbana, IL: National Council of Teachers of English.

Giroux, H.A. (1988). *Teachers as intellectuals: Toward a critical pedagogy of learning*. South Hadley, MA: Bergin & Garvey.

Giroux, H. A. (1993). Reclaiming the social: Pedagogy, resistance and politics in celluloid culture. In J. Collins, H. Radner, & A. P. Collins (Eds.), *Film theory goes to the movies* (pp. 37-55). London: Routledge.

Giroux, H.A., & Simon, R. (1989). *Popular culture, schooling, and everyday life*. New York: Bergin & Garvey.

Hall, S. (1996). *Representation: Cultural representations and their signifying practices*. London: Sage.

Hobbs, R. (1997). Literacy for the information age. In J. Flood, S. B. Heath, & D. Lapp (Eds.), *Handbook of research on teaching literacy through the communicative and visual arts* (pp. 7–14). New York: Simon & Schuster/Macmillan.

Hobbs, R. (1998). The seven great debates in the media literacy movement. *Journal of Communication, 48*(1), 16–32.

Kellner, D. (1995a). *Media culture*. London: Routledge.

Kellner, D. (1995b). Preface. In P. McLaren, R. Hammer, D. Sholle, & S. S. Reilly (Eds.), *Rethinking media literacy: A critical pedagogy of representation* (Vol. 4, pp. xiii–xvii). New York: Peter Lang.

Learning, W. S. C. o. S. (1996). *Revised essential learnings* .

Lehtonen, J. (1988). The information society and the new competence. *American Behavioral Scientist, 32*(2), 104-111.

Leu, D. J., Hillinger, M., Loseby, P. H., Balcom, M. L., Dinkin, J., Eckels, M. L., Johnson, J., Mathews, K., & Raegler, R. (1998). Grounding the design of new technologies for literacy and learning in teachers' instructional needs. In D. Reinking, M. C. McKenna, L. D. Labbo, & R. D. Kieffer (Eds.), *Handbook of literacy and technology: Transformations in a post-typographic world* (pp. 203–220). Mahwah, NJ: Lawrence Erlbaum.

Leveranz, D., & Tyner, K. (1996). What is media literacy? Two leading proponents offer an overview. *Media Spectrum, 23*(1), 10.

Masterman, L. (1980). *Teaching about television*. Hong Kong: MacMillan Education.

McKibben, B. (1992). *The age of missing information*. New York: Random House.

McLaren, P., Hammer, R., Sholle, D., & Reilly, S. (Eds.). (1995). *Rethinking media literacy: A critical pedagogy of representation*. New York: Peter Lang.

McLuhan, M. (1962). *The Gutenberg galaxy: The making of typographic man*. Toronto: University of Toronto Press.

McLuhan, M. (1964). *Understanding media: The extensions of man*. New York: McGraw–Hill.

McLuhan, M., & Fiore, Q. (1967). *The medium is the message*. New York: Random House.

McLuhan, M., & Fiore, Q. (1968). *War and peace in the global village*. New York: Bantam Books.

Messaris, P. (1994). *Visual literacy: Image, mind & reality*. Boulder, CO: Westview Press.

Mosenthal, P. B. (1983). Defining reading program effectiveness as an ideological approach. *Poetics, 13*, 195–216.

Mosenthal, P. B. (1993). Understanding agenda setting in reading research. In A. P. Sweet & J. I. Anderson (Eds.), *Reading research into the year 2,000* (pp. 115–128).

Neuman, S. B. (1991). *Literacy in the television age: The myth of the tv effect*. Norwood, NJ: Ablex Publishing Corporation.

Pierce, K. (1990). A feminist perspective on the socialization of teenage girls through Seventeen magazine. *Sex Roles, 23*(9/10), 491–500.

Postman, N. (1985). *Amusing ourselves to death*. New York: Elizabeth Sifton Books/Viking Press.

Regents, N. Y. S. (1991). *A new compact for learning* (government document). Albany: The University of the State of New York.

Reinking, D. (1995). Reading and writing with computers: Literacy research in a post-typographic world. In K. A. Hinchman, D. J. Leu, & C. K. Kinzer (Eds.), *Perspectives on literacy research and practice* (Vol. 44, pp. 17–33). Chicago: National Reading Conference.

Reinking, D., McKenna, M. C., Labbo, L. D., & Keiffer, R. D. (Eds.). (1998). *Handbook of literacy and technology: Transformations in a post-typographic world*. Mahwah, NJ: Lawrence Erlbaum.

Richins, M. (1991). Social comparison and the idealized images of advertising. *Journal of Consumer Research, 18*(June), 71–91.

Robinson, M. (1997). *Children reading print and television*. London: Falmer Press.

Semali, L. (1994). Rethinking media literacy in schools. *Pennsylvania Educational Leadership, 13*(2), 11–18.

Semali, L., & Watts Pailliotet, A. (Eds.). (1999a). *Intermediality: The teachers' handbook of critical media literacy*. Boulder, CO: Westview/Harper Collins.

Semali, L. M., & Watts Pailliotet, A. (1999b). Introduction: What is intermediality and why study it in U.S. schools? In L. M. Semali & A. Watts Pailliotet (Eds.), *Intermediality: The teachers' handbook of critical media literacy* (pp. 1–30). Boulder, CO: Westview.

Shenkman, H. (1985). Reversing the literacy decline by controlling the electronic demons. *Educational Leadership, 42*(5), 26–29.

Sholle, D., & Denski, S. (1993). Reading and writing the media: Critical media literacy and postmodernism. In C. Lankshear & P. L. McLaren (Eds.), *Critical literacy: Politics, praxis and the postmodern* (pp. 297–321). Albany: State University of New York Press.

Streibel, M. J. (1985). Visual literacy, television literacy, and computer literacy: Some parallels and a synthesis. *Journal of Visual/Verbal Languaging, 5*(2), 5–14.

Thoman, E. (1993). "Imagine": A media of meaning. *Media & Values, 63*(1), 22–25.

Thoman, E. (1998). Media literacy: A guided tour of selected resources. *English Journal, 87*(1), 34–37.

Thoman, E. (1999). Skills and strategies for media education. *Educational Leadership, 56*(5), 50–54.

Tyner, K. (1998). *Literacy in a digital world: Teaching and learning in the age of information*. Mahwah, NJ: Lawrence Erlbaum.

Watts Pailliotet, A. (1995). "I never saw that before." A deeper view of video analysis in teacher
    education. *The Teacher Educator, 31*(2), 138–156.
Watts Pailliotet, A. (1998). Deep viewing: A critical look at texts. In S. Steinberg & J. Kincheloe (Eds.),
    Unauthorized methods: Strategies for critical teaching (pp. 124–136). London: Routledge.
Weber, S., & Mitchell, C. (1995). *That's funny, you don't look like a teacher: Interrogating images and
    identity in popular culture.* London: Falmer Press.
Witkin, M. (1994). A defense of using pop media in the middle school classroom. *English Journal, 83*(1),
    30–33.
Wolf, N. (1991). *The beauty myth.* New York: Morrow.

SECTION I

IDENTITY: RECONCEPTUALIZING LITERACY
STANCES AND RELATIONS

USING MEDIA ETHNOGRAPHIES TO STUDY RESPONSE TO MEDIA AS ACTIVITY

Richard Beach

I am surfing the cable channels on television with a group of students in a media studies methods class. On TNT, two larger wrestlers in elaborate costumes are throwing chairs at each other, much to the delight of screaming fans. On CBS, some eager participants are competing for prize money on a quiz show. On PBS, a group of scholars are analyzing foreign policy implications of lack of funding for the United Nations. On NBC, a married couple in a situation comedy show is planning a cruise neither one wants to take. On ABC, a group of doctors and nurses on a hospital drama program are debating whether to maintain a dying man's life in the face of intense suffering. On the Christian network, a minister is preaching about the evils of "secular humanism." Given the largely critical, irreverent stance operating in this class, we construct the meaning of these different worlds not in terms of what is "in" these media worlds, nor what is simply "in" ourselves as viewers. Rather, the meaning of our response is constituted through our participation in an academic, classroom activity in which we adopt certain tools of critical analysis, identities, and ideological stances.

Advances in Reading/Language Research, Volume 7, pages 3–39.
Copyright © 2000 by JAI Press Inc.
All rights of reproduction in any form reserved.
ISBN: 0-7623-0264-X

If meaning resides in the *activity* of social participation with media texts, then media education needs to focus not simply on analyzing media texts but also on the social contexts constituting the meaning of response as an activity. As Grossberg, Wartella, and Whitney (1998) argue in defense of their model of "mediamaking":

> the media are *themselves being made* while they are simultaneously *making something else*. . . we must see the media and all of the relationships that the media are involved in as active relationships, producing the world at the same time that the world is producing the media. This means that the media *cannot* be studied apart from the active relationships in which they are always involved: We cannot study the media apart from the context of their economic, political, historical, and cultural relationships. (p. 7)

Moreover, the distinction between the activity of responding to the media and responding to written texts has become blurred with the increased use of hypertext and hypermedia texts. As Molly Travis (1998) notes: "The more interactive that hypertextual literature becomes and the closer it moves to virtual reality, the more the reader becomes a role-player in 'real-time' dramatic performance with other readers" (p. 12).

This suggests the need for media education to go beyond discussions of general uses or effects of media on audiences to examine particular viewers' or readers' responses in particular viewing or reading activities. Such instruction draws on the work of media ethnographers who study "the lived experiences of media consumers" (Moores, 1993, p. 32). Through observation and interviewing audience participation in responding to the media, media ethnographers (Ang, 1985; Bird, 1992; Brown, 1990; Buckingham, 1993, 1996; Davis, 1997; Harrington & Bielby, 1995; Jenkins, 1992; Lull, 1990; McKinley, 1997; McRobbie, 1990; Palmer, 1986; Provenzo, 1991; Radway, 1984, 1988; Riggs, 1998; Seiter, Borchers, Kreutzner, & Warth, 1989; Schwartz, 1998; Spigel & Mann, 1992; Turkle, 1995) attempt to understand an audience's perspective on their responses as a social activity (for summary analyses of media ethnographies, see Ang, 1991; Crawford & Hafsteinsson, 1997; Moores, 1993; Nightingale, 1996; Stevenson, 1995).

In this chapter, I argue for the value of conducting small-scale media ethnographies as part of media education. Rather than simply analyzing media texts—television programs, films, magazines, and so on—in a vacuum, it is also important to provide students with an understanding of how the meaning of media texts is constructed through participation in viewing or reading activities. I formulate a model for how meaning is constructed through viewer or reader participation in response activity, as illustrated through examples of published media ethnographies. Central to that model is the assumption that the primary unit of analysis is the response/viewing activity itself as driven by certain cultural values or discourses. As Donald Carbaugh (1996) notes:

> By foregrounding cultural communities and their messages, their own beliefs about communication, and using those beliefs to interpret mediated messages (and selves), one can conduct the

kind of audience research that is anchored . . . in a community's communication system (including television). (p. 86)

ACTIVITY THEORY OF LEARNING AND RESPONSE TO THE MEDIA

One limitation of much audience research is that the primary unit of analysis is the autonomous, individual viewer's own response studied in isolation from the activities and social contexts in which that viewer is responding. Sociocultural "activity theory" of learning posits that participants learn within the context the activity of viewing driven by the need to achieve a certain object or purpose (Cole, 1996; Engestrom, 1987; Cole & Engestrom, 1993; Leont'ev, 1981; Rogoff, 1995; Wertsch, 1991). Through their participation in an activity, participants transform the nature of the activity, and, in the process, are transformed by their participation. For example, a group of students in 1981–82 initiated a letter-writing campaign expressing opposition to nuclear war and making the case for nuclear disarmament (Engestrom, 1987). While their campaign lasted about a year, it precipitated the spread of other letter-writing activities, creating a new form of the original activity. Participation in the initial campaign provided these students with a sense of a "life goal" or "motive goal" defining the meaning of specific practices within the context of larger activities (Engestrom, 1987, p. 162). Similarly, a group producing the female zine magazine, "riot grrrl," engages in the activity of constructing an organizational network designed to promote their music. Marion Leonard (1998) describes the evolution of this social world as part of an expanding network of activities:

> Riot grrrl is a feminist network which developed in the underground music communities of Olympia, Washington, and Washington, D.C. The initiative was promoted by members of the bands Bratmobile and Bikini Kill who sought to challenge sexism in the underground music scene and encourage girls and women to assert themselves. . . . As women and girls began to identify with this idea, riot grrrl networks spread across the USA and Britain. The realization of this initiative took several forms. Female audience members began by challenging the traditional division of the gig environment into gendered spaces, where women were largely absent from front of stage. Others grrrls formed bands, wrote zines, arranged meetings and organized events to introduce girls to music making . . . Riot grrrl zines employ small scale production with issues sometimes numbering only twenty copies . . . Acquiring the addresses of zines involves tapping into the informal friendship networks active within riot grrrl. (Leonard, 1998, pp. 102, 103, 106)

In the case of riot grrrl, the participants were driven by the object or purpose of establishing the legitimacy of their own music within the context of a male-controlled world. That object or purpose served to define the meaning of the tools they employed—their publications and musical instruments, as well as the identities they assumed as organizers, writers, and performers. Recent work in the field of "distributed cognition" (Hutchins, 1993) posits that certain ways of thinking or knowing associated with an activity become embodied or "distributed" in certain physical or technological tools. For example, navigational instruments are used to capture what is known about navigating the seas. They serve as tools that guide a ship based on human knowledge about navigation. Similarly, expert computer systems are built on experts' knowledge about a certain phenomenon such as diagnosing a particular disease. Tools are therefore used within an activity to function as extensions of certain ways of thinking in an activity.

In conducting media ethnographies of viewer activities, students are examining viewers as participants constructing meaning through activity in which they employ certain tools and adopt certain identities within an activity constituted by certain conventions, codes, and discourses. They may study how, within response activities, viewers or readers are also positioned to perceive and experience media texts as representing certain kinds of activities driven by certain kinds of purposes. In their book, *Media Events*, Dayan and Katz (1992) argue that television viewers are socialized to perceive certain special or historical events—the Kennedy funeral; the Presidential debates; the Watergate, Iran-Contra, and Anita Hill hearings; the Super Bowl, Final Four, World Series, and the World Cup; the visits of the Pope; the Gulf War bombings; or the OJ Simpson ride on the freeway as extraordinary, unusual, even historical deviations from the norm. In contrast to the typical television news broadcast, in which events are chopped up into brief segments interrupted by commercials, media events are presented in a continuous flow without interruption. While news events are tightly framed, excluding viewer involvement, media events "allow their spectators to follow the event from within . . . to inhabit the event through the mediation of the primary audience in attendance" (p. 115).

These special media events often serve as the basis for viewing activities as special, festive, social events, as in groups gathering in homes or bars for Super Bowl parties (Schwartz, 1998). Within these activities, viewers learn certain ritual-like genres associated with celebrating a team's successes and enjoying each other's company.

Analyzing these activities involves examining various components of an activity or activity system (Russell, 1997). These components include the object or purpose, tools, genres, identities, conventions and codes, and discourses, components evident in media ethnography research. These different components provide a useful framework for analyzing viewer or reader activity, as illustrated in examples of media ethnography studies.

Object or Purpose

A particular group's activity of responding to the media is driven by certain objects or purpose. Studies of media fans' participation in fan clubs indicate that the fan club activities are driven by a number of different objects or purposes (Bacon-Smith, 1992; Harrington & Bielby, 1995; Jenkins, 1992; Penley, 1991). For example, Henry Jenkins's (1992) analysis of meetings of members of *Star Trek* fan clubs examined members' creation and sharing of their own versions of *Star Trek* programs in the form of edited videos or fanzine stories. These edited videos or fanzines often introduced interpersonal or erotic themes into the stories, in which, for example, Spock and Captain Kirk are engaged in a relationship. Jenkins found that one primary purpose for sharing the videos and fanzines was to create a social community for fans to share and legitimatize responses that the public-at-large would perceive as deviant. He also found that members compared evaluations of edited versions to determine which versions represented the most unusual, outlandish revision of the original programs.

Being an avid fan often involves exerting some influence on people involved with the production (Harrington & Bielby, 1995; Jenkins, 1992). In a study of soap opera fans and fan clubs, Harrington and Bielby (1995) found that producers and actors/actresses often lurked on fan club bulletin boards or participated in fan club meetings for the purposes of garnering evaluative comments about their program. Because the fans were aware of their participation, they assumed that their responses might have some influence on the program's production.

Fan participation is also driven by the need to publicly demonstrate their commitment to being more than simply casual viewers through displaying pictures of soap opera actors/actresses in one's home or attending fan club meetings (Harrington & Bielby, 1995). In doing so, they must also often cope with their peers' stereotypes of themselves as fans who are incapable of distinguishing between fiction and reality, stereotypes which, in some cases, created a sense of ambivalence about their own viewing habits.

Purposes for viewing may also be driven by psychological needs. Andrea Press's (1991) study of middle-class and working-class women's responses to television drama programs found that these two groups of women differed in their responses to portrayals of female characters. The middle-class women perceived middle-class female television characters as largely unrealistic. The working-class women perceived these middle-class female characters as realistic role models whom they sought to emulate. These different reactions represent two different purposes for viewing. The middle-class women were interested simply in enjoying the programs while the working-class women were interested in emulating the middle-class female characters' consumerist lifestyle.

Viewers' responses may also be driven by the need for a reassuring, ritual-like activity. Viewers may enjoy watching a weekly mystery program because of the reassurance of a predictable sense of closure provided by the final resolution of solving the crime. Based on her research on elderly viewers' responses to mystery programs, Karen Riggs (1998) argues that "the reassuring mystery presents a means to validate the self at a stage of life when one's identity is threatened in many ways by society as a whole" (p. 17).

Michael Real (1996) argues that these ritual participations in the media culture serve to connect viewers to larger, mythic dramas as well as other fans engaged in the same collective rituals. Rituals involve viewers in a collective experience that serves to unify their allegiance to a group. They engage viewers in the repetition of certain familiar narrative patterns. They structure time and space in ways that provide a sense of order and defined roles. Real cites the example of soccer fans' active engagement in viewing World Cup television broadcasts of soccer games. He draws a comparison between the rituals of the Balinese cockfight as described by Clifford Geertz (1973) and sports fans' participation with media sports:

> First, both the cockfight and sports provide double meanings and metaphor that reach out to other aspects of social life. Second, both are elaborately organized with written rules and umpires. . . . Third, betting plays a major role in each. . . . Fourth, violence heightens the drama of each. Fifth, the presence of status hierarchies surpasses money in importance in the event, with corporate and political elites assuming central roles. . . . Sixth, each of the two, the cockfight and the media sporting event, "makes nothing happen"; neither produces goods or directly affects the welfare of the people. (p. 60)

By perceiving viewers' responses as part of a larger ritual activity, students may understand how viewing is driven by larger cultural purposes. For example, analysis of television sports viewing found certain dimensions associated with purposes for viewing (Wenner & Gantz, 1998). Five basic dimensions emerged from analysis of the viewers' responses. A primary motive was a "fanship dimension and the desire to 'thrill in victory'" (p. 237). A "learning dimension" (p. 237) had to do with acquiring information about the teams and players. A "release dimension" refers to the "opportunity to 'let loose'" or "get psyched up" (p. 237). A "companionship dimension" (p. 237) has to do with the use of sports to share time with friends and family. A "filler dimension" relates to the use of sports viewing to "kill time" (p. 237). While these objects or purposes overlap, they suggest that understanding different objects and purposes requires an understanding of the activity in which viewers are engaged.

Tools and Genres

Within an activity, viewers employ various tools designed to achieve these purposes. Jenkins (1992) also studied the uses of various tools employed by *Star Trek* fans—video editing equipment, graphic art design, a *Star Trek* register, costumes, and so on. The meaning of these tools depends on their use in fulfilling an activity's purpose. Members would employ the editing equipment to clip together different scenes to create their own story versions, use artwork to illustrate their fanzine stories, or wear costumes and act out scenes at conferences. These tools mediate the relationship between an activity's object and identity. Their value can therefore only be understood in terms of the object they are being used to achieve. The video editing equipment has no meaning other than as a means to construct alternative story versions.

Media ethnographers are interested in how these tools are being employed within activities. As part of her study of the production of Super Bowl XXVI held in Minneapolis, Dona Schwartz (1998) examined the uses of photography as a tool within the activity of constructing the Super Bowl as a corporate and media extravaganza both for the actual participants and for television viewers. On the one hand, both still and television photography were being used by the Super Bowl promoters and publicists as public relations tools to glamorize the Super Bowl as a significant event in American society. On the other hand, within the context of her own study, Schwartz worked with a team of photographers to capture a more realistic, behind-the-scenes portrayal of the less glamorous, ironic side of this media event. Her study report therefore used photos of department store mannequins wearing football helmets or a group of Native Americans protesting the Washington Redskins' logo to represent the "behind-the-scenes" political issues associated with this media event.

One important tool within an activity is the use of genres (Bazerman, 1994; Berkenkotter & Ravotas, 1997). Current genre theory goes beyond analysis of genres as simply text forms to define genres as "forms of life, ways of being, frames for social action. They are environments for learning" (Bazerman, 1994, p. 1). For Russell (1997), genres "are ways of recognizing and predicting how certain tools . . . in certain typified—typical, reoccurring—conditions, may be used to help participants act together purposefully" (p. 513).

Genres serve as tools for coping with unusual events or conflicts and tensions that arise within and across different activity systems. Because they are familiar, predictable ways of framing action, genres can act as social glue for coping with conflicts or social disruptions. For example, when a family member dies, the surviving relatives employ the genres of grieving or funerals that help them cope with the death. Or, a blues singer lamenting the loss of a girlfriend or boyfriend draws on a familiar genre to define his/her identity within the activity of singing the blues. The singer may evoke a range of different links through song lyrics and music that are familiar to an audience, who identifies with the use of a tool for coping with conflict.

In his study, Jenkins (1992) examined the genres of various narrative forms represented in fanzine and video versions of the *Star Trek* programs as tools designed to mediate between multiple, competing objects. He studied how fans constructed and used genres of romance, erotic literature, and adventure stories to construct their own alternative versions reflecting their own often feminist/gay discourses and values. These genres served as ways of coping with the tensions in their own lives between their own values and those opposed to feminist/gay values.

In his analysis of the television production of professional wrestling, Jenkins (1997) posits that the staging of a melodramatic encounter between the "good guy" who ultimately seeks revenge on and overcomes the trickery of the underhanded, villainous "bad guy" is a genre tool that is highly appealing to a working-class male audience. Vicarious participation in this drama allows males to "confront their own feelings of vulnerability, their own frustrations at a world which promises them patriarchal authority but which is experienced through relations of economic subordination . . . WWF wrestling offers a utopian alternative to this situation, allowing a movement from victimization toward mastery" (p. 560).

Viewers and readers also acquire expertise in using certain response tools to achieve certain objects. One genre tool typically associated with a "female" gendered discourse is gossip (Ayim, 1994). As a genre, gossip is a social practice that contains elements of the fictional narrative in that it focuses on both concrete behaviors—"do you know what X did"—as well as shared knowledge of genre patterns—"we all know what she was really up to." As Jenkins (1992) notes: "This shift in the level of discourse traditionally allowed women room in which to speak about factors that shaped their assigned social roles and their experience of subordination . . . in a forum unpoliced by patriarchal authorities because it was seen as frivolous or silly" (p. 84).

As a genre, gossip can then be used to define one's identity in certain contexts. For example, in a study of avid readers' reasons for reading the newspaper tabloid, *The National Inquirer*, female readers often read the tabloid in order to obtain information about celebrities which they could then share with their friends as a form of gossip (Bird, 1992). Women who could cite the latest celebrity "insider story" from sources such as *The National Inquirer* and dramatize its relevance for their peer group assumed status within that peer group (Bird, 1992).

Viewers' and readers' responses are also shaped by various public relations and publicity campaigns that serve as tools to socialize viewers and readers to adopt certain stances favorable to a television program or film (Bennett & Woollacott, 1987). For example, campaigns associated with James Bond movies were based on magazine and television interviews with movie stars who played the Bond characters, press releases, newspaper articles, and previews designed to portray Bond as representative of masculine, anti-Communist, pro-Western values (Bennett & Woollacott, 1987). This portrayal invited viewers to adopt a "male-gaze" stance, a stance which appealed to many male viewers. Similarly, analysis of the public relations campaign, magazine articles, and reviews of the 1973 PBS documentary, *An American Family*, found that much of the success of the documentary was due to the interest developed through controversies associated with publicity and commentary about the program (Ruoff, 1997). Much of this publicity and commentary revolved around the issue of representation versus reality—the extent to which the series provided an authentic portrayal of the Loud family as opposed to portraying only glimpses of these lives in which they may have been "playing" for the camera.

Thus, in addition to studying viewers' and readers' responses to media texts, media ethnographers also study producers' own activity of constructing or selecting media texts as shaped by their own discourses or ideological stances. Janice Radway (1988) studied editors' decisions about selection of books for Book-of-the-Month Club members within the context of a corporate culture designed to provide books most likely to please book-club members. She found that editors preferred those books that did not offend or challenge what they perceived to be their members' middle-class values. They therefore often excluded experimental or controversial texts, despite their literary quality, preferring books consistent with what they assumed would be their readers' ideological preferences.

IDENTITIES

Within an activity system, participants define their identities within the context of an activity. As Lave & Wenger (1991) note: "Learning . . . is a process of becoming a member of a sustained community of practice. Developing an identity as a member of a community and becoming knowledgeably skillful are part of the same process" (p. 65). Fan-club members in Jenkins's (1992) study defined their identities as fans through their acquired expertise in using the Star Trek register, designing costumes, or displaying their knowledge of programs or the actors' and actresses' personal lives. Soap opera fans displaying pictures of soap opera actors/actresses in their bedrooms, wrote letters to the actors/actresses, or attended conferences to meet the actors/actresses, practices that served to mark their identities as avid fans (Harrington & Bielby, 1995).

For Virginia Nightingale (1996), the experiences of private everyday life have become controlled by a media culture in which the private experience is replaced by public performances and consumption in a range of different worlds. As a result, the ideal, unified self of the "'individual personality'" is now dispersed across a range of loosely defined, transitory alliances. As she notes:

> media engagement increasingly transposes everyday life to a public 'out there.' Everyday life has become synonymous with what's on television or radio, what's in the newspapers or magazines, what's on at the cinema or what's in the shops. All that is left is the person finding a way 'to be,' operating electronically and commercially programmed pathways. (p. 141)

In defining their own identities in a media culture, adolescents often perceive their everyday local experience and identities in terms of links to larger global media. Given the globalization of youth market consumer goods, adolescents throughout the world mark their identity as consumers though purchase of brand-name items or participation in homogenized global media. At the same time, they may also hold allegiances to the unique culture of their own local community, creating a tension between participation in global and local cultures. In a visit to an isolated village in the Yucatan in Mexico, geographer Doreen Massey (1998) discovered that the adolescents in the village were devoting much of their time to playing computer games housed in a small shack. Based on interviews with these adolescents, she found that they gravitated between connecting to their local community and connecting to the consumer images of the global market. The local aspects of the peer-group social world were evident in the "Mayan family relations, an understanding of an ancient cosmology, a particular attitude to the USA which comes from being its southern neighbor, [and] a vague consciousness of 'Latin

America'" (p. 122). The global aspects of their peer-group social world were evident in computer games as well as "the T-shirts with slogans in English, the baseball camps, the trainers, the endless litter of cola cans" (p. 122). Massey perceives this peer social world as a "hybrid culture" (p. 123) that evolves from an interaction of complex links between the local and the global. From this interaction, peer-group social worlds or youth culture is not "a closed system of social relations but a particular articulation of contacts and influences drawn from a variety of places scattered, according to power relations, fashion and habit, across many different parts of the globe" (p. 124). This suggests the need for studying the intertextual or intermedial connections (Semali & Watts Pailliotet, 1999) between local peer-group responses to media and the need for attachment to a larger global media culture.

Within response activities, viewers and readers therefore formulate their responses in ways that reflect values and cultural models shaping their identities, particularly in terms of gender (Brown, 1990; Joyrich, 1996; McKinley, 1997). For example, a group of adolescent males responding to a television program formulated their responses around a need to maintain their masculine identities (Buckingham, 1993). Given their fear of being perceived by their peers as unmasculine, they rarely expressed emotional reactions to characters and often ridiculed female characters as "stupid" or "ugly." Similarly, in her research on adolescent females' group responses, Meredith Cherland (1994) found that females applied cultural models of what was considered to be "female"—being outgoing and relating to others—and being "male"—managing events. They also responded to characters in terms of oppositions between "good girl" or "saintly" behaviors and "bad girl" or "sinful" behaviors. Both of these groups presupposed that the male stance is the privileged norm. By defining their identities in terms of this essentialist discourse of gender, both these males and females are adopting what Sandra Bem (1993) defines as a "gender polarization" lens that perceives males and females as distinct, dichotomous, categories.

In constructing their stances and identities, females may challenge these "good girl"/"bad girl" essentialist categories through recognizing and interrogating how they are positioned to adopt these roles. In a study of early adolescent females' responses to romance novels, Pat Ensico (1998) used cutout images to foster talk about identifications with "good" and "bad" characters in romance novels, a method she described as "symbolic representation interview." As the females moved through the story, they referred to the different cutouts to describe their responses to the text, particularly their positions and value stances in relationships to the characters. As Ensico notes, "through the SRI, I asked children 'What are you?' instead of only 'What are you thinking?' This shift invited the girls to consider relative positions and implied the possibility of reorchestrating positions that are otherwise settled by repetition and a drive for consistency" (p. 60). The females' responses reflected ways in which they were being positioned in terms of discourses of "good" versus "bad" girl behavior and gender attitudes: "The girls link good girls with neat rooms, forgiveness, and reserved anger; and bad girls with messiness, unleashed anger (hitting), meanness, and insincerity" (p. 51).

A central question in examining the construction of gender identity through discourses in responding activities is the extent to which participants accept or resist these discourses. In a widely cited study of women's responses to romance novels, Janice Radway (1984) found that women would often read romance novels for the purpose of making a statement within their own male-dominated homes against the patriarchal control of their spouses. In homes in which women are valued primarily for their work, the very act of reading romance novels as an enjoyable pastime served to assert their resistance to assumptions about their roles and status within their own home.

In her study of female adolescents' responses to the popular television program, *Beverly Hills, 90210*, McKinley (1997) found that the females rarely challenged the program's predominate narrative of employing a range of practices associated with being attractive to males. Through their talk about the characters' appearance and actions, they defined their own beliefs about gender identity in ways that were consistent with the program's traditional, consumerist values. As McGinley noted, "talk about fictional characters and situations both produces and makes possible certain ways of being in the world and relating to others, certain identities, and the same talk conceals and closes off other possibilities" (p. 52). They perceived themselves as experts on these topics, and gained pleasure and status from sharing their expertise. She found that "never did they question the media definition of 'pretty,' or their own unproblematic equating of appearance and identity" (p. 77). They "accepted the show's invitation to foreground appearance, then enthusiastically cycled that way of attending to female identity back toward their own lives" (p. 78).

The females in the study defined a virtual community through their relationships with the characters: "As viewers constructed a community with the characters, as they drew connections and disjunctions between the characters' personalities and their own, new meanings accrued to those traits that gave viewers important new ways to attend to their own lives" (p. 103). The females achieved status through responding in ways that demonstrated their expertise about the social practices of dating as portrayed in the program. As McKinley notes, "They constructed a pleasurable community with which they could be experts, and positioned themselves as authors of the female identity they constructed" (p. 215).

Media ethnography can therefore be used to examine how viewers or readers construct their identities within the competing contexts of their own immediate, local activity, as well as within the larger context of a virtual media world which attempts to blur the distinction between the private and the public, the local and the global.

CONVENTIONS AND CODES

Conventions constitute what is considered to be appropriate practices or behavior in a social world—the implicit "rules of the game." Media ethnographers are interested in how groups define and adhere to certain conventions within a response activity. This adherence is particularly evident when people violate conventions, and are reprimanded, scolded, or chastised for behaving in a certain manner. For example, in television program fans' computer newsgroup discussions, instances of "flaming" or ridicule of group members are considered a violation of "netiquette." While these norms and conventions are generally not explicitly stated, they are implied by members' comments or reactions to behaviors and talk per-ceived as appropriate or deviant. Within the context of online chat rooms of romance, participants construct themselves as romantic lovers or provocateurs, because, in these virtual worlds, they do not need to be concerned with actual social consequences (Turkle, 1995).

Codes define the meaning of images and social practices based on these conven-tions. While media texts portray certain codes, media ethnographers are interested in viewers' or readers' stances for interpreting those codes. As Stuart Hall (1980) argued, viewers or readers may adopt a stance of taking up or accepting, opposing or resisting, or negotiating the codes portrayed in a text. For example, female characters in romance novels, soap operas, romantic comedies, or song lyrics are portrayed according to "codes of beautification"—that being physically attractive contributes to building a love relationship within the activity of having a relation-ship with a male (Christian-Smith, 1993). These codes specify what it means to be beautiful as defined by the cosmetics, fashion, and hair-product "beauty industry" as defined in teenage magazine advice columns and articles on ways to attract males (McRobbie, 1990).

Viewers or readers accept, resist, or negotiate these codes based on their object or purpose for viewing or reading, the object or purpose being related to their ideological stances or discourses. In a study of responses to the annual *Sports Illustrated* swimsuit issue, Laurel Davis (1997) found that readers differed in their reactions due to their stances relative to the codes of gender and sexuality associated with the portrayal of female models in swimsuits. She found that the producers perceived the issue as primarily serving to provide a nonsexual portrayal of current swimsuit fashions. Some readers responded by accepting this invited stance, stating that they read the issue simply to acquire information about swimsuits, what Hall (1980) defines as taking up or accepting the codes endorsed by the producers. However, most male readers responded in terms of the sexual appeal of the models. These males frequently referred to the influence of male peer pressure in social contexts to adopt the stance that being attracted to sexual representation of females is a marker of male heterosexuality. This male peer pressure in turn influenced their public endorsement of and positive response to the swimsuit issue. Davis (1997) quotes one male participant's description of this peer pressure:

> A lot of [young male athletes] kind of go with the flow, you know, peer pressure. . . . Cause, like, their friend'll open up the magazine and show them a girl and they'll say, 'You don't like this girl? Oh, man, what's wrong with you? You should like this girl,' and that kind of thing. And the kid might not even like girls, you know. So, it's like peer pressure . . . all around. (p. 52)

In other cases, females responded critically given their resistance to the sexist portrayals of women, an opposing or resistant stance (Hall, 1980). Davis cites a female who objected to the larger "codes of beautification" she perceived operating in the issue that:

> shows how American society views women, as to how they *should* be and how they *should* look and they *should* act and what they *should* wear . . . I mean, they're supposed to look glamorous and sexy. And, I'm not. I don't like to be portrayed that way at all. . . . When I look at those magazines, it's like, 'I'm supposed to be this way?' And [this image] is so popularized . . . slim figure, not a stomach, long legs, and you know the rest. (p. 82)

This study suggests that both males and females adopt a range of different positions associated with their particular needs or purposes for reading the swimsuit issue. Rather than adopting the essentialist perspective that males and females respond differently, students therefore need to examine the range of different subjectivities associated with gender portrayals in the media.

Viewers or readers therefore often construct stances related to conventions and codes in opposition to other, opposing groups' stances. In Margaret Finders's (1997) study of two early adolescent female groups, the "social queens" and the "tough cookies," group members solidified their allegiance to their own group by deliberately responding in ways opposed to social practices of members of the other group. The "social queens" were actively engaged in social matters within and outside of school. They also defined their identities in opposition to the "tough cookies"— girls who were less socially involved in the school, through the use of exclusionary categories: "woof-woofs" (as not being physically attractive), "babies," "dogs," "little girls," and "kids." Finders cites the following example of the "social queens" responding to some teen magazines:

> *Lauren*: What do they [the "woof-woofs"] read? They probably just read books. They have nothing better to do.
> *Angie*: They probably don't even read these [holds up a copy of *Sassy*].
> *Tiffany*: Did you guys see this? God, I'm gonna get some of these [holds open a page from YM and points to a pair of pants]. Isn't this so cool? (p. 58)

This group also referred to the fact that their teachers and parents disapproved of their reading teen zines. "She [mother] wants me to read books, but I read *Sassy*" (p. 58). The very fact that they read these zines serves to display their defiance of adult authority. As Finders notes, "Zine readings serve adolescents to unite particular groups of peers and exclude others, serving as a powerful tool to mark insiders and outsiders" (p. 58). In themselves, the magazines have no meaning. However, as markers of social status, they serve to fulfill the group's objective of establishing their collective group identity. The "social queens" were using their responses to establish a set of conventions and codes associated with popularity in their peer-group world.

In studying group responses to the media, ethnographers are therefore interested in defining those conventions and codes constituting appropriate ways of responding to texts. They note instances in which responses are perceived to be deviant or inappropriate, suggesting that certain conventions and codes are operating. For example, in studying *Star Trek* fan clubs, Jenkins (1992) found that these clubs established certain norms for constructing their own edited video versions of programs to display at meetings or conferences.

DISCOURSES

Media ethnographers also examine adherence to certain conventions and codes as implying underlying ideological perspectives or discourses. These discourses of science, law, religion, business, romance, medicine, education, and so on constitute commonsense, taken-for-granted assumptions operating within a world (Fairclough, 1995; Gee, 1996; Lemke, 1995). They operate as "identity tool kits" (Gee, 1996) that define one's identity as a scientist, athlete, politician, teacher, historian, priest, union member, public relations person, or corporate executive. As van Dijk (1997) notes, a person's social identity is constituted by ideology or discourse as "a basic system that allows their members to act as such, to know what is good and bad for them, and what to do in situations of conflict, threat, or complication" (p. 27). Lawyers, plaintiffs, defendants, law enforcement officials, witnesses, and jury members construct their identities, rights, and responsibilities by acquiring and mastering practices constituted by a legal discourse. Future lawyers acquire this discourse through highly competitive, rigorous training in law school (Gee, 1996).

Media ethnographers are interested in how the discourses operating within an activity or social context shape viewers' or readers' responses to a media text (Beach, 1997). As Rose and Friedman (1997) posit, "while the discourses of film and television construct preferred positions for the spectator, each viewer is always simultaneously interpolated by a number of discourses (cultural, institutional, personal) which define him as a subject and have an impact on his reading of any text" (p. 12).

Positioning of Viewers or Readers through Discourses

Critical discourse analyses of media texts (Bell & Garrett, 1998; Fairclough, 1995; Hodge & Kress, 1988) theorize about how viewers are positioned by various discourses to adopt certain stances or ideological orientations, theorizing that often does not account for how actual viewers or readers respond in contexts shaped by various discourses. In a study of viewers' responses to the evening soap opera program, *Dallas*, Katz and Liebes (1990) found that viewers in the United States, Russia, Israel, and Saudi Arabia generated quite different responses to the same programs, differences reflecting different discourses or ideological perspectives. The Americans and the Israelis interpreted the characters' actions in terms of various psychological needs and themes. The Russians interpreted the characters' actions in terms of thematic beliefs. The Saudi Arabians interpreted the characters in terms of moral issues associated with family values. These different groups of viewers therefore constructed meanings of *Dallas* consistent with their own ideological orientation.

Media ethnographers also examine how viewers or readers are positioned to adopt certain stances consistent with the discourses or ideological forces operating within an activity. Viewers and readers adopt ideological stances in opposition to stances based on discourses they are resisting. In a study of a group of communication studies graduate students who met weekly to watch television as a social event, John Fiske (1994) examined the group's responses to *Married . . . With Children*, a Fox Network sitcom parody of family values with a focus on sexuality. Consistent with an academic discourse of critical analysis, these graduate students adopted their own critical stance in opposition to the discourses of merchandising and conservative religious values associated with viewer response to the program. Fiske analyzed the students' use of intertextual references to the discourse of merchandising inherent in the program's advertisements. Because the students often purchased McDonalds hamburgers to eat during the viewing of the program, they made comments about or parodied McDonalds ads' as representing an attempt to appeal to adolescents as consumers. The graduate students referred to a conservative group whose objections to the "immoral" portrayal of sexuality on the program led them to launch a campaign to boycott companies who advertise on the program, objections based on a "family values" discourse of conservative political and religious values. Through these intertextual references to discourses of merchandising and political conservatism, these students were constructing their own critical stance in opposition to these discourses.

Viewers may prefer to view programs consistent with their own ideological predispositions. A study of 25 elderly women representing a range of different socioeconomic groups who were fans of the program, *Murder, She Wrote*, found that the women responded positively to the familiar, predictable storyline whose values were consistent with their own (Riggs, 1998). At the same time, there was some variation in their responses due to differences in class background. The upper-middle-class women identified strongly with the Angela Lansbury character, whom they valued for her independence. These women also enjoyed participating in the problem-solving processes inherent in the plot development. A group of African-American women responded more to the program's portrayal of anxieties about youth and crime in their own urban setting. Thus, despite the similar, ritual-like participation with the program, there were distinct differences in their responses that represented differences in their own purposes for viewing.

How Discourses Define Emotions or Intersubjective Relationships

Discourses also define how emotions or intersubjective relationships are valued in a particular group or community. A discourse of therapy constitutes readers' "emotional roles" (Buckingham, 1996, p. 58) as being "in touch with" their "inner needs" through responding to texts. Discourses of spirituality/therapy are often couched as ideologically pure or "monologic." As Bakhtin (1981) states, "monologic," authoritative discourse "demands our unconditional allegiance, permitting no play with its borders, no gradual and flexible transitions, no spontaneously creative stylized variance on it" (p. 343). In sharing their responses to a text in a therapy group, participants value expression of their own and others' emotional needs. For example, in a study of a series of Oprah Winfrey programs on the topic of race, Janice Peck (1994) found that Winfrey and the studio audience defined racial attitudes primarily in individualistic as opposed to institutional terms. They frequently provided testimonials about their own experiences of racial conflict, leading them to espouse the belief that if people just recognized each other's humanity, there would be less racism. This discussion of racism as "cured" through confessions, release of anger, empathetic understanding of others, and positive human relations was assumed to have high appeal to the television audience. For Peck, this stance was constructed around a discourse of therapy in which racism is defined as an "illness" (Peck, 1994).

Similarly, a study of middle-class female readers' responses to self-help books (Grodin, 1991) found that these readers shared their empathy with portrayals of other women relying on their inner resources to cope with and solve problems. Then, in sharing their responses in groups, these women constructed their own narrative scenarios of transformation that celebrated the value of self-reliance. As Grodin (1991) argues, "women's stories about the use of self-help offered countless tales of what might be called the interruption of inherited social routines—everything from feeling freer to rejecting inappropriate dating partners to realizing that married women need not do all the cooking and cleaning" (p. 415).

On the other hand, some women in the study were bothered by what they perceived to be a contradictory message in these books—a tension between a rigid insistence on the need for self-reliance and the need for relationships with others. Admonitions against "women who love too much" were weighed against the idea of interdependence with others. As one woman commented:

> The book said that if you want to start a new relationship, you ought to be an eagle, alone, and enjoying life by yourself, and then find yourself another eagle, or you really aren't going to have a very good relationship. The problem is that there aren't that many people in the world who are just wonderful and perfect and whole, who are so independent and so happy. (p. 419)

In questioning the "individualistic" value assumptions inherent in the discourse of self-help, these women were recognizing that their own needs may not be met by calls for self-reliance. This created a tension between a therapeutic discourse of self-reliance and an alternative discourse of community and interdependence, a tension that led them to reflect on the limitations of therapeutic discourse.

In contrast to these therapeutic discourses, the largely male sports talk show is constituted by a discourse of masculine gender identity that values sharing of technical expertise about players, rules, and "stats" (Sabo & Jansen, 1998). Participants also celebrate the value of competitiveness and hard work, and generally avoid topics related to emotional, interpersonal matters associated with the "feminine". In their analysis of the discourses constituting television sports, Rose and Friedman (1997) found that male viewers often experienced a "distracted, identificatory, and dialogic spectatorship which may be understood as a masculine counterpart to soap opera's 'maternal gaze'" (p. 4).

Analyses of viewer/reader discourses may also examine conflicts between competing discourses regarding the meaning of media texts. One study of letters written by members of the *E.C. Comic Book* Fan Club during the 1950s found that these members would frequently parody the language and emotions of those who were engaged in a moral crusade to ban comic books for their effects on children (Adler-Kassner, 1997). These fan-club members were ridiculing the assumption that reading *E.C. Comic Books* would have a corrupting influence on their readers. For example, one letter stated:

> Your stories are the most revolting, the most repulsive, the most disgusting stories I have ever read. When I read your magazine, I get sick to my stomach. I'm not alone in this opinion. All my friends think the same thing. Keep up the good work. (p. 115)

Adler-Kassner (1997) posits that these letters parodied a discourse of moral outrage and fear prevalent during the 1950s regarding the seductive powers of these comic books. To counter this moral crusade, both fans and producers formulated their own defense of comic books as serving to create a tight-knit community of avid readers who were appreciative of the intelligence and wit of the writing in these comic books.

Television Viewing and a Discourse of Class

Another discourse shaping viewers' and readers' activity is that of socioeconomic class. In her study of the television viewing practices of retired persons living in an upscale retirement home, Karen Riggs (1998) found that its largely upper-middle-class residents selectively watched certain programs in order to be able to share their responses with other residents. Riggs describes their viewing practices:

> A man watches PBS's concert with the world's most famous tenors not because he particularly enjoys it but because he knows his dinner companions the next day will consider it worthy of

discussion. A women switches on Larry King Live in the evening because her neighbor mentions that she has read somewhere that attorney general nominee Zoe Baird will take phone calls from the public. (p. 95)

The residents preferred programs such as documentaries on PBS that provided them with a larger, global perspective on social and political issues. They perceived themselves as concerned, informed citizens who wanted to maintain an active involvement both in the retirement community and in national political affairs. They treated their viewing as an active investment of their time in acquiring useful information as opposed to passive consumption of television.

Programs that appealed to these viewers could be "characterized by an aesthetic element of 'class' that attracts the Woodglen residents. The urbane people on these programs use language well, display critical thinking skill, approach events and issues with a degree of emotional distance, and otherwise signify affluence" (p. 64). Drawing on Herbert Gans's notion of a "taste public," Riggs perceived the residents as a "taste public" "that exercises certain values with regard to cultural forms such as music, art, literature, drama, criticism, news and the media [that appeals to an] overlapping high and upper-middle-class taste culture occupied by Woodglenners [that] privileges the elite forms of television, such as Masterpiece Theater, as well as what Woodglenners take to be 'serious' nonfiction content" (pp. 64–65).

These, then, are the different components of a viewing activity that could serve as the basis of media ethnographies. I now turn to considering ways of implementing media ethnographies in the classroom.

APPLYING THE COMPONENTS OF ACTIVITY TO RESPONSE TO MEDIA

Prior to conducting media ethnographies of viewers' or readers' responses to media, students may discuss how the different components described in the previous section shape their responses to media. By learning to apply these different components as a framework for understanding their own responses, in conducting media ethnographies, they may then apply that framework to others' responses. Students may also begin to examine the interrelationships between the different components of activity.

Responding to the Film Genre of the Unemployed British Worker

One illustration of students' application of the components could be their responses to a series of films made in the 1990s about unemployed British workers— *The Full Monty*, *Brassed Off*, *The Van*, or *Scrapper*. In these films, the workers' tools/genres are perceived to be irrelevant to the new "service/information" economy. In their previous jobs, usually as steelworkers, they had acquired a set of tools/genres that served them well in their jobs. They could provide for their families at a modest standard of living. After they lose their jobs, they can no longer find equivalent jobs in their economically depressed towns. They lack tools or technological training necessary for acquiring new jobs. They begin to perceive little purpose in life, leading to a diminished sense of self-worth, depression, family conflicts, and attempted suicides.

In *Brassed Off*, the workers, whose coal mine is being shut down, continue to play in a brass band as they compete to earn a bid to the national championship. They are fighting a losing battle to keep the mine open by working against a vote to accept severance pay. They continue to practice in their band knowing that once the mine is closed down, they can no longer afford to continue to play in the band. One female band member, who works for management as a surveyor, is caught between her allegiance to these systems and is forced to leave the band. However, once she discovers that her work is fraudulent since management had always planned to shut down the mine, she quits her job. Meanwhile, the workers vote to accept the severance pay, the mine is shut down, and, despite winning a semifinal contest, the band can no longer participate in the final contest for lack of funds. The female band member then donates the funds and the band wins the final contest. After winning the contest, the band leader gives a speech in which he denounces the Thatcher capitalist economy that has led to the mine closures. While participation in their winning band provides a newly found sense of dignity, the sad irony of the film is that these tools will not transfer to the world of work, an illustration of the lack of transfer of tools from one activity to another.

Similarly, in *The Van*, two laid-off factory workers find an abandoned truck, which they transform into a mobile restaurant. This requires them to learn a set of new tools associated with managing their own business through collaborative decision making. It also requires them to redefine their identities around expressing their feelings about their close-knit relationships as friends versus co-workers. Their momentary success is short-lived because they fall back on previous tools—one of them decided to go on strike. Moreover, they are not aware of the need to comply with governmental sanitary regulations, and their business is shut down.

In *The Full Monty*, when a group of men lose their jobs, they begin to practice for a male-stripper show. They must rely on a totally different set of tools—their dancing ability and male sexuality, to achieve their object of appealing to a female audience. This requires them to adopt a different set of rules and community structure from those operating in their factory jobs, rules and structures based on their interpersonal skills and physical appearance. While they retain some of the hierarchical structure operating in the factory community, their former boss, a member of the group, must now assume a role involving equal status with other group members, and they construct a new egalitarian structure consistent with the principle that "we're all in this together." However, as in *Brassed Off*, their newly acquired tools have little relevance to succeeding in the workplace.

Students could apply the different components of activity as a framework for describing their responses to these films, drawing connections to similar activities in their own lives. Students may first identify the different components of the films:

- Object/purpose: the lack of a sense of purpose in life driving an activity, resulting in the need to create a new activity with a new sense of purpose. For example, the activity of organizing the male-stripper show gives the group of workers a sense of a shared mission and group camaraderie. In reflecting on their own experiences of engaging in activities, students may recall their experience of anxiety associated with activities in which they lacked a clear sense of purpose. They may then connect that sense of anxiety to the characters' own sense of helplessness in being unemployed.

- Tools/genres: the need to acquire new tools/genres to achieve new objects/purposes, for example, learning to use word-of-mouth advertising to lure customers to the mobile restaurant in *The Van*. Students may recall instances of acquiring new purpose-driven tools/genres, for example, learning to construct a class Web page to display their work on a study of their town's pollution record. Students may also focus their analyses of the particular uses of tools or genres within activities. In his communication class at the University of California, San Diego, Phil Agre asks students to conduct genre analyses of participants' uses and responses to genres within the contexts of communities, relationships, or activities. His students have written papers on rave posters, political advertisements, abstract expressionist paintings, graffiti, Filippino comedy films, how-to books, real estate ads, and anarchist propaganda posters (for sample student papers, see *http://communication.ucsd.edu/pagre/internet-papers.html*).

- Identities: the construction of new work identities that differ from their regular jobs, identities that require interpersonal skills or the use of new tools/genres. In *The Full Monty*, the male strippers learned to use music and dance to organize their production. Students may perceive connections with their own experience of moving from elementary school to middle or junior high school, and adopting the identity of students having to work with different teachers in different subject matter areas, requiring the use of new tools.

- Conventions/codes: the need to establish a set of conventions/codes for operating in a new activity, as portrayed in *Brassed Off*, in which the conductor established a strict set of rules for practice, rules that were difficult to follow once members lost their jobs. Students may describe similar experiences in having to adhere to a new set of conventions, for example, in becoming members of a youth organization or sports team.

- Discourses: the ideological tensions between discourses of management and economics that perceived the British plants, factories, or mines as inefficient, unproductive, and unprofitable versus the discourse of human labor that valued the work done in these plants, factories, or mines. Students may analyze the various discourses operating in media texts by, for example, moving through different television channels and describing the predominate discourses at work for each channel. For example:

Program	Discourses
Money Line/Wall Street Week	Economics/capitalism
Professional wrestling	Masculinity/war
Soap opera	Femininity/consumerism
Talk shows	Therapy
News analysis shows	Political analysis/management
Home Buyers Channel	Merchandising
Religious services	Religion/evangelical doctrine
Courtroom simulation	Legal
Local news	Community/medicine

Having applied these various concepts to their own responses, students can then turn to conducting media ethnographies of others' responses.

ETHNOGRAPHY AS INQUIRY: A PEDAGOGICAL JUSTIFICATION

One of the pedagogical values of ethnography is that it encourages students to engage in systematic, focused inquiry about the social world of viewers' media participation. Dennis Sumara (1996) argues that, in contrast to often superficial "touring" instructional approaches, a "dwelling" mode involves "living in a place with others with an attitude of caring and attention" (p. 160). In "dwelling" in a social world, students spend enough time in that world to get to know a world in some depth through the use of what Sumara defines as "hermeneutic inquiry" which "seeks to locate sites for inquiry that situate interpreters in the middle of the activities related to some topic of mutual interest" (p. 127). That is, students gain new insights into how viewers and readers actively respond to media and what readers and viewers learn through that experience about themselves and the world.

In planning their studies, rather than define a study simply in terms of predetermined hypotheses, students need to be open to acquiring new insights into viewer responses that emerge during the study, responses that may challenge students' predispositions and assumptions. As James Spradley (1980) notes, "Fieldwork involves the disciplined study of what the world is like to people who have learned to see, hear, speak, think and act in ways that are different. Rather than *studying people*, ethnography means *learning from people*" (p. 14).

For Sumara (1996), "hermeneutic inquiry" also "allows the path of inquiry to be 'laid while walking'. . . depending on interpretations given to questions that 'present themselves' rather than questions which are predetermined" (pp. 126–127). This suggests that students formulate their questions, concerns, problems, issues, or "wonderings" (Short & Harste, 1995) as they are studying viewers' construction of media. Students may identify certain questions, for example, whether young children, in viewing Saturday morning cartoons, articulate any responses to those cartoons to themselves or others. And, as they are observing a particular site, they continue to revise or formulate new questions, concerns, problems, or "wonderings," particularly when they note conflicting or competing social agendas (Mosenthal, 1998). They also use the different components of the activity model to generate questions.

In conducting these studies, students draw on some of the methods used in qualitative or ethnographic research on methods to study social contexts or sites. Glesne and Peshkin's (1992) *Becoming Qualitative Researchers* is a readable introduction appropriate for even high school students. Bruhn and Jankowski's (1991) *A Handbook of Qualitative Methodologies for Mass Communication Research* and Lindlof's (1995) *Qualitative Communication Research Methods* contain discussions of methods specific to qualitative research on response to media.

Students may select certain groups such as classes, computer newsgroups, book clubs, or other sites of viewer/reader activity for observation. They may observe previously formed groups. Or, they may create their own groups, asking students to share their responses with each other. Given the usual practice of a group of students renting a video, students may ask their friends to share their responses to the video. Or, students may want to study their younger siblings' response to television because they can observe and interview their siblings in their own home (for examples of ethnographic studies on children's responses to television, see Buckingham, 1996, and Palmer, 1986). It is important that students have easy access to groups. Students often find that studying an Internet chat group organized around a particular television program represents a convenient site to study participants' responses.

Students may also study instances in which participants are producing their own media, for example, a video documentary or school newspaper. In doing so, they may examine how producers assume the role of surrogate audiences, assessing their actual audiences' own potential responses (Radway, 1988).

It is also useful for students to have access to a "cultural broker" who provides the students with an "insider's," behind-the-scenes perspectives on a group's activities. For example, in studying the *Star Trek* fan clubs, Henry Jenkins (1992) worked with some key members of these clubs to gain access to their meetings or conferences. Similarly, in studying women's responses to romance novels, Janice Radway (1984) worked with a bookstore owner who sold romance novels to her customers and who was familiar with her customers' reading interests.

In some cases, students are members of the group they are studying. In assuming this role of a participant/observer, students need to reflect on how their own relationship toward that group—as an "outsider" or "insider"—shapes their perceptions of the group. As an "outsider," they may not be familiar with a group's inner workings and routines. As an "insider," they may be a fish in water, and may have difficulty standing back and assuming an "outsider's" stance required to perceive the group as a micro culture. They may therefore want to share their perceptions with someone who was not familiar with the group. Ideally, students should embrace both of these perspectives by experiencing what it is like to be a group member and by standing back to assume a spectator stance.

Students also need to reflect on their own assumptions or predispositions related to the group or media they are studying (Chiseri-Strater & Sunstein, 1997). Students often bring stereotypical beliefs and attitudes toward certain types of groups or media. If they simply impose those beliefs and attitudes onto their participants, they will only reconfirm those beliefs and attitudes. On the other hand, if they suspend or bracket their assumptions or predispositions and carefully attend to their participants' responses, they may then be open to changing their beliefs and attitudes. In her study, Radway (1984) initially assumed that the women in her study were passively accepting the patriarchal values portrayed in romance novels. However, after discovering that the women often used their reading of romance novels as a means of expressing their own individuality within the home, she shifted her attitudes toward these romance novel readers.

In cases where they are doing extensive observations and interviews with a selected group of participants, students should develop an informed consent form to be signed by the participants in their study. This form stipulates that participants will not be placed at risk in any way, that they can withdraw from the study at any time, that they will not be identified by name, that their confidentiality will be protected, and that field notes or interview tapes referring to them will be destroyed after completion of the study. By granting their informed consent, participants are more likely to cooperate in a study knowing that their confidentiality will be protected.

In observing groups, students use field notes, mapping, or photos to record perceptions of viewer activities (Glesne & Peshkin, 1992). They note specific instances of viewers' physical participation or social interaction, and then reflect on the meaning of that participation or interaction. For example, in observing their family's viewing habits, they may note that male adults attempt to dictate television program selection for a family, in some cases, by not letting others have the remote control (Morley, 1986). Or, they note that children or adolescents challenge parental authority by selecting music, programs, or Internet sites as a way of defining their own sense of independence (Moores, 1993).

Students also record group discussions of their viewing or reading, and then create a transcript of that discussion for further analysis of the participants' verbal responses. In analyzing these discussions, students determine the extent to which each person participates, the types of responses employed (engagement, description, interpretation, connection, analysis of context, or judgment), the degree of elaboration of responses, the use of intertextual links, the stances adopted, or the conventions and codes constituting appropriate responses (Beach & Hynds, 1991).

Interviewing also plays a central role in gaining insights into viewers' or readers' perceptions of a viewing or reading activity (Lindlof, 1995; Mishler, 1986). In some cases, "ethnographic" or "informal conversational interviews" (Patton, 1990, pp. 281–282) involve the use of casual conversation with participants often during the viewing or reading activity. The success of these informal interviews depends on the student's ability to note particular, momentary aspects of a participant's talk that peaks that student's interest. More formal interviews revolve around prepared questions designed to understand participants' perceptions of a viewing or reading activity. Based on previous analysis of participants' response transcripts, it is often useful to ask participants to elaborate on or explain particularly interesting re-sponses. Participants could also be asked to provide narrative recollections of their viewing or reading experiences, for example, recalling past instances of group viewing of a particular television program. Or, participants may respond in focus groups, which, in working with adolescents, often provides insights into how participants adopt certain shared group stances reflecting conventions, codes, or discourses.

In analyzing their data, students attempt to define consistent patterns that repre-sent certain practices for constructing the meaning of an activity. They may also apply the different components of the model in discussing strategies for construct-ing this meaning.

STUDENT ANALYSES OF COMPONENTS OF VIEWER ACTIVITIES

I now turn to some examples of my own university students' media ethnography studies to illustrate their use of the components to frame their own studies. These media ethnographies were conducted by students as an optional final project for a course entitled *Teaching Film, Television, and Media Studies*, a graduate course designed primarily for secondary English teachers. [The textbooks for the course included Teasley and Wilder's (1997) *Reel Conversations: Reading Films with Young Adults* and required handouts that include sample published media ethnog-raphies.] By conducting their own studies in this course, teachers may then model their use of various research techniques for their students.

The objectives of this course are to help teachers:

- Understand different theoretical justifications of film/media study

- Understand and apply different critical approaches to studying media: aesthetic, formalist, genre, technical, psychological, critical theory, cultural studies, feminist
- Understand the purpose for the use of different film/video techniques and techniques for teaching these techniques to students
- Use video production to teach students video/film technique
- Demonstrate the ability to conduct critical analysis of media representation, invited stances, value assignments, and genre characteristics
- Develop instructional activities to involve students in actively responding to and critically analyzing media texts
- Understand the economic and consumer forces shaping commercial media
- Critically analyze representations of gender, class, and race in the media
- Define similarities and differences between the experiences of different types of media and draw implications for instruction
- Determine the social uses of media by adolescents and ways of building on those social uses in order to motivate students

Topics and related activities included in this course are as follows:

- *Justifying film and television study* in the curriculum; response to film; social and cultural schemata and film meaning; the psychology of the film experience; the "image-sound skim."
- *Film/video techniques*: analysis of shots, angles, color, lighting, framing, rhythm, sound, music, editing. (Activity: pick a television program or movie of which you have a video copy. Analyze a couple of scenes and analyze the techniques being used in those scenes. Describe specific examples of camera shots, angles, color, lighting, framing, rhythm, sound, music, and editing techniques. Describe the purposes for the use of these techniques in terms of the program's or movie's larger purpose. Bring the tape to class for sharing of your analysis of those scenes.)
- *"Viewer-response approach"*: constructing viewer guides; facilitating discussions of viewing. Fostering critical response to the media: analyzing value assumptions and media representations. (Activity: select a certain phenomenon or type as portrayed in the media: teachers, men, women, nature, "the city," the elderly, crime, adolescents, "vacations," schools, love, religion, sex, sports, and so on, and describe how that phenomenon is portrayed in some television shows, films, magazines, or newspapers. Describe the value assumptions underlying these portrayals.)
- *Media ethnographies* and the components of viewing activities: objects/purpose, identities, conventions/codes, discourses. [Activity: observe or recall a group of persons who are/were viewing television, a video, or who are actively participating in constructing media. (You may also "lurk" on the Internet/newsgroups' responses to a television program.) Describe their re-

sponses and how their shared group stances or discourses shaped those responses.]

- *Methods for conducting media ethnographies*: acquiring participants' permissions; eliciting oral or written responses; analysis of responses; interviewing participants about their responses in terms of how their knowledge, attitudes, beliefs, purposes, gender, and so on influence their responses; writing final research reports describing participants, viewers, setting, tasks, and methods of analysis; reporting open-ended quotes that illustrate certain patterns of response.

- *Critical discourse analysis/genre analysis* of texts; analysis of discourses shaping responses to film/media; genre analysis of conventional media forms. [Activity: select a film or video that is representative of a certain genre type (comedy, detective, spy thriller, mystery, game show, sports broadcast, gangster, Western, musical, talk show, medical drama, news, and so on). Analyze the various discourse and/or genre characteristics: typical roles, settings, language/discourses, storyline features (what the typical problem is, who solves the problem, and how), and value assumptions.]

- *Semiotic/narrative analysis*: determining underlying value assumptions in images or storylines. [Activity: select some magazines for adolescents or adults and/or television ads and analyze the ads: images, representations, discourses, construction of target audience(s), invited stances, and your own responses.]

- *Intertextuality/intermediality/film/video adaptations*: organizing instruction around thematic or topical links between media experiences; defining differences between experiences of film, television, theater, radio, mixed media forms; teaching film adaptations of literature. [Activity: recall a film/video adaptation of literature and describe the differences in experiences of the two (e.g., "Clueless," "The Crucible," "Persuasion," "Emma," "Sense and Sensibility," "The English Patient," "Hamlet").]

- *Television news*: analysis of the purposes of news; economics of television news; creating a sense of shared community; viewing news as ritual. [Activity: keep a viewing log recording the stories covered and number of minutes per story. Then reflect on the experience of watching television news: discuss the rhetorical appeals or strategies employed to influence an audience's beliefs and attitudes; describe the use of techniques and editing (selection versus exclusion of material) designed to influence the audience.]

Each of these topics and activities provides teachers with some background concepts and experiences related to conducting their media ethnographies.

SAMPLE STUDENT MEDIA ETHNOGRAPHIES

To illustrate how students applied their understanding of the different components of viewing activity, I will now describe some of the studies my students conducted in this course.

Some students were interested in determining viewers' underlying purposes for viewing. In one study, Cheryl Reinertsen (1993) analyzed a group of her daughter's female friends' weekly viewing of two television programs, *Beverly Hills 90210* and *Melrose Place*. In planning her study, Reinertsen was interested in determining reasons for their willingness to meet weekly to discuss the program despite their otherwise busy schedule. She assumed that the activity of the weekly viewing meetings itself must hold some appeal. Having analyzed some selective shows of these two programs, she also had some assumptions about potential responses to the portrayal of gender identities and romantic relationships. Based on these assumptions, she formulated some interview questions to determine their purpose for their weekly meetings. She then taped all of the weekly meetings, and interviewed the participants separately regarding their perceptions of their responses.

She found that one of their primary purposes for the females' weekly meetings was to share their perceptions and judgments about the characters' actions as a means of reflecting on their own lives. Because the characters were involved in similar issues or dilemmas in their relationships, the participants could vicariously examine their own issues or dilemmas through talking about the characters' issues or dilemmas.

Reinertsen was also interested in her participants' interpretation of the "codes of beautification" (Christian-Smith, 1993) operating in their responses to the female characters. She found that, in some cases, participants accepted the prevailing focus on physical appearance as central to attracting males. In other cases, participants interrogated the female characters' obsession with their weight, dress, and makeup.

Reinertsen also examined how the participants applied their own values or discourses in responding to the two programs. She analyzed transcripts of the discussions and interviews by focusing on participants' judgments of characters' actions. She also focused on their explanations for characters' actions, explanations that reflected underlying value assumptions. She found that members applied their own beliefs and attitudes to judge the characters' actions. They "liked Donna because she is nice and she doesn't do anything wrong; Andrea because she doesn't care only about her clothes and appearance; Billy because he is true and the most caring, ideal, and sensitive; Jo because she is her own person and she stands up for herself; Matt because he is a peacemaker and serves other people" (Reinertsen, 1993, p. 8). They "disliked Amanda because she is anorexic, out for herself, and ruthless and arrogant and Kimberly because she's a weakling" (p. 9). Participants judged the characters as irresponsible for not being more concerned with their education or future career. For example, in one episode of *90210*, a female college student becomes engaged to an older man. The group shared their displeasure with her decision to become engaged: "'She likes him just because he's rich.' 'She should stay in college.' 'She's too young.' and 'Wait until her parents find out. They will really be mad'" (p. 14). As one participant noted, "college age students should not be engaged because they are too young. If they do get engaged, they will drop out. Education is important, love can wait" (p. 22).

For Reinertsen, these judgments of characters' actions consistently reflected a discourse of achievement-orientation and the value of long-term sacrifice of immediate emotional needs in order to obtain economic success. She linked this discourse of achievement-orientation to the participants' upper-middle-class backgrounds and concern with achieving success within the context of traditional institutional norms. She also concluded that this ritual-like gathering provided a forum for participants to express and verify their shared values or discourses regarding appropriate practices within male/female relationships.

In a related study, Aaron Cato (1996) examined the responses of two separate groups of viewers, a group of three black males' and a group of three black females' responses to the movie adaptation of Terry McMillan's novel, *Waiting to Exhale*, that features four, strong black women and their relationships with men. Cato recorded their responses and also interviewed participants about their perceptions of their own as well as their group's responses. He analyzed participants' uses of different types of responses, as well as the differences between the two groups in terms of gender-based stances and attitudes. He found that the females identified strongly with the female characters. In contrast, the males were more critical of the negative portrayals of males in the movie, perceiving the lack of positive characters as a personal attack on themselves: "'She portrayed us as no good men who were afraid of responsibility'" (Cato, 1996, p. 10). The females disagreed with the males' critique. As one noted, "'I don't think it was the down play of Black men in general; it was just those men in particular whom she chose to write about'" (p. 11). In response to Cato's question as to whether "the women were unhappy because they didn't have a man" (p. 11), the females argued that the women could achieve happiness without men, while the men argued that the women were unhappy "'because they could not find a man'" (p. 11). Cato concluded that the gender-based nature of the discourses operating in the two separate groups influenced the shared stances adopted in each group.

In another study, Rick Lybeck (1996) examined his own family members' responses to a televised baseball game. He recorded and took notes on his father's and brothers' responses to a series of baseball games. He analyzed these data in terms of what aspects of the game the participants focused on, their physical behaviors in responding together as a group, and any ritual-like patterns of response.

Lybeck found that his participants, all of whom were or had been baseball players, responded to the game by vicariously experiencing the actions of the players. They used their viewing to fulfill the purposes of a "companionship dimension" (Wenner & Gantz, 1998, p. 237) to share time with other family members. In some cases, the actual physical act of responding—of standing up and swinging as if they were a hitter or giving "high-fives" to each other as if they were on the field—was part of a shared drama of mutual engagement in the game. Through mimicking the ballplayers on the field, they were vicariously playing out their own enjoyment of the game as a form of male bonding. The participants also frequently adopted the "sports-talk" lingo of the television commentators to formulate their own descriptions of the game. Lybeck notes that this male sports talk serves to define their social identities as avid fans:

> The main feature of the ESPN update was Barry Bonds having hit his 300th and 301st home runs earlier that afternoon. The significance of this was that Bonds joined an elite group of three other players who have in their careers hit 300 or more home runs and stolen 300 or more bases. A trivia question was put: who are the other guys. There were three generations of ball players present, two father-and-son combinations, quizzing each other on father-and-son baseball trivia; it truly was a question made for them. The TV medium as focused on in this informal ethnography was something that was *integrated* into a male bonding setting, but not necessarily central to the bonding. TV enabled the males to extend their baseball enjoyment and to affirm their identities as baseball players following in the footsteps of baseball fathers. (Lybeck, 1996, p. 12)

Lybeck's analysis points to the need to understand television sports-viewing activity as central to constructing male relationships.

Some of my students have studied how adolescents define their identities through intertextual links between practices portrayed in the media and their own social practices. In one study, Louise Covert (1997) examined the intertextual links employed by four high school students. She analyzed intertextual links in students' writings and interviewed them about how these links reflected their experiences in the social worlds of peers, family, school, and work, as well as their reading and viewing activities. One of her students, Anna, employed a range of intertextual links associated with her "Dark-Sider" identity: those who wear only black clothes, color their hair, and wear dark red or black lipstick and heavy black eye makeup. Anna defined links between the gothic, macabre elements of Anne Rice's books and her own beliefs in the value of unconventional behavior. As Anna noted in an interview:

> Anne Rice is the idol of all the gothic and the children of darkness [Dark-Siders]. In *Gothic* magazine there's all these people with black make-up and hair and spikes. [My friends and I talk about] the *Vampire Chronicles*. We're like, "I can't believe he did that!" When I read these novels it's like I'm living in a fantasy world. Anne Rice is someone I would aspire to be like. I would like to be like her. (Covert, 1997, p. 23)

In writing short stories, Anna draws on her genre knowledge associated with narratives depicting gothic, supernatural worlds and alternative forms of society. One of her stories, "Melinda," is set in the early 1900s in a small town on the edge of a dark, haunted forest called "Witches Forest." Trevor, a young male, has been cast out of his home and, after days of going hungry, wanders into the forest, where he meets a witch who saves him. In an interview about the story, Anna comments that she is "more like Trevor" than Melinda. The character of Melinda seems to be derived from Anne Rice's female vampire characters. In resisting the stereotype of the evil witch, she portrays Melinda as benevolent, a parallel to her own experiences of being misperceived as "some devil worshipper . . . and I [think], 'Yeah, black means devil, I guess'" (Covert, 1997, p. 20). She also described a link between Trevor and a rock star, Trent Reznor, whom she perceived as someone who is "true to himself" (p. 21). The fact that Trevor is an outcast is connected to her own identity as a "Dark-Sider." Covert concluded that Anna, as well as her three other participants, frequently use intertextual links to their media experiences both in their writing and in their perceptions of their own experiences.

Some students also analyzed the conventions and codes constituting appropriate responses in a discussion. For example, Judy Ward (1996) studied computer newsgroup participants' responses to the television program, *X-Files*. Ward asked participants if they were interested in answering some questions, and 35 participants provided her with answers to her questions. When asked what they liked about the newsgroup, participants noted that they "enjoy the discussion threads concerning plot and character development, the 'far out' theories members propose, news about production issues, 'insider information you would otherwise never hear about,' and the stars' talk show appearances" (p. 12).

She found that certain types of postings that were considered inappropriate included making irrelevant, off-topic statements (considered as "dreck" or "drivel"), bashing or spreading false rumors about the two celebrity stars of the show, positing sexually explicit or violent messages, or misusing the newsgroup. When a participant began spreading false rumors about the female star of the show, she was immediately castigated and told "either get with it and get some netiquette or please keep your computer turned off" (p. 8).

Members gained status in the group by making frequent postings; being affiliated with the program; meeting one of the stars; selling magazines, scripts, autographs, or T-shirts; or sharing videos of programs. They also gained status by making intertextual links between the program and other television programs. The practices reflect the value group members place on assisting each other as group members. They also sought out verification of their feelings, asking each other if "someone feels this way" or "am I the only one who feels bad." Based on her analysis of the group members' adherence to certain norms and conventions, Judy inferred that "alt.tv.x-files is a micro culture with its own genre of literature, myths, and mores, embedded in larger cultures of paranoia and distrust of big government and a general fan culture which becomes deeply connected to entertainment icons."

Other students were interested in how discourses shaped responses. Timothy Rohde (1996) analyzed the responses of readers of romance novels produced by one publisher for an evangelical Christian audience, Heartsong Press. To examine the discourses portrayed in these novels' development, drawing on Christian-Smith (1993) and Radway (1984), he analyzed the plot development of 110 of these novels. He found that they contained few references to sexuality, a marked contrast to recent Harlequin and Silhouette romance novels. For evangelical Christians who objected to the trend toward "steamier" romance novels, these Christian romance novels provided a more "pure" alternative. In contrast to the typical romance novel plot development (Christian-Smith, 1993; Radway, 1984), the Heartsong romance novel heroine initially expresses doubt in her faith. She then meets a "good man," whom she believes is not a Christian. She subsequently experiences a conversion, removing her doubt in her faith. The heroine is then rescued from peril by the man, and she learns of his true nature as a Christian. It is only after they marry that they have sex. While the romance novel is designed to celebrate women's role as a nurturer who transforms a more impersonal hero into a more caring person (Radway, 1984), the Heartsong novels are designed to be more didactic and morally uplifting, serving to reify readers' allegiances to evangelical Christian beliefs.

Interviews with avid readers of these novels indicated that they did not have to be concerned about being 'on guard' when reading what they perceived to the "pure" subject matter in these novels. Some preferred the historical romance novels because they were set in a past perceived to be less corrupt than the current period. They also responded positively to the novels' didactic messages, noting that reading these books enhanced their Christian faith. These books also appealed to the conservative Christian's belief in the value of the past over the present. As Rohde (1996) notes:

> To the mind of many conservative Christians, the past represents a "golden" time when society was less immoral and generally safer. So, by reading about the exploits of these heroines in the past, these readers are safer than reading about contemporary heroines who would perceivably face the same immoral society the readers face. In this way, the past becomes even more romantic as these readers imagine a time when their conservative morality would not be challenged as stridently as they perceive society to challenge it today. (p. 14)

WHAT MY STUDENTS LEARNED FROM CONDUCTING MEDIA ETHNOGRAPHIES

In conducting these media ethnographies, my students learned several things about how viewers and readers construct meaning through participation in response activities.

- *Meaning as socially or culturally constituted through activity.* These students recognized that the meaning of media texts lies not simply in texts or in viewers or readers, but rather in the social or cultural activity itself as the primary unit of analysis. Because these students are teachers, they recognized that, rather than have their students analyze media texts in a social vacuum, they needed to encourage their own pupils to examine how participation in viewing or reading activities shapes the meaning of responses. They also used their own studies to model the use of specific research strategies in conducting media ethnographies. And, within the social context of their own classes, they promoted pupil reflexivity about their responses by asking them to reflect on

how the different components of activity shaped the meaning of their responses within their own classroom group activities.

- *Construction of identities through responses.* My students learned that viewers
and readers construct and experiment with certain identities through their
responses. Lybeck recognized that his participants established their identities
through their shared participation with other male family members watching
a baseball game. Ward noted how newsgroup participants adopted roles
associated with summarizing storylines or maintaining decorum in the newsgroup. And Rohde learned that his avid romance novel readers affirmed their
allegiance as church members through resisting "hot" romance novels and
responding positively to the "pure" Christian novels. Examining how viewers
or readers constructed these identities also led my students to consider the
postmodern question as to whether these identities vary or are relatively
consistent across different contexts.

- *The influence of discourses or ideologies on responses.* My students also
recognized the importance of discourses or ideological forces on constituting
the meaning of viewing or reading activities. Reinertsen's adolescent females,
Cato's gender-based groups, Lybeck's family television viewers, and Rohde's
readers drew on discourses of gender to construct their response stances. They
also recognized how these discourses of gender intersect with other discourses. Reinertsen's viewers drew on discourses of class to judge female
characters' behaviors. Rohde's readers applied discourses of religion in responding to romance novels.

Again, as teachers, these students formulated instructional strategies to help their
pupils infer the discourses or ideologies constituting viewing or reading activities.
For example, Lybeck recognized the need for his own pupils, who frequently watch
television sports, to reflect on how the discourses of gender shape their responses.
They also recognized the need to help pupils interrogate activities constituted by
rigid, "monologic" (Bakhtin, 1981) discourses associated with controlled media
events (Dayan & Katz, 1992).

- *Defining intertextual links between real-world and virtual-world activities.* My students noted that their own pupils operate within a complex
network of different, competing activities operating within peer, family,
school, workplace, and community worlds (Dillon & Moje, 1998; Russell,
1997). They know that their own pupils have difficulty negotiating the
competing demands of these different worlds (Phelan, Davidson, & Yu,
1998). While they may assume high status in their peer-group world, they
may have little status in their school or family worlds. They therefore
perceived the need to formulate curriculum for designing literacy curriculum around helping pupils infer intertextual links between activities operating in these different worlds. This includes having pupils compare their own

and others' participation in peer group, family, school, workplace, and community worlds with their participation in the "virtual worlds" of media participation. For example, pupils may study their own participation in social activities, and then compare that participation to their virtual or vicarious participation in responding to television program or literature portrayal of similar social activities. Or, pupils may analyze the activity of their own workplace, and compare that activity to a study of their peers' construction of the virtual workplaces portrayed in television or literature. Through defining links between real-world and virtual-world activity, pupils may then reflect on their uses of tools/genres and their construction of identities across different worlds.

WHAT I'VE LEARNED FROM HAVING STUDENTS CONDUCT MEDIA ETHNOGRAPHIES

In assigning these media ethnographies in my course, I have learned that it's important to give students a lot of leeway in letting them formulate their own questions and methods of analysis. At the same time, I try to show them how to conduct these studies by sharing my own research experiences, particularly if I'm conducting a study as I'm teaching the course. In sharing my own experiences, I emphasize the need to bracket out one's predispositions and to be open to surprises or unexpected phenomena. I also emphasize the need to be open to finding a range of individual differences and variety within a response community. Too often students begin their studies assuming that they will find what they are looking for, and therefore are not attending to novel, unusual responses.

I have also found that students are more likely to be open to deviations from expectations and to attending to individual differences when they share their results with peers or conduct these studies in collaboration with others. When several students are looking at the same data, they are more likely to apply different perspectives, resulting in different interpretations.

I also find that I can use responses within our own class discussions to illustrate ways of analyzing responses. Because students share written responses on a course Web-based discussion site, I can print out their responses and describe ways of analyzing these responses within the context of stances adopted within the classroom community.

In the future, I hope to have more students' reports on Web pages so that instructors from other institutions can share examples of these reports with their own students.

REFERENCES

Adler-Kassner, L. (1997). "Why won't you just read it?": *E.C. Comic Book* readers and community in the 1950s. *Reader, 38/39*, 101–127.

Ang, I. (1985). *Watching "Dallas": Soap opera and the melodramatic imagination.* London: Methuen.

Ang, I. (1991). *Desperately seeking the audience.* London: Routledge.

Ayim, M. (1994). Knowledge through the grapevine: Gossip as inquiry. In R. Goodman & A. Ben-Ze'ev (Eds.), *Good gossip* (pp. 85–99). Lawrence: University of Kansas Press.

Bacon-Smith, C. (1992). *Enterprising women.* Philadelphia: University of Pennsylvania Press.

Bakhtin, M. (1981). *The dialogic imagination* (M. Holquist, Ed.). Austin: University of Texas Press.

Bazerman, C. (1994). Where is the classroom? In A. Freedman & P. Medway (Eds.), *Learning and teaching genre* (pp. 25–30). Portsmouth, NH: Heinemann.

Beach, R. (1997). Critical discourse theory and reader response: How discourses constitute reader stances and social contexts. *Reader, 37,* 1–26.

Beach, R., & Hynds, S. (1991). Research on response to literature. In R. Barr, M. Kamil, P. Mosenthal, & P. D. Pearson (Eds.), *Handbook of reading research* (pp. 453–491). London: Longman.

Bell, A., & Garrett, P. (Eds.). (1998). *Approaches to media discourse* (pp. 220–250). Oxford: Blackwell.

Bem, S. (1993). *The lenses of gender: Transforming the debate on sexual inequality.* New Haven: Yale University Press.

Bennett, T., & Woollacott, J. (1987). *Bond and beyond: The political career of a popular hero.* London: Methuen.

Berkenkotter, C., & Ravotas, D. (1997). Genre as tool in the transmission of practice over time and across professional boundaries. *Mind, Culture, and Activity, 4* (4), 256–274.

Bird, E. (1992). *For enquiring minds: A cultural study of supermarket tabloids.* Knoxville: University of Tennessee Press.

Brown, M. (Ed.). (1990). *Television and women's culture: The politics of the popular.* Thousand Oaks, CA: Sage.

Bruhn, K., & Jankowski, N. (1991). *A handbook of qualitative methodologies for mass communication research.* London: Routledge.

Buckingham, D. (1993). Boys' talk: Television and the policing of masculinity. In D. Buckingham (Ed.), *Reading audiences: Young people and the media* (pp. 89–115). New York: Manchester University Press.

Buckingham, D. (1996). *Moving images: Understanding children's responses to television.* New York: Manchester University Press.

Carbaugh, D. (1996). Mediating cultural selves: Soviet and American cultures in a televised "space-bridge." In D. Grodin & T. Lindlof (Eds.), *Constructing the self in a mediated world* (pp. 84–106). Thousand Oaks, CA: Sage.

Cato, A. (1996). *Waiting to Exhale ethnography.* Unpublished paper, University of Minnesota.

Cherland, M. (1994). *Private practices: Girls reading fiction and constructing identities.* London: Taylor & Francis.

Chiseri-Strater, E., & Sunstein, B. (1997). *Fieldworking: Reading and writing research.* Upper Saddle River, NJ: Prentice-Hall.

Christian-Smith, L. (Ed.). (1993). *Texts of desire: Essays on fiction, femininity and schooling.* London: Falmer.

Cole, M. (1996). *Cultural psychology: A once and future discipline.* Cambridge, MA: Harvard University Press.

Cole, M., & Engestrom, Y. (1993). A cultural-historical approach to distributed cognition. In G. Salomon (Ed.), *Distributed cognitions: Psychological and educational considerations* (pp. 1–46). London: Cambridge University Press.

Covert, L. (1997). *High school students' intertextual links in reading and writing.* Unpublished paper, University of Minnesota.

Crawford, C., & Hafsteinsson, S.B. (1997). *The construction of the viewer: Media ethnography and the anthropology of audiences.* Hojbjerg, Denmark: Intervention Press.

Davis, L. (1997). *The swimsuit issue and sport: Hegemonic masculinity in Sports Illustrated.* Albany: SUNY Press.

Dayan, D., & Katz, E. (1992). *Media events: The live broadcasting of history.* Cambridge, MA: Harvard University Press.

Ensico, P. (1998). Good/bad girls read together: Pre-adolsecent girls' co-authorship of feminine subject positions during a shared reading event. *English Education, 30,* 44–62.

Dillon, D., & Moje, E. (1998). Listening to the talk of adolescent girls: Lessons about literacy, school, and life. In D. Alvermann, K. Hinchman, D. Moore, S. Phelps, & D. Waff (Eds.), *Reconceptualizing the literacies in adolescents' lives* (pp. 193–224). Mahwah, NJ: Erlbaum.

Engestrom, Y. (1987). *Learning by expanding.* Helsinki: Oy.

Fairclough, N. (1995). *Media discourse.* London: Edward Arnold.

Finders, M. (1997). *Just girls: The literate life and underlife of early adolescent girls.* New York: Teachers College Press.

Fiske, J. (1994). Audiencing: Cultural practice and cultural studies. In N. Denzin & Y. Lincoln (Eds.), *The handbook of qualitative research* (pp. 189–198). Thousand Oaks, CA: Sage.

Gee, J. P. (1996). *Social linguistics and literacies: Ideology in discourses.* London: Falmer.

Geertz, C. (1973). *The interpretation of cultures.* New York: Basic Books.

Glesne, C., & Peshkin, A. (1992). *Becoming qualitative researchers.* London: Longman.

Grodin, D. (1991). The interpreting audience: The therapeutics of self-help book reading. *Critical Studies in Mass Communication, 8,* 404–420.

Grossberg, L., Wartella, E., & Whitney, D. C. (1998). *MediaMaking: Mass media in a popular culture.* Thousand Oaks, CA: Sage.

Hall, S. (1980). Encoding/decoding. In S. Hall, D. Hobson, A. Lowe, & P. Willis (Eds.), *Culture, media, language* (pp. 124–139). London: Hutchinson.

Harrington, C. L., & Bielby, D. (1995). *Soap fans: Pursuing pleasure and making meaning in everyday life.* Philadelphia: Temple University Press.

Hodge, R., & Kress, G. (1988). *Social Semiotics.* Ithaca, NY: Cornell University Press.

Holland, D., & Eisenhart, M. (1990). *Educated in romance: Women, achievement, and college culture.* Chicago: University of Chicago Press.

Hutchins, E. (1993). Learning to navigate. In S. Chaiklin & J. Lave (Eds.), *Understanding practice: Perspectives on activity and context* (pp. 35–67). London: Cambridge University Press.

Jenkins, H. (1992). *Textual poachers: Television fans and participatory culture.* London: Routledge.

Jenkins, H. (1997). "Never trust a snake": WWF wrestling as masculine melodrama. In A. Baker & T. Boyd (Eds.), *Out of bounds: Sports, media, and the politics of identity* (pp. 48–80). Bloomington: Indiana University Press.

Joyrich, L. (1996). *Re-viewing reception: Television, gender, and postmodern culture.* Bloomington: Indiana University Press.

Katz, E., & Liebes, T. (1990). *The export of meaning: Cross-cultural readings of Dallas.* New York: Oxford University Press.

Lave, J., & Wenger, E. (1991). *Situated learning: Legitimate peripheral participation.* Cambridge, England: Cambridge University Press.

Lemke, J. (1995). *Textual politics.* London: Taylor & Francis.

Leonard, M. (1998). Paper planes: Travelling the New Grrrl geographies. In T. Skelton & G. Valentine (Eds.), *Cool places: Geographies of youth cultures* (pp. 101–120). London: Routledge.

Leont'ev, A. N. (1981). The problem of activity in psychology. In J. Wertsch (Ed.), *The concept of activity in Soviet psychology* (pp. 37–71). Armonk, NY: Sharpe.

Lindlof, T. (1995). *Qualitative communication research methods.* Thousand Oaks, CA: Sage.

Lull, J. (1990). *Inside family viewing: Ethnographic research on television's audiences.* New York: Routledge.

Lybeck, R. (1996). *Family members' responses to television news and sports.* Unpublished paper, University of Minnesota.

Massey, D. (1998). The spatial construction of youth cultures. In T. Skelton & G. Valentine (Eds.), *Cool places: Geographies of youth cultures* (pp. 121–129). London: Routledge.

McKinley, E. G. (1997). *Beverly Hills, 90210: Television, gender, and identity*. Philadelphia: University of Pennsylvania Press.

McRobbie, A. (1990). *Feminism and youth culture*. New York: Macmillan.

Mishler, E. (1986). *Research interviewing: Context and narrative*. Cambridge, MA: Harvard University Press.

Moores, S. (1993). *Interpreting audiences: The ethnography of media consumption*. Thousands Oaks, CA: Sage.

Morley, D. (1986). *Family television: Cultural power and domestic leisure*. London: Comedia.

Mosenthal, P. (1998). In D. Alvermann, *Reconceptualizing the literacies in adolescents' lives*. Hillsdale, NJ: Erlbaum.

Nightingale, V. (1996). *Studying audiences: The shock of the real*. London: Routledge.

Palmer, P. (1986). *The lively audience: A study of children around the TV set*. Sydney: Allen & Unwin.

Peck, J. (1994). Talk about racism: Framing a popular discourse of race on Oprah Winfrey. *Cultural Critique, 27*, 89–126.

Penley, C. (1991). Brownian motion: Women, tactics, and technology. In C. Penley & A. Ross (Eds.), *Technoculture* (pp. 135–161). Minneapolis: University of Minnesota Press.

Phelan, P., Davidson, A., & Yu, H. (1998). *Adolescents' worlds: Negotiating family, peers, and school*. New York: Teachers College Press.

Press, A. (1991). *Women watching television: Gender, class, and generation in the American television experience*. Philadelphia: University of Pennsylvania Press.

Provenzo, E. (1991). *Video kids: Making sense of Nintendo*. Cambridge, MA: Harvard University Press.

Radway, J. (1984). *Reading the romance: Women, patriarchy, and popular literature*. Chapel Hill: University of North Carolina Press.

Radway, J. (1988). The Book-of-the-Month Club and the general reader: On the uses of "serious" fiction. *Critical Inquiry, 14*, 516–538.

Real, M. (1996). *Exploring media culture*. Thousand Oaks, CA: Sage.

Reinertsen, C. (1993). *Wednesday night is girls' night*. Unpublished paper, University of Minnesota.

Riggs, K. (1998). *Mature audiences: Television in the lives of elders*. New Brunswick, NJ: Rutgers University Press.

Rogoff, B. (1995). Observing sociocultural activity on three planes: Participatory appropriation, guided participation, and apprenticeship. In J. Wertsch, P. Del Rio, & A. Alvarez (Eds.), *Sociocultural studies of mind* (pp. 129–164). London: Cambridge University Press.

Rohde, T. (1996). *"I love you; let's pray," The business and "ministry" of the Christian romance novel*. Unpublished paper, University of Minnesota.

Rose, A., & Friedman, J. (1997). Television sports as mas(s)culine cult of distraction. In A. Baker & T. Boyd (Eds.), *Out of bounds: Sports, media, and the politics of identity* (pp. 1–15). Bloomington: University of Indiana Press.

Ruoff, J. (1997). "Can a documentary be made of real life?": The reception of an American family. In C. Crawford & S. B. Hafsteinsson (Eds.), *The construction of the viewer: Media ethnography and the anthropology of audiences* (pp. 270–298). Hojbjerg, Denmark: Intervention Press.

Russell, D. (1997). Rethinking genre in school and society: An activity theory analysis. *Written Communication, 14*(4), 504–554.

Sabo, D., & Jansen, S. C. (1998). Prometheus unbound: Constructions of masculinity in sports media. In L. Wenner (Ed.), *Mediasport* (pp. 202–220). London: Routledge.

Schwartz, D. (1998). *Contesting the Super Bowl*. London: Routledge.

Seiter, E., Borchers, H., Kreutzner, G., & Warth, E. (Eds.). (1989). *Remote control: Television, audiences, and cultural power*. London: Routledge.

Semali, L., & Watts Pailliotet, A. (Eds.). (1999). *Intermediality: The teachers' handbook of critical media literacy*. Boulder, CO: Westview.

Spigel, L., & Mann, D. (Eds.). (1992). *Private screenings: Television and the female consumer*. Minneapolis: University of Minnesota Press.

Spradley, J. (1980). *Participant observation.* New York: Holt, Rinehart, & Winston.

Stevenson, N. (1995). *Understanding media cultures: Social theory and mass communication.* Thousand Oaks, CA: Sage.

Sumara, D. (1996). *Private reading in public: Schooling the literary imagination.* New York: Peter Lang.

Teasley, A., & Wilder, A. (1997). *Reel conversations: Reading films with young adults.* Portsmouth, NH: Heinemann.

Travis, M. (1998). *Reading cultures: The construction of readers in the twentieth century.* Carbondale: Southern Illinois University Press.

Turkle, S. (1995). *Life on the screen: Identity in the age of the Internet.* New York: Simon & Schuster.

van Dijk, T. (1997). Discourse as interaction in society. In T. van Dijk (Ed.), *Discourse as social interaction* (pp. 1–37). Thousand Oaks, CA: Sage.

Ward, J. (1996). *Don't watch it alone! An ethnography of the alt.tv.x-file newsgroup.* Unpublished paper, University of Minnesota.

Wenner, L., & Gantz, W. (1998). Watching sports on television: Audience experience, gender, fanship, and marriage. In L. Wenner (Ed.), *Mediasport* (pp. 233–251). London: Routledge.

Wertsch, J. (1991). *Voices of the mind: A sociocultural approach to mediated action.* Cambridge, MA: Harvard University Press.

THEORIZING THE INTERNET FOR THE PRACTICE, INSTRUCTION, AND STUDY OF DISCIPLINARY WRITING

Linn Bekins

Rapid changes in computer-based technology have had wide-ranging effects in the workplace, in schools, and in our home environments. Odyssey, a respected San Francisco research firm, states that 45% of U.S. homes have personal computers and about 27% are online (*Wall Street Journal*, 1998). A 1990 census report showed that over 38% of U.S. workers in all occupations used computers on the job; among workers with some college education the number is over 50% (U.S. Bureau of Census, 1991, p. 412). In addition, *Business Week's* report on recent trends in workplace technology notes a need for electronic literacy by calling it the "ability to 'mine' information—the process of quickly gathering and analyzing the millions of bits of data that a business generates each day—and steer various pieces to the right people within the organization" (*Business Week*, 1994, p. 104).

As such, communication skills are being redefined as the ability to handle vast amounts of information and to adapt it for a wide range of users. As Tebeaux (1989) notes, it follows that audience analysis (users) will increasingly become crucial to meet new, demanding communication situations. Indeed, technological changes

Advances in Reading/Language Research, Volume 7, pages 41–60.
Copyright © 2000 by JAI Press Inc.
All rights of reproduction in any form reserved.
ISBN: 0-7623-0264-X

have been so pervasive that the effective use of dominant reading and writing technologies has increasingly become a defining characteristic for literacy (Bruce, 1995).

Educators have cited these workplace needs to argue for computers in education. However, the response in many cases has been to increase access to computers and networks without making explicit the connections between reading, writing, and technology. In other words, computers in and of themselves often times do very little to aid learning. Their presence in a classroom does not automatically inspire teachers to rethink their pedagogy or students to adopt new modes of learning. Salomon and Perkins (1996) write, "learning depends crucially on the exact character of the activities that learners engage in with a program [or network], the kinds of tasks they try to accomplish, and the kinds of intellectual and social activity they become involved in, in interaction with that which computing affords" (p. 113). Instead of focusing on vital critical thinking skills, basic skill sets associated with functional literacy are often taught. Many times, such a pragmatic approach stresses assimilating into a system rather than assessing and possibly resisting it. The tension between workplace literacy, which is frequently associated with basic skills and/or vocational training, and academic literacy, which many associate with egalitarian exploration and critical thinking, is real and unfortunate because, as this chapter will illustrate, connections can be readily made. Throughout this chapter, I will argue along with Bruce and Hogan (1998) that literacy extends beyond reading and writing texts, to "reading" social communities and the technological artifacts within them.

Whether one is a technology enthusiast, voicing claims of increased empowerment, equality, and access to information, or a cautious critical observer giving out warnings of a potential loss of jobs, poor working conditions, and the general subordination of humanity to technology, technology has become embedded in our society. We have also become increasingly dependent on it to function in our everyday activities. Rather than conceptualizing the debate via these exclusive and deterministic structures, the purpose of this chapter is (1) to examine how the social theoretical perspective can be broadly used to inform the teaching and practice of written communication in a postsecondary computer-based classroom, and (2) to illustrate how teachers and students can utilize the Internet to enhance teaching and learning.

THE SOCIAL PERSPECTIVE IN DISCIPLINARY WRITING RESEARCH

The past two decades has seen a growing interest in socially based research for both writing and literacy studies. In conjunction with this increased interest, writing theorists have attempted to articulate the shared assumptions that form the basis for what Faigley (1985) termed the social perspective. Perhaps the most distinctive is the fundamental rejection of positivism. According to positivism, knowledge is a direct apprehension of reality, where the human mind merely acts as a mirror reflecting the outer world, and ideas are true to the degree that they correspond with the world. Such a view assumes that discourse is an arhetorical, unproblematic recording of thought or speech originating within an individual's mind (versus in society). Social theorists reject these positivistic notions, arguing instead that reality is unknowable apart from language. By further extension, discourse is treated as a manifestation of social context. Thus, a text is not an isolated utterance, but a moment in the continuous process of verbal and written communication.

Foundational to social theory is that language is developed and maintained in social contexts. Language and even thought, observes Vygotsky (1962), is not a private and individually driven enterprise:

> Thought development is determined by language, i.e., by the linguistic tools of thought, and by the sociocultural experiences of the child. . . . The child's intellectual growth is contingent on his [sic] mastering the social means of thought, that is, language. . . . Verbal thought is not an innate, natural form of behavior but is determined by a historical-cultural process. (p. 51)

Vygotsky states that in a sociocultural process, people learn words not just through memorization, but through hearing words in social situations to convey particular meanings. Words carry the particular contexts in which they have been used and people learn language as it is *embedded in* and *related to* a variety of contexts. Language, in this sense, is mediated to fit particular social contexts. As such, a text is not an isolated utterance, but a moment in the continuous process of verbal and written communication. Hence, a text is constructed in relation to previous texts; it is not an isolated linguistic form developed by an isolated mind of an individual writer.

Because language originates within social contexts, the discourse emerging out of particular contexts can be said to reflect the thoughts of a discourse community. The concept of discourse community is used here to refer to people using special-ized kinds of language competencies that enable them to participate in specialized groups (Faigley, 1985). Gee (1990) defines discourse as "a socially accepted association among ways of using language, of thinking, feeling, believing, valuing, and of acting that can be used to identify oneself as a member of a socially meaningful group or 'social network'" (p. 143). One might postulate, as Gee does, that literacy or literacies can be conceived as discourses because people conceptu-alize certain literacies to be appropriate to particular settings and purposes. As such, communities may be identified and defined by how members use language as a tool to shape the form and content of specific texts. For instance, the discourses of the hard sciences, such as biology or chemistry, are quite different from the discourses occurring in the humanities.

The concept of discourse is intimately connected to the concept of disciplinary community because such communities use discourse to communicate. According to the social perspective, language is a social construct and writing is viewed as a social act through which the writer uses language in such a way that it is reflective of their discourse community. This point may be extended further to assert that reality, knowledge, texts, selves, and so on are community-generated and community-maintained linguistic entities. Disciplinary communities, such as those within academia, are types of discourse communities, each having their own jargon, subject matter, and methods of argument which allow them to justify their beliefs socially and arrive at consensus about what they call knowledge (Bruffee, 1984). Hence, from this perspective, language is at the center of understanding knowledge.

The basic tenet of the social approach—language is developed and mediated within social contexts—can provide insight into disciplinary writing research and practice because the purposes, goals, and values of this perspective enable us to investigate the social roles, group purposes, and ideologies inherent to particular discourse communities. Such research is context sensitive and aims to make explicit the communication indices of community membership. This assumes, of course, that various disciplines and sites use discourse differently, a point which is well supported in disciplinary writing research (Ackerman, 1991; Bazerman, 1981, 1984, 1985, 1988; Berkenkotter, Huckin, & Ackerman, 1988; Gilbert & Mulkay, 1984; Haas, 1994; Knorr-Cetina, 1981; Latour & Woolgar, 1979; Myers, 1985; Reither & Vipond, 1989). Such studies examine the context in which communication occurs, the background and training of writers, the state of knowledge within the community, and the expectations of the readers.

Disciplinary writing research not only provides insight into how individuals within specific communities come together to produce and disseminate knowledge, but also provides an understanding of the form and content of the discourse individuals must acquire so that they can successfully participate in such communities. Thus, by making explicit the often intuitive recognition that disciplinary differences exist in written communication practices, disciplinary writing research is able to make explicit the language tools deemed necessary for community participation.

Composition scholars, in particular, have long argued that students entering academic disciplines must learn the genres and conventions that members of the disciplinary community employ (e.g., Bartholomae, 1985; Bizzell, 1982). Without such knowledge, they believe, students will remain outside of the community's discourse. Pedagogically, the demystification of what counts as effective discourse provides the overt conversational tools to help students think about planning, organizing, and presenting their ideas in discipline-specific ways. In addition to learning genres and conventions, Bazerman (1980, 1985) contends that students must also become aware of "the conversations of the discipline." The conversation metaphor refers to the issues under discussion within a community. While this argument for the research and teaching of disciplinary communication practices may be viewed by some as pragmatic and basic skills-oriented, it addresses academic literacy concerns for critical thinking. For instance, the articulation of the rhetorical features of argument that characterize disciplinary communication facilitates the development of individual agency; that is, as students become aware of and skilled in disciplinary practices, they become active, reactive, and proactive members of a disciplinary community. "Explicit teaching of discourse," states Bazerman (1992), "holds what is taught up for inspection. It provides the students with means to rethink the ends of discourse" (p. 64). Awareness that language is a fundamental tool of knowledge construction can lead students to analyze the function of language, whose interests it serves, and how it can be used to act on one's social desires. Such an awareness not only shows students that rhetoric is at the basis of all communicative acts, but it also makes apparent that their participation in communities helps shape the discourse of that community.

Unfortunately, writing instructors too often assume that instruction should train students to mimic observed, real-world practices without highlighting reasons for questioning them (Miller, 1989). While some scholars argue that learning a disciplinary community's "identity kit"—its ways of being–doing–thinking–valuing–speaking–listening–writing–reading (Gee, 1990)—enables a student to participate in a community, others assert that teaching such practices without attention to the theoretical and practical implications of such practices may actually constrain students (Bazerman, 1992). In keeping with the promotion of human agency within the composition classroom, this latter perspective argues that students need to be made aware of (and critical of) the social boundaries inherent in a text produced for particular purposes and within a particular context. Semali and Watts Pailliotet (1999) also note that texts are not value-neutral, unchanging, "objective" artifacts; they reflect cultural and discursive ideologies (Althusser, 1986; Derrida, 1986; Fiske, 1989). Taking a critical approach to texts enables students to develop and negotiate within a discipline effectively to "regain territory that may have been inappropriately enclosed within expert discourse" (Bazerman, 1992). If, on the other hand, teachers provide students with only the formal trappings of the communication practices (e.g., specific written and oral genres) they need as professionals, teachers offer them nothing more than "unreflecting slavery to current practices and no means to ride the change that inevitably will come in the forty or fifty years that they practice their professions" (Bazerman, 1988, p. 320).

I believe the social perspective offers a view of writing as a social action, which can be either enabling or constraining, depending on how writing is taught. To address such a potential problem, Spilka (1993) suggests that teachers explore issues of social accommodation and social innovation within texts as they instruct students in evaluating the implications of various texts. For me, such an approach not only recognizes agency, but it also can be used to promote change within disciplinary community conventions. In the text that follows, I will illustrate how the social approach informed the teaching and practice of disciplinary writing in a postsecondary technical writing classroom.

TEACHING CONTEXT: COURSE DESCRIPTION

The writing courses at this large Intermountain West university emphasize the development of problem-solving skills within organizational contexts and writing for multiple audiences. Students come from predominately middle-class, Caucasian, Mormon families, most commute to the school, and many hold part- or full-time jobs. The technical and professional writing classes offered to juniors and seniors are usually split evenly between males and females.

The courses' purposes are (1) to ensure that students understand the forms and processes used by successful college-level writers, and (2) to help students develop the written communication skills necessary to continue maturing as writers in undergraduate and postcollege settings. To meet such goals, the professional writing courses—business and technical—employ workplace-based projects whose purpose is to stress writing as a highly social process through which students learn about the symbiotic and systematic relationships between culture, themselves as individuals, and themselves as members of particular discourse groups. Such an approach is guided by the activity theory of learning (Lave, 1996; Leontiev, 1981; Wertsch, 1985, 1991), which perceives learning as occurring through what Rogoff (1995) describes as "participatory appropriation" of social practices. According to this perspective, learning occurs as the learner engages in an activity, and through participation in the activity, the learner internalizes skills. Such engagement not only enables a student to analyze and make explicit a disciplinary community's assumptions and communication patterns, but also enables them to have a better chance of critiquing and then communicating within a community. (For a further discussion of "gatekeeping" in disciplinary communications, see Berkenkotter & Huckin, 1995.)

SAMPLE CLASS ACTIVITIES

In these courses, students are required to use the Internet extensively as a means of doing research, collaborating on writing activities, and developing a dialogue outside of class with both class members and professionals within their major. As part of their assignments, students choose a discipline—usually their major—to research. They then utilize Internet search engines to locate information about the discipline and explore ways to "lurk about" or participate within the discipline's conversations. Through active research, students not only learn how to "surf the net," but they also learn "a socially accepted association among ways of using language, of thinking, feeling, believing, valuing, and of acting that can be used to identify oneself as a member of a socially meaningful group or 'social network'" (Gee, 1990, p. 143). Thus, within this activity, students explore one conception of literacy, that of practicing reading and writing used for particular purposes in specific contexts of use (Scribner & Cole, 1981). (See Appendix A for sample professional writing course syllabus.)

One of the core assignments common to the course asks students to investigate and report on the writing practices of a discipline of their choice. To complete the assignment, students are required to complete a five-step process (see Appendix B for sample disciplinary writing exercise). First, they must interview at least one professional in their chosen field with the purpose of understanding the goals and expectations of the discipline, the types of communication required, how writing functions within the discipline, and how specific types of thinking and conventions are associated with a discipline's learning and knowledge. Second, students are required to research a sample of the discipline's writing—typically, a journal or trade magazine—and analyze it for its key rhetorical components (e.g., purpose, audience, presentation, evidence, and language). Students then write up their results according to the discipline's submission guidelines. Next, the students give a formal oral presentation to the class on their findings. Lastly, the students each write an executive summary of a different discipline's writing practices. The purpose of each step within the exercise is for students to explore and then analyze how culture and cognition mutually construct one another (Wertsch, del Rio, & Alvarez, 1995) in writing. By examining how writing is conceived by (and in) a discipline, students not only come to understand the dynamic nature of how symbol systems, or signs, represent cultural systems (Vygotsky, 1978), but also learn to critique issues within disciplinary writing.

STUDENT EXAMPLE

The following excerpt is from "Morgan," a senior-level writing student studying premedicine. He was a competent writer and showed great interest in becoming an active member within his discipline. I choose to show his work because he followed the assignment guidelines and, I believe, successfully conveys what he learned about his discipline's criteria for participation. To complete the assignment, he reported using the research vehicles of his discipline; that is, he used the Internet extensively to locate and read online journals in his discipline and corresponded via email with professional contacts within the discipline. With this information, he then mimicked the genre, language, and conventions of the medical discipline. To document his findings, he again made use of the "tools of the trade," and included a screen shot (Fig. 1) of a medical and diagnostic treatment software package to illustrate how medical informaticists use visual aids in their writing. By extension, one could argue that Morgan's use of technology might be read by those within his discipline as an achievement of status because his expertise has become a mode of currency for achieving status and a sense of belonging to a community that highly values technology (Tierney & Damarin, 1998).

Within Morgan's assignment, we see him taking stock of what constitutes "standard" communication in his discipline (see Appendix C). He begins by noting his purpose, which is to provide the reader with "an introductory analysis of the structure and content of communication" in medical informatics, and to provide

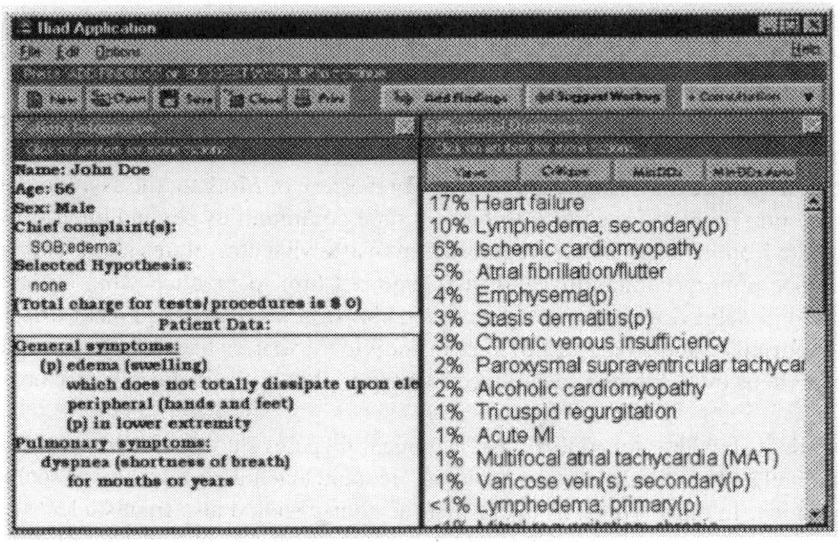

Iliad Application

File Edit Options Help

Name: John Doe
Age: 56
Sex: Male
Chief complaint(s):
  SOB;edema;
Selected Hypothesis:
  none
(Total charge for tests/procedures is $ 0)
        Patient Data:
General symptoms:
  (p) edema (swelling)
    which does not totally dissipate upon ele
    peripheral (hands and feet)
    (p) in lower extremity
Pulmonary symptoms:
  dyspnea (shortness of breath)
    for months or years

17% Heart failure
10% Lymphedema; secondary(p)
6% Ischemic cardiomyopathy
5% Atrial fibrillation/flutter
4% Emphysema(p)
3% Stasis dermatitis(p)
3% Chronic venous insufficiency
2% Paroxysmal supraventricular tachycar
2% Alcoholic cardiomyopathy
1% Tricuspid regurgitation
1% Acute MI
1% Multifocal atrial tachycardia (MAT)
1% Varicose vein(s); secondary(p)
<1% Lymphedema; primary(p)

Figure 1. Iliad—Consultation Screen Shot

"the subjective 'feel' for how professionals in the field of medical informatics perceive communication both within and beyond their discourse community." It is from within this stance that Morgan informs the reader of what constitutes effective written communication within his chosen discipline. It is interesting to note that the language and rhetorical moves made by Morgan within the assignment further illustrate his awareness of and his ability to "take on" the discipline's communication conventions. For instance, he follows the submission criteria for the journals he analyzed, he adheres to the traditional scientific reporting format of Introduction, Methods, Results, and Discussion (IMRD), and he effectively takes on the personae (as reflected in his language use) of scientific researcher reporting study results. Through his research, Morgan not only became more familiar with the IMRD format, but also reported becoming more conscious of the fact that there exists an internal ordering of the information presented in various sections of the research article. According to Morgan, developing this awareness made him more able to produce a clear, coherent, and logically organized research report.

In this case, technology also served as a set of means allowing Morgan to cultivate his writing-related metacognition. The activity of analyzing and practicing disciplinary writing provided the external guidance that was internalized to become self-guidance (Vygotsky, 1962). This observation is based on the assumption that self-regulation is crucial in learning. Morgan's active engagement in assembling, interpreting, extending, and in broad terms constructing knowledge out of the raw materials found in the disciplinary communication research served an enabling function for him. Within this classroom context where students are, for the most part, highly motivated, this open-ended, discovery learning environment facilitates knowledge construction.

Furthermore, this assignment maps out the process through which a writer can begin to learn the conventions and conversations for literate communication within a specific disciplinary framework. In the case of Morgan, the assignment helped him prepare for entry into professional communities beyond his immediate environment. As such, it required him to ask what constitutes membership in a disciplinary community and then required him to practice what he had learned to achieving disciplinary membership. In brief, this assignment offers an opportunity and a basic guideline for individual writers to actively research and perhaps even achieve specialized literacy within specific disciplinary contexts.

While it could be argued that this assignment prepares students for what Spilka (1993) refers to as "social accommodation," it could better address issues of social innovation. In other words, I believe that the course should also train students in social analysis so they can analyze and decide on which disciplinary communication practices to emulate and which to critique and attempt to change. To address this need, issues of social innovation were covered through "hands-on" critical discourse analysis (CDA) (Fairclough, 1989; Kress, 1989) of sample texts, both print and virtual. I regularly incorporated in-class exercises utilizing CDA on popular advertisements to help students develop the habit of approaching a wide variety of texts with a critical and analytical eye. I found such texts stimulated rich discussions about whether or not the text in question encouraged stasis or challenged social norms, and the exercises enabled the class to explore the role of visual rhetoric and technology in communication products. Here, I use the Aristotelian definition of rhetoric: "the ability in each particular case, to see the available means of persuasion" (1991, pp. 36–37). Practicing CDA forces students out of a passive reader/viewer mode of receiving texts and into an active involvement with textual production and dissemination. In addition, the Internet proved to be a good resource for CDA, as it offers access to an infinitely wide variety of public texts (e.g., newsgroups, job lines, journals).

IMPLICATIONS

The social perspective views language as developmental, socially and culturally mediated, and individually situated. Moreover, learning is understood as a self-regulated process of dealing with cognitive conflicts that become apparent through experience, interactive discourse, and reflection. In an effort to demystify the process of learning and development, such a perspective focuses on how people participate in sociocultural activities, such as particular discourse communities. The goal of such an approach, says Wertsch et al. (1995), is "to explicate the relationships between human mental functioning, on the one hand, and the cultural, institutional, and historical situations in which this occurs, on the other" (p. 3). As such, an individual thinking or the functioning of a community may be considered in the foreground without the assumption that they are all separate elements.

The notion that knowledge is personally constructed and socially mediated further reflects the idea that knowledge is no longer a result of an individual Cartesian privately examining the certainty of the contents of thought. Certainly, easy access to vast bodies of information, databases, discussion groups, and bulletin boards afforded by new technological developments has affected our conceptions of knowledge. "For if large bodies of information are so accessible," state Salomon and Perkins (1996), "and if the manipulation of the information so gathered is so easy, it may well be that knowledge stored in students' minds, as traditionally cherished and tested by school, is less valid today than in the past" (p. 127). Likewise, Simon (1992) has suggested that we reconsider our perceptions of knowledge as a noun denoting possession and more toward perceiving the concept of knowledge as a verb denoting access.

In the technical and workplace writing classrooms discussed, the Internet is used as a tool through which students can explore varying conceptions of literacy in multiple disciplines. In addition, the incorporation of in-class exercises using CDA to analyze written discourse practices helps develop students' sense of social innovation. In this case, as students learned to detect patterns of how social contexts influence what is written as well as how a text is written, they also learned to detect reliable patterns of composing that might influence social contexts. That is, students learned that in tracing the social interactions within a text, they might be able to effect needed social change in writing. CDA provides a powerful tool for developing agency among students and the teacher because it can help reveal certain social, cultural, and political interests that have been taken as truths and that have constructed individuals' subjectivities and identities.

The combination of these two teaching tools forces students out of a passive reader/viewer mode of receiving information and into a more active involvement with textual production and dissemination. The Internet and CDA work together not only to help students experience the modeled used of disciplinary communication and tool use, but also to help students critically explore disciplinary learning and knowledge. Thus, while the Internet offers students access to a wide variety of disciplinary texts to explore, analyze, and perhaps even model, they also learn to critique the theoretical and practical underpinnings of their respective disciplines' texts at the local, textual level and on a more global, societal level.

It is, however, important to note that just as teachers' and students' stances, interactions, and constructions are embedded in larger societal, cultural, and political structures, so is technology. In these courses, the use of the Internet and collaborative writing exercises encourages students to engage in naturalistic and ethnographic research of professional and disciplinary writing practices and to critically explore the "dialectical relationship between human thinking and culture, on the one hand, and technology on the other" (Haas, 1996, p. 230). Thus, we begin the course by exploring the textual practices of industry, government, and/or business, and then examine the ideological premises on which these practices are based both individually and collaboratively. Assignments might include interviewing a professional in their major to explore their writing practices and values, studying various genres or forms of professional writing, or examining how collaboration is used in certain industries to facilitate the development of a product or idea.

Throughout the course, we examine how each discipline uses technology to communicate, asking questions, such as: how and why the discipline utilizes certain channels of technology communication over others, and how a discipline's use of technology might reflect its knowledge-making practices. To explore technology uses, I use a hands-on approach and have students take an active part in the exploration by having them surf the Internet, participate in newsgroups, use email and voice mail, and so on as a part of their assigned work. Throughout this process, students are encouraged to take on critical stances in their examination of technology and the array of texts that stem from it to form the meaning-making and written communication processes of particular disciplines.

In taking this pedagogical approach, students are enculturated into a disciplinary discourse through their personal completion of the disciplinary writing assignment and they become critical readers of other disciplinary discourses through individual and collaborative exercises. By enculturated, I mean students consciously participate in a disciplinary culture in an effort to generate something that is acceptable to the norms of the community. This process of socialization, or the active mediation between a cognizing individual and sociocultural activities, infers that cognitive processes are subsumed by social and cultural processes (Cobb, 1994; Hull & Rose, 1990; Vygotsky, 1978).

Learning a discipline's "identity kit" (Gee, 1990) is a complex process involving an understanding of the social origins of higher mental functions (e.g., problem solving, appropriating knowledge) in a culture's practices and the role of more knowledgeable others, such as instructors, in providing opportunities for the learner to participate in knowledge-making activities. Such a process is an extension to the sociocultural learning and teaching theory developed by Vygotsky (1978). Rogoff (1995) takes the concept of apprenticeship beyond the expert–novice dyad introduced by Vygotsky by focusing instead on "a system of interpersonal involvements and arrangements in which people engage in a culturally organized activity in which apprentices become more responsible participants" (p. 143). (An example of this can be seen in the five-step disciplinary writing exercise in Appendix B.) In other words, by participating in the discursive activities of a culture, learners are socialized, or enculturated, into a culture's particular ways of knowing and communicating.

This emphasis on participatory appropriation and socialization views development as a dynamic, active, and mutual process, as opposed to the traditional internalization perspective which views development in terms of a static "acquisition" or "transmission" of knowledge. In these classrooms, students learned genres as well as discipline-specific communication values by participating in the construction of documents reflective of various disciplinary "identity kits." Students learn through direct experience that language, a cognitively constructed cultural tool, is a semiotic means that has the power to shape speaking and thinking (Vygotsky, 1978; Wertsch et. al., 1995). As such, students also learn that literacy events center around issues of what it means to read and write in relation to larger sociocultural patterns which they may exemplify or reflect (Heath, 1982; Hull & Rose, 1990).

An increase in academia and industry as well as cross-disciplinary cooperation to explore what constitutes quality in writing has shown that such experiences encourage writers "to consider such issues as social roles, group purposes, communal organization, ideology, and, finally, theories of culture" before writing (Faigley, 1985, p. 236). Such an assertion might logically lead instructors to consider teaching writing within the contexts of certain disciplines. In a university-wide study examining 24 professors' views on literacy across various disciplines, Bekins and Mathison (1996) found that there exist discipline-specific meanings of what constitutes good writing. Implications of this research indicate that learning how to write may be more realistically achieved through a disciplinary-centered curriculum that can facilitate in students the types of thinking and participating that occur through enculturation into the various practices that link writing to learning. To do so, however, means that instructors and students must not only develop an understanding of disciplinary specific issues and conventions, but also learn about the technological mediums through which the disciplines communicate. Such information is necessary to enable writers to become literate within specific disciplinary frameworks.

SUMMARY

In this chapter, I have described how the social theoretical perspective can inform the instruction and practice of disciplinary writing and have illustrated through example how classroom assignments were used to teach discourse conventions and conversations for literate communication within a specific disciplinary framework. The student example illustrates how a writer used the technological tools of his discipline to prepare himself for entry into a disciplinary community beyond his immediate environment.

I want to conclude by noting that I am an enthusiast (if a cautious one) about the potential of computer networks for accomplishing communicative acts. I generally support a basic-skills approach to teaching writing, driven by dealing directly with issues of social accommodation and social innovation. My point is to convey some of the many purposes and points of view that surround literacy and to connect computer networks clearly to the social contexts that affect and often define their use. Thus, while I share a sense of inevitability in regard to the growth of computer networking, I believe that as instructors we need to address the multiple social issues surrounding technology with our students and to encourage self-conscious, critical use. As Bowers (1988) notes, "the classroom is not only a microcosm of the larger society; it also contributes to the future direction the society will take" (p. 5). Indeed, there are some promising connections to be made between disciplinary writing research and technology/literacy studies of individual writers' efforts to achieve specialized literacy within specific disciplinary contexts.

APPENDIX A: SAMPLE PROFESSIONAL WRITING COURSE SYLLABUS

Course Goals:

1. To analyze firsthand the writing products, contexts, and processes found in area businesses or other real-world workplace settings.
2. To practice writing as a research activity and to include the use of:
    *   *Interviews and observations*: gathering firsthand information about writing processes, products, and contexts.
    *   *Text analyses*: comparing real-world writing with assumed standards for efficient and readable business communication.
    *   *Reader reviews*: analyzing how and why readers comprehend, interpret, and make use of transactional texts.
3. To examine assumptions about the differences between academic and non-academic writing, and your ability and potential as a writer of both.
4. To practice common forms of professional writing—proposals, reports, and letters—by designing them for specific audiences and purposes.
5. To practice collaboration and project management.

Required Texts:

Flower, L., & Ackerman, J. (1994). *Writers at work: Strategies for communicating in business and professional settings*. Fort Worth, TX: Harcourt Brace.
Flower, L., & Ackerman, J. (1994). *Writers at work casebook for teachers and students: Nine scenarios for discussion and practice*. Fort Worth, TX: Harcourt Brace.
Williams, R. (1994). *The non-designers design book: Design and typographic principles for the visual novice*. Berkeley, CA: Peachpit Press.

Assignments and Grading:

1. Career Research Memo (Individual)   10
2. Case Study of a Business Document (Individual)   10
3. Collaborative Research Project
    Confirmation Letter to Client (Group)   5
    Research Proposal (Group)   15
    Oral Presentation to Class (Group)   10

Progress Reports (Individual)	10
Final Report to Client (Group)	20
4. Memos & Exercises (Individual)	10
5. Class & Group Participation (Individual)	10
	100

Course Timeline:

Week 1.   **Understanding Context**

Introduction to computer lab.

Topics/Activities:	Assignments/Readings
Course and project introduction	In-class writing assignment
Studying writing in context	Read: Driskell article, Ch. 1
Genres of organizational writing: Memos	Read: Ch. 7
Collaboration & group work	Read: Ch. 6
	Read: Paradis et al. article

Week 2.   **Collaboration/Ethics**

Using the Internet as researching & writing tool.

Topics/Activities:	Assignments/Readings
Form research groups	Select possible clients using criteria
	Read: Project Description
Collaboration & group work	Read: Burnett article, Ch. 2
Practice textual analysis	Read: GMAT analysis of issue
Intro. research memo	
Ethics: Discourse as Social Action	Read: Case Study Handout, Reddick article

Choose & contact client; collect client documents.

Week 3.   **Ethics/Textual Analysis**

Exploring the Internet.

Topics/Activities:	Assignments/Readings
Business settings as rhetorical contexts	Read: Clark, Rentz, & Debs, Guidelines for nonsexist writing articles
Intro. to textual analysis	In-class writing assignment
	Read: Document Standards article
Genres of org. writing: Short letter	Read: Ch. 7, Casebook II

Week 4.   **Genres/Interviews**

Using email as a communication channel.

Topics/Activities:	Assignments/Readings
Introduction to case study assignment	Read: Case Study
Short correspondence	Draft client confirmation letter
	Read: Ch. 7, Email article
Interviews introduced	Read: Ch. 8, Conducting interviews, interview stages, formal interview

Week 5. Feb. 3–5	**Textual Analysis**

Using Web pages and newsgroups as information sources.

Topics/Activities:	Assignments/Readings
Textual analysis	Read: Redish, Casebook V
Bring: Client doc. to class for analysis	
Bring: Confirmation letter for approval	
Practice textual analysis	Read: GMAT analysis of an argument
Getting from interview 1 to 2	Group work on interview questions
Reader reviews introduced	Read: Ch. 5, Reader Reviews
Project planning and management	Read: Ch. 6, Review of project management software
Data analysis: Case building	Bring: Rough draft/outline of client case study to class

Week 6.	**Proposals/Client Reports**

Topics/Activities:	Assignments/Readings
Intro. proposal assignment	Read: Proposal (packet), Asner, Casebook IX
Intro. client report	

Week 7.	**Visual Rhetoric**

Topics/Activities:	Assignments/Readings
Resume: Controlling design & function	Read: New technologies article
Design issues	Read: Non-Designers Design Book

Week 8.	**Design Issues & Oral Pres.**

Topics/Activities:	Assignments/Readings
Design issues (continued)	Read: "Stepping lively," Writing visually articles
Intro. to oral presentations	Read: Preparing for oral article

Week 9.	**Writing Workshop**

Topics/Activities:	Assignments/Readings
Client reports	Group work
Writing/revising client reports	Group work

Week 10.	**Wrap up**

Topics/Activities:	Assignments/Readings
Oral presentations	
Review, evaluate course	

APPENDIX B: SAMPLE DISCIPLINARY WRITING
EXERCISE

In this course, you will be required to use the Internet extensively as a means of doing research, collaborating on writing activities, and developing a dialogue outside of class with both class members and professionals within your major. As part of your assignments, you will choose a discipline—usually your major—to research. You will then be asked to utilize Internet search engines to locate information about the discipline and explore ways to "lurk about" or participate within the discipline's conversations.

Through active research and learning how to "surf the net," you will learn "a socially accepted association among ways of using language, of thinking, feeling, believing, valuing, and of acting that can be used to identify oneself as a member of a socially meaningful group or 'social network'" (Gee, 1990, p. 143). Thus, within this activity, you will explore one conception of literacy, that of practicing reading and writing used for particular purposes in specific contexts of use (Scribner & Cole, 1981).

This course asks you to investigate and report on the writing practices of a discipline of your choice. To complete the assignment, you will be asked to complete the following five-step process:

Step One.

Interview at least one professional in your chosen field with the purpose of understanding the goals and expectations of the discipline, the types of communication required, how writing functions within the discipline, and how specific types of thinking and conventions are associated with a discipline's learning and knowledge.

Step Two.

Research a sample of the discipline's writing—typically, a journal or trade magazine—and analyze it for its key rhetorical components (e.g., purpose, audience, presentation, evidence, and language).

Step Three.

Write up your findings according to the discipline's submission guidelines.

Step Four.

Give a formal oral presentation to the class on your findings.

Step Five.

Using what you've learned during the oral presentations, write an executive summary of a different discipline's writing practices.

APPENDIX C: DISCIPLINARY WRITING ASSIGNMENT SAMPLE

An Introductory Analysis of Communication and Reasoning in Medical Informatics

INTRODUCTION

As one finds in most professional careers [1] communication is a fundamental component in medical informatics. This paper is an introductory analysis of the structure and content of communication following the research of standard written communication and focused interviews with professionals in the field. The research and interview data suggests a standard format for professional communication, and provides the subjective "feel" for how professionals in the field of medical informatics perceive communication both within and beyond their discourse community.

METHODS

An article [2] selected from a primary forum of communication in medical informatics, the Symposium on Computer Applications in Medical Care (SCAMC), [3] was evaluated with the following criteria: general layout requirements for article submission, usage of visual aids, usage of professional jargon, and rhetorical style. A full year (1995) of articles from SCAMC were then reviewed to determine the type of persons and groups submitting to that forum which were categorized as: student, non-healthcare professional, healthcare professional, then, as an independent variable, whether they were affiliated with a university, a healthcare organization, a corporation, or none of the above.

The data from this research and evaluation was then presented to Omar Bouhaddou, Ph.D., [4] and Joseph Lambert, M.D., [5] in separate interviews to evaluate their perception of the results and to have them comment on communication beyond the professional community of medical informatics. These expert reports are then compared and contrasted with the data and summarized.

RESULTS

General Layout. Table 1 shows the 1995 SCAMC research a neral layout criteria. Scope was limited to the area of medical informatics and depended on an annual theme. Formatting requirements were quite explicit and rightfully so since the papers were to be submitted in a photo-ready format. The Journal of American Medical Informatics (JAMIA), [6] another major publication in medical informatics, requests a more general format, and that the paper be submitted electronically so the final formatting is done by the journal staff.

Usage of Visual Aids. This SCAMC submission was entirely devoid of visual aids. One could reason that this is true in larae part due to the space limitations imposed by the proceedings chair. Other papers [7,8,9] from the same SCAMC proceedings and JAMIA [10,11] included both tables and figures to organize their findings or provided screen shots of computer applications. This is particularly useful if the author is trying to describe the flow and function of an application. Often times just presenting a screen shot of the user interface elucidates the purpose and method of a software. Figure 1 demonstrates a screen shot of Iliad®, a medical and diagnostic treatment software for physicians well documented in the literature [12,13,14,15,16,17]. Here we see the effectiveness of an image in conveying the functionality of a software. The differential window illustrates this is a diagnostic program, the percentages indicates it is a probabilistic model, the patient data window demonstrates the vocabulary being used, the patient demographics window always keeps the practitioner focused on a particular patient, and other functions of the program are clearly illustrated by depressable buttons.

Professional Jargon. Medical informatics is a highly technical synthesis between medicine and computer science. Most of the lead minds in the field are medical doctors with training in databases, programming, expert systems, artificial intelligence, network design, and more. Furthermore, most developers have coined phrases for their systems, or aspects of their systems. In the article reviewed for this paper [2] examples include: controlled medical terminology (CMT), and medical entities dictionary (MED). Professional medical and computer science jargon found in the article include: data repository, AP Chest x-ray, semantically equivalent terms, and medical concept.

ACKNOWLEDGMENTS

I thank Maureen Mathison, David Reinking, Ann Watts Pailliotet, Tom Huckin, John Ackerman, and Scott Harris for helpful criticism, suggestions, and other collegial contributions to this chapter. Portions of this chapter were presented at the annual meeting of the National Reading Conference in Scottsdale, Arizona (1997, December) and at the Western States Composition Conference in Salt Lake City, Utah (1998, October).

REFERENCES

Ackerman, J. M. (1991). Reading, writing, and knowing: The role of disciplinary knowledge i n comprehension and composing. *Research in the Teaching of English, 25*, 133–178.
Althusser, L. (1986). Ideology and ideological state apparatuses. In H. Adams & L. Searle (Ed s.), *Critical theory since 1965* (pp. 239–251). Tallahassee: Florida State University Press.
Aristotle (1991). *On rhetoric* (G.A. Kennedy, Trans.). London: Oxford University Press.
Bartholomae, D. (1985). Inventing the university. In M. Rose (Ed.), *When a writer can't write* (pp. 134–165). New York: Guilford.
Bazerman, C. (1980). A relationship between reading and writing: The conversational model . *College English, 41*, 556–661.
Bazerman, C. (1981). What written knowledge does: Three examples of academic discourse. *Philosophy of the Social Sciences, 11*, 361–382.

Bazerman, C. (1984). The writing of scientific non-fiction: Contexts, choices, constraints. *PRE/TEXT,* 5, 39–74.

Bazerman, C. (1985). Physicists reading physics: Schema-laden purposes and purpose-laden schema. *Written Communication, 2,* 39–74.

Bazerman, C. (1988). Writing well, scientifically and rhetorically: Practical consequences for writers of science and their teachers. In C. Bazerman, *Shaping written knowledge: The genre and activity of the experimental article in science* (pp. 318–332). Madison: University of Wisconsin Press.

Bazerman, C. (1992). From cultural criticism to disciplinary participation: Living with powerful words. In A. Herrington & C. Moran (Eds.), *Writing, teaching, and learning in the disciplines* (pp. 61–68). New York: MLA.

Bekins, L., & Mathison, M. (1996, April). *Constructing literacy across the university.* Paper presented at the meeting of the American Educational Research Association, New York.

Berkenkotter, C., & Huckin, T. (1995). *Genre knowledge in disciplinary communication.* Mahwah, NJ: Erlbaum.

Berkenkotter, C., Huckin, T., & Ackerman, J. (1988). Conventions, conversations, and the writer: Case study of a student in a rhetoric Ph.D. program. *Research in the Teaching of English, 22,* 9–44.

Bizzell, P. (1982). Cognition, convention, and certainty: What we need to know about writing. *PRE/TEXT, 3,* 213–243.

Bowers, C. A. (1988). *The cultural dimensions of educational computing: Understanding the non-neutrality of technology.* New York: Teachers College Press.

Bruce, B. C. (1995, November). *Twenty-first century literacy* (Tech. Rep. No. 624). Urbana: University of Illinois, Center for the Study of Reading.

Bruce, B. C., & Hogan, M. P. (1998). The disappearance of technology: Toward an ecological model of literacy. In D. Reinking, M. McKenna, L. Labbo, & R. Kieffer (Eds.), *Handbook of literacy and technology: Transformations in a post-typographic world* (pp. 269–281). Mahwah, NJ: Erlbaum.

Bruffee, K. A. (1984). Collaborative learning and the 'conversation of mankind.' *College English, 46,* 635–652.

Cobb, P. (1994). Where is the mind? Constructivist and sociocultural perspectives on mathematical development. *Educational Researcher, 23,* 13–20.

Derrida, J. (1986). Structure, sign, and play in the discourse of the human sciences; Of grammatology; Difference. In H. Adams & L. Searle (Eds.), *Critical theory since 1965* (pp. 83–137). Tallahassee: Florida State University Press.

Faigley, L. (1985). Nonacademic writing: The social perspective. In L. Odell & D. Goswami (Eds.), *Writing in nonacademic settings* (pp. 231–248). New York: Guilford.

Fairclough, N. (1989). *Language and power.* London: Longman.

Fiske, J. (1989). *Understanding popular culture.* Boston: Unwin Hyman.

Gee, J. P. (1990). *Social linguistics and literacies: Ideology in discourses.* London: Falmer.

Gilbert, N. G., & Mulkay, M. (1984). *Opening Pandora's box: A sociological analysis of scientists' discourse.* London: Cambridge University Press.

Haas, C. (1994). Learning to read biology: One student's rhetorical development in college. *Written Communication, 11,* 43–84.

Haas, C. (1996). *Writing technology: Studies on the materiality of literacy.* Mahwah, NJ: Erlbaum.

Heath, S. B. (1982). What no bedtime story means. *Langauge in Society, 11,* 49–76.

Hull, G., & Rose, M. (1990). Toward a social-cognitive understanding of problematic reading and writing. In A. Lunsford, H. Moglen, & J. Slevin (Eds.), *The right to literacy* (pp. 235–244). New York: Modern Language Association.

Knorr-Cetina, K. D. (1981). *The manufacture of knowledge: An essay on the constructivist and contextual nature of science.* Elmsford, NY: Pergamon.

Kress, G. (1989). *Linguistic processes in sociocultural practice* (2nd ed.). London: Oxford University Press.

Latour, B., & Woolgar, S. (1979). *Laboratory life: The social construction of scientific facts.* Beverly Hills: Sage.

Lave, J. (1996). Teaching as learning in practice. *Mind, Culture, and Activity, 3*, 149–164.

Leontiev, A. N. (1981). The problem of activity in psychology. In J. Wertsch (Ed.), *The concept of activity in Soviet psychology* (pp. 37–71). Armonk, NY: Sharpe.

Miller, C. R. (1989). What's practical about technical writing? In B. E. Fearing & W. K. Sparrow (Eds.), *Technical writing: Theory and practice* (pp. 14–24). New York: MLA.

Mossberg, W. S. (1998, October 10). Computing got easier last year, but it still has a long way to go. *Wall Street Journal*, p. B1.

Myers, G. (1985). The social construction of two biologists' proposals. *Written Communication, 2*, 219–245.

Reither, J. A., & Vipond, D. (1989). Writing as collaboration. *College English, 51*, 855–867.

Rogoff, B. (1995). Observing sociocultural activity on three places: Participatory appropriation, guided participation, and apprenticeship. In J. Wertsch, P. del Rio, & A. Alvarez (Eds.), *Sociocultural studies of mind* (pp. 139–164). London: Cambridge University Press.

Salomon, G., & Perkins, D. (1996). Learning in wonderland: What do computers really offer education? In S. T. Kerr & K. J. Rehage (Eds.), *Technology and the future of schooling: Ninety-fifth yearbook of the National Society for the Study of Education* (pp. 111–130). Chicago: University of Chicago Press.

Scribner, S., & Cole, M. (1981). *The psychology of literacy*. Cambridge, MA: Harvard University Press.

Semali, L., & Watts Pailliotet, A. (1999). Introduction: What is intermediality and why study it in U.S. classrooms? In L. Semali & A. Watts Pailliotet (Eds.), *Intermediality: The teachers' handbook of critical media literacy* (pp. 1–30). Boulder, CO: Westview.

Simon, H. (1982). *The science of the artificial*. Cambridge, MA: MIT Press.

Spilka, R. (1993). Influencing workplace practice: A challenge for professional writing specialists in academia. In R. Spilka (Ed.), *Writing in the workplace: New research perspectives* (pp. 207–219). Carbondale: Illinois University Press.

Tebeaux, E. (1989). The high-tech workplace: Implications for technical communication instruction. In B. E. Fearing & W. K. Sparrow (Eds.), *Technical writing: Theory and practice* (pp. 136–144). New York: MLA.

Tierney, R., & Damarin, S. (1998). Technology as enfranchisement and cultural development: Criss-crossing symbol systems, paradigm shifts, and social-cultural considerations. In D. Reinking, M. McKenna, L. Labbo, & R. Kieffer (Eds.), *Handbook of literacy and technology: Transformations in a post-typographic world* (pp. 253–268). Mahwah, NJ: Erlbaum.

U.S. Bureau of the Census. (1991). *Statistical abstract of the United States, 1991* (111th ed.). Washington, DC: U.S. Government Printing Office.

Vygotsky, L. S. (1962). *Thought and language* (E. Hanfmann & G. Vakar, Trans.). Cambridge, MA: MIT Press.

Vygotsky, L. S. (1978). *Mind in society*. Cambridge, MA: Harvard University Press.

Wertsch, J. V. (1985). *Vygotsky and the social formation of mind*. Cambridge, MA: Harvard University Press.

Wertsch, J. V. (1991). *Voices of the mind: A sociocultural approach to mediated action*. Cambridge, MA: Harvard University Press.

Wertsch, J. V., del Río, P., & Alvarez, A. (1995). Sociocultural studies: History, action, and mediation. In J. V. Wertsch, P. del Río, & A. Alvarez (Eds.), *Sociocultural studies of mind* (pp. 1–31). London: Cambridge University Press.

MEDIA LITERACY AND SPIRITUALITY

TALES FROM A UNIVERSITY WRITERS' CENTER

Lynn Briggs

Brussart and Brussart (1996) begin *Spiritual Literacy* with a story of how using media can enable one to be spiritually literate, or to "read the world" for meaning" (p. 27). The story is from the movie *Smoke*, in which one character, Auggie, takes photos of the same corner in Brooklyn every day. Looking at these photos, Auggie's friend, Paul, dismisses them as being the same. When Auggie tells him that "you'll never get it if you don't slow down" and calls his attention to the subtle differences—the changes in light, the different people, the weather—Paul "notices a detail in one of them that makes all the difference in the world to him" (p. 27).

Auggie's photographic chronicle of his corner allows him to hold the corner still, out of time, and to give it the kind of attention that makes all the difference in the world. Looking at his 4000 photos in albums, what he calls his "life's work," enables Auggie to study the scene in a manner that allows him to be wide awake to wonder, and to "read the world for meaning" (p. 27). Auggie's approach to life would be considered quintessentially spiritual by many scholars (Campbell, 1988; Frankl, 1997; Fox, 1994; Hillman, 1996; Moore, 1994). Careful study is the process that

Advances in Reading/Language Research, Volume 7, pages 61–87.
Copyright © 2000 by JAI Press Inc.
All rights of reproduction in any form reserved.
ISBN: 0-7623-0264-X

Auggie invokes as his ritual of spiritual practice, and study is what Auggie encouraged Paul to do to see past the sameness in the photos. The purpose of the ritual of study, according to Thomas Moore, is "[t]he manifestations of one's essence, the unfolding of one's capabilities, the revelation of one's heretofore hidden possibilities" (Moore, 1994, p. 59). Auggie's photographic study of his corner made his life meaningful; Paul's introduction to this method of studying the world changed his. Media made study possible for Auggie and Paul. Because the images were captured on film, media is what enabled Auggie and Paul to share the ritual.

In a world that encourages us to rush past wonder, the infinite repeatability of media allows us to study in times, spaces, and company conducive to spiritual awareness. Media, therefore, can support spiritual growth by slowing the world down enough to allow it to be studied. As important as media's ability to allow study, is media's ability to allow sharing of the study ritual, of the spiritual experience. The "aha" that occurs in the moment of epiphany can, through media, be a collective "aha." Such a shared experience can transform a community (Fleckenstein, 1997; Giroux, 1988). A community thus transformed will perpetuate an environment for the ritual and further enhance spiritual connections. However, such a perpetuation of the ritual will not be the only way in which the members of the community act differently as they become "transformative intellectuals" (Giroux in Semali & Watts Pailliotet, 1999, p. 15). Instead, their actions will resonate through their environments.

Therefore, study is a life-changing process. Auggie's deliberate photography suggests his understanding of study's potential. Through study, Auggie was able to make meaning out of the mundane. Concentration camp survivor Viktor Frankl's "logotherapy" describes the process of making sacred meaning out of horror. Frankl's work focuses on how meaning making is humanity's key to spiritual life. He described the "most important avenue" to a meaningful, spiritual life as "changing ourselves" (Frankl, 1997, pp. 141–142). Auggie's medium, photography, played a role in Paul's "aha" as he changed from someone who saw sameness to someone who saw significance.

Personal change is not the only way that Frankl says people create meaningful, spirit-filled lives; another approach to meaning and spirit is "encountering someone" (Frankl, 1997, pp. 141–142). Just as media played a role in the study that led to Paul's personal change, it also played a role in the quality of Auggie and Paul's personal encounter. The effect on Auggie and Paul's relationship demonstrates media's ability to enable shared spiritual experiences through transformative study and human encounters.

Even a popular television show can connect people with each other, as anyone who has ever attended a *Star Trek* convention knows. This show may be an extreme example of how the entertainment media can create a vibrant, actual, human community. People who have never met each other greet with the palm-forward, split-fingered signal that, on one level, says "live long and prosper," and on another level says "we share something with each other."

Media can also create virtual human encounters of great import, as Mitch Albom describes in *Tuesdays with Morrie*. The loving outpourings from "Nightline" viewers flooded Morrie Schwarz's home after he appeared on the show and described what living with ALS (Lou Gehrig's disease) had taught him. Viewers described how seeing Morrie had changed their lives. Encountering these viewers through their letters changed Morrie, as he dealt with the praise of being called a "prophet," or of being asked to contact a viewer's mother in the great beyond after his death (Albom, 1997, p. 85). Morrie Schwarz formed the hub of a spiritual community connected through "Nightline."

Given the abilities of popular media to enhance spirituality (Brussart & Brussart, 1996), it is not a tremendous stretch to imagine that media can be used to spiritual ends in academic settings. Although notions of spirituality are sometimes resisted in academe (Foehr & Schiller, 1997; J. Mullin, personal communication, 1998), recent publications in disciplines as diverse as psychology, management, education, and composition indicate that this resistance is crumbling (Briggs, 1998; Foehr & Schiller, 1997; Hillman, 1996; Marcic, 1997; O'Reilley, 1998).

This chapter will demonstrate how the use of a media-based heuristic enhanced the spiritual connections in a campus community. Comparing media literacy to print literacy may make it easier to see the relationship between such literacy and spirituality. The notion that print literacy could lead to spiritual enlightenment is as old as the sacred texts. The ability to read texts like the Bible or Koran spread spiritual ideas. Media technology—which requires "readers" to see, touch, and listen—can also enhance spirituality.

O'Reilley (1998) defines listening as a powerfully spiritual act. It is possible, she says, to "listen someone into existence" (p. 22). At our Writers' Center, listening is our primary offering, and our goal is to listen writers into an existence as confident, competent, more rhetorically aware and socially connected people. But before we can listen the writers who visit us into an enhanced existence, we must have others listen to us, and we must learn to listen to ourselves. We began the practice of deep viewing (Watts Pailliotet, 1998, 1999), a videotape-based heuristic, as a way to listen to ourselves and each other more critically, but have found that it enabled us to listen more humanely. This was a flip, for it started as an administrative strategy to reinforce center policies and procedures and ensure a particular type of profes-sional development, but it was fortuitously transformed by participants for their own more humane purposes. These purposes, it turns out, included becoming more humanely connected to each other and to the writers we work with, as well as more accepting of ourselves.

I am director of this center at a medium-sized, comprehensive university in the Pacific Northwest. I work with 8–12 Responders each year to support university community writers in their learning and communication. I have a healthy budget by writing center standards, and have pledged to the university that I will use some of the money to ensure that Responders will be professionals who continue to develop as they work in the center, and who regularly assess their own work. The "deep viewing" strategy was how I chose to spend some of our money on professional development, with an initial investment in equipment, and a continuing investment in Responder's time.

In our center we now tell stories about how using deep viewing helped us rid the center of lily pads, stand up to those who refuse to put fruit on pizza, and cleanse our dirty minds. These stories, some of them humorous, some of them touching, have become a part of the intertext (Beach & Hynds, 1991; Porter, 1986) and lore (North, 1987) of work in our center. We initiate our new members into center work by sharing such stories, and they know they are full-fledged members of the community when their stories enter the center canon.

Deep viewing has become a ritual of sorts—a process that we use to welcome members into our community, to renew our commitment to the work we do, to remember where our work comes from and why we do it. Our use of deep viewing in the Writers' Center involves many of the principles Fox (1994) describes in *The Reinvention of Work* as principles of effective ritual. These principles include elements of play, the use of silence, encouragement of risk-taking and sacrifice, and the involvement of community (pp. 265–266). Deep viewing allows what Fox describes as a key purpose of ritual, namely, remembering. By using deep viewing, we remember the writers we tape, the strategies used, points in our personal histories in the center, points in our evolution as a facility, what we claim to value, what we demonstrate we value, and what it means to be a member of a community. These memories help us make connections, a key goal of critical media literacy, described by Semali and Watts Pailliotet (1999) as "the bridge among ideas, disciplines, people, texts, processes, and contexts, educational purposes and outcomes, theory and praxis" (p. 4).

I will share six of these stories in this chapter—one story to illustrate each of the lenses that deep viewing provides for analyzing events. First, however, I'll use a story to describe deep viewing.

DEEP VIEWING

It is not often that I am privileged enough to be present at a stroke of genius, having limited access to this myself, but I was present when deep viewing was conceived. Its conception, like most conceptions, was the result of social relationships. I recall excitedly sharing the work of one brilliant friend—Margaret Himley—with another brilliant friend—Ann Watts Pailliotet. When Ann saw Margaret's description of how teachers at Pat Carini's Prospect school used a method called "deep talk" (Himley, 1991) to slowly examine, honor, and pay remarkable attention to students' works, her eyes lit up. "Ooh! That would be so good with media!" and she started talking too fast for me to understand about the *Wizard of Oz*. Before I knew it, she was explaining her analysis to me, drawing on dictionaries of signs and symbols,

Jung's archetypes, and Campbell's monomyths. While I didn't catch everything she said in those excited, breathy conversations, I learned that studying what had previously seemed like a familiar, even trite, movie, *The Wizard of Oz*, could tell me things about my epic journey and the fulfillment of dreams (and nightmares!). I was surprised that there was so much beneath the surface of something that had seemed so cliché to me (just as the photos had seemed pointless to Paul), and I realized how powerful a study technique such as deep viewing could be for slowing down and waking me up to wonder.

Like Himley's "deep talk," deep viewing involves addressing a text (read that broadly) at increasingly deeper levels. The first level requires remarkable attention to what is already there—summarizing, restating, examining the order. The second level involves making observations of patterns, noting themes in the material that has been summarized and restated. The final level is that of interpretation and evaluation, where the meanings and the value of the patterns and themes are considered (Himley, 1991; Watts Pailliotet, 1998, 1999). By examining the text in these concentric levels, a participant in deep talk or deep viewing becomes more aware of the deeper levels of meaning. Fox (1994) would view this as spiritual engagement, for "spirituality is about living life in depth" (p. 92).

Because Ann wished to use this process for media that were even more packed than children's writing and art projects, she felt she needed something to slow down the first part of the process, to make sure that viewers could summarize and restate. It would be difficult to simply summarize a commercial without breaking it apart—there is visual action, there is sound, there is spoken or sung discourse, colors and shapes used to create a mood, printed discourse, changes in camera angles, all wrapped in complex cultural cues—happening at once. So, Ann's idea was to view the text multiple times, each through a different lens, in order to enable a summary of the myriad messages possible.

The Deep Viewing Codes

The codes Ann developed for deep viewing analysis follow. These codes are used to collect the data from the medium—whether it is print or video (Watts Pailliotet, 1998, pp. 126–127):

1. Action/Sequence: When examining a segment of a videotaped session through this lens, Responders ask questions like "What happened? When do events occur? How long does each event last? Who initiates events? Who ends them?"

2. Semes/Forms: When examining a segment of a videotaped session through this lens, Responders ask questions like "What forms, shapes, patterns, textures, or objects are repeated or emphasized? What objects are seen? How are they positioned in relation to each other? What stands out?"

3. Actors/Discourse: When examining a segment of a videotaped session through this lens, Responders ask questions like "What are the tones of the voices used? What sounds are repeated? What words are repeated? What concepts stressed? Who talks the most? How is silence used?"

4. Proximity/Movement: When examining a segment of a videotaped session through this lens, Responders asked questions like "Where do objects and actors move? What motions are repeated? What people and objects are positioned near and far from each other?"

5. Culture/Context: When Responders examine a segment of a videotaped session through this lens, they ask questions like "What knowledge of culture is assumed? What symbols of culture and cultural values are present? What gaps in cultural knowledge are noticed?"

6. Effects/Process: When Responders view a videotaped session through this lens, they ask questions like "What did the camera angle and microphone position contribute to this video? What might I have heard or seen if camera and microphone were positioned elsewhere? What is the result of where the camera is placed? How different is what is seen and heard from what the participants saw and heard?"

Applications of Deep Viewing in the Writers' Center

In the center, we used the deep viewing procedure in numerous ways. First, Responders taped themselves and brought the tapes to group deep-viewing sessions; second, Responders taped themselves and deep-viewed in private. In addition, we added it as a strategy to help writers decode levels of discourse.

As center director—a position set up administratively, and described by Responders as a "benevolent dictatorship"—I introduced deep viewing as a strategy for quality control. I wanted Responders to have a means by which to develop professionally, and I wanted to instill the notion that I expected ongoing professional development as part of employment. I introduced deep viewing as a "critical pedagogy" that I hoped would lead to "reflection, learning, and praxis through positive personal and collective social action" (Watts Pailliotet, 1998, p. 32). My other goal was not so enlightened, however. Part of me also wished to have deep viewing reinforce and support the norms of philosophy and procedure. By watching these tapes, deep-viewing them, and listening to my learned commentary, Responders would get a sense of the more and less acceptable approaches, and would be frequently reminded about the direction the center was headed. These were managerial goals—goals to make me more powerful, more able to control quality, more able to enforce my values. They were not goals that assumed shared authority for center work or that trusted in the judgment and sense of Responders. In essence, I wanted to use deep viewing to help create a sense of what is "in" and "out" of center norms and expectations. Fortunately, this backfired. Instead of supporting the existing power structure, this heuristic for critical media literacy allowed Responders to "transform their newfound critical understandings into agency, positive acts and effects in themselves and others" (Semali & Watts Pailliotet, 1999, p. 8).

Before I explain the details of how this plan for control blew up in my face, and how the participants transformed the process, and, ultimately, the center, I will describe both the cultural climate in which deep viewing was introduced in the center, and delineate the center goals and assumptions.

Cultural Climate and Community Context

I was hired to direct a newly revised (budgetarily and administratively) center at a comprehensive university. The reconstructed center had been in "initial" operation for four months when I arrived. Prior to the revamping, the center had operated on a shoestring in a shoebox, with goodwill being the only source of support. As such, the center had a triage function, working to diagnose and remediate those in most serious trouble, who were often sent there, sometimes just to sit and do homework or worksheets. There was no time or money for training or materials, so the hope was that some good would be done by osmosis.

While the new version of the center had resources, it had no permanent director until I arrived, and thus it continued some practices of the previous establishment. I was attracted to the position because of the resources and support accorded the center, and was sure that with such things I could make great changes quickly. I intended, immediately, to change it from a culture of writing remediation to one of writers' engagement. And deep viewing was part of my plan. I knew that this switch in thinking would be difficult, and I knew that some of the staff would carry over from the previous incarnation, so I wanted to provide a means by which we could reflect, publicly, on whether we were changing appropriately. The appropriateness of those changes was to be gauged by the degree of compliance to the center's mission statement, which follows.

Deep Viewing and the Mission of the Writers' Center

Andrea Lunsford (1991) describes three types of writing centers: the Storehouse, the Garret, and the Burkean Parlor models. The Storehouse, she says, "operates as information station . . . prescribing and handing out skills and strategies to individual learners," while the Garret centers are "informed by a deep-seated belief in individual 'genius,' in the Romantic sense of the term" (p. 4). What she advocates is the Burkean Parlor center, in which true collaboration takes place, where writer and Responder really work together and don't just go through the motions. The Burkean Parlor center, according to Lunsford, could have for its motto: "For excellence, the presence of others is always required" (Hannah Arendt, as quoted in Lunsford, 1991, p. 6).

This view of work in the center is consistent with foundational ideas for deep viewing, including that "the reader is not a passive recipient of information, but actively engages in transactions with a text" and the writer of the text, "to create meaning" (Watts Pailliotet, 1998, p. 124). In addition, deep viewing creates social contexts in which participants' actions are tied to others (Semali & Watts Pailliotet, 1999). Being an active recipient and creating meaning require engagement. Writers and Responders can only collaborate if both are truly present. Deep viewing helped Responders become more radically present, and highly sensitized to their actions, wondering during sessions "what will this look like later?"

The goal of the Writers' Center is to help writers understand the influence and power of "others": those who are present in writing response in the person of the Responder, and those who are conjured by the talk of the writer and Responder. These others, present and imagined, fit into what Marilyn Cooper (1986) refers to as the web of readers in the ecological system that writers carry around. In essence, "understandings are developed through past and present experiences" (Watts Pailliotet, 1998, p. 124).

Response in the Writers' Center is collaborative in an even richer sense than Lunsford intended, for the collaboration occurs between more than those physically present—the writer and Responder are able to "collaborate" with others like authors, real readers, and imagined audiences who are discussed. These others influence writer and Responder perceptions of texts and enable the expansion of the writer–Responder system in discussions of these texts. The voices of others as they are anticipated, imagined, or recollected echo during Writers' Center sessions. These voices can populate a room.

In *Stories from the Center* (Briggs & Woolbright, 2000) I document how the room where response to writing took place "was very crowded with people we could not and did not abandon. The impact of the others in the web of readers that we spun was real, tangible, textual. It was not an ephemeral notion that our texts, our reading, our writing, was shaped by others to whose language we were connected" (p. 30).

In the deceptively simple system of response, Responders offer real responses to writers' texts—responses that have their roots in the intertextual world and web of readers. As Responders tap their own intertextual resources, they encourage, implicitly or explicitly, writers to do the same (Briggs, 2000). Hence, in a meeting between two people, the existence of many others is invoked, reminding writers and Responders that, whenever we read or write, we are always in the presence of others. Helping writers carry away a sense of how their current text fits into their own world of writers, readers, and texts is a goal of this center.

The name of this center is symbolic of the goals. Though many similar facilities across the country are called "Writing Centers," calling it the "Writ*ers*' Center" emphasizes its focus on people in their roles as writers, rather than simply on texts. We assume in the center that the writers and their texts are integrally connected. Responders intend that writers who come into the center will walk away aware of their own processes, the rhetorical concerns of writing, and the social, temporal, and academic realities that influence those processes and concerns. In addition, writers will get a sense of the rich and complex way that these elements—the psychological, rhetorical, contextual, and even spiritual—intertwine. While many writers who leave the center may not have an explicit understanding of these elements, most will have some sort of "aha" experience after sessions with a Responder. Data compiled in other centers suggest that writers often become aware later of the many intertextual (Beach & Hynds, 1991; Porter, 1986) influences on their writing.

It should be clear from this description that this is a non-"remedial" writing center. The idea in the center is to pay attention to *writers and their writing* instead of *writing problems*. This does not mean that "problems" are not addressed, but that they are not addressed as problems. What qualifies as a writing problem depends greatly on the perspective from which it is viewed. Responders in the Writers' Center recognize that the flip sides of problems are often strengths—like a writer who has an inconsistent voice in her text because she has so many strong writing voices to choose from, or the writer who cannot control conventions because he has devoted all of his energy to making the text conceptually sophisticated. The participants identify "problems" in a context that also celebrates the strengths of writer and text.

In addition, the goal is not to produce better writing, but better writers—rhetorically aware people who can make textual decisions from an informed, critical, and reflective place. Deep viewing is one of the elements of center work that would make it possible for Responders to make decisions from this place. It would be easier for Responders to help writers simply produce better texts—an admonition to add more examples, to clarify a thesis, to run a spell check—but that would create a population of writers dependent on Responders for feedback. Rather, Responders desire to help writers understand their writing processes so that they can independently make rhetorical decisions that will achieve their desired effects. It is akin to the well-worn metaphor of teaching someone how to fish rather than serving her a fish dinner. My plan for deep viewing initially was for it to show why Responders should be dependent on my view, but instead this process enabled independence in spite of me. The use of a critical literacy process with media resulted in self-empowerment (Considine & Haley, 1992; Semali & Watts Pailliotet, 1999) even though that wasn't the reason I employed it.

The term "Responder" reflects this view of working with writers. Responders offer reactions, visions, commentary, questions to writers' texts or the processes they describe. These strategies reflect beliefs in a writer's voice and sense of self, both of which are related to the spiritual. Since a "Responder" must have something to respond to, writers are encouraged to come in with an agenda. This agenda could center on a text, an assignment, a process, or an experience. "Responder" is capitalized as a rhetorical key to a political message. Just as "Writers' Center" is designed to send a message about who and what is privileged in the center, "Responder" emphasizes that it is a professional title, and not just a role. While many people in writers' lives may play the role of responder, the folks in the center are educated, committed, and engage in regular professional development to be

Responders. Remembering to capitalize that term has served often to remind me of the professionalism and value of my staff.

Writers who use the center are a varied group: from freshmen to faculty, artists to economists, writing assigned and self-sponsored texts. Some writers come in once, then disappear for a quarter, year, or forever; some come in at weekly, biweekly, or monthly intervals. All of them leave information about themselves, their writing, their reason for coming to the center. Writing Responders in the center believe that writers do and should have authority over their own texts, that responses to writing are contextually determined, and that writers benefit most from responses that detail readers' reactions and trace those reactions to the words on the page. The strategies Responders invoke reflect these beliefs.

Responders respect writers' authority over their texts and demonstrate their respect in the way that they treat the text—rarely handling it, never marking it up. Responders declare and remind writers that they are in charge of what happens to their texts in the sessions. This respect of boundaries is one concrete practice designed to honor the writer's humanity. It is designed to communicate that what is important is the writer's growth in ability and confidence, rather than the correction of a discrete text.

Responders recognize and celebrate that responses to writing are contextually bound and that different Responders to the same text may have very different reactions. Responders explicitly own all of their responses and ground them in their particular contextual milieu. Responders work to detail exactly what they thought, wondered, or felt in response to writers' texts. Responders trace these responses to the words on the page so that writers can weigh their words and make informed decisions based on their own goals and intentions.

While Responders work to help writers learn, they are not teachers in the traditional sense; they do not approach their work with writers as experts on subject matter, as evaluators of texts, as assigners of tasks. Rather, they are experienced and perceptive readers inviting writers into a literate conversation. Deep viewing invites Responders into a media literate conversation. Power relationships in the center are not static or clearly defined (Briggs, 2000). While Responders at the Writers' Center have some academic status—most have master's degrees, all have graduate course-work—they remain in a tenuous employment situation, officially classified as "temporary part-time."

Those who come to them for response sometimes have greater or equal social status in other venues or cultures. Many writers are ESL students who have been practicing lawyers, businesspeople, or educators in their native lands. Graduate students, faculty, and staff also use the center. Determining the social and academic status balance between writer and Responder is not an easy task. And so, because power relationships are unpredictable (even once a session has begun) Responders must enter each session assuming the writer is equally powerful. In taping sessions for deep viewing, the power relationship is tipped again, as the presence of the camera suggests the possibility of infinite others in the session. Those others may be people who hold lower status—new Responders using the tape to learn the ropes—or they may be people of higher status—the director, watching the tape to assess the session. The existence of the tape means that the power relationships surrounding the session will continue to shift.

In order to better describe the work of the center, the assumptions and procedures are outlined below.

Response Procedures

The response procedures grow out of the following assumptions:

1. Writing is a social activity.
2. Writers learn to write in order to make meaning for themselves and others.
3. Others can help writers write by providing detailed responses to the meaning of a text.

The procedures are simple; there are only four guidelines:

1. Always say "I."
2. Never touch the text.
3. Respond by paying attention to the reactions that the text creates and trace those reactions to the words on the page.
4. Be explicit with the writer about the reasons for using these methods.

While this mission statement is an internal document, shared externally only with those who have similar interests or are charged with regulating the center, the goals are shared with faculty and students, although usually in an informal, oral form. They are, officially, as follows:

Goals for Writers

1. Writers will be better able to critically analyze writing in different disciplines and situations. This ability to analyze writing situations will provide writers with the working knowledge necessary to perform successfully.

Writers will be supported in their attempts to understand the elements of writing situations like purpose, audience, and mode of discourse. Writers will be encouraged to see the requirements of a writing situation as indicative of the expectations and values of the discipline, profession, medium, or location. Writers will have an analysis of writing situations modeled for them by Responders when they bring papers, assignments, or ideas to response sessions. Writers will be able to use the knowledge gained through analysis of writing situations to make appropriate choices about style, sources of data, mechanics, and so on in their own writing.

Writers' ability to adapt to different discourse situations is heightened by the fact that they will also be expected to compose in different media. Responders' approaches are often metaphorically taken from media; they may ask a writer to describe the main point of her paper in a sound byte format, or ask questions that lead to a hypertext-like explication. Participants' familiarity with multimedia formats, while not actually operative in center sessions, comprise shared territory in which to communicate.

Deep Viewing and Goal 1:   In order for writers to be assisted to see how to analyze discourse situations so that they may successfully write to them, Responders must have such analytic skills as second nature. Deep viewing has helped Responders think in terms of analytical schemes and analytical heuristics. Some of the heuristic approaches Responders develop in their work with writers are connected to the habits of mind encouraged through deep viewing. Deep viewing sometimes jars Responders into looking beyond what they take for granted in a situation. A Responder who has become open to the possibility that things, once reflected on, may not be what they seem, can encourage writers to reflect as well. This might be manifest in sessions when Responders suggest that writers go back and problematize their assignments, or reconsider what their goals are for their university education. Discussions that diverge from the expected text-based talk often result in unexpected insights for writers. Deep viewing helps keep Responders open to the unexpected.

2.   Writers will be able to use writing to learn.

Writers will see writing used by Responders in response sessions as a means to record, connect, and synthesize information. Writers will be encouraged by Responders to use writing in this way themselves. Responders will support such practice by suggesting strategies such as freewriting, mapping, or outlining. Responders will also offer support to writers regarding ways to use writing to help understand, recall, and assimilate reading. Writers will transfer this knowledge to situations outside of the center.

Some writers come in a bit jaded about the use of writing to learn, having been admonished to take notes or write outlines from time immemorial. Occasionally, Responders suggest media-related strategies to support writing to learn, like the clustering software "Inspiration" available on some center computers, or an approach called a "meta" done using a Word document with two columns.

Deep Viewing and Goal 2:   Responders—well-educated people with good memories—can often understand complex concepts without writing anything down. Student writers may often not choose to write in order to learn, and it is easy for Responders, who can "get" what the writer is talking about without any notes, to forget how useful writing is as a way to learn new information, connect information, and evaluate information. The complex texts and the categorical lenses used in deep viewing demand writing to record and summarize. Through deep viewing, Responders were reminded of the value of using writing to learn, and so could honestly encourage writers to try it. Deep viewing requires Responders to take notes on the tapes they watch. As they do this, they often express surprise at how much they noticed after taking notes on a tape they had watched several times before. The process of deep viewing serves to reinforce the usefulness of using writing to learn.

The fact that the tapes must be replayed so many times in order for Responders to see what is going on in any one, short segment of a Response session emphasizes how packed with meaning their work is. The infinite repeatability of the medium of the videotape enables the writing that is done in relation to deep viewing to focus on analysis rather than simply recollection. The fact that the tape can be rewound to recapture a detail allows Responders the freedom of analysis in their writing. They can use the notes they take while watching the video to key into and analyze what they see, as they are inspired to do so, without fear that if they don't simply record, the events will slip away. The freedom to analyze as inspired is something that Responders pass on to writers. They often encourage writers to explore and explicate what the writers might feel is a tangent in the text as a way to consider whether a key point may be contained within.

3. **Writers will be able to engage in other learning communities as a result of their work in the center.**

   Writers will discover that in their work with Responders they are able to make connections, push beyond previous conceptual boundaries, and understand issues and strategies from different people's perspectives. Writers will be able to generalize the benefits of this learning community and establish and enhance other such interactions. Writers may do this by creating a network of classmates to respond to their writing, by visiting other campus facilities (like the Math Lab or Academic Support Center), and by becoming more adept at peer group work in classes.

   The media that writers are exposed to, particularly in the form of software, contribute to their ability to collaborate. Even software that Hawisher (1994, p. 39) would not define as "social" is collaborative. In order for a student to compose in Word, other writers have had to set up programs that expand or constrict possibilities. The common sight of someone yelling at a computer communicates how such media are viewed as collaborators, even if that role is not always considered a friendly one. The availability of a table tool in a word-processing program is a suggestion from a software engineer that can say to a writer, just as a peer working on the same project could: "Hey, let's display that data as a table!" As Hawisher says, "they simultaneously enable and constrain 'ways of seeing'" (p. 38).

Deep Viewing and Goal 3:   The tapes that are deep viewed always tell a story about a relationship between Responder and writer. Such attention to the dynamics of the relationship can enable Responders to reflect on the actions and elements that led to more and less successful collaborations. The categories provide a variety of lenses through which to view these collaborative relationships. Responders often find it useful to examine tensions that they discover between the elements of the categories—for example, movement that is distancing, like leaning away, or pushing books or papers between people, in a session with language that suggests closeness—lots of references to "we," or allusions to shared experiences. Deep viewing helps Responders see when and how connections are made with writers.

4.   **Writers will have an increased ability to assess their own writing.**
By participating in the response process—listening to Responders' feedback, considering their questions, and analyzing patterns of error—writers will develop an "internalized reader." This mechanism will aid writers in assessing their own work, for they will be able to ask the questions, raise the issues, and anticipate the intended reader's response. Writers will therefore be able to estimate how particular criteria apply to their writing as the criteria relate to the writing situation.

Writers who develop this "internalized reader" are able to "actively analyze" and "evaluate" their own "media messages" (Hobbs, 1998, p. 127). Writers who become able to adeptly self-assess realize that in their writing, as well as in other media, "meaning is derived from an intersection of reader, text, and culture, and that the messages have economic, political, social, and historic contexts" (Hobbs, 1998, p. 128). Becoming able to effectively critique one's own writing can take a writer to a place where she can more successfully "move beyond information and skills to meaning and interpretation" (Heath in LeBlanc, 1994, p. 24).

Deep Viewing and Goal 4:   Deep viewing creates a more careful and selective internalized reader by providing Responders with a heuristic through which they can check their response behaviors while they are happening. A Responder who notices through deep viewing that, though she allows enough silence after her questions, she moves her body in a way that suggests she has the answer, might be able to see herself doing this in the middle of a session, and change her approach while still working with the writer. The deep viewing categories give Responders the ability to quickly assess themselves in various ways—they can ask, as they are about to sit down in a session, "If I sit here, what will the writer be confronted with visually throughout our session?" or "What is the message that my writer's clothing is sending about her cultural understanding and expectations?"

For some Responders, deep viewing has resulted in a variety of changed behaviors—including everything from how they positioned themselves physically in a session to how long they waited before rephrasing a question (or whether they chose to use questions at all!). Such changes were the result of self-assessment sparked by deep viewing. By engaging in deep viewing, Responders were able to participate in the same challenging cognitive process that they ultimately encourage writers to attempt. Deep viewing changed lives in the Writers' Center. Work in the center became more than a cognitive process; Responders engaged in praxis, and the community was changed, not just socially, but spiritually (Semali & Watts Pailliotet, 1999).

DEEP VIEWING WRITERS' CENTER LIVES

In the sections that follow, I employ stories of key events that resulted from "deep viewing" to illustrate how media can rehumanize a facility and promote a literacy of meaningful interpersonal connection. Deep viewing worked in the center by helping Responders "connect. . . analytical skills to social or daily contexts" (Semali & Watts Pailliotet, 1999, p. 9). Each of the following stories will emphasize one of the categories of deep viewing.

The First Tale: Lily Pads into Art Gallery (Semes/Forms)

I arrived ten minutes late to the Writers' Center on a Monday morning, and was shocked to see that my staff had made a shambles of the place. Bookshelves were emptied, plants shoved into corners, chairs piled up against one another. "Just give us another hour," Aimee said, "and we'll be rid of all of those lily pads."

Those "lily pads" were patterns of visual meaning that we had noticed in our Friday "deep viewing" meeting. During our weekly 2-hour meeting we had viewed a tape of a Writers' Center session. On this video, the Responder sat with the writer at a round, gray table, while in the background three or four other round, gray tables were visible with other pairs working at them. The planes of the tables were broken only by the bodies, and the tables hovered above the plane of a blue-green floor. As we rewound and reviewed a section of tape that Friday, we were shocked to see the monochromatic, repetitive nature of our center. Monday the Responders conspired with each other to do something about it.

The Responders' embrace of deep viewing as a way to analyze, understand, and even change their environment was a bit of a surprise to me, for I had spent some of Friday's meeting nearly arguing (not quite, though, as we are very polite) for the value of this method. Ward, one of the Responders, asked plaintively (a tone unusual for him), "Please explain how studying a videotape for what forms are repeated, what colors dominate, what textures reappear, is going to help us work in the Writers' Center. I just don't get it." Ward was not alone, and, as the others joined Ward's questioning, I began to doubt as well.

But I'd used this method in the classroom; I'd adjusted my use of physical space because of analyzing the units of visual meaning, and I'd felt that my adjustments had been useful. So, I reiterated my desire for the Responders to watch the tape again (this time without sound) and note what they saw, perhaps metaphorically. And so, when we rolled that footage for the third or fourth time, someone said "lily pads." Someone else said "and we're the frogs." Someone got up and said, "look at all the flattened circles" and pointed to the shapes on the screen. Then they contrasted the colors—"but it's not richly colored like a pond, everything is so dull," "except for that evaluation form box, it's bright red, and the only thing in the room that stands out." "Ooh," said someone else, "what does it say that the center of attention is the place writers put their evaluations of us?"

Sometime between Friday happy hour and Monday at 9 the Responders hatched a plan, and I walked in to find them carrying it out. They had used the deep viewing heuristic to become more connected to the center and to each other. They were excited about their plans for redecorating (I saw that they had made drawings over the weekend), complimentary toward each other for their ideas, and they worked as a unit. I had only hoped that viewing the tape could help them think about where they position their chairs, or what section of the center they sit to face in a session. They had bigger plans.

While the rearranging was, in fact, finished in less than an hour, another decision that the Responders had made was that there be art on the walls. Since our budget didn't allow us to buy or rent from the university galleries, we decided to volunteer our space as a student gallery, and to have students apply for shows. The art department was happy to oblige, and we have had a series of student shows (complete with cocktail party openings and paintings sold) since we were first critical of the lily pads. We have since established some lasting relationships with these artists, some of whom have visited the center as writers since their art was displayed.

This art enabled many other connections to be formed. One important story is of a conversation that took place between me, the center's director, and a normally shy, Japanese student. When the student entered the center to make an appointment, she found Gail and me staring a painting. It depicted a boxer, in a ring, with various classical and religious figures (Jesus, scenes from the Sistine Chapel, traditionally hellish scenes, "The Thinker") portrayed around the edges in fuzzy, sort of dream-like renderings. Another figure outside was a woman in an American flag bikini, portrayed in the most realistic terms of anyone in the painting.

Gail and I were discussing our study of the painting, considering what the meaning was, particularly around the bikini-clad woman. We had a theory about how she was helping the boxer decide whether to engage in a heavenly or hellish way. The student had a different reading of the painting. She offered that she thought that the woman represented beauty and perhaps even innocence. She detailed how the woman's expression placed her above the various frays depicted in the painting.

The American flag on the bikini led us into a discussion of American culture, its worship of violence, reverence of beauty and youth.

The Japanese student had been in the center before. She had been quiet, reserved, and retiring during sessions. Our discussion of the art, however, was one in which she was animated, even opinionated. It was a discussion among equals. In our center, using media analysis led us to use media to connect to each other. The usually quiet student had found a voice to express herself in the presence of media. Perhaps it was the universality of the images that made her comfortable, perhaps it was her familiarity with visual texts, which seemed more manageable than the foreign language in which she had to write at the university. For whatever reason, the medium of the painting gave her something to say and a way to say it that allowed for more eloquence than in previous center interactions.

This story illustrates in a concrete and material way the usefulness of the deep viewing methodology. Deep viewing allowed us to honor the spirit of the center by reading its spaces and places for meaning. Through deep viewing we realized that the message our physical environment was sending wasn't what we wanted our writers to get. In a manner akin to the way we hoped our writers would understand the importance of context in discourse choices, we viewed our center as a text, and the placement of furniture as rhetoric. Through deep viewing we became able to adapt our rhetorical strategies to our audience and purpose.

We spent a great deal of time in the center discussing ways that we could welcome writers. The inconsistency of our welcoming words and unwelcoming environment wasn't apparent until we used deep viewing to look at the physical space of the center as a text. While the changes that resulted from this deep viewing session are obvious and dramatic, they are not the largest and most significant. Stories that follow will detail the other aspects of center life that deep viewing modified.

Moulthrop and Kaplan (1994) point out that through the use of media like "hypertext, student texts are no longer so easily subordinated to the bound volumes of revered authors" (in Johnson-Eilola, 1994, p. 213). This conceptualization of media expands the boundaries of "text," just as our deep viewing of the center allows us to see physical space as text. The heuristic of deep viewing enabled us to break the bounds of typical textuality, and read our environment for meaning, an act that Frankl (1997) and Brussart and Brussart (1996) would name "spiritual."

Deep viewing helped us realize that fulfilling the first goal of the center—helping writers understand and adapt to discourse communities—could begin with us understanding the messages the text of our physical space sent, and how that helped or hindered our attempt to develop community.

The Second Tale: Keeping Kathy (Movement/Proximity)

After her husband lost part of his hand in an accident, she had three car-totaling accidents in one year, and another bout with pneumonia, accomplished ESL teacher and Responder Kathy decided to leave the center staff. We had often depended on

Kathy to guide us in working with the 50% of our student population who are nonnative English-speaking students, and we missed her desperately. Then we remembered that Kathy had videotaped for deep viewing. All of the Responders had done deep viewing of their own sessions as part of their professional development, and Kathy had left us her tapes. We had a meeting and watched a tape of Kathy working with a Japanese student from the English Language Institute. We had often discussed and appreciated Kathy's gestures when she worked with us, so we watched her tape with particular attention to how things moved.

Kathy's gestures and expressions were instructive. We watched how her hands made larger movements at the beginning of the session, when she and the writer were getting acquainted, and smaller, more intimate movements later. Her movements were large, again, when there was a misunderstanding or a point of tension, and smaller when there was agreement. It was as if, in the more challenging moments in the session, Kathy used her hands to lasso the ideas and reign them in. Her large movements seemed to say "we are this much apart," and they required her to lean back from the writer, while her smaller movements required that both she and the writer focus on the close space between their bodies.

As we watched, and noticed, and reflected, we remembered fondly how she would talk like that in our midst and we began to discuss what we each do, when, and what others do. One Responder commented that she had begun to move like Kathy after watching her work with ESL students. She talked about how attending to Kathy's movements made her more aware of how individual fingers moved to emphasize an idea, rather than just the total movement of the whole hand. We started to talk about what kind of finger positions seemed inviting, and what kind seemed scary or "witchy"—like the stereotypical crooked finger on Halloween decorations. We talked about how hands moved from faces—noses, eyes, mouth—to the table, papers, and started to think about spreading germs. This piqued Joy's interest, and she reinitiated an academic study of nonverbal communication. We also put a bottle of antibacterial hand lotion on the front desk. The antibacterial lotion was a sign that we saw ourselves as woven tightly into the campus community. We were touchable, located close enough to each other to transmit illness.

Our attention to Kathy's tapes after she left reminded us of how important the members of our community are. What we saw in Kathy's actions was that collaboration was an activity that involved not just the mind or the voice, but also the body. Deep viewing made us aware of our wholeness, both as individuals and as a community. As we saw how Kathy's actions were connected to her words and to the affective messages she was sending, we were also reminded while watching Kathy on tape, together, how the members of our center community were linked. These links between "body, soul, spirit, and work" are elements that Fox suggests are necessary for a healthy adult life (1994, p. 11).

Deep viewing Kathy's tapes helped us remember that collaboration continued outside of the walls of the Writers' Center—a message that we hoped our work would ultimately send to writers.

Tale Three: Making Bread (Actors/Discourse)

Gail laughed when she watched her own hand movements—she described herself as "making bread" as she kneaded her ideas in the air. Her laugh was in stereo, for the video was full of her giggle as well. The other Responders watching laughed too, but a bit more tentatively. Everyone knew that Gail hadn't wanted to do this—not make the video, not watch the video. She was the last of the Responders to do so. She politely resisted, joked that she didn't want to see herself on video because of how she looked in the tape of her sister's shipboard wedding, and made excuses for nearly two quarters. When we finally got to see her first video, the people were distant from the camera, and the sound was low. However, one sound carried above the low talking—Gail's catchy laugh.

Without clear dialogue to distract us, the prevalence of this laugh was pointed. Both Gail and her Japanese writer found things funny frequently. As we viewed the tape, we were struck by how normal it seemed for Gail to be laughing with a writer. We mused about the fact that this would seem odd to many, especially those instructors who had sent students to the center as a punishment for being "bad writers." Gail's session didn't sound much like punishment. In fact, if viewed from the perspective of someone thinking of the center as a place to send student miscreants, Gail's session would look like rebellion. By reflecting on how typical a session filled with giggling was at the center, we were able to notice that typical university power relationships had been toppled.

Perhaps it is partly this ability at the center to subvert the dominant hierarchy that keeps Responders in their jobs even when higher paying, more regular, or benefit-carrying positions become available to them. The center Responders are generally a liberatory group, hoping to convince writers not only of the authority of their own voices, but also of the value of critical literacy, which "encourages a dialogue between teachers and students resulting in 'self-realization and self-direction, affecting not only [the students'] relations to school but also their relations to work, family, and community life'" (Johndan-Eilola, 1998, p. 211). Responders' work with writers may be similar in effect to the way that Moulthrop and Kaplan describe hypertext—beyond "the neutrality of academic theory and onto the livelier and more dangerous ground of social practice" (Moulthrop & Kaplan, 1998, p. 236). Real laughter between two people requires at least a momentary leveling of hierarchies. Successful collaboration can occur most easily when such distinctions between status are erased.

But deep viewing Gail's mirthful session did more than remind us of the virtue of a liberatory pedagogy, it allowed us to vicariously experience her sense of joy in the work, and for all of us to "rejoice in the good work that [we] do" (Aquinas in Fox, 1994, p. 91).

Viewing Gail's tape allowed us to conceptualize center work as both political and spiritual, a connection also made by Matthew Fox. In his book arguing for a new paradigm for work, Fox states that "[o]ur search for meaning in our work, for recognition, for astonishment or wonder or awe is another way of saying that our work deserves to be a mystical experience" (1994, p. 92).

Tale Four: Zyrtec and Gutterminds (Culture/Context)

While Gail was initially resistant to the idea of making a videotape of herself, she was attracted to deep viewing for use in her conversation groups full of nonnative English-speaking students. She taped television commercials and used the method to help her students learn not only the language, but also the cultural conventions that are commonplace. However, as it turned out, the most daunted by cultural conventions were not her Asian or Arab students, but her colleagues.

Gail's use of deep viewing with commercials in the conversation group became so popular with the students from the English Language Institute that instructors from the ELI began requesting that she do so with their classes. So at least once a quarter, Gail goes to ELI classes to do deep viewing of a commercial with the students. Gail had coopted the process of deep viewing for her own purposes for a different context. She was able to do with deep viewing what we hoped writers were better able to do once they left the center—adapt their texts for different audiences and purposes.

Before she goes to the ELI class, Gail previews the commercial at a Writers' Center meeting and we practice our deep viewing skills on it, as well as talk about the cultural messages that international students might need coaching to understand. Sometimes the commercials she tapes give us more than we have bargained for.

The visits Gail makes to the ELI are significant for another reason. While we work with many ELI students in the center, and while both the center and ELI profess to benefit from the collaboration, our pedagogy and philosophy usually diverge. Gail's guest lectures are the one instance in which the goals and approaches used by the ELI and the center intertwine.

One winter, she brought in a familiar Calvin Klein scent ad. We'd all seen it before, but when screened with regard to an unfamiliar audience, we were shocked at its overt sexual messages. We didn't know, however, how ingrained in our cultural mindset sexual reference was until the next quarter, when she brought in the Zyrtec commercial.

From the start of the ad it was clear that the product was a pharmaceutical. The name was emblazoned in the corner of the screen, and it showed a man in a suit walking out into a desert filled with tall, pointy rocks. The voiceover said something like "Feel better than you ever have before" and made some reference to being able to accomplish big feats. The announcer ended by repeating the name and saying "It's big; really BIG." In the meantime, the man in the suit had scaled one of the tall, tan, pointy rocks by pulling himself up on a rope, which dangled between his legs.

We had a field day exploring the cultural cues. Ray talked about the classic Freudian symbolism of the peaks, the more vulgar suggestiveness of the position and use of the rope, the locker room reference to "big." Even Joy, normally less likely to fall prey to our warped sensibilities, saw the phallic symbols.

An 800 number appeared on the screen. The ad never stated what Zyrtec did, so we were all convinced by our culturally informed reading that it was Viagra's precursor. All of us, that is, except Patrick, who sat at the meeting shaking his head, indicating that he was ashamed of our dirty minds. However, because the rest of us were so sure that we had read the cultural cues correctly, we called the 800 number and asked for the literature so that we could show Patrick that we were not oversexed, just culturally aware. We thought we'd have the little chat with Patrick once the literature arrived.

Gail, who had smugly gone to her ELI class and deep viewed this tape, came back reporting that most of the students thought it was something to keep people awake or an allergy medication. She noted that she had described what she had seen, and how those things were connected to Western literary and popular American male culture. The ELI students found her insights interesting and amusing, and began to share some of the symbols with similar meaning in their various cultures. Some students indicated that unlike our view of the actor's feat of climbing the rocks as sexual, the emphasis in other cultures would be on the accomplishment, not on the phallic imagery. The actor's subdued, professional suit would be viewed as a sign of responsibility and status, rather than pointing to his maleness, which for us reverberated with the shapes of the rocks.

Imagine, then, how stunned we were to see the literature, covered with pictures of sunflowers, that described the benefits of Zyrtec, a prescription antihistamine.

Taking deep viewing to the ELI not only enabled us to collaborate with colleagues with whom we often disagreed, it reminded us of the importance of respecting differences—both between the two facilities, and among the many cultures represented. The juxtaposition of differing viewpoints allowed us to gain a perspective that made it easier to read our world for meaning. Our Zyrtec experience reminded us of our naiveté, and reinforced the notion that we all had much to learn. Being so blatantly wrong in our reading emphasized our need for caution, respect for others' opinions, and suggested that we might need some strategies for reading cultural texts. These are the messages that we often hope to send to writers, and we offer writing as a strategy to learn about and sort through complex issues.

Tale Five: Who Puts Fruit on Pizza? (Action/Sequence)

Try as they may, Responders Vicki, Gail, and Karen couldn't get the pizza parlor to understand them. "Who puts fruit on pizza?" was the question that met their attempt to order a large Hawaiian for delivery to their hotel room. We had ventured to NYC to do a presentation at a Writing Center conference on their use of deep viewing. As the conference progressed, we found that the cultural differences were larger than fruits and vegetables—and that these differences rocked some of our assumptions about what was at stake in writing center sessions. This questioning of assumptions, however, eventually proved useful, for during the session in which we presented deep viewing, the audience was able to see something in the action sequence that emphasized some positive but largely unnoticed elements of our center life.

The presentation outlined the procedures for deep viewing, described how it was used in the center, showed a videotaped clip and how it was analyzed, and, finally, ran a three-minute segment that the participants were asked to deep-view themselves. The clip featured Vicki working with a young man who was writing a paper about feminism in Greek tragedy. From the tape, it was clear that Vicki was engrossed in the writer's paper, asking questions, making notes, closing her eyes, knitting her brow, smiling, laughing. We had planned for the analysis to focus on the pair, yet members of the audience seemed equally interested in the action in the background.

Behind the response pair much was going on. In fact, in that three-minute segment there was something like a parade; a couple of faculty members went by, then returned with a cart carrying a television and VCR, they stopped and backed up to converse with someone who was not yet on screen, then appeared to fiddle with the equipment; several people passed behind the cart and TV to open filing drawers and put in or take out fluorescent colored paper, someone offscreen called someone walking across the back, and she turned around and squeezed by the two faculty members and the TV cart. All the while, Vicki stayed focused on Grant, the writer, acting as if the circus was not filing by behind her.

In this tape, folks who were used to work in the center hardly noticed the parade—the activity seemed normal. They started to deep view, talking only about Vicki and Grant. For those used to life in our center, the scene looked something like this:

- Grant reads
- Vicki takes notes
- She looks up a couple of times and scratches her head
- Grant stops reading and looks expectantly at her while she finishes some notes
- She looks up and smiles and comments on a part that she liked
- He asks her if she really liked it
- She nods
- They discuss the decision he made to include that information, the clip ends.

Folks unused to the level of background activity, however, described entirely different action. Their descriptions of the action sounded were as follows:

- TV cart rolls by
- Stops
- Someone comes out of back room, talks to people with cart
- Cart moves back

- Something is taken off the cart by the person from the back
- Another person crosses behind the cart and opens a file cabinet, the cart finally rolls out.

The conference participants who engaged in deep viewing with us did find the level of activity unusual, and Responders got many questions about whether this was "normal." Notably, the "action" in the video didn't seem to outsiders to include the response session!

As we looked at the notes that the audience had made about the action and then evaluated the normalcy of the presence of faculty, the camaraderie of staff, the modernness of equipment, we began to appreciate the richness of our environment. Other centers, apparently, weren't as vibrant, busy, or popular. We had taken these conditions for granted, even found things about them to grouse about, and yet, others looked on them with envy. Taking deep viewing on the road showed us how welcoming home was. Our view of home from a distance showed us how vital our center was. We became aware of what a lively environment we have. The attention that those participating in our session paid to the action in our center helped to positively reshape our perspective. Participants were able to pay such careful attention to the events in the session because of their media literacy—the notion of a session on tape was not unusual—the medium itself became invisible to the participants, just as the action outside of the session had become invisible to the people who worked in that center.

Tale Six: "A Little to the Left" (Effects/Process)

I had never imagined that the videotape would record anything but the "truth," but poet-Responder Ray immediately thought otherwise. As he watched Kathy's tape, he was critical of the camera and microphone position, unwilling to commit to any interpretation until he had more fully explored the role that effects played. I found him, one afternoon, lying on the floor, lowering the camera to its lowest angle, pointing it at a writer who was clearly awaiting Ray's return to the table. The ridiculous angle would catch a bunny's-eye view of the session. Ray had previously taped a session from the opposite angle—with the camera above the participants. After watching these tapes he noticed distinctly different results, not because of the angles involved, but because of the levels of engagement. These vast differences led Ray to ask himself, "how can we bring our core being to sessions?" Ray wanted to know how he could manage to be "centered" in all of his Writers' Center work, to be, as O'Reilley (1998) suggests, "radically present" (title page).

Like many of the writers who visit the center, Ray was ready to self-assess his work. In the center, we hope to facilitate this by responding in a way that provides writers with our detailed reactions to specific sections of text. Deep viewing provided that kind of response for Ray.

Ray's searching question was the result of observing the vast differences between the two sessions. In the high-camera angle interaction, Ray worked with Roger, a criminal justice major whom he had come to know in four previous visits. Even though the camera angle made for odd viewing, there was a great deal of motion. Though the lens window only allowed for Ray's body to be seen when he leaned forward, Roger's face was always in the picture, as were Ray's hands. His hands rarely stopped moving, and Roger's face was animated.

The session taped from the low-camera angle was entirely different. Ray described it as "static." It was his first session with a writer—a woman who spoke English as her second language. During deep viewing, Ray watched himself lean in and speak softly, rarely moving, becoming nearly inanimate. He said that what he saw on tape contrasted oddly with what he knew had happened before the tape—there was an animated discussion of the process of taping. Ray worked to convince this writer to allow him to videotape the session. She didn't seem reluctant when she agreed, but he remembers thinking that she was self-conscious about the camera during the session. He recalled thinking at one point during the session "She's forgotten the camera," but she never became as animated in the session as she was in the presession taping negotiation.

Ray began his "effects" experiment intending to look microcosmically at the way that a camera angle changes perceptions of events. What he ended up considering was the effect of the whole videotaping process on a session.

While Ray felt that the differences in levels of engagement in the sessions may have been due to many factors—including gender, familiarity, maturity—he also had a sense that choosing to videotape requires some sacrifice. As he looked back at the tapes, he felt that in the session with Roger the "essence of the people comes through," but in the low-camera angle session, with a writer whose name he can no longer recall, he "didn't see the people." He recalled feeling that he was not present in that session, that he was only there on the surface, only playing a role.

Ray's sense that something might be sacrificed in choosing to videotape for deep viewing is consistent with deep viewing as a ritual practice. Fox (1994) describes a need for sacrifice in ritual, and, indeed, Ray decided that his need for the reflective community ritual of deep viewing was worth the sacrifice of discomfort in a static session.

CONCLUSION: MEDIA LITERACY AND SPIRITUAL LITERACY

Our experience with deep viewing had profound effects on our work in the Writers' Center. Through our practice of deep viewing, we learned to better pay attention, to appreciate that the essence of center work involves being intellectually and affectively present, that we could become more connected to each other and the writers we work with, that the art of deep listening is one that needs to be nurtured, that by being open to each other's interpretations we may learn something valuable, that play is possible even when the work is serious, that silence can be instructive, and that transformation is possible. These are characteristics Brussart and Brussart (1996) attribute to spiritual literacy. Such literacy is not primarily or necessarily connected to religious traditions, though most religions include practices that encourage spiritual literacy.

Deep viewing contributed to our spiritual understanding of both writing and our work in the center. By enabling us to internalize a way of understanding our work more deeply, deep viewing has enabled us to come closer to a spiritual approach to literacy instruction. Many of the elements described above are thought of by scholars as "spiritual." Noted literacy scholars Wendy Bishop (1997), Richard Graves (1997), James Moffet (1997), and Mary Rose O'Reilly (1998) all posit that an understanding of pedagogy that includes elements of the spiritual is not only possible, but necessary. More broadly based academic writers—from Viktor Frankl (1997) and Matthew Fox (1994) to Mihkail Czisksenmihalyi (1991) to James Hillman (1996)—argue that spiritual elements must imbue our work.

The definitions offered by these writers for what is "spiritual" do not stray far from the descriptions that I provide here about humane interactions. Spiritual understandings do not mean religious understandings or practices. Rather, spiritual understandings are those things that people use to make life meaningful. A synthesized definition of this is "for a meaningful life, people must be able to see and feel daily events as experiences that connect them to themselves, to others, and to larger forces in the universe" (Briggs, 1998). The stories included here describe situations in which Responders and writers became more connected to others, and more confident in the sensibility of the universe.

The final piece of evidence that I offer that deep viewing has enhanced, ritualized, and helped us remember a practice in which we read meaning is Campbell's (1988) notion of following one's bliss. Responders must be following their bliss in their work in the center, for they are qualified in the world of commerce for much better paying, higher status jobs, yet they choose to do part-time work with no benefits. There seems no other explanation than the meaningfulness of the experience. Perhaps deep viewing is a critical reading process that has helped the center and those in it "connect aspects of their lives" (Semali & Watts Pailliotet, 1999, p. 7) and uncover the "hidden wholeness," a concept that Palmer (1998) attributes to Thomas Merton. Palmer describes the process of finding the spiritual nature, the "hidden wholeness," by saying "It's easy to look on the surface of things and judge that there is no community here at all. But if you go deep, as you do when you seek the sacred, you find the community that a good teacher evokes and invites students into, which somehow weaves the fragmented life back together" (p. 27).

REFERENCES

Albom, M. (1997). *Tuesdays with Morrie*. New York: Doubleday.

Beach, R., & Hynds, S. (1991). Research in response to literature. In R. Barr, M. Kamil, P. Mosenthal, & P. D. Pearson (Eds.), *Handbook on reading research* (pp. 453–491). New York: Longman.

Bishop, W. (1997). Teaching lives: Thoughts on reweaving our spirits. In R. Foehr & S. Schiller (Eds.), *The spiritual side of writing* (pp. 129–136). Portsmouth, NH: Heinemann Boynton/Cook.

Briggs, L. (1998). Understanding spirit in the writing center. *Writing Center Journal, 19*, 87–98.

Briggs, L. (2000). A story from the center about intertextuality and incoherence. In L. Briggs & M. Woolbright (Eds), *Stories from the Center* (pp. 13–34). Urbana: NCTE.

Briggs, L., & Woolbright, M. (Eds.). (2000). *Stories from the Center*. Urbana: NCTE.

Brussart, F., & Brussart, M. A. (1996). *Spiritual literacy: Reading the sacred in everyday life*. New York: Scribner's.

Campbell, J. (1988). *The power of myth*. New York: Doubleday.

Considine, D. M., & Haley, G. E. (1992). *Visual messages: Integrating imagery into instruction*. Englewood, CO: Teacher Ideas Press.

Cooper, M. (1986). The ecology of writing. *College English, 48*, 364–375.

Csikszentmihalyi, M. (1991). *Flow: The psychology of optimal experience*. New York: Harper Perennial.

Fleckenstein, K. S. (1997). Creating a center that holds; spirituality through exploratory pedagogy. In R. Foehr & S. Schiller (Eds.), *The spiritual side of writing* (pp. 24–33). Portsmouth, NH: Heinemann Boynton/Cook.

Foehr, R. P., & Schiller, S. (Eds.). (1997). *The spiritual side of writing: Releasing the learner's whole potential*. Portsmouth, NH: Heinemann Boynton/Cook.

Fox, M. (1994). *The reinvention of work: A new vision of livelihood for our time*. San Francisco: Harper.

Frankl, V. E. (1997). *Man's search for ultimate meaning*. New York: Insight Books/Penguin Press.

Giroux, H. (1988). *Teachers as intellectuals: Toward a critical pedagogy of learning*. South Hadley, MA: Bergin & Garvey.

Graves, R. (1997). Grace, in pedagogy. In R. Foehr & S. Schiller (Eds.), *The spiritual side of writing* (pp. 15–24) . Portsmouth, NH: Heinemann Boynton/Cook.

Hawisher, G. (1994). Blinding insights: Classification schemes and software for literacy instruction. In C. Selfe & C. Hilligoss (Eds.), *Literacy and computers* (pp. 37–56). New York: MLA.

Heilker, P. (1997). The rhetoric of spirituality in popular meditation books." In R. Foehr & S. Schiller (Eds.), *The spiritual side of writing* (pp. 107–117). Portsmouth, NH Heinemann Boynton/Cook.

Hillman, J. (1996). *The soul's code*. New York: Random House.

Himley, M. (1991). *Shared territory: Understanding children's writing as works*. London: Oxford University Press.

Hobbs, R. (1998). Media literacy in Massachusetts. In A. Hart (Ed.), *Teaching the media* (pp. 127–144). Mahwah, NJ: Erlbaum.

Johnson-Eilola, J. (1998). Reading and writing in hypertext: Vertigo and euphoria. In C. Selfe & C. Hilligoss (Eds.), *Literacy and computers* (pp. 195–219). New York: MLA.

LeBlanc, P. (1994). The politics of literacy and technology in secondary school classrooms. In C. Selfe & S. Hilligoss (Eds.), *Literacy and computers* (pp. 22–36). New York: MLA.

Lunsford, A. (1991). Collaboration, control and the idea of a writing center. *The Writing Center Journal, 12*, 3–10.

Marcic, D. (1997). *Managing with the wisdom of love: Uncovering virtue in people and organizations*. San Francisco: Jossey–Bass.

Moffet, J. (1997). Soul school. In R. P. Foehr & S. Schiller (Eds.), *The spiritual side of writing: Releasing the learner's whole potential*. Portsmouth, NH: Heinemann Boynton/Cook.

Moore, T. (1994). *Meditations: On the monk who dwells in everyday life*. New York: HarperCollins.

Mouthrop, S., & Kaplan, N. (1994). They became what they beheld: The futility of resistance in the space of electronic writing. In C. Selfe & C. Hilligoss (Eds.), *Literacy and computers* (pp. 220–237). New York: MLA.

North, S. (1984). The idea of a writing center. *College English, 46*, 433–446.

North, S. (1987). *The making of knowledge in composition*. Montclair, NJ: Boynton/Cook.

O'Reilley, M. R. (1998). *Radical presence: Teaching as contemplative practice*. Portsmouth, NH: Heinemann Boynton/Cook.

Palmer, P. (1998, September). The grace of great things. *The Sun*, pp. 24–28.

Porter, J. (1986). Intertextuality in the discourse community. *Rhetoric Review, 5*, 34–47.

Schiller, S. (1997). Writing: A natural site for spirituality. In R. Foehr & S. Schiller (Eds.), *The spiritual side of writing* (pp. 34–43). Portsmouth, NH: Heinemann Boynton/Cook.

Semali, L., & Watts Pailliotet. A. (Eds.). (1999). *Intermediality: The teachers' handbook of critical media literacy*. Boulder, CO: Westview.

Watts Pailliotet, A. (1998). Deep viewing: A critical look at texts. In S. Steinberg & J. Kincheloe (Eds.), *Unauthorized methods: Strategies for critical teaching*: (pp. 124–136). London: Routledge.

Watts Pailliotet, A. (1999). Deep viewing: Intermediality in preservice teacher education. In L. Semali & A. Watts Pailliotet (Eds.), *Intermediality: The teachers' handbook of critical media literacy* (pp. 31–51). Boulder, CO: Westview.

SECTION II

INTERMEDIALITY: RECONCEPTUALIZING LITERACY TEXTS AND PROCESSES

PREPARING TEACHERS TO TEACH WITH UNDERSTANDING

Victoria J. Risko

As we enter the 21st century, there is much speculation about reforms in education at all levels, but most particularly about changes that are proposed for the preparation of teachers. Reform efforts are characterized by major shifts away from traditional forms of pedagogy and directed toward helping future teachers engage in a systematic study of their own learning and teaching practices (Zeichner, 1998). The pedagogy of telling (Sizer, 1985) and teaching to simplify complex concepts as described by Grossman (1992), following a positivist tradition, is being replaced with methods that engage future teachers in active and generative learning. Rather than viewing learning as an "additive" process (Feiman-Nemser & Buchmann, 1985) that is linear and directed by the college professor, learning is viewed as multidimensional and enhanced by students' own inquiry, problem solving, and critical thinking. Reform is directed toward developing a pedagogy that encourages learning that applies to life (Wiske, 1999), that is guided rather than transmitted, that invites reflection and critical thinking, and that is situated in the study of "real" problems.

This chapter is organized around two themes. One focuses on the compatibility of teacher education reforms and current applications of multimedia. Both empha-

Advances in Reading/Language Research, Volume 7, pages 91–104.
Copyright © 2000 by JAI Press Inc.
All rights of reproduction in any form reserved.
ISBN: 0-7623-0264-X

size students' active and generative learning, problem solving and inquiry-based instruction, collaborative and shared-learning environments in classrooms, and in-depth analysis and synthesis of multiple views of learning and teaching. A second theme identifies issues and problems that need to be addressed if we are going to develop optimal applications of multimedia as a tool to support teacher preparation.

While there is much excitement about both realized and potential benefits of multimedia designs for enhancing teacher preparation, there are issues and questions that I believe require more thought. These issues and questions go beyond concerns typically identified, such as difficulties associated with integrating technology into existing teacher education courses, educating college instructors, limited college financial and personnel resources to support technology acquisitions and software development, teacher educators' limited preparation for modeling creative uses of technology, and the amount of time required to change teacher education curriculum (OTA, 1995; Pellegrino & Altman, 1997). There is no doubt that these concerns must be addressed if we expect to use multimedia to enhance college instruction as described above.

The main thesis of the concerns described within this chapter, however, is centered on a distinction between uses of multimedia that engage prospective teachers in actions that are *reflective* rather than *routine* (Zeichner & Liston, 1985). This discussion calls for preparing teachers who can teach with understanding as described by Wiske (1999) and others. Within this chapter, this notion is used to represent teachers who are active, persistent, and reflective learners, and who carefully consider their ideas and consequences of their decisions. Teaching with understanding within the context of this chapter is consistent with Giroux's (1988) description of "teachers as intellectuals."

LEARNING ABOUT TEACHING AND UNDERSTANDING WITH MULTIMEDIA

As has been discussed by Pellegrino and Altman (1997) and others, learning environments that are enhanced with multimedia have a tremendous power to create dynamic learning events in which future teachers are involved in the analysis of authentic pedagogical dilemmas that invite critical thinking and flexible use of newly acquired knowledge for achieving problem resolution. The goal is to enhance future teachers' deep understandings of disciplinary information, theories of teaching and learning, and scientific pedagogical concepts.

Changing the "Authority" within Teacher Preparation

Multimedia has the power to change both the *structure* and the *substance* of teacher preparation programs. Structural changes involve transitions from teacher-directed instruction to student-initiated and collaborative learning, access to multiple sources of information via Web browsers and CD-ROM materials, and so on.

These structural changes can support prospective teachers' strategic learning, independent thinking, and ability to access a broad range of information. Substantive changes place an emphasis on using multiple sources of information (e.g., written text supported with video and audio representations of "authentic" happenings) to inform decisions, provide opportunities to revisit concepts to examine them from different theoretical viewpoints, and require reflection and synthesis. Such changes are consistent with current efforts to reform teacher education on a policy level (e.g., the Report to the President on the Use of Technology to Strengthen K–12 Education in the United States, March 1997 [President's Committee, 1997]; recommendations from the National Council for Accreditation of Teacher Education, NCATE, 1997), and as guided by social-cultural and critical pedagogy theories aimed at changing the "tradition and authority" within teacher preparation programs.

Optimal applications of multimedia should stimulate the kind of persistence in inquiry that helps future teachers rework misconceptions, reposition their own experiences as students within classrooms, and develop as reflective and intellectual scholars (Calderhead, 1989; Giroux, 1988; Sparks-Langer, Simmons, Pasch, Colton, & Starko, 1991; Tom, 1995). And this inquiry can be used to help prospective teachers develop reasoned decisions that are grounded in their understanding of theoretical and practical knowledge, and the ability to "care" about the impact of these decisions on their students' development (Darling-Hammond, 1996).

Potential Power of Multimedia

I draw on the work conducted at Vanderbilt University to illustrate how we are using multimedia to reform our teacher education methodology courses. Several faculty are exploring the use of multimedia to enhance our problem-based instruction as an alternative to lecture-based pedagogy (e.g., Barron & Goldman, 1996; Risko & Kinzer, 1999). We use video-based case materials, supported with CD-ROM technology, to display real classroom situations. Embedded in these situations are multiple teaching and learning dilemmas and information (e.g., interviews, student performance data, management procedures) that can be used for resolving these dilemmas.

These projects have several common features. First, they are designed to enhance prospective teachers' active and generative learning, and to demonstrate strategies that preservice teachers might choose to implement when they develop their own classrooms in which inquiry and problem solving are valued. The prospective teachers are invited to analyze the embedded problems and these interpretations are shared and examined during class discussions. The prospective teachers are encouraged to formulate and reflect on their proposed resolutions of embedded problems. They use case content to support their inquiry.

Second, our prospective teachers access multiple data sources, available on the CD-ROMs we have developed and on the Internet. Videos (of classroom scenes, students' performance), audiotapes (of interviews with parents, students, administrators, and teachers), and hypertext that can be accessed for various reasons provide many opportunities for our prospective teachers to construct relationships among multiple and divergent sources of information. Opportunities to observe the complexities associated with teaching and learning increase the possibility of identifying and solving problems. As students analyze the various options and factors that influence teachers' decision making, they are learning how to use disparate sources of information as tools to aid their problem solving (CTGV, 1990). Requiring students to frame questions and solve problems encourages them to apply and modify newly acquired concepts based on situational and contextual information.

Third, a community that acknowledges and encourages diverse beliefs and interpretations is formed within our college classes. When students are invited to generate issues and problems associated with case content, learning is shared and facilitated by the members of the classroom community. This direction for teaching within such environments is influenced greatly by sociocultural research that is grounded in demonstrations of how teachers and students collaborate and mediate each other's learning (Gavelek, 1986; Tharp & Gallimore, 1988; Vygotsky, 1978), and a belief that knowledge is best constructed through multiple opportunities for interactions among the instructor and students (Cazden, 1988; Eeds & Wells, 1989; Hynds, 1994).

Overall, this instruction is designed to enhance the possibility of preparing teachers to understand that teaching is complex and problem-laden. Future teachers are learning how multimedia enhances their ability to access many sources of information and to study ideas from multiple perspectives. These experiences demonstrate the benefits of active learning and reflective practice (Calderhead, 1989). They signal the importance of problem-based, generative, and collaborative learning. Taken together, these experiences provide a rich demonstration of what these future teachers can accomplish in their own classrooms—classrooms that are developed by teachers who teach with an understanding of the power of multimedia-based teaching environments.

AND YET WE HAVE MUCH TO UNDERSTAND ABOUT TEACHING AND MULTIMEDIA

While applications of multimedia provide many opportunities to advance teachers' intellectual and imaginative development, there is much to be learned about its particular impact on learning and teaching. Applications of multimedia may change our forms of content delivery, but unless we analyze carefully our practices, we may be replacing one set of "routines" (traditional, lecture methods) with another (computer- or multimedia-based methods) that can be just as mechanistic and inhibiting of intellectual development. Or as Wideen, Mayer-Smith, and Moon (1998) argue, we may be simply "rearranging the deck chairs on the Titanic" (p. 167).

As we apply new technologies to our teaching methods, we must scrutinize very carefully our practices. Are these applications providing an "illusion" of substantive change or are they providing "real differences" in teacher scholarship and understandings? Are these applications helping teacher educators solve dilemmas they have faced for decades? Are they helping future teachers acquire knowledge that is usable and useful for their future teaching? Are they aiding in our quest to develop "thinking" teachers who teach with understanding? Learning to teach is influenced by many factors. Before we can feel confident about multimedia as a tool to reform teacher education programs we need to address conditions that may inhibit its power. Some of these will be addressed in the material that follows.

First, there is the complexity of goals set for teacher education—the goals of building both theoretical wisdom and practical wisdom, as described by Aristotle and others. When we separate the two we fail to make explicit how each informs the other; informed actions are grounded in world knowledge *and* knowledge of the world is deepened by reflecting on practical actions. Too often we engage future teachers in "custodial forays" (Fenstermacher, 1986) that result in suggestions for quick fixes rather than inviting deep analysis of complex problems. As has been discussed previously, deep forms of learning can be fostered when prospective teachers learn to access multiple sources of theoretical and practical knowledge to support their problem solving. When prospective teachers are asked to analyze teaching and learning events displayed in video and audio presentations, they can be coached to draw on their beliefs, theories, and practical actions to help them frame issues and resolve dilemmas they identify. Revisiting the video and audio information to cross-reference multiple perspectives can help prospective teachers acquire a depth of knowledge that is required for building analytical thinking.

Deep analysis is especially needed if we are going to help future teachers move beyond the narrow frameworks they bring to their teacher preparation programs. We know that it is very difficult to change firmly held beliefs about teaching (Johnston, 1994; Loflin Smith, 1993; Richardson, 1996; Stofflett & Stoddart, 1992), and traditional teacher education methods are often ineffectual in helping future teachers confront the contradictions that exist between their beliefs and experiences, and the realities of teaching they are learning about in teacher education programs (Cochran-Smith, 1994).

Multimedia presentations of classroom situations can be inviting, but we must still ask whether these presentations are sufficiently "more compelling, more memorable, and more powerful in the minds and hearts of prospective teachers" (Roskos, 1998, p. 4) than their own prior experiences. Uses of multimedia must provide a method for revisiting novel content, encourage sustained reflection and evaluation of personal beliefs, and enable teacher educators to assess their students' interpretations and assumptions about teaching. Learning must occur for the individual as well as the group. Programs where mentoring is provided are needed to sustain each student's continued development.

Several years ago, we learned firsthand about the importance of conferences to help our students revisit content embedded in our multimedia materials, class discussions, and course readings (Risko, Peter, & McAllister, 1996). During our classes, we noticed that our students adopted additional perspectives as they analyzed teaching situations embedded in our materials and demonstrated argumentation strategies as they referred to multiple sources of information to discuss their problem-solving approach. Yet when our students experienced similar problems later in their own teaching, they had difficulty accessing the information they had discussed previously. Peer-led discussions and conferences with the college instructor and supervisors were useful for inviting reflection on course content and reinstituting previously developed problem-solving strategies.

From this experience, we learned that even with applications of multimedia within courses, these courses may be perceived as disconnected and too far removed from the life of real classrooms. Simulations and video representations are far superior to verbal descriptions, but they are still something that "happens" in the college classroom. Also, if the content is embedded within separate classes, there may be no mechanisms in place to help students make the much needed connections across the classes *and* between these classes and their teaching experiences. The structural fragmentation and competing agendas that typify college programs may prevent the applications that are the aim of these programs. Even innovative courses may be "nullified" within programs that are fragmented (Zeichner & Gore, 1990) or when the experiences within one course are not related explicitly to themes promoted within other courses and/or across the program. From a constructivist perspective, it may be impossible to develop deep thinking about complex concepts unless there is consistent and intense study of these concepts within a program that is conceptually coherent (Mayer-Smith & Mitchell, 1997). More importantly, it is impossible to prepare teachers to teach with an understanding of the relationships between theory and practice unless these understandings are mediated during the learning and teaching experiences.

A second problem relates to our limited knowledge about our role as mediators in teacher education programs. Instructional scaffolds are extremely important for helping students assimilate and apply what they are learning. Reform efforts support notions of mediated learning associated with theories generated by Vygotsky (1978) and Tharp and Gallimore (1988). Within such a paradigm, instructors model strategies students can adopt to assist their learning and thinking and then coach their students in the learning process. Since the learning goal is to develop students' independent learning, students are taught strategies for monitoring their own learning. Such forms of educating, preferred over transmission approaches, invite students to generate their own understandings as they are building conceptual knowledge.

As described above, we learned that our students made progress in building concepts about teaching literacy and literacy development when they were involved in multimedia case analyses. We learned, though, that the instructor was needed to continue these forms of mediation when students were teaching in the schools to prevent them from dismissing these perspectives when they were confronted with similar problems in another context. Mediating in ways that helped the prospective teachers form connections with the class content helped them return to their ability to draw on multiple resources and strategies that aided their earlier problem solving.

Specifying how instructors should mediate learning is difficult, especially when thinking about this responsibility within multimedia environments. Earlier in this chapter, I described how interactive technologies can be used to invite analysis of content and dilemmas displayed within real classroom happenings. Our goal for teaching within such environments is to afford students' active learning and critical thinking. Such affordances are supported by the instructor who invites students to puzzle over ideas, construct interpretations and problem resolutions, and seek multiple ways to examine issues (Doll, 1993). Yet, as I described in an earlier paper (Risko, 1996), teaching with multimedia has many challenges. There is much to organize and manage. Instructors need to be immersed in the range and depth of the course content so they can encourage students to think more deeply about issues that may be generated during class discussions. They need to be able to "go with the flow" of the conversations while accessing particular segments that are most relevant to the students' inquiry and reflections. During class discussions, the instructor needs to acknowledge the many voices of the class, help students draw connections across individual contributions, and encourage them to examine their own misconceptions. The role of the instructor is extremely important for the success of discussions that are both interesting and meaningful, and that allow instructors to shift flexibly across the many roles they assume as facilitator and leader.

Developing meaningful discussions as an instructional strategy is challenging. We have noticed, for example, that discussions around our multimedia cases help our students adopt novel ways to frame and analyze instructional problems and integrate class readings in ways that help them generate contextually appropriate and informed problem resolutions (Risko, Yount, & McAllister, 1992). Yet meaningful learning may not always be the outcome of such discussions. Moje, Remillard, Southerland, and Wade (in press) describe how their (nonmultimedia) case-based classroom discussions seemed to help their prospective teachers understand complex aspects of teaching but were ineffective for helping these teachers adopt new perspectives about teaching and learning; earlier beliefs were not changed. When Moje and her colleagues analyzed their own teaching they concluded that their energy and attention were often diverted away from building concepts and critical thinking and instead directed more toward facilitating engaging and "lively" discussions.

Their observation is extremely important to consider when thinking about the complex role of the instructor who is also using multimedia to support such discussions. Given the necessary demands of accessing the multimedia information to support discussion points, there is even a greater chance that the instructor will be more drawn to technical procedures instead of strategies that support deep learning. To accommodate this challenge, instructors must become facile with their navigating skills so they are prepared to revisit scenes and other multimedia sources of information that can support students' thinking and comprehensive analysis of issues being discussed. Additionally, when instructors publicly acknowledge how they are managing these conditions they are more likely to prepare future teachers to teach with an understanding of how they may do the same in their own classrooms.

Another related challenge is what Herrmann and Saracino (1993) describe as "finding middle ground" between direct forms of teaching and those that invite discovery learning within mediated formats. Even though these two instructors were enthusiastic about their efforts to create student-centered instruction within their teaching methods courses, they were disappointed with their initial applications. Quickly they learned that their students expected them to lecture on content that was predetermined and clearly identified. They learned how difficult it is to adjust their instruction to help their students understand the value of generative learning activities and active problem solving. Similarly, Macgillivray (1997) analyzed her attempt to implement critical pedagogy in her undergraduate literacy methods courses. While committed to this approach, she describes the conflict she experienced between her roles as the "professor" who was responsible for grading and directing the learning experiences of her students, and the "nurturer" who supported their independent thinking and actions. She concluded that her students, who seemed distrustful of her intent for the course, displayed little ownership of the content during class discussions and the conversations they had were limited in depth.

The problems experienced by these instructors are not unexpected. Changes in methodology often are uncomfortable for both the instructor and the students. A way to build comfort for both may require instructors to implement change gradually and state expectations explicitly. In the spirit of building shared knowledge about what is occurring in the college class, it is important for instructors and students to jointly specify their goals for the class, identify explicitly what they are learning while attending to the video material and other resources (Ball, 1992), and draw conclusions about how this information is advancing their knowledge. Such an approach demonstrates methods of mediating learning and problem resolution.

A third problem, closely related to the former two, is that events inviting active learning may defy the expectations students bring to their college classes, for they have a history and a culture that may mitigate such expectations. Fox (1994), for example, describes his difficulty with inviting undergraduates to participate in literature-response groups because of their reluctance to voice their personal opinions due to their "fear of being wrong." Feeling comfortable with personal interpretations shared openly was a major cultural shift for his students. Others suggest, in similar ways, how difficult it is to make more dominate the "silent and muted voices" of our undergraduates who are preparing to teach.

For example, Souza Lima (1998) found she had difficulty communicating with students whose culture was different from her own and whose ideas about what constitutes "good instruction" differed from hers. Her strategy to bridge cultural differences through the use of instructional narratives was unappreciated and interpreted as ineffective by her students who wanted "real content" and not stories. She found that even with extensive attempts to explain the intent and purpose, her methods were met with "silent subversion" by students who would not participate. Her students were distrustful about her choice of content and the structures of her lessons were viewed as inadequate. Finally, she realized that the lack of communication and trust was the result of a difference in language experiences between herself and her students. She made this difference public and the group reflected on the many functions of language and its use in teaching. This group sharing helped shape subsequent interactions and created new ways of "seeing and evaluating reality" (p. 156), and new ways of "talking" about teaching and learning.

Such discussions may be extremely useful for the instructor and students whose learning is situated within multimedia materials, especially when classroom happenings are often represented in contextually rich narratives about the classroom, teacher, students, parents, and other school personnel. Expectations about multimedia and student involvement may differ. The contribution of narratives to support inquiry may be undervalued (Egan, 1989). Students may have difficulty recognizing the importance of information embedded within the materials. Striving to develop shared expectations and understandings could enhance communication and demonstrate the value of multiple viewpoints. Additionally, explicit heuristics, such as reflective guides (Watts Pailliotet, 1999) that are used to guide discussion at multiple levels, can be useful for signaling the usefulness of ideas that are generated. These efforts prepare teachers to understand the value of communication and the importance of delineating specific learning goals.

Fourth, there is the problem associated with what Giroux (1988) refers to as "immediacy with the text." The concern is that in-depth analysis of problems embedded within "local texts," such as the situated problems presented within our multimedia cases, may not transfer in ways that support prospective teachers own teaching unless they learn from the beginning how to apply what they are learning to broader issues and contrasting situations. Wolf, Mieras, and Carey (1996) addressed this issue in their study with 43 preservice teachers. Their use of a field note component within the tutorial activity of an undergraduate children's literature class helped their future teachers identify explicitly information that was guiding their teaching. The authors concluded that this requirement helped their students "provide enough detailed information [field notes] to write the story of where they were and what they did" (p. 464) during times when the preservice teachers read to their case-study children. Over a year's time, Wolf asked the preservice teachers to examine the substance of their guided discussions and their use of questions. These data then were discussed extensively within the college classes. The prospective teachers reported better understandings of course content (e.g., purposes and design of higher-order questioning). The process of asking students to record field notes and use this information to guide their interpretation of what they are learning provides a way to draw connections between theory and practice (Lave & Wenger, 1991). Similarly, Au and Carroll (1997) used a checklist for preservice teachers to self-report and monitor their own teaching behaviors and reflect on the relationship between these behaviors and constructivist notions of teaching.

Such frameworks can be extremely useful for helping prospective teachers think critically about issues they will face as teachers, understand the importance of what they are learning in their college classes, and build usable knowledge for responding to complicated situations. Such instruction is grounded in notions associated with teaching for conceptual change (Beeth, 1998), mediated teaching that invites reflection, and analysis of inconsistencies in reasoning. These frameworks can be initiated during class sessions where prospective teachers are exploring multimedia materials and continued in use during teaching to support sustained interaction with course content (Hollingsworth, Dybdahl, & Minarek, 1993). Providing such connections can help teachers form "smart" decisions (CTGV, 1993, 1996, 1997) and sound reasoning for their instruction. Furthermore, these strategies signal the "compelling authority" (Fenstermacher, 1986) of knowledge domains that are addressed within the college program.

Fifth, there is the issue of authenticity. Corresponding to the thesis that new technologies allow us to situate learning in the analysis of actual classroom happenings (as displayed in the video and audio content and other multimedia resources), could be a concern about whether this content is viewed as "authentic" by the prospective teachers. Could it be that undergraduates who are preparing to be teachers will dismiss these "authentic problems" portrayed "for" them as trivial and inconsequential? Will they fail to understand their importance and "disconnect" from serious study of these issues in a way that is similar to what Slattery (1995) describes in his analysis of why prospective teachers fail to value education philosophy?

Related to this issue is the consideration of what constitutes a "critical mass" of information that may be needed to substantiate authenticity of issues for individual study. Sufficient representations of information must be displayed within the multimedia materials so that we are not representing mere snapshots of "fragments of human awareness" (Tuthill & Ashton, 1983). We learned, for example, that the study of one case alone is not sufficient to determine action or study in depth related literature. Contrast sets and reasons to cross-reference information are needed to sharpen students' understandings of broad issues and complexity.

Multimedia environments can provide more controlled environments, which may be helpful for sustaining learning about complex teaching situations "rather than in the highly unpredictable setting of the live classroom" Gliesman (1984, p. 109). This protected environment (Graber, 1996) may be needed to help future teachers "stand in place" while they examine and question their beliefs. Yet, careful scaffolds and robust discussions are needed to support teachers' transition to classrooms, to help them understand the usefulness of information they are learning for classroom teaching. The monitoring guides as suggested above may be useful here. Sometimes, though, a total redesign of teacher education programs is needed to provide teaching experiences for students while they are completing their coursework (the design of many fifth-year certification programs and professional development schools). Alternatively, methods courses could be extended beyond the typical one semester, such as the year-long format suggested by Hermann and Sarracino (1993), to provide many opportunities to revisit course content while reflecting on teaching experiences.

CONCLUDING THOUGHTS

Throughout this chapter, I describe benefits of using multimedia to situate prospective teachers' analysis of teaching and learning issues and dilemmas. As teachers examine the problems that are posed within authentic happenings, they are required to integrate theoretical and pedagogical information to formulate plausible resolutions that are context-specific and that can be generalized, with guidance, to their own teaching. They are developing as critical thinkers whose reflections are enhanced by persistent inquiry and careful study of different viewpoints. Optimal applications of multimedia, as described in this chapter, can transform traditional preparation programs in substance and structure. And yet, these applications can be enhanced greatly by considering issues such as *authenticity* (Are the problems under study viewed as important by the prospective teachers?), *what is needed for effective mediation* (Is learning mediated in ways that are comfortable for the instructor and students and enhance understandings?), and *how to demonstrate a synergistic relationship between theory and practice* (How can we prepare future teachers to use theory to guide their teaching and their teaching to guide their theories and beliefs?). Attention to these issues is critical for developing the vision of teacher education that is described throughout this chapter.

REFERENCES

Au, K., & Carroll, J. (1997). Improving literacy achievement through a constructivist approach: The KEEP demonstration classroom project. *The Elementary School Journal, 97*, 203–221.

Ball, D. (1992). Magical hopes: Manipulatives and the reform of math education. *American Educator, 16*(2), 14–18, 46–47.

Barron, L., & Goldman, E. S. (1996). *Introducing new perspectives on teaching and learning mathematics to preservice teachers.* Paper presented at the annual meeting of the American Educational Research Association, New York.

Beeth, M. (1998). Teaching for conceptual change: Using status as a metacognitive tool. *Science Education, 82*, 1–14.

Calderhead, J. (1989). Reflective teaching and teacher education. *Teacher and Teacher Education, 5*(1), 43–51.

Cazden, C. (1988). *Classroom discourse: The language of teaching and learning.* Portsmouth, NH: Heinemann.

Cochran-Smith, M. (1994). The power of teacher research in teacher education. In S. Hollingsworth & H. Sockett (Eds.), *Teacher research and education reform* (pp. 142–165). Chicago: University of Chicago Press.

Cognition and Technology Group at Vanderbilt. (1990). Anchored Instruction and its relationship to situated cognition. *Educational Researcher, 19*, 2–10.

Cognition and Technology Group at Vanderbilt. (1993). The Jasper series. Theoretical foundations and data on problem solving and transfer. In L. A. Penner, G. M. Batsche, H. M. Knoff, & D. L. Nelson (Eds.), *The challenge in mathematics and science education: Psychology's response* (pp. 113–152). Washington, DC: American Psychological Association.

Cognition and Technology Group at Vanderbilt. (1996). Looking at technology in context: A framework for understanding technology and education research. In D. C. Berliner & R. Calfee (Eds.), *Handbook of education psychology* (pp. 807–840). New York: Simon & Schuster.

Cognition and Technology Group at Vanderbilt. (1997). *Building on strengths: Accelerated, integrated curriculum and its effects on children, teachers, and parents*. Year Two Report to the James S. McDonnell Foundation.

Darling-Hammond, L. (1996). The right to learn and the advancement of teaching: Research, policy, and practice for democratic education. *Educational Research, 25*, 5–17.

Doll, W. E., Jr. (1993). *A post-modern perspective on curriculum*. New York: Teachers College Press.

Eeds, M., & Wells, D. (1989). Grand conversations: An explanation of meaning construction in literature study groups. *Research in the Teaching of English, 19*, 2–10.

Egan, K. (1989, February). Memory, imagination, and learning. Connected by the story. *Phi Delta Kappa*, 455–459.

Feiman-Nemser, S., & Buchmann, M. (1985). Pitfalls of experience in teacher education. *Teachers College Record, 87*, 49–65.

Fenstermacher, G. D. (1986). Philosophy of research on teaching: Three aspects. In M. Wittrock (Ed.), *Handbook of research on teaching* (3rd ed., pp. 37–49). New York: Macmillan.

Fox, D. (1994). What is literature? Two preservice teachers' conceptions of literature and the teaching of literature. In C. K. Kinzer & D. J. Leu (Eds.), *Multidimensional aspects of literacy research, theory, and practice*. Forty-third yearbook of the National Reading Conference (pp. 394–406). Chicago: National Reading Conference.

Gavelek, J. R. (1986). The social context of literacy and schooling: A development perspective. In T. E. Raphael (Ed.), *The contexts of school-based literacy* (pp. 3–26). New York: Random House.

Giroux, H. A. (1988). *Teachers as intellectuals*. New York: Bergin & Garvey.

Gliesman, D. H. (1984). Changing teacher performance. In L. Katz & J. Raths (Eds.), *Advances in Teacher Education* (Vol. 1, pp. 95–111). Norwood, NJ: Ablex.

Graber, K. C. (1996). Influencing student beliefs. The design of a "high impact" teacher education program. *Teaching and Teacher Education, 12*(5), 451–466.

Grossman, P. L. (1992). Teaching and learning with cases: Unanswered questions. In J. S. Shulman (Ed.), *Case methods in teacher education* (pp. 222–239). New York: Teachers College Press.

Herrmann, B. A., & Saracino, J. (1993). Restructuring a preservice literacy methods course: Dilemmas and lessons learned. *Journal of Teacher Education, 44*(2), 96–106.

Hollingsworth, S., Dybdahl, M., & Minarek, L. T. (1993). By chart and chance and passion: The importance of relational knowing in learning to teach. *Curriculum Inquiry, 23*(1), 5–35.

Hynds, S. (1994). *Making connections: Language and learning in the classroom*. Norwood, MA: Christopher Gordon.

Johnston, S. (1994). Conversations with student teachers—Enhancing the dialogue of learning to teach. *Teaching and Teacher Education, 10*(1), 71–82.

Lave, J., & Wenger, E. (1991). *Situated learning*. London: Cambridge University Press.

Loflin Smith, R. (1993, April). *The evolution of preservice teachers' orientations during early field experiences and initial teacher education course work*. Paper presented at the annual meeting of the American Educational Research Association, Atlanta.

Macgillivray, L. (1997). Do what I say, not what I do: An instructor rethinks her own teaching and research. *Curriculum Inquiry, 27*(4), 469–488.

Mayer-Smith, J., & Mitchell, I. (1997). Teaching about constructivism using approaches informed by constructivism. In V. Richardson (Ed.), *Constructivist teacher education: Building a world of new understandings* (pp. 129–153). London: Falmer Press.

Moje, E., Remillard, J., Southerland, S., & Wade, S. (in press). Researching case pedagogies to inform our teaching. In M. Lundeberg, B. Levin, & H. Harrington (Eds.), *Who learns what from cases and how? The research base for teaching with cases*. Mahwah, NJ: Erlbaum.

Office of Technology Assessment. (1995). *Teachers and technology: Making the connection*. Washington, DC: U.S. Government Printing Office.

Pellegrino, J. W., & Altman, J. E. (1997). Information technology and teacher preparation: Some critical issues and illustrative solutions. *Peabody Journal of Education, 72*(1), 89–121.

President's Committee of Advisors on Science and Technology, Panel on Educational Technology. (1997). *Report to the President on the use of technology to strenghten K–12 education in the United States*. Washington, DC: Author.

Richardson, V. (1996). The case for formal research and practical inquiry in teacher education. In F. B. Murray (Ed.), *The teacher educator's handbook* (pp. 715–738). Washington, DC: AACTE.

Risko, V. J. (1996). Creating a community of thinkers within a preservice literacy education methods course. In K. Camperell, B. Hayes, & R. Telfer (Eds.), *Literacy: The information superhighway to success* (pp. 3–15). Logan: Utah State University Press.

Risko, V. J., & Kinzer, C. K. (1999). *Multimedia cases in reading education*. New York: McGraw–Hill.

Risko, V. J., Peter, J., & McAllister, D. (1996). Conceptual changes: Preservice teacher's pathways to providing literacy transaction. In E. Sturtevant & W. Linek (Eds.), *Literacy grows* (pp. 103–119). Eighteenth Yearbook of the College Reading Association. Pittsburgh, KS: College Reading Association.

Risko, V. J., Yount, D., & McAllister, D. (1992). Preparing preservice teachers for remedial instruction: Teaching problem solving and use of content and pedagogical knowledge. In N. Padak, T. Rasinski, & J. Logan (Eds.), *Literacy research and practice: Foundations for the year 2000* (pp. 37–50). Fourteenth Yearbook of the College Reading Association. Pittsburgh, KS: College Reading Association.

Roskos, K. (1998, November). *A brief summary of teacher education and the learning to teach process*. Paper presented at the annual meeting of the College Reading Association, Myrtle Beach, SC.

Sizer, T. R. (1985). *Horace's compromise: The dilemma of the American high school*. Boston: Houghton Mifflin.

Slattery, P. (1995). *Curriculum development in the postmodern era*. New York: Garland.

Souza Lima, E. (1998). Teachers as learners: The dialectics of improving pedagogical practice in Brazil. In G. L. Anderson & M. Montero-Sieburth (Ed.), *Education qualitative research in Latin America: The struggle of a new paradigm* (pp. 141–160). New York: Garland.

Sparks-Langer, G. M., Simmons, J. M., Pasch, M., Colton, A., & Starko, A. (1991). Reflective pedagogical thinking: How can we promote it and measure it? *Journal of Teacher Education, 41*(4), 23–32.

Stofflett, R., & Stoddart, T. (1992, April). *Patterns of assimilation and accommodation in traditional and conceptual change teacher education courses*. Paper presented at the annual meeting of the American Educational Research Association, San Francisco.

Tharp, R. G., & Gallimore, R. (1988). *Rousing minds to life: Teaching and learning in social contexts*. London: Cambridge University Press.

Tom, A. R. (1995). Inquiry into inquiry-oriented teacher education. *Journal of Teacher Education, 36*, 35–44.

Tuthill, D., & Ashton, P. (1983). Improving educational research through the development of educational paradigms. *Educational Research, 12*(10), 6–14.

Vygotsky, L. (1978). *Mind in society*. Cambridge, MA: Harvard University Press.

Watts Pailliotet, A. (1999). Deep viewing: Intermediality in preservice teacher education. In L. Semali
    & A. Watts Pailliotet (Eds.), *Intermediality: The teachers' handbook of critical media literacy* (pp.
    31–51). Boulder, CO: Westview.
Wideen, M., Mayer-Smith, J., & Moon, B. (1998). A critical analysis of the research on learning to
    teach: Making the case for an ecological perspective on inquiry. *Review of Educational Research,*
    68(2), 130–178.
Wiske, M. S. (Ed.). (1999). *Teaching for understanding*. San Francisco: Jossey–Bass.
Wolf, S., Mieras, E., & Carey, A. (1996). What's after "What's that?": Preservice teachers learning to
    ask literacy questions. *Journal of Literacy Research, 28*, 459–498.
Zeichner, K. (1998, April). *The new scholarship in teacher education*. Vice-presidential address at the
    annual meeting of the American Educational Research Association, San Diego.
Zeichner, K., & Gore, J. (1990). Teacher socialization. In W. R. Houston (Ed.), *Handbook of research*
    on teacher education (pp. 329–348). New York: Macmillan.
Zeichner, K., & Liston, D. (1985). Varieties of discourse in supervisory conferences. *Teaching and*
    Teacher Education, 1(2), 155–174.

GIRLFRIEND IN A COMA:
RESPONDING TO LITERATURE THROUGH HYPERMEDIA

Roberta F. Hammett

TEACHING HIGH SCHOOL ENGLISH LANGUAGE ARTS

By this time most teachers of secondary English have read and been influenced by the reader response theories of Louise M. Rosenblatt (1938, 1978), followed by Wolfgang Iser (1974) and Robert Probst (1986), among others. Thus, teachers have adjusted to a pedagogical pattern for reading texts in the English language arts classroom that begins with an evocation of the text—the experience of reading and imaging the text in a personal way. This evocation, which occurs during silent reading or while listening to the text being read aloud, involves giving oneself up to the experience of the work, consciously or unconsciously making connections and meaning of the words on the page, and drawing on memories and personal and previous literary experiences (Rosenblatt, 1978, p. 10). In a classroom, students may be invited to close their eyes as the teacher reads a poem aloud so that each person experiences the mood or feeling or memory conjured up by the work. Second, there is a response, a conversation with or about the text, with self or with

Advances in Reading/Language Research, Volume 7, pages 105–127.
Copyright © 2000 by JAI Press Inc.
All rights of reproduction in any form reserved.
ISBN: 0-7623-0264-X

others, that is, as Rosenblatt (1978) suggests, "active, self-ordering, and self-corrective" (p. 11). Writing responses in reading journals is commonly part of this engagement. In the classroom, the discussion of individual responses to the text continues to encourage the broadening of the response, with each reader incorporating ideas and responses from others that illuminate and enhance her or his own readings, but that do not necessarily result in rejecting or radically changing it. Third, there is an efferent reading (Rosenblatt, 1978, p. 69), when the student explores textual significance, interprets the text, "concentrates on what the symbols designate" (p. 27), decides what to "carry away" from it, and creates texts about it. This interpretation may be poststructuralist, archetypal, deconstructionist, or new critical, or may involve other possibilities of critique. In a classroom, a teacher may, for example, invite students to develop a feminist critique of a poem. The focus during this third reading is no longer on the text or the individual reader, but on the interpretive community. This focus attempts to place the work in larger contexts—to define its place in social discourses or the history of ideas, to evaluate its significance and meaning in relation to any number of established or newly proposed criteria, to test the worldview it embodies, to use it as the focal point for questioning one's assumptions about human experience or the sense of values prevalent in one's society, and to analyze the adequacy of its language and literacy devices to achieve effects deemed appropriate for its genre or theme. The reading and knowledge at this stage tend to move the response from the control of the student to that of the teacher and into a realm that may be more public, distant, and rational.

These approaches to teaching English language arts and the text practices each embodies are my starting point for more detailed descriptions of other literacy theories and practices. I would like to suggest that reader response may serve as a point from which to step to other textual practices and literacy theories, including personal literacy, intertextuality, and critical literacy. Furthermore, I believe that the contexts and practices of hypermedia composing can help to push reader response into other, more critical, realms.

WHAT IS HYPERMEDIA?

Before detailing specific critical literacy practices that I am suggesting can grow out of reader response, in combination with hypermedia composing, I will provide a brief description of hypermedia. Hypermedia, also called multimedia hypertexts, refer to the combining in one window or space, potentially, of a variety of texts and links to other windows. Generally, hypermedia have little linear organization. Rather, the reader moves from one space to the next in a random pattern, using links provided by the author as well as the program's opportunities to close windows and go back to opening screens to select and open different windows and thus pathways. A familiar example of hypermedia is the World Wide Web, particularly its sites that combine print text, images, sounds, and video clips, as well as multiple links within and without the site. CD-ROMs, which incorporate the same features in order to provide information in exciting and realistic ways, are other well-known examples of hypermedia. In this chapter, I will be describing hypermedia that were created using Storyspace™ (Eastgate, 1994) software in a Macintosh platform. Storyspace™ provides means for exporting the texts to HTML, but it is not necessary to do this; the Romeo and Juliet hypermedia being discussed here were not thus exported.

PERSONAL LITERACY

Reading a text aesthetically, as Rosenblatt (1978) describes it, means entering into the experience of the text. It also means bringing one's personal history to the transaction with the text. That personal history includes one's lived experiences and one's previous reading experiences. "Literature, when reader response is allowed and encouraged," says Stover (1996), "helps us not only expand our view of the world, but to rethink our own place in it and our relationship to it and others as well" (p. 120). Thus, personal literacy involves exploring the self, connecting the self, and exposing the self (Myers, Hammett, & McKillop, in press) during practices of both reading and writing. In these social acts, identities are constructed and reconstructed (Heath, 1986; Christian-Smith, 1993). Identities, like the readings of texts, are context-dependent, multiple, and shifting (Orner, 1992). As Rosenblatt (1978) suggests, "The relation between the reader and the text is not linear. It is a situation, an event at a particular time and place in which each element conditions the other" (p. 16). Rosenblatt further explains that a reading can never be repeated, for each reading is "an event occurring at a particular time in a particular environment in a particular moment in the life history of the reader" (p. 20). The readers of a text, *Romeo and Juliet*, for instance, and the composers of the hypermedia or any other response, in making connections, explore and expose their identities, as was demonstrated in the hypermedia being discussed in this chapter. When I invited students to compose the *Romeo and Juliet* hypermedia, adding and creating texts they connected with Shakespeare's play, I was asking them to reveal both their personal readings of the play and aspects of their personal lives, like the music they listened to and the movies and videos they watched.

INTERTEXTUALITY

Central to many intermediate and secondary language arts curricula is the concept of intertextuality (see Beach, 1993). This intertextuality has been incorporated in many different forms, not the least of which is the thematic approach. Anthologies and literature textbooks use the thematic approach to assist students in understanding issues and phenomena through intertextual connections. In another sense, the intertextuality of one text is sometimes explored, particularly in relation to a Shakepearean text like *Romeo and Juliet*, whereby Shakespeare's multiple sources are investigated, often by the text's editor who presents his or her findings to the student in the form of an introductory essay or line notes. A somewhat broader notion of intertextuality, for me, is articulated in Foucault's (cited in Talbot, 1995) description:

> The frontiers of a book are never clear-cut: beyond the title, the first lines, and the last full stop, beyond its internal configuration and its autonomous form, it is caught up in a system of references to other books, other texts, other sentences... it indicates itself, constructs itself, only on the basis of a complex field of discourse. (p. 45)

As Talbot explains, "Any text contains, is part of and is constituted by, the society which produced it and that society's history. Intertextuality expresses the rather dizzying concept of a text as a bundle of points of intersection of other texts" (Talbot, 1995, p. 45).

What I might call a third conception of intertextuality incorporates both the thematic and Foucaultian versions and Rosenblatt's reader response theory. Rosenblatt's theory moves the understanding of intertextuality from the text to the reading, bringing the reader's previous experiences, both lived and textual, into the transaction with the text. Thus, asking students to explore and represent the intertextuality of a text asks them to identify, as much as possible, the texts they connect with the current text—in genre, theme, character, situation—whatever aspects occur to them as they consider the text within the discourses of English language arts.

Providing a set of thematically connected texts as well as the opportunity and encouragement to identify, share, discuss, and produce personally connected texts ensures a rich environment for textual (and self) exploration. The text set concept (Short, 1992) generally involves at least one core or class text considered through teacher-directed learning activities, a few texts that several students read and discuss, and a number of texts for individual selection and response. All of the texts are related in some way, usually in theme and situation. Such an instructional consideration of multiple texts provides opportunities for students to make comparisons, develop understandings based on several viewpoints, consider contradictions and opposing opinions and perspectives, and thus generate inquiry topics. As well, teachers may strive to meet individual students' needs and interests by providing a selection of texts that are thematically interrelated, from which students select the text each will read and discuss in collaborative groups. Generally, intertextual connections are then explored and shared in whole class discussions.

I implemented this pedagogical approach to teaching English language arts in the course I am discussing in this chapter. With Shakespeare's *Romeo and Juliet* as the "main" text, the education students read, shared, and discussed several popular adolescent novels. *Lucy* (Kincaid, 1990), *My Darling, My Hamburger* (Zindel, 1969), and *Only Earth and Sky Last Forever* (Benchley, 1974) are three of the texts subsequently included in the hypermedia.

RESISTING TEXTS AND READING POSITIONS

Texts, reading practices, and pedagogical contexts all position readers, encouraging them to assume and construct particular viewpoints, sympathies, interpretations, and readings (O'Neil, 1990). This positioning is accomplished through a variety of discourses, experiences, and textual practices. Rosenblatt (1978), for example, describes how "past literary experiences serve as subliminal guides as to the genre to be anticipated, the details to be attended to, the kinds of organizing patterns to be evolved." The argument has been made (Fairclough, 1992; Peim, 1993) in the contexts of critical literacy practices that readers can resist this positioning. One aspect of resisting texts is resisting the genre expectations that, as Rosenblatt (1978) suggests, subliminally overwhelm us. In this sense, hypermedia's structure resists traditional genres, particularly their linear nature. As well, composers of hyperme- dia (in the Romeo and Juliet project, for example) incorporate a wide variety of texts from media culture. This use of popular culture texts seems to resist the canonical and potentially elitist meanings of Shakespeare's plays and other classics. On still another level, the resistance may be toward the ideology of the text, as connections are made that present alternative values and viewpoints to question those represented in the original. A student who juxtaposes, as one did in this hypermedia, Shakespeare's portrayal of young aristocrat's romance with Blessid Union of Souls' (1995) depiction of an interracial relationship brings ideology into question.

CRITICAL LITERACY

In response to Freire's challenge to the banking concept of education (Freire, 1970, p. 60), secondary English language arts teachers have increasingly attempted to deemphasize lecture and knowledge transfer methodologies and incorporate teach- ing strategies that provide students with opportunities to construct knowledge in social contexts. In these contexts, students collaboratively pose the questions and bases for inquiry and engage in the activities they and their teacher devise to assemble and integrate the knowledge necessary to satisfy the questions, solve the problems, and potentially act on the personal and social situations that give rise to the inquiry. Students may, for example, engage in research in their communities, and then write letters or publish articles and stories that share their findings. The knowledge which is thus socially constructed is constituted in and of language and culture. Bruner's (1986) constructivism, for example, views culture as "a *forum* for negotiating and renegotiating meaning" (p. 123, original emphasis), though it does not, as Willinsky (1990) points out, contest "the uneven balance of power in this negotiation of meaning" (p. 207). Critical literacy, as conceptualized by Freire and other Freirean theorists, "incorporates both critical thought and critical action" (Myers, Hammett, & McKillop, 1998, p. 77), as readers of the world and the word develop and act on critical projects that are transformative, emancipatory, and democratic (Freire & Macedo, 1987). I see a potential in hypermedia composing for resisting cultural reproduction, and for bringing "students' cultural capital—i.e. their life experience, history, and language" to canonical texts, so that they are "able to engage in thorough critical reflection, regarding their own practical experience and the ends that motivate them in order, in the end, to organize the findings and thus replace mere opinion about facts with increasingly rigorous understanding of their significance" (Freire & Macedo, 1987, p. 148).

COMPOSING THIS HYPERMEDIA: THE CLASSROOM CONTEXTS

The hypermedia project described and discussed in this chapter was composed by 13 secondary English education students. Most of the students were taking their second block of education courses as part of an integrated degree and were juniors or seniors; three were graduate students doing education courses after completing an undergraduate degree. Most were in their early 20s, single, white, and from working-class backgrounds; three were in their late 20s, and were married. Two had young children. There were eight women and five men. The students were familiar with basic computer commands and with word processor software. None were familiar with HTML, digitizing (audio, video, or images), or hypertext. They learned each of these skills as needed by observing a demonstration, following written step-by-step directions with expert and nonexpert observation and assistance, and by collaborative trial and error. The hypermedia project was produced as a collaborative enterprise after a classroom introduction to hypertext. It evolved from a basic conception (organized around basic themes of love at first sight, suicide, death, and so on) agreed on by consensus.

The education students were enrolled in two courses, Teaching Adolescent Literature and Secondary English Methods I, which were being taught collaboratively by three instructors (myself and another doctoral student and our supervising professor) in a local high school setting. The education students spent each morning (5 hours) for 4 weeks in various areas of the school. They met in the school library for the course classes, which were taught by me and my colleague; they received computer instruction and assistance from all three of us in the Mac computer lab; they observed and worked with Grade 9 students in two classrooms; and, finally, they met with the classroom teachers to discuss their observations and plan the next day's activities. One of these ninth-grade classes was taught by a "regular" teacher and the other, by a team consisting of another teacher and our supervising professor. Sometimes the education students worked individually with a small group of ninth graders, other times they observed from the back of the room, and on other occasions they moved about the room assisting individuals. In both high school classes the unit of study was Shakespeare's *Romeo and Juliet*. In both classes the variety of activities in which the ninth graders engaged included reading portions of the play aloud, viewing Zefferelli's (1968) movie version, viewing scenes from Roxanne (Schepisi, 1987), acting scenes in small groups, writing response journals, and answering teacher-devised questions in group and whole class discussions.

During the hypermedia workshop, we provided the undergraduates with instruction, demonstration, and assistance in digitizing images, audio, and video; in creating quicktime movies; and in combining the various electronic texts in the hypermedia environment. The 13 university students worked collaboratively to create one hypermedia composition. As the hypermedia project developed, they organized and reorganized it to accommodate the various texts, deciding the main organizing feature should be thematic.

Another course enterprise involved selecting and reading two adolescent novels and sharing a summary and critique of each novel and its themes with classmates. Because they were reading these texts simultaneously with the study of *Romeo and Juliet*, students were able (even encouraged) to make connections between the novels and the play.

My description of the hypermedia, which follows next, will focus on the kinds of responses outlined earlier in this chapter: reader response, personal literacy, intertextuality, resistant readings, and critical literacy. As a former teacher of senior high school English and as a student of Language and Literacy Education, I was familiar with these concepts and was (am) interested in ways that computer technologies can be used in classrooms to facilitate their implementation in high school English language arts classrooms.

THE *ROMEO AND JULIET* HYPERMEDIA

The Romeo and Juliet hypermedia composition consists of 74 spaces and 249 links. It is divided by themes into several subfields, each of which is introduced with a "menu." The "Suicide" menu, for example, provides links to a variety of texts in the "Suicide" strand and in other strands or sections, including the Shakespeare spaces. The following Storyspace^{TM} view (Figure 1) demonstrates the physical organization of the spaces on the computer screen; the semantic links are indicated by the arrows.

Shakespeare's words are incorporated in the hypermedia in two ways. One section of the hypertext includes spaces that quote various portions of the play which the composers were connecting with other texts; for example, the "Despair" texts are linked to quoted lines from Act III, Scene v, in which Romeo and Juliet part after their wedding night. Other students chose to place the relevant Shakespeare quotation in the same space as the connected text, as is illustrated by the following quoted texts in the space "Despair":

> A raindrop just splashed on my forehead and it was like a tear from heaven. Are the clouds and the skies really weeping over me? Am I really alone in the whole wide gray world? Is it possible that even God is crying for me? Oh no. . . no. . . no. . . I'm losing my mind. Please God, help me.
> *Go Ask Alice*, Anonymous

> "Romeo is banished," to speak that word,
> Is father, mother, Tybalt, Romeo, Juliet,

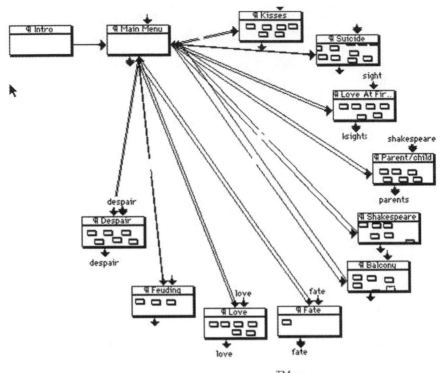

Figure 1. The Storyspace™ View

All slain, all dead. "Romeo is banished!"
There is no end, no limit, measure, bound,
In that word's death; no words can that woe sound.
   Juliet (Act III, Scene ii)

This juxtaposition of texts within a window makes explicit the absolute despair the two women share and perhaps suggests or foreshadows their similar use of drugs as a desperate and regretful solution to their problems. One text thus represents a response to the other, as well as an intertextual connection between them.

THE DESPAIR STRAND

There is a great deal of flexibility for linking and juxtaposing texts inherent in the Storyspace™ program. The descriptions above introduce two potential arrangements: linking between spaces and putting more than one text in the same space. The possibility of linking spaces to be followed by the reader in a preset sequence and arranging them to stay open in specific areas of the monitor screen is another potentiality, one which allows for simultaneous viewing and thus particular intertextual readings, as illustrated in Figure 2. On this screen there are four texts visible; in actuality there are six texts represented.

Rosenblatt (1978) says, "We are not usually aware of the organizing or constructive process—the fitting together and interpretation of visual clues—which results in the act of perception" (p. 50). In composing their hypermedia, the students tried to capture in the somewhat concrete form of the hypertext the experiences that informed their reading of *Romeo and Juliet,* selecting out, synthesizing, and interinanimating (Rosenblatt, 1978) textual experiences—for the hyperactive quality of hypermedia does interinanimate the readings. The set of texts described in the following section illustrates this quality.

Texts in the *Romeo and Juliet* hypermedia open from main menus—in this case the "Despair" menu, with the "Babe" space. The visible commentary can be read on the screen while the opening verse of the Styx (1987) song, describing a sad parting but professing continuing devotion, is heard:

Babe I'm leaving
I must be on my way. . .
I'll be missing you.

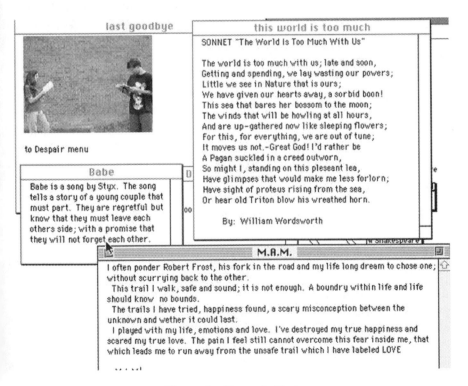

Figure 2. Despair Texts

The next potential space for the reader to access is the "Separate Lives" window, which again presents commentary while the lyrics are heard. The commentary is: "Separate lives was a song used in the movie *White Nights*. The song tells the story of two people in love; due to their circumstances they are not able to be together and have realized it." The phrase "separate lives" provides a link to the "M. A. M." space (which will be discussed in more detail below). Its link is to the "this world is too much with us" space, which presents Wordsworth's sonnet. Finally the links lead to the "last goodbye" space which includes a quicktime movie constructed from three still electronic photographs of ninth graders reading Shakespeare's Act III, Scene v and a clip from "Last Goodbye" by Jeff Buckley (1994):

> This is our last goodbye
> I hate to feel the love between us die. . .
> this is our last goodbye.[1]

Not only is an overwhelming emotional impression created here by the juxtaposition of texts, but also an interinanimated experience of regret and despair, reflection and pain, and remorse and apathy. This interinanimation of the associated texts broadens the representation of the experience from single to complex, from one dimensional to multidimensional; but it also creates a particular reading of the Shakespeare scene, one which questions the lovers' agency in their situation. As Rosenblatt (1978) explains: "The reader, assuming the aesthetic stance, selects out and synthesizes—interinanimates—his [or her] responses to the author's pattern of words. This requires the reader to carry on a continuing, constructive, 'shaping' activity" (p. 53). The hypermedia represent this reader response (of the composers) while at the same time functioning as a text that invites or evokes a response in its readers. In this section or strand of the hypermedia, a particular and intentional interpretation is represented by the composers, one that is not in any way questioned or contradicted. Should this "Despair" strand of the hypermedia have included alternative texts that do illustrate agency and resistance as an alternative for star-crossed lovers? Should I have intervened to raise this possibility or suggestion? These sorts of questions will be explored in discussions of other strands and literacies and of critical pedagogy in upcoming sections of this chapter.

Other texts in the "Despair" section of the hypermedia ably demonstrate the concept of personal literacy. Two students included texts they wrote in response to the play and the hypermedia they were composing collaboratively. Stan (a pseudonym), who was called away from classes to join his family at his grandmother's bedside and then at her funeral, wrote this haiku, entitled OLD AGE:

> The hospital bed,
> holds an old woman I love.
> The gates are open.

Stan included a link to the Ann Sexton poem, "Wanting to Die," linking specifically to the phrase "wanting to die" from the words "Old Age." The composer of the "Wanting to Die" space explained her inclusion of the text (Ann Sexton's poem) in a commentary at the end of the poem (see below). Another student also included an original text in the "Despair" strand:

> I often ponder Robert Frost, his fork in the road and my life long dream to chose one; without scurrying back to the other.
> This trail I walk, safe and sound; it is not enough. A boundry within life and life should know no bounds.
> The trails I have tried, happiness found, a scary misconception between the unknown and whether it could last.
> I played with my life, emotions and love. I've destroyed my true happiness and scared my true love. The pain I feel still cannot overcome this fear inside me, that which leads me to run away from the unsafe trail which I have labeled LOVE.

These students have been prompted by the textual practices involved in hypermedia composing to explore their own lived experiences, to make connections with the texts that they and others have chosen to include in the hypermedia, and to share and expose their own emotional responses and experiences—all personal literacy practices.

Another opportunity for original writing in this hypermedia is illustrated by the commentary on the Ann Sexton poem:

> Justification: It's quite evident the poem is about suicide but it's so much more than that. Desperation and longing can be linked to the theme of *Romeo and Juliet* and "suicides sometimes meet" shows the hopelessness that the couple feels. That's why I chose the poem.

In this text, Ellen reveals that, as Probst (1988) suggests, students engage best with literature that "deals with issues that are significant to them" and that "stimulate[s] the effort to 'actualize' or make meaning out of the text" (p. 35). Exploring the issues like teen suicide through a variety of texts, students themselves having chosen both issue and texts, is likely to lead to a committed and purposeful effort to understand and internalize the issue and the texts—a critical literacy practice.

THE KISSES STRAND

Readers of this hypermedia can begin where they wish, for the creators have saved the hypertext in such a way that it opens with the Storyspace™ view (illustrated in Figure 1). Alternatively, the hypertext might have been saved to open to a particular text window, presenting links to other windows in a predetermined sequence. As this composition is left open, the reader decides the starting point by double clicking on any one of the boxes visible on the screen. The choice of the "Kisses" menu window, for example, holds links to six spaces, each of which presents at least one text. One window opens with quoted lines from *Only Earth and Sky Last Forever* (Benchley, 1974), one of the text set novels; another, with a quotation from Catullus

("A thousand kisses grant me sweet . . . "); and another, with the words "'With a kiss let us set out on an unknown world' by Alfred de Musset (1810–1857), French Poet." Still another space presents a quotation: "'. . . then I did the simplest thing in the world. I leaned down . . . and kissed him. And the world cracked open.' Agnes de Mille (b. 1905 American choreographer and dancer)" and a song clip from "Groovy Kind of Love" (Collins, 1988):

> When I kiss your lips, ooh I start to shiver
> Can't control the quivering inside
> Wouldn't you agree, baby, you and me got a groovy kind of love.

Thus, the interconnected windows layer meaning between and in spaces, creating an intertext of meanings that amplify the meanings of Shakespeare's text (the meeting of Romeo and Juliet at the Capulet ball) and introduce additional possibilities of meaning. As Barthes (1977) asserts and hypermedia ably demonstrate, a text is "not a line of words releasing a single 'theological' meaning but a multi-dimensional space in which a variety of writings . . . blend and clash. The text is a tissue of quotations drawn from innumerable centers of culture" (p. 146). The "centers of culture" or discourses, though in some senses incongruous, do blend to create and represent an experience of love that crosses borders of time, geography, culture, race, nationality, and sensibility.

This strand of the hypermedia also offers two stanzas of a poem by Emily Dickinson ("For each ecstatic moment . . . ") and this explanation by the composer of the space: "This poem by Emily Dickinson illustrates how intense passion has a price. This can be compared to Romeo and Juliet because with their passion came the ultimate price—death." Thus, the intertextual connection extends beyond the present theme to other themes and strands, both in the explanation of the composer and the physical links that take the reader, if selected, to another space that adds to the meaning. The word "death" links the reader to the suicide menu, the organizer for the spaces that relate to the deaths of Romeo and Juliet.

THE SUICIDE STRAND

The texts in the "Suicide" section are equally diverse, ranging from an Ann Sexton poem "Wanting to Die," to a quoted passage from *My Darling, My Hamburger* (Zindel, 1969), and to a poem "How Did You Die?" by Edmund Vance Cooke. In this section, the composers took advantage of the software program Adobe Premiere 4.2^{TM} (1994) to digitize the Juliet funeral scene from the Zefferelli (1968) video, which was presented in a space without comment. Linked to this space through the words "another version" was a quicktime movie clip with the same visual track but a replaced audio track. The composer had digitized the Alice in Chains (1995) song "Grind" to replace the original background music of the scene. After a long opening instrumental section, the words "In the darkest hole, you'd be well advised/Not to plan my funeral before the body dies . . . " are heard. These words are provided below the movie clip, with a link to a third movie version. Again the same visual track is presented with the song,

> Girlfriend in a coma, I know
> I know—it's serious
> Girlfriend in a coma, I know
> I know—it's really serious. . . . (The Smiths, 1987, Strangeways, Here We Come)

Finally, there is a fourth quicktime movie in the series. This one depicts students reading the Shakespeare funeral scene, with accompanying audio,

> Came into my life, made me think that I was really something
> Took me by surprise, someone with your charm, looking my way.
> Am I in heaven? . . .

These audio and visual combinations are interesting for a number of reasons. First, they illustrate the production capability students can achieve with software like Adobe Premiere 4.2™ (1992), which manages the production of quicktime movies. Students can select visual images from any one of many sources and can combine them with audio from multiple sources, including original audio and visual creations, if desired. Buckingham, Grahame, and Sefton-Green (1995) argue that, in the same way reading and writing are linked in traditional literacy learning, so must producing other media texts be linked with viewing in other visual and media literacies. Important, too, is that students have a means to "actively construct and explore their own cultural identities" (p. 81). Using media texts to produce their own meanings and to resist the dominant readings gives students opportunities to be producers rather than consumers of texts and meanings.

Second, replacing the audio permits the presentation of a different mood. In the case of the Alice in Chains/Zefferelli combination, the peppier soundtrack seems to speed up the action, and different visual images seem to be highlighted—like the Friar's cagey smile. Thus, the reader/viewer is reminded that Juliet is not dead, despite the solemnity of the original Zefferelli (1968) video version, by the new auditory experience and, at the end of the clip, the song lyrics. Similarly, in a third quicktime movie version, the repeated lines "Girlfriend in a coma/It's really serious" serve to refocus our attention—on Balthazar as he witnesses the funeral believing Juliet to be dead and on the Friar, who stops his grin and saddens his face just at the phrase, "I know, it's serious" is heard. This multimedia tool provides students with the chance to experiment, in a constructivist learning activity, with film conventions like music soundtrack and to observe very specifically their uses and effects.

Third, this space is an example of an intertextual creation which demonstrates how readers and composers can resist the authorial meaning and aesthetic experience of a text. By changing the soundtrack, the composer resists the position assigned by the Zefferelli text, repositioning herself and her readers/viewers in relation to the visual text.

Hypermedia composing opens up possibilities for resisting texts in ways that were not necessarily demonstrated by the education students but which might have been made available as an extension of what the students did do. Other popular songs might have challenged the gender or class ideologies, for example, inherent in either the Shakespeare or Zefferelli text. Responsibility for raising this possibility lies with me, the teacher, for these education students, even though they were discussing and reading about critical literacy and pedagogy (as Freire, 1970, and Shor & Freire, 1987, were listed resource texts), did not create this kind of textual resistance on their own. These data, viewed in retrospect, suggest that hypermedia composing alone is not a sufficient intervention to challenge the preferred response or the constructedness of the text (O'Neil, 1990); the intervention or molesting, to use O'Neil's term, must be purposeful, with hypermedia composing as the means.

PARENTAL CONFLICT SECTION

The "Parental Conflict" strand of the hypermedia opens with Kahlil Gibran's (1968) poem "Your Children Are Not Your Children." It seems appropriate that these education students, generally caught between the roles of parent and child, between student and teacher, should focus on this theme in their hypermedia. It is interesting, however, that their texts seem to represent the point of view of children (who desire independence).

The Gibran text links back to the strand menu, where the second listed text, "deadpoets," links to a video clip from *Dead Poets Society* (Weir, 1989). The viewers see and hear Neil's father tell his son that there will be no more "defying us . . . tomorrow I'm withdrawing you from Welton and enrolling you in. . . Military School." The offered links take the hypermedia reader to a very similar confrontation scene between Juliet and her parents (Act III, Scene v) when they order her to prepare to marry Paris and to the suicide strand and the digitized clip of Neil's suicide. The intertextual connections continue as the offered links move back to the Shakespeare text and Juliet's (fake) suicide scene when she is similarly discovered by her parents (Act IV, Scene v). These linked texts are provided without comment, with the hypermedia composers seeming to point out the similarities or parallel meanings. The more contemporary scenes seem to be offered as introductions to the Shakespeare scenes and as aids to understanding the more challenging Elizabethan English by providing a more familiar context for its reading. Highlighted lines in the target (Shakespearean) text emphasize this aspect.

The "deadpoets" space also offers a link to a video clip from *The Little Mermaid* (Musker & Clements, 1989), again a scene depicting an argument between father and daughter, and also to the Shakespeare text described above.

Also in this strand is the space "10,000 lyrics," which displays the words to the song under the heading "You and Me of the 10,000 Wars words and music by Emily

Saliers." At midpoint of the text the words are interrupted to present a quicktime movie which combines still pictures of ninth graders reading the Shakespeare text while the song is heard. Although the words for the entire song are presented, the final lines offer a promise that seems to add a different element to the theme:

> After the battle and we're still around
> everything once up in the air has settled down
> sweep the ashes, let the silence find us
> a moment of peace is worth every war behind us.
> you and me of the 10,000 wars. (Indigo Girls, 1990)

Another space in this section, labeled "ham lov/fam," presents a quotation from *My Darling, My Hamburger* (Zindel, 1969, p. 42):

LOVE/FAMILY:

> I [Liz] need you, Sean, more than anything in the world. The only time I feel alive is when I'm with you. Even when we fight, I don't care as long as we make up. My stepfather thinks I have loose morals. He thinks a lot of dirty things, and he's turned my mother against me. She used to stick up for me, but now she does whatever he says. I think she's scared of him. Either that, or I'm no good and not worth worrying about. I'm glad my father is dead because if he could see what she married, he'd be ashamed. They don't trust me at all.

The last space in the Parent/child menu is "I believe." In this space the song lyrics of "I believe" (Blessid Union of Souls, 1995) are heard. The song expresses the belief that adversaries are not that different, and that love can bridge the gap between them and can cure societal ills like violence, drugs, and racial prejudices. The song concludes with a reference to the parent of an interracial couple realizing he's lost his daughter unless he understands and sees the lover "as a person not just a black man." The clip ends midsong with the words "black man." The space also provides a link to a Shakespeare text, Act II Prologue, highlighting the words: "That fair for which love groan'd for and would die/With tender Juliet match'd is now not fair." Thus, multiple spaces in the strand, with links offered to several spaces in other sections of the hypermedia, create a rich intertextual experience on the theme of parents and children, focusing particularly on the conflicts among them and taking the viewpoint (largely singular) of the child.

As the intent is to create an intertextual experience for the hypermedia reader, no explanations for, or comments on, the connections made and illustrated are provided by the composers. In combination, the texts create meanings, and the identities of the composers are revealed and articulated in the intertext. When meaning is shifted to the intertext, and can be represented by the arrangement of texts in a hypermedia project, then the cultural values and personal identities of the readers/composers can be signified and examined.

Hypermedia also offer the opportunity to juxtapose alternative texts which raise questions and challenge omissions and biases and thus create resistant readings. Consider Annette Kolodny's assertion (cited in Flynn & Schweickhart, 1986):

> *Insofar as we are taught to read, what we engage are not texts, but paradigms. . . .* Insofar as literature is itself a social institution, so, too, is reading a highly socialized—or learned—activity. . . . We read well, and with pleasure, what we already know how to read; and what we know how to read is to a large extent dependent on what we have already read [works from which we have developed our expectations and learned our interpretive strategies]. What we choose to read—and, by extension, teach and thereby 'canonize'—usually follows upon our previous reading. (p. 45, italics and insertions original)

By challenging students to illuminate a text (like *Romeo and Juliet*), we disrupt both the canonical text and the canonizing reading practice. Popular culture texts, which students often select in composing their hypermedia (as is illustrated here), bring with them different interpretive assumptions and strategies which shift the authority for meaning from the text into the reading community. These reading practices reframe the purpose for texts in school as an opportunity to explore personal identity, and social values and relationships, instead of getting the right interpretation and learning the correct moral lesson.

We also open up possibilities for critical examinations of the texts and their ideologies, as illustrated by the above references to "I believe" (Blessid Union of Souls, 1995). A teacher could ask students to discuss dating rules constructed by both parents and peer groups and to think about the simplistic solution ("love is the answer") offered by the song. Students could try to uncover underlying ideologies for the rules and prejudices and suggest other solutions or ways to address these societal problems.

FEUDING STRAND

One of the smallest (in number of spaces) sections of the hypermedia is "Feuding." There are three spaces, the first being the "feud/cliques" space. When this window opens, the viewer/reader may read parts of Act I, Scene v, the conflict between Capulet and Tybalt over the presence of Romeo at the ball. From this space, the words "this is a Montague, our foe" provide a link to the "breakfast club" space. In this window a digitized portion of *The Breakfast Club* (Hughes, 1985) video can be viewed. In the scene the diverse group of students, who have struggled through many conflicts to a relationship of mutual respect and even caring, begin to wonder what will happen to their new friendship in school on Monday. The Molly Ringwold character lays out the reality of cliques and peer pressure to convince them they will have to ignore one another. This clip is followed by a commentary by the students:

Many of the ideas Shakespeare employs in his plays deal with events and concepts that are alien to today's youth. For example, young people today do not understand the importance and the severity of the two families feuding in *Romeo and Juliet*. In an effort to make this more accessible to students, we thought this clip from *The Breakfast Club* is a good modern-day example of group conflict and segregation. Cliques have taken the place of family for many youths in American culture. To understand why, for example, Tybalt is so enraged that Romeo dared to come to a Capulet party, is difficult for students unless we can somehow relate it to their world and experience. This clip, we feel, does this. The link is to Act I, Scene v of *Romeo and Juliet*. Students had a lot of questions about why Tybalt was so upset about Romeo being there. In answer we asked them how they would feel if another student from another clique just crashed one of their parties. By placing the scene in a scenario they understood, students were able to grasp what the conflict was about.

One of the links from this space is to the last window in this series—a quicktime movie and the printed lyrics of "Brothers in Arms" (Dire Straits, 1987). The quicktime movie is constructed of six still pictures of students acting out the fight scene between Romeo and Tybalt. Two of the images and some of the lyrics are shown here (see Figure 3). The song asserts that their enemies are not that different, are in fact "brothers in arms," and they are foolish to suffer and die in a battle with them. Thus, "brothers in arms" are both companions and adversaries.

In this link I see some resistance in relation to the feuding theme, although it is not made explicit. What it does provide, however, is the space in the classroom to take up the issues through the kind of "dialogical" teaching advocated by Shor and Freire (1987) that "disconfirms domination and illuminates while affirming the freedom of the participants to re-make their culture" (p. 99). Students in their commentary of *The Breakfast Club* (Hughes, 1985) might have referred to a critical reading of student experience around issues of social class inequities and conflicts. The comments by the characters in *The Breakfast Club* scene are not taken up, nor

You did not desert me
My brothers in arms

There's so many different worlds
So many different suns

Figure 3. Fight Scenes

are their meanings resisted or disrupted. The futility of conflict is suggested in the Dire Straits (1987) song (see Figure 3), but the class issue is not raised specifically and the war issue is not explicitly political. This portion of the hypermedia demonstrates the potential for popular media texts to raise issues and provide openings for students to articulate and examine their own experiences. This must be taken up, however, within a critical pedagogy which challenges students to name the differences. Kelly (1997) discusses these "contested discourses" and "discourses of difference" (p. 106), going on to quote Chantra Mohanty (1994):

> The central issue, then, is not one of merely *acknowledging* difference; rather, the more difficult question concerns the kind of difference that is acknowledged and engaged. Difference seen as a benign variation (diversity), for instance, rather than conflict, struggle, or the threat of disruption bypasses power as well as history to suggest a harmonious, empty pluralism. (Mohanty, p. 146 in Kelly, 1997, p. 106)

Hypermedia composing is thus viewed as one part of a critical pedagogy that intends to "understand how reading can be democratized, how students can be given the keys to unlock or open up the literature they read" (Corcoran, 1988, p. 43). Students select the texts, and often present them in such a way that confirms the statement by Shor and Freire (1987): "Traditional discourse confirms the dominant mass culture and the inherited, official shape of knowledge" (p. 99). But they also reveal gaps and silences, raise questions and demonstrate resistance, and open up spaces for dialogue and further critical reading. A teacher, given more time than I had in this course, could ask students to discuss these sorts of issues as they are revealed in their hypermedia composing, and challenge them to write or select and link other texts that would make them explicit.

OTHER STRANDS

There are many more strands and texts in this hypermedia that provide additional examples of the kinds of personal and critical literacies, intertextuality, and textual resistance. I will discuss only a few more texts to raise an additional pedagogical issue. Much of my discussion of intertextuality addresses the connections to the play as though Shakespeare's work is the foundational text. For most of our students, the media culture texts are the foundational texts, which illuminate the "new" text, *Romeo and Juliet*. Most students come to the play with multiple previous balcony scenes (for example) in their experience. They do not see *Roxanne* (Schepisi, 1987) and think of *Romeo and Juliet*; they read *Romeo and Juliet* and understand it in relation to *Roxanne* or *Valley Girl* (Coolidge, 1983) or "Come to my window" (Etheridge, 1993). Multiple images, characters, plot lines, and songs inform and influence their reading and viewing of the play as is illustrated by the hypermedia strands, particularly "Balcony," "Love," and "Love at First Sight." In "Balcony," for example, the Zefferelli (1968) balcony scene video clip is shared along with the lyrics of Carole King's (1987) "Will You Still Love Me Tomorrow?" Another space replaces the Zefferelli soundtrack with "Come to my Window"

(Etheridge, 1993). Another space shows the *Aladdin* (Clements, Musker, & Pell, 1992) balcony scene and the end of the movie's theme song, "A Whole New World" (Kane & Salonga, 1992) which re-creates, in another example of intertextuality, Romeo's exultant departure from Juliet's balcony in the Zefferelli (1968) film. Another video balcony scene, "Serenade," has replaced the soundtrack with the Indigo Girls's version of the song "Romeo and Juliet" by Mark Knopfler (1980a) of Dire Straits. Also in this strand are a quoted passage from *Only Earth and Sky Last Forever* (Benchley, 1974) and *Lucy* (Kincaid, 1990), both text set novels; and Deville Willy's (Knopfler, 1987b) "Storybook Love"; and the song "Somewhere" (Sondheim, *West Side Story*, 1961). Thus, the hypermedia composers achieve multiple layerings of meaning both by replacing one video soundtrack with another, again and again, and by presenting other lyrics and print texts in the window. Links to other related spaces layer still more meanings.

Additional versions of the Romeo and Juliet story, in song form, are introduced in other strands of the hypermedia, including Lou Reed's (1989) "Romeo Had Juliette." This song picks up Shakespeare's themes of star-crossed love, forbidden desire, drugs, and conflict. Its text, like many others, raises issues of diversity and cultural representation that can then be taken up critically in the classroom, for the students did incorporate a wide range of cultural representations in their hypermedia. If, as Kelly (1993) and others (Peim, 1993; Willinsky, 1990) suggest, we should be about the business of remaking English as a subject, hypermedia composing illustrates one way to jump in. Consider Kelly's explanation:

> Reformulating English. . . and in so doing, hopefully enhancing the possibilities for remaking the human subject of English, demands 'a pedagogy of possibility' (Simon, 1987, 370) in which the bias of all forms of literary knowledge is acknowledged and critiqued and in which multiple realities are celebrated and interrogated. It is a pedagogy in which students may come to see more clearly the forces that work to make them who they are, in which they imagine greater possibilities for what they may become, and in which they can discern those qualities they no longer desire. Such an informed citizenry might well strike a resounding commitment to social justice once the conditions of injustice are more fully realized. (p. 210)

Hypermedia provides a tool that can open up spaces for literacy practices that push the edges of reader response into critical literacy and textual resistance. These practices encourage students to read, question, and resist school texts and all the texts that comprise their world; they invite them to create texts that express and enact possibilities of a different world they might envision. I will summarize these pedagogical practices in the next section.

THE POTENTIAL OF HYPERMEDIA

The possibilities of hypermedia and its diverse texts have led to new forms of knowledge production and new rhetorical conventions. Opportunities for collaboration, nonlinear arrangement, flexibility of movement between texts (or spaces in the hypermedia), new genres, new types of language, and juxtaposition and simultaneous presenting of different, even contradictory texts, are all appropriate examples of these phenomena. Hypermedia technology provides students with other ways of representing knowledge and ideas, an objective of many new curricula (Foundation for the Atlantic Canada English Language Arts Curriculum, 1996, p. 13; Western Canadian Protocol for Collaboration in Basic Education, 1998, p. 3). Hypermedia technology provides the means to demonstrate connections between words and ideas in texts by: allowing the display of several different texts in the same space and in spaces side by side on the screen, showing linked words through highlighting and contrasting font colors, and facilitating links between texts. It allows composers to set up texts so that they can be examined and possibly contested, as in the case of *Romeo and Juliet* and "Romeo Had Juliette" (Reed, 1989). If nothing else, the portrayals of different classes and related values can be discussed.

Hypermedia technology presents possibilities for intersecting school literacies (the traditional literacies of reading and writing) and popular literacies (related to culture and identity) (Kelly, 1997, p. 8). Students read texts and write explanations and introductions as they select and incorporate a wide variety of texts in their hypermedia. They choose quotations and images from their favorite songs and movies, thus representing their identities and engaging in personal literacy practices (Hammett, 1997). The juxtaposition of such texts offers an opportunity to critique media images and ideologies in a way that is not so threatening to the pleasures and desires of media enthusiasts. As C. Luke (1997) states, "Media studies scholars have noted that the relocation of children's and adolescents' 'leisure/pleasure' texts into the classroom for formal intellectual scrutiny potentially subverts and belittles whatever pleasure kids derive from such texts and the social relations within which such texts are consumed" (p. 43). In contrast, the arguably pleasurable activities of selecting, digitizing, and placing the texts in computer windows during the generally independent composing of hypermedia may lead students to a self- or teacher-directed consideration of the ideologies (Myers et al., 1998; Hammett, 1999). The teacher can ask students to articulate the similarities and differences in the texts they juxtapose, thus helping to expose the underlying values and worldviews.

Unlike the use or reading of commercial multimedia products, which position readers as consumers, hypermedia composition allows students to actively bring their worlds to bear on the texts under consideration and to create a literacy experience for themselves and for others. The process provides the opportunity for reinterpretation of both the "school" text and the many other "popular" texts juxtaposed with it. It encourages alternative reading and writing practices that challenge traditional texts' constructedness. Various texts, set side by side or morphed together, provide space for reinterpretations and the construction of new meaning. Instead of talking about a connection one might make to another text, the electronic space of hypermedia provides firsthand concreteness, as has been illustrated in my descriptions and the figures provided in the sections above.

This lived experience with texts generates more possible meanings for students, some of which may well be critical in the Freirean sense. Janks (1993), discussing her Critical Language Awareness Series, explains:

> The processes of de-naturalizing and de-constructing [and here I would add "re-constructing"] offer students changed discursive perspective which has a disruptive potential. Offering students other subject positions from which to read the world has "implications for affecting new identities and disorganizing old ones." (Simon, 1992, p. 92 in Janks, 1993, p. 64)

A pedagogical pattern for reading texts in the classroom that invites students to consider their choices in relation to approved curricular resources, and to manipulate both kinds of texts in ways I have described above (like replacing soundtracks in videos), positions students as authors of new texts.

In an English language arts classroom committed to critical reading and pedagogy, the evocation and initial personal response to texts, represented in whatever form (writing, hypermedia composing, and so on), can be secondly shared and discussed in critical dialogue. It can then be considered carefully, analyzed, subjected to efferent readings—all within a critical pedagogy that aims at offering both active engagement with texts and additional identities for students involved in the process of constructing and reconstructing texts, themselves, and their world.

ACKNOWLEDGMENT

I gratefully acknowledge the contribution of Dr. Jamie Myers, the Pennsylvania State University, and Dr. Ann Margaret McKillop, University of Maryland, to this research. I also thank the education students for their enthusiastic and insightful composing of hypermedia.

NOTE

1. Lyrics for these songs are often available on the Internet sites like *http://www.lyrics.ch/*, which at the time of writing recently was shut down for copyright litigation.

REFERENCES

Adobe Premiere 4.2™. (1994). Mountain View, CA: Adobe Systems, Inc.

Alice in Chains (Cantrell, J.). (1995). Grind. *Tripod*. Nashville, TN: Columbia Records.

Anonymous. (1967). *Go ask Alice*. Toronto: Prentice–Hall.

Barthes, R. (1977). *Image music text*. New York: Noonday Press.

Beach, R. (1993). *A teacher's introduction to reader-response theories*. Urbana, IL: National Council of Teachers of English.

Benchley, N. (1974). *Only earth and sky last forever*. New York: Harper Trophy.

Blessid Union of Souls. (1995). I believe. *Home*. New York: Capitol Records.

Bruner, J. (1986). *Actual minds, possible worlds*. Cambridge, MA: Harvard University Press.

Buckingham, D., Grahame, J., & Sefton-Green, J. (1995). *Making media: Practical production in media education*. London: English and Media Centre.

Buckley, J. (1994). Last goodbye. *Grace*. Nashville, TN: Sony Music.

Christian-Smith, L. (1993). Constituting and reconstituting desire: Fiction, fantasy, and femininity. In L. Christian-Smith (Ed.), *Texts of desire: Essays in fiction, femininity and schooling* (pp. 1–8). London: Falmer Press.

Clements, R., Musker, J., & Pell, A. (1992). *Aladdin*. Burbank, CA: Walt Disney Productions.

Collins, P. (1990). Groovy kind of love. *Serious hits . . . live*. Burbank, CA: Wea/Atlantic.

Coolidge, M. (1983). *Valley girl*. San Monica, CA: Vestron Video.

Corcoran, B. (1988). Spiders, surgeons, and anxious aliens: Three classroom aliens. *English Journal, 77*(1), 39–44.

Dire Straits. (1987). Brothers in arms. *Brothers in arms*. Burbank, CA: Wea/Warner Brothers.

Etheridge, M. (1993). Come to my window. *Yes I am*. New York: Polygram.

Fairclough, N. (1992). *Discourse and social change*. Cambridge, UK: Polity Press.

Flynn, E., & Schweickhart, P. (1986). *Gender and reading: Essays on readers, texts, and contexts*. Baltimore: Johns Hopkins University Press.

Foundation for the Atlantic Canada English Language Arts Curriculum. (1996). *English language arts foundation*.

Freire, P. (1970). *Pedagogy of the oppressed* (M. B. Ramos, Trans.). New York: Continuum.

Freire, P., & Macedo, D. (1987). *Literacy: Reading the word and the world*. South Hadley, MA: Bergin & Garvey.

Gibran, K. (1968). *The prophet*. New York: Random House.

Hammett, R. (1997). *Adolescent women, identity, and hypermedia composing*. Unpublished doctoral thesis, The Pennsylvania State University.

Hammett, R. (1999). Intermediality, hypermedia, and critical media literacy. In L. Semali & A. Watts Pailliotet (Eds.), *Intermediality: Teachers' handbook of critical media literacy* (pp. 306–328). Boulder, CO: Westview Press.

Heath, S. B. (1986). The functions and uses of literacy. In S. de Castell, A. Luke, & D. MacLennan (Eds.), *Literacy, society, and schooling* (pp. 15–26). London: Cambridge University Press.

Hughes, J. (Director). (1985). *The breakfast club*. New York: MCA.

Indigo Girls. (1990). You and me of the 10,000 wars. *Nomads Indians Saints*. Nashville, TN: Sony Music.

Iser, W. (1974). *The implied reader: Patterns of communication in prose fiction from Bunyon to Becket*. Baltimore: Johns Hopkins University Press.

Janks, H. (1993). Developing critical language awareness materials for a post-apartheid South Africa. *English in Australia, 106*, 55–67.

Kane, B., & Salonga, L. (1992). A whole new world. *Aladdin: Original Motion Picture Soundtrack*. Burbank, CA: Walt Disney Productions.

Kelly, U. (1993). Teaching English: Who's subject to what? In S. Straw & D. Bogdan (Eds.), *Constructive reading: Teaching beyond communication* (pp. 205–213). Portsmouth, NH: Boynton/Cook.

Kelly, U. (1997). *Schooling desire: Literacy, cultural politics, and pedagogy*. London: Routledge.

Kincaid, J. (1990). *Lucy*. New York: Farrar, Strauss, & Giroux.

King, C. (1987). Will you still love me tomorrow? *Tapestry*. Nashville, TN: Sony Music.

Knopfler, M. (1987a). Romeo and Juliet. *Making Movies*. Burbank, CA: Wea/Warner Brothers.

Knopfler, M. (1987b). Story book love. Princess Bride Soundtrack. Burbank, CA: Wea/Warner Brothers.

Luke, C. (1997). Media literacy and cultural studies. In S. Muspratt, A. Luke, & P. Freebody (Eds.), *Constructing critical literacies: Teaching and learning textual practice* (pp. 19–49). Cresskill, NJ: Hampton Press.

Mohanty, C. (1994). On race and voice: Challenges for liberal education in the 1990s. In H. Giroux & P. McLaren (Eds.), *Between borders: Pedagogy and the politics of cultural studies* (pp. 145–166). London: Routledge.

Musker, J., & Clements, R. (Directors). (1989). *The little mermaid*. Burbank, CA: Walt Disney Productions.

Myers, J., Hammett, R., & McKillop, A. M. (1998). Opportunites for critical literacy and pedagogy in student-authored hypermedia. In D. Reinking, M. McKenna, L. Labbo, & R. Keiffer (Eds.), *Handbook of literacy and technology: Transformations in a post-typographic world* (pp. 63–78). Mahwah, NJ: Erlbaum.

Myers, J., Hammett, R., & McKillop, A. M. (in press). Connecting, exploring and exposing self in hypermedia projects. In M. A. Gallego & S. Hollingsworth (Eds.), *Challenging a single standard: Perspectives in multiple literacies.*

O'Neil, M. (1990). Molesting the text: Promoting resistant readings. In M. Hayhoe & S. Parker (Eds.), *Reading and response* (pp. 84–93). Philadelphia: Open University Press.

Orner, M. (1992). Interrupting the calls for student voice in "liberatory" education: A feminist poststructuralist perspective. In C. Luke & J. Gore (Eds.), *Feminisms and critical pedagogy* (pp. 74–89). London: Routledge.

Peim, N. (1993). *Critical theory and the English teacher: Transforming the subject.* London: Routledge.

Probst, R. (1988). *Response and analysis: Teaching literature in junior and senior high school.* Portsmouth, NH: Boynton/Cook–Heinemann.

Reed, L. (1989). Romeo had Juliette. *New York.* Burbank, CA: Wea/Warner Brothers.

Rosenblatt, L. (1938/1983). *Literature as exploration* (4th ed.). New York: Modern Language Association.

Rosenblatt, L. (1978). *The reader, the text, the poem: The transactional theory of the literary work.* Carbondale: Southern Illinois University Press.

Schepisi, F. (Director). (1987). *Roxanne.* Los Angeles: Columbia Pictures.

Shor, I., & Freire, P. (1987). *A pedagogy for liberation: Dialogues on transforming education.* Granby, MA: Bergin & Garvey.

Short, K. (1992). Making connections across literature and life. In K. Holland, R. Hungerford, & S. Ernst (Eds.), *Journeying: Children responding to literature* (pp. 284–301). Portsmouth, NH: Heinemann.

Simon, R. (1987). Empowerment as a pedagogy of possibility. *Language Arts, 64*(4), 370–382.

Sondheim, S. (1961/1992). Somewhere. *West Side Story.* Nashville, TN: Sony Music.

Storyspace[TM]. (1994). Watertown, MA: Eastgate Systems, Inc.

Stover, L. T. (1996). *Young adult literature: The heart of the middle school curriculum.* Portsmouth, NH: Boynton/Cook–Heinemann.

Styx. (1987). Babe. *Cornerstone.* Pgd/A&M.

Talbot, M. (1995). *Fictions at work: Language and social practice in fiction.* London: Longman.

The Smiths. (1987). Girlfriend in a coma. *Strangeways, here we come.* Burbank, CA: Wea/Warner Brothers.

Weir, P. (Director). (1989). *Dead poets society.* Touchstone Pictures.

Western Canadian Protocol for collaboration in Basic Education. (1998). *The common curriculum framework for English language arts kindergarten to grade 12.*

Willinsky, J. (1990). *The new literacy: Redefining reading and writing in the schools.* London: Routledge.

Zefferelli, F. (Director). (1968). *Romeo and Juliet.* Los Angeles: Paramount Pictures.

Zindel, P. (1969). *My darling, my hamburger.* New York: Bantam Books.

RESPONSE TO LITERARY TEXT THROUGH MEDIA:
REVISITING CONCEPTUALIZATIONS OF LITERATURE AND ARTISTIC EXPRESSION

Patricia I. Mulcahy-Ernt

Moved by the sense of loss, the spirit of tragic desperation, yet the realization of idealism and beauty of two forsaken lovers who come to their deaths too early, the artist in response casts a dark line, then a rising pink hue on the page. The story the artist is interpreting is the classic tale of the Montagues and Capulets in Shakespeare's *Romeo and Juliet*. It is the final scene, and Capulet declares, "O brother Montague, give me thy hand." Responds Montague, the grieving father of Romeo who too late recognizes the love Juliet has sworn to his son, "But I can give thee more: For I will raise her a statue in pure gold." The artist chooses this final scene of reconciliation as the subject for the painting and attempts to represent it through color, shape, line, and movement. The artist creates a towering monument with soft hues and strikingly sharp lines, symbolizing the joining together of two families finally at peace after bitter war.

Often it is such inspiration from literature that an artist, musician, dancer, or sculptor uses as fuel for creative expression. The artist may choose a pivotal literary

Advances in Reading/Language Research, Volume 7, pages 129–154.
Copyright © 2000 by JAI Press Inc.
All rights of reproduction in any form reserved.
ISBN: 0-7623-0264-X

scene, sense of mood, or expression of character, then through the medium of paint, or music, or dance transform it into a new artistic creation that has its own unique form, beauty, and interpretation. Such artistic expression provides nuance, new life, and a unique response to the original literary text. The goal of such expression is not to copy the original text but to render a personal response that now becomes available for public viewing.

The scenario described above is real. However, its context was not situated in an art class but a course for secondary-level preservice English language arts teachers which focused on strategies for teaching language and literature. The "artist," whose work will be discussed later in this chapter, does not claim to be so from a professional stance; as a preservice English language arts teacher, she was interested in learning instructional approaches for the teaching of language and literature. Through the medium of art in an original response to literature she deeply thought about her text as well as her own approaches for learning and teaching literature. Through her own aesthetic expression of a personal response to text using the medium of art, she entered the artistic community, viewing literature from a fresh perspective.

In this chapter I will take the position that reader response to literature can be reconceptualized to include text that utilizes media in both print and nonprint forms, inclusive of artistic expression, utilizing a variety of old and new technologies. Such response does not require sophisticated training in art, dance, or music. On the other hand, such response does require a deep analysis of text, a personal connection to the text, and a rethinking of text in creative, abstract, and meaningful ways.

READER RESPONSE TO LITERATURE

Understanding literature in personal, meaningful ways is a process Langer (1995) believes incorporates "envisionment building" (p. 9), allowing the reader to create an understanding of the text and to connect to the text by making sense of it in relation to one's own life. This process allows the reader to explore the horizon of possibilities (p. 26) that promotes inquiry, curiosity, risk-taking, and creativity throughout the literary experience. The aesthetic literary experience (Rosenblatt, 1978) allows for a personal construction of the text; depending on the reader's stance, however, the reader may consciously choose to analyze, respond to, evaluate, or appreciate the text from a social, cultural, topical, or textual perspective (Beach & Marshall, 1991; Beach, 1993). Similarly, other reader response theorists (Purves, 1977; Probst, 1981, 1988; Karolides, 1992; Cox & Many, 1992; Smagorinsky, 1996; Hynds, 1997; Smagorinsky & O'Donnell-Allen, 1998) support the view that when reading literature, the process is a complex negotiation of meaning that occurs on many levels; the reader's own interpretation of the text allows for a literary experience that goes beyond the text itself.

Such personal construction of meaning prompts cognitively complex expressions in written, verbal, or nonverbal formats. When readers are prompted through open-ended questioning and discussion about the text and their own interpretations, readers not only discuss essential textual elements, but they also make connections of the text to their own lives, become more aware of the centrality of the literary experience to their own personal issues, pose critical questions, speculate and hypothesize about characters and the plot, infer important relationships within the text, make critical judgments, and pose and then solve problems that are relevant to both the text and to their own lives (Mulcahy-Ernt & Ryshkewitch, 1994).

However, in most discussions of reader response activities for literature class-rooms, the assumption is that the reader's response is in written form, typically through expressive journal writing, or through class discussion. Rarely does the research literature describe literary response in the form of nonprint media. New conceptualizations and definitions of literacy, however, consider both print and nonprint sources. Literacy broadly defined includes media. Particularly in the current definition of language arts, the expanding notion of literacy entails the processes of reading, writing, listening, speaking, viewing, and visually repre-senting language (National Council of Teachers of English & International Reading Association, 1996). Thus, responding to literary text need not be limited to written or spoken platforms.

The expanded perspectives of literacy endorsed by national and state standards have had important implications for the pedagogy of English and language arts education. As noted by the work of preservice teachers represented in this chapter, media responses to literature use artistic platforms for visually representing lan-guage and the literary aspects often discussed in literature circles. The reader's media response to literature may take the form of the visual arts: photography, painting, sculpture, or other artistic rendering. Or, students may choose television or computer images to combine graphics with sound or text in order to create a multimedia response. On the other hand, students who choose performing arts as media may interpret text through a variety of forms: dance, pantomime, drama, reader's theater, music, or other such forms that may be collaborative expressions involving the leadership and coordination of small groups of students.

MEDIA LITERACY IN THE LANGUAGE ARTS

Responding to literary text with genuine involvement on cognitive, emotional, philosophical, ethical, and aesthetic levels promotes an understanding of the human experience and the complexities inherent in the broader issues of life. Recent curricular efforts to promote such literary engagement have called for classroom activities that encourage reader response to literature. These curricular goals are stressed by national standards (National Council of Teachers of English & Interna-tional Reading Association, 1996) and by state or province standards. These curricular goals emphasize the use of media as essential for communication and central to instructional goals for literacy and the English language arts. How these national standards translate into actual classroom practice in elementary (Cox,

1999), middle school (Macaul, Giles, & Rodenberg, 1999; Wilhelm, 1996), and secondary-level contexts (Smagorinsky, 1996) is a recent challenge for educators.

The goal of responding to both print and nonprint sources, as cited by these standards, broadens the definition of literacy to include media in the language arts, as noted in Cox's (1999) definition:

> Media literacy refers to composing, comprehending, interpreting, analyzing, and appreciating the language and texts of the multiple symbol systems of both print and nonprint media. The use of media presupposes an expanded definition of "text" in the English arts classroom. Print media include books, magazines, and newspapers. Nonprint media include photography, recordings, radio, film, television, videotape, videogames, computers, the performing arts, and virtual reality. On the full range of media channels, all these types of text constantly interact. They are all texts to be experienced, appreciated, and analyzed and created by students. (p. 451)

In this definition of media literacy for the language arts there lies the underlying purpose of language and literacy: communication. The technological tools now available for embracing and expressing literacy allow us to move our conceptualization beyond the technology of pre-20th-century societies. The emerging technologies for 21st-century societies allow for multiple platforms for expression, inclusive of nonprint sources. Such technologies now require a deeper need for inquiry, for critical viewing, and for an understanding of the intermediality of multiple sign systems (Semali & Pailliotet, 1999); this process of reading multiple texts requires the construction of meaning that builds connections across print and nonprint sources.

An aesthetic understanding of the world and of the literary texts representing our human experiences will remain a critical curricular goal for instilling a shared sense of human values, particularly as emerging technologies threaten to isolate individuals in their technological communities. So, on the one hand, technology threatens to dehumanize the societies in which we live, but on the other hand, the communicative potential of expressing our deepest selves through multiple sign systems and multiple media platforms expands our potential for creativity, thereby enriching our abilities to communicate with one another and promote the human spirit.

This expanded definition of literacy impacts curricular goals in the teaching and learning of language and literature and challenges traditional thinking about "text." The use of media in the language arts creates multiple forms of expression and communication, creating new forms of "text." As shown through the work of the preservice teachers included in this chapter, their aesthetic responses to literature strove to use a variety of technologies both old and new: paper cutout graphic design, pastel line drawings, water color, and digital photography. Their media texts were created after a thoughtful analysis of a choice of literature, after a deliberate selection of media to best represent their perspectives, after much time on the task of creating their media responses (for some students this was a novice attempt), and after a critical overview of their work in order to make final touches. Such engagement with literature occurred on many levels: cognitive, aesthetic, and emotional. The process of creating these new texts employed many aspects of the goals for a language arts class: active student involvement with literary text, deep analysis and critical inquiry of literature, and communication of ideas in both print and nonprint forms. As preservice teachers, they also learned firsthand the pedagogy of teaching through media literacy; these lessons learned were exemplars that they could use in their own classrooms with secondary-level students.

THE ABSTRACTION OF MEANING THROUGH MEDIA RESPONSE

Multiple media platforms provide a repertoire of choices for responding to a text and for constructing nonverbal abstractions of meaning. Nonprint pictorial formats, such as photography, pottery, sculpture, paintings, and drawings, allow the reader to use color, shape, form, line, texture, depth, contrast, and similar artistic conventions to create symbols, represent themes or moods, create settings, represent characters, make a social statement, or evoke a feeling. Artistic formats, such as music, creative dramatics, and dance, provide a fluid, dynamic opportunity for expressing a range of responses, which can tell a story, describe the characters' emotional or psychological responses, and give life form to the human experience. Other media, such as computer technology, film, newspapers, and television, can provide a platform that integrates pictorial information with verbal text in order to tell a story, present an opinion, explore a theme, present an argument, provide historical background, or report information. These examples are just a few of the choices that media formats give the reader in responding to literature; media formats provide a vast repertoire of choices, each with their own unique characteristics, limitations, and options. Table 1 provides an overview of these formats.

In my graduate course for preservice secondary-level English and language arts teachers, students choose their own media platforms to respond to a novel or classic work. Their reasons of choice vary greatly: Sometimes they want to venture into a medium new to their experience, sometimes they want to use a medium in which they have artistic talent or familiarity, or sometimes they choose a certain medium because they have pragmatic reasons due to time and available resources. From my stance as the course instructor I do not constrain the type of choice of media. My goal is to provide the type of experiences that encourage divergent thinking, a deep analysis of literary text, and a personal connection to the text. As illustrated by the student work in this chapter, students become involved with both their own media texts and their original literary selections. This is evident through several outcomes. In the classroom context each student presents, discusses, and elaborates his or her media responses; this public viewing of media responses simulates a showing at an art gallery and prompts students to take such work seriously. There is much classroom talk that accompanies each media response; other students raise questions about the media responses, thereby promoting conversation that requires the reader to field questions about his or her literary selection and media representation.

Table 1. Media Responses to Literature

Media Forms	Examples	Illustrative Literary Goal
Visual arts	Painting	Create mood
	Drawing	Depict character
	Photography	Represent symbols
	Pottery	Represent theme
	Sculpture	Show conflict
	Film	Evoke a response
	Collage	Make a social statement
		Portray a point of view
		Represent conflict
Performing arts	Dance	(All the above)
	Music	Show a range of emotions
	Reader's theater	Tell a story
	Pantomine	Portray character change
		Give life form to the human experience
Combined technologies	Computer images	Present an argument
	Television	Explore an opinion
	Newspapers	Present different types of images and texts
		Provide historical and geographical background

The Beach and Marshall (1991) classification of reader responses provides a framework that I use for describing media responses; in this classification reader responses are based from the perspectives of the reader's textual, social, cultural, or topical knowledge base. In the following sections these perspectives will be explored more fully, then illustrated with student examples.

Textual Stances in Media Responses

Readers using a textual stance focus primarily on literary elements, such as mood, tone, characterization, theme, plot, conflict, imagery, and symbolism. According to Beach and Marshall (1991), readers taking a textual stance "are defining the ways in which the separate parts of the text are related to its overall form or structure" (p. 248). Media formats give the reader a wide variety of choices to convey these literary elements and to use symbols to communicate their abstractions. For instance, highly contrasted black-and-white photography can convey conflict and emphasize strife between protagonists and antagonists. Soft pastel hues in a painting can symbolize a peaceful mood. Slow, long reaches coupled with wide, arching leaps in a ballet can create a romantic mood. A collage of pictures of historical events related to the theme of injustice can be juxtaposed with essays and quotes related to the same theme. A social, cultural, psychological, and physical portrait of a character in a novel can be presented on a hypertext program. The main storyline can be represented through several different media formats: a dance, a pantomime, a video, a computer storyboard, and the characters and the conflicts they encounter can be represented through sculpture, drawing, painting, or film.

Reading literature from a textual perspective is a predominant approach often required by curricular frameworks. Most English language arts programs require students to be familiar with the concepts of characterization, setting, plot, conflict, theme, imagery, and symbolism. Media representations, however, allow students to present their conceptualizations of these literary elements in rich and powerful ways without the fear of failing to write about them in sophisticated verbal forms. Particularly for the student who has not acquired the written proficiency needed to describe literary aspects, media responses provide the option of demonstrating rich understandings of literature. Then, if the student is given the opportunity to talk about his or her artistic response and to describe how it was created in relation to the text, the student has a firm base for creating a written response that describes and elaborates the media response, describes the student's reason for choosing the medium, and describes the student's perspective in relation to the text. The instructional approach of first providing options of media responses, inclusive of nonverbal ones, followed by discussion, then followed by a written reflection about the student's media response creates the instructional scaffolding for reader responses that have depth, complexity, and personal relevance to the student.

Encouraging students to talk about their own artwork as a literary response is similar to the discussion approach in art circles. Discussions about artworks in relation to their aesthetic qualities and their own artistic elements, such as character, scene, theme, or mood, have a long history in the arena of art history. For example, Gombrich's (1998) *The Story of Art* describes Leonardo's *Mona Lisa* in terms of her intriguing character:

> What strikes us first is the amazing degree to which Lisa looks alive. She really seems to look at us and to have a mind of her own. Like a living being, she seems to change before our eyes and to look a little different every time we come back to her. Even in photographs of the picture we experience this strange effect, but in front of the original in the Louvre it is almost uncanny. Sometimes she seems to mock us, and then again we seem to catch something like sadness in her smile. All this sounds rather mysterious, and so it is: that is so often the effect of a great work of art. (p. 300)

Thus, as art critics, art historians, art consumers, as well as artists, the reader as responder can delve into literature and analyze the many literary qualities of its masterpieces. Often many of the subjects of classical art are routed in classical literature. For example, the story of Achilles, the myths about the Greek gods and goddesses, the heroics of Hercules, and scenes from the journey of Homer's Ulysses are subjects of many famous sculptures, drawings, and pictures on pottery of the Hellenistic time period (Gombrich, 1998). With a media literacy approach to contemporary literary works, readers can complement the textual works with contemporary visual-aesthetic works that likewise bring characters, settings, and stories to life.

When creating a media representation of a literary element, the reader views literature from the perspective of an artist who uses symbolism and sign systems instead of verbal tools to convey a message. The reader attempts to represent some aspect of the text and achieve a unified, aesthetic whole; it is this fresh perspective that encourages abstract thought, visual imagery, fostering what Gardner (1985) views as spatial intelligence. It is a popular belief that teachers can support the development of multiple intelligences by linking the visual arts and musical arts to the language arts (Campbell, Campbell, & Dickinson, 1996). In so doing students also develop an aesthetic appreciation of literature.

Social Stances in Media Response

A social stance when reading literature occurs when the reader draws on his or her knowledge of social relationships to reflect on the text and the characters in the text, his or her relation to the text, and the author's assumptions about the audience (Beach & Marshall, 1991). Readers using a social perspective analyze the social relationships of the characters, particularly in reference to their own social attitudes, experiences, and values. For instance, the reader's own conception of friendship will influence responses to open-ended prompts such as, "Is the main character a good friend—Why or why not? What evidence from the story indicates this?" "What would you tell the main character if you were his friend?" "If you were one of the characters in the story, what would you like your relationship to be in relation to the main character?" "What type of writing techniques did the author use to convince you about the moral character of the protagonist?"

The reader's response to a literary work can depict through a media format the conflicts, the emotional and psychological characteristics, and the social relationships of the main characters in the text. The reader can also make a social statement about these relationships. For instance, one could note approval of the main characters and disapproval of the antagonists and their actions through the use of lighting, color, and tone. In music heavy, discordant tones can convey conflict, while contrasting light, airy harmonies can convey peacefulness.

McLuhan's (1997) perspective that "the medium is the message" (p. 7) also points to the personal and social consequences of choosing a medium. The chosen medium, as an extension of the writer or artist or dancer or musician, represents a point of view about the subject. The critical viewer needs to understand that the artist, too, has a position relative to the topic. In classroom contexts teachers and students could practice "deep viewing" (Watts Pailliotet, 1999) in order to be informed and critical consumers of media; through this process the viewer observes, describes, examines, and analyzes the media representation and asks critical questions that guide the viewer's own interpretation. However, the process of becoming a critical viewer is much more deeply understood when the reader as responder ponders the multiple ways meaning can be represented in media formats.

Cultural Stances in Media Responses

Cultural attitudes and values also influence the reader in terms of a response to literature (Beach & Marshall, 1991). The norms, cultural context, roles, and inherent values represented in the text, but also held by the reader, influence the type of response. Often in a media response the reader takes a stance that reveals his or her own value system. Examples of such perspectives can include experiences, beliefs, and attitudes about gender roles, social class, habits, and routines.

How the reader regards money, sex, power, food, religion, politics, drugs, education, war, freedom, children, censorship, animals, personal hygiene, the environment, cars, privacy, work, play, home ownership, and medical technology are but a few of the topics that are laden with cultural perspectives. A reader may choose to consider the historical context of a literary work and contrast that with a contemporary perspective. For example, present perspectives of the value of Shakespeare's play are vastly different from the perspectives of the 16th-century Puritans who viewed such work as corrupt. The concept of "childhood" is also a relatively recent phenomenon, dating only to the mid-19th century. The idea of owning land and property is not a universal one. These are just a few examples that illustrate cultural perspectives.

Effective media representations that illustrate the reader's cultural perspectives through the use of visual imagery can communicate themes that are highly significant and powerful. The reader's choice of images can reveal beliefs and biases, sometimes representing perspectives unexamined by the reader (Serrano & Myers, 1999). Unlike reader responses that are only print-based text, media responses can use pictures, film, drawings, and other graphic images. For instance, a reader's response to the novel *To Kill a Mockingbird* can use film clips, photographs, pictures, and headlines from newspapers to illustrate the theme of racism and intolerance; the connection to current events can make a social statement that links the characters and conflict in the novel to contemporary cultural issues.

Readers of science fiction and stories of societies cast in futuristic worlds can use their imagination to create a media representation of the culture, characters, and setting. For instance, how a futuristic society views death, child rearing, and marriage can provide a sharp contrast to contemporary norms. Each of these concepts is culturally laden with highly relevant notions of appropriateness. Other themes that could be represented include cooperation versus competition, innocence versus corruption, and beauty versus ugliness.

Topical Stances in Media Responses

Specialized knowledge of different academic fields or topics gives the reader a level of expertise that can be represented through print and media responses.

Examples include literature, history, science, math, art, music, or even topics such as architecture, sports, gardening, or cooking. When responding to text through a topical stance, the reader assumes the role of the expert and shows the connections between the text to a specialized field (Beach & Marshall, 1991).

Media representations require a level of expertise in visually representing the text and the reader's response to it; they are interdisciplinary in nature. However, the reader as responder must make cross-connections among disciplines. For instance, the reader may choose to represent a scene from a historical novel through a painting, a collage, dance, or authentic costuming for a theatrical piece. Music from a specific time period can also create the mood for the setting.

However, even though the reader may choose to use background knowledge from a specific discipline, my objective of using a media literary approach for a reader response to literature is not to judge the merits of the response on the reader's expertise in a discipline nor with the reader's technical proficiency in creating a work of art. Such background knowledge adds to the overall quality of elaboration. However, as an instructional approach to teaching and learning literature, I believe media responses should encourage students' risk-taking, creativity, and critical understanding of the texts they encounter.

MEDIA RESPONSES TO LITERATURE

Media responses to literature share similar characteristics to print-based responses in that both prompt the reader to think deeply about literary text, to reflect on his or her stance in relation to the text, to apply his or her textual, social, cultural, and topical perspectives, and to share those reflections with others (Considine & Haley, 1991). Both media and print-based responses foster critical inquiry and reflection (Sinatra, 1986). Both engage the reader in cognitive and affective activities; they prompt the reader to describe the text, to make personal connections internal to the text and external to the text by linking values, attitudes, and beliefs presented in the literary text to those held by the reader and the viewer (Flood & Lapp, 1995). Both prompt the reader to ask questions that guide future learning. Both prompt the reader to explore new connections. Both encourage the reader to examine the assumptions held by the author, the audience, even the characters in the story. Both challenge the reader to examine literary techniques, including the use of metaphor, dialogue, symbolism, allusion, and foreshadowing. Both require a close examination of central themes and issues inherent in the text, particularly in relation to those universal to the human condition. Both permit the expression of emotional responses. Both encourage the aesthetic experience.

Media responses allow for choices of expression that are aesthetically visual as well as print-based. Since students have a repertoire of choices of media, these options foster a creative outlet that is comfortable to the personality of the student and is often one that is of interest to the student. The reason for choosing a particular medium is of itself an important aspect of the response. Consequently, in instructional contexts I believe it is important for my students to share not only their media products but also their processes in creating them.

In the following sections I present three examples of responses to literature through media formats. These examples illustrate the various textual, social, cultural, and topical perspectives, as well as the reader's own unique rationale for creating the media response. (See the Appendix.)

The following sections contain examples from the graduate-level course I teach for preservice secondary-level English language arts teachers. The specific assignment required that students choose a literature selection currently used in secondary-level (7–12) classrooms. Students could pick an adolescent novel or a literary classic.

Students were asked to read their selection, then to create a media response to the text as a whole or to some aspect of the text (such as the theme, a character, the setting, the central conflict, the essential plot elements, or the use of symbols in the text). The students had the option of using visual formats (such as drawings or paintings), electronic formats (such as videotaped or computer images), or responses utilizing the performing arts (such as music, dance, or drama).

Students also wrote accompanying papers that briefly described their media and elaborated their responses. The students wrote their responses to a series of statements, such as the following:

- Describe your reason for choosing this book.
- Write a brief synopsis of your book.
- Describe your personal written response to this book, using a prompt such as the following:
  a. While reading this book, I learned. . . .
  b. This book changed my thinking about . . . because . . .
  c. I identified with (name of character) because . . .
- Describe your multimedia format and reason for choosing this format.
- Describe what you are communicating through your original work.
- Write an explanation of the most important aspects of your book for teaching secondary-level school students.

On a due date discussed in class, students gave oral presentations for both their media responses and their written responses. Students, therefore, had the opportunity to display their media responses, talk about them, and respond to questions from the viewers. In this way other class members could learn about other literary selections, view unique interpretations, and appreciate their classmates' artistic endeavors.

Sample student written responses are included in the Appendix. Their media responses are presented and discussed in the following sections. Both the media and textual responses give students the opportunity to connect to the literary text on a personal level, to construct their own interpretations of the text, and to illustrate their perspectives. Often the textual responses clarify the intent of the media responses and voice feelings and ideas that move beyond the original literary piece.

Students in my course presented a range of responses inclusive of the visual and performing arts, and I have selected three examples to illustrate the use of media as reader response. The sample media responses were created by three graduate students enrolled in a Master of Science program in Education; all three are white, female students in the 25–45 age range; all expressed the goal of learning good instructional strategies for teaching the English language arts.

Textual Response to *Romeo and Juliet*

At the time she enrolled in the course, Zhanna had just started her graduate Master of Science program in Education. She had just arrived in the United States, formerly living in Belarus. She spoke fluent English, Russian, and French and planned to teach English after graduation. The literary text that she chose was *Romeo and Juliet*, a universal classic.

Adopting a textual stance for her media response, Zhanna chose to focus on the plot and the character's emotional responses to the events in the storyline. She used abstract art to describe three pivotal places in the plot: the coming together of the two lovers during the balcony scene, the warring conflict between the two families, and the final scene of reconciliation of the two household heads.

Zhanna uses color, line, balance and imbalance, and symbolism to communicate the emotion of the two lovers, the strife of the families, and the action leading to the final tragic yet inspirational scene. She describes her work in terms of contrasting color and lines:

> The paper arrangement "Two Lovers Meet" shows the culmination point of love. The photograph that illustrates "Broken Love" follows it. The pastel drawing "A Monument to Love" demonstrates the resolution. The hues and shades of the passionate red color (yellow, yellow-orange, orange, orange-red, and red) are used in the first drawing to give the notion of love growing. Warm colors were chosen to express saturation, love and passion. In Shakespeare's work Juliet is associated with a "sunlight, starlight, daylight, and heaven light." To my mind the colors used to create the image of love are stronger than words. The black and white photograph illustrates the irregular pieces of paper cut by scissors and scattered about. This is a symbolic representation of broken love. The pastel shows a monument. Straight, vertical lines are used to express nobel and exalted feelings. Black and white colors are used to contrast death and life, hatred and love. Red color symbolizes the blood shed by two young souls who sacrifice their lives to bring about reconciliation.

Zhanna's multimedia classroom presentation of her media response included her own rehearsed discussion of her art, accompanied with background music from Tchaikovsky's symphony *Romeo and Juliet*. The choice of color, shape, and symbolism displayed in her artwork powerfully conveyed the drama, the conflict, and the tragedy of Shakespeare's masterpiece.

Figure 1. Photograph of Original Drawing as Response to *Romeo and Juliet* by Zhanna Tubis. "Two Lovers Meet."

As a new international student immediately and totally immersed in an English-speaking environment, Zhanna struggled with the language demands of her graduate classes. In her media response, on the other hand, she had a different outlet for expression. From my perspective as the course instructor, I was impressed with her thoughtful and creative analysis, with her concern with artistic detail, and with her sophisticated presentation.

Figure 2. Photograph of Original Drawing as Response to *Romeo and Juliet* by Zhanna Tubis. "Broken Love."

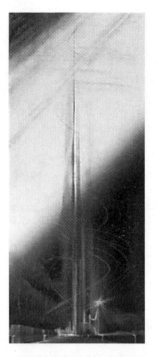

Figure 3. Photograph of Original Drawing as Response to *Romeo and Juliet* by Zhanna Tubis. "A Monument to Love."

Social Response to *Their Eyes Were Watching God*

Carla, a graduate-level intern in the Master of Science program in Education, was pursuing her certification as a secondary-level English teacher. Her love of poetry and creative writing was evident in her choices of text. Carla chose Zora Neale Hurston's (1990) novel *Their Eyes Were Watching God* because she was moved by the language, the poetic voice, and the imagery the author uses in the novel. In her media responses Carla uses as her focal image the symbolism of the tree to represent Janie's (the main character's) maturation and her awakening social consciousness.

Carla's paintings are heavy and rich with browns and deep greens. Carla chooses the image of trees, the roundness of the moon, and the darkness of the earth; these were used to symbolize Janie's life. Her paintings use feminine forms and symbols; for instance, the lines of the tree (see Figure 5) are contoured to the full shape of a woman. Carla writes, "Hurston uses images from nature to describe the characters and their life journey, so it was easy for me to decide on an oil painting as my multimedia format. The images are so detailed that I felt as if I were watching a mental movie while reading the story." Carla additionally writes:

Figure 4. Photograph of Original Oil Painting as Response to *Their Eyes Were Watching God* by Carla Pinto

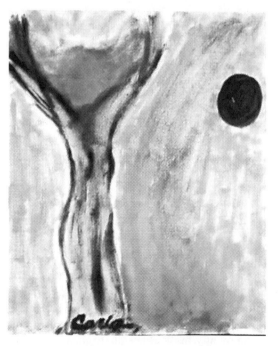

Figure 5. Photograph of Original Oil Painting as Response to *Their Eyes Were Watching God* by Carla Pinto

> Although Janie continuously seems to be searching for springtime, I see her in the autumn of
> her life throughout the story. My painting attempts to characterize Janie using the symbolism of
> a tree in autumn. At the beginning of the story Janie is looking back on her life about to tell her
> story. Hurston writes, "Janie saw her life like a great tree in leaf with the things suffered, things
> done and undone. Dawn and doom was in the branches" (p. 8). This is how I pictured Janie with
> the "dawn and doom" of autumn leaves.

In her textual interpretation of this novel, Carla stresses that this is a novel about
the voice of an African American woman, a voice often silenced. In her written
response Carla also explores Hurston's use of imagery, use of dialect, and relationships with others. As a reader, Carla responds that "I identified with Janie because
I can also see my life as continuous search for self discovery, happiness and love.
The desire to have these things carry Janie on a journey through life."

These media responses were Carla's first experience in painting. She took the
risk in trying a new format for her response and in creating an original, personal
statement. Carla's new venture into the world of painting gave her a new voice for
her own perspective; it was precisely the theme of voice that created the power of
Hurston's work and impressed Carla.

Cultural Response to *The Giver*

One of the more popular adolescent novels that is currently in use in school
settings is Lois Lowry's *The Giver.* The setting for the novel is a utopian society in
which there are highly scripted norms and rules for the members. In this society no
one can see color, hear music, or experience other emotions, such as love, common
to the world of the reader. Mary Beth, a graduate student seeking additional teaching
endorsements in the field of Reading and Language Arts, chose to explore the
medium of photography and to represent the theme and setting of her book. She
created a series of black-and-white images, using a digital camera to photograph
common objects.

Mary Beth's media response was based on the cultural conventions of this utopian
society. She notes:

> My multimedia format is black and white photography. I used a digital camera and took pictures
> of everyday things. I downloaded the images onto the computer and then printed them. The
> reason I used black and white photography is because this "community" was colorless and
> everything was the same.

Mary Beth's depiction of a black-and-white world was similar to the setting in
the text; furthermore, the use of black-and-white photography made a significant
commentary about the theme of the book. In the beginning of the novel the setting
was starkly black and white. However, as Jonas, the main character, learns the
"memories" of the community, his world begins to change; he realizes that the world
has shades of gray. Mary Beth depicts this change in her photography. By the end
of the novel Jonas begins to see subtle shades of color. The notable change to a

Figure 6. Photograph of Original Photograph as Response to *The Giver* by Mary Beth Jarvis

Figures 7. Photograph of Original Photograph as Response to *The Giver* by Mary Beth Jarvis

world of color at the end of the novel symbolizes Jonas's breaking away from the community and the development of his own independence. Mary Beth likewise includes color at the end of her photographic collection.

Mary Beth chose to tell her story through pictures of everyday objects. Her choice of photography allowed her to see her world in contrast to the world described by *The Giver*. In her class presentation she indicated that she enjoyed creating her photographic essay, especially since she had the opportunity to experiment using a digital camera.

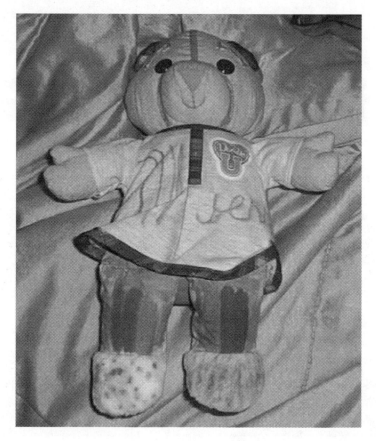

Figure 8. Photograph of Original Photograph as Response to *The Giver*
by Mary Beth Jarvis

Figure 9. Photograph of Original Photograph as Response to *The Giver* by Mary Beth Jarvis

CONCLUSION

Media literacy, broadly defined, includes print-based text and non-print text, expanding the notion of text to include visual images. The tools and technologies of the 21st century will require increasingly more sophisticated applications of technology and will require a broader knowledge base for understanding the interconnections among the disciplines using those technologies. The goal of literacy will be for readers to be proficient in working with multiple sign systems, to be critical viewers, but also to be proficient in using media representations to represent opinions as well as facts. Furthermore, as readers become more proficient in using written and visual symbols for expressing their responses to literature, the notion of "text" will expand to become more complex, thus promoting critical inquiry and reflection.

The complexity of using multiple sign systems will have an impact on curricular goals for the teaching and assessment of language and literature. Yet, there are still many unanswered questions for the use of multiple media platforms in the classroom. For instance, how should students be evaluated? What will be fair assessments of literacy development? What will be the curricular roles of language arts teachers and media specialists, particularly in the development of multiple litera-cies?

As teachers explore the use of multiple media platforms for reader response to literary text, the options of choice for students provide multiple forms of expression. Students who lack proficiency in English language expression can still produce powerful and sophisticated works that illustrate deep analysis of literary text and meaningful connections of the text to their own lives. Media responses as multiple ways of expression also support multiple ways of viewing. Students' work in the visual and performing arts adds dimensionality to classroom conversations about literature. Finally, media responses to literature bridge disciplines of art, dance, and music with disciplines of computer technology, education, language, and literature, and encourage readers and writers to make connections in novel, creative, and inspirational ways.

APPENDIX: SAMPLE RESPONSES TO TEXT

Response to *Romeo and Juliet*
by Zhanna Tubis

There are several important reasons that I took in consideration for choosing this book. First of all, Shakespeare is one of my favorite writers. I personally admire the language of Shakespeare and love the noble characters he created in his immortal works. Second, *Romeo and Juliet* is one of the most popular classical works appropriate for high school settings. This multimedia presentation can be applied to teaching Shakespeare to students.

Romeo and Juliet is a play about two lovers of Verona. There was an ongoing feud between the houses of Montague and Capulet. The main characters of the tragedy *Romeo and Juliet* belonged to hostile families. Lady Capulet was anxious to get her daughter off her hands. Juliet's parents wanted their daughter to marry Count Paris. Juliet's response was lukewarm. The turning point for Romeo was the moment when he first saw Juliet at the family feast and fell instantly in love with her. Romeo and Juliet learned to their dismay that they were sundered by the Montague–Capulet feud. Regardless of this the lovers exchanged their vows and decided to get married. The marriage was secretly performed by Friar Lawrence. But Romeo slew Tybalt who was the nephew of Lady Capulet. As a result of this he was banished from Verona. Juliet suffered because Old Capulet had strong intentions to persuade his daughter to marry Paris. She was willing to take her own life if no other way were found. Friar Lawrence provided Juliet with a potion of poison that would induce for forty-two hours the symptoms of death. They planned that Romeo and the Friar would be present at the moment of her recovery and rescue her from the tomb. Juliet drank the poison the night before the arranged marriage. Romeo was told that Juliet had died. Friar Lawrence's letter to Romeo informing him of the true facts about Juliet's death remained undelivered. So Romeo drank the poison at the Capulet Tomb. Juliet awoke and slew herself with a dagger. The members of the Montague and Capulet households repented, and each resolved to erect a golden monument to the memory of the other's child.

While reading *Romeo and Juliet* I had not only an intellectual understanding of the play but also a strong emotional experience. I read in fascination and awe this dramatic reminder of our own inevitable mortality. The tragedy evoked tears. I sympathized with the tragic and noble characters of Romeo and Juliet. I was exalted in witnessing the high human aspirations of self-sacrificial love. One of the most moving moments for me was the "balcony scene." I enjoyed the expressive language of Shakespeare. I liked the comparison of love to "lightening, sudden and violent." I changed my thinking about the interpretation of the end of that tragedy. Even though the lovers died, reconciliation between the enemies was achieved.

My multimedia format is based on visual and auditory perceptions. I have presented a sequence of original art works: a paper arrangement based on image making, a black and white photograph and a pastel drawing. (See Figures 1–3.) I used the art works because art is the best means of communicating feelings. Tchaikovsky's symphony *Romeo and Juliet* played at the time of presenting the art works intensified the aesthetic experience.

Through the sequence of art works I present the development of plot: a rising action, leading to culmination, a falling action, and a final resolution. The paper arrangement "Two Lovers Meet" (Figure 1) shows the culmination point of love. The photograph that illustrates "Broken Love" (Figure 2) follows it. The pastel drawing "A Monument to Love" (Figure 3) demonstrates the resolution. The hues and shades of the passionate red color (yellow, yellow-orange, orange, orange-red, and red) are used in the first drawing (Figure 1) to give the notion of love growing. Warm colors were chosen to express saturation, love, and passion. In Shakespeare's work Juliet is associated with a "sunlight, starlight, daylight, and heaven light." To my mind the colors used to create the image of love are stronger than words. The black and white photograph (Figure 2) illustrates the irregular pieces of paper cut by scissors and scattered about. This is a symbolic representation of broken love. The pastel drawing shows a monument (Figure 3). Straight, vertical lines are used to express noble and exalted feelings. Black and white colors are used to contrast death and life, hatred and love. The red color symbolizes the blood shed by two young souls who sacrifice their lives to bring about reconciliation.

Romeo and Juliet is of high appeal regarding its subject matter—love. We draw students' attention to the fact that the plot has a good deal of action and clearly defined causal links between events. The fact that Shakespeare's *Romeo and Juliet* has a modern version can grab students' attention. We have to introduce William Shakespeare as an actor, writer, and an outstanding person. We need to help students to comprehend the language and the peculiar style of Shakespeare's writing. We teach the concept of tragedy to the students. We inform students that dreams rely on dialogue and description and take the form of stage directions. This play is good for staging and the actual process of acting may be of interest to students.

Response to *Their Eyes Were Watching God*
by Carla Pinto

Zora Neale Hurston's (1990) *Their Eyes Were Watching God* is one of those books that changes the way a person views literature. Originally published in 1937 by Harper & Row Publishers in New York, Hurston's novel gave a voice to the African American female. Written in dialect, it is a story rich with culture. I chose this book because of the language. Hurston's voice is poetry. Her images and descriptions are rich with emotion and meaning. The book opens with these words:

> Ships at a distance have every man's wish on board. For some they come in with the tide. For others they sail forever on the horizon, never out of sight, never landing until the Watcher turns his eyes away in resignation, his dreams mocked to death by Time. That is the life of men.
>   Now, women forget all those things they don't want to remember, and remember all those things they don't want to forget. The dream is the truth.
>   (Hurston, 1990, p. 1)

Hurston weaves these and other specific images throughout the story. I also chose this novel to become more familiar with dialect. Hopefully, I will have the opportunity to use sections of this story in my internship. I feel as if the students could relate to the characters and feel comfortable with the language.

I am currently an intern at Harding High School in Bridgeport where the students in one class are reading Nathaniel Hawthorne's *The Scarlet Letter*. When I ask them how they like the story, the students' response is that it is hard to understand the language. It often seems to me that the students, who are not all African American, are speaking a different language. It is sometimes difficult for me to interpret the meaning of their words.

There were times while I was reading *Their Eyes Were Watching God* when I had difficulty cutting through the dialect to find meaning. I wondered if this is what some of the students meant when they said they can't understand the language in Hawthorne's novel. Perhaps it is difficult for them to relate to the character's voice.

Hurston's *Their Eyes Were Watching God* is a woman's personal journey through life. The imagery carries the story through Janie's experiences, which Hurston describes as "years that ask questions and years that answer" (p. 20). The story briefly delves into Janie's childhood, when she first realizes that she is not white, to her early adolescence when she feels the first stirrings of love. But the story really begins with Janie's first marriage that was set up by her grandmother. Hurston views this turning point in Janie's life as "Janie's first dream was dead, so she became a woman" (p. 24).

Janie leaves her first husband to marry Joe Starks. Hurston writes, "Janie pulled back a long time because he (Joe) did not represent sun-up and pollen and blooming trees" (p. 28). Janie feels stifled in this marriage; she expresses this to Joe by saying, "Ah feels lak Ah'm jus markin' time. Hope it soon gits over" (p. 43). Finally, Janie finds freedom in her love for Tea Cake. Although the story does not have a happy ending, Janie's journey is complete in that she has finally found the "flower dust and springtime" (p. 31) of her life which she has been searching for throughout the story. I identified with Janie because I can also see my life as continuous search for self discovery, happiness, and love. The desire to have these things carry Janie on a journey through life.

Hurston uses images from nature to describe the characters and their life journey, so it was easy for me to decide on an oil painting as my multimedia format. The images are so detailed that I felt as if I were watching a mental movie while reading the story. The image of trees is seen throughout the whole story. When Janie visits with Joe Starks before they are married, they would always meet in the scrub oaks. Chapter Five, the chapter in which Janie and Joe begin their life together, is filled with references to oak trees. As the marriage between Joe and Janie drags on, Janie begins to see herself in relation to trees. Hurston writes, "Then one day she sat and watched the shadow of herself going about tending store and prostrating itself before Jody (Joe), while all the time she herself sat under a shady tree with the wind blowing through her hair" (p. 73). When Janie begins a relationship with Tea Cake, her third husband, one of the first things he does is to "chop down that tree she never did like by the dining room window" of Joe and Janie's home (p. 105).

When Janie was sixteen and feeling the first pangs of love, Hurston associates Janie with a tree. She writes, "Oh to be a pear tree—any tree in bloom" (p. 11). This is what drives Janie through her life. Although Janie continuously seems to be searching for springtime, I see her in the autumn of her life throughout the story. My painting attempts to characterize Janie using the symbolism of a tree in autumn. At the beginning of the story Janie is looking back on her life about to tell her story. Hurston writes, "Janie saw her life like a great tree in leaf with the things suffered, things done and undone. Dawn and doom was in the branches" (p. 8). This is how I pictured Janie with the "dawn and doom" of autumn leaves.

Tea Cake, whom Janie describes as "the son of Evening Sun," often makes references to the moon. One of the first times Janie meets Tea Cake, she sits on the porch enjoying the moon after he has left. Hurston writes, "So she sat on the porch and watched the moon rise. Soon its amber fluid was drenching the earth, and quenching the thirst of the day" (p. 95). The next day Tea Cake addresses Janie saying, "Moon's too pretty fuh anybody tuh be sleepin' it away" (p. 98). After Tea Cake's death, Janie finds "a package of garden seeds that Tea Cake had brought to plant. The planting never got done because he had been waitin for the right time of the moon. . . . The seeds reminded Janie of Tea Cake more than anything else" (p. 182). It is through her relationship with Tea Cake that Janie is finally alive. My painting symbolically displays the union of Tea Cake and Janie.

Response to *The Giver*
by Mary Beth Jarvis

I chose *The Giver* (Lowry, 1993) because of a recommendation by my professor in the course Reading in the Content Areas. She recommended it as a good selection for 7 to 10th graders. *The Giver* is an intriguing science fiction novel about a town in the future, known as the "community." This place is a utopia with no war, hate, disease, poverty, or fear. The community has rules for everything and every member has certain privileges and responsibilities.

Family rituals are part of the rules of the community. Everyone does volunteer hours, no bragging is allowed, no rudeness is allowed. "Birthmothers" give birth to three children then become "laborers." "Family units" get two children—one male and one female. Children born during the current year are named and given to their chosen family at the "Ones" ceremony. "Nines" get their bicycles.

Jonas, the main character, is impatiently awaiting his "Ceremony of Twelve," when the twelve year olds receive their lifelong career assignment. He is selected to become the Receiver of Memories. This means he receives all the memories of the past, including pain, grief, and love. He learns about war, misery, and neglect. He also learns about pleasures the community never experiences. No one can see color, hear music, or experience love. Jonas receives all the memories from the mind of the Old Receiver, whom he names "The Giver." As Jonas learns more from *The Giver*, he decides he wants more from life than rules and security. He desires color and choices. He wishes all members could have memories. The book has a surprise ending.

While reading this book, I learned to appreciate life more. Sometimes life seems crazy or out of control, but I have choices. I may experience pain sometimes, but I can also heal. I need to look at each day and not take it for granted. We can see colors, hear beautiful music, smell flowers, and use all of our senses.

This book changed my thinking about living in a perfect world. The community seemed perfect on the surface, but at what price? These people did not realize what they were missing. This book reminded me of the *Stepford Wives*; the people were like robots. Everybody followed the rules, asked no questions, and performed their assigned positions.

I identified with *The Giver* because he reminded me of a parent. He wanted to help everyone in the community, but could not reveal too much. He followed all the rules in his society. Like a good parent he loved Jonas and encouraged him to take the final step, the one he himself could not find the courage to take. He helped Jonas plan the escape. As a good father, he stayed back to help the community members as they adapted to the "new" memories.

My multi-media format is black and white photography. I used a digital camera and took pictures of everyday things. I downloaded the images onto the camera and then printed them. The reason I used black and white photography was that this "community" was colorless and everything was the same. Through my photography

I show a place where everything is on black and white. Everyone follows the rules and has the same things. One day is the same as the next. Everyone's house, bicycle, even family life is the same. Nothing is original. Finally, Jonas starts noticing gray, then some shades of colors slowly appear. In the end Jonas sees colors everywhere. This is the mood shown in the book. I show this transition through my pictures. First everything is all black and white, then has some color, and finally has bright, beautiful colors!

When using this book in secondary schools, I would stress how this story compares to our own lives. I would have students keep a response journal as they read through the chapters. We would compare and contrast our life with the community's life. I would also have the students finish the book. In the response journals students could write down their feelings while they read. I would provide questions to focus their reading and help them give more thoughtful responses, both written and graphic. I would have students compare what they read with life as they know it and express feelings about situations they have experienced. Some possible topics are: My idea of a perfect community. . . . If everyone was the same. . . . If I lived in a "controlled community" I would. . . . After the final chapter I would ask the students to write down what happened to Jonas. I would have them describe how the "community" is changing and adapting to the memories. We would discuss how important life is and suggest that possibly, the way we wish life to be might not be the best after all.

REFERENCES

Beach, R. (1993). *Reader-response theories.* Urbana, IL: National Council of Teachers of English.

Beach, R., & Marshall, J. (1991). *Teaching literature in the secondary school.* San Diego: Harcourt Brace Jovanovich.

Campbell, L., Campbell, B., & Dickinson, D. (1996). *Teaching and learning through multiple intelligences.* Needham Heights, MA: Allyn & Bacon.

Considine, D. M., & Haley, G. E. (1992). *Visual images: Integrating imagery into instruction.* Englewood, CO: Teacher Ideas Press.

Cox, C. (1999). *Teaching language arts: A student- and response-centered classroom.* Needham Heights, MA: Allyn & Bacon.

Cox, C., & Many, J. (1992). Toward an understanding of the aesthetic response to literature. *Language Arts, 66,* 28–33.

Flood, J., & Lapp, D. (1995). Broadening the lens: Toward an expanded conceptualization of literacy. In K. A. Hinchmann, D. J. Leu, & C. K. Kinzer (Eds.), *Perspectives on literacy research and practice: Forty-fourth yearbook of the National Reading Conference* (pp. 1–16). Chicago: National Reading Conference.

Gardner, H. (1985). *Frames of mind: The theory of multiple intelligences.* New York: Basic Books.

Gombrich, E. H. (1998). *The story of art.* London: Phaidon Press.

Hurston, Z. N. (1990). *Their eyes were watching God.* New York: Harper & Row.

Hynds, S. (1997). *On the brink: Negotiating literature and life with adolescents.* Newark, DE: International Reading Association.

Karolides, N. (1992). *Reader response in the classroom: Evoking and interpreting meaning in literature.* New York: Longman.

Langer, J. (1995). *Envisioning literature: Literary understanding and literature instruction.* Newark, DE: International Reading Association.

Lowry, L. (1993). *The giver.* Boston: Houghton Mifflin.

Macaul, S. L., Giles, J. K., & Rodenberg, R. K. (1999). Intermediality in the classroom: Learners constructing meaning through deep viewing. In L. Semali & A. Watts Pailliotet (Eds.), *Intermediality: The teachers' handbook of critical media literacy* (pp. 53–74). Boulder, CO: Westview.

McLuhan, M. (1997). *Understanding media: The extensions of man.* Cambridge, MA: MIT Press.

Minister of Education and Training, Manitoba. (1996). *Manitoba curriculum framework of outcomes and senior 1 standards.* Winnipeg, Manitoba: Author.

Mulcahy-Ernt, P. I., & Ryshkewitch, S. (1994). Expressive journal writing for comprehending literature: A strategy for evoking cognitive complexity. *Reading and Writing Quarterly: Overcoming Learning Difficulties, 10*(4), 325–342.

National Council of Teachers of English & International Reading Association. (1996). *Standards for the English language arts.* Urbana, IL: Author.

Probst, R. E. (1981). Response-based teaching of literature. *English Journal, 70*(7), 43–47.

Probst, R. E. (1988). *Response and analysis: Teaching literature in junior and senior high school.* Portsmouth, NH: Boynton Cook.

Purves, A. (1977). *How porcupines make love.* New York: Wiley.

Rosenblatt, L. (1978). *The reader, the text, the poem.* Carbondale: Southern Illinois University Press.

Semali, L., & Watts Pailliotet, A. (Eds.). (1999). *Intermediality: The teachers' handbook of critical media literacy.* Boulder, CO: Westview.

Serrano, R. A., & Myers, J. (1999). Preservice teachers' collages of multicultural education. In L. Semali & A. Watts Pailliotet (Eds.), *Intermediality: The teachers' handbook of critical media literacy* (pp. 75–96). Boulder, CO: Westview.

Shakespeare, W. (1996). *Romeo and Juliet.* Waltham, MA: Blaisdell.

Sinatra, R. (1986). *Visual literacy connections to thinking, reading, and writing.* Springfield, IL: Charles C. Thomas.

Smagorinsky, P. (1996). *Standards in practice, Grades 9–12.* Urbana, IL: National Council of Teachers of English.

Smagorinsky, P., & O'Donnell-Allen, C. (1998). The depth and dynamics of context: Tracing the sources and channels of engagement and disengagement in student's response to literature. *Journal of Literacy Research, 30*(4), 515–559.

State of Connecticut Department of Education. (1998). *The Connecticut framework: K–12 curricular goals and standards.* Hartford, CT: Author.

Watts Pailliotet, A. (1999). Deep viewing: Intermediality in preservice teacher education. In L. Semali & A. Watts Pailliotet (Eds.), *Intermediality: The teachers' handbook of critical media literacy* (pp. 31–51). Boulder, CO: Westview.

Wilhelm, J. D. (1996). *Standards in practice, Grades 6–8.* Urbana, IL: National Council of Teachers of English.

INQUIRY-BASED LEARNING AND THE NEW LITERACIES:
MEDIA, MULTIMEDIA, AND HYPERMEDIA

Jackie K. Giles, Sherry L. Macaul, and
Rita K. Rodenberg

INTRODUCTION

This chapter is the result of a study entitled "Critical Viewing and Visual Representation: The Impact of Intermedia Links on the Interpretation and Design of Messages" conducted during the 1997–98 academic year. The study was conducted with seventh and eighth graders in a multiage classroom. The purposes of the study were to:

1. Assist learners in becoming critical consumers and producers of media
2. Engage in structured and nonstructured viewing and media design experiences
3. Critically interpret, design, and evaluate messages produced by a variety of print and nonprint media and hypermedia

Advances in Reading/Language Research, Volume 7, pages 155–183.
Copyright © 2000 by JAI Press Inc.
All rights of reproduction in any form reserved.
ISBN: 0-7623-0264-X

4. Evaluate ways in which the integration of a variety of media influences meaning and impacts on the interpretation of a message

The students in this study were male and female seventh and eighth graders of white Anglo-Saxon and Hmong descent. The segment of the study reported here was conducted during the second semester of 1997–98 in a Midwest town with a population of 60,000. The students in the study represent mostly middle-class families. Their experiences with computers varied; approximately half had computers in their homes.

This chapter describes the second half of a study undertaken during the 1997–98 academic year. In a previous publication (Semali & Watts Pailliotet, 1999) we share our findings about students' use of deep viewing and their interpretation of intermedia links. In this chapter we will discuss the impact of deep and critical viewing on the design of student representations.

LEARNING LITERACY THROUGH SOCIAL INTERACTION WITH TECHNOLOGY

The current literature on technology, media literacy, and learning advocates a constructivist approach to learning in which technology is considered as a tool for learning. Reinking (1998) suggests that the "expanding boundaries of literacy exist on two parallel yet interacting levels." He notes "electronic forms of communication as one level of communication that promises to transform acts of reading and writing" through "digital texts" (p. xvi). The other level he perceives to be "how diverse perspectives and fields of study enrich understandings of literacy" (p. xvi) such as social constructivist and semiotic theories of learning. The literature tells us that students need to learn by applying technology rather than learning about how technology works. For instance, as we will find in the next section of this chapter, national case studies on educational technology highlight the importance of learning and applying technology through group projects (Gooden, 1996; Raizen, Sellwood, Todd, & Vickers, 1995). A review of the national standards in the areas of English/Language Arts (International Reading Association & National Council of Teachers of English, 1996) and Educational Technology (International Society for Technology in Education, 2000) reveals the important and extensive role that technology plays in the teaching and learning process. Literacy and learning across the K–12 English Language Arts curriculum have become and continue to be more widely represented through media, multimedia, and hypermedia learning experiences. In this study, we will examine how such an increased attention to new technologies may be applied in middle-level classrooms. We will explore how middle-level learners view and interpret various types of media. In addition, we will investigate how students work in teams to select, learn, and apply different media to suit their purposes while involved in inquiry-based learning projects.

Hobbs (1997) emphasizes how the representations of language have changed during the past century (p. 165). She further suggests that we consider a new definition of literacy proposed by educator-advocates of media literacy and documented by (Aufderheide, 1993) which states that "literacy is the ability to access, analyze, evaluate and communicate messages in a variety of forms" (p. 166). She asserts that "media literacy incorporates the theoretical traditions of semiotics, literary criticism, media studies, communication theory, research on arts education, as well as language and literacy development" (p. 169). Our study will consider how students incorporate and integrate components and processes from a variety of the communicative arts.

In a book documenting how teachers apply technology to transform instruction, Gooden (1996) related that elementary school teacher Kathleen Duplantier chose HyperCard as useful software for students to use to represent their learning. HyperCard was chosen because "students could combine text, graphics, animation, and sound, to create interactive documents with multiple layers of information" (p. 35). She found the software to be versatile allowing for adaptability to a diverse range of abilities and learning styles. Duplantier's philosophy is to "maintain a balance between technology and curriculum seeing the computer as a tool to enhance hands-on learning experiences" (Gooden, 1996, p. 43). In the Apple ASCOT case studies (Fisher, Dwyer, & Yocam, 1996) Tierney (1996) "indicated that when students interacted and collaborated with others in a variety of ways, including joint construction of projects" (p. 177). In our study we found collaboration and social interaction to be critical components of the learning process.

Sandholtz and Ringstaff (in Fisher et al., 1996) also conclude that "technology-rich classrooms resulted in higher levels of student interaction and peer collaboration" (p. 288). These researchers found that the social interaction among learners applying literacy and technology had an important impact on what students learned and applied. In addition, Tierney (1996) found that while learning with technology, "students improved their ability to solve problems and communicate ideas effectively, use alternative symbol systems, establish goals for themselves, and perceive strengths and weaknesses of their work" (p. 180). In the same series of technology case studies, Yocam (1996), like Tierney, perceived the importance of conversation in learning. In addition, Yocam found evidence of teacher change to be important. He concludes, "only when each individual teacher can have the opportunity to reflect on and learn about teaching will there be meaningful reform in classroom practice giving rise to new opportunities for student-centered learning" (p. 276). In our study, we found that the teacher's knowledge of the learners as well as day-to-day reflection on one's teaching, led to a greater degree of student empowerment and student self-initiated, collaborative learning. Through observations and conversations with students, we discovered that the teacher is better prepared to support rather than to direct student learning.

Referring to the findings of the ASCOT case studies, Sandholtz and Ringstaff (1996) found that "throughout their careers, teachers had assumed the role of expert in the classroom. But technology-rich classrooms undermined that role as some students quickly became more knowledgeable than both their peers and their teachers in using particular computer applications or hardware" (pp. 283–284). In the study described in this chapter, we discovered that if we insisted on teaching our middle-level learners everything that they wanted to do with technology before they applied it, we would have held them back from moving ahead in designing their presentations. We may also have inhibited the creative combinations of media that they explored and constructed independently as well as in teams that were subsequently incorporated into their projects.

In the lessons learned section of the Apple Computer Education grant recipient projects, Gooden (1996) concludes, "with computers, students can assume greater control of their learning. They are able to take risks in problem solving, engage in computer-generated simulations, experiments, exhibit understanding through the creation of multimedia products, visualize abstract concepts, and conduct independent and collaborative research using electronic communications" (p. 156). To our amazement, our study found that students were capable of much more than we first anticipated.

Reigeluth and Miller-Nelson (1997) addressing the paradigm of instructional systems design, especially in nonprofit institutions, advance the importance of transformation through introduction of "teams that are being given considerable autonomy to manage themselves within the purview of the corporate vision, rather than being directed from above" (p. 24). They also suggest moving toward a "learning-focused paradigm" (p. 26) and instruction that is "customized" (p. 25) to the individual learner or team. According to Reigeluth and Miller-Nelson, "Learning-Focused Instructional Theory" must follow "flexible guidelines" that include "working in teams," on "authentic real world tasks," applying "features of powerful advanced technologies," and "persevering until they reach appropriate standards." They see "learning-focused theory" as including "variable methods of instruction such as problem-based learning, simulations, tutorials, and team-based learning" (p. 27). Their "Instructional Systems Design" reflects a constructivist approach to learning (p. 24). Our study of ways middle-level learners view and represent ideas using diverse technologies parallels the Reigeluth and Miller-Nelson (1997) "learning-focused instructional" model in that we focus on inquiry-based learning framed around topics of historical interest to students and related to their local community.

Salomon and Perkins (1998) "clarify the idea of distinctive meanings of the notion of social learning vis-à-vis individual learning" (p. 2). They assert that learning involves collectives of learners as well as individual learners. They perceive "well-designed instruction" as "involving different learning systems at different moments in synergistic interaction" (p. 20). In the current study we will address how several of our students reflected, during our interviews with them, on the benefits of working in small groups as well as needing time to work alone to explore and develop their own ideas.

RECONCEPTUALIZING LITERACY REPRESENTATIONS

As we broaden our notions of what literacy is becoming, we must also reconceptualize how literacy may be expressed. In the 1996 IRA/NCTE English Language Arts Standards our field moved well beyond the traditional communication modes of reading, writing, speaking, and listening to acknowledging viewing and representing as the two newly recognized areas of interest. IRA/NCTE English Language Arts Standard number 8 states that "students use a variety of technological and informational resources (e.g., libraries, databases, computer networks, video) to gather and synthesize information and to create and communicate knowledge" (p. 25). Standard number 12, also addressing new literacy representations, states that "students use spoken, written, and visual language to accomplish their own purposes (e.g., for learning enjoyment, persuasion, and the exchange of information" (p. 25). In the present study we will explore how the English/language arts, visual literacy, and informational literacy standards all play a part in the ways in which our students interpret and represent their thoughts and ideas.

Bolter (1998) refers to hypertext as "fluid text" (p. 5). He states that "the reader's decisions in following links determine the order of presentation for those pages. A rich hypertext can and probably will be different for each reader and each act of reading." He asserts that "hypertexts are multilinear" (p. 5). He believes that "the author constructs the text so that it can be read in a variety of orders and that the reader approaches the text with that assumption" (p. 5). Kommers (1996), addressing hypertext, recognizes "the paradigm of knowledge engineering" as important to analyzing information for teaching and learning. He perceives many opportunities for teachers and learners to engage in what he refers to as "knowledge representation" (p. 36). Lemke (1998) sees new literacies such as "multimedia literacies" (p. 288), and "informatic literacies" (p. 289) as transforming literacy and literacy education. He believes we need to teach students how to integrate a wide variety of media into writing and suggests that "text may or may not form the organizing spine of multimedia work" (p. 288). He asserts that "what we really need to teach, and to understand before we can teach it is how various literacies and various cultural traditions combine different semiotic modalities to make meanings that are more than the sum of what each could mean separately" (p. 288). He sees this type of construction as "multiplying meaning," and refers to it as "cross-multiplying" as a "combinatorial explosion leading to "meaning possibilities that are not merely additive" (p. 288). In our study, when the middle-level students were interviewed about their media and multimedia projects the teachers learned so much more than what the teachers could construct for themselves through viewing projects.

Roth and McGinn (1998) have recently introduced the concept of "inscriptions" often used in science, social studies, and technology. They define "inscriptions as signs that are materially embodied in some medium" (p. 37) such as paper or white board drawings, charts, diagrams, or photos. These researchers assert that "focusing on inscriptions leads to a change in the location of representing activity from individual minds to social arenas" (p. 37). In our investigation it was noted that individual students shared their own unique views and perceptions of meaning with the peers in their group. They indicated that they often needed to substantiate their ideas and negotiate to create a collaborative representation. Roth and McGinn (1998) contend that "inscriptions occur in a medium such as paper or computer monitors and are readily available forms as opposed to representations which tend to refer to graphical displays and mental forms" (p. 35). They further state that the meaning of any inscription is dependent on the other information or signs that surround it and agreement by others in the field. According to Roth and McGinn (1998), "to be a representationally literate individual means being able to participate in the practices of producing, comprehending, comparing, and critiquing inscriptions" (p. 45). They further suggest that we need to explore the "transformations that inscriptions undergo and the roles they play in social situations as well as the rhetorical purposes for which they are deployed" (p. 35). They seem to view this as "deemphasizing individual mental activity" and focusing more on "the social practices of inscription users" (p. 35). Such new conceptions of literacy involve multiple participants applying multiple media to create meaning that is interpreted differently by a variety of reader/viewers. In our study, middle-level learners were encouraged to work in groups to select their own media. After completing their first drafts, student teams shared their media productions and conferenced with other classmates to gather feedback to enhance their designs.

MULTIPLE TOOLS AND MULTIPLE INTERPRETATIONS

Bruce (1998) uses the term "hybrid" to describe combinations of new and old technologies (p. 37). According to Bruce, as we move into uses of newer and "multiple technologies," we reconceive and redefine how we "make and interpret texts, changing the occasions for these practices" (p. 136). Bruce refers to these new forms of literacy as "hybrid literacies" (p. 137) and believes they involve inquiry as well as use of new communications and information access such as email and Web searches. He refers to this as "knowledge work" (p. 138). In the present study, students combined multimedia, CD-ROM encyclopedias, Internet images and music; and student-created images.

Gilster (1997) refers to such new forms of representations as "digital literacy" defined as "the ability to understand and use information in multiple formats from a wide range of sources when it is presented via computers" (p. 1). He states that "the concept of literacy goes beyond simply being able to read; it has always meant the ability to read with meaning, and to understand. It places demands upon you that were always present, though less visible, in the analog media of newspaper and TV" (p. 2). He refers to "digital literacy as the ability to understand and use information in multiple formats from a wide range of sources when it is presented via computers" (p. 33). Indicating that "the NET is a study in the myriad of uses of rhetoric," he advocates that "forming a balanced assessment by distinguishing between content and its presentation is the key" (pp. 2–3). Gilster views the use of these new resources as becoming more responsive and asserts that "one of the most important competencies is being able to critically evaluate and interpret information in a variety of formats that the computer can deliver. In our study we encouraged students to critically analyze media that they viewed as well as media that they created" (Pool, 1997, p. 6). Gilster (1997) uses the term "digital convergence" to refer to "a collage of media" (p. 7). As have Kommers (1997) and Lemke (1997), Gilster (1997) too has coined a phrase for construction involving media that he refers to as "knowledge assembly" (p. 195). His term describes the process of accessing and evaluating a multiplicity of reports, data feeds, and resources from the Internet and beyond to "build a perspective critical to an issue."

Kinneavey (1991) addresses rhetoric as "the study of persuasive discourse," which he sees as being communicated through reading, writing, speaking, and listening (pp. 633–634). Viewing and representing are also applied as persuasive means of communicating. Gilster (1997) claims that "the dynamics of writing for an online newspaper do not change, but the dynamics of editing for the reader do by revealing links and suggested sources." He further reminds us that "no medium is so complete that it cannot be complemented by another" (p. 223).

Inquiry-based learning and new technologies create a suitable match for learning. According to Raizen et al. (1995), "technology education provides a natural opportunity for students to generate and articulate questions and communicate hypotheses; identify problems and design solutions; and generate ideas for building, testing and improving protopypes and products" (p. 128).

Perkins (1992) advises us to address our content via higher levels of under-standing. Through thoughtful teaching he suggests we engage learners at four levels, namely, the "content level" of clarifying ideas and terms, the "problem-solving level" of raising questions, the "epistemic level" of seeking evidence and arguments, and finally at the "inquiry level" where students pose their own questions and pursue issues of interest to them (pp. 86–87). The present study, based on an inquiry-based learning model, encouraged students to address all four levels in terms of both content and process.

Finally, Raizen et al. (1995) suggest that "teachers should use authentic, and where possible, embedded assessments to accompany curriculum" (p. 141). In the final section of this study we discuss how student work was assessed by both students and teacher-researchers.

COLLABORATIVE INQUIRY

Our team of teacher-researchers was comprised of a classroom teacher, who is also a certified Reading Specialist; a Newspaper in Education Coordinator from the local newspaper and former teacher; and a university literacy faculty member, certified

Reading Specialist, and former teacher. Two of the three teacher-researchers have engaged in training in critical viewing through the National Parent Teacher Association and National Cable Television Association. All three teacher-researchers read, shared, and discussed studies, applied articles, books, educational materials such as NIE teachers' guides (Garrett et al. 1995 & 1996) along with state and national standards related to literacy, inquiry, media, and technology focusing on viewing and representing. We established a study group that met every two to three weeks to discuss and apply ideas from the recent literature related to literacy, inquiry/media, and technology. We, much like our students, learned individually as well as collaboratively. Each of us read common articles/studies and then circulated various books, technology handbooks, and materials creating copies and note cards of sections, citations, and quotes that guided our processes and practices. We also created an agenda of what we hoped to accomplish but guided our next steps by our observations of students and our readings.

The newly built school in which the study was conducted housed a computer lab with 18 Windows computers with Microsoft Software, Windows 95, and Encarta software. Students had access to one computer in each of their previous grades and were provided with keyboarding classes in the upper elementary grades. The students in this study were 18 male and female seventh and eighth graders from a multiage classroom of white Anglo-Saxon and Hmong descent from mostly middle-class families.

Encarta was available on the computers in the lab. Jackie Giles, from the *Leader-Telegram*, provided a laptop Windows computer with Internet access and a video projector for activities requiring Internet demonstrations. Through grant monies provided by Sherry Macaul, the university faculty member, the school was able to purchase and install HyperStudio 3.1 as well as a color scanner. This equipment was used for the creation of group projects. With teacher facilitation by Rita Rodenberg, several students who were particularly adept with computers, studied the HyperStudio training handbooks and learned the applications for creating hyperstacks. The group then formed four new groups. Each of the original four students demonstrated the process for applying HyperStudio to the other students in their group using a peers-teaching-peers model. The computer coordinator taught the students how to use the scanner to create and import images into their hyperstacks and Web projects. One student, who had created his own Web site at home, taught several other students in his group how to design a Web site.

In the next section, we will share how we engaged middle-level learners in collaborative and critical viewing of a variety of media representations. First we will present activities used to involve our learners in deep viewing. Next we will present the outcomes that we noted from the learning experiences.

MEDIA LITERACY ACTIVITY 1: DEEP VIEWING

This part of the study began during the fall when students were introduced to the deep viewing model (Watts Pailliotet, 1995). Students viewed a video advertisement and responded individually and in small groups to what they viewed under each of the six elements of deep viewing, namely, (1) Action & Sequence, (2) Semes/Forms, (3) Actors/Words, (4) Closeness/Distance, (5) Culture & Context, and (6) Effects/Process (Appendix A). Next, students viewed the newspaper advertisement for the same product and responded to the same six elements. Finally, students were shown the Web site for the same product and were asked once again to express their thoughts and perceptions of how the six elements of deep viewing were depicted. In small groups and then as a whole class, students compared and contrasted how the product was presented in each of the three types of media. Finally, we asked students to critically reflect and analyze how accurately the company represented the product to consumers. We found that students were, for the most part, taken in by the advertisements that they saw. Through our work with them it became evident to us that the students required more experience in critically reviewing and analyzing media (Macaul, Giles, & Rodenberg, 1999).

MEDIA LITERACY ACTIVITY 2: LINKING THE PAST TO THE FUTURE

In this activity, Jackie first introduced students to the daily local newspaper, The *Leader-Telegram*, in its traditional paper format. Next, the students were provided with a Venn diagram (Figure 1) with traditional newspaper printed above the left

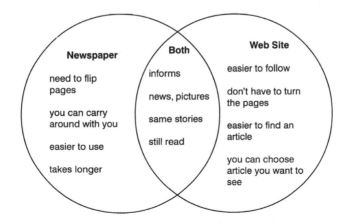

Figure 1. Comparison and Contrast of Traditional Newspapers versus Web-Based Newspapers

circle, and Web site (online) newspaper printed above the right circle. In the middle intersecting section was written both. Jackie then used the Internet to demonstrate how that day's *Leader-Telegram* appeared in its online Web-based version. She asked the students to write down the features that someone reading/viewing the paper might attend to while reading to learn and locate information for each of the two sources in the large parts of the circles. In the overlapping area, students were asked to indicate what the two forms had in common. Students worked with a partner and then shared their responses with the group.

Students' responses indicated that they were able to perceive differences between the two types of media. They liked the portability of the traditional newspaper as well as the ease of moving through the daily online edition on the Web site. Jackie pointed out how they could print out articles and coupons. She then explained how students could enter the online archive to access past articles of interest.

MEDIA LITERACY ACTIVITY 3: ANALYZING AND CRITIQUING AN EVENT DEPICTED IN THREE REPRESENTATIONS

This activity and those that follow, represent the second segment of our yearlong study which occurred in the spring and focused on how students design messages or representations using a variety of media. After one of our teacher-researcher planning meetings, we decided to identify a local event of interest to our students as a basis for viewing and critiquing media about the same story yet from the perspective of three different media. Trying to promote an inquiry issue/problem focus and at the same time appeal to the interests of middle-level learners, we discussed the White Pine Nature Reserve as well as Beaver Creek Reserve located in our community. Many students had visited Beaver Creek Reserve nature center on field trips. The site was celebrating 50 Years of Service to the community. Jackie had access to the special supplement and was able to receive permission from the local TV station to use the video clip. We decided to select that event to explore Beaver Creek Reserve's 50th anniversary celebration across three prominent types of media as follows:

- *Leader-Telegram* newspaper supplement entitled "Beaver Creek Reserve: 50 Years of Educating the Community 1947–1997."
  Leader-Telegram photo by Dan Reiland (Figure 2a)
- *WEAU TV-13* three-minute video newscast of a reporter interviewing the director of the Beaver Creek Reserve, Rick Koziel, about the gala celebration held onsite at the reserve and featuring children and adults of all ages engaged in outdoor learning experiences and reflecting on the value of the site's service to the greater community. (Figure 2b)
  Courtesy of WEAU TV-13

Figure 2a. From: Leader-Telegram special supplement, Beaver Creek Reserve: 50 Years of Educating the Community. Photo by Dan Reiland

Figure 2b. Beaver Creek Reserve's 50th Anniversary Media Promotions. Eau Claire Leader-Telegram Supplement. WEAU TV-13 3-Minute Video Newscast. Beaver Creek Reserve Website

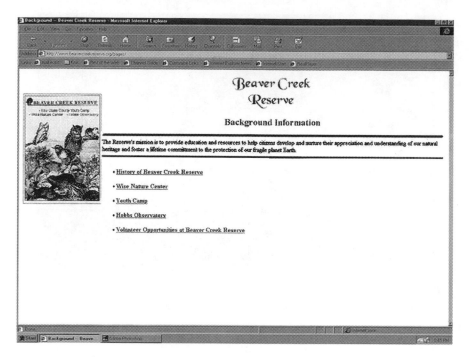

Figure 2c.

- *Beaver Creek Reserve Web site* featuring segments about its events and background including the history of the reserve, its camp, nature center, educational projects, its observatory, and volunteer opportunities. (Figure 2c)

Jackie introduced the Beaver Creek Anniversary event to the students through the three types of media discussed above. Sherry and Rita reintroduced the students to the deep viewing guide (Appendix B) used in Media Activity 1 in the fall, and asked them to respond in writing as to what elements of deep viewing they noted to be apparent in each of the three media as the media were introduced.

Next, students worked in five small groups to complete a Venn diagram comparing and contrasting what they noticed about the same event as it was depicted in three different media. Students responded in their small groups by comparing, contrasting, and critiquing each of the three representations. They responded based on what they knew about each type of media and its purpose. The familiar event, Beaver Creek Reserve's 50th Anniversary, was selected so that students could concentrate on the specific type of mass media, its development, effectiveness, and impact on the featured event.

In Figure 3, Beaver Creek Reserve's 50th Anniversary media comparison, Jackie has depicted just what the five teams of seventh and eighth graders observed when

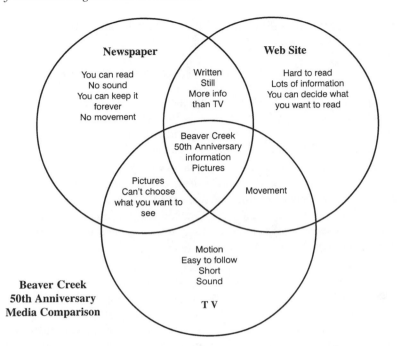

Figure 3. Comparison and Contrast of Beaver Creek Reserve's 50th Anniversary as Depicted in the Newspaper, on TV, and on a Web Site

they viewed the same feature story from the vantage point of three different media. They worked in small groups to critique the depiction of the same event, Beaver Creek Reserve's 50th Anniversary celebration as represented in three different media. We found that students were aware of the unique elements of each type of media and were able to detect the advantages of each medium. It was noted that students were also observant of the effective and least effective design features.

Uniquenesses among Media Representing the Same Event

Students noticed a few of the obvious deep viewing elements of each media although not all as indicated in Figure 3. Students indicated that the traditional print form of the newspaper is "read." When addressing TV, students noticed the inclusion of "motion and sound." They saw that the segment was brief and "easy to follow." This was largely due to an exceptionally good match between the images/events and the dialogue supporting each part of the featured interview. Student interpretations of the Web site representation of the celebration were perceptive and critical. Students noticed that the page was "hard to read" due to the combination of background texture, color, as well as the print used in the construction of the page. Students did comment that the Web site allowed readers to "decide" what they wanted to read.

Commonalities across Media Representing the Same Event

Comparisons of student deep viewing, across the newspaper and TV newscast representations of Beaver Creek Reserve's 50th gala event, indicated that there are "pictures" in each of the two media. They indicated that you cannot "choose what you want to see." The notion of selectivity seemed to be a known concept for them.

Student perceptions of comparisons of deep viewing across the TV newscast and the Web site indicated that the written formats in the newspaper and on the Web site seem to provide more information than on TV. Student comparisons of the Web site and the TV newscast indicated that "movement" was a salient feature that these two representations shared. Finally, students commented that "information and pictures about Beaver Creek Reserve" were key components that all three forms of media shared.

After studying students' interpretations of their viewing of various media, we wanted to see how they chose to apply the various types of media and express their perceptions and interpretations of viewing when designing their own media and multimedia presentations. Examination of student responses makes it apparent that middle-level students could benefit from instructional programs and experiences focused on the uniquenesses as well as the strengths and benefits of applying each type of media. Many national and state standards address not only technology but also media literacy. Inviting guest speakers from the local media industry is one way of exposing students to actual applications in each type of media as well as career opportunities. Such experts may also serve as resources or mentors to students undertaking projects involving the expert's area of media expertise.

MEDIA LITERACY ACTIVITY 4: PEERS-TEACHING-PEERS MULTIMEDIA

Next, in this segment of our study, the middle-level students explored HyperStudio, a multimedia software package created for students. Sherry provided copies of the HyperStudio mini-workbooks for use in preparing HyperStudio applications. With Rita's assistance, a small core of students adept with computers taught themselves to use the program by reading and exploring the workbook. Then, each member of the initial student training group taught another group of three or four students to implement the applications of the multimedia package. Students then applied their understandings of deep viewing and multimedia design by creating HyperStudio slide shows and in one case a Web site for their science project reports and presentations.

An exploratorium of multimedia science presentations was set up in the computer lab. Students and teacher-researchers rotated through each station where team members talked through and demonstrated their project stack. The collaboration afforded many more students with opportunities to learn how to apply the various effects available in the multimedia software. Examples of the projects included a stack featuring information about El Niño and another on the recent flooding in the Midwest.

Our review of student group-designed hyperstacks indicated that the middle-level learners in this study were able to

- Apply hot buttons to connect information using HyperStudio
- Access and import images from Encarta into their HyperStudio stacks to complement and support their purposes
- Activate sound and, in two group projects, animation
- Document information obtained, provide credit to sources consulted
- Experiment with a variety of backgrounds, colors, and print forms to express their findings legibly with an audience and purpose in mind

In reflecting on this learning activity and student stacks, we learned that we need to observe and monitor how well female members in the groups assume an active role in the direct hands-on opportunities with the multimedia. It was evident that the groups were highly motivated by the media and the multiple ways it allowed them to represent their ideas and discover just how the process of representing ideas in paths worked. Students learned with and from one another. Many opportunities were provided for teams of students to work in the computer lab and share their questions and victories with one another. This was a component of the design process that Rita believes is essential.

MEDIA LITERACY ACTIVITY 5: INQUIRY/RESEARCH THROUGH MEDIA

We met and decided to move toward a theme for the final learning experience that would involve students in the use of varied media. After viewing the WI Sesquicentennial 150th Anniversary newspaper supplement that Jackie provided and helped design, Rita decided that we should follow the 150th Anniversary theme. Jackie provided each student with a copy of the WI Sesquicentennial newspaper supplement, created by newspaper NIE Coordinators from across the state of Wisconsin. She gave them time to explore the special edition which provided a collage of original stories and images on a wide variety of Wisconsin events and topics from the past 150 years. Next the students were asked to identify topics or issues for their inquiry projects. We decided to follow the structure of the Wisconsin Sesquicentennial issue, which was a Wisconsin Then and Now format. Students decided to research topics and issues related to Eau Claire using an Eau Claire Then and Now focus.

One week later, Jackie and Rita shared books with the students pertaining to the history of Eau Claire. Jackie provided one created by the *Leader-Telegram* and others from the L. E. Phillips Library. Students worked in groups to select topics and issues of interest related to Eau Claire to investigate. Sherry met with two groups to brainstorm possible community resources to contact. One group contacted the University Archivist and set up an appointment to review artifacts from the 1800s and 1990s in Eau Claire related to their topic, Fashion in Eau Claire, Then and Now. The team interested in transportation connected to the State Transportation Web site.

During the next session, Sherry and Rita introduced the inquiry cycle to the students. The version passed out to students was entitled Technology and Inquiry Learning (Appendix C), a version adapted from Harste's Inquiry-Based Learning model (in Ruddell, Ruddell, & Singer, 1994, p. 1221, and Short et al., 1996, p. 18). We adapted the Harste model with an emphasis on applying a variety of new technologies.

We asked the student groups to maintain an Inquiry Learning Log (Appendix D) or keep track of the inquiry process that they followed right on their Technology and Inquiry Learning sheets while investigating their projects and preparing their media presentations. The students shared the topics they had chosen such as the history of the Green Bay Packers Then and Now, Transportation in Eau Claire Then and Now, and Farming in Eau Claire Then and Now. We asked students to identify the type of media they would use to create their representations and to share what they learned with their classmates. Two groups selected video, two selected posters, two others selected multimedia, and another team selected a Web site. From this point on, students worked daily in teams for the next 2 weeks for 45 minutes a day to research the questions that they posed and to plan and prepare visual media representations of what they learned. Groups inquired about the questions that they posed during class as well as outside of school. Rita consulted with the students as they refined their questions, and began to seek sources, contacts, and materials to broaden their perspectives. She also dialogued with students daily as they adapted their media choices to suit their purposes and findings. Students negotiated within their groups to select an appropriate focus and media that would compliment what they learned. Groups created posters, videos, hyperstacks, and Web pages to portray what they learned about their inquiry topics and issues.

GROUP PRESENTATIONS AND EDITING THROUGH PEER INQUIRY CONFERENCING—DRAFT #1

Approximately 2–3 weeks after students began their projects, we set aside a 45-minute period for students to share their project drafts with the rest of the class. They elaborated on and showed what they had developed to date. Their classmates responded on Peer Inquiry Conferencing feedback sheets (Appendix E). We saw this step as synonymous with the peer editing which occurs during the writing process. Sherry designed a PQIM format, which stands for Praise, Question, Ideas, and Suggestions for Media Representations. The purpose was to provide positive feedback as well as ideas for clarification and for enhancing the representations. As we circulated, we noted that most of the feedback to peers was positive. We did not collect the feedback sheets but instead asked that students hand the feedback sheets directly to the members of each group for their consideration. Student groups then used the feedback to refine their representations.

FACILITATOR INTERVIEWS

In a debriefing session, approximately 2–3 weeks later, and late in the spring semester, we met with the students in their small groups to conduct an interview using the Facilitator Interview form (Appendix F) with each group. The purpose of the interviews was to debrief about the processes they used in exploring their inquiry topics and issues. Questions were designed to examine students' use of the inquiry cycle, probe collaborative efforts and decision making, and tap applications of new literacies and technologies. Students' articulated responses helped make visible to us the ways in which they collaborated, the processes they used, and the media and technology applied to construct meaning.

Each of us interviewed two project teams. The Agriculture group, when interviewed, expressed some particularly reflective remarks about their learning experiences. With respect to the first question relating to how they applied the inquiry cycle, this group indicated that they first posed questions. Next they gathered information exploring such sources as Encarta, Internet, encyclopedias, magazines, and interviews with people in the community. They then revised their stack based on peer feedback during the conferencing sessions. In particular, they changed their background and buttons on their hyperstack. They realized that their choices of background and lettering would be difficult for their audience to read. Students began to view their own representations with the same critical eye they used to view local media productions earlier in the term. The students also extended their stack to provide further helpful information. This team of four students interviewed one student's grandfather whose farm had been passed down through generations. The theme that they saw running through their inquiry was how much technology has changed farming and the equipment used by farmers. In terms of collaboration, students worked on their inquiry project during time provided in school and also via phone at home. With respect to designing their presentations using media and technology applications, the students enjoyed using the HyperStudio because they said, "there is no right or wrong way to create. It is all done with your imagination." When we asked students what types of media and technology they had used and were planning to add, they indicated sound, pictures, animation, voices, and words. Students planned to explore a multitude of ways to represent their ideas. Finally, when asked about the criteria they planned to use to self-evaluate their project, this group enumerated the following:

- Information
- Creativity
- Approaches and applications

- Collaborative efforts

A final comment by the Agriculture Then and Now team was, "We were excited about how it turned out! It was better than we expected."

Summary of Facilitator Interviews of Projects

Agriculture Then and Now

Use of Inquiry Approach: gathered, organized, constructed, presented, got more information, revised and presented final draft
Choice of Topic/Issue: one member of team lives on a farm
Sources: Encarta, Internet, encyclopedias, magazines, interviews of farmers (dad, grandpa)
Audience: anyone interested in farming technology and its development
Themes or Ideas: machinery, time frame of jobs and how they have evolved
Media/Technology Applied: computer, HyperStudio program
Presentation: sound, picture, animation, words both written and spoken
Criteria for Self-Evaluation: information presented, creativity, cooperation of group

Packers Then and Now

Use of Inquiry Approach: chose topic, present history of team, gathered information, used HyperStudio to record information, revised, presented, and revised
Choice of Topic: interest in sports particularly the Packers
Sources: own knowledge, books, encyclopedias, Encarta
Audience: Packer fans and anyone interested in the team history
Themes or Ideas: history of the Packers
Media/Technology Used: computer, HyperStudio, Encarta
Presentation: sound, pictures, written and spoken words, hyperlinks
Criteria for Self-Evaluation: information included, design and effort

Transportation Then and Now (computer Web page)

Use of Inquiry Approach: choose topic, find information, develop Web page, revise, and present
Choice of Topic: brainstormed as a class and chose this topic
Sources: books, Internet
Audience: middle school students and up (learn about history of transportation)
Themes or Ideas: evolution of transportation in Eau Claire

Media/Technology Applied: Microsoft Front Page, books, Paint Shop, Pro 5, Microsoft Animator, computer Web page
Presentation: hyperlinks, sound color and background
Criteria for Self-Evaluation: information, creativity, and cooperation

Entertainment Then and Now (picture ad)

Use of Inquiry Approach: choose topic, gather information, decide on method of presentation, organize material, present and revise final draft
Choice of Topic: interest in entertainment
Sources: UWEC archives, library, books, newspaper
Audience: people interested in history of entertainment in Eau Claire
Media/Technology Applications: computer, copy machine
Presentation: organization of material into a picture ad
Criteria for Self-Evaluation: layout, organization, presentation of information, and overall effort

Evaluation of Student Inquiry and Media Representations via Group Interviews

The students shared their final projects with one another in either the classroom or the computer lab depending on the media involved. Students provided a verbal explanation of their inquiries and the design processes undertaken to answer their inquiry questions.

The students in the Packer group created a HyperStudio stack incorporating the Then and Now format. Their stacks depicted the coach then and now, the quarterback then and now, and an animated full-screen poster-type graphic with a goal post that read "Go Green Bay Packers." Students incorporated Encarta 96, and images from the Milwaukee Sentinel Newspaper Web site. The group self-evaluation and whole group share was based on

- Decision-making process as to choices of media
- Application of inquiry and technology standards
- Evolution of the process of working collaboratively
- Applying new technologies

Deep Viewing Evidenced in the Design of the Packers Then and Now Web Site

The students who designed the Packers Then and Now Web site included many of the characteristics that were apparent in the deep viewing media that they observed earlier in the year. They included multiple types of interactive media.

The teacher-researchers in this project noted the following while viewing their representation:

Action & Sequence—the students created a hypermedia path for then and another for now. They also created a path for the coaches in a parallel manner. They chose to import several action photos.

Semes/Forms—students retrieved images from the Packers home page as well as Encarta. They included a green and yellow background and letters to represent the team's colors, logo using the Word Art on Microsoft. They created a goal post with a shadow and included a cheer. They chose to highlight the coaches and most favored players. They incorporated the team's colors in a uniform and accurate manner and critically selected important ideas and images due to space constraints. They selected media appropriate to their intended message.

Actors/Words—students read and recorded audio for part of the content. They condensed their message into a few words, a summary of available information.

Closeness/Distance—they created closeups and considered the purpose of their site which was to inform viewers.

Effects/Process—visual, audio, and a high-quality layout with accurate information. They applied effects from the Internet in terms of sound and visuals. They attempted to credit their sources. According to Jackie who knows about newspaper layout, they used some good principles of representing ideas but also could use some feedback from a *Leader-Telegram* sports editor and layout person on how to depict photos with the images pointing toward the center of the page or text.

EVALUATING STUDENT WORK

Student work was evaluated in several ways. First, Rita provided students with a rubric when they began their media responses to inquiry that considered such components as content/information, layout, use of pictures and fonts, appropriate title, and effectiveness of portraying the message. Second, students indicated how they thought that their projects should be evaluated, as indicated in the student responses to the Facilitator Interview question, "What criteria will you use to self-evaluate your project?" One area that was important to the students in terms of evaluation was collaboration. Third, we as educators evaluated student projects in terms of the state standards that we found embedded in students' projects. In the Packers Then and Now media response to inquiry, we found that students were able to apply many standards from both of the WI English Language Arts Standards, (Fortier, Grady, Karbon and Last, 1998) namely:

E.   Media & Technology

E.8.1   Use of computers to acquire, organize, analyze, and communicate information

- Use manuals and on-screen help in connection with computer applications
- Collect information from various online sources, such as Web pages (and they used CD-ROM encyclopedias)

E.8.2   Make informed judgments about media and products

- Recognize common structural features found in print and broadcast advertising

E.8.5   Analyze and edit media work as appropriate to audience and purpose

- Revise media productions by adding, deleting, and adjusting the sequence and arrangement of information, images, or other content as necessary to improve focus, clarity, and effect
- Develop criteria for comprehensive feedback on the quality of media work and use it during production

F.   Research & Inquiry

F.8.1   Conduct research and inquiry on self-selected or assigned topics, issues, or problems and use an appropriate form to communicate their findings.

(Students in this group accomplished all but one of the six performance standards in research and inquiry) which in abbreviated format include

- Formulate research questions and focus on relevant information
- Use multiple sources to identify/locate information from a variety of resources including encyclopedias, and various electronic search engines
- Compile, organize, and evaluate information
- Review and evaluate the usefulness of the information gathered
- Produce an organized written and oral report that reflects and presents the findings, draws conclusions, adheres to conventions, and gives proper credit to sources

as well as the WI Information & Technology Literacy Standards (Fortier, Potter, Grady, Lohr and Klein, 1998) at the eighth grade level, which included:

1.   Media & Technology

A.8.1   Use common media and technology terminology and equipment

- Scan, crop, and save a graphic using a scanner

A.8.2   Identify and use common media formats

- Describe the operating and file management software of a computer (e.g., desktop, file, window, folder, directory, pull-down menu, dialog box)

A.8.3   Use a computer and productivity software to organize and create information
- Move textual and graphics data from one document to another
- Use graphics software to incorporate pictures, images, and charts into document

A.8.4   Use a computer and communication software to access and transmit

- Access information using a modem to connect to Internet
- Use electronic encyclopedias to retrieve and select information

A.8.5   Use media and technology to create and present information

- Use multimedia technology tools and software to design, produce, and present a multimedia program
- Plan and deliver a presentation to inform, persuade, or entertain

A.8.6   Evaluate the use of media and technology in a presentation
Students accomplished four of six criteria here briefly summarized:

- Ascertaining the purpose of the presentation
- Describing the effectiveness of the media
- Identifying criteria for judging the technical quality
- Specifying ways to improve future presentations

Review of this sample student inquiry project, Packers Then and Now, indicates to us that middle-level students are able to work collaboratively using a variety of integrated media to create their own media representations. Students learned both from and with us as well as from each other. What is most evident is that we learned from them. It became evident to us that students who are critical media viewers also are capable of becoming critical media creators. In the final section, we will summarize what we learned about middle-level learners' literacy, learning, and new technologies.

FINDINGS/CONCLUSIONS OF THE STUDY

As we reflect on our purposes for conducting this study, it becomes evident to us that we were able to engage middle-level learners in activities that assisted them in becoming critical consumers, decision makers, as well as designers of various types of media. We found that the student-designed group representations that emerged from their inquiry, reflected their understanding and thoughtful application of deep viewing and possibly what might be called deep media representations. Students applied a wide variety of print and nonprint media. They were able to self-reflect on their work as well as generate criteria for evaluating their own presentations.

Watching our middle-level learners has helped us to realize how Reinking's (1998) notion of "expanding the boundaries of literacy" is occurring in classrooms every day as students make choices about how they wish to represent their ideas. The world around them is filled with "digital texts" and thus digital literacies (Gilster, 1997, p. 33, and Reinking, 1998, p. xvi). As Gooden (1996), Fisher et al. (1996), and Tierney (1996) point out, students are eager to work together and gain much more when they explore the possibilities of the new technologies together. As Reigeluth and Miller-Nelson (1997, p. 26) have suggested, students succeed in learning environments where "learning-focused instruction abides." Results of our facilitator interviews helped us to see what Salomon and Perkins (1998, p. 20) asserted, namely, that different learning systems are at work in group projects, the learning of individuals as well as the "collective." Finally, the work of Kommers (1996, p. 288) has helped us to realize the importance of recognizing media as opposed to only writing as a possible "organizing spine" of teaching and learning. As we viewed the various student creations, we realized the unique ways in which learners individually and in a collaborative manner express themselves and their ideas.

As teacher-researchers, we discovered that we also discovered much more through collaborative inquiry than we would have on our own. We had the benefits of hearing each other's questions and sharing one another's strengths and areas of expertise. It broadened our understanding and insights. The collaborative inquiry caused us to question our own practices and revise our plans for the good of the learners as well as our profession. There is always more to learn and apply and we have ideas of where we would like to proceed next. We perceive many of our findings and conclusions as purposes for our next study into media, literacy, and learning.

CONCLUSIONS

1. Students became critical consumers, decision makers, as well as designers of messages incorporating a variety of media.
2. Students applied inquiry to create media messages and representations that reflected an understanding of deep viewing.
3. Students were capable of generating criteria to self-evaluate their own presentations.
4. Students selected and presented media representations that demonstrated stylistic and persuasive rhetoric.
5. More males than females chose to design their representations using multi-media and computer technologies.

6. Students naturally incorporated many state English Language Arts and Information Technology Standards.
7. Students sometimes prefer to work alone and at other times in collaborative groups; they find negotiating to be challenging at times.

REFERENCES

Bolter, D. (1998). Hypertext and the question of visual literacy. In D. Reinking, M. McKenna, L. Labbo, & R. Kieffer (Eds.), *Handbook of literacy and technology: Transformations in a post-typographic world* (pp. 3–13). Mahwah, NJ: Erlbaum.

Bruce, B. (1998). Mixing old technologies with new. *Journal of Adolescent & Adult Literacy. 42*(2), 136–139.

Fisher, C., Dwyer, D. C., & Yocam, K. (Eds.). (1996). *Educating and technology: Reflections on computing in classrooms.* San Francisco: Jossey–Bass & Apple Press.

Fortier, J., Grady, S., Karbon, J., & Last, E. (1998a). Wisconsin's Model Academic Standards for English Language Arts. Madison: Wisconsin Department of Public Instruction.

Fortier, J., Potter, C., Grady S., Lohr, N., & Klein, J. (1998b). Wisconsin's Model Academic Standards for Information and Technology Literacy. Madison: Wisconsin Department of Public Instruction.

Garrett, S. D., Frey, J., Wildasin, M., & Hobbs, R. (1996). *Messages and meaning: A guide to understanding media.* Newark, DE: Newspaper Association of America Foundation, International Reading Association, and National Council for the Social Studies.

Garrett, S. D., McCallum, S., Yoder, M. E., & Hobbs, R. (1996). *Mastering the message: Performance assessment activities for understanding media.* Newark, DE: Newspaper Association of America Foundation, International Reading Association, and National Council for the Social Studies.

Gilster, P. (1997). *Digital literacy.* New York: Wiley.

Gooden, A. R. (1996). *Computers in the classroom: How teachers and students are using technology to transform learning.* San Francisco: Jossey–Bass & Apple Press.

Harste, J. (1994). Literacy as curricular conversations about knowledge, inquiry, and morality. In R. B. Ruddell, M. R. Ruddell, & H. Singer (Eds.) Newark, Delaware: International Reading Association, *Theoretical models and processes of reading* (4th ed., pp. 1220–1242).

Hobbs, R. (1997). Expanding the concept of literacy. In R. Kubey (Ed.), *Media literacy in the information age* (pp. 163–183). New Brunswick, NJ: Transaction.

International Reading Association and National Council of Teachers of English. (1996). *Standards for the English language arts.* Newark, DE and Urbana, IL.

Kinneavey, J. L. (1991). Rhetoric. In J. Flood, J. M. Jensen, D. Lapp, & J. R. Squire (Eds.), *Handbook of research on teaching the English language arts* (pp. 633–642). New York: Macmillan.

Kommers, P., Grabinger, S., & Dunlap, J. (Eds.). (1996). *Hypermedia learning environments: Instructional design and integration.* Mahwah, NJ: Erlbaum.

Lemke, J. (1998). Metamedia literacy: Transforming meanings and media. In D. Reinking, M. McKenna, L. Labbo, & R. Kieffer (Eds.), *Handbook of literacy and technology: Transformations in a post-typographic world* (pp. 283–301). Mahwah, NJ: Erlbaum.

Macaul, S., Giles, K., & Rodenberg, R. (1999). Intermediality in the classroom: Learners constructing meaning through deep viewing. In L. Semali & A. Watts Pailliotet (Eds.), *Intermediality: Teaching critical media literacy* (pp. 53–74). Boulder, CO: Westview.

Perkins, D. (1992). *Smart schools: From training memories to educating minds.* New York: The Free Press.

Raizen, S. A., Sellwood, P., Todd, R., & Vickers, M. (1995). *Technology education in the classroom: Understanding the designed world.* San Francisco: Jossey–Bass.

Reigeluth, C. M., & Miller-Nelson, L. (1997). A new paradigm of instructional systems design? In R. M. Branch & B. B. Minor (Eds.) with D. P. Ely, *Educational media and technology yearbook.* (Vol. 22, pp. 24–36). Englewood, CO: ERIC Clearinghouse on Information & Technology and the Association for Educational Communications & Technology.

Reinking, D. (1998). Synthesizing technological transformations of literacy in a post-typographic world. In D. Reinking, M. McKenna, L. Labbo, & R. Kieffer (Eds.), *Handbook of literacy and technology: Transformations in a post-typographic world* (pp. xi–xxx). Mahwah, NJ: Erlbaum.

Roth, W.-M., & McGinn, M. (1998). Inscriptions: Toward a theory of representing as social practice. *Review of Educational Research. 68*(1), 35–59.

Salomon, G., & Perkins, D. N. (1998). Individual and social aspects of learning. In P. D. Pearson & A. Iran-Nejad (Eds.), *Review of Research in Education* #23, 1–24.

Sandholtz, J., & Ringstaff, C. (1996). Teacher change in technology rich classrooms. In C. Fisher, D. Dwyer, & K. Yocam (Eds.), *Education and technology: Reflections on computing in classrooms* (pp. 281–299). San Francisco: Jossey–Bass.

Semali, L., & Watts Pailliotet, A. (Eds.). (1999). *Intermediality: The teachers' handbook of critical media literacy.* Boulder, CO: Westview.

Short, K., Schroeder, J., Laird, J., Kauffman, G., Ferguson, M., & Crawford, K. (1996). *Learning together through inquiry.* Portsmouth, NH: Heinemann Books.

Tierney, R. (1996). Redefining computer appropriation: A five-year study of ACOT students. In C. Fisher, D. Dwyer, & K. Yocam (Eds.), *Education and technology: Reflections on computing in classrooms* (pp. 169–183). San Francisco: Jossey–Bass.

Watts Pailliotet, A. (1995). "I never saw that before." A deeper view of video analysis in teacher education. *The Teacher Educator, 31*(2), 138–156.

Yocam, K. (1996). Conversation: An essential element of teacher development. In C. Fisher, D. Dwyer, & K. Yocam (Eds.), *Education and technology: Reflections on computing in classrooms* (pp. 265–279). San Francisco: Jossey–Bass.

RESOURCES

Badger times: A collection of newspaper pages and activities celebrating the Wisconsin sesquicentennial (1848–1998). (1998). Wisconsin Newspaper Association.

Eau Claire and the valley, where the rivers meet. (1997). Eau Claire, WI: Leader-Telegram.

Our story: The Chippewa Valley and beyond. (1976). Eau Claire, WI: Leader-Telegram.

Settlement and survival. (1994). Eau Claire, WI: Chippewa Valley Museum Press.

HyperStudio (Version 3.1). El Cajon, CA: Roger Wagner Publishing, Inc.

APPENDIX A: DEEP VIEWING GUIDE

Group Members

Deep Viewing Guide

View the video and record your thoughts and observations through writing and drawings for each category.

6 Areas of Analysis

1. Action & Sequence:
   (time relationships)

What happens?
When & how long?
2. Semes/Forms:
(visual meaning units)
What objects are seen?
What are their characteristics?

3. Actors/Words?
What is said and by whom?
How is it said & heard?

4. Closeness/Farness
& Movement:
(directionality and relationships of movement)
What types of movements occur?

5. Culture & Context:
To whom might this video be targeted?
What symbols do you notice?

6. Effects/Process:
(artistic devices—visual & audio)
What is seen?
What is missing?
What is the quality?

Comments & Questions:
What impact does this video have on you? Why?
What effects influenced you most?
What do you want to know about this video?

Adapted from Watts Pailliotet, A. (1995). "I never saw that before." A deeper view of video analysis in teacher education. *The Teacher Educator*, *31*(2), 138–156.

APPENDIX B: DEEP VIEWING GUIDE FOR VIDEO, NEWSPAPER, AND WEB SITE

Deep Viewing Guide

*Name*_____

	Video Ad	*Newspaper Ad*	*Web site Ad*

1. Action & Sequence: (time relationships)
    What happens?
    When & how long?
2. Semes/Forms: (visual meaning units)
    What objects are seen?
    What are their characteristics?
3. Actors/Words:
    What is said and by whom?
    How is it said & heard?
4. Closeness/Farness & Movement:
    (directionality and relationships of movement)
    What types of movements occur?
5. Culture & Context:
    To whom might this video be targeted?
    What symbols do you notice?
6. Effects/Process: (artistic devices—visual & audio)
    What is seen?
    What is missing?
    What is the quality?

Note: Adapted from Watts Pailliotet, A. (1995). "I never saw that before." A deeper view of video analysis in teacher education. *The Teacher Educator, 31*(2), 138–156.

APPENDIX C: TECHNOLOGY AND INQUIRY LEARNING
Technology & Inquiry Learning

Note: Adapted from Short, R., Schroeder, G., Laird, J., Kauffman, G., Ferguson, M., Crawford, K. (1996). *Learning Together Through Language.* York, ME: Stenhouse Publishers.

APPENDIX D: INQUIRY LEARNING LOG

Written Accounts & Sketches of Collaborative Thinking & Planning

Date: _____

Date: _____

Date: _____

APPENDIX E: PEER INQUIRY CONFERENCING

Inquiry Focus _____

Team Members _____

P   Praise

Q   Question

I   Ideas

M   Media Representations

Peer Team _____
_____
_____

APPENDIX F: FACILITATOR INTERVIEWS

Tell me/us about your inquiry and technology project. (Have them take you through the inquiry cycle as they applied it and show you what they have created to date.)

Probing Questions:

What have you explored and designed thus far and what do you plan to do next?

Who is your audience? What do you hope you and others will learn from viewing your project and presentation?

Are there any themes or big ideas running through your project?

How is your team collaborating?

What media/technology are you incorporating into our inquiry?

What will your presentation involve?

What criteria will you use to self-evaluate your project?

SECTION III

ISSUES: RECONCEPTUALIZING CHANGING LITERACY CONTEXTS

IN THE BELLY OF THE BEAST:
PROPOSING A CRITICAL MEDIA LITERACY COURSE FOR A NEW GENERAL EDUCATION PROGRAM AT A COMPREHENSIVE STATE UNIVERSITY

Arnold S. Wolfe

INTRODUCTION

Americans and peoples in other developed nations are being overrun by claims about the so-called "information society" (see, e.g., Crandall, 1991; Dizard, 1989, 1994; Egan, 1991; Horowitz, 1991; Masuda, 1980; Mosco & Wasko, 1988; Slack & Fejes, 1987; Sussman, 1990; Traber, 1988). Critics contend that no current definition of this phrase presents a fundamentally new way of structuring collective human interaction. Some even argue that the information society portends the end of public discourse historically thought to be constitutive of democracy. Contrarily information society advocates claim that the new opportunities for accessing and exchanging information that the information society makes possible represent the preservation, even the salvation, of democracy. Inventions of the motion picture, radio, television, and cable television called forth similar claims.

Advances in Reading/Language Research, Volume 7, pages 187–218.
Copyright © 2000 by JAI Press Inc.
All rights of reproduction in any form reserved.
ISBN: 0-7623-0264-X

Prompted by a call for course proposals from a universitywide committee charged with reforming the General Education Program (GEP) at Illinois State University, I recently developed a course that treats these issues in a particular—and interdisciplinary—way. I am an associate professor of communication at Illinois State. I believed then, and continue to, that a course that problematizes "the information society" both as linguistic signifier and social signified should be part of the general education of all undergraduates. I called the course *The Changing Role of Mass Communication in the Information Society*. Its focal purposes are:

1. To describe how the information society has *changed* mass communication and how information technology *may change* mass communication in the future
2. To assess the impact of such changes on democracy in the United States (or in other nation-states, depending on the instructor's interest and expertise)

The course invites students to:

1. Think seriously and critically about "the information society" and how that phrase may be defined
2. Define the traditional media of mass communication and consider the multiple and reciprocal relationships between those media and the information society. (The course will describe and detail the media's historic role as society's information distributor. The historic formation of the "mass" audience and its subsequent fragmentation into multiple audiences and publics with varied and specialized information needs will be discussed.)
3. Assess the extent to which the information society—and the media's role in creating, maintaining, and transforming it—have either enlarged or diminished the possibilities for public discourse constitutive of democracy. [Observers as varied as John Berger (1972), Arthur Asa Berger (1991), and Richard Brown (1989) have argued that the media's broad circulation of both information and entertainment has maintained and even expanded democracy in the Western democracies. The U.S. Supreme Court regards the World Wide Web as democratic and democratizing (*Reno v. American Civil Liberties Union*). Others, such as Mosco and Wasco (1988), are not as sure.]

GENESIS

In order to be considered by the Illinois State powers-that-be, the proposal for *The Changing Role of Mass Communication in the Information Society* had to address highly specific criteria beyond those required in conventional course proposals. I contend that these GEP criteria are not matters of mere local concern. They are the product of institutionwide research, debate, and experimentation of a decade's duration, informed by an exhaustive review of the higher education literature in general and the literature on general education in particular. That review revealed that often, students view general education requirements as "obstacles to be overcome before the door to coveted courses in the major [can] be opened." Illinois State University (ISU), however, has undertaken an institutional "commitment to make general education a meaningful, strong, and common foundation for all undergraduates" (Illinois State University, 1997, p. 1). A comprehensive discussion of ISU's GEP would take us far afield. By presenting the following argument about how the proposal meets the program's pertinent criteria, this chapter will give readers a strong sense of a GEP that in the "lean and mean" 1990s has garnered nearly three-quarters of a million dollars of supplemental state revenue for its development and implementation (Illinois State University, 1997, p. 3). The Illinois state legislature is notoriously political, but I choose to believe that the appropriated funds represent some continuing commitment to advance the democratic values that spurred Lincoln to found ISU during his term as Illinois governor.

This chapter will proceed by detailing how the proposed course

1. Meets the GEP standards as expressed in its synoptic "Philosophy" of general education (Illinois State University Academic Senate, 1991)
2. Builds on the course category-specific learning "objectives and student outcomes" (Illinois State University Academic Senate, 1997b, p. 1) for its three "Inner Core" courses (Illinois State University Academic Senate, 1997a, p. 4)
3. Addresses the "description," "content and goals," "criteria" (pp. 15–16), and "designated [learning] objectives and student outcomes" (Illinois State University Academic Senate, 1997b, p. 13) for courses in the social sciences in the advanced GEP course category the course was designed to embrace

Elements of the "Philosophy" of General Education met by *The Changing Role of Mass Communication in the Information Society*

The course was crafted to build on the common foundation of interpretive skills students acquire in a new General Education course, Foundations of Inquiry, and written and oral communication skills students acquire in Language and Composition and Language and Communication, ISU's names for the freshman composition and public speaking courses, respectively (Illinois State University Academic Senate, 1997a, p. 3).

Foundations of Inquiry (Foundations) is a freshman seminar that is designed to help students negotiate the intellectual transition from high school to college. 'Foundations' addresses the idea of what it means to engage in the disciplined inquiry which characterizes the University. [It] is designed to help students become more critical and reflective in their reading and reasoning skills, requiring that they defend their viewpoint[s] through extensive writing assignments (Illinois State University, 1997, p. 2).

The Changing Role of Mass Communication in the Information Society builds
on Foundations of Inquiry and the composition and public speaking courses,
because it stresses how "technological, social and political" changes (Illinois State
University Academic Senate, 1997a, p. 15) mandate commitment to "learning as
an active, continuous, and life-long process." Such active learning strategies as
collaborative learning groups and group presentations twined with question-and-
answer opportunities are featured prominently in the syllabus (see pp. xxx–xxx).

Consonant with the "Philosophy of University Studies" approved by ISU's
Academic Senate (1991), *The Changing Role of Mass Communication in the
Information Society* is "liberal" in its view of knowledge, "interdisciplinary" and
"global" in its orientation. Each of these three terms will be defined and elaborated
in turn. According to the "Philosophy" (1991), the liberal view emphasizes "self-
development with regard to the individual's ability to initiate and adapt to change
[and] civic fulfillment with regard to the individual's human and communal
responsibilities." As Brown (1989, p. 1) reminds us, "knowledge is power"; one's
power "to initiate and adapt to change" in the information society can be aided and
abetted by the knowledge the course aims to provide. Whether students who have
mastered this knowledge apply it in efforts to "fulfill" their personal human
potential or that of the larger social units to which they claim membership is up to
them. But course instructors can surely describe, and even model, ways certain
persons have used the knowledge the course presents to "fulfill" their personal
human potential, their "self-development." Contrastingly, course instructors can
describe and model ways persons have used the knowledge the course presents to
"fulfill" the "responsibilities," or goals, of larger social units of which those persons
are a part (Illinois State University Academic Senate, 1991).

Members of the ISU chapter of the American Association of University Professors (AAUP), for instance, recently scoured the Internet for matter on candidates
for ISU president who had been chosen for campus interviews. When one member
found a disquieting report on a candidate that was posted on a Texas newspaper's
Web site, she "downloaded" the story and reposted it on the chapter membership's
email "listserv." The report was (literally) news to the (few) faculty on the presidential search committee; the candidate had not submitted the newspaper report
along with his vita and cover letter. In this instance an "information society"-literate
colleague skillfully used "information society" media to supply at least 700 faculty
with information that potentially empowers them to make a better decision about
a critical choice that is sure to affect their lives.

There can be no doubt, however, that "technological developments, social and
political forces" (Illinois State University Academic Senate, 1997a, p. 15) and other
cultural contexts, including economic ones, have radically changed the nature and
experience of mass communication for all Americans and citizens of the developed
world. Less than 20 years ago, for example, long after broadcast television had
eclipsed all other communication media in ubiquity, a social scientist defined
culture as "the subjective basis of all doing and making among an organized group

of people sharing adjacent space" (Nieberg, 1984, pp. 50–51). But even by then, broadcast television had fundamentally changed human culture, perhaps forever. Due to the invention and spread of broadcast television, spatial adjacency was no longer required for either the production or consumption of culture; in 1967, the Beatles performed "All You Need Is Love" before an estimated 400 million people in 24 spatially discontiguous nations on the first live, worldwide telecast (Dowlding, 1989, p. 185). More recently, live television transmission of the funeral of Diana, Princess of Wales, was shared by an estimated 2 billion viewers.

"The technological, social, political" (Illinois State University Academic Senate, 1997a, p. 15) and economic changes that have wrought a new medium of communication, the World Wide Web, are now reconfiguring to redefine culture again. The very notion of culture itself—along with the individuals and groups invested and embedded in it—is undergoing yet another paradigm shift. Boon or bane, the changes the phrase "information society" attempts to reference are altering the "entire constellation of beliefs, values . . . and so on, shared by the members of [the Internetworked] community" (Kuhn, 1970, p. 175). Because that community is global and Kuhn's phrase his definition of paradigm, the information society can be said to be altering the very paradigm of what being human means.

Rosovsky declares that "it is no longer possible to conduct our lives without reference to the wider world or to the historical forces that have shaped the present and will shape the future" (quoted in Illinois State University Academic Senate, 1991). For much of the 20th century, America and much of the developed world could not be adequately understood apart from the growing centrality first of the mass communication media, then of computers, to virtually every significant cultural context shaping civilization. But the disciplines of communication have hardly "resolv[ed] issues" of how broadcast television affects "individual and social life" (Illinois State University Academic Senate, 1997a, p. 16; see also DeFleur & Ball-Rokeach, 1989, and Semali & Watts Pailliotet, 1999b), let alone how the invention and spread of cable television may have shattered previous understandings. Few responsible students of media in the age of cable television and the fragmentation of the "mass audience" cable begat would concur today with C. Wright Mills's 1957 declaration that "the media tell man [sic] in the mass who he is." Even if "the media" were monolithic four decades ago, the consensus today is that "they" are no longer.

Today, the invention and spread of computer-generated communication media threatens to shatter status quo understandings once again. Educators such as Henry Giroux (1987) and Semali and Watts Pailliotet (1995, 1999a,b) have introduced the notion of an expanded "school literacy" to enable educational institutions at all levels to address these developments. They call on these institutions, and others, to install in students "a critical media literacy," an end to be achieved by "expand[ing] the notion of school literacy, which [has been traditionally defined as] principally the ability to read the printed text, to include a critical reading of all media texts" (Semali & Watts Pailliotet, 1995, p. 9). Elaborating the notion of critical media literacy, Semali and Watts Pailliotet (1999b, p. 5) write that the critically media literate can "function competently in the 'communicative arts'," which are here grasped most expansively as "the language arts as well as the visual arts of [graphics,] film, video, and television" (quoting Flood and Lapp). *The Changing Role of Mass Communication in the Information Society* is designed to be a critical media literacy course, aimed at developing critical media literacy "competencies," in the words of Illinois State's Philosophy of University Studies, "essential in a technological age" (Illinois State University Academic Senate, 1991). Among these competencies is the capacity to intelligently engage with mass media both as technologies and as institutions in a continuing "struggle" over their "democratic potential and cultural devolution" (Chambers, 1985, p. 211; see also Semali & Watts Pailliotet, 1999b, p. 8).

To these ends, some of the proposed course will be delivered as a series of dichotomies, or conflicts, that students will not be expected to resolve but be conscious of, sensitized to, and to research, write about, and discuss. Put in question form, among those conflicts are:

The individual vs. society:

    a.   To what extent have the mass media enhanced the quality of life for the individual at the expense of the quality of life of the surrounding society?

    b.   To what extent have the mass media done the opposite?

    c.   To what extent has the information society enhanced the quality of life for the individual at the expense of the quality of life of the surrounding society?

    d.   To what extent has the information society done the opposite?

(See the Sample Syllabus, pp. xxx–xxx, below, for a more complete discussion of other thematic dichotomies the course will treat.)

The Changing Role of Mass Communication in the Information Society is also liberal in "its view of knowledge [that] supports the development of . . . a cultural awareness stressing the heritage of values which earmark civilization" (Illinois State University Academic Senate, 1991). It is to this topic of civilized values that this chapter now turns.

How the Course Is Interdisciplinary and Global

The Changing Role of Mass Communication in the Information Society addresses requirements that GEP courses value and use what the ISU Academic Senate (1991) calls "interdisciplinary" approaches, because they "allow . . . faculty and students to treat [the course's] subject matter in terms of thematic [and] practical connections." *The Changing Role of Mass Communication in the Information Society* is designed to be what the Senate calls "global" insofar as it both "engenders an understanding and a critical appreciation of *democratic* values and institutions" (italics added; Illinois State University Academic Senate, 1991). By means of its semester-long inquiry into how mass communication and the information society have affected democracy and how developments in information technology are likely to affect democracy in the near future, the course proposes to deepen the understanding and appreciation of democratic values and institutions, for which the Philosophy of University Studies calls. ISU has identified democracy as the globally preferred governmental form.

The course invites students to view the specialty fields of communication, mass communication, and computer-mediated communication in the same "larger context" (Boyer, quoted in Illinois State University Academic Senate, 1991) that America's founders used to evaluate the communication and mass communication of their day. James Madison himself called the communication media one of the great bulwarks of liberty and democracy, and he wanted to make freedom of the press "inviolable" (Tedford, 1993, p. 25). One wonders if Madison would have called "inviolable" the right of a recent ISU student newspaper editor to respond to the Lewinsky scandal by speculating on the size and shape of the Presidential privates.

The larger, Madisonian context of maximizing communication technology's utility to preserve and extend democracy is no less applicable today. To mobilize Rosovsky's apt distinction (quoted in Illinois State University Academic Senate, 1991), *The Changing Role of Mass Communication in the Information Society* seeks to motivate students to "leap from informed acquaintance to critical appreciation" of the interrelations among mass communication, computer-mediated communication, and democratic values. Of Rosovsky's two forms of knowledge, "critical appreciation . . . is more important and more difficult" to develop (Rosovsky, 1990). Moreover, as the forces that have formed the information society institutionalize, and particularly, as Internet firms such as America Online absorb others, "critical appreciation" of the role communication plays in democracy is what America needs as much as, if not more than, ever. Educator Ernest Boyer (quoted in Illinois State University Academic Senate, 1991) writes, "What we need today [and forever, I believe] are groups of well-informed, caring individuals who band together in the spirit of community to learn from one another, to participate, as citizens, in the democratic process."

It is the purpose of *The Changing Role of Mass Communication in the Information Society* to inform students and to unify students and faculty—not only from the University's Department of Communication but from other departments, such as History, Philosophy, and Sociology—to "band together in the spirit of community to learn from one another, to participate, as citizens, in the . . . process" of understanding

a. How mass communication and the information society have affected democracy
b. How developments in information technology are likely to affect democracy in the near future

c. How the democratic potential of these technological and market develop-
    ments can be preserved, if not optimized. The problems addressed in *The
    Changing Role of Mass Communication in the Information Society* "demand
    insight," in educator Jerry Gaff's phrase, "from several disciplines" (quoted
    in Illinois State University Academic Senate, 1991).

The Changing Role of Mass Communication in the Information Society is also
global for an allied reason: It "stresses the social nature of knowledge and learning"
(Illinois State University Academic Senate, 1991). Group projects and in-class
treatment of the above-mentioned dichotomies are designed to prompt "active
student involvement" ("Vision for the Year 2007," quoted in Illinois State University Academic Senate, 1991) that promotes social, rather than individual, exchange
of thought and action. Semali and Watts Pailliotet (1999b) remind us that "critical
analysis of diverse media . . . *promotes* student empowerment, interest [and] active
learning" (p. 8, italics added). Referencing Kellner they mark collaborative learning
as a set of "behaviors needed [for the development of] a truly democratic nation"
(p. 24).

<h2 style="text-align:center">Ways that the Course Category-Specific Objectives of the GEP Are
Addressed by The Changing Role of Mass Communication
in the Information Society</h2>

The proposed course builds on the course category-specific objectives of Foundations of Inquiry (FOI) because *The Changing Role of Mass Communication in
the Information Society* "gives students an[other] opportunity to investigate what
it means to be educated and to develop [their] desire for learning" (Illinois State
University Academic Senate, 1997a, p. 4). Educators "focus[ing] on the multiple
ways in which learners gain access to knowledge and skills" have argued that "by
broadening our" definition of literacy to include the sort of media literacy the course
is designed to advance, "a greater number of students will be motivated to see
themselves as learners" (Semali & Watts Pailliotet, 1995, p. 7). *The Changing Role
of Mass Communication in the Information Society* is proposed as a GEP option
designed to deepen the "sense [students acquire by completing FOI] of the value
and importance of acquiring knowedge [and] the idea of what it means to engage
in the disciplined inquiry which characterizes the university" (Illinois State University Academic Senate, 1997, p. 4). By banding students and faculty "together in
the spirit of community to learn from one another, to participate, as citizens, in
the . . . process" (Boyer, quoted in Illinois State University Academic Senate, 1991)
of understanding

a. How mass communication and the information society have affected democ-
    racy

b. How developments in information technology are likely to affect democracy in the near future

c. How the democratic potential of these developments can be preserved, if not optimized;

faculty who teach the course will enact "the value and importance of acquiring knowledge [and] the idea of what it means to engage in the disciplined inquiry which characterizes the university" (Illinois State University Academic Senate, 1997a, p. 4).

In *The Changing Role of Mass Communication in the Information Society*, students will also build on FOI by "learn[ing] to become [even] more critical and reflective in the activities of reading, listening to the views of others, and presenting their own views" (Illinois State University Academic Senate, 1997a, p. 5). Students will further "develop . . . their reasoning skills, by learning to identify the authors['] conclusion[s] and supporting evidence, and evaluating the strength of that evidence." They will build on FOI as well by undertaking more intensive "research projects, in the library and sometimes in the field," than they were assigned in FOI. In the proposed course, students will add to their FOI experiences of "gathering, analyzing, and evaluating data as evidence." They will build on their FOI experiences of "practicing reasoning by defending their own point of view in extensive writing, including short informal essays and longer position papers."

Like FOI, *The Changing Role of Mass Communication in the Information Society* will "ask students to be actively involved in their own learning" (Illinois State University Academic Senate, 1997a, p. 5). Like faculty teaching FOI, faculty who teach the proposed course will "seek to create a classroom atmosphere which fosters open communication and includes frequent discussions" and often assign students to "work in small groups discussing and attempting to resolve issues raised in the readings." Through such efforts, among others, faculty teaching *The Changing Role of Mass Communication in the Information Society* will also meet course category-specific objectives for Language and Communication, the GEP's public speaking course. Like FOI faculty, faculty teaching *The Changing Role of Mass Communication in the Information Society* will

a. Assign students to do "research, and [to] evaluate each other's written work."

b. "[A]sk students to use email to enhance communication with other students and with their instructor."

c. "[U]se the Internet to locate information resources" (Illinois State University Academic Senate, 1997a, p. 5).

By such efforts, among others already discussed, faculty teaching *The Changing Role of Mass Communication in the Information Society* will also meet course category-specific objectives for Language and Composition, the GEP's "freshman comp" course. Even more, the class discussions that will examine the series of dichotomies discussed above constitute but one way *The Changing Role of Mass*

Communication in the Information Society will replicate the pedagogies students experienced in FOI.

The proposed course will also build on FOI by "incorporating readings which introduce" a variety of "historical perspective[s]" (Illinois State University Academic Senate, 1997a, p. 5) on how mass communication and the information society affected democracy and how developments in information technology are likely to affect democracy in the near future (see Dizard, 1994; Lipsitz, 1988; and Sample Syllabus below). Finally, *The Changing Role of Mass Communication in the Information Society* aims to build on other course category-specific goals of FOI. Like FOI, by requiring that students engage in research and produce reasoned oral and written discourse, the proposed course addresses FOI goals of deepening students'

a. Knowledge of "the intellectual life of the university"
b. "[I]ntellectual confidence and skills in reading, in the use of technology, in research, in written and oral expression, and in analytical reasoning skills"
c. Zeal for "life-long learning and active inquiry"
d. Comprehension of "approaches that a variety of disciplines take to discussing issues and generating knowledge" (Illinois State University Academic Senate, 1997a, p. 5).

In addition to FOI, Language of Communication, and Language and Composition, ISU's GEP requires students to take a mathematics and a natural sciences course to complete the "Inner Core" (Illinois State University, 1997, p. 2). I proposed *The Changing Role of Mass Communication in the Information Society* as a course that addresses one of two approved "Outer Core," or advanced general education, course categories, namely, "Disciplinary Knowledge in Cultural Contexts." I'll next explain how the course meets the requirements of that course category.

ELEMENTS OF THE OUTER CORE COURSE CATEGORY DESCRIPTION MET BY *THE CHANGING ROLE OF MASS COMMUNICATION IN THE INFORMATION SOCIETY*

The Changing Role of Mass Communication in the Information Society better addresses the specific objectives of the "Disciplinary Knowledge in Cultural Contexts" Outer Core Course category than the objectives of the "Knowing in the Disciplines" Outer Core Course category primarily because the focal problem the proposed course aims to investigate flows beyond the boundaries of the communication discipline. Both the *industries* of mass communication and the academic *discipline* of mass communication interact with and have helped constitute the information society (Dizard, 1994). But the cultural contexts of technological, social, political, and economic development have changed in no predictable relation to changes in the discipline of mass communication. As media historian George Lipsitz (1988, p. 150) reminds us, "Historians investigating . . . electronic mass media cannot rely upon standards of evidence and methods of inquiry developed to study printed documents alone." In the discipline of history, such documents have been the privileged form of evidence in the "dominant model of historical scholarship." Lipsitz's claim can be contested. What cannot is the proposition that for the problems *The Changing Role of Mass Communication in the Information Society* will examine, "mass communication texts provide indispensable information, serving as historical evidence even when the texts display no overt consciousness of their own historicity" (p. 150).

Outer Core Course Category "Content and Goals" the
Proposed Course Addresses

"Utilizing methodological," if not substantive, "knowledge from outside" mass communications, "the discipline being investigated," students in the proposed course will

a.	"[D]evelop a familiarity with how disciplinary tools" from the disciplines of History, Sociology, and from multiple subdisciplines within Communication, "can shape [such] individual and social practices" as the production of knowledge about the history and possible futures of mass communication.

b.	"[L]earn to think critically about the role . . . disciplinary knowledge" can play "in resolving [such] issues of individual and social life." Examples of such issues are:

   1.	In what ways did the invention and spread of broadcast television technology "shape disciplines" of communication "and the knowledge they produce[d]?" and

   2.	In what ways, if any, have the invention and spread of computer-mediated communication, and particularly such technologies as the Internet and the World Wide Web, re-"shaped disciplines" of communication and reshaped—even obsolesced—the knowledge they once produced?

c.	"[L]earn to identify values that shape a cultural context, and how these may affect disciplinary knowledge" (Illinois State University Academic Senate, 1997a, p. 16). In *The Changing Role of Mass Communication in the Information Society* students will understand how the "emergence of motion pictures and commercial radio created new possibilities for realizing [Walt] Whitman's vision" (Lipsitz, 1988, p. 151) of a free and democratic system of expression. Students will also understand how capitalist values conflicted with democratic ones and eventually prevailed to "inscribe . . . commodity form and commercial exchange within every [motion pictorial and radio] communication." Students will know how the conflicts among scientific/technological values, politically democratic ones, and economically capitalistic values—conflicts that have shaped and continue to shape American civilization—gave form to the knowledge the communication discipline produced, including historical knowledge about the development of mass communication, particularly in the United States. In *The Changing Role of Mass Communication in the Information Society*, students will also

d.   "[L]earn to perceive an issue from a variety of perspectives . . . and reflect critically on how those perspectives differ" (Illinois State University Academic Senate, 1997a, p. 16). In the course, students will identify "a variety of . . . and reflect critically on . . . perspectives" from which they can view communication technology development. Those perspectives that privilege technological development over all other values, or the maintenance and extension of democracy over others, or economic profit over others, or that lionize only the best and the beautiful in culture will be discussed and clash in all the issues and debates on dichotomies *The Changing Role of Mass Communication in the Information Society* will specify.

Outer Core Course Category "Criteria" the Proposed
Course "Attend[s] To"

1.   As stated above, the proposed course does "utilize knowledge from outside [Mass Communication,] the discipline being investigated."

2.   The proposed course "address[es] disciplinary perspectives from [the] Social Sciences" (Illinois State University Academic Senate, 1997a, p. 16), particularly from Sociology and History, as well as social science perspectives, such as media economics, from within the discipline of Communication. Wolfe and Kapoor's (1996) examination of the effects on "freedom of expression in motion pictorial communication" of Matsushita's buyout of Hollywood major MCA exemplifies research that deploys knowledge from within one Social Science discipline— namely, economics—to address a question historically posed by humanist communication scholars (p. 1; see, e.g., Emerson, 1970; Jacklin, 1978).

3.   *The Changing Role of Mass Communication in the Information Society* "encourage[s] students in actively applying disciplinary theories, tools and creations to the shaping of individual and social practices." Students will be asked to apply to the social practices that constitute mass communication *production* "theories, tools and creations" (Illinois State University Academic Senate, 1997a, p. 16) from within three disciplines: Communication, History, and the Production of Culture perspective from within Sociology. Wolfe's (1985) Production of Culture account of the post-World War II U.S. recording industry exemplifies one study that combines such communication, historical, and industrial sociological perspectives. From within the Communication discipline, "apparatus centered" histories (Lipsitz, 1988, p. 149) will help students account for the mass media's role as society's information distributor. Also from within Communication, textual ana-

lytic approaches will help students describe and analyze the changing image of the newspaper in media creations such as *Citizen Kane* and *All the President's Men*, of television in *Network* and *Broadcast News*, and of high technology in any number of films, such as *Bladerunner* and *The Right Stuff*. Rushing's (1986) analysis of *Bladerunner* and *The Right Stuff* as mythic expressions of American ambivalence toward technology stands as an exemplar of such textual approaches.

From within History, *The Changing Role of Mass Communication in the Information Society* will stress "the importance of historical thinking as an organic and necessary way of understanding human experience . . . that is as indispensable to everyday life as it is in scholarly research" (Lipsitz, 1988, p. 148). And from the perspective within History that insists that the everyday lives of ordinary people are as significant as public events, the proposed course will examine those "individual and social practices" (Illinois State University Academic Senate, 1997a, p. 15) of mass communication consumption that have been largely ignored by conventional histories and historians. Wolfe, Miller, and O'Donnell's (1999) inquiry into the lasting popularity of Cream's 1968 song-recording, "Sunshine Of Your Love," aims to legitimate such "events without prestige" (LeFebvre, quoted in Chambers, 1985, p. 2) as *contemporary* consumption of a "psychedelic oldie." To a review of critical discourse dating from the song's release, Wolfe et al. immix reports of interviews with U.S. and European adults who were approximately college-age when the song was first released. Consistent with what could be called the demotic historical perspective Lipsitz (1988) describes, Wolfe et al. argue that the published responses of popular music critics may be "no more significant than the heretofore unpublished responses of members of other, perhaps less literate—or at least less published (or, alternately, more silenced)—living social groups." In a methodological move influenced by historians Lipsitz (1988) lauds, Wolfe et al. interviewed the adults in an effort to discover meanings they made of the song more than 30 years ago and meanings they make of it today. Interviews with contemporary radio station executives aim to account for the song's continued airplay, and a focus group of current college students attempts to determine the song's meanings to them.

By virtue of a method of data collection inspired by both demotic historians and qualitative sociologists (Pauly, 1991), Wolfe et al. "democratize what once would have been presumed to have been a critical task wholly and solely responsive to humanities disciplinary approaches: In order to 'explain' the enduring appeal of a text, one analyzes the text (by using theoretic tools recognized within such humanities disciplines as literary criticism, [history,] and musicology)" (Wolfe & Haefner, 1996, p. 136). Wolfe et al. (1999), however, make space for living social groups *other than* critics to account for their consumption of the text under study—and in group members' "own words" (MacGregor & Morrison, 1995, p. 142) to boot.

From within the discipline of Sociology, *The Changing Role of Mass Communication in the Information Society* will familiarize students with Production of Culture approaches to such issues as the adoption of information technology by mass media organizations. From one such Production of Culture study, students will learn to distinguish the differing *cultural* functions of news and entertainment content from the strikingly similar *"social forces* that determine" the use of identical information technology by both news and entertainment producers and consumers (italics added; Pietila, Malberg, & Nordenstreng, 1990, p. 172).

4.   Finally, *The Changing Role of Mass Communication in the Information Society* will "encourage students to reflect on ways in which the theories, tools and creations produced by a discipline are responsive to individual and social practices from the larger social context" (Illinois State University Academic Senate, 1997a, p. 15). From sources such as Jensen and Rosengren (1990, p. 209), students will see how so many of the disciplinary theories and tools used and esteemed in communication owe their origin not to value-neutral social scientific curiosity but to fear—"widespread fear," voiced with the popularization of "each new medium . . . that its effects might be deleterious, especially to supposedly weak minds, such as those of children, women and uneducated people." But as James Carey (1985), former dean of the University of Illinois' College of Communication and current professor at Columbia University's Graduate School of Journalism, insists, the tradition of social scientistic communication research that was founded to quell the fears of those "panicked" by the rise of each new medium "has been a failure." The media effects research tradition "has not generated any agreement on the laws of behavior or the functions of [mass] communications of sufficient power and pertinence to signal to us that success has been achieved" (p. 28). Broader social contexts of cultural politics and technological development may still clamor for "The Holy Grail . . . a positive science of communication" (p. 27). But the

a.   Epistemological and social failures of the effects tradition
b.   Growing ideological opposition to greater government regulation twined with the growing ideological promotion of greater freedom of expression, and
c.   Discovery that the individual media consumer is less accurately grasped as "a passive recipient of powerful[ly influential] messages" than as "a much more active and selective user of media" (Jensen & Rosengren, 1990, p. 209)

have combined to forge a new "context" that has "influenced" the "creation" of what gets called "knowledge" (Illinois State University Academic Senate, 1997b, p. 15) by mass communication disciplinarians. Knowledge forged in this new context has shown how mass communication consumers actively make meaning of the variety of mass communication texts they consume. *The Changing Role of Mass Communication in the Information Society* will trace this disciplinary history.

Courses proposed for the GEP must also meet "Designated Program Objectives and Student Outcomes" for Outer Core courses. My initial proposal positioned *The Changing Role of Mass Communication in the Information Society* as meeting the GEP's "Designated Program Objectives and Student Outcomes" for "Courses in the Humanities" in the program's "Disciplinary Knowledge in Cultural Contexts"

Outer Core Course Category (Illinois State University Academic Senate, 1997b, pp. 13–14). The Department of Communication Curriculum Committee, the Communication faculty as a whole, and the College of Arts and Sciences Curriculum Committee each approved my proposal in turn. To the program's chief gatekeeping committee, however, the proposal's preoccupation with the effects of technology on democracy drove the course toward the social sciences rather than the humanities. For the first time anywhere, then, I present the following:

How the Proposed Course Meets Designated Program Objectives and Student Outcomes for Courses in the *Social Sciences* in the Disciplinary Knowledge in Cultural Contexts Outer Core Course Category of the Illinois State University GEP

The Changing Role of Mass Communication in the Information Society will meet Primary Designated Program Objective #1 for *Social Science* Courses in the Disciplinary Knowledge in Cultural Contexts Outer Core Course Category, because it will "focus on the acquisition and application of a common core of knowledge, from the humanities, sciences, and social sciences" (Illinois State University Academic Senate, 1997b, p. 15) in ways described above. As a result of their common Inner Core experiences, students who successfully complete the proposed course will be able to "recognize the key events, ideas, individuals, and institutions that have shaped the world." Guilliermo Marconi, inventor of radio; David Sarnoff, inventor of television; William Paley, founder of the Columbia Broadcast System; Hollywood's Louis B. Mayer; Microsoft's Bill Gates—and their innovations—will be among "the key events, ideas, individuals, and institutions that have shaped the world" that students will come to "recognize" (p. 15).

Communication majors who successfully complete *The Changing Role of Mass Communication in the Information Society* will meet Primary Designated Program Objective #3 for *Social Science* Courses in the *Disciplinary Knowledge in Cultural Contexts* Outer Core Course Category, because they will "integrate [their] general education" (Illinois State University Academic Senate, 1997b, p. 15) in critical thinking, in "gathering, analyzing, and evaluating data," in "defending their . . . reason[ed] point[s] of view in extensive writing" (Illinois State University Academic Senate, 1997a, p. 5), and in oral presentations with their major in Communication "through the identification, exploration, and development of common dimensions. As a result, students [who successfully complete the course] will be able to:

a. "[U]nderstand how disciplinary knowledge is amplified and enriched by [such] general knowledge" (Illinois State University Academic Senate, 1997b, p. 15) as "gathering, analyzing, and evaluating data" and "recogniz[ing] the key events, ideas, individuals, and institutions that have shaped the world" (Illinois State University Academic Senate, 1997a, p. 5).

b.   "[I]ncorporate those skills developed in general education to activities and
     course work within their majors" (Illinois State University Academic Senate,
     1997b, p. 15).

The Changing Role of Mass Communication in the Information Society will meet
Primary Designated Program Objective #7 for *Social Science* Courses in the
Disciplinary Knowledge in Cultural Contexts Outer Core Course Category, because
the course is designed to develop each student's "ability to function as a responsible
participant in the social, economic, [and] technological . . . dimensions of life within
[her or his] local, national, and global communities" (Illinois State University
Academic Senate, 1997b, p. 15). In order "to function as a responsible participant
in the social, economic, [and] technological . . . dimensions of [contemporary] life,"
students in the proposed course will:

a.   Think seriously and critically about "the information society" and how that
     phrase may be defined
b.   Define the traditional media of mass communication and consider the mul-
     tiple "social, economic, technological and political" relationships between
     those media and the information society (Illinois State University Academic
     Senate, 1997b, p. 15).

The course will describe and detail the media's historic role as society's information distributor and some of the focal social, economic, technological, and
political reasons both the mass media and the information society developed as they
did. The knowledge the course will present on the historic formation of the "mass"
audience and its subsequent fragmentation into multiple audiences with varied and
specialized information needs is aimed at deepening the student's understanding of
social, economic, technological and political forces that have shaped and continue
to shape the mass media and the information society.

And, again, the course requires students to:

c.   Assess the extent to which the information society and the media's role in
creating, maintaining, and transforming it have either enlarged or diminished the
possibilities for public discourse constitutive of democracy.

"As a result," the proposed course meets Primary Designated Program Objective
#7 a for *Social Science* Courses in the *Disciplinary Knowledge in Cultural Contexts*
Outer Core Course Category, because the students who successfully complete *The
Changing Role of Mass Communication in the Information Society* will be able to
"describe different ways in which the social, economic, technological, and political
dimensions of life" in a mass mediated society such as the United States "are
known." Students who successfully complete the course will also be able to
"describe different ways in which [some of the] social, economic, technological,
and political dimensions of life" in a mass mediated society such as the United
States have been "conducted" (Illinois State University Academic Senate, 1997b,

p. 15). Of course, depending on the instructor's interest and expertise, the social, economic, technological, and political dimensions of life in nation-states other than the United States may be examined or compared to those dimensions in the United States or other nation-states or regions.

Similarly, students who successfully complete *The Changing Role of Mass Communication in the Information Society* will be able to "describe different ways in which the social, economic, technological, and political dimensions of life" in an *information society* such as the United States are coming to be known. Students will also be able to "describe different ways in which [some of the] social, economic, technological, and political dimensions of life" in an information society such as the United States are being "conducted" (Illinois State University Academic Senate, 1997b, p. 15). The explosive popularity of "on-line" securities trading, for instance, expresses all of these dimensions (Weigel Broadcasting, 1999).

The Changing Role of Mass Communication in the Information Society will also meet Primary Designated Program Objective #10 for *Social Science* Courses in the *Disciplinary Knowledge in Cultural Contexts* Outer Core Course Category, because the course develops students' "acquaintance with the civilizations of the world," particularly with those information societies that are forging an "emerging common civilization . . . of the contemporary world community" (Illinois State University Academic Senate, 1997b, p. 16). By successfully completing the proposed course, students "will be able to":

a. "[I]dentify and critically reflect upon the major institutions, movements, ideas, and values which characterize the past and present culture in the United States.
b. "[I]dentify and critically reflect upon the major institutions, movements, ideas, and values which characterize the past and present of culture in [those] Western cultures" that are transforming into information societies, and, especially,
c. "[I]dentify and critically reflect upon the major institutions, movements, ideas, and values which characterize the past" book and newspaper dominant societies and those which characterize the fewer "present . . . world cultures" in which electronic mass communication dominate.

By studying the invention and diffusion of radio, television, film, and computer communications, students will be able to "identify and critically reflect upon major institutions, movements, ideas, and values" such as the broadcast industries, the idea and value of entertainment, and the computing movement as they have manifested themselves in the United States, other Western cultures, and in those non-Western societies, such as Japan, that are now relying heavily on information technology.

Students who successfully complete *The Changing Role of Mass Communication in the Information Society* will also meet Secondary Designated Program Objective

#10 d for *Social Science* Courses in the *Disciplinary Knowledge in Cultural Contexts* Outer Core Course Category, because they will "investigate [the at least] cross-[sub]cultural issues, including human rights," such as freedom of expression, that have been threatened by worldwide attempts to restrain both mass mediated- and computer-assisted communication.

Students who successfully complete *The Changing Role of Mass Communication in the Information Society* will also meet Secondary Designated Program Objective #10 e for *Social Science* Courses in the *Disciplinary Knowledge in Cultural Contexts* Outer Core Course Category, because they will "discuss events, values, and ideals that [are] contribut[ing] to an emerging world civilization," the information society (Illinois State University Academic Senate, 1997b, p. 16).

WAYS *THE CHANGING ROLE OF MASS COMMUNICATION IN THE INFORMATION SOCIETY* WILL ADDRESS THE PEDAGOGICAL REQUIREMENTS OF GEP COURSES

The proposed course will "ask students to be actively involved in their own learning" (Illinois State University Academic Senate, 1997a, p. 5). Like faculty teaching FOI, faculty who will teach the proposed course will

a. "[S]eek to create a classroom atmosphere which fosters open communication and includes frequent discussions"
b. Often assign students to "work in small groups discussing and attempting to resolve issues raised in the readings."

The Changing Role of Mass Communication in the Information Society will be writing intensive. Students will be expected to write papers that discuss, in a critical way, issues germane to the assessment of the performance of the mass media in preserving democratic institutions. They will also be asked to write micro essays that require them to critically read or view such material as "hi-tech" magazine reports, broadcast news programs, and scholarly articles and to analyze the ideas being expressed. In addition, students will be required to critique each other's work. They will also be expected to write persuasively, preparing letters of support for a legislative position. These letters will be sent to their local senators or to members of Congress. Students will be asked to write collaboratively as part of assigned group projects.

Instructors will guide students through the assigned material in such a way that they can begin to critically evaluate the main arguments and develop their own positions. Classroom activities supporting this goal will include lectures, organized discussions, student-led presentations, guided in-class analysis, and use of micro essay assignments.

In their group projects, students will select a policy issue—for example, whether parents should be required to have technological means to prevent their children from being exposed to certain kinds of content on the Internet. Students will work in groups to prepare a well-argued position, consistent with one of no fewer than five First Amendment theories, for or against a proposal. They will then send the proposal to the U.S. senator or congressperson representing their congressional districts. To help prepare their position paper, students will access scholarly and popular periodical articles, congressional proceedings, government documents, and the like using Internet search engines as well as other search techniques.

Students will also role-play: They will convene a mock broadcast license renewal hearing, with some students representing the FCC commissioners, some the incumbent licensee (the firm operating the TV station whose license is expiring), and others special interest and citizens' groups. Prior to holding the hearing, students will act out their assigned roles by researching a conflict pitting citizens' groups against the incumbent licensee. Students will come to the hearing prepared to defend, or persuade others to adopt, their point of view. Students might also participate in "virtual communities," contacting various Internet sites or newsgroups about issues that arise in the course.

Course approval processes at various colleges and universities may be shaped by institution-specific idiosyncrasies. But my experiences at three higher education institutions persuade me that some issues are common. The next section is intended to help those who wish to propose this course or one like it jump some of the hoops they'll likely have to surmount in order to teach it.

Q & A: FREQUENTLY ASKED COURSE PROPOSAL QUESTIONS

Are courses similar to the proposed course offered at comparable institutions of higher education? Developments in new communication technologies have emerged recently and rapidly, so courses such as this one are not commonly offered at major universities around the country. A few more farsighted communication departments are recognizing the importance of providing majors with a grounding in new communication technologies, and more are adding such courses to their curriculum every year. The proposed course would put Illinois State University (or yours!) and the Department of Communication (or yours!) at the forefront of this trend.

Is the proposed course required or elective? The course is designed as an elective for all communication majors who could also use it, as could all other majors, to partially satisfy the University's Outer Core General Education requirements.

Does the addition of the proposed course affect staffing or other courses in the proposing department? No. The author's department has a tenure-track faculty line with a specialty in communication technologies. This line and others specializing in mass communication law and mass media history would provide the primary staffing for the proposed course.

Does the course overlap or conflict with any course offered in other university departments? No.

The GEP committee at Illinois State concurred with the argument presented in my initial proposal that the proposed course aptly fits into the Disciplinary Knowledge in Cultural Contexts Outer Core Course Category. But, as I have noted, committee members were not convinced that focal issues *The Changing Role of Mass Communication in the Information Society* addresses are matters of the "humanities," as my initial proposal argued, rather than the social sciences, as the GEP defines them. At the committee hearing during which that proposal was reviewed, a committee member (and a humanities department chair) remarked that he "fail[ed] to see how a Supreme Court opinion [in such a case as *Reno v. American Civil Liberties Union* (1997)] could be a humanities." The "mmm-hmm"s and other less verbal signs of assent from other committee members, plus a strong prehearing warning from my department chair to "avoid being perceived as defensive," compelled me to refrain from verbalizing my response to the remark: "Well, what would *you* call the High Court ruling that declared the Communication Decency Act of 1996 unconstitutional, a survey study?" I agreed to revise the proposal in order to explain how the proposed course meets designated program objectives and student outcomes for courses in the *social sciences*, rather than the humanities, in the Disciplinary Knowledge in Cultural Contexts Outer Core Course Category. In academia as in life, you not only have to choose your battles. You also have to know when you're licked.

The committee completed its work in May 1998, and its replacement has not yet formed, let alone called for new or revised proposals. In anticipation of that moment, I have prepared and will present the following (revised) syllabus.

SAMPLE SYLLABUS

The Changing Role of Mass Communication in the Information Society

"Theories [that attempt] to explain the role of the media in the social construction of individual and shared meanings are . . . moving to the forefront of mass communication research."
—Mass communication theorists Melvin L. DeFleur & Sandra J. Ball-Rokeach (1989)

COURSE DESCRIPTION (from catalogue):

COM 2XX The Changing Role of Mass Communication in the Information Society

Prerequisites: Foundations of Inquiry, Language and Composition, Language and Communication

How information technology has changed and may change mass communication products and processes; the impact of such changes on democracy.

INTRODUCTION:

Americans and peoples in other developed nations have been overrun by claims about what has been called "the information society." Critics contend that no current definition of that phrase presents a fundamentally new way of structuring collective human interaction. Some even argue that the information society portends the end of public discourse historically thought to be constitutive of democracy. Information society advocates claim that the new opportunities for accessing and exchanging information that the information society makes possible can preserve, even save, democracy. History reveals that the inventions of the motion picture, radio, television, and cable television called forth similar claims.

The fundamental purposes of *The Changing Role of Mass Communication in the Information Society* are:

1. to describe how the information society *has changed* mass communication and how information technology *may change* mass communication in the future, and
2. to assess the impact of such changes on democracy.

In *The Changing Role of Mass Communication in the Information Society*, you will be encouraged to:

1. think seriously and critically about "the information society" and how that phrase may be defined.
2. define the traditional media of mass communication and consider the multiple and reciprocal relationships between those media and the information society.

   The course will describe and detail the media's historic role as society's information distributor. The historic formation of the "mass" audience and its subsequent fragmentation into multiple audiences and publics with varied and specialized information needs will be discussed.

3. assess the extent to which the information society and the media's role in creating, maintaining, and transforming it have either enlarged or diminished the possibilities for public discourse constitutive of democracy.

How This Course Meets the Designated Program Objectives and Student Outcomes for Courses in the Social Sciences in the Disciplinary Knowledge in Cultural Contexts Outer Core Course Category

The Changing Role of Mass Communication in the Information Society will meet **Primary Designated Program Objective #1 for Social Science Courses in the *Disciplinary Knowledge in Cultural Contexts* Outer Core Course Category**, because it will "focus on the acquisition and application of a common core of knowledge, from the humanities, sciences, and social sciences" (Illinois State University Academic Senate, 1997b, p. 15) in several ways.

In *The Changing Role of Mass Communication in the Information Society* you will build upon your Foundations of Inquiry (FOI) prerequisite by "learn[ing] to become [even] more critical and reflective in the activities of reading, listening to the views of others, and presenting [your] own views" (Illinois State University Academic Senate, 1997a, p. 5).

You will further "develop . . . reasoning skills, by learning to identify the authors['] conclusion[s] and supporting evidence, and evaluating the strength of that evidence." You will build upon your FOI experience as well by undertaking more intensive "research projects, in the library and sometimes in the field," than you were assigned in FOI. In the proposed course, you will add to your FOI experiences of "gathering, analyzing, and evaluating data as evidence" (Illinois State University Academic Senate, 1997a, p. 5).

As a result, you will be able to "recognize the key events, ideas, individuals, and institutions that have shaped the world." Guilliermo Marconi, inventor of radio; David Sarnoff, inventor of television; William Paley, founder of the Columbia Broadcast System; Hollywood's Louis B. Mayer; Microsoft's Bill Gates—and their innovations—will be among "the key events, ideas, individuals, and institutions that have shaped the world" that you will come to "recognize" (Illinois State University Academic Senate, 1997b, p. 15).

The Changing Role of Mass Communication in the Information Society **will build upon the common foundation of interpretive skills you acquired in Foundations of Inquiry and written and oral communication skills you acquired in Language and Composition, and Language and Communication.**

Communication majors who successfully complete *The Changing Role of Mass Communication in the Information Society* will meet **Primary Designated Program Objective #3 for Social Science Courses in the** *Disciplinary Knowledge in Cultural Contexts* **Outer Core Course Category**, because they will "integrate [their] general education" (Illinois State University Academic Senate, 1997b, p. 15) backgrounds in critical thinking, in "gathering, analyzing, and evaluating data," in "defending . . . reason[ed] point[s] of view in extensive writing" (Illinois State University Academic Senate, 1997a, p. 5) and oral presentations *with* their major in Communication through the identification, exploration, and development of common dimensions. As a result, upon successful completion of the course, Communication majors will be able to:

a. "understand how disciplinary knowledge is amplified and enriched by [such] general knowledge" (Illinois State University Academic Senate, 1997b, p. 15) as "gathering, analyzing, and evaluating data" (Illinois State University

Academic Senate, 1997a, p. 5) and "recogniz[ing] the key events, ideas, individuals, and institutions that have shaped the world."

In *The Changing Role of Mass Communication in the Information Society* Communication majors will also be able to:

b. "incorporate those skills developed in general education to activities and course work within [your] majors" (Illinois State University Academic Senate, 1997b, p. 15).

The Changing Role of Mass Communication in the Information Society will meet **Primary Designated Program Objective #7 for Social Science Courses in the** *Disciplinary Knowledge in Cultural Contexts* **Outer Core Course Category**, because the course is designed to develop your ability, regardless of major, "to function as a responsible participant in the social, economic, [and] technological . . . dimensions of life within [your] local, national, and global communities" (Illinois State University Academic Senate, 1997b, p. 15). Again, the course requires you to:

1. think seriously and critically about "the information society" and how that phrase may be defined,
2. define the traditional media of mass communication and consider the multiple "social, economic, technological and political" relationships between those media and the information society (Illinois State University Academic Senate, 1997b, p. 15).

The knowledge the course will present on the historic formation of the "mass" audience and its subsequent fragmentation into multiple audiences with varied and specialized information needs is aimed at deepening your understanding of "social, economic, technological and political" forces that have shaped and continue to shape the mass media and the information society.

And, again, the course will require you to:
3. assess the extent to which the information society and the media's role in creating, maintaining, and transforming it have either enlarged or diminished the possibilities for public discourse constitutive of democracy.

"As a result," the proposed course meets **Primary Designated Program Objective #7a. for Social Science Courses in the** *Disciplinary Knowledge in Cultural Contexts* **Outer Core Course Category**, because those of you who successfully complete *The Changing Role of Mass Communication in the Information Society* will be able to "describe different ways in which the social, economic, technological, and political dimensions of life" in a mass mediated society such as the United States "are known." Students who successfully complete the course will also be

able to "describe different ways in which [some of the] social, economic, technological, and political dimensions of life" in a mass mediated society such as the
United States have been "conducted" (Illinois State University Academic Senate,
1997b, p. 15).

Similarly, students who successfully complete *The Changing Role of Mass
Communication in the Information Society* will be able to "describe different ways
in which the social, economic, technological, and political dimensions of life" in
an *information society* such as the United States are coming to be known. They will
also be able to "describe different ways in which [some of the] social, economic,
technological, and political dimensions of life" in an information society such as
the United States are being "conducted" (Illinois State University Academic Senate,
1997b, p. 15).

The Changing Role of Mass Communication in the Information Society will meet
Primary Designated Program Objective #10 for Social Science Courses in the
Disciplinary Knowledge in Cultural Contexts **Outer Core Course Category**,
because the course aims to develops your "acquaintance with the civilizations of
the world," particularly with those information societies that are forging an "emerging common civilization . . . of the contemporary world community" (Illinois State
University Academic Senate, 1997b, p. 16). By successfully completing the proposed course, you will be able to:

a.   "identify and critically reflect upon the major institutions, movements, ideas,
     and values which characterize the past and present culture in the United
     States.
b.   "identify and critically reflect upon the major institutions, movements, ideas,
     and values which characterize the past and present of culture in [those]
     Western cultures" that are transforming into information societies, and,
     especially,
c.   "identify and critically reflect upon the major institutions, movements, ideas,
     and values which characterize the past" book and newspaper dominant
     societies and those which characterize the fewer "present . . . world cultures"
     (16) in which electronic mass communication dominate.

Students who successfully complete *The Changing Role of Mass Communication
in the Information Society* will also meet Secondary Designated Program Objective
#10e. for Social Science Courses in the *Disciplinary Knowledge in Cultural
Contexts* Outer Core Course Category, because they will

d.   "discuss events, values, and ideals that [are] contribut[ing] to an emerging
     world civilization," the information society.

HOW OBJECTIVES AND OUTCOMES WILL BE ACHIEVED:

You learn and retain more when you are actively engaged in the learning process. Through readings, discussions, and course activities, the course will attempt, in the phrase of one media scholar, to "provide civil defense against media fallout." Some course matter will be presented as a series of dichotomies, or conflicts, that you will not be expected to resolve but be conscious of and sensitized to. Put in question form, among those conflicts are:

1. *The individual vs. society*:
   a. To what extent has the information society enhanced the quality of life for the individual at the expense of the quality of life of the surrounding society?
   b. To what extent has the information society done the opposite?
   c. To what extent have the mass media enhanced the quality of life for the individual at the expense of the quality of life of the surrounding society?
   d. To what extent have the mass media done the opposite?
2. *Commodity vs. public resource*:
   a. Are the products of the mass media best conceived as commodities or public resources?
   b. Which label more accurately captures the products of the information society?
   c. Can information be owned and, if so, who owns it?
3. *Information vs. entertainment*:
   a. Is the information supplied by the information society more accurately characterized as entertainment?
   b. Is the entertainment supplied by the mass media more accurately characterized as information?
   c. Do the historically-grounded distinctions between information vs. entertainment remain useful in the information society?
4. *Mass vs. Class*:
   a. Is the production and transmission of *specialized* content for relatively small groups of consumers, or classes, more characteristic of the information society than of mass communication?
   b. Is the production and transmission of *conventionalized* content for relatively large groups of consumers, or masses, more characteristic of the mass communication than of the information society?
   c. Does the information society portend the eventual eclipse of mass communication?
   d. Because the *channel* of communication shapes the *character* of the communication it carries, do the channels of the information society distribute merely a greater *quantity* of information than the traditional

mass media historically did or, rather, a distinctly different *quality* of information?

e. What are the consequences for public discourse constitutive of democracy if the current trends toward increased specialization continue?

GENERAL EDUCATION ORIENTATION

The Changing Role of Mass Communication in the Information Society is neither an introduction to mass communication course nor a survey of a *facet* of mass communication course. Introduction to mass communication courses expose you to a variety of traditional issues in mass communication and to a variety of methods used to examine those issues. These issues or topics are different in kind depending on the nature of the course. One intermediate-level—or survey of a *facet* of mass communication—course, such as COM 260, "Mass Communication: Cultural Criticism & Problems," focuses on a variety of approaches to issues of meaning in mass communicated texts. COM 360, "Mass Communication: Theory and Effects," exposes students to a variety of ways mass media *effects* can be conceptualized and determined. Still other courses, such as COM 165, "Reporting I," teach students the conventions of that form of mass-communicated storytelling known as journalism.

All of the above-noted courses stand in marked contrast to *The Changing Role of Mass Communication in the Information Society,* which will provide an in-depth analysis and critique of a comparatively far more narrow range of topics. In this course, you will study ways in which the mass communication and information technologies have been affected not only by scientific, or technological, change but by economic, social, and political forces as well.

This *global* educational perspective is designed to engender an understanding and a critical appreciation of democratic values and institutions.

You will "examine the interplay [among] disciplined inquiry" within communication and allied fields, such as history and sociology, "and the larger world" of the information society (Illinois State University Academic Senate, 1997a, p. 15). *The Changing Role of Mass Communication in the Information Society* will also focus on how factors in the context of industrial and postindustrial culture, "such as technological developments, social and political forces" are helping to shape the academic discipline of communication and the knowledge it produces (Illinois State University Academic Senate, 1997a, p. 15).

"Utilizing methodological," if not substantive "knowledge from outside" mass communication, "the discipline being investigated," you will

1. "develop a familiarity with how disciplinary tools," from the disciplines of history and sociology and from plural disciplines within communication, "can shape [such] individual and social practices" as the production of knowledge about the history and possible futures of mass communication;

2. "learn to think critically about the role . . . disciplinary knowledge" can play "in resolving [such] issues of individual and social life" (Illinois State University Academic Senate, 1997a, p. 16). Examples of such issues are:
   (a) In what ways did the invention and spread of broadcast television technology "shape disciplines" of communication "and the knowledge they produced?" and
   (b) In what ways, if any, have the invention and spread of computer-mediated communication, and particularly such technologies as the Internet and the World Wide Web, re-"shaped disciplines" of communication and obsolesce the knowledge they once produced?

READINGS

Dizard, W., Jr. (1994). *Old media/new media: Mass communications in the information age.* New York: Longman.
Jensen, K. B., & Rosengren, K. E. (1990, June). Five traditions in search of the audience. *European Journal of Communication, 5,* 207–238.
Lipsitz, G. (1988, June). "This ain't no sideshow": Historians and media studies. *Critical Studies in Mass Communication, 5,* 147–161.
Turow, J. (1992). *Media systems in society.* New York: Longman. (excerpts)

GRADING BASIS:

Quizzes:[a]   210 POINTS
7 quizzes × 27 [max.] op-scan points = 189
3 "application" essays @ 3 points ea. = 9
3 conventional essays @ 4 points ea. = 12
Group Research Participation:[b]   100 POINTS
Group Research Paper   100 POINTS
Other Class Participation: 40 POINTS
Total   450 POINTS

Note: [a]*Quizzes*: Approximately every other week, starting Week 3, you will take a mostly op-scan quiz. Questions will test your knowledge of the readings *and* class presentations. Each quiz will pose nine (9) op-scan questions, each of which will be worth 3 points.

Three (3) *quizzes* will include the same single essay question:

"Describe how the knowledge to which you've been exposed in this course these past two weeks could be applied in the work *you* wish to do."

You can earn up to *three* (3) *points* for each answer to this question that I view as particularly thoughtful.

At least *three* (3) *quizzes* will include **an essay** question **of variable content**. You can earn up to *four* (4) *points* for correct answers to each one of these essay questions.

Your *lowest* quiz *score* will be *dropped*. If you miss a quiz, a zero will be counted as the dropped score. **It will not be possible to permit make-ups on any quiz.**

ANY MATERIAL DISCUSSED IN CLASS IS TESTABLE UNLESS
OTHERWISE INDICATED.

[b]**The Group Research Participation grade is comprised of grades for "pre-writing" assignments and a peer evaluation by your Group (G) of your** *individual* **contribution to your G Project**. The two *pre-writing* assignments are:

a) *ten* (10) *points* for a bibliography that communicates matter you wish to access in order to compose your Individual Research Paper. Print, audio, video, and Internet sources may be included. And

b) an outline for your proposed Individual Research Paper. That outline will be worth *fifteen* (15) *points*.

Failure to turn in a G assignment on the due date will result in **5 points off** your Group Research Participation grade for the first incident, **10 points** for the second, **15** for the third, etc. "Free riding" on others' work will be severely penalized.

Each G member is required to submit *copies* **of each assignment to** *all* **other members of his/her G. Failure** to meet this requirement will result in **1 point off** your Group Research Participation grade **for each G member not supplied with a copy** *each* time a copy is due (higher with Reports). The Department of Communication cannot defray your copying costs.

Week

1. Introduction: The development of human communication:
    Human communication from the Dawn of Speech to the Discovery of Radio Waves.

2. History, Part II: The development of human communication:
    Wave theory—Analog to digital. Radio, Television, Satellite communication.

3. History: The development of human communication, Part III: The origins of the information age. Cable television and the information highway.

4. Issue Discussion I:
    a. The extent to which the mass media enhanced the quality of life for the individual at the expense of the quality of life of the surrounding society.
    b. The extent to which the mass media did the opposite.

5. Issue Discussion II:
    a. The extent to which the information society has enhanced the quality of life for the individual at the expense of the quality of life of the surrounding society.
    b. The extent to which the information society is doing the opposite.

6. The convergence of mass communication & information technology.

7. Economics of new technologies—tokens for the tollbooths on the information highway.

8. Midterm
9. Issue Discussion III: *Commodity vs. public resource*:
   a. Are the products of the mass media best conceived as commodities or public resources?
   b. Which label more accurately captures the products of the information society?
   c. Can information be owned and, if so, who owns it?
10. Patterns of adoption and diffusion of new technologies.
11. Regulation of new media.
12. Social effects of new technologies.
13. Issue Discussion IV: *Information vs. entertainment*:
   a. Is the information supplied by the information society more accurately characterized as entertainment?
   b. Is the entertainment supplied by the mass media more accurately characterized as information?
   c. Do the historically-grounded distinctions between information vs. entertainment remain useful in the information society?
14. Issue Discussion V: *Mass vs. Class & the Implications for Democracy*:
   a. Is the production and transmission of *specialized* content for relatively small groups of consumers, or classes, more characteristic of the information society than of mass communication?
   b. Is the production and transmission of *conventionalized* content for relatively large groups of consumers, or masses, more characteristic of the mass communication than of the information society?
   c. Does the information society portend the eventual eclipse of mass communication?
   d. Because the *channel* of communication shapes the *character* of the communication it carries, do the channels of the information society distribute merely a greater *quantity* of information than the traditional mass media historically did or, rather, a distinctly different *quality* of information?
   e. What are the consequences for public discourse constitutive of democracy if the current trends toward increased specialization continue?
15. Information technology presentations.
16. Date of the Final Exam TBA.

COURSE BIBLIOGRAPHY

Abramson, J. B., Arterton, C., & Orren, G. (1988). *The electric commonwealth*. New York: Basic Books.
Bagdikian, B. (1987). *Media monopoly*. Boston: Beacon.
Barnouw, E. (1990). *Tube of plenty: The evolution of American television*. London: Oxford University Press.
Bell, D. (1973). *The coming of the post-industrial society*. New York: Basic Books.
Beniger, J. (1986). *The control revolution*. Cambridge, MA: Harvard University Press.

Benjamin, G. (1982). *The communications revolution in politics*. New York: Academy of Political Science.

Berger, A. A. (1991). *Media USA*. New York: Longman.

Besen, S. (1984). *Misregulating television: Network dominance and the FCC*. Chicago: University of Chicago Press.

Brand, S. (1988). *The media lab: Inventing the future at MIT*. New York: Penguin Books.

Brown, R. D. (1989) *Knowledge is power: The diffusion of information in early America*. London: Oxford University Press.

Crandall, R. W. (1991). *After the breakup: U.S. telecommunications in a more competitive era*. Washington, DC: The Brookings Institution.

Dahlgren, P., & Sparks, C. (1992). *Journalism and popular culture*. Thousand Oaks, CA: Sage.

DeSonne, M. (1990). *Spectrum of new broadcast/media technologies*. Washington, DC: National Association of Broadcasters.

Dizard, W. P. (1989). *The coming of the information age*. New York: Longman.

Dutton, W., Blumler, J., & Kraemer, K. (1987). *Wired cities: Shaping the future of communications*. Boston: G.K. Hall.

Egan, B. L. (1991). *Information superhighways: The economics of advanced public communication networks*. Norwood, MA: Artech House.

Eisenstein, E. (1980). *The printing press as an agent for change*. London: Cambridge University Press.

Ellul, J. (1964). *The technological society*. New York: Knopf.

Ellul, J. (1968). *Propaganda*. New York: Knopf.

Gumpert, G. (1987). *Talking tombstones and other tales of the media age*. London: Oxford University Press.

Horowitz, I. L. (1991). *Communicating ideas: The politics of publishing in a post-industrial society*. New Brunswick, NJ: Transaction.

Innis, H. (1972). *Empire and communications*. Toronto: University of Toronto Press.

Kellner, D. (1990). *Television and the crisis of democracy*. Boulder, CO: Westview.

Lippman, W. (1922). *Public opinion*. New York: Harcourt, Brace.

Marvin, C. (1988). *When old technologies were new*. London: Oxford University Press.

Masuda, Y. (1980). *The information society as post-industrial society*. Tokyo: Institute for the Information Society.

McLuhan, M. (1962). *The Gutenberg galaxy*. Toronto: University of Toronto Press.

Mosco, V., & Wasco, J. (1988). *The political economy of information*. Madison: University of Wisconsin Press.

Neuman, W. R. (1992). *The future of the mass audience*. London: Cambridge University Press.

Postman, N., & Powers, S. (1992). *How to watch tv news*. London: Penguin.

Real, M. R. (1989). *Supermedia*. Thousand Oaks, CA: Sage.

Slack, J. D., & Fejes, F. (1987). *The ideology of the information age*. Norwood, NJ: Ablex.

Smith, A. (1980). *The geopolitics of information*. London: Oxford University Press.

Sussman, L. (1990). *Power, the press and the technology of freedom: The coming age of ISDN*. Lanham, MD: University Press of America.

Traber, M. (1988). *The myth of the information revolution: Social and ethical implications of information technology*. Thousand Oaks, CA: Sage.

Turow, J. (1992). *Media systems in society*. New York: Longman.

REFERENCES

American Civil Liberties Union, et al. v. Reno. (1996). Online. Available: http://www.aclu.org/court/cda-com2.html (April 14, 1997).

Berger, A. A. (1991). *Media USA*. New York: Longman.

Berger, J. (1972). *Ways of seeing*. London: Penguin & British Broadcasting Corp.

Boyer, E. L. (1987). *College: The undergraduate experience in America*. New York: Harper & Row.

Brown, R. D. (1989). *Knowledge is power: The diffusion of information in early America*. London: Oxford University Press.

Carey, J. W. (1985). Overcoming resistance to cultural studies. *Mass Communication Review Yearbook, 5*, 27–39.

Chambers, I. (1985). *Urban rhythms: Popular music and popular culture*. New York: St. Martin's.

Crandall, R. W. (1991). *After the breakup: U.S. telecommunications in a more competitive era*. Washington, DC: The Brookings Institution.

DeFleur, M. L., & Ball-Rokeach, S. (1989). *Theories of mass communication* (5th ed.). New York: Longman.

Dizard, W. P. (1989). *The coming of the information age*. New York: Longman.

Dizard, W., Jr. (1994). *Old media/new media: Mass communications in the information age*. New York: Longman.

Dowlding, W. J. (1989). *Beatlesongs*. New York: Simon & Schuster.

Egan, B. L. (1991). *Information superhighways: The economics of advanced public communication networks*. Norwood, MA: Artech House.

Emerson, T. I. (1970). *The system of freedom of expression*. New York: Random House.

Gaff, J. G. (1983). *General education today: A critical analysis of controversies, practices, and reform*. San Francisco: Jossey–Bass.

Giroux, H. (1987). Critical literacy and student experience: Donald Graves' approach to literacy. *Language Arts, 64*, 175–181.

Horowitz, I. L. (1991). *Communicating ideas: The politics of publishing in a post-industrial society*. New Brunswick, NJ: Transaction.

Illinois State University. (1997, Fall). General education reform: Ahead of the national curve. *Illinois State Today, 32*(1), 1–3.

Illinois State University Academic Senate. (1991, March 13). Philosophy of university studies. Available: http://orathost.cfa.istu.edu/pic/ (February 1, 1998).

Illinois State University Academic Senate. (1997a, March 5). *A new general education program for Illinois State University*. Normal: Illinois State University.

Illinois State University Academic Senate. (1997b, December 3). A writing aid for course proposals prepared for the new general education program (outer core). Normal: Illinois State University.

Jacklin, P. (1978, Spring). Representative diversity. *Journal of Communication, 28*(2), 85–88.

Jensen, K. B., & Rosengren, K. E. (1990, June). Five traditions in search of the audience. *European Journal of Communication, 5*, 207–238.

Kuhn, T. S. (1970). *The structure of scientific revolutions*. Chicago: University of Chicago Press.

Lipsitz, G. (1988, June). "This ain't no sideshow": Historians and media studies. *Critical Studies in Mass Communication, 5*, 147–161.

MacGregor, B., & Morrison, D. E. (1995). From focus groups to editing groups: A new method of reception analysis. *Media, Culture & Society, 17*, 141–150.

Masuda, Y. (1980). *The information society as post-industrial society*. Tokyo: Institute for the Information Society.

Mosco, V., & Wasco, J. (1988). *The political economy of information*. Madison: University of Wisconsin Press.

Nieberg, H. L. (1984, Fall). Structure of the American public. *Journal of American Culture, 7*(4), 50–51.

Pietila, V., Malberg, T., & Nordenstreng, K. (1990, June). Theoretic convergences and constraints: A view from Finland. *European Journal of Communication, 5*, 165–185.

Rosovsky, H. (1990). *The university: An owner's manual*. New York: Norton.

Rushing, J. H. (1986). Mythic evolution of the "New Frontier" in mass mediated rhetoric. *Critical Studies in Mass Communication, 3*, 265–296.

Semali, L., & Watts Pailliotet, A. (1995). *Prospectus for Intermediality: Teaching critical media literacy*. Unpublished manuscript.

Semali, L., & Watts Pailliotet, A. (1999a). *Intermediality: Teaching critical media literacy.* Boulder, CO: Westview.

Semali, L., & Watts Pailliotet, A. (1999b). Introduction: What is intermediality and why study it in U.S. classrooms? In L. Semali & A. Watts Pailliotet (Eds.), *Intermediality: Teaching critical media literacy* (pp. 1–29). Boulder, CO: Westview.

Slack, J. D., & Fejes, F. (1987). *The ideology of the information age.* Norwood, NJ: Ablex.

Sussman, L. (1990). *Power, the press and the technology of freedom: The coming age of ISDN.* Lanham, MD: University Press of America.

Tedford, T. L. (1993). *Freedom of speech in the United States* (2nd ed.). New York: McGraw–Hill.

Traber, M. (1988). *The myth of the information revolution: Social and ethical implications of information technology.* Thousand Oaks, CA: Sage.

Weigel Broadcasting (Producer). (1999, March 8). *Stock market observer* [Television program]. Chicago: WCIU, Channel 26.

Wolfe, A. S. (1985, Fall). Reward systems in popular music: Rock as industrial output in the fifties, sixties, and now. *Onetwothreefour: A Rock 'n' Roll Quarterly, 1*(2), 35–52.

Wolfe, A. S. (1999). A late-'60s leftie's lessons in media literacy: A collaborative learning group project for a mass communication course. In L. Semali & A. Watts Pailliotet (Eds.), *Intermediality: Teaching critical media literacy* (pp. 97–128). Boulder, CO: Westview.

Wolfe, A. S., & Haefner, M. J. (1996). Taste cultures, culture classes, affective alliances, and popular music reception: Theory, methodology and an application to a Beatles' song. *Popular Music and Society, 20*(4), 127–155.

Wolfe, A. S., & Kapoor, S. (1996). The Matsushita takeover of MCA: A critical, materialist, historical, and First Amendment view. *Journal of Media Economics, 9*(4), 1–21.

Wolfe, A. S., Miller, C., & O'Donnell, H. (1999). On the enduring popularity of Cream's 'Sunshine Of Your Love': Sonic synecdoche of the 'Psychedelic '60s.' *Popular Music, 18*(2), 259–276.

INTEGRATING STANDARDS IN K–5 MEDIA LITERACY

Lyn Lacy

The school year 1998–99 in Minneapolis Public Schools (MPS) started off as usual with a districtwide Staff Development Day for all employees downtown at the convention center. We had messages from our superintendent, two guest speakers, presidents of the teachers' union and principals' forum. Then, without warning or any introduction whatsoever, a live band began to belt out a medley, the last song of which was the Three Dog Night hit from 1971, "Joy To The World." The chorus was changed to a rousing chant, "Standards for the world/Standards for the students in MPS/We expect the best!"

The surprising—and darned good—little rock-and-roll band was made up of half a dozen well-known members of our Teacher and Instructional Services (TIS). Over-the-hill employees like me who remember the days of "Jeremiah was a bullfrog"—as well as disco, Earth Day, smiley faces, and the first VCRs—rose to our feet, laughing and singing and clapping along. Remaining seated were most of our younger colleagues, stoic, unmoved, their sidelong glances saying, "What IS this song? And why are these guys dancing?"

Another school year had begun.

Advances in Reading/Language Research, Volume 7, pages 219–275.
Copyright © 2000 by JAI Press Inc.
All rights of reproduction in any form reserved.
ISBN: 0-7623-0264-X

How could we have guessed that within a few short weeks we would elect a governor—former "bad guy" wrestler-turned-actor and radio talk-show host Jesse Ventura—whose performance at his inauguration party could top a Three Dog Night reprise? At his "People's Celebration," our new state leader wore a Jimi Hendrix T-shirt, buckskin jacket, bandana, and earrings, and joined Warren Zevon on stage to sing "Werewolves of London." As I watched on TV, I admit wondering, "What IS this song? And why are these guys dancing?" as 4 years of Jesse "Our-Governor-Can-Beat-Up-Your-Governor" Ventura began. He expressed it himself after his inauguration speech at the state capitol with the battle cry from his days as a Navy SEAL—"Hoo Yah!"

A few days later, the Commentary page of our Twin Cities newspaper, *Star Tribune*, ran an essay by a guy who "never attended a Star Trek convention" but explained convincingly anyway that Jesse is in fact a Klingon. The writer concluded that perhaps the prologue for this governor's term should read "Minnesota—the frozen frontier. These are the voyageurs of the Ventura administration, their four-year mission to Bodily go where no state has gone before. . . . Thank the stars we didn't elect Xena" (Swalm, 1999, p. A19).

The afternoon after Jesse's inauguration party, our Vikings—the highest scoring team in the history of the NFL—lost their bid for the Super Bowl in overtime on home turf to the Atlanta Falcons. A few days later, I took the photo below on the way home from work. It appears that, after wailing and beating our breasts, we resilient Minnesotans were expected to shrug it off. After all (battle cry!) we still have Jesse.

Returning for a moment to Jeremiah Bullfrog, I guess, as with other things in the 1960s and 1970s, you had to have been there. Those of us who were there then—and were there teaching and writing curriculum—loved the dejà vu inspired by our little TIS band last fall, and I don't mean just revisiting a good friend of mine. Not only have we been there, designing instruction over several decades, we are still here and are still writing curriculum.

In the 1960s, we wrote what learners needed to know and called them "behavioral objectives." In the 1970s, they became "competency goals" and we wrote them again, and in the 1980s, "exit outcomes," rewritten. Changes in semantics and definitions have been accompanied by curriculum refinements that reflected each decade, much of which thankfully remain into the 1990s—the first widespread inclusion of thinking skills comes to mind, as do real-world, authentic tasks (sometimes called "survival skills"), cooperative learning, whole brain learning, open education, interdisciplinary studies, and the baby steps of multiculturalism.

The birth of media literacy in this country was even earlier—critical viewing skills began showing up in the 1950s—and it too has seen changes in nomenclature and definition. The National Telemedia Council (NTC), founded in 1953 in Madison, Wisconsin, was the earliest nationwide organization that recognized the electronic media as a powerful form of expression to be studied with children. Media literacy was described by NTC as an expanded view of traditional literacy—

Figure 1. One way to look at the Vikings' lost bid for Super Bowl Sunday was to go ice fishing instead, as exhibited by a sign in the photo
above—"Hoo Yah!" (we still have Jesse). However, proving the adage
that a coded message is ineffective when you don't know the code, fifth-
grade Keewaydin students misinterpreted the sign to mean (1) no Vikings are allowed inside the bait and tackle store because (2) the store is
owned by Green Bay Packer fans and (3) "Hoo Yah" must be a mistaken
inversion of "Yahoo." Once students were told the date the photo was
taken (a few days after the team's loss to the Falcons) and background of
a battle cry of the Navy SEALs (branch of the Armed Forces in which
Jesse served), they could "identify contextual clues and inference for
meaning behind a media message," a fifth-grade IMT expectation in media literacy, and could "understand particular cultural and historical contexts," a media arts expectation in media literacy at the fifth grade.

critically viewing and then producing visual messages was equal in importance to critically reading and then writing or critically listening and then speaking.

As a newly hired elementary media specialist in the early 1970s, I found NTC materials, like the "Look—Listen—Think" program, that offered me ways to empower elementary students to analyze and interpret what they see, hear, think, and feel. Into the 1980s, classroom activities in NTC's "Teacher Idea Exchange" were useful also, like a news game, video letters by Larry Johnson of MPS, checklists for political ads, and guidelines for family viewing.

Over the years, Action for Children's Television in Newtonville, Massachusetts, also worked to upgrade television for children and eliminate commercialism from children's TV. Center for Media Literacy in Los Angeles has a long history as a clearinghouse for teacher training and valuable materials, including theme-related books and information packets like "What Is Media Literacy?" The New Mexico Media Literacy Project is now five years old and in addition to providing training and materials, is in the process of developing a scope and sequence/standards framework for K–12 media literacy as a guide for teachers and administrators.

The National PTA joins with the National Cable Television Association and Cable in the Classroom each year to sponsor "National Critical Viewing Day" with suggested special events and PSA scripts to place special focus on media literacy. The Twin Cities newspaper *Star Tribune* offers "Learning Works" programs and products in its Newspaper In Education project, like "Close Encounters of the Comic Kind" and "Reading Realities." These organizations have provided me invaluable guidance and teaching ideas as media literacy instruction grows increasingly sophisticated.

Today, elementary media programs such as mine in MPS have expanded their instructional responsibilities to include computers, interactive multimedia, telecommunications, and emerging technologies in addition to the books, newspapers, magazines, movies, still photography, audio, and video we have taught in the past. It is no secret among most of the elementary Information Media and Technology (IMT) specialists I know that to achieve a balanced program among all of these forms of media is not easy, especially in elementary schools where we usually see students only once a week for a 55-minute class (providing contractual preparation time for classroom teachers).

Ever since personal computers were introduced in our elementary schools in the late 1970s, hardware and software advancements have come at an accelerated pace, and students' acquisition of computer skills increasingly requires more and more time for them on task in the media center. Administrators, classroom teachers, and resource personnel in the building also rely on us to be computer experts in addition to other duties of maintaining the media center and its instructional program. I am not alone in feeling that trying to keep up with computers has become a formidable task often performed to the neglect of print and film/video.

As the school year rolled around in 1998, I vowed once again to try to reinstate a balance in my instruction among the three forms of information media and technology—print, computer, and film/video—in other words, to return to what I consider to be the true meaning of literacy. After so many years involved with curriculum development, I was hopeful that standards-based reform envisioned by Minnesota's Department of Children, Families and Learning (CFL) was going to support my plans better than any of my previous efforts.

STANDARDS AND MEDIA LITERACY

Many of us who have been designing instruction over several decades are indeed still here—only this time, it's called standards, a new term replacing the objectives, competencies, and outcomes we were writing in the past. In 1994, responding to concerns documented in the "Nation at Risk" report, the *Goals 2000: Educate America Act* made standards-based reform national policy. Dramatic differences exist between these standards and our past efforts in curriculum development, and these differences directly influence how media literacy may now be incorporated into a school's curriculum. Because of the way our standards in Minnesota are presently written, I believe that media literacy can have a firmer toehold than ever before in public school curricula.

One influential difference from earlier movements is that creating standards has been nationwide, involving not only educators, parents, and community members as before but additionally the President, governors of all 50 states, legislators, and leaders of big business representing employers. This broad-based approach, with input from so many quarters, has meant that the movement itself has changed over time.

For instance, standards began as requirements solely focused on academics in the core disciplines of English, math, science, and social studies, and for some standards experts and for some states that remains the goal. However, by mid-1996, subjects covered at the national level had expanded to include the arts, foreign languages, and communications, which included not only new areas of speaking and listening but also media literacy. Standards in several states, including Minnesota, began to be written across this broader base for students headed for the 21st century, because public groups as well as educators demanded that it happen.

Input from such a wide array of interested parties meant that the standards movement in many states like mine did not become a move back to basics. As the executive director of our Association of Metropolitan School Districts said in 1995, his fear was that "we'd end up with a couple of basic-skills tests and . . . minimum competencies. For that to be the cornerstone of our education system in this state, with its reputation for good education, I think, is misguided" (Mallander, 1995, p. A1).

Another difference from the past is that standards exhibit two interwoven parts, content standards (what students are to know and be able to do) and performance standards (how well learners demonstrate their fulfillment of the content standards). These two aspects reflect the best research about teaching and learning, including

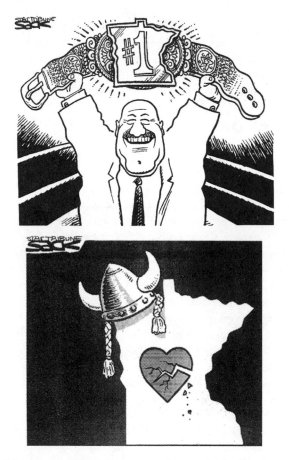

Figures 2 and 3. Two editorial cartoons by Steve Sack appeared within a week of each other in the Twin Cities *Star Tribune* newspaper. Both were wordless, and they each made use of symbols which Keewaydin Community School fourth and fifth graders were asked to interpret. In one, Jesse Ventura holds up a wrestling belt with "#1" on the outline of Minnesota after his inauguration as governor, and in the other, a Vikings' helmet is hung up on the corner of the state with a broken heart after the NFL defeat by the Falcons. No better examples than these needed to be found for young Vikings' and Jesse Fans to fulfill IMT expectations in standards-based lessons about media literacy: "identify symbols or devices used in a persuasive message" and "identify the main idea and inference." When students were asked to cover up the belt on one cartoon and the helmet on the other, they came up with other things Jesse could be holding up (his opponents) and other events that "broke the heart" of Minnesotans (Hubert Humphrey's death). Reprinted with permission, *Star Tribune*, Minneapolis.

what we know about different kinds of literacies, different ways of knowing, and nonlinear versus linear thinking. Since students today no longer rely solely for learning and doing on pen and paper but also on computers and camcorders, meaningful standards in states around the country include concepts and skills in media literacy. However, this emphasis on performance and more than one way of learning is still controversial with many parents, because it is simply not the way they learned when they went to school. "Take, for example," wrote a disgruntled reporter, "the insistence on using fuzzy-sounding names, such as 'inquiry', 'decision-making' and 'number sense'" (Draper, 1999, p. B1).

A third difference is that standards written today are also to be internationally competitive or "world" standards comparable to what students in high-achieving countries are expected to master. In the area of media literacy, Canada, Australia, and Great Britain lead the world with their national curricula and predetermined courses of study. Since the United States has no nationwide curriculum, our national standards instead set competency goals or statements of desired results that establish frameworks for states and districts to follow. These standards are deliberately broad statements about areas of content, expectations for student experience, and levels of student achievement, leaving philosophies, implementation methods, and points of view to states, districts, and teachers. One unhappy result is that across the nation, media literacy may indeed be incorporated but in an uneven manner from state to state.

At the national level, however, standards have been put in place which identify specific learning competencies and processes for evaluation in the areas of media and information literacy. The International Reading Association and National Council for Teachers of English have identified for the English Language Arts standards which include the use of nonprint media and technology. The American Association of School Librarians and Association for Educational Communications and Technology, both of the American Library Association, have written Information Literacy Standards for Student Learning as well as a guide describing standards which are the foundation stones of media literacy. For example, the first three standards that define a student who is information literate read together like the definition of a media literate: "accesses information [add media] efficiently and effectively," "evaluates information critically and competently," and "uses information accurately and creatively" (ALA, 1998, p. 4).

The National Communication Association (formerly Speech Communication Association) has re-released its Speaking, Listening, and Media Literacy Standards for K–12 Education which provide a set of guidelines for state and local educators to use in designing their own curriculum and assessment plans to improve communication. The International Society for Technology in Education has begun work on Technology Foundation Standards for pre-K–12 students that include domains outlining basic proficiency in use of technology; social, ethical, and societal issues related to technology; and use of productivity, communication, research, and problem-solving/decision-making tools. A standard in the National Health Education Standards states that students will analyze the influence of culture, media, technology, and other factors on health. The National Standards for Arts Education document, however, regrettably does not include Media Arts as one of its content areas.

In standards documents from several states, media literacy is interwoven throughout many different learning areas, such as Library Arts; English Language Arts; The Arts; Inquiry and Read, Listen, View. For example, Washington has established State Essential Learnings in communication, writing, and the arts, with media literacy implied in several contexts. Massachusetts has a Media Strand in which standards set the expectation that students will become effective users of electronic media. The Oregon Information Literacy Guidelines are related to English, Media and Technology. Within the English Language Arts standards of Texas, Viewing/Representing is included for Grades 4–12 and encompasses media interpretation, analysis, and production now required in all English classes. Utah includes media literacy inside the English Language Arts core for secondary education and inside Library Arts for its elementary students. North Carolina released standards related to Visual Literacy or the ability to comprehend, evaluate, and compose visual messages as well as translate from visual to verbal and vice versa.

MEDIA LITERACY IN MINNESOTA'S HIGH STANDARDS

As in other states, media literacy in Minnesota is not considered a separate standard, but rather it appears in most of the state's High Standards or what is called the Profile of Learning, a set of challenging standards for students in addition to basic requirements in reading, writing, and math. These standards stress practical skills and call for a shift from textbooks and lectures to experimental projects and teamwork. Rather than articulating standards in subject areas, the Profile categorizes ten types of learning below—like Inquiry and Resource Management—which are needed for students to achieve five comprehensive goals of Purposeful Thinker, Effective Communicator, Self-Directed Learner, Productive Group Participant, and Responsible Citizen (CFL, 1997).

A suburban school board member has said, " I believe the Profile is one of the best things to happen to Minnesota education in a long time . . . not just because business and post secondary schools want higher levels of student achievement—but because these high expectations will better prepare our children for the world they will live in" (Rummel, 1998, p. A19). In addition to high school standards, a series of preparatory standards are for primary, intermediate, and middle grades. The italics below are mine to indicate emphases placed on media literacy in my paraphrasings for seven of the High Standards:

- Read, Listen, *View*: A student shall demonstrate comprehension of literal meaning through *viewing nonfiction and fiction* selections; and shall interpret and evaluate information such as effects of *persuasive visual messages.*

- Write and Speak: A student shall demonstrate *public speaking strategies and techniques* (and) shall demonstrate *effective communication skills.*
- Literature and the Arts: A student shall demonstrate the ability to communicate ideas effectively through *at least three different media and techniques.*
- Inquiry: A student shall demonstrate the ability to gather information from *electronic media, print, interviews, and other sources.*
- People and Cultures: A student shall describe *how technology has changed the lives of people in the home, at work,* in transportation, and *communication.*
- Decision Making: A student shall *use information to . . . make healthy choices* in real or simulated situations.
- Resource Management: A student shall *use computer software* (graphics, word processing, and basic desktop publishing techniques) *to access information and produce products.*

Of particular note about the Read, Listen, View standard is that Technology Specialist Mary Dalbotten of CFL has convened a task force of a dozen high school teachers charged with the design of statewide tenth-grade assessments in listening and viewing to complement the assessment in reading. Facilitator for the View component of the standard is Karon Sherarts, Twin Cities media arts educator, and David Considine of the Media Studies Department at Appalachia State University in North Carolina serves as the national expert for critical viewing skills.

Also important is Minnesota's inclusion of Visual or Media Arts in standards for Literature and the Arts, with the following examples in media literacy:

- Artistic Creativity, Performance and Expression (Primary):
  —Use *appropriate tools and processes* of at least three different media to communicate ideas.
  —Use elements of visual/*media arts* to communicate ideas.
- Artistic Creativity, Performance and Expression (Intermediate):
  —Communicate ideas effectively through *at least three different media and techniques.*
  —Describe selected works of art in terms of the elements and principles of visual/*media art.*
- Creative Technology (High School):
  —Know *contemporary technological principles, concepts, and tools.*
  —Know legal, environmental, and ethical *issues concerning production.*
  —Apply technology to create an *original, complex production* that meets quality standards of performance, *broadcast,* publication, business, or industry.
  —Demonstrate an advanced level of *technological skill.*
  —Communicate effectively to accomplish the creative purpose for *target audience.*

—Apply principles of *media aesthetics.*
—Analyze how images both *convey information and persuade.*

Three areas of learning in the Profile that are not as specifically related to media literacy for elementary students are Mathematical Applications, Applied Scientific Methods, and World Languages. However, in Math, Science, Inquiry, and Write and Speak, high school students are to complete an application of technology.

My own curricular planning for kindergarten through fifth grades evolves from the media literacy concepts in the High Standards from CFL. My school district labels areas and organizes standards differently, but concepts at the local level are in alignment with the state and thus, as I will show later in this chapter, my individual school's media literacy program refers directly to MPS standards and ultimately to Minnesota's High Standards as well.

CFL also mandated that teachers use Performance Packages, which are lengthy and prescriptive units with assessment tools (perhaps better called performance assessments of the content standards). Many Packages were written by CFL and Minnesota teachers as examples, and they may also be written and approved at a district level (MPS has just begun to provide training in developing Packages for district approval). A suburban curriculum director who has presented the Profile and Packages to many diverse groups, including representatives of business and industry, said that "this is indeed a major retooling of education of exactly the sort we need as a state and nation" (Partridge, 1998, p. A19).

Only a few Packages from CFL for kindergarten through Grade 5 directly address media literacy. For example, at the primary level one Package involves watching TV news, another analyzes fact and fiction, and two others analyze book illustrations and author/illustrators. At the intermediate level is analysis of media technology, photographic observation, and expert interviewing. However, teachers are reminded always to teach to the standard, not to the Package, and tasks and products in all Packages may be changed to lend themselves to media literacy. Some tasks or products might become videotaped interviews, collections of photographs, scripts written from different perspectives, comparisons of movie and TV genres, domestic comedies rewritten, or graphic designing for Home Pages.

At this writing in winter 1999, after more than 10 years of planning and only 5 months of implementation, Minnesota's Profile of Learning has been declared seriously flawed by some teachers, parents, and legislators. In January the state's teachers union conducted a poll of its members in which only 30% supported the Profile and, after other alarming and discouraging reports from teachers, union co-presidents called for immediate halt to full implementation of the Profile and suspension of the state mandate to use Performance Packages (*Minnesota Educator*, p. 1). Recently, more than 900 parents and teachers met at a suburban church for a daylong conference called "an all-out assault" on the Profile, "most of them united by fears that it will change education in ways they don't want to see" (Draper, 1999, p. B1).

Figures 4–6. A "frame of mind" advertising campaign in the *Star Tribune* is comprised of a dozen informal portraits of columnists, feature writers, and reporters posed with a picture frame and sometimes props as clues to their individual journalistic perspective. These excellent visual metaphors help third-, fourth-, and fifth-grade Keewaydin students with IMT expectations such as "analyze the concept of viewpoint" and "identify techniques used to create point of view." They also help students "differentiate among news articles, opinions and features," which is an English language arts fourth-grade media literacy expectation. One observation by fifth graders is that the ad campaign should use a variety of picture frame styles rather than one that always looks the same—after all, they say, "Aren't the writers supposed to have *different* frames of mind?" Reprinted with permission, *Star Tribune*, Minneapolis.

Figure 5.

Finally, the House of Representatives voted 92–35 on February 11 to "replace the fledgling system with one grounded in basics and local control. . . . The Senate, which has yet to take up the matter, also is expected to advocate repairing the practical-skills-based system of learning" (Lonetree, 1999a, p. B1).

Repair rather than repeal of the Profile is the desire of some of us in Minnesota. Repairs are needed regarding record-keeping in Packages; a preponderance of standards at middle and high school levels; the scarcity of time, tools, and training teachers have had for implementation; and the lack of practical ways to address standards for special-needs students (such as 8600 English Language Learners in

More good sports stories than you can shake a stick at.

PAT REUSSE ON SPORTS, EVERY TUESDAY, THURSDAY, SATURDAY AND SUNDAY.

You've always enjoyed sports. But you've never enjoyed it like this: lively, entertaining commentary from the true master of sports storytelling, Pat Reusse. Timely and relevant, Pat's column always gives you more than the score. And as with all Star Tribune columnists, you can turn to Pat for insight, opinion, and a new angle for your frame of mind.

StarTribune
It's where you live.

For home delivery, call (612) 673-4343 or 1-800-775-4344.

Figure 6.

MPS who speak 80 different languages). Lt. Governor Mae Schunk, a former St. Paul schoolteacher, believes the Profile "should be preserved as a means of preparing students for a changing, competitive society. . . . But the show-what-you-know schools initiative received only a tepid endorsement from the governor himself, who said that to 'throw it out . . . [would be] a great waste of time and effort.' If legislators decide to 'scrap it, they scrap it,' he said" (Lonetree, 1999, pp. B1, B3).

However the Profile is altered, MPS remains committed to a standards-based system and continues to move forward with implementation (Vana, 1999, p. 1). In a published letter to Governor Ventura, MPS Graduate Standards Coordinator Bev

Lillquist wrote, "We believe that standards need to guide our instruction, be embedded in our curriculum and be measured by our assessments" (Lillquist, 1999). She offered recommendations from the district's school- , parent-, and community-based Implementation Committee: Keep ten learning areas in the Profile but integrate them somewhat to reduce the number of standards, eliminate state Packages and replace them with locally developed performance assessments, provide for local recordkeeping, eliminate a high-stakes eleventh grade test, and establish strategies for students who fail to meet graduation requirements.

MEDIA LITERACY IN MINNESOTA'S FACS

An important document in the state's media literacy movement is the Minnesota Frameworks for Arts Curriculum Strategies (FACS), a supplement to the state's Literature and the Arts standards. The FACS project, funded by a U.S. Department of Education grant, was a joint project of CFL, Minnesota Center for Arts Education, Minnesota Alliance for Arts in Education, and Minnesota State Arts Board. The FACS document is used statewide to develop and implement curriculum for students to meet state standards in Dance, Literary Arts, Music, Theater, Visual Arts, and Media Arts.

The FACS definition of Media Arts is "the study of human communication through film, photography, video, audio, computer/digital arts, and interactive media. Creatively, students employ the elements of space, time, light, motion, color, and sound to express their perspectives, feelings, and ideas. Critically, they learn to interpret and evaluate media within aesthetic, cultural, and historical contexts to become more enlightened consumers and effective citizens" (FACS, 1996, p. 1).

The FACS Media Arts writing team constructed these guidelines:

- Students explore, generate, and develop ideas and feelings through creating media productions.
- Students apply the media arts genres and their aesthetics to media productions.
- Students employ skills and techniques of a chosen medium.
- Students collaborate effectively in group media production and presentation.
- Students acquire knowledge of the genres, techniques, and aesthetics in the media arts.
- Students utilize critical thinking skills in the study of media messages.
- Students demonstrate understanding and respect for personal, cultural, and historical contexts and the effects of media in shaping and extending human communication.
- Students experience presenting the media arts to a wider community.
- Students demonstrate the ability to actively participate as a discriminating consumer of the media arts to maintain a healthy media environment.
- Student demonstrate the skills to become self-directed lifelong learners in the media arts.

The team was led by Nancy Norwood, media arts instructor at the Lola and Rudy Perpich Minnesota Center for Arts Education, who has developed a comprehensive 2-year standards-based production curriculum for the arts high school that is truly state-of-the-media-arts. Her Level 1 units offer experiences for students to meet

Figure 7. Books, trumpet, and computer surround a boy with a friendly smile and waving hand. Using *Kid Art* stamps for *Kid Pix Studio* software, fifth-grader Caleb adopts the *Star Tribune*'s "Frame of Mind" theme to fulfill a grade-level expectation in media Arts: "use subjects, themes and symbols to communicate intended meaning" about how he sees himself. Pizzas, cola cans, puppies, rainbows, skateboards, sports equipment, and motorcycles are the most popular icons in computer creations by other fifth graders. Sometimes boys at this age opt for threatening portrayals of macho violence—flames, skulls, or a big eyeball.

state standards by applying media arts forms, such as Basic Black and White Photography, Location Photography, Experimental Photographic Techniques, Photography Book with Creative Writing, Digital Photography, Computer Design and Animation, Experimental Video, Film Narrative with Sound Collage, and Video Documentary. Level 2 units offer standards-based experiences in Film Animation, Film History, Screenwriting for Film, Alternative Photographic Process, Exhibition, Portrait Photography, Performance Video, Color Digital Photography, Public Service Announcement, and compilation of a student portfolio for the two levels. In both levels, Norwood teaches history of photography, book design and computer graphics, radio, video art, avant-garde cinema, film critiques, documentary film and video, screenplays, and the historical evolution of portraiture.

I served on the FACS team as writer of the kindergarten through fourth-grade expectations for the guidelines above, such as sequencing pictures, using the basic media elements and techniques, collaborating in group production, distinguishing among types of media arts forms and media genres, relating media messages to daily life, and analyzing the mass media's influence on society and the individual. Much of my media literacy program today is based on concepts I learned while working for a stimulating year with Norwood and the rest of the FACS Media Arts team, Diane Remington, Ron Rogosheske, and John Schott. For instance, one of Norwood's student production ideas I have used with great results in fifth grade is the creation of television crossovers, in which students must analyze content and design of two genres and then script one of them (such as content of a weather forecast) using the design of the other (such as a music video). To do one, they must know two.

"ROUND ONE" OF MPS CONTENT STANDARDS

In fall 1995, MPS introduced content standards for English Language Arts (Reading and Writing), Fine Arts, Social Studies, Mathematics, and Science, all of which are aligned with the Minnesota standards. To provide additional direction for teaching and learning, the district also developed grade-level expectations. Integration of media literacy expectations from the following three of these standards is one goal of my media program, which I will describe later in this chapter:

1. English Language Arts (Reading and Writing): Regrettably, listening and viewing in the state's Read, Listen, View standard are not included for primary and intermediate grades in the district's English Language Arts standards. However, the MPS document about reading and writing has a few media literacy expectations for primary students: collecting information from videos, arranging pictures in a logical sequence, labeling objects, writing captions for pictures, and a story for pictures arranged in order. In intermediate grades, student expectations in media literacy are using media sources, presenting findings in more than one form (written, visual, oral), comparing objectivity in two news accounts of the same controversial event, and writing a video script, a sketch of a favorite TV character,

a jingle for a commercial, an examination of bias in a news story, a movie review, an opinion for a school newspaper, and an editorial on a current issue. More tasks will be added in this chapter for reading and writing from the new Houghton Mifflin reading series, to be discussed later.

2. Fine Arts: The MPS Fine Arts document includes standards in Media Arts that are basically organized and worded the same as in the FACS document written at the state level. However, the district omits one from FACS that expects students "to acquire knowledge of the genres, techniques and aesthetics in the media arts." Embedded elsewhere in the MPS Fine Arts document are most of the sub-standards in media literacy from the FACS document. Grade-level expectations have not been written yet by teachers in MPS for Media Arts, so I have used the state Literature and the Arts as well as the FACS document for my planning.

3. Social Studies: An important MPS Social Studies media literacy standard to note is for Grade 9: Students become informed consumers by understanding the techniques producers use to sell products. Regarding the elementary level, I am still in the process of deciding how to integrate—rather than compartmentalize as totally separate units of study—the following standards related to media literacy (except the last one, which is already included in my planning):

- Students identify and describe ways in which science and technology have changed and will continue to change the lives of children and their families.
- Students describe and analyze the effects of changing technologies on the local, national, and global community.
- Students seek reasonable and ethical solutions to problems that arise when scientific and technological advancements and social norms or values come into conflict.
- Students demonstrate proficiency at using available technology in school, community, and global settings; students analyze the implications of inequities in availability of technology resources and instruction.
- Students use critical thinking skills when interpreting information.

"ROUND TWO" OF MPS CONTENT STANDARDS

In fall 1996, MPS standards were introduced in five more areas: Health Education; Information Media and Technology; Physical Education; Technology Education; and World Languages. An integration of media literacy standards from the first two with the English Language Arts, Fine Arts, and (next year) Social Studies standards outlined earlier describes my plan for creating a standards-based media program.

1. Health Education: Three of the six MPS Health Education standards include media literacy:
    - Health and Consumer Information: Students access and analyze information about products and services that promote healthy life (example: analyze the effects of advertising on personal health choices).

- Health Promotion and Disease Prevention: Students understand concepts related to health promotion and disease prevention (example:
  classify violent and nonviolent TV).
- Influences (Media/Peers/Culture): Students analyze the influence of
  culture, media, technology, and other factors on health, personal, and
  family relationships (example: evaluate the idealized body image and
  elite performance levels portrayed by the media and the influence on a young
  adult's self-concept, goal-setting, and health decisions).

2. Information and Media Technology (IMT) Content Standards: In MPS media
literacy is the most comprehensively addressed in the IMT standards, and the
grade-level expectations (see Appendix) are specifically what I use for curriculum
development at my school. The preface to these standards defines media literacy as
"the ability to access, analyze, evaluate, and produce communication in a variety
of forms. To achieve this goal, the IMT standards set forth the principles of media
ethics, equal access to information, critical thinking skills for processing information, and flexibility in use of tools and techniques for presenting or reporting to
diverse audiences" (IMT Content Standards, p. 1).

Throughout each of five broad standards and their sub-standards is an interwoven
"strand" of concepts in media literacy, which I include below with age-level
focuses:

- IMT Ethics: Students demonstrate understanding of rights, responsibilities,
  ethics, and equality of use of IMT (ages 5–18).
  —Demonstrate responsibilities and encourage responsible actions by all people in appropriate and equitable use of IMT (ages 5–18).
  —Understand copyright and abide by legal restrictions on copying and using
  copyrighted works (ages 5–18).
  —Compare and evaluate quantity and quality of information in available
  media about diverse cultures (ages 5–9)/Evaluate effects on diverse
  cultures of cultural exclusiveness in IMT (ages 9–14)/Communicate
  with producers of IMT concerning cultural exclusiveness in their work.
  —Participate in schoolwide/community planning for equitable access to IMT
  (ages 5A–18).
- IMT Accessing: Students locate, access, and use IMT to suit various purposes (ages 5–18).
  —Compare and contrast types of print fiction and nonfiction (ages 5–18).
  —Identify print and nonprint IMT about same topic (ages 5–9)/ Compare
  types of nonprint (ages 9–14)/Compare and contrast types of print and
  nonprint media crossovers (ages 14–18).
  —Use and compare features of print and nonprint IMT (ages 5–18).
  —Use a variety of technologies for educational purposes, multicultural awareness, enjoyment, and appreciation (ages 5–18).

—Identify available IMT at home, in the community, nationally, and internationally, and connect accessing skills used at school with skills used elsewhere (ages 5–18).

- IMT Processing: Students research study topics, and analyze content and design of a variety of resources, including the mass media, which reflect/influence diverse perspectives (ages 5–18).

    —Analyze real, realistic, and unreal content from various viewpoints (ages 5–9)/Compare and contrast information with real-life situations (ages 9–14)/Recognize diverse points of view or purposes (ages 14–18).

    —Recognize works by author, illustrator, nonprint media creator (ages 5–9)/Identify and evaluate the role and perspective of the author (ages 9–14)/Interpret purpose or cultural perspective of the author (ages 14–18).

    —Recognize main idea, details, sequencing, cause and effect, inference in content (ages 5–9)/Recognize differences between facts and opinions in content (ages 9–14)/Recognize propaganda and other persuasive approaches in content (ages 14–18).

    —Compare the same topic from a variety of cultural perspectives (ages 5–9)/Evaluate similarities and differences in news reports and reporting techniques from various perspectives (ages 9–14)/Evaluate how amount and type of information can distort perceptions of an event (ages 14–18).

    —Interpret influence of audio in nonprint IMT (ages 5–9)/Analyze influence of editing in print and nonprint IMT (ages 9–14)/Relate script, soundtrack, and visuals to the purpose in nonprint IMT (ages 14–18).

    —Interpret influence of visuals and special features in print IMT (ages 5–9)/Interpret influence of visuals in nonprint IMT (ages 9–14)/Interpret commercial influences on creation of IMT (ages 14–18).

    —Identify contributions to IMT by many people in various cultures throughout history (ages 5–18).

    —Establish criteria to distinguish best IMT to suit purposes (ages 5–18).

    —Evaluate impact of time spent daily on mass media and entertainment technologies (ages 5–9)/Analyze advantages and limitations of mass media (ages 9–14)/Evaluate power of mass media to create opinion about various cultures (ages 14–18).

    —Recognize motive and appeal of persuasive mass media messages (ages 5–9)/Interpret inferences of words, visuals, and sounds in mass media and evaluate impact on various cultures (ages 9–14)/Analyze long-range effects of mass media messages on diverse cultures (ages 14–18).

- IMT Reporting, Presenting, and Exhibiting: Students plan a report, presentation, or exhibition that takes into account how diverse audiences may receive the information (ages 5–18).

    —Work cooperatively, develop a presentation plan, and select a mode of delivery that suits an intended audience and takes into account cultural similarities and differences (ages 5–18).

—Select various forms of print and nonprint IMT that fit content (ages 5–18).

—Demonstrate sensitivity to cultural similarities and differences when selecting verbal and nonverbal presentation techniques (ages 5–18).

—Demonstrate technical skills necessary to report in more than one form of technology to reach diverse audiences and learning styles (ages 5–18).

—Develop revision strategies and develop criteria from diverse perspectives (ages 5–18).

• Digital IMT: Students use information digital technology applications to access, process, and report (ages 5–18).

—Use computer, video, and audio to create multimedia presentations (ages 5–18).

—Operate word processing, graphic, telecommunications, and presentation software (ages 5–18).

—Program computer operations to create interactive projects (ages 5–18).

The standards document from the Media Technology (MT) department has been a work in progress since 1996 under the directorship of Kay Sack and Coleen Kosloski. It provides direction for the district's media programs. An overview of the MT department's supportive 20-year advocacy for media literacy curricula is instructive at this point, because such a history places the development of today's standards and media programs into perspective. As I felt at the beginning of the school year when we were singing "Jeremiah was a bullfrog," I now take pleasure in applauding the impact of some other old but very worthwhile documents.

DEVELOPMENT OF K–5 MEDIA LITERACY CURRICULA IN MPS

The group process for curriculum development is the process of choice in MPS, with dynamic results. Our district's curricula have been written by teachers themselves, and the evolution of our media curricular efforts over 20 years is no exception. Many media specialists have been involved in these efforts, and I am proud to be one of them, proud of being a member of the team. I am also a published writer and, as such, am often off on my own time writing about topics dear to my heart, like kids, children's books, and video. For this chapter, I have been asked to write not only about our group process of media literacy curriculum development in MPS but also to give my own personal experiences and points of view as one teacher of and writer about kids and the media. My hope is that I have fulfilled my assignment well enough for the reader to recognize the strong, supportive group environment in MPS that exists behind the individual endeavors I have been asked to mention here.

Revisiting our group history in media literacy curriculum development is instructive to see just how long ago we began our effort and far we have come together since then as a profession in MPS. Our curriculum reflects our historic roles in the

Figure 8. "Speculate about what may have been Left Out," "Interpret the Main Idea and Inference," and "Identify Motives and Appeals of Different Types of Ads" are third-grade IMT media literacy expectations, and a classified ad campaign by the *Star Tribune* again offers fine visual metaphors for these concepts, as in the example above. In English language arts, third graders are also expected to "Understand Ideas Not Explicitly Stated," and in health education they are expected to "Identify Techniques (i.e., humor) Used to Sell Products." The students' favorite follow-up to a study of these ads is to create frozen poses of their own, and the ads also segue nicely into video editing. Reprinted with permission, *Star Tribune*, Minneapolis.

schools as primary providers of library/media skills for students and, in most elementary schools, as providers of preparation time for classroom teachers. As such, most of my elementary media colleagues and I provide 55 minutes of instruction for every classroom at least once a week without the room's teacher present. We think of our media centers as classrooms or learning laboratories, where students explore all that is to be found in information centers and prepare themselves for the public library resources in the outside world. The most recent revision of our job description as IMT Specialists includes program administrator, instructional collaborator with teachers, information specialist in support of the school curriculum, computer instructor, and teacher of IMT skills for students and staff. The last jobs on the list are the reason why my friend and IMT colleague Rosemary Carlson suggested in the 1970s that we should write a scope and sequence of a media curriculum.

The first MPS Elementary Media Curriculum was written in 1979 and included Visual Literacy as one of eight competency goals. For this eighth goal, the curriculum writing team devised expectations in Visual Recognition (use of details, body language, colors, and so on), Critical Discrimination (interpreting style, type, intent), and Production of Visual Messages (which were defined as "visual actions, objects and symbols natural or man-made which the student encounters in his/her environment"; Elementary Media Curriculum, 1979). Directed and guided by Gladys Sheehan, then director of the MT department, I chaired this four-member writing team, with members Carlson, Sue Krueger (now Sue Sandstede), and Pat Schumacher. We each wrote about 20 grade-level lesson plans intended to enable students to achieve one of the competency goals. For the Visual Literacy goal, I wrote lessons about still visuals (differences among photos, drawings, and diagrams, uses of symbols and colors in illustrations). Sandstede was already writing television literacy curriculum, and her video lessons about camera angles and storyboarding were the first TV lessons I had seen that fit within my time constraints seeing students only once a week. Combining Sandstede's lessons with NTC's "Look–Listen–Think" material began my enthusiasm for teaching and learning about film/video.

One ambitious production project I remember for Mickey Mouse's 50th birthday (Lacy, 1978) was to organize my two classes of fifth graders at Laura Ingalls Wilder School into the seven departments then typically found in a production studio, in this case an animation studio. The departments were story editors, animators, background artists, photographers, sound engineers, public relations people, and projectionists, and once a week over several weeks, students created everything needed for a schoolwide premiere of an original 3-minute Super 8 cartoon. Along the way, they experienced the behind-the-scenes necessities related to mounting a production but sad to say, only one student of all those involved reported to me years later that he continued to study animation through high school.

Another favorite movie-and-book unit (Lacy, 1980) from the late 1970s was a comparison of the movie *Star Wars* with the book/movie *The Wizard of Oz*. Twenty years ago, Wilder's students and I discovered three dozen similarities between the two stories in our study of classic fantasy literature and science fiction. From this analysis, the fifth graders generalized ideas about characters, setting, and plot to create an outline called "What Makes A Good Story?" that they used for book reports and movie/television reviews. Needless to say, I have already started plans to revive parts of this unit when Lucas' *The Phantom Menace* is released on May 21, 1999.

Back in 1985, the Elementary Media Curriculum was expanded to include middle and high school and was revised by Sheehan, Sack, and Kosloski as the K–12 Information Technology Curriculum with learner outcomes based on critical thinking skills of Knowledge, Application, Analysis, Synthesis, and Evaluation. Additional lessons were contributed by over a dozen media specialists in Audio Technology, Video Technology, Photography, Computers, even Robotics and Teleconferencing. The district was going through a serious technological transition at this time, and many of us in MPS elementary media centers were confused about our changing role from print and film/video specialist to computer specialist. In addition, not all schools had budgets for the new technology, so the MT department circulated hardware, software, kits of materials with lesson plans, and yes, even TOPO the robot, to those of us who were struggling with the new direction our profession was going.

The next year, the Minnesota State Department of Education published its *Model Learner Outcomes for Media and Technology* (Dalbotten, 1986) to aid in the formulation of local media goals and objectives across the state. Visual and media literacy skills were for the first time included as "strands" throughout Information Accessing, Processing, and Reporting. This interweaving of media literacy throughout a scope and sequence was reflected in a 1987 rewriting of our district's media curriculum by Sheehan, Kosloski, Sandstede, Jean Doolittle, Norma Anderson, Sandra Clarke, and Renea Roach.

This "strand" approach was far more dramatic for many of us who taught elementary media in the 1980s than it may seem at first glance, for it validated what we desired for students—a balance among the old and new technologies in our media centers. At the time, media forms were considered more or less as discrete subjects for study; our lesson plans and units were too compartmentalized and lopsided in favor of whatever was new and trendy—an example was my own animation-studio experience at the fifth grade. When only one student was interested in pursuing a study of animation, I began to question whether spending a quarter of the school year making a 3-minute Super 8 cartoon was a life skill my students needed. (Perhaps "Mickey Mouse" described my project only too well.) I was determined not to spend an inordinate amount of time with TOPO, fun as he was.

Then, in the mid-1980s, according to both state and district curriculum documents, Information Accessing meant understanding *equally* all of the different forms of media; Information Processing required *equal* analysis and evaluation of all media messages; and Information Reporting encouraged student communication using all media forms *equally*. With the time constraints of weekly media classes, this meant finding ways to connect, combine, integrate instruction about the forms of media, rather than separating them. As a result, students and I began to make more connections among books, film, TV, and even robotics, instead of isolating each as its separate unit of study.

For instance, in a chapter "Visual Literacy, Children, and Picture Books," I presented a rationale for applying fine art criticism to Caldecott Award-winning picture books to foster visual and media literacy: "Generally speaking, the basic skills that need to be taught for evaluation of visual material are: to distinguish between reality and unreality, to appreciate use of details that contribute to the whole, to identify unique properties of the medium used, and to understand the main idea intended by the visual message. . . . Most children today can learn these concepts quickly because they are visually oriented due to the amount of time spent watching television" (Lacy, 1986, pp. 1–2). Indeed, the idea for media literacy through appreciation of the Caldecotts had come from my staff and students, when first-grade teacher Mary Gilbertson advised me to "give them the best" in my media

Figure 9. Periodically during the school year, Keewaydin kindergart-ners, first and second graders are confronted with "TV as a Guest in Our Homes" when they come to media classes. Students freely explore what this "guest" has to offer them—entertainment, information, opinion, and advertising, in video clips or with the camcorder hooked up to the TV. This leads to discussions about why they watch what they watch, adults' versus children's programming, reality versus fantasy, and other topics in their grade-level expectations for IMT, media arts, health education, and English language arts standards. Older students also enjoy coming up with other metaphors for TV—as babysitter, as magic carpet, as win-dow, as mirror.

classes and students themselves were saying, "Look. This picture book is just like a cartoon" or "I figured out the story in this wordless book all by myself."

The MT department funded publication of several projects to help MPS media specialists teach about television, such as *Children and Television: Critical Viewing Skills* (1985, 1988) and *Video Production with Kids* (1987, 1990), both written by Clarke and Sandstede. Sandstede also continued to contribute exemplary television units like "News Coverage: Predicting Cause and Effect," "Fact and Opinion," "The 5 'W' Questions: Commercials," and her own master's dissertation which used video clips to test students on television advertising techniques. Another publication was *Visual Education: An Interdisciplinary Approach for Students K–12 Using Visuals of All Kinds* (MPS,1987), in which I outlined goals and objectives and presented critical and creative thinking questions used already in the fine arts:

- "What do you see?" (Identification)
- "How is it put together?" (Analysis)
- "Why is it as it is?" (Interpretation)
- "How successful is it?" (Evaluation)
- "Can you make one?" (Production)

Eight forms of visual media were described in the book with their potential uses in the classroom—live action, objects, print graphics, visual fine arts, film, video, computer graphics, and holography/emerging technologies. A decade later, I still use the same questions as an approach to visual information—with exciting results now with digital photography and other computerized special effects.

In 1987 Cooper Elementary School, where I was IMT specialist, received a district grant to pilot a program in visual awareness and thinking skills called "Look, Think, Act" (a name inspired by the NTC "Look, Listen, Think" materials I had used for over a decade). In the school's yearlong program, students in kindergarten through third grade were offered a variety of visual experiences outlined in *Visual Education* to help them become better critical analyzers of visual messages and to encourage them to imagine and produce better visual projects. Cooper students made connections among visual messages not only found in video, picture-book art, and computers but also in dance, theater, body language, color-coded music, cartoons, architecture, storytelling, musical instruments, and holograms. Students also produced their own original work—such as a video of the alphabet featuring toys found at a department store—with help from artists-in-residence like Norwood, mentioned earlier as FACS writing team leader, who was then teaching media arts at a local organization, Film In The Cities.

Adults as well as the children at Cooper learned a great deal that year about the impact of visual imagery on our lives. For several years afterward the school hosted touring exhibitions from the University of Minnesota Art Museum, after which Cooper students' own visual responses were exhibited at a public event to demonstrate what students had learned. While teaching at Cooper, I also became an educator facilitator for the Discovery Networks, conducting workshops for teachers in the use of television in the classroom. I consulted with the Networks about the need for television literacy, and the company designed its "Know TV" program for students about analyzing documentaries. During a yearlong Teacher Fellowship from the American Council of Learned Societies, I also constructed a visual education program featuring auditory and visual cues to prompt children as participants in storytelling.

Media literacy as an interwoven "strand" in information accessing, processing, and reporting remained in a 1991 revision of the IMT curriculum. Another "strand" throughout curriculum writing by MPS media specialists has always been to foster awareness and appreciation of multiculturalism as a media literacy skill. For example, I worked with the Indian Education and MT departments to produce a staff-development videotape, "Indian Stereotypes in Children's Books" (Lacy, 1988), to demonstrate how visual clichés of Native Americans are the result of many insensitive images over time not only in movies but also in children's picture books.

In 1991 Native stereotyping achieved national attention with the sports mascot debate during the World Series. Fans of the Atlanta Braves fans arrived with their "Tomahawk Chop" to play the Minnesota Twins at the Minneapolis Metrodome and were bemused and angry to find protesters demanding "Stop the Chop! The Chop stops here!" The mascot issue as media illiteracy as well as cultural illiteracy is explored fully in *Imagine That: Developing Critical Thinking and Critical Viewing Through Children's Literature* (Considine, Haley, & Lacey, 1994, pp. 175–183), as are distorted media views of diverse cultures that diminish us all by their perpetuation of "isms" ("tokenism," "classism," and so on) and "PWADs" ("People Who Are Different").

Elsewhere in the book is presented student experiences at Cooper using mechanical or "pop-up" books as a connection to animation, special effects, and interactive media (pp. 107–122). In a study of action verbs, some third graders made "animated" books in which paper objects "popped" up, out, over, or around according to actions described in a simplified rendering of *Little Red Riding Hood*. Other students re-created illustrations from picture books as three-dimensional scenes to demonstrate Considine and Haley's "5P Approach to Analyzing Pictures: Point of View, Position, Proportion, Posture and Props" (pp. 61–74), parts of the "visual language of the picture book [that] is related to other visual media, including advertising, motion pictures, and television" (p. 60). Caldecott Award-winner Haley visited Cooper and showed students how she used this visual language to create her exemplary picture books.

In 1993, the MPS K–6 Student Progress Report included media literacy for the first time as an expected competency in media education: "The student uses critical viewing skills for television and other media." This is the only known instance in the nation of media literacy on an elementary report card and was accomplished, after input from IMT specialists, by Doolittle, our representative on a task force assigned to revise the specialists' Progress Report.

To grade this new line on the Progress Report, I presented six concepts that I use in a 10-page booklet entitled "About TV: What Do You Know About, Think About, Do About Television?" (1994). The concepts are intentionally worded simply for youngsters, but the adult dialogue starters that accompany the concepts encourage sophisticated appreciation of television:

- Use tools of TV and video. (What are tools that allow you to control what you watch on TV as well as when and how you watch it? How do they influence your viewing? What are your rights and responsibilities regarding use of these tools?)
- Define mass media. (How are mass media outlets different from two-way communication like talking on the telephone? What would you say if you could interact with messages in the mass media?)

Figure 10. After studying television commercials that feature celebrities endorsing products, fourth grader Kyle Chooses clip art, speech balloons, and word processing using *ClarisWorks for Kids* software to create the ad above that offers his interpretation of *Jurassic Park* meets *King Kong* to promote the school store. In an exercise intended to help students "Identify the Influence of Culture on Text" (fourth-grade media literacy expectation in English language arts) and "Analyze the Influence of Visuals Used in Advertising" (IMT fourth-grade expectation in media literacy), other ads created by students feature "celebrities" in clip art such as the American presidents, Santa Claus, the Taco Bell Chihuahua, an astronaut, planet Earth, and the Easter Bunny who all think the school store is cool.

- Analyze the impact of TV on daily life. (How do you describe your TV viewing habits? What kind of target audience are you? What type of TV user are you? What positive and negative effects does TV have on you personally?)
- Contrast some types of TV messages. (How are types of TV programs and ads alike and different? Why are they produced? Who are they for?)
- Interpret some TV production techniques. (Who constructs TV programs and ads? How? Why? Who for?)
- Produce a video message. (What do you have to say to others? How and why do you want to say it? What do you need? Who is your audience? How effective are you?)

The booklet offers suggestions for lessons, products, and grading, as well as a brief dictionary for students of common TV terms categorized under a few simple concepts in media education—"TV Is A Mass Medium (Interested In Making Money)," "TV Targets Audiences (With Value Messages)," "TV Offers Variety (Which Are Constructions of Reality)," "TV Is Teamwork (Performed By Various People)," and "TV Has A Language (With Techniques That Can Be De-Constructed)."

To aid in marking the Progress Report, a checklist for a whole class is used during media instruction to indicate how well individual students (1) contribute to a discussion (declarative knowledge) and (2) contribute to a process or product (procedural knowledge). Progress Reports are in the process of being rewritten to reflect standards in the school district, and media literacy is expected to remain in some form on the IMT report to families.

IMT STANDARDS DEVELOPMENT IN MPS

Today's IMT standards document with its "strand" in media literacy is the direct result of the role the MT department and IMT specialists in MPS have played in media curriculum development. When reform of standards was federally mandated, the MT department once again took the lead, conducting in 1995 a series of monthly discussions with a 30-member IMT Content Advisory Committee comprised of parents, students, teachers, principals, media specialists, computer teachers, and members of the community, business sector, and higher education. The Committee worked in small groups, with at least one member in every group from each of the noneducator areas, and input about what these members wanted for their children, graduates, and employees was most instructive to MPS educators. In addition to knowledge of the media, they expressed the most interest in demonstration by students of inquiry skills, problem-solving skills, multimedia communication skills, and collaborative group skills.

Also in fall 1995, two focus discussions were held to gather input for the standards process from all of the district's media specialists. From that large group of over 100 professionals, 14 media specialists volunteered to serve as a writing team representing primary, intermediate, middle, and high school media programs. Team members were Sack, Kosloski, Clarke, Doolittle, Jesness, Margaret Axt, Diane Wallace-Reid, Frank Dewey, Juanita James, Nancy Fowler, Barb Risken, Coreen Blau, Lisa Finsness, and myself. We worked throughout winter and spring 1996 to produce the first draft of the standards document, meeting periodically after school in the district's computer lab. Some of the standards were written by the entire team, while others were written by small groups, usually pairs of us working on each of the five broad standards.

In fall 1996, all media specialists K–12 met in small study groups to react to these standards. The common responses to the standards as a whole were that the content was appropriate for the age levels. However, the wording at the time was not teacher- or parent-friendly, such as excessive use of "multicultural" (which had been my overzealous addition in every other sentence throughout the document). The team rewrote a preface in which broad goals were explained (including multiculturalism) and subject-specific terminology was defined for the lay reader.

Each IMT specialist joined a study group for one of the five standards, and on a student release day the groups brainstormed grade-level expectations. The expectations were compiled as a databank organized by grade level and at MT meetings throughout the rest of the school year, we suggested sample activities and strategies that would help students fulfill standards at those grade levels. Reactions to these meetings were generally positive, with colleagues reporting that they appreciated the opportunity to suggest activities they were already doing with students as well as suggesting what students should be doing at grade levels below their own. By August 1997 both the revised IMT standards and K–9 grade-level expectations with examples of activities were in place for designing standards-based media programs in the district.

The members of the IMT standards writing team were joined in fall 1997 by 10 other IMT specialists who wanted to write or adapt existing grade-level curriculum units that would teach to the standards. A template was designed using *Filemaker Pro 4.0v1* as a format. These units would be activities and strategies rather than Performance Packages, since MPS was still in the process of establishing guidelines for the writing and adoption of packages.

Three members of this curriculum writing team met together throughout winter 1997–98 to specifically devise units in media literacy: myself (for Grades K–1), Sandstede (for Grades 2–3), and Doolittle (for Grades 4–5). We used many resources, such as Level 5 of *Techworks: A Program That Integrates Technology Skills into the Curriculum* (Teacher Created Materials, 1997), which had been purchased by the MT department for every elementary media center in the district, and our own publications from the past. In addition, I had gleaned from the grade-level databank those expectations that I felt applied to media literacy—and added some from my booklet "About TV"—making a list of K–5 expectations (see Appendix) that gave direction for the units I wrote. For instance, I reprised primary units I had written in 1994 about use of TV tools, one-way versus two-way communication, home viewing habits, types of TV programs, and TV as a "guest in our homes" (see Figure 9).

The media literacy units, as well as others written by members of the IMT curriculum writing team, were distributed to IMT specialists for implementation at staff development training in May and September 1998. Also in fall 1998, K–9 grade-level expectations were updated to correlate with the scope and sequence of skills from *TechWorks*. Starting in fall 1998, Wallace-Reid became the IMT Curriculum Standards Specialist, coordinating the implementation of IMT standards, grade-level expectations, and assessments districtwide. She works with all IMT specialists to develop delivery models for standards, curriculum units, activities, and technological documentation of student work.

As it has for a quarter of a century, the MT department again today gives support, guidance, and direction as we work together to build a standards-based media literacy program at Keewaydin Community School, where I now teach.

KEEWAYDIN COMMUNITY SCHOOL

Keewaydin is located in a small red-brick building in a modest neighborhood of post-WWII bungalows in southeast Minneapolis, not far from the famed Minnehaha Falls in Longfellow's poem "Song of Hiawatha." "Keewaydin" is the Ojibway's word for "home wind," the wind that propelled Hiawatha off into the sunset in his canoe as he said farewell at the end of the bard's epic.

Many things in this part of the city are named after Longfellow and his characters or ideas, even though the poet never visited Minnesota and he mixed up Lake Superior Ojibway legends about Nanabozho with heroic accounts of the Iroquois leader Hiawatha on the east coast. One street that leads to Keewaydin is Nokomis Avenue, named after Nanabozho's grandmother, and in this city of beautiful lakes, both Lake Nokomis and Hiawatha Lake are just blocks away, fed by Minnehaha Creek that meanders alongside Minnehaha Parkway before it spills over Minnehaha Falls.

The area is richly redundant with such historic place names.

The neighborhood is primarily residential, and is in transition, with younger families moving in as seniors retire and move elsewhere. Keewaydin was designated as a community school in 1995, which means it serves families in the immediate area and reflects their needs and interests. Registration is guaranteed to students who live in the neighborhood, and students outside the area are bused to the school. Keewaydin has 355 students in High 5 through fifth grade. Racial demographics include 22% African American, 3% American Indian, 28% Asian American, 44% European American, and 3% Hispanic American.

The school is a site for English Language Learners, serving 106 Hmong-speaking students, and seven other non-English languages are also spoken. We have two special education classrooms, a PALS/SIMS (Program for Academic and Language Services/Systematic Instructional Management Strategies) with 15 students, and

SPEN (Special Program for Elementary Needs) with 10 students. Free and reduced lunch eligibility is 58%. Over the 2-year period from 1996 through 1997, the number of continuously enrolled students was 148 and the turnover rate was consistent at 33%.

The student environment in a community school like Keewaydin consists of children placed in graded classrooms by age level. For some instructional purposes, groups may be made by achievement levels from children in more than one classroom. Team teaching or other cooperative arrangements may also be utilized during the school year. Students spend most of their time in subject activities scheduled by the teacher, with the help of resource teachers and educational assistants. Students participate weekly in areas of visual arts, music, physical education, and IMT, each of which is taught by a specialist in that area.

THE MEDIA CENTER AT KEEWAYDIN

Almost 20 years ago, Keewaydin's old two-story building underwent a unique renovation—a 3700-square-foot media center was built in the only space available, down two flights of stairs in a huge, high-ceilinged basement area that had been the warming house for an ice-skating rink in the neighborhood park.

Two decades have seen many changes in this large media center. Today it provides space for library bookshelves, multicultural displays, and professional materials; tables and chairs for IMT classes, staff, and community meetings; and three computer labs of 20–25 locally networked PowerMacs each. Two of the labs are for the Computer Curriculum Corporation (CCC) daily program in individualized computer-assisted instruction, one for primary students and one for intermediate. The third lab is the IMT facility for student and staff word processing, reference, curriculum support, and graphics creation. The media labs and computers elsewhere in the building are in the process of being networked with a hub at our closest high school, but for now only one PowerMac in the center is online, severely limiting all that can be taught and learned using such a resource.

As many as 75 students at a time may be found working in the media center, arriving and departing on a staggered schedule so that traffic jams are not a problem on the stairs up to the first floor. The media center also provides office space for the school social worker; the Title I lead teacher; the Special Education Resource Teacher; an educational assistant who is transportation director as well as coordinator for the two CCC labs; a half-time technical assistant; and me, the IMT Specialist. I do not have or want an office, frankly preferring the view from my "desk" on a 3-foot-high, freestanding bookshelf.

I conduct large-group instruction in Keewaydin's media center at least once a week for each of the school's 17 classrooms. Students in Grades 1 through 5 usually have 20 minutes of instruction and 35 minutes for book selection and computer or video practice or assignments. High 5 and kindergarten students have 30 minutes of media class, usually spent on one topic at a time each week. I also conduct

30-minute keyboarding units for fourth- and fifth-grade classrooms. I am available to team teach with teachers when they schedule additional use of the computer lab, and small groups will in the future be scheduled to work with me in a video studio.

The principal Don Genereux and I began to plan a video production studio in fall 1998 in a room that had been at various times a teachers' work area and the art room. Not an ideal space for production, it is open to the rest of the media center, has a door leading to the engineers' office, and is near two bathrooms. The low-ceilinged little alcove is only 300 square feet, is shelved on two walls, and on one side has a counter with cupboards and two sinks as the only thing separating it from the walkway to the bathrooms. The cabinet for the computer network was recently installed on the fourth wall, occupying precious space. Despite these spatial and acoustical drawbacks, the area will become a studio where up to six students at a time may work.

We plan for small groups of students to videotape other students' reports and projects in media literacy, sometimes narrowcasting the productions over our

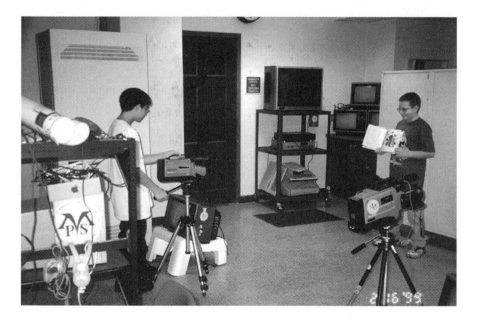

Figure 11. This small space affectionately known as "the cave" is in the process of becoming Keewaydin's video studio. Funds from the PTA, school budget, and a business partner are being put together to purchase a computer video-editing station, video and audio mixers, dolly, industrial-grade vcrs, monitors, microphones, and a video blue backdrop. Until the studio is ready, students work elsewhere in the media center and around the school with a camcorder, both hand-held and on a tripod.

schoolwide cable system. Intermediate students will also be trained in hand-held camera work and have videotaping assignments around the school and community. An ambitious project planned for fifth graders is to storyboard, create graphics, and tape a map-study tour of all of the neighborhood sites named after those characters and ideas in "Song of Hiawatha."

THE MEDIA PROGRAM AT KEEWAYDIN

My goal for an elementary media program has been to provide a balance of education in print materials; computer skills and applications; and film/video analysis and production at progressive levels of sophistication for students with a wide range of ages and abilities. More specifically, my media literacy objectives are:

- To raise students' awareness of a need for balance in their uses of three forms of media resources: print, computers, and film/video
- To identify what is alike and different among the three forms of media resources
- To understand the strengths and limitations of unique properties, conventions, and formal features of each form of media
- To differentiate among fantasy and reality; fact and opinion; unreal, realistic, and real content in media resources
- To recognize various effects used by creators of media resources to entice us as consumers of information and entertainment
- To understand how all forms of media influence our feelings about and knowledge of ourselves, society, and relationships with others and to identify subtle, as well as obvious, messages in all forms of media
- To explore the implications of freedom of the press, freedom of speech, freedom of expression, and freedom of access to information and the responsibilities attendant to those freedoms

When I explained to colleagues at Keewaydin that balance was my primary goal for students this year, fellow teacher Sue Larsen loaned me an antique brass balance scale which I began using immediately as a teaching aid the first weeks of school. Even though lessons were devoted to orientation and the use of applications in our new computer lab, students were required to pour beans on one side of the scale to represent minutes spent at computers and on the other side, they were asked to balance the scale with beans representing criteria for good book selection (i.e., fits their reading levels and interests or classroom assignment).

For later lessons during the rest of the year, I planned that we would balance the scale in a variety of ways to represent minutes students spent involved in activities at home: reading books versus watching videos or playing Nintendo; playing outside versus TV or computers; playing computer games versus word processing or creating original graphics; watching fantasy versus reality on TV.

At different grade levels, I made some of the following other connections the first weeks of school among books, computers, and film/video:

- Ads from magazines and newspapers that use computer language—"Back To School @ Dayton's," "www.elcome to Fall Savings!"—were analyzed by fifth graders, who then created graphics and their own back-to-school captions using *ClarisWorks for Kids* (Claris) software for such media crossovers.
- Computer software menus and our lab's management system were introduced to all grades by comparing and contrasting them to TV guides and tables of contents in various books.
- All grades contrasted CD-ROMs that include video clips and animations to photographs and graphic art in print volumes.
- Connections were shown between new TV programs—*Anatole, Franklin, Dumb Bunnies, Animorphs*—and the children's books they are based on. First graders watched clips I had taped from these shows and discussed such questions as:
  —What's alike and different about TV versions of book characters?
  —What are value and/or literary considerations of changing book plots and characters in order to make a TV series?
  —Which do you like better, book or TV? How might you like both but for different reasons? What would be the reasons?
  —Which book character(s) would you like to see made into TV shows? Why?
  —What TV shows do you regularly watch? Why?
  —What else do you like to do besides watch TV?
  —What could you do to change or improve what's on TV?
- First and second graders used *Kid Pix Studio* (Broderbund) software to create graphics and word processing for alphabet and math-related booklets reproduced to take home.
- Kindergartners were introduced on videotape as they demonstrated rules for taking care of books.
- Fairy tale and nursery rhyme variants were studied in books and video versions, then third graders created their own variants using *ClarisWorks for Kids*.
- Fiction and nonfiction adventure stories were researched and compared in books, on CD-ROM encyclopedias, television, and the movies by fifth graders.
- Mythological backgrounds were studied by third graders for shape-shifters like character Odo in *Star Trek: Deep Space Nine*.
- Digitized ads in newspaper and magazine were analyzed, and fourth-grade students combined, transformed, or resized two or more images using *ClarisWorks for Kids* to create their own versions.

As I continued plans for teaching balance in media literacy the rest of the year, at least four other influences guided my decisions:

1. A schoolwide committee chose "Connections" as the Keewaydin theme for the year, which nicely dovetailed with my own goal. I met with the three other specialists—Nancy Paxson in music, Jan Braaten in physical education, and Sheila Farrell-McFarland in art—to plan how we might connect our instructional concepts. Our plans focused on grade-level expectations for standards in each of our content areas that complement each other. Especially helpful were media-related Health Education standards, which Braaten had written for MPS, as well as elements of design in the visual arts that have similarities to those in media arts. We agreed that as students saw the connections among our specialist areas, each of our programs would be strengthened.

2. The district implemented a new Houghton Mifflin (HM) thematic reading series *Invitations to Literacy* (1999) at the elementary grades. The series' scope and sequence of skills is correlated with state standards, and the district designated HM Integrated Theme Tests as Performance Packages at Grades 3 and 5. To integrate my IMT standards with classroom reading themes, concepts, skills, strategies, titles,

come to the wacky store
of mixed heads and bodies
where every weird creature
buys pencils and erasers!

Figure 12. Another eye-catching way to advertise the school store is a "Weird Creature" ad campaign by Keewaydin fourth graders. A study of digitized photography and computerized effects in film/video leads students like Nicole to experiment with the toolbox in *ClarisWorks for Kids* software in order to subtract part of an animal and add on a part from another animal to create a third "weird" animal. This media literacy unit of study offers students hands-on experience to work toward the IMT grade-level expectation, "Analyze the Design and Content of Ads and Programs, Including Use of Special Effects" and ultimately, "Recognize Real, Realistic and Unreal Content."

and author/illustrators was one more instructional piece I needed to create balance throughout a standards-based media program.

As I looked through the HM teacher resource books for each grade level, I saw how media literacy could play a strong role in improving many themes for students. The resource books encourage visual literacy instruction of illustrated print material and occasionally media literacy also. This seemed to offer me exciting opportunities to connect to the English Language Arts curriculum by integrating my program with that in the classroom to encourage a balanced use of print, computer, and film/video forms of media.

3. Using a manuscript in progress that I call my *Creative Planning Resource (CPR) for Teachers* (Lacy, 1999) helps me think of new ways to teach old things—or perhaps old ways to teach new things—in my media program. It is a flip book like the ones in which children flip cut-apart pages of heads, torsos, and feet "to create 1001 monsters." My flip book has four sections that I use to create 1001 lesson plans:

- "Why" (grade-level expectations and assessment tools)
- "Who" (large group, small groups, or individual students—and when to change during a lesson)
- "What" (kinds of experiences to offer students)
- "How" (strategies and process-based activities)

This flip-book tool helps me break down my plans into categories to consider. For example, kinds of experiences to offer are in eight categories of audio, computer, the environment, film/video, people, objects, print, and still visuals. This includes Social Studies concepts of learning from other people and learning from the environment, which I will now find better ways to fit into my plans. The flip book idea has helped me in this and countless other ways over the years to dramatically balance my repertoire of uses of different experiences, grouping arrangements, and instructional strategies to meet standards.

4. Resources in my professional library prove invaluable so that I do not reinvent the wheel. I use the *Star Tribune* (see Figures 2–6 and 8) and its "Learning Works" programs and products to introduce the news media to my students. I have shown in this chapter some of my uses in the classroom for Jesse-coverage in the newspaper, as well as samplings from some of its newest advertising campaigns that provide me with excellent visual metaphors for teaching media literacy. Computer applications like *Kid Pix Studio* and *ClarisWorks for Kids* and videos like the *Buy Me That!* three-part series (1990, 1992, 1993, 30 minutes each, $169.95 for all three) and *Kids Talk TV: Inside/Out* (1996, 45 minutes, 140-page guidebook, $79.95) are crucial in my curriculum.

Books that continue to guide my approach are *Media & You: An Elementary Media Literacy Curriculum* by Donna Lloyd-Kolkin and Kathleen R. Tyner (1991, 170 pages, $29.95) and *Visual Messages: Integrating Imagery into Instruction* by

David M. Considine and Gail E. Haley (1992, 267 pages, $29.00). Considine and Haley have revised their book, to come out in 1999, with gratifying mention of the development of media literacy in MPS, and Tyner also had a new book out in fall 1998, *Literacy in a Digital World: Teaching and Learning in the Age of Information* (1998, Erlbaum, $32.95) that mentions the IMT standards and media literacy grade-level expectations. These authors are people I have worked closely with over the years, and our work—in classrooms and workshops as well as in publications—reflects our similar approaches to media literacy instruction.

Keewaydin's media center subscribes to professional magazines *Cable in the Classroom* (monthly, CCI/Crosby Publishing), *Better Viewing* (bimonthly, CCI/Crosby Publishing), *Telemedium* (quarterly, National Telemedia Council), and *Zillions* (bimonthly, Consumers Union) for students, all of which have excellent articles about media literacy. *Techworks* has been mentioned as a comprehensive media instructional program. *Reading Rainbow* (GPN/Nebraska ETV Network) videotapes are excellent examples to use with children for a balance between print and nonprint as well as fiction and nonfiction.

What follows is an example of how such planning using standards, a school theme, a new reading series, a professional library, and my own little flip book works for me—and pays off in the long run—as I search for better ways to connect print, computers, and film/video to make a balanced, standards-based media literacy program.

AN EXAMPLE OF GRADE-LEVEL PLANNING IN MEDIA LITERACY

The following integrated package in media literacy for a year at the third grade level is similar to ones I am continuing to develop for all grade levels at Keewaydin. Although this example is school-, program-, grade-, and reading series-specific, any one of the fundamental ideas behind it could be adapted to fit other situations. It is also media title-specific—using movies like *Titanic*—because I believe that popular culture must be used in teaching media literacy. This means that parts of the following plan are soon outdated, and I will be replacing those titles with new ones, just as all curriculum developers do to fit the times. However, classics like *The Wizard of Oz* and *Make Way for Ducklings* are never out-of-date, so I will continue using them. Gone are the youthful days when I dressed up as Princess Leia for my students, but my unabashed enthusiasm for a good story—whether movie *Babe* or book series *Animorphs* or Governor Jesse—spills over still today in the classroom.

Software-specific references, like *ClarisWorks for Kids*, are also unavoidable but hopefully are substitutable at least to some degree by those who do not have the same computer capabilities. In sharing ideas for teaching media literacy, the media specifics are all too often confining, if not impossible to replicate. My hope is that the ideas given here are important enough so that others can see their way clear to

Figure 13. Keewaydin fourth graders work in pairs on storyboards for humorous pet-food commercials using animal hand puppets or plastic toy characters from the popular *Pokemon* cartoon series. Students are instructed to use one of the food advertising techniques demonstrated in the *Buy Me That!* video series, and they study food-related episodes in comic strips like "Garfield" and "Buckles" for storyboard ideas. Working in teams of four, each pair then videotapes the other pair's commercial. Hands-on production like this is crucial for fourth-grade media literacy expectations, too many to name here (see Appendix), in IMT, media arts, health education, and English language arts.

adjustments that use other media titles and can overcome what appear to be media-specific drawbacks.

At this writing, I use simple assessment tools that are feasible with my schedule of seeing over 300 children a week—mainly class checklists to show growth in a standard, on which I note the quality and amount of individual students' contributions to discussions and projects. I have yet to develop an alignment of IMT standards with the MT Progress Report, and I plan to attend training soon in writing performance assessments with rubrics.

Third-Grade Media Literacy: Integration of Standards

In the outline that follows, third-grade expectations have been listed in media literacy for four content standards: IMT, Media Arts, Health Education, and English Language Arts. All MPS grade-level expectations in media literacy from these four standards for kindergarten through fifth grade are found in the Appendix. I plan to include standards in Social Studies next year.

Third-Grade IMT Expectations in Media Literacy:

- Find examples of copyright on a book and on a video.
- Share something you know about media to help another student.
- Find information from a specific cultural perspective.
- Compare aspects of book production and film/video.
- Use a TV, VCR, CD/audiotape player.
- Use a video production studio or set up a production area.
- Recognize real, realistic, and unreal content in print and film/video.
- Interpret main idea and inference.
- Analyze effects of eye-level viewpoints.
- Determine whether fiction or nonfiction best suits purpose.
- Compare information resources inside and outside the school.
- Sequence a story line that demonstrates cause and effect.
- Compare works by illustrators and nonprint media creators.
- Compare photo, drawing, and film/video about the same topic.
- Analyze influence of sound effects in film/video.
- Evaluate the effects of details in illustrations.
- Speculate about what may have been left out.
- Identify motives and appeals of different types of advertisements.
- Evaluate time spent daily on entertainment media.
- Work cooperatively in a group to videotape a presentation.
- Demonstrate technical skills in use of materials and equipment.
- Select appropriate presentation plan and techniques.
- Devise revision strategies for the videotape.

Ages 5–9 Media Arts Expectations in Media Literacy:

- Sequence images and sounds to tell a story.
- Create images and sounds to represent a series of events.
- Choose media elements to focus attention, suggest a mood, or communicate an idea (e.g., color, sound, viewpoint).
- Demonstrate an ability to lead or contribute significantly to group productions.
- Explore a variety of skills and techniques for developing a given topic (e.g., videotaping a subject).
- Communicate information using effective presentation techniques incorporating media equipment (e.g., audiotaping).
- Recognize the differences among media genre.
- Interpret and evaluate media messages.
- Describe how a media message relates to one's own beliefs, values, and needs.
- Analyze and evaluate the influences of media messages.

- Plan and present a production for others.
- Analyze and evaluate an effective production.
- Discuss the impact of media on daily life.
- Set a goal and complete a media arts project.

Third-Grade Health Education Expectations in Media Literacy:

- Discuss media's influence on our spending decisions.
- Develop time management skills.

Third-Grade English Language Arts Expectations in Media Literacy:

- Identify main ideas and some supporting details.
- Retell main events or ideas in sequence.
- Understand ideas not explicitly stated.
- Make predictions and draw conclusions.
- Distinguish among fact, fiction, and opinion.
- Compare and contrast elements of characters, setting, plot.
- Identify tone in persuasive and fictional texts.
- Identify media sources.
- Use appropriate technology to handle and display information.

THIRD-GRADE MEDIA LITERACY: INTEGRATION ALSO OF READING SERIES

In addition to the concepts and skills from the four subject areas above are additional media literacy concepts and skills in the HM *Invitations to Literacy* reading series for third grade. HM themes like "Disasters," "Community Ties," and "Weather Watch" were useful as foundations on which to base my plans. As I read the HM Teacher's Books, I flagged pages that offered possibilities for media literacy instruction, especially looking for ideas using visuals that could be helpful for those of our English Language Learners who are emergent readers. I then made lists of those ideas and communicated my findings to classroom teachers for their input. Each of the six themes is for a 6-week unit, so creatively planning that many is extremely time-consuming, and sometimes everything planned cannot be accomplished. However, once done, the plans could be modified and used every year, with rubrics developed for assessments.

Whereas many of the expectations above often apply to planning for more than one lesson, what follows are the specific themes with media literacy concepts and skills in HM for each theme. My ideas then follow for integrating these specifics with third-grade expectations from the four standards documents.

HM Third-Grade Theme 1: "Oink Oink Oink"

- Conduct an interview.
- Differentiate between reading a story and watching it on TV.
- Recognize real versus fictional wolves and pigs.
- Analyze facial expressions and body language.
- Use a K-W-L chart before watching a video.
- Give a persuasive speech.
- Analyze details of costumes and makeup.
- Compare and contrast two videos about the same topic.

Media Literacy Integration of Theme 1

Use the electronic catalog to find fiction and nonfiction resources in the media center about animals and contribute to a class bibliography of available materials, pointing out copyright for each. *Media literacy focus*: What are the kinds of media found? Which animals did you find the most? Why are certain animals good subjects for fiction and folklore as well as for nonfiction?

Read aloud *Perfect, the Pig* by Susan Jeschke (1980, Holt) and compare it to the *Reading Rainbow* read-aloud video of the same title; compare both to claymation adaptation of a book in *Reading Rainbow: Piggy In A Puddle. Media literacy focus*: what are strengths and limitations of these three different kinds of storytelling? Which was done first (compare copyright dates)? Which do you like best? Why?

Make a K-T-W-L (Know–Think I Know–Want To Know–Learned) chart about pigs for comparing the remaining documentary clips in the *Reading Rainbow* video with a clip from the movie *Babe. Media literacy focus*: What did you learn and what is still left to find out? What is sometimes left out in documentaries and stories? Who left them out? Why?

View other clips from *Babe*, with different directions what to look for in each clip (i.e., facial expressions, body language, obvious editing, special effects) and compare to photographs and drawings of animals. *Media literacy focus*: What are ways filmmakers make fantasy stories appear real? How could you tell?

Videotape persuasive speeches during a pretend talk-show in which a student representing Babe is the host, another student representing a real pig is the guest, and other students are either the movie's barnyard characters or real pigs acting as the audience; participants are to attempt to persuade viewers to favor real, realistic, or unreal portrayals of animals in film/video. *Media literacy focus*: When trying to persuade, why is it important to know who your audience is, state opinions clearly, give supportive reasons or examples, and use effective presentation techniques in front of the camera?

Ongoing Assessments: Checklists for contribution to bibliography and to discussions; rubrics planned for participants who give persuasive speeches; checklist for cooperative group work in the video studio.

HM Third-Grade Theme 2: "Community Ties"

- Recognize supermarket slogans, signs, arrays.
- Compare fiction versus nonfiction.
- Create food icons.
- Create city images.
- Recognize fact versus opinion.
- Combine celebratory photos and speech balloons.
- Create a picture book dummy.
- Interpret paintings of community celebrations.
- Create a two-page magazine ad.

Media Literacy Integration of Theme 2

Compare the media center's fiction and nonfiction collections to products on display in a supermarket, then create a sign with slogan for a section of materials. *Media literacy focus*: How is the media center arranged like familiar places outside the school? How might the media center better "advertise its products" to reach its consumers? What is the motive for this advertisement and who would it appeal to? Who are they and what do they need or want? What are elements of an effective sign for these consumers?

Replicate an effective design used to convey information elsewhere in the community for presenting information about materials in the media center. *Media literacy focus*: How might display techniques used in other familiar places (i.e., fast-food menu boards, TV guides, public icons or symbols) be replicated to direct students, staff, and visitors to areas inside school?

Make a K-T-W-L chart of fact versus opinion about what your downtown community is like from your perspective, then study about your community and create a cardboard building to add to a three-dimensional model of the downtown area. *Media literacy focus*: How does our constructed environment reflect who we are as a community and what we need, desire, and value? Are the needs, desires, and values of any members of the community ignored or left out of the constructed environment? How could that be remedied?

Find a magazine photo of people that infers they are having a good time and write a story or description of them as if they were people in your community; add such things as speech balloons or captions, and make your text and photo into a double-page spread for a class picture book. *Media literacy focus*: What are genres of photographs? Of advertisements? What kinds of inferences do they make? How is the class book like a storyboard for a little movie? In what ways are book and film/video production alike and different?

Put together what you have learned about images and words to make a magazine ad for your community in which you write original text and incorporate graphic ideas from the building you made and the photo you described. *Media literacy focus*: How do text and graphics go together to promote an idea like "Our Community Is the Best!" in advertising?

Ongoing Assessments: I plan rubrics for sign, display, double-page spread, and magazine ad; checklist for contribution of cardboard building.

HM Third-Grade Theme 3: "Disaster!"

- Recognize magnification.
- Analyze details that establish a time period.
- Analyze viewpoint in illustrations—above, below, at eye level.
- Identify features of newspapers.

Media Literacy Integration of Theme 3

Analyze nonfiction books about the Titanic as background for the movie. *Media literacy focus*: Note details in photos and drawings of the disaster that establish the time period as 1912. Sequence the event to show cause and effect. How is reality of the event alike and different from the movie version?

Use computer graphics of ships and people in *ClarisWorks for Kids* to create a scene reminiscent of the Titanic disaster; create a second graphic that is a magnification of one detail in the first scene; add both with added sound to a class multimedia *ClarisWorks* slideshow. *Media literacy focus*: What are purposes behind establishing shots and closeups in film/video? For which of these kinds of shots can computer enhancement be most effectively used today to "fool the eye"? What examples do you remember from the movie *Titanic*?

Contrast uses of above-, below-, and eye-level viewpoints in the movie *Titanic* to illustrations in Caldecott Award-winning picture books *Make Way for Ducklings* (1941, Viking) by Robert McCloskey; *The Fool of the World and the Flying Ship* (1968, Farrar) by Uri Shulevitz; *Jumanji* (1981, Houghton) and *The Polar Express* (1985, Houghton) by Chris Van Allsburg. *Media literacy focus*: What is the effect on the audience of different viewpoints used by moviemakers and illustrators? Why?

Working in small groups, take turns videotaping above-, below-, and eye-level viewpoints of students playing board games. *Media literacy focus*: What are the best camera angles to understand what is going on? How could the different angles be used for storytelling purposes, as in *Jumanji*?

Contrast features of newspapers of the past with those of today; contribute to original front-page news and art about the movie *Titanic* using *Student Writing Center* (Learning Company) software. *Media literacy focus*: What is newsworthy about the movie? Why? When are pictures or words better to convey the news to the public? What details can be used to establish the time period for the movie as the present day?

Ongoing Assessments: Checklists for contribution to discussions; rubrics are needed for computer graphics and newspaper contribution.

Figures 14 and 15. Student interest in the Titanic after release of the movie is increased for Keewaydin's third graders when the thematic unit "Disasters" in the Houghton Mifflin reading series suggests the study of eye-level viewpoints of the disaster—below, above, and normal eye-level—as well as magnification. Students use extra sets of stamps for *Kid Pix Studio* software to create an establishing scene of the sinking ship and a magnification, closeup, or "zoom in" of one detail. Other activities to help students with the grade-level expectations in media literacy, "evaluate the effects of details in illustrations" and "analyze effects of eye-level viewpoints," are to experiment with binoculars, a magnifying glass, and the camcorder's tight and wide features.

HM Third-Grade Theme 4: "What's Cooking?"

- Compare books by the same illustrator.
- Recognize signs and symbols.
- Analyze animals in comic strips.
- Analyze fast food commercials.

Media Literacy Integration of Theme 4

In small groups, compare illustrations of the same characters in different titles by picture book illustrators (i.e., Tomie dePaola, Patricia Polacco, Ezra Jack Keats) and create original segues that tie the stories together chronologically as one long story. *Media literacy*: Why do illustrators sometimes use the same characters? Who are the characters? How do they change from book to book? When did the changes occur? What has been left out in between the books?

Make signs for the school that incorporate only symbols for nonreaders and non-English speakers. *Media literacy focus*: What are different kinds of universal icons?

Study animal comic strips and use *ClarisWorks for Kids* software to create animal cartoons that include speech or thought balloons as advertisements for the school store, lunchroom, or upcoming schoolwide event. *Media literacy focus*: How and why are animals interesting in comic strips? How do they attract our attention? Who are the audiences for different types of cartoons?

Study food commercials; then plan, practice, and produce original videotaped TV commercials for the school store or lunchroom that are parodies of fast food commercials. *Media literacy focus*: What is a parody? How, when, and why can they be funny? When and how do food commercials persuade? What presentation techniques are needed in front of the camera? What technological skills are needed behind the scenes?

Establish criteria for improving the videotaping of original commercials. *Media literacy focus*: What presentation techniques and technological skills need improvement? How may they be improved?

Ongoing Assessments: Checklists for contribution to discussions, small group work on segues, and cooperative group work in video studio; rubrics planned for sign, cartoon, presentation techniques, and technological skills.

HM Third-Grade Theme 5: "Weather Watch"

- Compare sights and sounds in film/video.
- Analyze newspaper weather reports.
- Analyze TV weather maps.
- Recognize uses of lighting to establish mood.
- Create sound effects for a storm.
- Create captions and descriptions for photos.
- Compare information in two newspapers or magazines.

Media Literacy Integration of Theme 5

Study the Kansas twister episode in the movie *The Wizard of Oz* and list details about sights and sounds that are realistic and unrealistic. *Media literacy focus*: What can we learn from fiction about lifelike events? What are clues that help us recognize when something lifelike is really make-believe? What is meant by "suspension of disbelief"?

Replay the twister episode from *The Wizard of Oz*, first without the audio and then without the video, and discuss effectiveness of each replay. *Media literacy focus*: Without the audio, is the episode as frightening? Why or why not? Without the visuals, do you know what's going on? Why or why not? How do sounds and visuals work together to make this episode a successful part of the story?

Replay the twister episode from *The Wizard of Oz* with half the class analyzing audio elements/attributes and the other half analyzing visual elements/attributes, then both groups report back to the whole class. *Media literacy focus*: About the audio, what are moods created by the sounds, how do they change, and how do you think they were produced? About the visuals, what are moods created by images and lighting, how many and what kinds of scenes are there, and what kinds of camera angles are used? In what specific instances do sounds and visuals work together? How? Name at least two intended messages of this episode.

Use a Venn diagram to compare/contrast symbols and colors used in newspaper weather reports with those used on TV weather news, then use *ClarisWorks for Kids* to re-create as many of those symbols and colors as possible for a weather-related storytelling picture; add to a class multimedia *ClarisWorks* slideshow, complete with recorded sound effects. *Media literacy focus*: What are strengths and limitations of newspaper weather reports? Of TV weather reports? Where do you think their weather symbology and uses of color originated?

Study the history and art of weather-related things such as weather vanes and lighthouses and how they are used in real life as well as in children's literature [i.e., *The Silver Pony* (1956, Houghton) by Lynd Ward, *Tuesday* (1991, Clarion) by David Wiesner, *Keep the Lights Burning, Abbie* (1985, Carolrhoda) by Peter and Connie Roop]. *Media literacy focus*: How and why do some things become symbols for people, places, institutions, companies, ideas, or events? When, where, and why can this kind of symbolism be positive or negative?

Read *Kate Shelley and the Midnight Express* (1990, Carolrhoda) by Margaret K. Wetterer, and use your own words as well as words in the text to write captions for photographs of kindergartners taken from different eye-levels as in the book; compare to *Reading Rainbow* video read-aloud of the same title. *Media literacy focus*: What are descriptive words and phrases that best capture specific action and moods in visuals? How does the video version add to the story with its closeups of details, sound effects, and occasional special effects?

Ongoing Assessments:　Checklists for contribution to list, discussions, half-class group work, and Venn diagram; rubrics needed for computer picture and captions.

HM Third-Grade Theme 6: "What A Day!"

- Compare film and book versions of a story.
- Analyze commercials for hair-care products.

Figure 16. Kindergartners pose for photos to demonstrate five angles (the above example of an overhead viewpoint) that artist Karen Ritz used to illustrate *Kate Shelley and the Midnight Express,* a story in the third-grade Houghton Mifflin reading series of a real girl who saved an express train in 1881 by crawling across a trestle bridge in a raging storm. Ritz took photos of a friend from different angles to help her draw pictures of Kate, and third graders write captions for our photos of kindergartners, fulfilling their grade-level media arts expectation in media literacy: "choose media elements (i.e., color, sound, viewpoint) to focus attention, suggest a mood or communicate an idea."

- Analyze photos of hairstyles in the past.
- Analyze videos that bring history to life.
- Recognize symbols of America.
- Study pet photographs.

Media Literacy Integration of Theme 6

Read aloud selected expository scenes from the *Ramona* series by Beverly Cleary and compare to re-creations of them in the movie *Ramona*. *Media literacy focus*: How is the description of something in a book alike and different from its visual re-creation in a movie? What is meant by "poetic license"? Which do you enjoy more, the written description or someone's visual interpretation of it? How can you enjoy both but for different reasons? What can you learn from each?

In the yellow pages of the telephone book, list how many suppliers and services there are under such headings as "beauty," "cosmetics," "hair," and the like, then add to that the numbers of (1) ads in one metropolitan newspaper, (2) ads in one general-audience magazine, and (3) TV commercials during one evening for products related to these topics. *Media literacy focus*: Why are these services and products so popular? Do you think they are as popular with people in other parts of the world? Do all people everywhere have "advertising"? How might "advertising" elsewhere be alike or different? Why or why not?

Study advertising for topics above in old magazines or catalogs, and analyze fashion details in photographs and videos of the past, then create a poster for a thing, idea, or universality that portrays the opposite (i.e., something that stays the same, lasts from generation to generation, never goes out of style). *Media literacy focus*: How does advertising reflect and influence attitudes and desires people have during a specific period of time? What are concepts that resist changes over time? What are meanings behind quotes "Beauty is in the eye of the beholder," "Beauty is as beauty does," and "A thing of beauty is a joy forever"?

Bring in photographs, drawings, or stuffed toys representing pets for a pretend "pet show"; using a balance scale, put beans in one side that represent time spent watching entertainment TV and beans in the other side that represent time spent doing other things, like caring for pets, doing homework and chores, exercising and playing. *Media literacy focus*: What balance exists in your life among the things you do daily? Is the time you spend on entertainment TV as productive as the time spent on other activities?

Compare individual time management plans for a future daily schedule with those of other students, focusing on the need to have a balance among activities. *Media literacy focus*: Why and how will you accomplish a balance of activities in the future? Who and/or what do you need to help you?

Ongoing Assessments: Checklists for contribution to discussions and list; rubric planned for poster.

HOO YAH!

This is the course set for me and others like me around the state who believe that Minnesota's Profile of Learning offers opportunities to design instruction that is higher, wider, and deeper than before. Much needs to be done by thoughtful educators within the system to repair the problems inherent in any new process. Those of us who have begun to use it and find worth in it have internalized much of it and will be loathe to repeal it. The administration of Minneapolis Public Schools had said, "These standards will not go away" (Vana, 1999), and we applaud that commitment.

The Profile offers a way to integrate media literacy instruction with the classroom curriculum and validates my personal desire for balanced use of print, computers, and film/video by my students. Without the High Standards, standards in media literacy may not exist.

None of us can know now how Jesse will govern but as for media literacy, this governor has given educators in Minnesota—and perhaps across the nation—more copy during his first few months than they can ever find time to explore properly with students. In addition, he may undoubtedly play a crucial role in deciding how the state's standards reform movement will look. At the end of the 1998–99 legislative session (about the same time our school year ends), the future of the Profile of Learning—including standards that involve media literacy—will be placed on his desk and his well-advertised broad shoulders.

We can only hope that our media-savvy governor is media literacy-savvy as well.

APPENDIX

Listed below are grade-level expectations for the end of kindergarten through the end of fifth grade in media literacy for Information Media and Technology (IMT), Health Education, English Language Arts, and Media Arts in Minneapolis Public Schools. In IMT the expectations are found throughout the MT department's standards document, but especially in IMT Processing. In Health Education, the expectations are found in Influences (Media/Peers/Culture) of the Physical Education/ Health document from TIS.

In English Language Arts, several of the same expectations are found for kindergarten through fifth grade, and I have listed them only at the initial grade level where they are mentioned in the document from Reading (Elementary) of TIS. In Media Arts, grade-level expectations have not been written, so I have chosen to place standard statements from the Fine Arts K–12 document from TIS for ages 5 through 9 at the end of third grade and for ages 9 through 14 at the end of fifth grade.

K–5 Cross-Curricular Expectations in Media Literacy

Kindergarten IMT Expectations in Media Literacy:

- Demonstrate proper care of media technology.
- Recognize the same story in different formats (book and video).
- Gather meaning from illustrations.
- Define nonprint-related vocabulary (audio and video).
- Operate a TV and an audio cassette player.
- Contrast animated and live-action film/video.
- Compare TV with other tools at home and school.
- Differentiate between adults' and children's TV programming.
- Sequence details in a film/video story line.
- Differentiate between reality and fantasy.
- Identify a variety of sounds used for storytelling purposes.
- Recognize visual storytelling in wordless books.
- Explain what is liked and disliked about TV and why.
- Differentiate between TV ads and stories.
- Relate simple information in front of a video camera.

Kindergarten Health Education Expectations in Media Literacy:

- Identify advertising messages that affect children.
- Describe personal TV watching habits.

Kindergarten English Language Arts Expectations in Media Literacy:

- Attend to illustrations.
- Draw pictures to illustrate sentences or stories.
- Preview text by looking at illustrations.
- Compare illustrations.

First-Grade IMT Expectations in Media Literacy:

- Define authorship.
- Analyze the same story in different formats (book and video).
- Produce a voice recording.
- Retell information presented on TV or video.
- Describe something about another culture shown on TV or video.
- Describe the main idea behind information, entertainment, and advertisement on TV.
- Recognize works by the same illustrator/media creator.
- Distinguish feelings and emotions in sounds.
- Recognize visuals that tell a story apart from words.
- Determine needs for fiction or nonfiction to suit purposes.
- Name TV shows they regularly watch and explain why.
- List reasons for watching film/video.
- Contrast one-way and two-way communication.
- Work cooperatively in a group to present a simple story on video.
- Devise revision strategies for the videotape.

First-Grade Health Education Expectations in Media Literacy:

- Identify an ad and discuss why the ad appeals to children.
- Define media as TV, news, magazines, books, music, and the Internet.
- Calculate time spent watching TV in a time period.

First-Grade English Language Arts Expectations in Media Literacy:

- Construct visual images to represent meaning.
- Compare stories with own experiences.

Second-Grade IMT Expectations in Media Literacy:

- Identify copyright symbols and dates on media materials.

- Evaluate print and nonprint versions of a story.
- Identify features of video (title frame, credits).
- Compare film/video available at school with those at home and at the theaters and explain different uses.
- Choose a single topic to research using video.
- Formulate questions and take simple notes using video.
- Organize information in a video in an appropriate manner (alphabetically, chronologically, numerically).
- Differentiate among real, realistic, and unreal content.
- Recognize illustrative media (drawing, painting, collage).
- Describe how audio influences video.
- Identify unique elements in books with special features (pop-ups).
- Explain changes that might be made in a story.
- Compare amount of time spent watching TV to other activities.
- Recognize advertised products, when and for whom advertised.
- Work cooperatively in a group to present a simple report on video.
- Devise revision strategies for the videotape.

Second-Grade Health Education Expectations in Media Literacy:

- Discuss how commercials influence our decisions.
- Classify violent and nonviolent TV.
- Identify ways the media makes products appealing.
- Identify how your time is spent.

Second-Grade English Language Arts Expectations in Media Literacy:

- Identify main ideas and some supporting details.
- Retell main events or ideas in sequence.
- Distinguish fact from opinion.

Third-Grade IMT Expectations in Media Literacy:

(see chapter for an example of planning at this grade level)
- Find examples of copyright on a book and on a video.
- Share something you know about media to help another student.
- Find information from a specific cultural perspective.
- Compare aspects of book production and film/video.
- Use a TV, VCR, CD/audiotape player.
- Use a video production studio or set up a production area.
- Recognize real, realistic, and unreal content in print and film/video.
- Interpret main idea and inference.
- Determine whether fiction or nonfiction best suits purpose.
- Compare information resources inside and outside the school.

- Sequence a story line that demonstrates cause and effect.
- Compare works by illustrators and nonprint media creators.
- Compare photo, drawing, and film/video about the same topic.
- Analyze influence of sound effects in film/video.
- Evaluate the effects of details in illustrations.
- Analyze effects of different eye-level viewpoints.
- Speculate about what may have been left out of a media presentation.
- Identify motives and appeals of different types of ads.
- Evaluate time spent daily on entertainment media.
- Work cooperatively in a group to videotape a presentation.
- Demonstrate technical skills in use of materials and equipment.
- Select appropriate presentation plan and techniques.
- Devise revision strategies for the videotape.

Third-Grade Health Education Expectations in Media Literacy:

- Discuss media's influence on our spending decisions.
- Develop time management skills.

Third-Grade English Language Arts Expectations in Media Literacy:

- Identify main ideas and some supporting details.
- Retell main events or ideas in sequence.
- Interpret presentations of data.
- Understand ideas not explicitly stated.
- Make predictions and draw conclusions.
- Distinguish among fact, fiction, and opinion.
- Compare and contrast elements of characters, setting, and plot.
- Identify tone in persuasive and fictional texts.
- Identify media sources.
- Use appropriate technology to handle and display information.

Ages 5–9 Media Arts Expectations in Media Literacy:

- Sequence images and sounds to tell a story.
- Create images and sounds to represent a series of events.
- Choose media elements to focus attention, suggest a mood, or communicate an idea (e.g., color, sound, viewpoint).
- Demonstrate an ability to lead or contribute significantly to group productions.
- Explore a variety of skills and techniques for developing a given topic (e.g., videotaping a subject).
- Communicate information using effective presentation techniques incorporating media equipment (e.g., audiotaping).
- Recognize the differences among media genre.

- Interpret and evaluate media messages.
- Describe how a media message relates to one's own beliefs, values, and needs.
- Analyze and evaluate the influences of media messages on families.
- Plan and present a production for others.
- Analyze and evaluate an effective production.
- Discuss the impact of media on daily life.
- Set a goal and complete a media arts project.

Fourth-Grade IMT Expectations in Media Literacy:

- Explain copyright infringements of pirated videos and off-air taping.
- Describe the same current event from different new sources.
- Differentiate among broadcast, cable, closed-circuit TV, and video.
- Compare a documentary to print information about the same topic.
- Differentiate among an article, opinion, and feature.
- Zoom, pan, and tilt using a camcorder.
- Analyze the design and content of an ad, TV show, or movie, including use of special effects.
- Contrast national and local perspectives in news outlets.
- Contrast TV violence with real-life situations.
- Analyze TV language and visuals to identify fact or opinion.
- Analyze the influence of visuals and sounds in commercials.
- List advantages and limitations of TV.
- Analyze social propaganda on TV and its impact on groups.
- Work cooperatively in a group to videotape a TV commercial.
- Devise revision strategies for the videotape.

Fourth-Grade Health Education Expectations in Media Literacy:

- Identify advertising messages.
- Discuss how gender roles, sexuality, and body image are portrayed in media.
- Analyze health messages in media ads.
- Analyze how violence in media influences behavior.
- Explore how Internet influences health.

Fourth-Grade English Language Arts Expectations in Media Literacy:

- Recognize diverse viewpoints on the same topic.
- Use illustrations as supplementary parts of texts.
- Compare and contrast characteristics of genre.
- Identify the influence of culture on text.
- Use a variety of electronic media.
- Identify plagiarism.
- Write in a persuasive form.

Table 1.

Teacher Name _____	Room Number:_____												

Performance Rubric
1 Not yet progressing toward outcome
2 Steady progress toward outcome
3 Achieved outcome
4 Exceeds outcome

Assessment Modes
Recorded Observation
Checklist
Oral or Written Test
Project, Performance/Demo.
Conferencing/Feedback
Portfolio
Student Self-Assessment
Journal
Pre and post Testing
Other

Student Names:

Student Activities						Work Habit Skills (Check & Describe all that apply)	Resource Management	Time Management	Persistence/Perseverance	Goal Setting	Group Work/Team Work	Independent Work

Note: A checklist such as the one above (created using a specially made template on FileMaker Pro 4.0v1) is necessarily used at Keewaydin to record students' progress when an entire classroom engages in activities during a short amount of time. Created by Sue Sandstede for an MPS performance package in primary-level critical viewing skills, this checklist uses a rubric of Excellent, Satisfactory, and Needs Improvement as performance criteria and distinguishes between performances that indicate declarative knowledge (what students say they know) and procedural knowledge (what students show they can do). Sandstede leaves room to add other activities, comments, and/or student self-evaluation.

Fifth-Grade IMT Expectations in Media Literacy:

- Explain issues of equitable access to and reporting of information.
- Choose relevant information in a video to include in an oral report.
- Edit a video (in-camera, VCR to VCR, deck, software).
- Identify intent, perspective, or bias in a news outlet.
- Identify audio techniques used to influence a listener.
- Identify techniques used to create a point of view.
- Investigate how cultures are represented in the mass media.
- Define media literacy and give examples of its skills.
- Analyze realistic content from various viewpoints.
- Identify contextual clues and inference for meaning behind a media message.
- Cite examples from documentaries of creative treatments of reality.
- Analyze stereotyping on TV and its impact on groups.
- Work cooperatively in a group to videotape an original program.
- Describe the audience and select appropriate techniques.
- Make a storyboard and prop list.
- Demonstrate technical skills (camera angles, in-camera editing).
- Devise revision strategies for the videotape.

Fifth-Grade Health Education Expectations in Media Literacy:

- Discuss how advertising techniques influence consumer decisions.
- Identify techniques used to sell products.
- Define entertainment addiction.

Fifth-Grade English Language Arts Expectations in Media Literacy:

- Identify purpose, point of view, allusion, tone.
- Recognize diverse viewpoints used to persuade.
- Identify symbols or devices used in a persuasive message.
- Identify examples of stereotypes.

Ages 9–14 Media Arts Expectations in Media Literacy:

- Create a media production that tells an original story, expresses personal feeling, or reports information.
- Use subjects, themes, and symbols to communicate intended meaning.
- Use media elements and aesthetics to develop media productions appropriate to one or more chosen styles and forms.
- Participate in more than one defined role in a group production or presentation.
- Accept responsibility for the goals of the group.
- Demonstrate basic technical skills necessary to complete works in more than one media form.

- Select and operate media equipment that is appropriate for developing a given topic (e.g., photographing a subject).
- Experiment with unconventional ideas and techniques.
- Analyze and evaluate technical aspects of a media production.
- Use the visual and verbal vocabulary of the medium.
- Identify features of media productions that locate them in time, space, and culture.
- Understand the ways media products are made within particular cultural and historical contexts.
- Experiment with different formats to reach a larger community.
- Plan, prepare, and present media productions for particular occasions, taking into account factors such as purpose, space, materials, and equipment.
- Judge the impact of various media messages on society.
- Influence media producers.
- Develop strategies to organize and revise ideas and plans.

REFERENCES

American Library Association. (1998). *Information power: Building partnerships for learning.* Chicago: Author.

Better viewing. Peterborough, NH: CCI/Crosby Publishing.

Buy me that! (1990). Chicago: Films Incorporated Video.

Buy me that too. (1992). Chicago: Films Incorporated Video.

Buy me that 3! (1993). Chicago: Films Incorporated Video.

Cable in the classroom. Peterborough, NH: CCI/Crosby Publishing.

Considine, D. M., & Haley G. E. (1992, rev ed. 1999). *Visual messages: Integrating imagery into instruction.* Englewood, CO: Teacher Ideas Press.

Considine, D. M., Haley, G. E., & Lacy, L. E. (1994). *Imagine that: Developing critical thinking and critical viewing through children's literature.* Englewood, CO: Teacher Ideas Press.

Dalbotten, M. (Ed). (1986). *Model learner outcomes for media and technology.* St. Paul: Department of Education.

Draper, N. (1999a, February 21). Group wants to end Profile. *Star Tribune,* p. B1.

Draper, N. (1999b, February 28). Why is Profile of Learning in danger of failing? *Star Tribune,* p. B1.

Elementary media curriculum. (1979). Minneapolis Public Schools: Educational Media Services.

Information media and technology content standards. (1997, August 27). Minneapolis, MN: Minneapolis Public Schools.

Invitations to literacy. (1999). Boston: Houghton Mifflin.

Jeschke, S. (1980). *Perfect, the Pig.* New York: Holt.

Kids talk TV: Inside/out. (1996). United Church of Christ: Office of Communications.

Lacy, L. (1978, May/June). Happy birthday, Mickey! *Teacher,* pp. 41–43.

Lacy, L. (1980, January). From Oz to the Death Star. *Teacher,* pp. 36–38.

Lacy, L. (1994). *About TV: What do you know about, think about, do about television?* Minneapolis, MN: Minneapolis Public Schools.

Lacy, L. E. (1986). *Art and design in children's picture books: An analysis of Caldecott award-winning illustrations.* Chicago: American Library Association.

Lacy, L. E. (1987). *Visual education: An interdisciplinary approach for students K–12 using visuals of all kinds.* Minneapolis, MN: Minneapolis Public Schools.

Lacy, L. E. (1999). *Creative planning resource (CPR) for teachers.* Manuscript in progress.

Lillquist, B. (1999, February 11). Correspondence to Governor Jesse Ventura. Minneapolis Public Schools: Teacher and Instructional Services.

Lloyd-Kolkin, D. & Tyner, K. R. (1991). *Media & you: An elementary media literacy curriculum.* Englewood Cliffs, NJ: Educational Technology Publications.

Lonetree, A. (1999a, February 12). House votes to unseat grad profile. *Star Tribune*, p. B1.

Lonetree, A. (1999b, February 16). Forum forecasts lively debate. *Star Tribune*, p. B3.

Mallander, M. (1995, September 24). Work on graduation rules fails to deliver. *Star Tribune*, p. A1.

McCloskey, R. (1941). *Make way for ducklings.* New York: Viking.

Minnesota Department of Children, Families and Learning. (1997). *The profile of learning . . . Minnesota's high standards, April 1997.* St. Paul, MN: Office of Graduation Standards.

Minnesota Educator. (1999, February 12). The Profile is not working! St. Paul: Education Minnesota, p. 1.

Minnesota frameworks for arts curriculum strategies. (1996). Golden Valley: Minnesota Center for Arts Education.

Partridge, L. (1998, March 28). There's academic rigor in state's Profile of Learning. *Star Tribune*, p. A19.

Ransome, A. (1968). *The fool of the world and the flying ship.* New York: Farrar Straus.

Reading Rainbow: Kate Shelley and the midnight express. Omaha: GPN/Nebraska ETV Network.

Reading Rainbow: Perfect the pig. Omaha: GPN/Nebraska ETV Network.

Reading Rainbow: Piggy in a puddle. Omaha: GPN/Nebraska ETV Network.

Roop, P., & Roop, C. (1985). *Keep the lights burning, Abbie.* Minneapolis, MN: Carolrhoda.

Rummel, S. (1998, March 28). Curriculum changes bringing new excitement to the classroom. *Star Tribune*, p. A19.

Sandstede, S. & Clarke, S. (1985, rev. ed. 1987). *Children and television: Critical viewing skills.* Minneapolis, MN: Minneapolis Public Schools.

Sandstede, S. & Clarke, S. (1987). *Video production with kids.* Minneapolis, MN: Minneapolis Public Schools.

Swalm, D. (1999, January 28). There's bit of Klingon in Gov. Jesse Ventura. *Star Tribune*, p. A19.

Techworks: A program that integrates technology skills into the curriculum (1997). Westminster, CA: Teacher Created Materials.

Tyner, K. (1998). *Literacy in a digital world: Teaching and learning in the age of information.* Mahwah, NJ: Erlbaum.

Vana, C. (1999, February 15). Director's notes. MPS: *TIS Express*, p. 1.

Van Allsburg, C. (1981). *Jumanji.* Boston: Houghton Mifflin.

Van Allsburg, C. (1985). *The polar express.* Boston: Houghton Mifflin.

Ward, L. (1956). *The silver pony.* Boston: Houghton Mifflin.

Wetterer, M. K. (1990). *Kate Shelley and the midnight express.* Minneapolis, MN: Carolrhoda.

Wiesner, D. (1991). *Tuesday.* Boston: Clarion.

Zillions. Yonkers, NY: Consumers Union of U.S.

IMPLEMENTING CRITICAL MEDIA LITERACY IN SCHOOL CURRICULUM

Ladi Semali

This chapter presents a case study in which I describe a classroom of preservice teachers attempting to develop and implement a curriculum of critical media literacy. Critical media literacy teaches students and teachers to take a critical stance when they read, view, or think about textual or media representations. To illustrate this process, I present two examples from local daily newspapers which explore ways to detect and understand bias. In this process, I encourage students and teachers to (1) scrutinize their initial understandings of textual and media representations; (2) engage in a critique of their own ideologically mediated perceptions of the situation described or inscribed in the text in question; and (3) sort out "truths" from half-truths, accuracies from inaccuracies, facts from fiction, reality from myth, and objectivity from bias.

This practice aims to help demystify the dictates of media culture and its ideologies of biased representations of women, and the use of racist representations of people of color and various minority groups, to reproduce social relations of domination and subordination. Through critical media analysis students learn to

Advances in Reading/Language Research, Volume 7, pages 277–298.
Copyright © 2000 by JAI Press Inc.
All rights of reproduction in any form reserved.
ISBN: 0-7623-0264-X

detect bias by examining its construction, production, and the meaning-making processes by which media imagery and popular representations of people help shape students' personal, social, and political worlds. Our goal is to increase awareness, question hegemonic cultural practices, and seek action toward social change, social justice, and social equality (Semali & Pailliotet, 1999).

However, to accomplish this goal in American classrooms is not an easy task. Learning to detect and understand media bias in U.S. classrooms today is one of the most difficult, but most important tasks for media literacy education. While students find it easy to surf the Internet and TV channels, it is harder to convince them why and how bias in the media they access everyday can be a powerful determinant of how they view themselves, others, and the world around them. Most students, having been raised with *Sesame Street* and having seen 5000 hours of TV programming before they ever came to school (Lutz, 1989), are reluctant to accept that the media contain biases of all kinds—racial, economic, gender, political, moral, and others.

Critical theorists like Stuart Hall (1997) and John Fiske (1987) argue that bias presented through the media does not merely reflect or reinforce culture but in fact shapes the thinking, attitudes, and values by promoting dominant ideology of a culture. This fact is daunting to some parents. A majority would wish to shield their children from such onslaught of ideology embedded in the daily barrage of media messages, especially those laden with sex, violence, and ideological lies. Others would like to know where to find the much needed antidote to bias, false representation, emotional appeals, and the power of language in manipulating myths, stereotypes, and values.

Teachers are equally perplexed by the dawning of new media like the information superhighway and the new literacies these media have introduced to us in such a short time. These new literacies which are rooted in the literacy traditions of oral/aural, visual, and alphabetic text modalities, have been called different names: print literacy, technology literacy, information literacy, visual literacy, media literacy, and so on. Teachers and parents are becoming increasingly aware of the impact of the new media on children's social, emotional, and cognitive functions. For parents who wish to become mediators or teachers of critical media literacy, how best to teach young children and adolescents about the messages relayed by television and the Internet and how to avoid biased viewpoints at odds with a family's ethics and moral concerns are difficult decisions.

More now than ever, prevailing social conditions and technologies require teachers to view literacy through broader, more critical lenses (Flood & Lapp, 1995). Such critical media literacy makes possible a more adequate and accurate reading of the world, on the basis of which, as Freire and others put it, "people can enter into 'rewriting' the world into a formation in which their interests, identities and legitimate aspirations are more fully present and are present more equally" (cited in Morgan, 1997, p. 6).

Perhaps the most crucial aspect of studying bias in the media is helping students understand that while many different kinds of people and situations are represented (fairly or unfairly) in the media, many people and their viewpoints are not. The selection process of who and what will be shown, or not shown, is a complicated one and most relevant to understanding how bias is created. Teaching students to understand this process and factors which affect selection decisions, is critical to their knowledge of media influence in all areas of discourse. My goal is to enable students to understand how our emotions, positive and negative, are influenced by the content of the media programs and to be aware of what in the program causes such feelings.

Understanding how media bias confines and defines public discourse on diverse issues is a key concept of media literacy education at the Pennsylvania State University. Media literacy education teaches students to take a critical stance when they read, view, or think about textual or media representations (Semali & Watts Pailliotet, 1999). The broader goal of such critical education is to enable students to understand and critique the insidious curriculum of media and to conceptualize social/economic justice more clearly and consequently celebrate diversity, develop a sense of fairness in the distribution of our society's cultural and economic resources, and therefore challenge the exclusionary aspect of the Eurocentric one-way view of the world (Dines & Humez, 1995, p. xviii). For my students, therefore, media literacy becomes a competency to read, interpret, and understand how meaning is made and derived from print, photographs, and other electronic visuals. Media literacy consists of understanding connotative messages embedded in the text of the visual and media messages, as well as interaction of pictures to words, the context of the viewer, and related messages obtained from the maker of the image.

FOUNDATIONS OF MEDIA LITERACY

The rationale for helping students study and understand bias is founded on theories and praxis of critical literacy. Critical literacy stands in contrast to works far removed from the students' experiences. As a pedagogical approach, critical literacy draws its practice from "constructivist" approaches to teaching and to learning, from social theory studies of popular culture. It has grown out of a number of social philosophies such as Latin American theologies of liberation, the philosophy of liberation of Brazilian educator Paulo Freire, Marxist revolutionary theory, and neo-Marxist cultural criticism and has been taken up in more recent years by educators influenced by new social theories such as deconstruction and poststructuralism and analyses of the media in its many forms, literature, the role of the state in the struggles over race, class, and gender relations, national and international economic structures, and the cultural politics of imperialism, postcolonialism, and poststructuralism.

Growing out of cultural studies literature, the core issue of media literacy is that reality—our worldview—is socially constructed significantly by media. The many strategies for media literacy are drawn from the cultural studies discipline and fit into the rationale of cultural studies as a cross-disciplinary subject and are concerned with institutions, representations, systems of beliefs, and communicative processes. In the past two decades, cultural studies has provided a new set of approaches to the study of culture and society as represented by media industries. The project was inaugurated by the University of Birmingham Centre for Contemporary Cultural Studies, which developed a variety of critical approaches for the analysis, interpretation, and criticism of cultural artifacts. Through a set of internal debates, and responding to social struggles and movements of the 1960s and 1970s, the Birmingham group came to focus on how various audiences interpreted and used media culture differently, analyzing the factors that made different audiences respond in contrasting ways to various media texts. In youth subcultures, British cultural studies demonstrated how culture came to constitute distinct forms of identity and group membership. For cultural studies, media culture provides the materials for constructing identities, behavior, and views of the world. Those who uncritically follow the dictates of media culture tend to "mainstream" themselves following the dominant fashion, beliefs, values, and behavior (Kellner, 1995, p. 97).

For media literacy, as it is the case for cultural studies, the concept of ideology is of central importance. Institutions like the media corporations are part of the dominant means of ideological production. As noted by Hall (1997), what these media industries produce is "representations of the social world, images, descriptions, explanations and frames for understanding how the world is and why it works as it is said and shown to work" (p. 20). Thus, dominant ideologies serve to reproduce social relations of domination and subordination. Kellner (1995) illustrates the formation of worldview by describing how ideologies of class, for instance, celebrate upper-class life and denigrate the working class. Ideologies of gender promote sexist and biased representations of women, and ideologies of race use racist representations of people of color and various minority groups. "Ideologies make inequalities and subordination appear natural and just, and thus, induce consent to relations of domination" (Kellner, 1995, p. 95). Because we tend to be unaware of how ideologies naturalize human relations (relations between races, sexes, or with older people, and so on), we can unconsciously be lulled to believing that what we see or know is natural or simply the way things are, and it becomes difficult to detect bias or manipulations which may occur within the way statements about these relationships are framed or formulated. In such circumstances, "ideologies tend to disappear from view into the taken-for-granted 'naturalized' world of common sense" (Hall, 1997, p. 19).

Doug Kellner and Stuart Hall are among several scholars who have contributed to the emerging field of cultural studies, in particular by laying out the dynamics of media culture. Their seminal works have been applied to critical inquiry in various disciplines. Drawing largely from these works, I have developed frameworks of critical media literacy within the broad concept of critical literacy. The frameworks I develop are clearly critical approaches which prompt students and teachers to carry out a critique of existing systems "in the context of how they relate to structure of domination and forces of resistance and which ideological positions they advance within the context of current debates and social struggles for a more democratic and egalitarian society" (Kellner, 1995, p. 95). By taking up a social critical theory as a pedagogical strategy, my students and I analyze and evaluate texts using the conceptual and methodological work of people like Norman Fair-clough (1989), Paulo Freire (1974), James Gee (1996), Gunther Kress (1988), Courtney Cazden and Judith Green (1992), among others, in conjunction with examples of classroom pedagogies provided by Catherine Wallace (1992), Chris Searle and the students of Earl Marshal School (1995), and Hillary Janks (1993). For example, I urge my students to examine newspapers or magazines of their choice and to select one article or picture that represents people. They must be prepared to explain why they chose a particular article or picture, the perceived bias, manipulation, stereotyping, or distortion in the way people are represented. By writing a paragraph describing the picture or article of their choice and the perceived bias, these students immerse themselves in critical reading, critical listening to their peers' points of view, and critical thinking of the texts they initially thought were innocent or neutral. Through this process they also make explicit the framework they use to arrive at their conclusions.

While the pedagogical strategies of authors like Fairclough, Freire, and Gee are by no means the only perspectives and approaches consistent with the ideal of critical media literacy, they are exemplary developments of that ideal. And if they are not the end point of our quest, they certainly provide points from which to begin a critical inquiry. By using an inquiry method in which I engage teachers in focus groups, I have also been able to generate themes, pilot-test course readings, and experiment with a variety of pedagogical strategies (Krueger, 1994; Stewart, 1990). This idea of using focus groups in curriculum inquiry to generate curriculum and instructional themes was first operationalized by Bradley and West (1994). By teasing out information gleaned from focus group members, I was able to engage teachers in a curriculum inquiry which was adept in generating content for in-service training workshops and summer institutes. Although this emerging model showed promise for curriculum reform, it was often disrupted by in-service teachers not attending regularly workshops and institutes.

Typically, curriculum inquiry is a conversation between disciplines, sign systems, and personalized knowing which provides teachers who practice it with curricular possibilities of a specific topic. It also provides them a process vehicle for readying themselves for handling an emerging curriculum. Thus, curriculum becomes a meaning-making potential where knowledge is created, acted on, and re-created at the point of experience in order to learn more, gain deeper meaning, critique, and transcend their present realities. My reason for focusing on media texts is to dispel the notion that critical literacy is best applied to literary works rather than to social practice. Critical literacy can be applied to all texts in multiple forms read by children of all age groups, whether in print, visual, or graphic format. The ideas I explore with my students have been developed during my college teaching. Over the years, I have experimented with several models of critical literacy.

My rationale for this method was to facilitate the inclusion of media literacy across the English curriculum, in response to some of the concerns raised by critics of media literacy: that teaching media literacy is difficult for practical reasons and therefore the basis of precluding wider acceptance in U.S schools today (Leveranz & Tyner, 1966). Some of these concerns have been documented by Milton Anderson and James Ploghoft (1993). They include: (1) lack of adequate models (many existing models of teaching media literacy aim at selling workshop kits and demonstration videotapes instead of illustrating the pedagogy of media literacy: how to teach it); (2) the difficulty of fitting a media literacy project (in competition with sex education, career education, art education, physical education, and so on) into a tight academic schedule; and (3) that basal readers from major publishers fail to include concepts dealing with media literacy (a situation which is beginning to change) along with the inadequate teacher preparation in schools of education concerning the role critical media literacy can play in the curriculum. These reasons have inspired me to examine the foundations of media literacy and seek out nontraditional methods to integrate media literacy across the curriculum instead of teaching it as a separate subject.

My reflective practice has been guided by two important questions: How can teachers help students sift through the heaps of messages, sometimes conflicting and contradictory, coming from textbooks, popular media, the Internet, and so on? What literacy competencies do students need to manage the influx of this information? In recent years, these concerns seem to have captured educators nationwide. At the annual meetings of the National Reading Conference, the International Literacy Association, and the National Council of Teachers of English, media literacy now occupies a place in their programs as keynote speaker topics, concurrent sessions and symposia.

Gradually educators are recognizing that media literacy has the potential to change the way we think, feel, and react to the world around us, and particularly in classrooms. Here is why. When a media literacy teacher who doesn't share the culture, language, race, or socioeconomic backgrounds of students enters a classroom, he or she becomes not an information provider but an explorer who works with students to analyze, evaluate, and produce mutually understood texts. Based on their explorations, teachers and students create new learning materials full of mutually generated meanings and shared interpretations. At a time when educational dilemmas resulting from the rapid increase of diverse students in schools portend the future of North American education, teachers' and students' explorations become extremely important (Kincheloe & Steinberg, 1998). If teachers are unable to meet the challenges issued by this expanding diversity, disastrous consequences will result. To meet these challenges, the Pennsylvania legislature mandated educational goals related to communication. These standards define knowledge and skills required for students to learn before graduating from public schools in Pennsylvania. Two of the eight goals specifically target critical pedagogy of media literacy stating that: (1) all students will write for a variety of purposes, including to narrate, inform, and persuade, in all subject areas; and (2) all students will analyze and make *critical judgments* about all forms of communication, as well as separating fact from opinion, distinguishing propaganda from the truth, recognizing stereotypes and *statements of bias*, recognizing inconsistencies and judging the validity of evidence (italics added; *Pennsylvania Education*, February 1993). The goals were approved by the State Board of Education and have been in effect since fall 1995, revised in 1998.

CRITICAL LITERACY IN TEACHER EDUCATION

Pennsylvania State University faculty grapple with these state mandates as they prepare elementary and secondary school teachers. The framework for secondary school teacher education with which the faculty work, is built on a model of teaching as reflective inquiry. In reflective inquiry, teachers make collective and individual decisions about life in classrooms in order to help students develop into active, knowledgeable citizens of a multicultural world. These decisions are based on teachers' understanding of self and prior experiences, their students, human development and diversity, subject matter, educational theory, curricular design, instructional methods, federal, state, and institutional regulations, and political, social, and moral relationships between education and community and world affairs. Teachers develop their understanding through continual, systematic, intensive inquiry involving problem posing, data gathering through educational literature, product analysis, observations, discussion, probing the historical conditions which produced the present circumstances, and acting on this new knowledge (Zeichner & Liston, 1996). As reflective inquirers, secondary school teachers bring personal, social, and theoretical knowledge to bear to promote curriculum change and school improvement. Clearly, reflecting critically and taking action on one's daily work is the hallmark of a profession engaged in self-improvement.

The new approaches to curriculum and instruction being implemented at the Pennsylvania State University are significantly different from traditional ones, in that they include the following assumptions: (1) all subjects are interconnected and interrelated with one another; (2) there is no "real" truth or no one correct method of doing or explaining things (i.e., it makes it possible to integrate critical analysis of social and cultural contexts and to analyze the multiple perspectives imbedded in multiple truths and that what is learned is based on points of view and experiences of the dominant groups in society; see, e.g., Bourdieu's notions of cultural capital); (3) learning involves creating knowledge and learning through our own lived experiences (as opposed to rote memorization of facts; see, e.g., Freire's notion of banking theory of knowledge); (4) curriculum is not fixed, rather it is seen as a "context specific" process changing with the evolving needs of society and individuals; and (5) finally, the new approach stresses the importance of focusing on the whole rather than the parts (i.e., administrative and bureaucratic constraints, classroom setup, and so on) (Kincheloe & Steinberg, 1998, pp. 4–5).

Within our teacher education classrooms we aim to develop students' critical awareness of oppressive social forces, including school structures and knowledges. Grounded in critical pedagogy, our teaching practices systematically undermine the dominant ideologies, institutions, and material conditions of society which maintain socioeconomic inequality. This is to say that we embrace a critical literacy approach in which our teaching practices strive to analyze all texts including printed and visual texts, by looking for class bias, gender bias, and racial bias. Even though this assignment has been difficult, we believe that this is an important task because all texts are constructions and contain a point of view of the writer or producer.

Masterman (1992) found good sense in such critical inquiry when he warned educators not to concentrate on or degenerate into laborious accumulation of facts or busywork but to motivate students to formulate their own opinions and ideas through examination of the evidence and through inquiry, reflection, and response. Hopefully, by applying the frameworks of inquiry, reflection, and action, students will be transformed through this language of critique and through social action. Equally and rightly, as Lankshear and McLaren (1993) put it:

> In addressing *critical* literacy we are concerned with the extent to which, the ways in which, actual and possible social practices and conceptions of reading and writing enable human subjects to understand and engage the politics of daily life in the quest for more truly democratic social order. Among other things, critical literacy makes possible a more adequate and accurate 'reading' of the world, on the basis of which, as Freire and others put it, people can enter into 'rewriting' the world into a formation in which their interests, identities and legitimate aspirations are more fully present and are present more equally. (p. xviii)

The practice I describe in this chapter embraces much of Lankshear and McLaren's notions of critical literacy with special attention to social practices. By problematizing the texts students read everyday in the classroom, students embark on a path of social consciousness which examines texts beyond surface impressions, traditional myths, and clichés. My process involves: (1) inquiry (research); (2) reflection (examining and questioning prevalent contradictions, constructions, conventions, codes, and practices and minority nonmainstream culture—and applying the meaning to one's own social context); and (3) action (formulating a response based on the resolve to change social order, injustices, unequal access to resources, or existing worldview). While reviewing the literature of critical literacy, Barbara Comber (1993) clarifies the objectives of reading media texts as social practice by insisting on (1) helping students to reposition themselves as researchers of language, (2) pushing students to understand and respect their resistance to mainstream interpretations of text and exploring minority culture constructions of literacy and language use, and (3) problematizing classroom and public texts.

CRITICAL MEDIA LITERACY IN AN
ENGLISH CLASSROOM

As future English teachers, preservice teachers grapple with the ideas that English in all its forms and uses can never be a matter of neutral communication of factual information or fictional truths. The English textbook is not factual or objective maxims valid for all times to be learned. In fact, many meanings evolve as readers/viewers interact with texts and construct meaning from them (Barthes, 1974; Derrida, 1986). Constructing textual understanding, therefore, is a recursive and ongoing process, not a linear or static one (Barthes, 1974). Through a cultural critique as represented in the multiple genres of the mass media, our students learn how forms of knowledge and the power they bring to the classroom, are created in language and taken up by those who use such texts. We broadly define "text" beyond referring to a verbal/written artifact (such as a story, play, or song lyrics). As used by cultural critics, a text can refer to any communicative or expressive artifact produced by media industries. Textual analysis, therefore, is a close examination of how particular media texts generate meaning. However, Kellner (1995) warns that audience reception and political economy approaches are also needed to locate texts in their social and political contexts. Through media literacy, therefore, students continually question how language might be put to different, more equitable uses, and how texts might be re-created in a way that would tell a different *unbiased* story.

The selected readings of the media literacy course, which I teach in the teacher education program, introduce the participants to curriculum inquiry methods, theories, critical media pedagogy, analytical schemes, and techniques of building bridges between school and society and between students and teachers. These bridges are key components of the holistic teaching and learning implicit in an integrated approach to education. The overall intent of the course is to seek ways to integrate the world of the classroom with the world of the child and society as a whole. Participants begin their inquiry by exploring general questions: What is the role of critical teaching in a world in which culture can no longer be understood as providing the normative integration and common values which cement together democratic social life? Is there a common or shared language, knowledge, history, and stories that identify us as "American"?

Critics of cultural literacy (Henry Giroux, Barbara Herstein, Donald Macedo, etc.) reject notions of monoculturalism because there is no single, comprehensive, common, or "national" culture in pluralistic societies like the United States. Students, particularly future teachers, must constantly question representational attempts to establish such monocultural visions of America. Are the visions of America represented in history books, in secondary English textbooks, in documentary films, in newspaper articles, in television genres, and so on, a fair, accurate representation of all Americans?

It is my desire that teachers use this method of inquiry to initiate a process for their own learning and professional growth. I also hope they will become committed to a critical pedagogy which promotes social critique, reimagining the common good in a diverse culture, and create classroom learning environments that support students in their inquiries. The immediate goal of inquiry implied in my media literacy curriculum is to expand the notion of literacy to include ability to read, analyze, evaluate, and produce communications through a variety of media texts (Hobbs, 1994). In this context, therefore, inquiry involves immersing oneself in a media text or topic and taking *time* to explore the text in order to find questions that are significant to the learner and then systematically investigating those questions.

PRINCIPLES AND PRACTICES OF CRITICAL MEDIA LITERACY

When implementing a critical media literacy, I encourage students to examine more thoroughly the role that beliefs and values play in our "knowing" and "doing" as teachers, particularly those beliefs, actions, and values shaped by our media culture (biased or not). Specifically, we examine how economic resources, advantages, and privileges are distributed inequitably in part because of power dynamics involving beliefs in racial, gender, and class divisions. Such analysis is not limited to TV and films only but is extended to other multimedia forms of representation including textbooks, book-covers, and other school-related materials. In this course, we seek to address issues such as the destructive effects of hegemonic language forms borrowed and legitimated by the mass media, particularly when they become the sole lingua franca of the classroom; the canonical provision of notions of knowledge, truth, and beauty without regard to the grounds of their construction; the violence perpetrated by an educational practice that inadequately addresses the reproduction of sexism and racism; the scientism of science that constructs a powerful and excluding ideology regarding what it means to do science; or the forms of work education that reduce valued labor to that which fits existing economic arrangements (Kincheloe & Steinberg, 1998).

This expanded approach to literacy has been referred to by others as "genuine literacy" (Walmsley & Walp, 1990). Being genuinely literate entails more than simply scoring well on a standardized test, or learning a narrow range of reading and editing skills. Instead, it entails actively engaging in literate behavior (Walmsley & Walp, 1990). Rather than merely preparing students for eventual literate behavior, teachers engage them in genuine acts of literacy right from the beginning and throughout the school career. It also implies that the language arts curriculum will not be fragmented into separate components for reading, composing, and editing, but will integrate these in meaningful ways. Further, it implies that skills will be taught within the context of genuine reading, writing, speaking, and listening, rather than as separate or prerequisite components of the program. Advocates of genuine literacy would have us pay attention to how our society is marked by a multiplicity of cultures, meanings, and values. By guiding students' attention to how powerful groups define their own particular meanings, values, experiences, and forms of writing and reading as the *valued* ones in society, students will better understand the inequalities and violations of social justice the mass media continue to peddle through their production of culture products. Through this reflective approach, we hope to illustrate how theory and practice of a critical pedagogy when applied to English texts helps students to engage in the social struggle over meaning and to navigate today's classrooms, which have become inundated by diverse and multiple layers of printed and electronic texts. To implement the vision of critical media literacy illustrated in this chapter, students will be able to (1) analyze the hierarchical positioning of individuals within the social order on the basis of race, class, gender, and sexuality and (2) acknowledge the multiple and insidious ways in which power operates in the larger society "to reproduce the interests of the dominant culture" (Hammer, 1995, p. 79).

Clearly, teaching critical media literacy must aspire to teach the youth in our classrooms, particularly those impressionable groups or individuals in desperate search of an identity and a place in the adult world. Critical media literacy will bolster skills and knowledge they need to be able to consciously reflect on their interactions with media. It will enable them to address injustices; become critical actors committed to combat problems of youth apathy, violence, substance abuse, rampant consumerism; and to generate a strong commitment to developing a world free of oppression and exploitation. Linking what students read/view with social concerns affirms what it means to be educated and to be media literate in a media-saturated milieu, in which information gathering and distribution processes thrive on the manipulation of seductive media spectacles.

Because reading, writing, speaking, listening, thinking, acting, and viewing are synergistic, interdependent, and interactive processes (Barthes, 1971), it is important to note that when readers/writers/audiences read, produce, or receive media messages, they do not create meanings in isolation. Instead they draw from experiences of other texts, connecting past and present understandings. Strategies and understandings developed in one form of communication interact and support others. As heavy media consumers, students bring an enormous quantity of information to the media literacy classroom. In fact, their information about the media usually exceeds that of the teacher. The role of the teacher will be that of co-learner and *facilitator* while discussing and contextualizing the media and clarifying value messages in media texts. Stuart Hall (1997) warns that meaning does not simply reside in a media text's codes but is the result of a complex *negotiation* between specific audiences and texts. This view contrasts with former critical media theorists who assumed that audiences had very little control over meaning and were vulnerable to being "brainwashed" by the media. Hall proposes three possible audience responses to the dominant ideology (bias) contained in the media text's codes or three distinct reading positions, corresponding to audiences' different social situations: (1) *dominant* reading (accepting the preferred meaning), (2) *negotiated* reading (accepting aspects of the preferred meaning but rejecting others), and (3) *oppositional* reading (rejecting the preferred meaning).

Thinking about reading positions is important. Often audiences are not aware of the literary devices, codes, or conventions used in producing media messages as a technique to tell stories. Such devices are not always obvious as students read stories in literature or view films and television. The way the stories are told and the person doing the telling play important roles in formulating the motive of the telling as well as making the story entertaining and at the same time believable. Recent developments in digital imaging of videos and the use of computer graphics in the morphing of images (changing parts of an image using digitized editing) make deceptions and bias much easier and faster to accomplish and much harder to detect.

The ways of telling media stories explain the coded genres of situation comedy, soaps, action adventures, and so on, that define the system of commercial television and the movie industry in the United States. Therefore, we no longer can deny the fact that some of these conventions are continually used in telling mythic stories that allow bias, overt manipulation of the characterization or plot, stereotyping, ethnic jokes, and comedic entertainment to "creep in" to the story being told. By the same token, a particular worldview is portrayed as a value, a better way of being or doing, superior culture, morally good, a better person, race, gender, or simply put, the acceptable norm—the measure of success, beauty, sexual orientation, and so on. Such normative worldview represented in the story is often influenced by the attitude and background of its storyteller, its interviews, writers, photographers, and editors.

The danger presented by these mythic realities such as those found in popular Disney movies and television situation comedy shows is that audiences sometimes make decisions or judgments on the basis of these myths. The conventions used in advancing the plot or resolving the conflict seem so believable and yet are oversimplified. It is important, therefore, that teachers and students examine critically their worldviews and come to the realization that media representations of race, gender, class, age, or sexual orientation are creations of producers, writers, and artists. Furthermore, it is essential to recognize that the end of this construction is to persuade, to render "natural" or "innocent" what is profoundly "constructed," motivated, and biased. Constructions offer positions for us, in terms of what we know, how we came to know it, and the attitudes or assumptions we can make of the reality being described or represented, through which we recognize images as similar or different from ourselves and those around us. A crucial step in any media literacy program according to Art Silverblatt (1995) is the awareness that one receives numerous messages daily through the media and that these messages can affect one's behavior, attitudes, and values. In the overview of media literacy, he examines the process of communication, which involves "receiving a message, selecting relevant information, forming appropriate responses, and responding to the message" (p. 14). In the next section, I will illustrate how my students apply these principles and practices in reading, viewing, and thinking about media texts.

APPLYING CRITICAL MEDIA LITERACY
TO STUDY BIAS

To illustrate how bias affects the content of media and confines public discourse, I encourage my undergraduate preservice teachers who enroll in my Media Literacy class every semester to learn to detect bias in all texts they read, view, or produce. My assumption is that by modeling this process for them, they will in turn expand and replicate the model in their own classrooms as future teachers. Activities which help students to come to terms or start to understand what I am talking about follow in this section to demonstrate how one might go about investigating the insidious cultural pedagogy of the media, particularly in the daily press. I encourage students to explore a text from the daily press in order to find questions that are significant to the learner, and then to systematically investigate and critically analyze the values embedded in those questions. As an introduction into this process of studying bias, I ask them to begin watching a movie such as *The Paper*. After they watch this movie on their own, they come to class prepared to design their own newspaper for their school. Students must make decisions about who and what pictures will be shown or written about, what information or message they are trying to communicate, how to fit it into the allotted space or time, and how to get all of this done on a deadline. They must take notes on the ethical dilemmas they encounter, the viewpoint(s) they take, and the moral stand they choose to uphold in the stories or opinions they select to publish.

As each group presents its version of a newspaper, peers are encouraged to note what has been included, what excluded, what message is being put forth, how people and events are portrayed, and what the overall effect might be on viewers and readers. The outcome of this exercise is that students gain firsthand experience with the way bias in the media system affects the content of media. We accomplish this by assisting students to identify their mental, sensory, and emotional positions, to develop new methods and stances, then to choose appropriate courses of action when engaging with texts.

In the next step, students examine literature texts they are reading in their English classes. They quickly realize how bias permeates the pages of these books: gender bias, racial bias, and how the characters in the stories they read have been manipulated by the authors to suit a certain moral stand or to perpetuate a myth or value system. Such discoveries are an important realization for these future English teachers, because they soon will be standing in front of impressionable minds looking up to them for firsthand interpretations of texts from literature and the media, from Hamlet and Chaucer to popular educational movies like *Stand and Deliver* and *Dead Poets Society*. Their opinions, values, or biases, which might reinforce myths, stereotypes, or clichés, will become primary examples these students will take away as valid ways of seeing the world. If we want our students to function and thrive in modern communicational environments, we must help them develop the means to critically read, write, and connect aspects of their lives.

By introducing students to critical media literacy enterprises such as these, they are able to bridge existing learning contexts and build new ones.

In taking up media literacy in a classroom, it is not enough to simply decode or understand existing biases in texts. Students and teachers must transform their newly found critical understandings into agency: positive acts and effects in themselves and others. This might transpire through generation of new texts and knowledge, developing ways of thinking and acting, or working toward alterations of unjust social conditions. Such activities might well include writing to the radio/TV station, writing letters to the editor, or encouraging students to voice their opinions or comment on detected media bias in the school newspaper. In the past, students have visited local newspaper publishing houses and a radio station, and met with community radio anchorpersons. These encounters generated lots of questions and follow-up community actions produced by students on their own.

LEARNING TO DETECT BIAS FROM THE NEWS

To help students understand and detect bias in media representations is not easy. This is so partly because bias is difficult to detect when embedded in everyday information using commonsense practices. When I encourage my students to understand and detect bias, I ask them to apply a familiar framework. For example, I prompt them to examine the motives of media producers and the techniques used to construct the messages conveyed. I ask them to consider what role they, as media consumers, may be able to play in changing the media messages and representations they find offensive or oppressive. They also need to be aware that not all bias is deliberate but nonetheless insidious in spite of the journalistic ideal of "objectivity." Every news story is influenced by the attitudes and background of its interviews, writers, photographers, and editors. However, students can develop awareness in reading or viewing the news by watching for specific journalistic techniques which allow bias to "creep" into news stories. As summarized by Newskit (1994), in the consumer guide to news media, some of the techniques are: (1) bias through selection and omission; (2) bias through placement; (3) bias by headline; (4) bias by photos, captions, and camera angles; (5) bias through use of names and titles; (6) bias through statistics and crowd counts; (7) bias by source control; (8) word choice and tone. This consumer guide is a useful tool to examine both literal and surface meanings produced by journalistic styles and techniques designed to attract readers' or viewers' attention.

ANALYSIS OF TWO NEWSPAPER ARTICLES

Activities that help students to come to terms with or start to understand what I am talking about follow in this section to illustrate how one might go about investigating bias, particularly in the daily press. As they began to examine newspaper articles, these students realized that bias is found not only in the news media, but also in textbooks, films, and more recently in the Internet. I encouraged them to explore a text from the daily press using the consumer guide to news media in order to find questions that are significant to the learner, and then systematically investigate and critically analyze the biases, manipulations, distortions, and stereotypes embedded in those questions. In the following paragraphs I provide a comparison of two newspaper articles: (1) Study angers relatives of dead children (*The Philadelphia Inquirer*, October 27, 1994) and (2) Malaria vaccine successful in Africa test, study says (*Center Daily Times*, State College, Pennsylvania, October 28, 1994). These articles have two things in common. They were published around the same time, and the stories tell about research on children. They revolve around the broader issue of life—particularly of little children—how to enhance it and prevent death from trauma in victims of sudden infant death syndrome (SIDS) and from malaria infection. The two articles were used in my classroom setting with preservice students studying critical media literacy. Because of space constraints, I will outline the central themes of the two articles separately and present the comments and reactions of these students with a short discussion.

Study Angers Relatives: Eyes Taken from Dead Children
Philadelphia Inquirer Staff Writer

> *Relatives of the 19 youngsters, all under 3 at death, were not told. The city*
> *Medical Examiner's office removed the eyes.*
> Without seeking permission from families of the dead, the Philadelphia Medical Examiner's Office permanently removed eyes and optic nerves from 19 deceased infants and young children—most of them abuse victims—as part of a study. According to a published scientific report, the study, which covered a 23-month period ending in August 1990, was a joint effort of the city Medical Examiner's office and the Scheie Eye Institute in West Philadelphia. The report was co-authored by two city medical examiners and two physicians from Scheie.
>
> The study involved three categories of children: nine who died from blunt trauma to the head, four victims of shaken baby syndrome and six victims of sudden infant death syndrome, or SIDS. City officials declined to identify any of the children but the Inquirer was able to obtain records that identify some of them.

When one of the children's grandmothers was interviewed, she said that she had never been told about her grandchild's involvement in the study. "They asked me about transplanting his organs and I said definitely not," she said. "They never asked me about his eyes. Never."

The reporter continued in the story to say:

> The purpose of the eye study was to compare the brain and optic nerve damage suffered by the shaken child with the damage suffered by children who had visible head injuries. The study focused on intracranial damage and optic nerve hemorrhages in the three study groups.

An article published in March 1994 in *Ophthalmology* Magazine, according to the *Inquirer* reporter, stated that the study concluded that the victims of shaken baby syndrome, despite the absence of visible injury, suffered fatal damage similar to victims of blunt trauma. Those injuries were not present in the six SIDS victims of the study.

The second article, published in the *Center Daily Times*, reads as follows:

Malaria Vaccine Successful in Africa Test, Study Says
London, the Associated Press.

Malaria kills between one million and three million children every year.
An experimental malaria vaccine reduced illness among African children by about a third, offering a glimmer of hope that doctors may one day conquer the global killer. Malaria, caused by a parasite transmitted to humans by mosquito bites, kills one million to three million children every year, the vast majority in Africa. The bug bursts red blood cells and hobbles the immune system, leaving many survivors, particularly those who have suffered several bouts, chronically fatigued and highly susceptible to other infections.

The London-based AP wire service continued to provide details in this article of where in Africa this study took place and under what circumstances. The specifics included:

The trial included 586 children between ages 1 and 5 in Idete village in Tanzania. Scientists gave 274 children three doses of the vaccine. The rest got placebos. After a year, investigators found that the vaccinated children were 31 percent less likely to suffer from malaria. The results are encouraging, but further work is necessary to boost the vaccine's effectiveness, wrote Dr. Nicholas J. White, a researcher at the Oxford Tropical Medicine Research Programme in Bangkok, Thailand.

The AP writer made sure that readers got some background information about malaria research worldwide, particularly in those places where malaria is rampant. The writer adds:

For decades, scientists have tried to create an effective vaccine. The research has been fraught with dashed hopes over test-tube experiments that did not pan out in animal or human trials. The new findings suggest that one experimental vaccine, called SPf66, is just as effective in Africa, where malaria is rampant, as it has been shown to be in South America. The vaccine reduced the rate of infection by nearly 40 percent in a South American study of 1,500 volunteers. Skeptics had thought the promising South American results, first published in March 1993, could be replicated because malaria is much more intense in Africa.

The reporter concludes this story by adding that the results of the African study were published in Saturday's issue of the *Lancet*, a medical journal. There were no details given as to the exact date or place of this publication.

Critical Thinking and Reading of Articles

How might students begin to unravel the insidious cultural pedagogy embedded in these two articles? What kinds of global values or biases are depicted? Do these articles present an optimistic view of life? The critical issues raised in the two articles reflect the standpoint of the social context from which they were written and equally implicate the social contexts of class, gender, and race of the audience for whom they were written. Readers of the *Inquirer* and the *Center Daily Times* (both owned by Knight-Ridder Corporation) are typically residents of metropolitan Philadelphia and State College, respectively, mostly working-class or middle-class to upper-middle-class Americans. For my students, the debate ensuing from the articles seemed to revolve around the larger issues of doing research on children, the sacredness of life, objectivity in reporting, and misreporting about Africa and South America. Their critique was informed and shaped by their views and attitudes about life, especially for little children and consent issues. In the Philadelphia story, the students noted these important issues of contention:

1. Tampering with cadavers of 19 children for medical science research seemed to bother students. Images from the movie *Sexist* were associated with this story.
2. Parents/relatives of these infants were justified to be enraged because they did not give consent to the research objectives.
3. The point of view of the journalist is biased in favor of medical research and seems to indicate that there were some benefits derived from such research. There was knowledge gained about the nature of trauma sustained by the infants as a cause of death.

By comparison, the malaria story seemed to raise more questions for my students rather than critical comments. Lack of details in the information given by the story may have contributed to this kind of response. However, some of the specific comments and questions resulting from the malaria story were:

1. The malaria study was pure research. In order to accomplish such research a researcher must establish experimental and control groups.
2. What happened to those infants who got placebos? Did they die? Were they treated after they contracted malaria?
3. How can an experiment having a 31 percent success rate be claimed to be successful?
4. Was Dr. White the principal investigator of this malaria experiment? What's the connection between the dateline (London), the research program where Dr. White is located (Bangkok), and Idete village in Tanzania? Were there no doctors in Tanzania or South America to comment on the results? Why are African doctors silent in this article? Wouldn't these doctors be more knowledgeable, as they work in the countries where this fatal disease is prevalent? Why is a doctor in Bangkok being sought out as a spokesperson?
5. What do estimates like "kills one million to three million children every year, the vast majority in Africa" mean?

6. Do comments from the journalist such as "in Africa, where malaria is rampant," and "malaria is much more intense in Africa" build on the stereotype about Africa being the "dark continent"?

Students were challenged to examine the reporting in these two articles, including the use of language, the descriptions of emotions, the value-laden statements, like "permanently removed eyes," "young children—most of them abuse victims," and the lack of human appeal or human interest in the use of names of continents (Africa, South America) instead of specific countries. The malaria story did not seem to bother these middle-class students of central Pennsylvania as much as the Philadelphia story. Their comments about the "Africa" story were limited because, as they claimed, they knew little about malaria and about Africa. They admitted, however, that whatever they knew about Africa came from the media. When pressed they did not have an answer to explain why they did not know much about malaria when it is a deadly disease, killing more that a million children every year—more than the AIDS epidemic. Unfortunately, the malaria story must take its place within the continuum of many other disaster stories coming out of Africa and South America—continents seen as "jungles" by many Americans—that show us the "dark other" from the standpoint of whiteness.

Notice that the reader is not told who invented the vaccine—it was, in fact, a doctor from Colombia. Instead, the reader is left to wonder and probably wrongly guess the inventor to be the Oxford Tropical Medicine Center in Bangkok or a European or North American lab. As noted by Ukadike (1990), much of the image Americans have about Africa has come from movies and for most Americans there is no motive to challenge these images. "It is amazing how, when films with exotic images reach Western screens, their hollow contents do nothing to diminish their anthropological value or rating. Nor is the audience inclined to seek detailed and accurate information for a true anthropological rendition of the culture or an attempt to point out when authors display latent prejudice abetted by careless research, poor writing, and inadequate editing" (p. 42). This point of view reiterates what we have known for quite some time and what Stuart Hall (1997) confirms in his analysis about the images of athletes of color, especially blacks in films. It is therefore true that the commercial cinema system has continued to stock its productions with themes and formulas dealing with black issues and characters that are reassuring to the sensibilities and expectations of an easy white audience. These filmic images tend to "mediate the dysfunctions and delusions of a society unable to deal honestly with its inequalities and racial conflicts, a society that operates in a profound state of racial denial on a daily basis" (Guerrero, 1993). Other scholars agree with Guerrero. Allen (1993), for example, states, "The print and the electronic media, and especially cinema and television, have shown African people and other people of color in comedic stances and in degrading ways. The depictions have suggested that African peoples are not interested in and do not care about serious matters, are frivolous and irresponsible, and are unable to participate in the mainstream of U.S.

society. Television has been notably powerful in implying, suggesting, and maintaining this myth" (p. 156). These accounts simply confirm what many media executives' attitudes are: Americans have never paid much attention to news from Africa.

It is also important to note how interpretations of the two articles were framed by the context of the students' assumptions, general knowledge, and widespread beliefs about scientific research and about Africa. Their discussion quickly degenerated into U.S. "values" of life, posing contradictions—from rights of the unborn child, protecting minors, abuse of children, partial fetal abortions, to the death penalty. These two examples illustrate how "values" about life are contested issues. Furthermore, their value for the lives of children in other countries, particularly far from home, was shaped by their Eurocentric view of holding to the tenets of science as more important than life. This view clouded over the fact that the Philadelphia children were dead corpses (19 of them) while the Tanzanian children (586 of them) were alive and their lives were threatened by both a deadly disease and medical science.

The critical reading of these two articles provided students with an opportunity to sit back and try to reconstruct the processes of their critical thinking. After their analysis, they worked in groups as they developed frameworks for teaching critical reading of texts to be used by teachers of English in secondary schools. Some of these frameworks advocated for the introduction of alternative explanations to phenomena, particularly those described in narratives read, viewed, and discussed in classrooms. Alternative explanations can be found in multiple texts containing different viewpoints and multicultural perspectives. Students presented with such multiple perspectives can take one of three positions as described by Fiske (1987) to select (1) the dominant reading (accepting the preferred meaning), (2) the negotiated reading (accepting aspects of the preferred meaning but rejecting others, or (3) the oppositional reading (rejecting the preferred meaning) (p. 260).

WAYS TO COMBAT BIAS

To help students critique bias and their own cultural stances, I ask them to read oppositional texts and employ the language of criticism. This allows students and teachers to move beyond "commonsense" readings of daily life narratives. If teachers continue to ask the same questions on social issues, they will simply recycle prevailing views or biases. Through *questioning, reflection,* and *action,* students get to know their social context, evaluate it, and plan action to take to make changes. McMahon and Quin (1993) list "alternative questions" I employ. I ask these questions to help students identify social issues raised by the text (literature or visuals related to them): (1) Through whose eyes or perspective do we get the information? (2) What assumptions are being made in the view presented? (3) What representations are there of the group concerned? (4) Whose voices are not being heard? (5) If a key piece of information were changed, how would the meaning change? (6) Why has this group been singled out for depiction in this manner? Who gains from this representation? (7) What would be the effect if the various depictions were reversed? (p. 18).

I also advocate and teach the language of criticism to detect biases. This process coincides with what John Dewey (1933) called the creation of an articulate public and its attendant concerns with these issues, institutions, and public spheres that are attentive to human suffering, pain, and oppression. Taking such a critical stance on media representations will effectively take reading and viewing of texts a step beyond surface impressions, traditional myths, and clichés.

As far as taking action is concerned, I encourage students to engage in an interdisciplinary unit about the local environment, examining varied media to understand and detect bias. They create public service announcements, research reports, Web sites, newsletters, and actions plans to address issues. In secondary social studies or English/language arts classrooms, they apply critical analysis of content and points of view represented in their content area. After identifying missing information, students employ community interview, oral histories, original documents, and mass media or artistic resources to build broader pictures of events or texts. As a culminating activity, these students choose to write their own books, create a newspaper, a Web site, a mural, or a dramatic presentation to convey their new understandings which are then displayed. They invite the public (usually peers, students from other disciplines, or high school students from nearby schools) for comment and critique. By using readings, observations, personal interviews, artifacts in their own lives, videos, and listserve discussions, these students access, articulate, examine, and adapt their beliefs about teaching, make professional changes, and formulate plans for their own future growth, as well as that of their respective communities.

These activities confirm one of the key concepts of critical media literacy—that all media are constructions. Because all texts are creations with potential bias, we need to bring a critical stance to all texts that inform our worldview, a competency gained through critical media literacy education. Within this perspective, the mass media are no longer viewed as windows of the world or objective representations of our world, but rather as subjective and sometimes loaded with social biases regarding race, class, sexual orientation, gender, and ethnic differences. In critical media literacy, teachers must ask students to take a hard look at what the media tell them about the world—as media continue to be a major source of information, culture, and entertainment. The media are not neutral conduits of messages but rather, they actively create notions of what constitutes truth, values, racial relations, bias, stereotypes, and representations of people. In sum, critical viewing, critical reading, and critical authoring are pivotal components by which to integrate media literacy across the school curriculum.

REFERENCES

Allen, R. L. (1993). Conceptual models of an African-American belief system: A program of research. In G. L. Berry & J. K. Asamen (Eds.), *Children and television: Images in a changing sociocultural world.* pp. 112–140. Thousand Oaks, CA: Sage.

Anderson, J., & Ploghoft, M. (1993). Children and media in media education. In G. L. Berry & J. K. Asamen (Eds.), *Children and television: Images in a changing sociocultural world.* pp. 27–60. Thousand Oaks, CA: Sage.

Barthes, R. (1971). *Image, music, text* (S. Heath, Trans.). New York: Hill & Wang.

Barthes, R. (1974). *S/Z* (R. Miller, Trans.). New York: Hill & Wang/The Noonday Press.

Bradley, D. F., & West, J. F. (1994). Staff training for the inclusion of students with disabilities: Visions from school-based education. *Teachers Education and Special Education, 17*(2), 117–128.

Comber, B. (1993). Classroom explorations in critical literacy. *The Australian Journal of Language and Literacy, 16*(1).

Derrida, J. (1986). Structure, sign, and play in the discourse of the human sciences; Of grammatology; Difference. In H. Adams & L. Searle (Eds.), *Critical theory since 1965* (pp. 83–137). Tallahassee: Florida State University Press.

Cazden, C., & Green, J., (1992). Critical language awareness in the ESL classroom. In N. Fairclough (Ed.), *Critical language awareness* (pp. 52–92). Harlow: Longman.

Dewey, J. (1933). *How we think.* Chicago: Henry Regnery.

Dines, G., & Humez, J. M. (1995). *Gender, race and class in media.* Thousand Oaks, CA: Sage.

Fairclough, N. (1989). *Language and power.* London: Longman.

Fiske, J. (1987). *Television culture.* London: Methuen.

Flood, J., & Lapp, D. (1995). Broadening the lens: Toward an expanded conceptualization of literacy. In K. A. Hinchman, D. J. Leu, & C. K. Kinzer (Eds.), *Perspectives on literacy research and practice: Forty-fourth yearbook of the National Reading Conference* (pp. 1–16). Chicago: National Reading Conference.

Freire, P. (1974). *Education for critical consciousness.* London: Sheed & Ward.

Gee, J. (1996). *Social linguistics and literacies: Ideology in discourses* (2nd ed.). London: Taylor & Francis.

Guerrero, E. (1993). *Framing blackness: The African-American image in film.* Philadelphia: Temple University Press.

Hall, S. (1997). *Representation. Cultural representations and signifying practices.* London: The Open University.

Hammer, R. (1995). Rethinking the dialectic: A critical semiotic meta-theoretical approach for the pedagogy of media literacy. In P. McLaren, R. Hammer, D. Sholle, & S. Reilly, *Rethinking media literacy: A critical pedagogy of representation* (pp. 33–85). New York: Peter Lang.

Hirsch, E. (1987). *Cultural literacy: What every American needs to know.* Boston: Houghton Mifflin.

Hobbs, R. (1994). Teaching media literacy—Are you hip to this? *Media Studies Journal* (Winter).

Janks, H. (1993). *Language, identity and power.* Johannesburg and Rundburg: Witwatersrand University Press and Hodder and Stoughton Educational.

Kellner D. (1995). *Media culture: Cultural studies, identity, and politics between the modern and the postmodern.* London: Routledge.

Kincheloe, J., & Steinberg, S. (1998). *Unauthorized methods. Strategies for critical teaching.* New York: Routledge.

Kress, G. (1988). *Communication and culture.* Kensington: University of New South Wales Press.

Krueger, R. A. (1994). *Focus groups. A practical guide for applied research.* Thousand Oaks, CA: Sage.

Lankshear, C., & McLaren, P. (Eds.). (1993). *Critical literacy: Politics, praxis, and the postmodern.* Albany: State University of New York Press.

Leveranz, D., & Tyner, K. (1966). What is media literacy? Two leading proponents offer an overview. *Media Spectrum, 23*(1), 10.

Lutz, W. (1989). *Doublespeak*. New York: Harper Perennial.

Masterman, L. (1992). *Teaching the media*. London: Routledge.

McMahon, B., & Quin, R. (1993). Knowledge power and pleasure: Direction in media education. *Telemedium, 39*(1-2), 18–22.

Morgan, W. (1997). *Critical literacy in the classroom*. London: Routledge.

Newskit. (1994). *How to detect bias in the news*. A consumers guide to News Media. Lake Zurich, IL: The Learning Seed Company.

Pennsylvania Education (1993, February). Volume 24, No. 5, pp. 3–5.

Searle, C. (Ed.). (1994). *Lives of love and hope: A Sheffield Herstory*. Sheffield: Earl Marshal School.

Searle, C. (Ed.). (1995). *Heart of Sheffield*. Sheffield: Earl Marshal School.

Semali, L., & Watts Pailliotet, A. (1999). Introduction. What is intermediality and why study it in U.S. schools? In L. Semali & A. Watts Pailliotet (Eds.), *Intermediality: The teachers' handbook of critical media literacy* (pp. 1–30). Boulder, CO: Westview.

Silverblatt, A. (1995). *Media literacy. Keys to interpreting media messages*. New York: Praeger.

Stewart, D. (1990). *Focus groups: Theory and practice*. Thousand Oaks, CA: Sage.

Ukadike, N. F. (1990). Western images of Africa: Genealogy of an ideological formulation. *Black Scholar, 21*(2), 30–48.

Walmsley, S. A., & Walp, T. P. (1990). Integrating literature and composing into the language arts. *The Elementary School Journal, 1*(3), 251–274.

Zeichner, K., & Liston, D. (1996). *Reflective teaching*. Mahwah, NJ: Erlbaum.

MEDIA LITERACY AS EVOLUTION AND REVOLUTION:
IN THE CULTURE, CLIMATE, AND CONTEXT OF AMERICAN EDUCATION

David M. Considine

> You can have the most creative, compellingly valid, educationally productive idea in the world, but whether it can be embedded and sustained in a socially complex setting, will be primarily a function of how you conceptualize the implementation-change process. (Sacason, 1994, p. 78).

On the surface, the 1990s were good years for the media literacy movement in the United States. National conferences were held in North Carolina, California, Colorado, and Minnesota. In less than a decade, media literacy had progressed from a dot on the horizon of American education, to a movement that had been embraced by the White House, the Office of National Drug Control Policy, the Secretary of Education, the Secretary of Health and Human Services, and prestigious campuses like Harvard and Penn State. In 1998 both the *English Journal* and the *Journal of Communication* devoted entire issues to media literacy. Nonetheless, despite such heady times, one could well ask whether the media literacy glass was half empty or half full. Beneath the surface of success, there was troubling evidence from the

Advances in Reading/Language Research, Volume 7, pages 299–327.
Copyright © 2000 by JAI Press Inc.
All rights of reproduction in any form reserved.
ISBN: 0-7623-0264-X

schools, which indicated that even traditional approaches to media and technology in education were experiencing difficulty.

In 1997, for example, the *Report to the President on the Use of Technology to Strengthen K–12 Education* commented that "while information technologies have had an enormous impact within America's offices, factories and stores over the past several decades... [the nation's schools] have thus far been only minimally affected by the information revolution" (p. 113).

This may seem a reasonably esoteric fact to media literacy proponents who might well wonder what schools and technology have to do with media literacy. The answer becomes abundantly clear when we stop dealing with media literacy as a discrete concept, competency, or subject area, and instead recognize that one of its primary characteristics is change. As such, for media literacy to succeed in the perilous journey from innovation, to implementation and integration, its advocates will have to focus on the nature of school as institutions, and the organizational response (often less than enthusiastic) to change itself.

Further, the terms media and literacy are neither neutral nor new. Introducing a concept like media literacy to our schools requires that we take into account existing attitudes and assumptions about both literacy and media. That process is complex and complicated. Though we tend to think about the relative merit of individual innovations, success or failure requires an understanding of schools as organizations. Robert Muffoletto has said that "education is a social institution, it has a purpose and a history that is full of contests and compromises, contradictions and agreements." Tellingly he adds, "any discussion on reforming education and technology, must situate itself within and against those discourses" (Muffoletto, 1994, p. 24).

Media literacy cannot isolate itself from the traditional discourse regarding media that has taken place in our schools. While we may know what we are talking about, administrators and other teachers are likely to filter any reference to media through the lens of their own experiences. For some that means the failure of each successive technology of instruction to transform the classroom as promised. For others, the term media means technology which in turn means computers. In an era of multimedia and hypermedia, how do we identify media literacy as a related but separate concept and make a case for its inclusion in our schools? How can media literacy, as a relatively new kid on the block, hope to succeed when the federal funding, legislative mandates, and an infusion of hardware and software have not changed our schools after almost two decades of initiatives and promises?

The answer to that question might well be that media literacy's weakness is also its strength. That is to say, for the most part, it is fed at the grass-roots level by classroom teachers, not by centralized bureaucracies. In fact, far from being unexpected or unanticipated, technology's failure to transform education is highly predictable based on the fact that for the most part, teachers have experienced the changes associated with technology, as something that happens *to them, not through them.*

As the recipients of top-down change, typically mandated externally, teachers as individuals and schools as institutions have responded by assuming the characteristics of change-resistant organizations. Hence, when innovation is imposed on an institution, when it evolves from external political realities rather than from the nature and needs of those who must implement the innovation, it is subverted by the very system it seeks to change. Externally mandated change can never substitute for internally motivated change.

Though it is argued that the new technologies are revolutionary, it is also true that they grow out of "a technocratic world view" and function as a detached, cold, scientific "means for controlling the educational experience" (Muffoletto, 1994). Perhaps it is the mechanistic relationship between means and ends, a process that seems to dehumanize education, that has resulted in teacher resistance to technology and transformation. What it is not, as Terry Woronov pointed out in *The Harvard Education Letter*, is technophobia. A phobia, is an irrational fear. There is, however, "nothing irrational about teachers being afraid of looking stupid in front of students" especially when they have had little training and little systems support Woronov (1994, p. 1).

For any change, including media literacy, to therefore succeed in our schools, as much attention must be given to the institutional context in which the change will be subverted or supported, as is given to the change itself. Yet as Jerome Bruner (1996) has noted, it is "astonishing how little systematic study is devoted to the institutional anthropology of schooling" (p. 29).

In fact, the operation, organization, modes of representation, and ideology of schools and the mass media remain for the average citizen or student, obfuscated and unexplained, a process made all the more extraordinary by our day-to-day contact with these agents of socialization, information, and entertainment. Like McLuhan's fish who could not recognize the water in which they swam, teachers frequently spend their lives in an organizational environment that they have never been helped to recognize let alone reject or reform. Under conditions such as these, based as they are on control and conformity, it is little wonder that technological tools promising individual, self-paced learning have failed to transform the curriculum and classroom.

It is ironic indeed, that those foisting technology on the nation's schools fail to perceive the most obvious fact that *tools don't change schools; teachers do.* To make those changes they need to be active partners in the transformation process.

Unfortunately, there is little if anything about traditional teacher preparation, at the in-service or preservice level, to indicate that teachers are encouraged to see themselves as transformers, not just transmitters of culture. In *Schoolteacher: A Sociological Study*, Lortie (1975) concluded that "they see themselves as constrained, under-supplied and under-appreciated; their aims and their context do not jibe; . . . but they apparently accept the terms imposed by the organization" (pp. 185–186). Almost a quarter century later, the alienated teacher is still a fixture in our schools. "How and why," asks Parker Palmer (1998), "does academic culture discourage us from living connected lives. . . encourage us to distance ourselves from our students and our subjects?" (p. 35). How might this sense of alienation and powerlessness affect the way teachers respond to media literacy? Of greater importance is the question of how media literacy might affect the way teachers see themselves, their students, and their schools. These are not inconsequential questions, for the principles of media literacy lead logically to a pedagogical Pandora's box, which once opened, is difficult indeed to close again.

At once evolutionary and revolutionary in nature, media literacy constitutes both a subject of study and a method or process of teaching. As both content and delivery system, media literacy challenges much of traditional education by exposing many of its inherent tensions and contradictions. Recognized, valued, and applied, the principles of media literacy and the critical pedagogy that grows logically from them, challenge and confront not only the controlling power of mass media, but also that corollary power within our schools, including the selection and rejection of curricula, which teachers, like television audiences, have been falsely conditioned to regard as neutral knowledge.

Despite this perception, school knowledge determines the way we prepare students to see themselves, the world, and their place in that world. "What counts as legitimate knowledge is the result of complex power relations and struggles among identifiable class, race, gender and religious groups" (Apple, 1993, p. 46). Textbooks, technologies, and the entire apparatus of instruction "signify through their content and form, particular constructions of reality, particular ways of selecting and organizing the vast universe of possible knowledge" (p. 49).

Teachers as individuals and schools as institutions function as carriers and conveyors of culture. But they do not assign equal time and weight to all cultures. As such, what they teach and how they teach it play an active role in selecting some cultures, while rejecting others. Recognizing their role in that process is a necessary stage in the movement toward a more equitable curriculum. Again, the context in which instruction occurs is crucial. "The designers of an empowering pedagogy have to study the shape of disempowering forces . . . the teacher's own critical learning prefigures the knowledge the class as a whole will gain" (Shor & Paulo, 1987, p. 47).

LOOKING AT LITERACY

Before moving on to a consideration of what media literacy is, has been, or is in the process of becoming, it might be beneficial to look at traditional literacy and its place in the classroom. Today, the phrase is so widely used that it is possible to talk not only about media literacy, computer literacy, information literacy, and visual literacy, but also an array of other areas including health literacy, cultural literacy (Hirsch, 1988), multicultural literacy (Simonson & Walker, 1988), television literacy (Buckingham, 1993), and even Amish literacy (Fishman, 1988).

Which if any of these conceptions of literacy schools value and validate, will depend of course on what teachers, administrators, legislators, textbook publishers, parents, and other stakeholders perceive as having legitimate value. Those perceptions are frequently based on a rather shortsighted view of both learning and literacy. As Elliot Eisner (1991) put it, "we continue to think about literacy in the tightest most constipated terms" (p. 15). What was needed, he added, was a wider sense of what it means to know and understand.

Once again, we must recognize from the outset that any attempt to define literacy, like any attempt to define knowing and understanding, must have at its heart the issue of power. Yet as Michael Apple (1993) points out, most people tend to believe that "literacy has a nonpolitical function" (p. 44). In reality of course, "the process of both defining what counts as literacy and how it should be gained has always had links to particular regimes of morality" (p. 44).

Just as proponents of media literacy will need to examine the organizational culture and climate of the schools where they wish to implement media literacy, the cultural conditions that have traditionally surrounded literacy itself must also be considered. Hence, one sees immediately the value judgments implicit in the statement: "Being literate has always referred to having mastery over the processes by means of which culturally significant information is coded" (de Castell & Luke, 1983, p. 159).

For media literacy advocates, one of the great battles of course is trying to convince parents, administrators, and other teachers that film, television, advertising, and other media not only are "culturally significant," but also that the messages they contain and convey should in fact be regarded as information, not simply entertainment.

While such a case can be credibly mounted, making that case has been made all the more difficult, ironically enough, by the way print journalism and broadcast news have affected public perception of the nation's schools. In a time when these perceptions suggest that students are "passive....unempowered... certainly unable to write" (Resnick, 1991), it is an uphill battle indeed to suggest that schools should turn their attention to media literacy rather than concentrating on the basics. Nonetheless, that is the challenge that now confronts us. Though the task and problems sometimes appear insurmountable, it may well be that media literacy provides a window of opportunity for engaging our students and linking the literacies.

This bridge building exercise would bring together the curriculum of the classroom and the curriculum of the living room, or as Vygotsky (1962) described it, the scientific knowledge of school and the spontaneous experience of the child. It might well be argued that those who express alarm about declining literacy rates, should not ignore the cold cognitive culture of the classroom, narrowly focused on school knowledge, while failing to recognize and respect the nature and needs of the very students it expects to value this knowledge. When students fail to perceive the value of such teaching, they are labeled dropouts. In reality of course, they are push outs, expelled from a system that they find meaningless. "It is not that students cannot learn; it is that they do not wish to. If educators invested a fraction of the energy they now spend trying to transmit information in trying to stimulate the students' enjoyment of learning, we could achieve much better results" (Csikszent-mihalyi, 1991, p. 115).

Experienced media educators know firsthand that student enjoyment of learning is greatly enhanced when popular culture comes into the classroom. Though there may be a hue and cry from various stakeholders when teachers talk about reading, analyzing, comprehending, or interpreting such products or programs, a successful strategy for defusing such objections is to concentrate on the process of making meaning (encoding and decoding) while downplaying the nature of the text being studied. *School Library Journal*, a bastion of literacy and books, has validated such an approach with a January 1994 cover story on media literacy (Considine) and by arguing earlier that "the skills and abilities needed to decode and interpret visual messages are probably as demanding as those required for reading print" (Vander-grift & Hannigan, 1993, p. 20).

This belief has already been validated by progressive school systems. In North Carolina, for example, viewing has been featured prominently for many years in the *Communication Skills* K–12 curriculum. "In a visually oriented world, the skills of viewing have assumed increasing importance. Visuals shape actions, promote thoughts and occasionally warp meaning" (North Carolina Department of Public Instruction, 1985, p. 29). North Carolina's 1992 *Information Skills* framework places images and information in context. Not only are students expected to "recognize the power of the media to influence" they are expected to "recognize how the presentation of information and ideas is influenced by social, cultural, political and historical events." In late 1998, Minnesota began developing a state-wide test for year ten students as part of their reading, viewing, and listening skills. The same year Utah developed *The Elementary Library Media Core Curriculum*. Among other things, students were required to recognize special effects, illustra-tions, perspective, and color in picture books, and the use of shot, camera angles, zoom, cuts, color, and graphics in other visual media.

LEARNING TO LOOK

There are certainly no shortage of tools, techniques, or frameworks teachers can utilize in the process of helping students recognize and read the language of visuals whether in movies, television, news, or advertising. Lester (1995) provides a series of perspectives for reading any type of image, including the personal, historical, technical, ethical, and critical perspective. In the case of motion pictures, Monaco (1977) explores the language, signs, and syntax of the medium, while Giannetti (1976) examines elements such as the frame, composition, shots, and angles. Drawing on concepts of *mise en scene*, Considine and Haley (1992, 1999) suggest ways in which classroom teachers can work with films such as *Mission Impossible*,

Rebel Without a Cause, *Ordinary People*, and *Forest Gump* to enhance student understanding and appreciation of film form and content.

Utilizing visual literacy research, film theory, and children's literature, the same authors provided a series of tools (prop, posture, position, point of view) to help children and teachers understand the content, form, and organization of children's picture books (Considine, Haley, & Lacy, 1994). Tellingly, they relied on the words of the authors and illustrators of these works to establish a link between the process of both creating and comprehending words and images. Don Wood (1986), for example, said that "the picture book is as close to drama or a 32 page movie as it is to either literature or art" (p. 556). In the chapter Painting with Words: Writing with Pictures (Considine, Haley, & Lacy, 1994), the authors open with Jane Yolen's comment: "There are two views of a picture book. The first is that it is a palette with words. The second is that it is a story with illustrations" (p. 123).

Visual modes of storytelling do of course share much in common with the codes and conventions of traditional narrative, so a study of visual storytelling like movies can represent a continuation and variation of narrative forms rather than a radical disruption or departure from such forms. First-person narrative accounts and cinematic voice-overs link the worlds of *Moby Dick*, *The Great Gatsby*, and *Catcher in the Rye* to contemporary films including *Inventing the Abbotts*, *How to Make an American Quilt*, *Stand By Me*, *A Civil Action*, and *The Education of Little Tree*. Such cinematic stories share common elements with literature including conflict, resolution, dilemma, motif, and theme.

Even nonvisual forms of storytelling like popular music can also be studied for common characteristics. The isolated state of mind of the central character, along with the lonely setting are instantly established in the first line of "Eleanor Rigby" as she "picks up the rice in a church where a wedding has been." Paul McCartney's reminiscences of childhood also skillfully create the urban setting and workday environment of "Penny Lane" inhabited by banker, fireman, nurse, and barber. The lyrics reinforce Yolen's conception of the different levels of storytelling. Penny Lane, we are told, "is in my ears and in my eyes."

The simple pleasures of the children's picture book or the intriguing words and music of Lennon McCartney are of course no substitute for comprehending a culture so saturated with visual messages. One of the most salient features of the so called information age is the fact that much of that information is carried by pictures not print, through television not textbooks. Occasionally when ethical boundaries are crossed and established practices ignored, the public becomes fleetingly aware of the changing nature of this information. *Time*'s now notorious "enhancement" of the Los Angeles Police Department mug shot of O. J. Simpson is a contemporary example. The short-lived firestorm about the media's role in covering and/or causing the death of Princess Diana is another. CNN's 1998 retraction of their story claiming the U.S. government used chemical weapons against deserters during the Vietnam War was one of many unhappy incidents undermining the credibility of the press that year, each of which compels us to reexamine our conception of literacy. At the very least they challenge us to think about how we know what we think we know.

Such images and incidents can become catalysts for change, providing teachable moments not just in our classrooms with our students, but in the wider community where we can draw on such controversies to make the case for a wider understanding of literacy. This wider understanding links literacy to the changing communication forms of our society. The shift from the oral tradition to traditional notions of literacy cannot, for example, be divorced from the technology of the times, most notably the printing press and movable type. Similarly the computer revolution fueled a call for computer literacy.

But hands-on skills with the computer, while potentially providing employment opportunities, is not in and of itself a guarantee that impressionable children and teens surfing the Net will have the skills to distinguish information from advertising or reject the spurious claims of sites suggesting, for example, that the Holocaust never happened. Access to information, so celebrated by schools, legislatures, and business, should not be equated with successfully understanding that information. That can only come from a critical criterion that recognizes the relationship between literacy and liberty by fostering independent thought and methods of inquiry. As such "literacy is only a first step in the empowerment of the mind, albeit a crucial one. . . it also shapes the way in which the mind is used. . . . Simply knowing how to write, or how to decipher what has been written, does not guarantee that these powers will be used" (Bruner, 1991, p. 111).

Nor can literacy be confined to simply recognizing or comprehending ideas contained in a text including media texts. Too frequently, as David Buckingham tells us, English teachers have used this approach in such a way that students were left trying to guess "the correct meaning," rather than actively constructing their own interpretation or reading of the text. Such a process, while employing novel and evolving technologies and texts, remains repressive in its approach to reading. It also isolates text, from context, including the cultural, social, political, and economic conditions in which it is both produced and consumed.

Yet these considerations are deeply interwoven with the traditional American value of responsible citizenship in a democratic society. How responsible is a citizen who does not understand the organization and ownership of society's information forms? Can we truly understand media messages if we do not equally understand the media messengers, who "fix the premises of discourse . . .decide what the general populace is allowed to see, hear and think about?" (Herman & Chomsky, 1988, p. 1]. Such a conception of literacy recognizes that literacy is liberatory. It is a "critical literacy, powerful literacy, political literacy which enables the growth of genuine understanding and of all the spheres of social life in which we participate" (Apple, 1993, p. 44). Though many of its supporters may not know it, or want to know it, media literacy in its origins and outcomes clearly embraces such ideals.

MEDIA LITERACY: EVOLUTION AND REVOLUTION

Debate and disagreement about the goals of media literacy in the United States was evident in the special issue of the *Journal of Communication*. Arguing that the approach of Hobbs and other advocates "avoids thorny political territory," and "sidesteps widespread citizen concerns," Lewis and Jhally (1998) said that media literacy must be "more than a question of comprehension." What was needed, they suggested, was a shift from "a text-focused form of media literacy" to a "contextual approach" that examines and critiques the institutional and industrial ownership and organization of the media and the messages they produce (p. 123).

Although this may seem profoundly radical within the context of traditional literacy where texts are studied for meaning, appreciation, and merit, critical pedagogy has begun to move us inexorably to a more rigorous reading of text. Hence, we find it argued that "it's no longer a celebration of children learning to read by reading, or students being authors, but rather concern over what it is that students are learning to read and write, what they do with that reading and writing, and what that reading and writing does to them and their world" (Comber & O'Brien, 1993, p. 2).

Jerome Bruner (1996) also believes that literacy is more than a series of coping or survival skills and strategies, aimed at enabling students and citizens to process the information forms of the contemporary world. While comprehension and communication are clearly part of literacy, Bruner sees a wider purpose for education. That purpose, he believes, "is aiding young humans in learning to use the tools of meaning-making and reality construction, to better adapt to the world in which they find themselves, and *to help in the process of changing it as required.*" (p. 20). As such the teacher and the classroom are no longer simply present to transmit culture, rather they exist to transform culture. Reading now includes the possibility of resistance. Literacy, including media literacy, becomes not simply an evolutionary response to the changing information technologies of an age, but a revolutionary response, which profoundly transforms subject matter and the student–teacher relationship.

Understanding this requires some sense of the origins of media literacy. For the most part those origins are in Australia and the United Kingdom where media literacy in one manifestation or another has been in place since the 1960s and 1970s. As an academic discipline media literacy can be seen to include content or the subject of study; instructional methods, modes, or techniques of teaching; and the intellectual and theoretical traditions on which it is based. Buckingham (1998) traces the evolution of media education in England through a series of stages including critical awareness, cultural studies, screen education, democratization, and defensiveness.

Under the auspices of the British Film Institute, contemporary media education is now concerned with "developing students' understanding of and participation in the media" (Buckingham, 1998, p. 99). Areas of study include media agencies, media categories, media technologies, media languages, media audiences, and media representations.

At an ATOM (Australian Teachers of Media) conference, Australian media educators were told the purpose of their work. Students, it was said, "should be able to locate their own experience of the media in relation to the larger context in which it occurs. . . . They should be self-reflexive consumers and producers of media—they should know what turns them on and why—and the political and cultural implications of that pleasure" (Turnbull, 1996, pp. 7, 8). Interestingly, the audience was also told that without being atheoretical, they should "not feel the need to adopt a single theoretical or political position."

Leaders of the Canadian and American media literacy movements met in December 1992, as part of the Aspen Institute's Communications and Society Program. The Canadians more specifically, Ontario had introduced media literacy as part of the high school English curriculum in the late 1980s. Supported by their Ministry of Education, they argued that media was "an essential ingredient of all curricula" (Ontario Ministry, 1989, p. 20) and that it needed to be studied "in a critical and coherent way" (p. 5). Their efforts would serve as a catalyst in the United States. At the Aspen conference, the leadership accepted a definition of media literacy as the *ability to access, analyze, evaluate, and communicate information in a variety of forms*. That definition is now widely accepted by organizations such as the Wisconsin-based National Telemedia Council and the Center for Media Literacy in Los Angeles. It has been repeated and reinforced in articles (Considine, 1995; Hobbs, 1997) and in books (Considine & Haley, 1999) which have found their way onto college reading lists and entered the domain of teacher preparation.

Less commonly held, as we have seen, is the purpose of media literacy. "Like many areas of education," writes David Buckingham, "it has been characterized by on-going debate about its aims" (1998a, p. 33). This ever-changing evolution of media education within the United Kingdom should be noted by American advocates. It cautions us against slavishly adopting a "foreign" model that may not be suited to the organizational or social context of the United States. It alerts us to the fact that the British approach has itself changed over several decades based on the experiences of those who have taught it. Surely this suggests that local ownership by American teachers rather than replication of external philosophies and approaches will be a criterion for the success of media literacy in this country.

Writing in *Beyond Radical Pedagogy*, Buckingham also provides a warning for those who advocate radical goals for media literacy in the United States. In England, he tells us, "this has led to the government's attempt to sever the connection between higher education and schools; and to replace teacher education with a form of instrumental on the job training" (1998b, pp. 1, 2). Such policies, despite opposition from the educational establishment, "have gained widespread popular support" (1998b, pp. 1, 2). Traditions of Labour, the intellectual Left, and an active union movement in Great Britain cannot be separated from the directions media education has taken. Since such conditions are not, however, historically present in the United

States, a more cautious agenda, more in keeping with this social conservatism, might initially at least be more productive and encounter less resistance. Before it can be revolutionary, media literacy must first be evolutionary, which is to say it will evolve out of the traditional aims and goals of American education.

MEDIA LITERACY PURPOSES: PREPARATION, PROTECTION, AND PLEASURE

This conservative context provided much of the introduction for what has been described as the first comprehensive media literacy text in the United States. First published in 1992, *Visual Messages: Integrating Imagery into Instruction* (Considine & Haley) argued that rather than isolating media literacy as an innovation, it should and could be shown to be compatible with key components of the curriculum; with broad goals like responsible citizenship, and with emerging trends and research such as cooperative learning, multicultural education, and critical thinking skills.

Pointing to the *Turning Points* report on middle schools (Carnegie Council, 1989), the authors argued that media literacy was compatible with the report's recommendations that schools should create students who "are literate. . . who know how to think critically. . . lead a healthy life, behave ethically and assume the responsibilities of citizenship in a pluralistic society" (p. 91). By the end of the decade, the second edition furthered the argument, drawing heavily on national standards and existing state frameworks in areas such as Language Arts, Communication, Social Studies, Art, Health, and Information Technology. Media literacy, they said, while both evolutionary and revolutionary, was also compatible with curriculum objectives already in place.

In Washington State where both authors conducted in-service teacher training, they used the state's 1997 *Essential Academic Learning Requirements* document to make their case (Washington State Department of Education, 1997). In the Communication component of the curriculum, students were expected among other objectives to "interpret visual texts such as illustrations, comics and video"; "analyze and interpret the influence of media sources." History, Social Studies, and Civics objectives were similarly compatible. Students were expected to use media and technology to "locate, gather and process information" and to "explain how cultural communication contributes to societal cohesion and/or division, for example through television, books and movies." The Health and Fitness curriculum asked students not only to resist harmful substances but also to "identify messages about safe and unsafe behaviors, such as tobacco or alcohol advertising."

Underlying such interdisciplinary content and objectives, one can identify three purposes that have been traditional components of American education. Linking media literacy to these existing goals and roles, it is argued, is a management strategy to curtail opposition and facilitate change.

PURPOSE #1: PREPARATION

One of the most fundamental and often-stated goals of American education has been the desire to create responsible citizens for a democratic society. Closely related to that goal has been the desire to create productive workers. In a high-tech world of digital data and image-based information forms, students, citizens, and workers will have to learn to discern. They will need a wide range of skills with a wide range of technologies. This not only includes hands-on skills or operator proficiency, but also the higher order thinking skills necessary to analyze and evaluate information whether it is located on a television news broadcast, a newspaper, or a Web site.

The need for these skills was evident at the start of the 1990s in the report the *Secretary's Commission on Achieving Necessary Skills* (SCANS, 1991). Presented to then Secretary of Labor Lyn Martin, the document pinpointed skills the commission believed U.S. workers would need in the 21st century. Among the skills was the ability to evaluate, process, and use information as well as the ability to use and understand technology.

Though the media including ABC News and the 1998 story in the inaugural issue of *Brills Comment* have frequently framed media literacy as little more than an exercise in television viewing or the deconstruction of commercials, it frequently includes the type of design, production, and teamwork skills addressed by the SCANS report.

Media literacy supports traditional skills in reading and writing, while recognizing that students have access to wider and different forms of information and therefore require wider and different understandings of literacy. Once again, rather than isolating this perception or realization to the media literacy community, a successful management strategy includes linking the literacies by demonstrating that these ideas are also held outside of the field.

One simple example of this can be found in *The Reading Teacher*. Though traditionally the province of the print and page purists, one now finds the publication exploring wider forms of both reading and writing. "We came to realize that we needed to broaden our conceptualization of literacy from a narrow focus on reading and writing skills to a definition that included all forms of the communicative and visual arts from reading, writing, speaking, and listening, to viewing and producing various modes of visual displays" (Flood et al., 1998, p. 343).

Preparation for employment is of course just one component of the productive responsible citizen. Surely the definition of a responsible citizen has always implied one who participates in that democracy, which in turn has been understood as informed participation whether exercising that privilege at a town meeting, in the PTA, or during a local, state, or national election. Exercising that vote today is not an easy matter. The media, as Kathleen Jamieson (Capella & Hall-Jamieson, 1997) has demonstrated, have created or contributed to a "spiral of cynicism" that among other things contributes to low voter turnout, thus undermining participation in the democratic process.

We live in tabloid times when press excesses, the ratings race, and the feeding frenzy drive stories more than truth or fact. Commenting on this process in coverage of the Clinton–Lewinsky scandal, the *American Journalism Review* said: "standards were the first casualty. Innuendo quickly replaced hard facts. . . . Have the media become a kind of journalistic vacuum cleaner, sweeping up the dirt, without worrying about the details?" (Ricchiardi, 1998, p. 31). Making the stories harder to understand and evaluate is the speed at which they now come at us from sources no longer restricted to newspapers, magazines, and the networks. In fact, the Lewinsky affair, while similar in some ways to the excessive coverage of Diana's death and the O.J. Simpson trial, marked the presence of new major players including the Internet (Drudge Report) and 24-hour cable services like MSNBC and The Fox News Channel.

One is reminded in such times of John Naisbitt's (1982) warning in *Megatrends* that we are drowning in information but starved for knowledge. The news excesses both predicted and parodied in Paddy Chayefsky's *Network* (1976) have unfortunately become reality. Making sense of these stories now requires much more than the ability to read the text in our newspapers and magazines. It requires "understanding how the events are framed for the public" and an awareness of how this coverage might affect "public cynicism about leaders and their performance" (Capella & Hall-Jamieson, 1997, p. 229). Such understanding is a key component of media literacy which not only accesses information, but also analyzes and evaluates the industries that create and disseminate that information, and the influence the selling and the telling has on public perceptions and public policy.

PURPOSE #2: PROTECTION

If the health of the body politic is threatened by the cancer of cynicism, the health of individual citizens including our impressionable children and teens may be threatened by the daily diet of sex, violence, materialism, and substance abuse evident in much of the media they are exposed to. It should also be noted, as the Harvard School of Public Health has said, that while the mass media has the power "to change social norms and individual behaviors" (De Jong & Winsten, 1998, p. 1), that power can also be harnessed for prosocial messages whether urging citizens to become physically fit, encouraging drivers to buckle up, or alerting us that "this is your brain; this is your brain on drugs."

While many parents, teachers, and administrators are no doubt aware of high-profile drug and substance abuse programs such as DARE and AODA, the public as a whole has not yet realized that media literacy may well have a role to play in such prevention/protection initiatives. This is clearly the belief of the Office of National Drug Control Policy, which began in 1995 to include media literacy as part of its annual report, *The National Drug Control Strategy*. The documents refer to "the pervasive power of the media, which collectively affects young people through words, actions and narrative portrayals" (1997, p. 41). Further, they have argued, such impressionable young people need media literacy which is a critical thinking tool that "empowers individuals to modify their internal environment by affecting the way they see and hear" (p. 43).

Whether dealing with advertising, stereotyping, propaganda, eating disorders, school violence, teen pregnancy, alcohol, tobacco, or other substance abuse, media literacy can play a role in helping young people detect and reject inappropriate messages and values. This can be especially effective when teens themselves are permitted to create countermessages, or adbusting as it is sometimes called. One successful example of the role for media literacy in the protection process is evident in the interagency approach of the Teen Futures Media Network at the University of Washington with its focus on teen sexuality. Another potentially promising project is Flashpoint, developed by the District Attorney's Office in Salem, Massachusetts. Preliminary data from the project indicate that it has achieved some success in using media literacy as a lens to provide lifetime skills for juvenile offenders. Concentrating on changing behaviors and attitudes related to aggression, gangs, and racism, the program uses media messages and media literacy skills to help the teenagers explore alternative behaviors and recognize their own flashpoints.

Although the National Health Education Standards agree that media messages affect our physical and psychological health and despite similar support from prestigious groups like the Carnegie Council on Adolescent Development, public school textbooks in health education and teacher preparation still lag behind in thoroughly recognizing the role of media messages and media literacy in the protection/prevention process. Greater cooperation between schools, communities, and prevention professionals is necessary for this role to be fully recognized and implemented.

PURPOSE #3: PLEASURE

Anyone who has ever seen the video of Pink Floyd's "Another Brick In the Wall," or read *Learning to Labour* (Willis, 1981), could be forgiven for dismissing the whole idea of associating pleasure with schools, as some cruel and monstrous joke. While it is true that some schools are painful and that most of us at one point or other as students, found the process and the place to be painful, it is also true that schools can nurture both creativity and sensitivity. Appreciation has always been an integral part of our classes in literature, music, and art. Exposing students to a wide range of these arts, it is argued, broadens their horizons, exposes them to culture (as school defines it), and potentially provides them with standards and criteria to make judgments about such works.

Adobe Photoshop and other sophisticated software now offer staggering new means of creativity and self-expression. As our information and entertainment increasingly come to us through a combination of sight and sound, training in the arts and crafts, including music, video, photography, computer graphics, drama, and dance, strengthens our ability to both encode and decode communication in a variety of forms. At the same time, of course, it stimulates our imaginations, offers us a forum for self-discovery and expression, and remains consistent with learning styles and multiple intelligences research. Though the initial Goals 2000 ignored the place of the arts in schools, it was later added. In the revised report, *The Arts and Education*, it was argued that "literacy should be redefined to include media and symbol literacy" (National Endowment for the Arts, 1995, p. 15).

Teachers who have engaged students in media production in England, Canada, Australia, and the United States will readily report the transformation they perceived in many of these students. Average and below-average students suddenly became A students. Absenteeism and behavior problems began to be reduced. Provided with tools and techniques, youngsters who had previously been silently submissive or aggressively disruptive, now became cooperative members of production teams capable of creating and sharing their own voices and visions.

This point was made explicit to participants at the "School Improvement Through Media in Education" conference sponsored by the Bertelsmann Foundation. "Stories abound of troubled students who suddenly come to life as their peers recognize talents they express in graphic programming, multimedia compositions, in video editing, or in building simulations" (Pea, 1995, p. 47). While experiencing pleasure, such students are of course also learning marketable job skills, not the least of which is the ability to work cooperatively with others.

PUTTING THE "ME" IN MEDIA LITERACY: PRINCIPLES AND PEDAGOGY

Ownership and autonomy have for the most part been absent from the way most of us as first students and then teachers have experienced education. Too often it felt like something being done to us rather than for us. This sense of alienation has been well documented. The Coleman Report, *Youth: Transition to Adulthood*, noted in 1972 that schools deny students responsibility, as a result of which they become irresponsible. The following year, *Inside High School* said school "has systematically denied their involvement in basic educational processes and relegated them to the position of watchers, waiters, order-followers and passive receptacles for the depositing of disconnected bits of information" (Cusick, 1973, p. 222). When students retreat from a process they perceive as irrelevant to their lives, we label them dropouts.

Ira Shor and Paulo Freire (1987) reject such labels, arguing instead that student responses are in fact "a performance strike" against a system that ignores their nature and needs. In *A Pedagogy for Liberation* they elaborate on the gap between the world in which our students live and the schools in which we educate them: "The world of American education is increasing the separation of the words we read and the world we live in. . . the world of reading is only the world of the schooling process, a closed world, cut off from the world we live where we have experiences but do not read about those experiences" (p. 135).

In both its subject matter and its methodology, media literacy confronts this alienation, addresses kid culture, builds a bridge between school and society, and moves rapidly away from the traditional teacher-centered classroom where subject matter experts function as information dispensers. While it is of course possible for media literacy to be taught in a traditional classroom environment, with students dutifully memorizing the definition of media literacy and its key principles, it would be a remarkable example of cognitive dissonance, with teacher and student alike making no connections between what they studied and how they studied it.

Observing the relationship between media literacy and the changing dynamics of the classroom in the United Kingdom, Len Masterman (1989) said, "first of all, and most remarkably, it de-centered the teacher in a number of ways which many found unsettling. Teachers were no longer the licensed arbiters of truth or taste. . . . The expertise which existed in the classroom was much more widely dispersed" (p. 13). Further he added, "teachers no longer possess an approved body of knowledge." The subject matter of media studies was being provided by the media. Classroom communication occurred laterally, not hierarchically, "speaking across not down to their audience." In terms of power and authority the result of these exchanges was significant. "The media equalized students and teachers" who became "co-investigators of media images and texts" (p. 14).

The reasons for this pedagogical shift are inherent in some of the most basic principles of media literacy. Perhaps the most important of these are the notions that "all media are constructions," that "media constructions or representations construct reality," and that "audiences negotiate their own meaning" (Ontario Ministry of Education, 1989). Engaging students in a discussion of how media assemble, edit, select, reject, design, construct, and deliver their messages is an eye-opening experience. Once they have learned to question the window on the world that the mass media construct, it does not require a quantum leap for them to realize that their textbooks, their curriculum, and their schools also construct a lens or frame, which is only a partial picture. The question, whose stories are sold and told, cannot easily be isolated to the mass media but applies equally to our school system. In short, media literacy offers them tools for deconstructing the ideological apparatus called education.

Though some may never make this link, reveling instead in the special pleasure of discussing their favorite soap or music video, the discussion in and of itself, as Masterman has indicated, represents a transformation of the traditional classroom. At the most obvious level this occurs with the subject matter. Having so long rejected the tasteless excesses of pop culture, the classroom now opens its doors to the electronic environment in which our students live. Their culture is validated. But the transformation is more profound than subject matter, which many critics would no doubt continue to dismiss as watering down the curriculum.

The transformation hinges on the idea that audiences negotiate meaning, which is to say, it validates how students perceive media rather than trying to impose a single, correct or teacher-driven reading on the text. It acknowledges clearly that just as gender, race, and class distinctions affect the way media audiences perceive media messages, these same distinctions will affect the way our students process education.

Central to this realization is a social constructivist perspective on how learning takes place. With this perspective comes an arsenal of classroom tools and techniques, all giving voice to the students who are no longer passive, watchers, listeners, waiters, or subordinates. Spontaneity and candor now manifest themselves in the teaching profession that has historically feared the personal and sought sanctuary "in the technical, the distant, the abstract" (Palmer, 1998, p. 16). Subjectivity, and the academic bias against it is at last banished. But its consequences have been great. It has, as Parker Palmer suggests, not only forced our students to write poorly but has "deformed their thinking about themselves and their world" (p. 18).

Though this student-centered classroom and curriculum may strike some as revolutionary, it is, on the surface at least, winning mainstream support and recognition. The 1997 President's Committee of Advisors on Science and Technology commented, for example, that "the teacher's traditional role as font of knowledge is likely to become less relevant" (p. 38). Education, it argued, should be individualized to the learning styles, interests, needs, and proclivities of students who will become "architects of their learning" (p. 34). Of course, most of that report is a celebration of tools, emphasizing skills necessary to create productive workers for the 21st century. One hardly imagines that its authors would consider a discussion of the Spice Girls or *Dawson's Creek* to be adequately addressing those goals.

TEACHER TRAINING: PUT ON AN "APPIE" FACE

One place that is building the bridge between teachers, tools, and media literacy is North Carolina's Appalachian State University. Having hosted the first national media literacy conference in 1995, the Reich College of Education is at the forefront of preservice teacher preparation in media literacy. Each semester more than 200 students begin this encounter in a required class called Literacy, Technology and Instruction. Throughout the semester they learn to design and create a Web page, Powerpoint presentation, videotape, or other project. They also look deeply at what it means to be literate in a media age. The course is far from a blanket endorsement of tools in the schools. Rather it raises critical questions about technology in education, including the state's new technology test for teachers. In the process, the students might well be forced to ask themselves if the technological tail is wagging the educational dog. The mass media components of the course include, among other tasks, in-depth analysis of broadcast news, the study of advertising including

Channel One's role in the state's schools, and the interdisciplinary use of motion pictures in education.

Central to course communication is the Listserve that maintains reflection and dialogue between instructors, students, administrators, former students, and public school teachers. In the classroom in both large-group and small-group format, discovery, reflection, and personal experience are also validated through conversation and dialogue. It is for many students a difficult experience, since so much of their high school writing has conditioned them to avoid the first person. Deeply committed to creating teachers who function responsibly as a community of practice (COP) Appalachian believes, as Jonathan Kozol (1981) argues, that "teachers need to feel they have the right, the license and sanction to speak out in the first person plural: 'we.' People however, cannot easily say 'we', if they do not first achieve the self-possession to say I" (p. 10).

One relatively easy way to facilitate this process is the early exploration of media representations. Rather than isolating this aspect of media literacy to some theoretical or abstract principle, it is connected immediately to personal experience of how the media represent schools as institutions, education as a process, and teaching as a profession. That includes studies of school in the mass media (Considine, 1985; Ayers, 1994) as well as consideration of how press coverage of education shapes community perceptions which in turn affect the fate of local bond issues. The relevance of these representations is not lost on these students. One participant in ASU's summer media literacy institute returned to her school and faxed her instructor:

> This really hit home because our school recently was listed as one of the top 25 in North Carolina. The city paper, reported our scores only—not exemplary—not school of distinction—not top 25, but they wrote on and on about the one city school that scored well. Whereas the newspaper based in the same town as our school system's office, gave us much credit." (8/18/1998 Moorseville, NC)

While traditional lecture or teacher-centered format is evident some of the time in some of these classes, observers will quickly note the reliance on conversation and dialogue. This emphasis reflects the Reich College of Education's commitment to the idea that knowledge is socially constructed. Early in each semester, students are introduced to the concept of Instructional Conversation (ICs). Deceptively simple from the outside, the IC engages the teacher and students in "a substantive and extended conversation, weaving individual participants' comments into a larger tapestry of meaning" (Goldenberg, 1992–93, p. 318).

The key components of this process include a challenging nonthreatening environment, responsivity to student contributions, less emphasis on known answers, clarification of student language, and general participation (Goldenberg, 1992–93, p. 318). Whether discussing their favorite teacher, analyzing a clip from *Square One*, or debating the validity of Ebonics, the class comes to understand ICs not as abstract theory, but as classroom practice. It is the type of practice inherent in the belief that audiences negotiate meaning.

This type of dialogue is also deeply democratic. It is a process, a conversational interaction, that does not push resolutely to a single outcome or conclusion. Rather it involves participation, commitment, and reciprocity. It "catches them up in a spirit of interaction" through engagement that is "creative, spontaneous, enjoyable" (Burbules, 1993, p. 1).

SYSTEMS, SYMPTOMS, AND ORGANIZATIONAL CONSTRAINTS

In an ideal world, perhaps all teachers would embrace the use of dialogue and instructional conversation as a valid classroom technique. In reality, of course, the organizational culture and climate of our schools often mitigates against such methods. Nicholas Burbules (1993) argues that "we must be able to identify and criticize the power relations and ideological barriers that undermine dialogical possibilities in schools" (p. 18). Among these constraints are content-driven curriculum, test driven institutions, and a management model based on discipline and control. In such an environment, spontaneity and conversation run the risk of being perceived as both disruptive and time-wasting. Trying to force media literacy into such an environment inevitably exposes what Linda McNeil (1985) refers to as "contradictions of control." In fact, much of what constitutes the content and practice of media literacy cannot successfully exist in such a setting. Its presence reveals the crossroads of schools "as agents of either education or social control" (p. 16).

Put more simply, "vegetation can survive only in a suitable climate and soil; programs take root and thrive only in a supportive setting" (Gibbons, 1976, p. 136). The comment can be located in the Phi Delta Kappa Task Force Report, *The New Secondary Education*. Published nearly a quarter century ago, it continues to offer insight into the issue of how innovations fare within traditional institutions. In the words of the study's author, "New Program Into Old Systems Won't Go." Unless they wish to run up against institutional brick walls, media literacy advocates need to know more than their subject matter, or its pedagogical past. They need to have a firm gasp on the culture and climate of the institution they expect to host the innovation.

At its most basic level, organizational culture is defined as the beliefs, value system, norms, or mores of the institution. One does not need to spend more than a few minutes talking to a teacher or school library media specialist to see this culture at work. Expressions like "my door is always open," "that's the way we've always done it," and "don't make waves" quickly resonant with those who spend their workday lives in schools. Far more than clichés, these expressions constitute the underlying culture of the organization. As such they will shape the debate about and fate of any innovation, including media literacy.

As we noted earlier in this chapter, this culture has subtly undermined the promise and potential of the new technologies. Only recently have we come to understand that the characteristics and attributes of the new technology constitute a culture clash with the traditional classroom. Technology predicated on individual self-paced learning represents an implicit threat to a chalk and talk, teacher-centered classroom. Recognizing and reconciling these cultures is a necessary step if we expect tools to change schools. "Innovation in any component of the system almost invariably requires modification of the entire system. The basic law of ecology applies: everything is connected to everything else" (Perelman, 1988, p. 21).

What then are the characteristics, components, and organizational patterns of traditional education and how might they affect the prospects for successfully introducing media literacy to our schools? In a McLuhanist sense, the envelope is part of the message. That is to say, "content is shaped by its context; the school program is controlled by the system which is its context" (Gibbons, 1976, p. 49). From the perspective of Linda McNeil, schools are, in fact, self-defeating institutions daily engaged in a civil war with themselves, for the most part without even knowing it. This internal conflict, she argues, has its origins in two historically different goals. These goals, it is argued, have been to educate citizens and to prepare them for economic production. The provision of information and skills, implicit in the first goal, is as unpredictable as the learning patterns and personalities of different children. Achievement of the second goal, however, hinges on predictability, credentialing, and stratified steps, denying the very individuality of those children. "Thus," she concludes, "the school is organized to be in conflict with itself" (p. 3).

This structure and stratification manifests itself in a number of social-cultural characteristics. The first is subject matter specialization (compartmentalization of knowledge). This knowledge is passed on in a downward flow of knowledge, or through vertical organization of the system. Teachers are dispensers and students are receivers. As we have already seen, both media literacy and technological innovation assault this tradition. Strongly related to the first two characteristics is the concept of adolescent inferiority, which devalues the experience and expertise our students have. Growing out of these concepts is the practice of batch processing of students and the routinization of activity. All of this occurs within a physical structure or building design that does not easily welcome disruption or alternative patterns of teaching and learning. As Cusick (1973) has noted, these characteristics "are not discrete entities, rather they depend on, reinforce and take their identity from one another" (p. 207).

At the head of it all is the office of the principal. Far more than a numbers cruncher or paper pusher, the principal through personality, practice, and politics asserts an enormous influence on what does or does not happen in the school. In the worse case scenarios, principals are engaged in open warfare with their teachers. In the final plenary session of the first National Media Literacy Conference, in 1995, this author raised the issue of principal power and the need to actively court their support to promote media literacy. A New England teacher stood to announce, somewhat angrily, that where he came from, if principals were for an idea, the teachers would be opposed to it.

Despite such sentiments, research on innovation within education continues to validate the support of the principal as a crucial ingredient. Schools that are receptive to change tend to house principals who support teacher intimacy, who manifest principal supportiveness, and create a climate of social cohesiveness as distinct from institutional discord and disaffiliation (Brady, 1988).

It should also be noted that the failure to require principals to take courses related to technology as part of their own professional preparation, severely undermines their ability to model anything other than the most tacit support for the new technologies. Their response most frequently is to assign such issues to the library media specialist. Since research suggests that teachers are often neutral or even negative in the way they perceive this group, there is a triangulation of the three professional groups necessary to create a common and cohesive policy toward technology in the schools. It is a formula for failure. When principals seek to assert power in the area but lack any real understanding of technology, it is a case of the blind leading the blind. When media specialists attempt to establish policy for acquiring and applying technology, but lack the power to enforce those policies, it is a case of the bland leading the blind.

Reforming such a system requires that we first recognize it. The success of both media literacy and technology necessitates this process of transformation. This transformation requires a systemic overhaul of education as we have known it. It must also be a transformation in reality, not just rhetoric. Far too many teachers have already been burnt by innovations like site-based management, only to find that when it came to actually allowing them to make and implement decisions, their principals were reluctant to relinquish power. Talking the talk, without walking the walk, does nothing but breed teacher cynicism, making the next innovation all the harder to promote. Real transformation requires changes in learning events, materials and methods, roles and relationships, educational environments and organizational patterns (Gibbons, 1976).

The shift from conventional classroom to innovational instruction implicit in both media literacy and technological development has been characterized in the following way (Means et al., 1993):

- From Teacher-Directed   To Student Exploration
- From Didactic Teaching   To Interactive Instruction
- From Short Blocks of Fixed Lesson Time   To Extended Blocks of Interdisciplinary Work
- From Individual Work   To Collaborative Work

- From Teacher as   To Learning Facilitator
  Knowledge Dispenser

- From Testing Facts and   To Performance Based Portfolio Assessment
  Discrete Skills

The question, of course, is can we get there from here?

WE CAN, WE WILL, WE MUST: WHAT WORKS AND WHY?

In 1993, *The Canadian Journal of Educational Communication* reported that a study of successful media education initiatives around the world, revealed nine common characteristics. These characteristics, hereafter known as the Pungente Principles, after the author of the study, made the role of the teacher a paramount factor. "Media education, like other innovative programs, must be a grassroots movement and teachers need to take a major initiative in lobbying for this" (p. 59). Further, it noted, as did the Presidential report on teachers and technology some 4 years later, that "in-service training at the school district level must be an integral part of program implementation" (p. 59).

But the nature of this training is crucial. Far too much time, money, and effort have been wasted on poorly implemented training. As witness to more than a few of these failed attempts, teachers have a tendency to be gun-shy and to eschew externally imposed change. Pungente's claim that media literacy must start with teachers certainly can be validated by research concerning change. Innovation diffusion theory (Hall, 1979; Rogers & Shoemaker, 1971) and the Concerns Based Adoption Model (Naidu, 1988) have already been linked to media literacy management strategies (Considine, 1997). These approaches recognize various levels of acceptance on the part of organization members. They identify aspects such as the career stages of those charged with implementing change, and they build the change around the nature and needs of the stakeholders, rather than on the nature of the innovation itself.

In describing the success or failure of federal educational projects, Sarason (1994) comments that "the adoption of projects did not insure successful implementation" (p. 74). Further, no matter how valid the concept, research indicated that "what the project was, mattered less than how it was done" (p. 76). What was crucial in supporting or subverting the innovation was the local characteristics such as school climate, leadership, teacher attributes, and district support. Again, it is worth stepping back to link the findings from these federal programs to Pungente's conclusions. In addition to teacher-initiated change and teacher training that we have already noted, Pungente also described the need for district level support. The federal research unequivocably demonstrates that local ownership, autonomy, and involvement are crucial to the success of any change including not only its implementation, but also its continuation. Among the key characteristics were "the quality of working relationships among teachers, the active support of principals and the effectiveness of project directors" (p. 77).

The emphasis on local concerns and characteristics as key ingredients to success-fully managing change in education, should give pause to those who wish to impose their own view of media literacy on a site or system. Unless the teachers themselves buy into this vision, intellectual integrity and academic approval will not bring about change. First, last, and always, the change must start with the teacher. Again, there is a dangerous tendency to talk about teacher preparation and faculty development in generalized terms, lumping all teachers together in a single category. Once more the research makes it apparent that this fails to perceive the complexity of how teachers confront change. The federal projects indicate that our secondary schools are harder to change than elementary education. Further, there are key characteristics or teacher attributes at work in how teachers respond to change. "Teachers with many years on the job were less likely to change their own practices" (p. 77). The teachers' sense of efficacy, or their belief that they could bring about change for their students was also a key determinant of their willingness to embrace innovation. At the very least, this suggests that a form of triage might be necessary whether we are trying to bring media literacy to our schools or the transformations associated with technology. Trying to change all teachers, at the same time in the same way is destined to be an exercise in futility.

Moving from theory to practice, we can see successful management strategies at work at Athens Academy in Georgia. Fusing media literacy (teaching about media) with technology infusion (teaching through media) the school made teachers the center of the process. The administrators understood that "a new Idea cannot be mandated. It must be understood, absorbed, evaluated and reflected upon by the individual who will implement it" (Chambers & Ridlehuber, 1994, p. 29). The teacher's willingness and receptivity were seen as key components in facilitating change. As such they were provided freedom and opportunity for exploration, communication, cooperation, and collaboration. "If true integration of media education is to occur," said the school administrators, "it needs to become part of each teacher's presentations. Each teacher needs to feel ownership of the goals of media education as applied in that teacher's classroom" (Chambers & Ridlehuber, 1994, p. 31).

As a private school, the academy is clearly less prone to external mandates and directives than the nation's public schools. Nonetheless, the principles they applied in implementing their project can be transferred to other sites. In addition to putting the primary focus on the teacher, the plan involved other important characteristics. These included (1) linking the project to the mission of the school, (2) a research phase to formulate specific goals, (3) integration across the curriculum, (4) phasing in the technology, (5) faculty visits to other sites, and (6) evaluation connected to the institution's mission statement.

Similarly, as we have already seen, the media literacy initiatives at Appalachian State University's Reich College of Education have not grown out of the isolated efforts of one or two individuals, but have achieved consensus by growing out of the values expressed in the college's model and mission statement. With more than 200 students in more than 10 different sections taking the key course each semester, it would not be possible for one or two faculty members to assume responsibility for the course. The community of practice (COP) and the social constructivist methods imbedded in the course are valued and practiced by a team of teachers, often working two, three, or four to a class. In short, "Literacy, Technology and Instruction" represents a team effort. It also reflects the dynamics of teamwork which is to say elements such as environmental factors, design factors, group processes, and the psychological traits of the group members (Cohen & Bailey, 1991).

Once again, these efforts need to be seen as much more than an attempt to push content or impose ideas. The management model behind the initiatives is consistent with research related to successful collaborations and partnerships. Among the components that have been identified as characteristics of successful collaborations are: (1) shared vision and goals of members, (2) mutual trust and respect, (3) shared decision making, (4) commitment from top leadership, (5) fiscal support, and (6) information sharing (Robinson & Darling-Hammond, 1994).

Going into its third year, the course continues to add new faculty, rotate team members, and modify both content and competencies. Student participation through the Listserve and their journal commentaries provide insight into the validation and relevance many of them find in the course. On any given week one may find them debating the relative merits of the Teletubbies and the Cookie Monster; expressing their fears about school violence, and concerns about media coverage of it; or wrestling with issues of censorship and the Internet. While the content of the class clearly provides a focus and forum for discussion, events from the real world both macro and micro, somehow have a way of intruding into the instruction, providing what educators refer to as teachable moments. Their response to the class and the critical lens through which it explores literacy, is like a pendulum swinging back and forth from resistance to revelation. One term that appears repeatedly in their writing is "eye-opening."

In May 1998 with the semester drawing to a close, Jennifer wrote:

> I hope that as we teach our students to be literate in the media, that we also teach them to take what they absorb and decide for themselves, how much information they want to take at face value, and how much they want to disregard. My hope is that we teach students to understand context and independently access media messages. . . and communicate through these complex technologies.

MARY AS A CASE STUDY

In the summer of the same year, Appalachian State University provided free media literacy sessions for teachers and media specialists already in the schools. One of them began that experience with the prospect of a little bit of work while enjoying an idyllic mountain summer. Her final journal reflected her journey:

> Media Literacy—From Television to Telling-vision began as an innocent attempt to earn some "free" continuing education hours, while learning 'a little something' which might prove useful in my school media center. This was all to take place while I enjoyed the beauty of the North Carolina Mountains. . . . Little did I know how little I knew. I have to admit that I did not even truly understand what media literacy was and frankly I didn't care.

Mary's journal describes the master's degree she earned in Library Science; a degree just 5 years old but with no reference to media literacy. She describes her rural elementary school, with its increasingly diverse population, a growing number of "transient students," "non-English speaking students," "more single parent students," "more BAD attitude students," "more poverty stricken students," "even a few crack babies." While acknowledging that it sounds like a bad place to work, Mary rejects the idea and says instead that the school is making a difference, especially with the reading level improvements in many students.

She also was motivated to bring media literacy to her students. "I want to say how excited I am about the possibilities which we have for improving the situation. Many of the issues we have discussed this week have been ones that have concerned me for many years. . . . Our discussions have not been negative or hopeless; we have been encouraged to look at both the contributions and consequences of advertising and other media."

In August of that year, Mary returned to her media center armed with a knowledge of media literacy. She was also armed with a curriculum context. North Carolina's Standard Course of Study Information Skills was compatible with what she had been exposed to that summer. She began the work of developing a fifth-grade media literacy unit to be implemented in the media center. She also began to face the prospect of preparing parents, teachers, and administrators to embrace media literacy. The final sentence in her journal reads, "My sincere thanks. . . it would have all been worth it, even if it had not been free."

The day-to-day constraints of the school may impede Mary's progress. Time will always be short and no doubt the state will always find new mandates to impose on schools. But many of the key determinants for success identified by John Pungente are now in place for Mary. She is not alone. She knows, that other teachers and other media specialists throughout the state are engaged in pioneering media literacy within their classrooms and schools. She knows too, that while the phrase may be unfamiliar to many of her stakeholders, what she is trying to do is consistent with state standards.

She knows that there is a university and a college faculty to call on if she needs support. She also knows that there are resources and materials and she knows there is a Web site at the college, reflecting the experiences of her peers (www.ci.appstate.edu/programs/edmedia/media lit/), available for her to implement media literacy in her classroom; not the least of which is *Telemedium: The Journal of Media Literacy*. A decade ago, these materials were largely unavailable. Today Theatre Books in Toronto and the Center for Media Literacy in Los Angeles provide a one-stop shopping experience. Textbooks like *Visual Messages* (Considine & Haley, 1999) model interdisciplinary classroom practice supported by a solid body of research. The case for media literacy is made in videotapes like *Media Literacy: The New Basic?*, *The Glitter: Sex, Drugs and the Media*, and *The Ad and the Ego*.

Of equal importance is the growing literature of the field. Three important components of this are the series of media-technology publications created by the Bertelsmann Foundation (1993a,b, 1994, 1995), the ongoing communication/technology series from the Aspen Institute (1993, 1995a,b, 1996a,b, 1997a,b, 1998a,b), and the recent series published by Taylor and Francis in London. This latter group includes *Digital Diversions: Youth Culture in the Age of Multimedia* (Sefton-Green, 1998), *Wired-Up: Young People and the Electronic Media* (Howard, 1998), and *Teaching Popular Culture: Beyond Radical Pedagogy* (Buckingham, 1998b).

Those of us who labor in education and who love it, know that it is a constant compromise between our individual integrity and identity as teachers, and the institutional edicts and imperatives that confront us daily. Reconciling the two, building a bridge between the self we are and the schools we work in, is not an easy task, but it is the work that must be done if we are to construct the conditions that will support media literacy. As Sarason has warned us, simply having a good idea is no guarantee that it will be received warmly. Within the realms of traditional literacy, new ideas have also generated controversy and we need to take notice of this parallel. The best defense against being exploited, misunderstood, or misrepresented by our opponents, said advocates of whole language, is "knowledgeable teachers. . . who know about language and learning. . . who develop an articulate coherent framework. . . who measure their practice against that framework" (Edelsky et al., 1991, p. 3). So it is with media literacy. Now is no time for complacency. A lurch to the right, or an economic downturn can quickly undermine budgets for equipment, progressive ideas, or opportunities for staff development.

We have a long way yet to go before we can truly say that media literacy is both visible and viable. We will know that day has arrived when we talk simply about literacy, taking it as a given, that its meaning embraces what we now call media literacy. Until then we need to be vigilant advocates, keenly aware of the culture and context in which we work. "Educational innovations have not fared well in the United States. With its materialist, consumer culture, the United States tends to consume innovations—to gobble the latest new idea, not tasting or digesting the substance, using it, spitting it out and on to the next" (Edelsky et al., 1991, p. 2). A decade from now, let that not be the obituary for media literacy in this country.

REFERENCES

Apple, M. (1993). *Official knowledge: Democratic education in a conservative age.* London: Routledge.

Aspen Institute. (1993). *A National Media Literacy Leadership Conference.* Communications and Society Program. Washington, DC: Author.

Aspen Institute. (1995a). *The future of community and personal identity in the coming electronic culture.* Communications and Society Program. Washington, DC: Author.

Aspen Institute. (1995b). *Toward an information bill of rights and responsibilities.* Communications and Society Program. Washington, DC: Author.

Aspen Institute. (1996a). *Creating a learning society: Initiatives for education and technology.* Communications and Society Program. Washington, DC: Author.

Aspen Institute. (1996b). *Elections in cyberspace: Toward a new era in American politics. Communications and Society Program. Washington, DC: Author.*

Aspen Institute. (1997a). *The future of advertising: New approaches to the attention economy.* Communications and Society Program. Washington, DC: Author.

Aspen Institute. (1997b). *Market journalism: New highs, new lows.* Communications and Society Program. Washington, DC: Author.

Aspen Institute. (1998a). *The global advance of electronic commerce.* Communications and Society Program. Washington, DC: Author.

Aspen Institute. (1998b). *Investing in diversity: Advancing opportunities for minorities and the media.* Communications and Society Program. Washington, DC: Author.

Ayers, W. (1994). *A teacher ain't nothin but a hero: Teachers and teaching in film in images of schoolteachers in twentieth century America.* New York: St. Martin's Press.

Bertelsmann Foundation. (1993a). *The pedagogical challenge of multimedia—abundance for what purpose?* Germany: Gutersloh.

Bertelsmann Foundation. (1993b). *Media competency as a challenge to school and education.* Germany: Gutersloh.

Bertelsmann Foundation. (1994). *Media as a challenge—education as a task.* Germany: Gutersloh.

Bertelsmann Foundation. (1995). *School improvement through media in education.* Germany: Gutersloh.

Brady, L. (1988). The principal as climate factor in Australian schools: A review of studies. *The Journal of Educational Administration, 26,* 73–81.

Bruner, J. (1991). Introduction. In S. Graubard (Ed.), *Literacy: An overview by 14 experts.* New York: Noonday Press. vii–xi.

Bruner, J. (1996). *The culture of education.* Cambridge, MA: Harvard University Press.

Burbules, N. (1993). *Dialogue in teaching: Theory and practice.* New York: Teachers College Press, Columbia University.

Buckingham, D. (1993). *Children talking television: The making of television literacy.* London: Falmer Press.

Buckingham, D. (1998a). Media education in the uk; moving beyond protectionism. *Journal of Communication, 48,* 33–43.

Buckingham, D. (1998b). *Teaching popular culture: Beyond radical pedagogy.* London: UCLS Press.

Capella, J., & Hall-Jamieson, K. (1997). *Spiral of cynicism: The press and the public good.* New York: Oxford University Press.

Carnegie Council on Adolescent Development. (1989). *Turning points: Preparing American youth for the 21st century.* New York: Author.

Chambers, R., & Ridelhuber, C. (1994). *Creating innovation in media as a challenge—education as a task.* Germany: Gutersloh & Bertelsmann Foundation.

Cohen, S., & Bailey, D. (1991). What makes teams work: Group effectiveness research from the shop floor to the executive suite. *Journal of Management, 23*, 239–290.

Coleman, J. (1972). *Youth: Transition to adulthood. Report of the panel on youth of the President's science advisory committee*. Chicago: University of Chicago Press.

Comber, B., & O'Brien, J. (1993). Critical literacy: Classroom explorations. *Critical Pedagogy Networker, 6*, 2–6.

Considine, D. M. (1985). *School on the screen: In the cinema of adolescence*. Jefferson, NC: McFarland.

Considine, D. M. (1995). An introduction to media literacy: The what, why's and how to's. *Telemedium: The Journal of Media Literacy, 41*, 1–6.

Considine, D. M. (1997). Media literacy: A compelling component of school reform and restructuring. In R. Kubey (Ed.), *Media literacy in the information age* (pp. 243–262). New Brunswick, NJ: Transaction.

Considine, D. M., & Haley, G. (1992). *Visual messages: Integrating imagery into instruction*. Englewood, CO: Libraries Unlimited.

Considine, D. M. & Haley, G. (1999). Visual messages: Integrating imagery into instruction (2nd edition). Englewood, Colorado: Libraries Unlimited.

Considine, D. M., Haley, G., & Lacy, L. (1994). *Imagine that: Developing critical viewing and thinking through children's literature*. Englewood, CO: Libraries Unlimited.

Csikszentmihalyi, M. (1991). Literacy and intrinsic motivation. In S. Graubard (Ed.), *Literacy: An overview by 14 experts* (pp.115–140). New York: Noonday Press.

Cusick, P. (1973). *Inside high school*. New York: Holt.

de Castell, S., & Luke, A . (1983). Defining literacy in North American schools: Social and historical conditions and consequences. *Journal of Curriculum Studies, 15*, 373–389.

De Jong, W., & Winsten, J. (1998). *National campaign to prevent teen pregnancy. The media and the message: Lessons learned from past public service campaigns*. Report for National Campaign to Prevent Teen Pregnancy. Washington, DC.

Edelsky, C., Altwerger, B., & Flores, B. (1991). *Whole language: What's the difference?* Portsmouth, NH: Heinemann.

Eisner, E. (1991). What really counts in schools? *Educational Leadership, 48*, 10–11, 14–17.

Fishman, A. (1988). *Amish literacy: What and how it means*. Portsmouth, NH: Heinemann.

Flood, J., & Lapp, D. (1998). Broadening conceptualizations of literacy: The visual and communicative arts. *The Reading Teacher, 51*, 342–344.

Giannetti, L. D. (1916). *Understanding movies*. Englewood Cliffs, NJ: Prentice–Hall.

Gibbons, M. (1976). *The new secondary education: A Phi Delta Kappa task force report*. Bloomington, IN: Phi Delta Kappa.

Goldenberg, C. (1992–93). Instructional conversations: Promoting comprehension through discussion. *The Reading Teacher, 46*, 316–325.

Hall, G. E. (1979). Developmental conceptualization of the adoption process in educational institutions. *Australian Educational Researcher, 7*, 5–32.

Herman, E., & Chomsky, N. (1988). *Manufacturing consent: The political economy of the mass media*. New York: Pantheon Books.

Hirsch, E. D. (1988). *Cultural literacy: What every American needs to know*. New York: Vintage.

Hobbs, R. (1997). Expanding the concept of literacy. In R. Kubey (Ed.), *Media literacy in the information age*. New Brunswick, NJ: Transaction.

Howard, S. (1998). *Wired-up: Young people and the electronic media*. London: Taylor & Francis.

Kozol, J. (1981). *On being a teacher*. Oxford University Press, Oxford: England.

Lester, P. M. (1995). *Visual communication: Images with messages*. Belmont, CA: Wadsworth.

Lewis, J., & Jhally, S. (1998). The struggle over media literacy. *Journal of Communication, 48*, 109–119.

Lortie, D. (1975). *Schoolteacher: A sociological study*. Chicago: University of Chicago Press.

Masterman, L. (1989). The development of media education in Europe in the 1980's. *Metro, 79*, 13–17.

McNeil, L. (1985). *Contradictions of control: School structure and school knowledge*. London: Routledge & Kegan Paul.

Means, B., et al. (1993). *Using technology to support school reform*. Washington, DC: U.S. Dept. of Educational Research and Improvement.

Monaco, J. (1977). *How to read a film*. New York: Oxford University Press.

Muffoletto, R. (1994, February). Technology and restructuring education: Constructing context. *Educational Technology*, pp. 24–28.

Naidu, S. (1988). Developing instructional materials for distance education: A concerns based approach. *Canadian Journal of Educational Communication, 17*, 167–179.

Naisbitt, J. (1982). *Megatrends*. New York: Time Warner.

National Endowment for the Arts. (1995). *The arts and education: Partners in achieving our national goals*. Washington, DC: Author.

North Carolina Department of Public Instruction. (1985). *Communication skills curriculum*. Raleigh.

North Carolina Department of Public Instruction. (1992). *Information skills curriculum*. Raleigh.

Office of National Drug Control Policy. (1997). *Executive summary*. Washington, DC: Executive Office of the President.

Ontario Ministry of Education. (1989). *Media literacy: Intermediate and senior divisions*. Canada: Queens Printer.

Palmer, P. (1998). *The courage to teach: Exploring the inner landscape of a teacher's life*. San Francisco: Jossey–Bass.

Pea, R. (1995). *The emergence and challenges of distributed multimedia learning environments in school improvement through media in education: A German/American dialogue*. Germany: Gutersloh & Bertelsmann Foundation.

Perelman, L. (1988, September). *Restructuring the system is the solution*. Phi Delta Kappan.

President's Committee of Advisors on Science and Technology. (1997). *Report to the President on the use of technology to strengthen K–12 education in the United States*. Washington, DC.

Pungente, J. (1993). The second spring: Media education in Canada's secondary schools. *Canadian Journal of Educational Communication, 22*, 47–60.

Resnick, D. (1991). Historical perspectives on literacy and schooling. In S. Graubard (Ed.), *Literacy: An overview by 14 experts*. New York: Noonday Press.

Ricchiardi, S. (1998). Standards are the first casualty. *American Journalism Review, 1*, March, 30–35.

Robinson, S., & Darling-Hammond, L. (1994). Change for collaboration and collaboration for change: Transforming teaching through school–university partnerships. In L. Darling-Hammond (Ed.), *Professional development schools*. New York: Teachers College Press, Columbia University.

Rogers, E. M.. & Shoemaker, F. (1971). *Communications of innovations: A cross cultural approach*. New York: Free Press.

Sarason, S. (1994). *Revisiting the culture of the school and the problem of change*. New York: Teachers College Press, Columbia University.

Sefton-Green, J. (1998). *Digital diversions: Youth culture in the age of multimedia*. London: Taylor and Francis.

Shor, I., Freire, P. (1987). *A pedagogy for liberation*. South Hadley, MA: Bergin & Garvey.

Simonson, P., & Walker, S. (1988). *Multicultural literacy*. St. Paul, MN: Graywolf Press.

Turnbull, S. (1996). Missionary positions: The state of media education. *Metro Education, 7*, 3–8.

United States Department of Labor. (1991). *Secretary's commission on achieving necessary skills*. Washington, D.C.: U.S. Government Printing Office.

Vandergrift, K., & Hannigan, J. A. (1993, January). Reading the image. *School Library Journal*, pp. 20–25.

Vygotsky, L. S. (1962). *Thought and language*. Cambridge, MA: MIT Press.

Washington State Department of Education. (1997). *Essential academic learning requirements*. Olympia.

Willis, P. (1981). *Learning to labour: How working class kids get working class jobs*. Boulder: University of Colorado Press.

Woronov, T. (1994). Six myths and five promising truths about the uses of educational technology. *The Harvard Education Letter, 5*, 1–3.

SECTION IV

RECONCEPTUALIZING FUTURE LITERACY THEORIES AND DIRECTIONS

ASSESSING KNOWLEDGE RESTRUCTURING IN VISUALLY RICH, PROCEDURAL DOMAINS:
THE CASE OF GARBAGE-DISPOSAL REPAIR WRIT/SKETCHED LARGE

Peter B. Mosenthal

INTRODUCTION

The Inception of the "How-To" Literacy Genre

In his book, *The Americans: The Democratic Experience*, Daniel Boorstin (1973) argues that America became a great nation because of its "know-how." Underlying Boorstin's argument is that, however we might think about progress, it is largely tied to doing things more effectively and efficiently. This, in turn, streamlines effort, cuts costs, increases productivity, enhances accessibility and, ultimately, raises the quality of life.

In developing his argument, Boorstin introduces us to Frederick Taylor, a man preoccupied with time and never without a stopwatch. When Taylor went to work

Advances in Reading/Language Research, Volume 7, pages 331–362.
Copyright © 2000 by JAI Press Inc.
All rights of reproduction in any form reserved.
ISBN: 0-7623-0264-X

for the Bethlehem Steel Company in 1898, he undertook a series of experiments "to find out how quickly the various kinds of work that went into the shop ought to be done." Taylor's prescription for a proper time study to determine the "best way to shovel possible" was the following:

> First find, say, 10 to 15 different men (preferably in as many separate establishments and different parts of the country) who are especially skillful in doing the particular work to be analyzed. Second, study the exact series of elementary operations or motions which each of these men use in doing the work which is being investigated, as well as the implements each man uses. Third, study with a stop watch the time required to make each of these elementary movements and then select the quickest way of doing each element of work. Fourth, eliminate all false movements, slow movements, and useless movements. Fifth, after doing away with all unnecessary movements, collect into one series the quickest and best movements, as well as the best implements.

This new method, involving that series of motions which can be made quickest and best, is then substituted in place of the 10 to 15 inferior series which were formerly in use. (Boorstin, 1973, p. 365)

By pursuing this kind of study, Taylor found that the best results for shoveling, as a whole, were obtained when workers used different kinds of shovels for different purposes—ranging from small flat shovels for handling ore, up to immense scoops for handling rice coal. In addition, he also defined the proper technique for using each type of shovel:

> There is one right way of forcing a shovel into material of this sort and many wrong ways. Now, the way to shovel refractory stuff is to press the forearm hard against the upper part of the right leg just below the thigh, like this [indicating], take the end of the shovel in your right hand and when you push the shovel into the pile, instead of using the muscular effort of the arms, which is tiresome, throw the weight of your body on the shovel like this [indicating]; that pushes your shovel in the pile with hardly an exertion and without tiring the arms in the least. Nine out of ten workmen who try to push a shovel in a pile of that sort will use the strength of their arms, which involves more than twice the necessary exertion. (Boorstin, 1973, p. 366)

Notes Boorstin, it was largely due to Taylor's influence that Americans became preoccupied with the idea of "mass-producing know how" that was conducted in the most effective and efficient manner possible. This preoccupation gave rise to people, in all endeavors in life, creating and disseminating how-to information to the public at large on every possible procedure—from cooking and child rearing to gardening and golfing. Much of America's magazine industry has since grown up around informing the public how to ski, run, knit, play tennis, eat healthy, buy cars, program computers, plan a wedding, and choose the ideal vacation. Along with the growth of the how-to magazine industry has been the growth of how-to books, ranging from ideal diets and home repair, to financial investing and finding one's true inner self.

The Problem of "How-To" in Instructional Domains

Despite the prevalence of "how-to information" as found in magazines and books, little attention has been paid to teaching this genre of information processing in elementary, secondary, and postsecondary schools. In short, the major emphasis in elementary schools has been and continues to be on teaching and assessing "learning to read and write." In these settings, the elements and rules of the linguistic system make up the principal content of the instructional curriculum. In addition, generic strategies (or processes) for comprehending and composing are usually taught. In many (if not most) cases, narratives constitute the primary structural units by which students learn to organize their knowledge (Guthrie & Greaney, 1991).

In secondary and postsecondary school settings, the emphasis shifts from learning to read and write to "reading and writing to learn" (Schumacher & Nash, 1991). In these settings, the elements of academic disciplines (e.g., chemistry, history, sociology, and economics) make up the basic content of the high school and postsecondary curricula. In some instances, study skills and more advanced rhetorical strategies are taught to provide students with better capabilities for organizing and processing larger units of content information (Mosenthal & Kirsch, 1991c). In most cases, exposition now serves as the primary means for structuring knowledge.

It is only when we turn to nonschool settings, such as the workplace, that the emphasis shifts to "reading and writing to do" (with substantial attention being paid to "how-to" information processing) (Kirsch, Jungeblut, & Campbell, 1992; Sticht, 1977). In these settings, instructions for performing various operations tend to make up the content of training curricula. As a consequence, procedural (or "how-to") strategies are taught to help learners master instructions as stated, as well as to help learners apply these instructions in innovative ways to new and novel problems as they may arise (Bovair & Kieras, 1991). In many instances, exposition as well as documents and other visual arrays are used as the means for conveying information in such applied domains (Guthrie, Seifert, & Kirsch, 1986). In these instances, readers are required to comprehend information displayed in text format as well as in matrix, pictorial, diagrammatic, and schematic formats (Mosenthal & Kirsch, 1992b).

While instruction in middle school settings often helps to ease the transition from "learning to read and write" to "reading and writing to learn," there are few such settings that ease the transition from "reading and writing to learn" to "reading and writing to do" (Gurthrie & Greaney, 1991; Resnick, 1987; Venezky, 1982). More often than not, this is accomplished through specific job training or through school-to-work transition programs, such as Job Training Programs (Kirsch et al., 1992). Although the range of individual performance levels in these programs tends to be extremely large (Mikulecky & Drew, 1991), training is carried out under the assumption that all learners are more or less homogeneous (Mosenthal, 1988).

In part, this stems from the fact that these programs lack assessment frameworks that are *relevant,* such that the structure and content of text and visual materials (as well as the procedural strategies for engaging these materials) are the same in an assessment as they are in actual job performance (Kirsch & Jungeblut, 1992; Resnick, 1987); *comparable,* such that different levels of expertise among individuals can be identified relative to the different difficulty levels of tasks which comprise a domain (Spiro, Vispoel, Schmitz, Samarapungavan, & Boerger, 1987); and *interpretable,* such that differences between experts and novices can be explained in a manner useful for designing more effective training programs (Mosenthal & Kirsch, 1989, 1991e).

Given the absence of such assessment frameworks as they might apply to visually rich, "how-to" information-processing domains, the primary purpose of this paper was to describe and illustrate such a framework as it applies to a specific procedure for fixing garbage disposals. This domain is particularly applicable, in part, because the format of its problem representation (see Figures 1 and 2 below) is one commonly found in "how-to-do" books and training manuals (Mosenthal & Kirsch, 1991b). Also, I chose this domain assuming that it would be familiar enough to this book's readers so they might more easily understand the notion of "knowledge models" as a way of representing both visual and textual information.

While this chapter's proposed assessment framework is useful for profiling the knowledge states that experts and novices maintain relative to a given domain, it is also useful for showing how learners update their knowledge using both text and visual information (Kirsch & Mosenthal, 1991a; Mosenthal & Kirsch, 1992a). As such, the proposed framework likewise serves as a useful tool for understanding how learners become more proficient in performing "how-to" tasks. Rather than focusing on discrete competencies that learners bring to such tasks, the proposed framework enables researchers and practitioners to understand how learners systematically increase their procedural knowledge proficiency (Mosenthal & Kirsch, 1992b; Schumacher & Nash, 1991).

In sum, this chapter is an attempt to build on Frederick Taylor's earlier efforts to distinguish between those with expert "know-how" versus those with novice "know-how." In examining the domain of garbage disposal repair, I recruited 18 individuals who were studying home repair as part of an adult basic training program. These individuals ranged in age from 24 to 42 and included 13 males and 5 females. The training session on garbage disposal repair lasted two classes (approximately 4 hours of instruction). The instructional materials included primarily a text, along with tables, pictures, diagrams, and process schematics.

This chapter is organized as follows. First, I introduce a taxonomy of knowledge types (Mosenthal & Kirsch, 1992b) and their corresponding representation formats (called "knowledge models"). In this section, I illustrate how these representational models can be used to profile novices' and experts' knowledge of garbage disposals. Second, I describe and illustrate how knowledge models also can be used to assess the way that novices and experts revise and update their knowledge of a domain.

Finally, I conclude by discussing how the proposed knowledge assessment framework can be used to design multimedia instructional systems to enhance learning in visually rich, "how-to" information domains.

TYPES OF KNOWLEDGE

Pictorial Knowledge

Building on the work of Anderson (1983), Mosenthal and Kirsch (1992b) have identified four levels of knowledge, each of which can be represented by a different type of "knowledge model." According to their taxonomy, the most basic level of knowledge is "pictorial" (Kirsch & Mosenthal, 1990a; Mosenthal & Kirsch, 1991d). *Pictorial knowledge* of a phenomenon involves understanding this phenomenon's "steady state." This includes understanding the phenomenon's use or function (in the event that the phenomenon is mechanical, such as a garbage disposal), its physical and operational characteristics, and its position in time and space. In addition, this includes understanding the conditions under which a phenomenon functions or fails to function, as the case may be. In many instances, pictorial knowledge is conveyed by a photograph or an illustration of a phenomenon. In other instances, it is conveyed by definition, description, and comparison and contrast.

To illustrate the concept of pictorial knowledge, consider the picture of a garbage disposal shown in Figure 1. Now imagine that associated with this figure, we find the following text:

A. (1) There are two types of disposals. (2) One runs continuously when the switch is turned on. (3) The second type is activated by twisting the cover after each batch of food has been entered. (4) Both types require running cold water (5) to flush food wastes through the holes in the turntable and out through the drainpipe.

(6) Both types of garbage disposals are useful in that they grind up leftover food and pass the remains out through the central sewage system. (7) Over the past decade, one or the other type of garbage disposals can be found in almost every house (8) which is equipped with sewage lines which are large enough to accommodate the disposal waste. (9) Today's modern disposals have built-in overload devices (10) which cut the motor off should it jam or overheat. (11) For the most part, both types of garbage disposals are cylindrical in shape and are quite durable, (12) capable of grinding the toughest bones. (13) The units can be found suspended from the sink bottom.

The information in *A* can be arrayed in terms of the pictorial knowledge model shown in Table 1. (Note that the sentence and phrase numbers used in the above paragraph correspond to the numbers in Table 1.)

From Table 1, we see that pictorial information presented in *A* contrasts two types of garbage disposals in terms of their "conditions of function and use." In addition, the information in *A* compares the "function or use" of the two types of disposals.

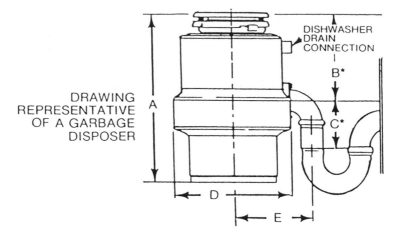

Figure 1. Pictorial Representation of a Garbage Disposal

Little information is provided in terms of the disposals' physical characteristics. The remaining information found in *A* tends to be "temporal and location conditions" related to specific "conditions of function and use" of the two types of disposals.

Diagrammatic Knowledge

Diagrammatic knowledge of a phenomenon also involves understanding a phenomenon's "steady state"; this, however, includes understanding a phenomenon's parts, their physical characteristics, their uses or functions, their physical and operational characteristics, their temporal and locational characteristics, and the conditions under which a phenomenon's parts operate or function (Kirsch & Mosenthal, 1990b; Mosenthal & Kirsch, 1991d). In many instances, diagrammatic knowledge is conveyed by a diagram which illustrates a phenomenon's parts. In other instances, it, like pictorial knowledge, is conveyed by definition, description, and, in some instances, comparison and contrast.

In Figures 2, 3, and 4, diagrammatic knowledge about garbage disposals is conveyed by diagrams which label the parts of the garbage disposal and illustrate pictorially the physical characteristics of each part. Note that each of the diagrams illustrates a different view of the garbage disposal. Figure 2 illustrates the outside of a garbage disposal while Figure 3 shows the inside of a garbage disposal with the insulated cover removed. Finally, Figure 4 shows the parts of the turntable in relation to the motor housing of a disposal.

Imagine the following text accompanying these three illustrations:

B. (1) The working mechanisms of garbage disposals are protected by an insulated cover (shown in Figure 2). (2) This cover can be opened at the seam. This reveals the parts of the disposal

Table 1. Pictorial Knowledge Model of Garbage Disposals as Described in *A*

Sentence Number and Type of Phenomenon	Function or Use	Physical Characteristics	Temporal and Location Conditions	Conditions of Function and Use
(1) There are two kinds of disposals.				
(2) Type 1 garbage disposal				Type 1 garbage disposals run continuously when the switch is turned on
(3) Type 2 garbage disposal				Type 2 is activated by twisting the cover after each batch of food has been entered
(4) Both types of garbage disposals				(Both types) require running cold water
(5) Cold water	to flush food wastes		(wastes) through the holes in the turntable and out through the drainpipe	
(6) Both types of garbage disposals	grind up leftover food wastes and pass the remains		out through the central sewage system	

(continued)

Table 1. Continued

Sentence Number and Type of Phenomenon	Function or Use	Physical Characteristics	Temporal and Location Conditions	Conditions of Function and Use
(7) Both types of garbage disposals			Over the past decade, (garbage disposals) can be found in almost every house	
(8) House				house is equipped with sewage lines which are large enough to accommodate the disposal waste
(9) Both types of garbage disposals			Today's (garbage disposals)	have built-in overload devices
(10) Overload devices	cut the motor off			should motor jam or overheat
(11) Both types of garbage disposals		are cylindrical in shape and are quite durable		capable of grinding the toughest bones
(12) Both types of garbage disposals			are suspended from the sink bottom.	

338

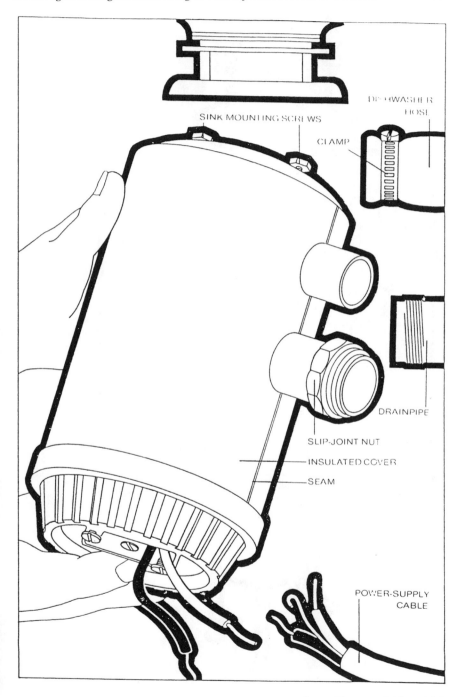

Figure 2. Diagrammatic Representation of a Garbage Disposal (Outside)

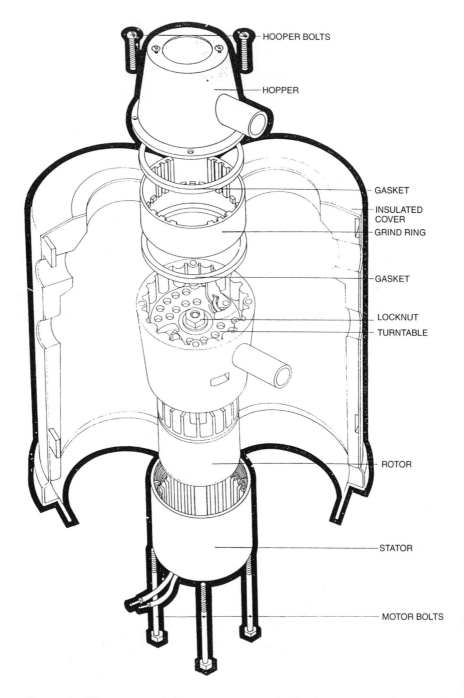

HOOPER BOLTS

HOPPER

GASKET

INSULATED COVER

GRIND RING

GASKET

LOCKNUT

TURNTABLE

ROTOR

STATOR

MOTOR BOLTS

Figure 3. Diagrammatic Representation of a Garbage Disposal (Inside)

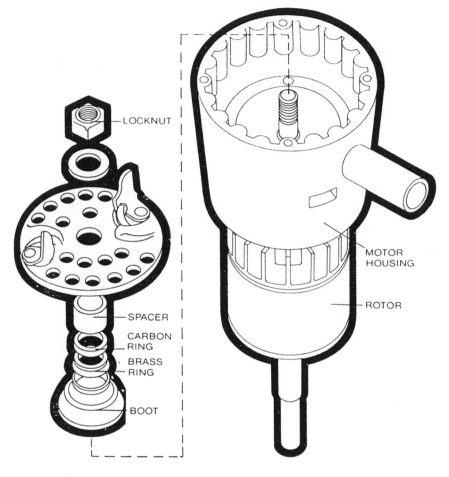

Figure 4. Diagrammatic Representation of a Garbage
Disposal's Turntable

shown in Figure 3. (3) Here we find the motor housing which consists of a turntable (4) which does the main work of the disposal. (5) The turntable is a perforated metal disk with two impeller blades. (6) The turntable is fastened to the motor shaft by a locknut, as shown in Figure 4. (7) The turntable connects to the motor housing by a motor housing bolt which connects through a boot, two rings, and a spacer. (8) These parts together make up the seal which prevents water and food particles from leaking from the weep hole.

This information is represented in the format of the diagrammatic knowledge model shown in Table 2.

From Table 2, we see that the diagrammatic knowledge of the garbage disposal focuses primarily on the "turntable" and the parts immediately associated with it.

Table 2. Diagrammatic Knowledge Model of Garbage Disposals
as Described in *B*

Sentence Number and Parts of Phenomenon	Function or Use	Physical Characteristics	Temporal and Location Conditions	Conditions of Function and Use
(1) insulated cover	protects the working mechanisms of garbage disposals			
(2) seam	allows insulated cover to be opened			
(3) motor housing	houses turntable			
(4) turntable	does the main work of the disposal			
(5) turntable		perforated metal disk with two impeller blades		
(6) locknut	fastens turntable to motor shaft			
(7) motor housing bolt	connects turntable to motor housing through a boot, two rings, and a spacer			
(8) seal (made up of a boot, two rings, and a spacer)	prevents water and food particles from leaking from the weep hole			

Most of the information represents "function or use," with little mention being made of "physical characteristics." Finally, note that no information representing "temporal and location conditions" or "conditions of function and use" is provided in *B*.

Process Knowledge

A third type of knowledge is called "process knowledge," which involves definition and description of changes in states of a phenomenon (Kirsch & Mosenthal, 1992; Mosenthal & Kirsch, 1991a). This type of knowledge is made up of 10 types of information. Six of these types include: an "agent" (e.g., steam) which is a thing that acts on one or more "objects" (e.g., piston) through an "action" (e.g., pushes). Both agents and objects have two types of components that have "physical characteristics" (e.g., large metal flywheel). There is an "effect," which is a consequence of the agent's acting on an object (e.g., the piston moves to the right), and this represents a change in some steady state. In some instances, the "function" (purpose, goal) of the agent, object, or action may be specified (e.g., the purpose of the piston rod is to turn the flywheel).

In addition to these six types of information, there are four others which commonly comprise process information. "Location"—such as one side of the piston—refers to the place where a change in state occurs, either in the initial, medial, or final stages. "Direction path" describes both the direction, say, to the right, of a change in state and the intermediate points of location through which an action occurs—such as from the first part of the cylinder to the second part. "Time" refers to the point in the time when an action transpires (e.g., at noon) or the interval that it takes to complete an action (e.g., 120 milliseconds). These times may be explicit or they may have to be inferred from the information given in a text. Finally, there is "condition," which is information that qualifies the other types of information. An example of a condition might be that, in order to operate a steam engine, we must heat the water to 100 degrees centigrade.

In many instances, process knowledge is conveyed by a "process schematic" (Mosenthal & Kirsch, 1991a). In such illustrations, we typically find the direction path of objects represented by arrows as these objects pass between various parts of the phenomenon. In addition, we often find a direction path signaled by arrows depicting the direction in which one or more parts of a phenomenon operate. An example of such process schematic appears in Figure 5 where we see food entering the garbage disposal, being ground to bits by the impeller blades, and passing through the holes in the turntable out the drainpipe.

To illustrate a typical example of process description, consider the text in C.

C. (Stage 1) Food waste is dropped through the mounting into the hopper which, in the installation type in Figure 5, is also connected to the dishwasher outflow. (Stage 2) Waste from the sink and food excess from the dishwasher fall onto the turntable. (Stage 3) Centrifugal force flings the food excess outward (Stage 4) where it is caught between the impeller blades and the cutting edges of the grind ring. (Stage 5) This process shreds and grinds food waste into small particles which (Stage 6) then are flushed by cold water from the tap through the holes in the turntable and out the drainpipe.

Following Mosenthal and Kirsch (1992a), this information can be arrayed in the stage process knowledge model representation shown in Table 3.

From Table 3, we see that the process of shredding and grinding the food is described in six stages. The types of information best represented in this process knowledge model include "agent," "object," "action," "location," and "direction path." One "effect" is identified, as is one set of "conditional information."

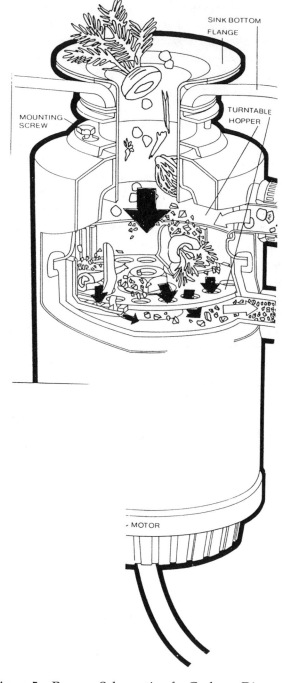

Figure 5. Process Schematic of a Garbage Disposal

Table 3. Stage Process Knowledge Model of Garbage Disposals as Described in C

Stages	Agent	Object	Action	Effect	Physical Characteristics	Function	Location	Direction Path	Time	Condition
Stage 1		Food waste	is dropped					through the mounting into the hopper		
		hopper	is connected				to the dishwasher outflow			in the installation illustrated
Stage 2		Waste and food excess	fall				waste from the sink; food excess from dish washer	onto the turntable		
Stage 3	Centrifugal force	the food excess	flings					outward		

(continued)

345

Table 3. Continued

Stages	Agent	Object	Action	Effect	Physical Characteristics	Function	Location	Direction Path	Time	Condition
Stage 4		food	is caught				between the impeller blades and the cutting edges of the grind ring			
Stage 5				Stage 4 shreds and grinds food waste into small particles						
Stage 6	Cold water	food waste	flushes				water from the tap	through the holes in the turntable and out the drainpipe		

346

Procedural Knowledge

Finally, a fourth type of knowledge is called "procedural knowledge," which involves a person as an agent performing instructions for the purpose of bringing about a desired effect (such as remedying a problem) (Mosenthal & Kirsch, 1991b). (In this regard, procedural knowledge represents the classic "how-to" knowledge type.) In essence, procedural knowledge is made up of basically the same types of information that comprise process knowledge. However, the principal difference between procedural and process knowledge is that, in the former, the implied "you" is always the control agent who carries out processes stated as instructions; in process knowledge, the agent is someone other than an "implied you."

In addition, agents always engage in procedural knowledge for the specific purpose of achieving a goal or solving a problem; in process knowledge, stages of change are described with reference to "effects" but not with reference to goal attainment or problem solving. Instead of the "implied you," parts of phenomena are the agents which bring about changes in a phenomenon's states. While parts may function as agents, they usually are not imbued teleologically with motives and problems. On the other hand, in procedural knowledge, we often find mention of "goal" or "purpose" information. This type of information usually replaces "direction path" in process knowledge.

To illustrate procedural knowledge, imagine that we had the problem of water leaking from the weep hole of our garbage disposal. Also, imagine that, based on our diagrammatic knowledge model in Table 2, we recall that such leakage is usually prevented by the seal which connects the turntable to the motor housing. To correct this problem, we must follow three major procedures, the first of which involves disconnecting the disposal which is illustrated, in part, in Figure 2. The second requires that we dismantle the disposal as illustrated partially in Figure 3. And the third requires us to disassemble the seal, as is reflected in Figure 4. The descriptions of these three major procedures might be as follows:

D. *Disconnecting the disposal*. (Procedure 1) First, turn off the power to the disposal circuit and then (Procedure 2) disconnect the wires at the base of the disposal. (Procedure 3) Proceed by loosening the screw on the clamp around the dishwasher hose, (Procedure 4) unscrewing the slip-joint nut on the drainpipe connection. Be sure to keep a firm hand under the disposal as you loosen the screws from the sink mounting. Otherwise, the disposal will fall. (Procedure 5) Once the unit is free from the sink, use a screwdriver to open the insulated cover at the seam.

Dismantling the disposal. Once the insulated covering is off, (Procedure 6) unscrew the hopper bolts and (Procedure 7) remove the hopper from the motor housing. As you do this, (Procedure 8) place the gaskets and grind ring in the proper sequence for easy reassembly. (Procedure 9) Remove the motor bolts from the bottom of the stator and (Procedure 10) lift out the motor housing and rotor.

Disassembling the seal. Because the rotor and the turntable turn together, (Procedure 11) you need to immobilize the rotor with one hand before (Procedure 12) unscrewing the locknut. (Procedure 13) Proceed by taking off the turntable, exposing spacer and the seal unit directly beneath it. (Procedure 14) Take off the spacer and (Procedure 15) lift out the seal unit. (Procedure

Table 4. Procedural Knowledge Model of "Troubleshooting a Damaged Seal" as Described in D

Procedures	Agent	Object	Action	Effect	Physical Characteristics	Function	Goal/ Purpose	Location	Time	Condition
Major Procedure 1: Disconnecting the disposal										
Procedure 1	you	power to the disposal circuit	turn off							
Procedure 2	you	the wires	disconnect					at the base of the disposal		
Procedure 3	you	the screw	loosen					on the clamp around the dishwasher hose		
Procedure 4	you	the slipjoint nut	unscrew					on the drainpipe connection under the disposal		
	you	a firm hand	keep	the disposal will fall						As you loosen the screws from the sink mounting
Procedure 5	you	screw driver	use			to open the insulated cover		at the seam		Once the unit is free from the sink

348

Major Procedure 2: Dismantling the disposal

Procedure 6	you	unscrew	the hopper bolts	Once the insulated covering is off from the motor housing in the proper sequence
Procedure 7	you	remove	the hopper	
Procedure 8	you	place	the gaskets and grind ring	for easy reassembly
Procedure 9	you	remove	the motor bolts	from the bottom of the stator
Procedure 10	you	lift out	the motor housing and rotor	

(continued)

349

Table 4. Continued

Procedures	Agent	Object	Action	Effect	Physical Characteristics	Function	Goal/ Purpose	Location	Time	Condition
Major Procedure 3: Disassembling the seal										
Procedure 11	you			need to immobilize the rotor						Because the rotor and the turntable turn together with one hand
Procedure 12	you	the turntable	unscrew the locknut							Do procedure 1 before 2
Procedure 13	you	the turntable	take off				exposing the spacer and the seal unit	directly beneath the turntable		
Procedure 14	you	the spacer	take off							
Procedure 15	you	the seal unit	lift out							
Procedure 16	you	the surfaces of the rings	examine				to see if there is dirt or disrepair			
Procedure 17	you	the entire seal unit	should be replaced							If there is any damage

350

16) Examine the surfaces of the rings for dirt or disrepair. (Procedure 17) If there is any damage, the entire seal unit should be replaced.

Following Mosenthal and Kirsch (1991b), this information can be arrayed in the procedural knowledge model representation shown in Table 4.

The above 17 procedures complete the steps for dismantling and troubleshooting the seal unit. Note that most of the information in the above procedural knowledge model includes "action," "object," and "condition" information primarily. Throughout the knowledge model, "you" is the understood "agent."

In sum, each of the above four levels of knowledge represents a hierarchy of complexity. Diagrammatic knowledge tends to include all of the same types of information that pictorial knowledge includes; but, in addition, diagrammatic knowledge includes information about a phenomenon's individual parts which, in turn, includes smaller units of pictorial knowledge.

Process knowledge builds on diagrammatic knowledge by including information about parts, their functions and their physical characteristics. Moreover, process knowledge further distinguishes between parts as being either agents or objects. These agents and objects are said to interact at times such that they produce various effects. In procedural knowledge, the implied "you" becomes the agent who carries out actions on objects to produce different effects for different goals or purposes (which may include solving a problem such as a leaky weep hole in a garbage disposal).

ASSESSING LEARNERS' KNOWLEDGE STATES

Profiling Levels of Prior Knowledge

By understanding the preceding four knowledge types and their corresponding knowledge models, we now have a basis for profiling learners' knowledge states. To illustrate this, I collected protocols from 18 students in an adult education class on home repair. The age range of these adults was from 23 to 42 years. Of the 18 adults, 13 were male and 5 were female. All of the adults had a high school diploma (or the equivalent); nine had associate's degrees. The adult education class was required for individuals seeking employment as salespersons in a large appliance discount store.

To profile these adults' pictorial prior knowledge of garbage disposals, I followed the assessment procedures proposed by Mosenthal and Kirsch (199b) and Mosenthal and Cavallo (1998). In this regard, I first asked the students to "Describe what a garbage disposal is and does." To profile their diagrammatic prior knowledge, I then presented them with Figures 2, 3, and 4 without their parts labeled. The students were asked to label the parts indicated by the identification lines. In addition, students were asked to identify and describe as many parts of the garbage disposal as they could. To assess students' process prior knowledge, I next presented them with the process schematic shown in Figure 5 (without the parts labeled) and asked them to describe the way garbage disposals work. Finally, to assess procedural prior knowledge, I presented them with Figures 2, 3, and 4, and asked them to list the procedures for replacing a damaged disposal seal.

After collecting these data, I analyzed the students' responses by first re-representing the content of students' written protocols in terms of the structures of pictorial, diagrammatic, process, and procedural knowledge models identified above. I then matched the content in each student's protocols with the content in terms of the above knowledge models.

For instance, Student 1 wrote the following pictorial description of a garbage disposal:

> E. Garbage disposals are located under the kitchen sink. They grind up leftovers. They make a lot of noise when they run. They are also quite dangerous.

Since Student 1's initial knowledge state of garbage disposals included only pictorial knowledge, I matched the content of her knowledge recall against the information in the pictorial knowledge model represented in Table 1. I highlighted the information that was the same and inserted in italics newly added information. Consequently, Student 1's initial knowledge state had the following representation:

In another instance, Student 2 provided the following process description of how garbage disposals work:

> F. Garbage is put into the disposal. Next, water is turned on to help mix the garbage while the disposal grinds it into bits. Finally, the water washes the garbage out of the disposal.

After re-representing this student's protocol in terms of its knowledge model and matching its content against the original, this was the resulting knowledge model that describes this student's prior process knowledge about disposals:

Once students' initial knowledge states had been represented, I created a knowledge hierarchy following Mosenthal and Kirsch (1992b) and Mosenthal and Cavallo (1998). This hierarchy is shown in Table 7. Here we find that initial students' recall of prior pictorial knowledge represented three levels of complexity (numbers not boldfaced). The simplest level included the case where students (i.e.,

Table 5. Student 1's Pictorial Knowledge Model of Garbage Disposals as Described in *E*

Phenomenon	Function or Use	Physical Characteristics	Temporal and Location Conditions	Conditions of Function and Use
Both types of garbage disposals	grind up leftover food wastes		are located under the kitchen sink	Can be dangerous; make alot of noise when they run

Table 6. Students 2's Process Knowledge Model of Garbage Disposals as Described in G

Stages	Agent	Object	Action	Effect	Physical Charac-teristics	Function	Location	Direction Path	Time	Condition
Stage 1		Garbage	is put					into the disposal		
Stage 2			water	turn on	to help mix the food					while the disposal grinds the garbages into bits
Stage 3	Water	garbage	washes					out of disposal		

Students 14 to 18) only described garbage disposals by mentioning their function or use (e.g., "to grind up food," "get rid of food wastes").

A slightly more complex level of difficulty included the case where students (i.e., Students 5 to 13) mentioned at least a single function or use of garbage disposals, as well as identified one other point of reference (e.g., a physical characteristic, a temporal or location condition, or a condition of function and use) (e.g., "garbage disposals grind up food as water pushes the food through the disposal").

Finally, the most complex level of knowledge represented by the 18 students included the case where they mentioned the function or use of disposals and identified information representing two points of reference. This level, in particular, was reflected in the recalls of Students 1 to 4 (where Student 4 noted that "in grinding up uneaten food, water from the tap washes the food through a grinder and out through the central sewage system of houses equipped with big enough sewage pipes"). Note that none of the students in my sample included information in their prior knowledge recalls that contained information about both types of disposals.

In terms of diagrammatic knowledge, nine of the students were unable to identify a single part on the diagrams provided (i.e., Students 10 to 18). Six students (i.e., Students 4 to 9) were able to identify and label one to three parts, while only three students (i.e., Students 1 to 3) were able to identify and label four to six parts. No students were able to label more than six parts.

In terms of process knowledge, all students identified one stage of how disposals work. Students 1 to 6 were able to identify two to three specific stages. None of the students identified more than three stages, as they were listed in Table 3.

Finally, in terms of procedural knowledge, none of the 18 students had any knowledge of the procedures for replacing a damaged disposal seal.

Table 7. Profile Distribution of Students' Levels of Prior Knowledge Related to Garbage Disposals

Pictorial Knowledge	Students Identified by Number
Function/Use	14, 15, 16, 17, 18
Function/Use + 1 Other Point of Reference	5, 6, 7, 8, 9, 10, 11, 12, 13/**13*, 14*+, 15*+, 16*+**
Function/Use + 2 Other Points of Reference	1, 2, 3, 4/**17*+, 18*+**
Type 1 + Type 2 + Function/Use + 1 Other Point of Reference	**1*+, 2*+, 4*+, 5*+, 6*+, 7*+, 8*+, 9*+, 10*+**
Type 1 + Type 2+ Function/Use + 2 Other Points of Reference	**3*+**
Diagrammatic Knowledge	
Identified no parts	10, 11, 12, 13, 14, 15, 16, 17, 18
Identified 1–3 parts	4, 5, 6, 7, 8, 9/**10*+, 11*+, 13*+, 14*+, 15*+, 16*+, 17*+, 18*+**
Identified 4–6 parts	1, 2, 3/**5*+, 6*+, 7*+, 9*+**
Identified all labeled parts	**1*+, 2*+, 3*+,12*+**
Process Knowledge	
Identified 1 stage	7, 8, 9, 10, 11, 12, 13, 14, 15, 16, 17, 18
Identified 2–3 stages	1, 2, 3, 4, 5, 6/**10*, 11*, 12*, 13*, 14*, 15*, 16*, 17*, 18***
Identified 4–5 stages	**5*, 6*, 7*, 8*, 9***
Identified 6 stages	**1*+, 2*+, 3*+, 4*+, 12*+**
Procedural Knowledge	
Disconnecting the disposal	
Identified 1–2 procedures	**10, 11, 12, 13, 14, 15, 16, 17, 18**
Identified 3–4 procedures	**5, 6, 7, 8, 9, 12**
Identified all 5	**1, 2, 3, 4**
Dismantling the disposal	
Identified 1–2 procedures	**10, 11, 12**
Identified 3–4 procedures	**1, 2, 4, 5, 6, 7, 8, 9**
Identified all 5	**3**
Disassembling the seal	
Identified 1–2 procedures	**5, 6, 7, 8, 9,10, 11, 12, 13, 14,15, 16, 17, 18**
Identified 3–4 procedures	**1, 2, 4**
Identified 5–6 procedures	**3**
Identified all 7 procedures	

In terms of the limited sample of 18, Students 1 to 3 tended to be the most knowledgeable students in the group, with Student 4 being a close fourth. These students' responses consistently reflected somewhat higher levels in terms of pictorial, diagrammatic, and process knowledge of disposals. Students 14 to 18 tended to be the least knowledgeable in the group; their responses consistently reflected the lowest levels in terms of pictorial, diagrammatic, and procedural knowledge. Students 5 to 9 had a somewhat higher level of knowledge than Students 10 to 13 who, in turn, had a higher level of knowledge than Students 14 to 18 (see Table 7).

Profiling Levels of Knowledge after Initial Reading

Building on the work of Vosniadou and Brewer (1987), Mosenthal and Kirsch (1992b) (see also Mosenthal & Cavallo, 1998) have identified three ways by which people can update (or revise) their knowledge: by "accretion," "tuning," and/or "restructuring." In terms of a knowledge model, *accretion* is the process whereby learners acquire more features descriptive of a phenomenon (or type of phenomenon) in a pictorial knowledge model. For instance, this might involve learning a second use of disposals or yet another physical characteristic about disposals. In diagrammatic knowledge, accretion is the process whereby learners acquire more features descriptive of a phenomenon's known part (or parts). In process knowledge, accretion involves learners adding more features to their understanding about a known stage (or stages) of a process. Finally, in procedural knowledge, accretion involves learners adding more features to their understanding about a known procedure or procedures. In all such cases, accretion occurs where learners add new information inside the knowledge model matrix.

In contrast, *tuning* is the process whereby learners acquire the concepts about a new type (or types) of a phenomenon in pictorial knowledge models. In diagrammatic knowledge, tuning is the process whereby learners acquire the concepts about a new part (or parts) which make up a phenomenon. In process knowledge, tuning is the process whereby learners acquire understanding of a new stage (or stages) of a process. Finally, in procedural knowledge, tuning is the process whereby learners acquire understanding of a new procedure (or procedures). In all such cases, tuning occurs where learners identify information that relates to an organizing feature (such as type, stage, temporal condition) that previously was not identified.

Restructuring is the process whereby learners reframe their understanding of a phenomenon in terms of a different type of knowledge model. For instance, learners who understand a phenomenon primarily in terms of parts but who then come to understand this phenomenon in terms of its process are said to restructure their knowledge model from one that is diagrammatic to one that is process.

Changes in Students' Knowledge States

To illustrate these three types of knowledge revision, the study's original 18 students read the information contained in paragraphs *A* to *D* above as well as viewed Figures 1 through 5 as illustrations accompanying the four sections (as part of their classroom instruction). Students were given the assignment to study the text and illustrations for as long as they wanted to until they thought they understood the information "thoroughly." After this time, students were then required to repeat the same procedures that they followed in representing their prior knowledge.

Again, the content of the students' written protocols were matched against those in the knowledge model templates represented by Tables 1 to 4. These templates were then matched against the students' original prior knowledge templates to determine the extent that students had either accredited, tuned, and/or restructured their knowledge about disposals.

The results are shown in Table 7 with the new scorings in bold. The numbers in roman type represent the students' original prior knowledge level. The numbers in bold represent the students' updated knowledge level. An asterisk (*) denotes that a student's knowledge had changed by accretion. A plus (+) denotes that a student's knowledge had changed by tuning. Finally, note that all students demonstrated some knowledge of restructuring as they acquired some procedural knowledge related to replacing the garbage disposal's seal unit. This is shown by fact that none of the students registered responses in the procedural knowledge section of Table 7.

Changes in Pictorial Knowledge: Accretion

As shown in Table 7 with recall responses in bold, all students accreted information by identifying more information as it related to a single point of reference. Most notable in this category was Student 13 who added new temporal and location information but did not add information related to any new points of reference. In particular, Student 13 added the information that "food got passed from the disposal to the house's sewage system to the central sewage system"). Initially, Student 13 had mentioned that "disposals attached to the bottom of the sink grind up food."

Changes in Pictorial Knowledge: Fine-Tuning

In assessing students before reading about garbage disposal repair, Students 14 to 18 could identify only a single use of function for disposals. After their reading, Students 14 to 16 shifted one knowledge level, such that they then included information from one other point of reference (e.g., Student 14 included information that "garbage disposals are placed underneath sinks in the kitchen"; Student 15 noted that "the food waste was washed out through the central sewage system of the house"; Student 16 added the information that "disposals are round in shape").

Students 17 and 18 went further than Students 14 to 16 in that they were able to not only identify one function but also were able to identify information related to two points of reference. In particular, Student 17 wrote that "garbage disposals have become more popular" and "are generally placed under sinks in modern homes." Student 18 noted that "cold water is used to flush food wastes through the holes in the disposal out through the drainpipe."

In their updating of information, Students 1 to 10 and 12 also included new information with points of reference. In addition, these students included mention that there were two types of disposals. Student 3 went on to distinguish how these two types of disposals are operated. As such, Student 3 represented the highest level of "expert knowledge" among the group.

Changes in Diagrammatic Knowledge: Accretion

As shown in Table 7, all students accreted diagrammatic information (as shown by the asterisk) by identifying more information as it related to defining parts and their functions. Students 10 to 18 identified one to three parts; Students 5 to 9 identified four to six parts; and Students 1 to 4 and 12 identified all seven parts.

Changes in Diagrammatic Knowledge: Fine-Tuning

While all of the students accreted some diagrammatic knowledge by identifying more parts, few fine-tuned this knowledge by updating the function of these different parts. As noted in Table 7 (and as signaled by the plus sign), only Students 1 to 4 and 12 actually identified functions for two or more of the seven parts identified. All of these students identified the function of the insulated cover (i.e., to protect the working mechanisms of the garbage disposal). Students 1 and 3 identified that the motor housing "houses the turntable." Finally, Students 3 and 12 identified that the seal "prevents water and food from leaking out of the weep hole."

Changes in Process Knowledge: Accretion and Fine-Tuning

As noted in Table 3, the instructional text that the students used did not convey much detailed information for any one point of reference. This, in turn, made if difficult for students to accrete information by elaborating or extending knowledge within a single point of reference (such as agent, object, or action). As a consequence, changes in students' knowledge of stages primarily were analyzed in terms of fine-tuning.

As shown in Table 7, the pattern for fine-tuning resembled the pattern of accretion. In short, Students 10 to 18 identified two to three stages; Students 5 to 9 identified four to five stages; and Students 1 to 4 and 12 identified all six stages correctly.

Changes in Procedural Knowledge: Restructuring

As noted earlier, none of the students demonstrated prior knowledge of how to fix a damaged garbage disposal seal. However, after reading and viewing the information related to this procedure, students were able to restructure their knowledge such that they were able to bring pictorial, diagrammatic, and process knowledge to bear in understanding some or most aspects of how to accomplish this goal.

As shown in Table 7, there was a wide discrepancy in terms of students' ability to construct valid procedural models for fixing a seal. Note that Students 10 to 18 demonstrated a minimal understanding of how to disconnect the disposal (identifying only one or two procedures for how this was to be accomplished). Students

5 to 9 and 12 could identify three to four procedures. Finally, Students 1 to 4 could identify and describe all five procedures.

In terms of dismantling the disposal, Students 10 to 12 recalled information related to only one or two of the procedures, whereas Students 1, 2, and 4 to 9 identified three or four procedures. Outstanding here was Student 3, who was able to identify all five procedures.

In terms of the final procedure for disassembling the seal, most students were limited in their knowledge update in this area. Students 5 to 18 were able to identify only one or two procedures. Students 1, 2, and 4 were able to identify three to four procedures. The standout here was Student 3, who identified five to six procedures correctly for disassembling the seal. In describing how to disassemble the seal, Student 3 forgot to mention that one should "immobilize the rotor" before unscrewing the locknut. Otherwise this student identified all of the information shown in Table 4 related to disassembling the seal.

Following this exercise, students received a lecture and demonstration on how to replace the seal of a switch-run disposal. Following this, each student was given an opportunity to disconnect and dismantle the disposal followed by replacing the brass ring component of the seal. Students were asked to explain each of the procedures as they went. As the procedural knowledge models would predict, students' ability to disconnect the disposal from the sink, dismantle the disposal, and disassemble the seal corresponded with the level of complexity of their procedural knowledge model. In short, Students 10 to 18 (with the exception of 12) were able to disconnect the disposal from the sink but needed information clarification in carrying out one or two procedures in dismantling the disposal. They needed information clarification in three or four procedures in disassembling the seal and replacing its brass ring. Students 5 to 9 easily disconnected the disposal from the sink; only Student 6 needed information clarification in carrying out one procedure in dismantling the disposal. These students each needed information clarification in no more than one procedure in disassembling the brass ring. These results stood in contrast to Students 1 to 4 and 12 who were able to complete all of the major and minor procedures without any assistance of any kind.

DISCUSSION

The purpose of this chapter has been to illustrate a procedure for profiling how learners update their knowledge in an applied domain that is represented both linguistically and visually. In particular, the case that I have illustrated was garbage disposal repair. The underlying assumption of this profiling procedure is that both linguistic and visual information can be represented at a common "deep-structure level" by the use of one of four knowledge models. These knowledge models include: pictorial, diagrammatic, process, and procedural. Pictorial knowledge models define a phenomenon's state largely in terms of its parts, attributes, and functions. When representing a phenomenon in terms of pictorial knowledge, one traditionally uses a single picture or a picture list (Kirsch & Mosenthal, 1990a) comprised of multiple pictures. The purpose of picture lists is to illustrate those parts and attributes that are common to a phenomenon and those that are different.

Diagrammatic knowledge models go one step further than pictorial knowledge models: They specifically label key parts of a phenomenon. Often these parts are then portrayed as phenomena themselves and defined pictorially or diagrammatically. When representing a phenomenon in terms of diagrammatic knowledge, one most commonly uses a diagram (Kirsch & Mosenthal, 1990b). The importance of diagrammatic knowledge is that it highlights the structural relations between and among a phenomenon's parts (much as does a general reference map).

Process knowledge models focus on changes in a phenomenon's states. In many instances, this knowledge involves understanding how change takes place chronologically at different parts of a phenomenon (e.g., something happens first in part one, then in part two, and finally in part three). In other instances, this knowledge involves understanding how change take place causally, as change in one part (e.g., water is heated to 220 degrees and turns to steam in the holding chamber) produces change in a second part (e.g., steam moves the turbines). When representing process knowledge, one most often uses some version of a process schematic that illustrates the direction path of change from one part of a phenomenon to another (Mosenthal & Kirsch, 1991a).

Note that these three types of knowledge represent an "implication hierarchy" such that diagrammatic knowledge builds on pictorial knowledge and process schematic knowledge builds on diagrammatic knowledge. In short, one must understand what comprises a phenomenon's parts and their structural relations before one can understand how changes occur within and between these parts. It is at the level of procedural knowledge where this implication hierarchy is brought to bear before someone him or herself can effect change.

Procedural knowledge consists of understanding the parts, their structural relations, and how these parts function in relation to one another in an operation so that, when an operation breaks down (or there is need to enhance efficiency of the operation), one is able to intervene and repair (or enhance) the operation (Mosenthal & Kirsch, 1991d). In this sense, it would be expected that individuals with greater pictorial, diagrammatic, and process knowledge would be more likely to have higher procedural knowledge and, in turn, be more effective in repairing (or carrying out) procedural operations. This, in fact, was what I found in the above-reported study of how adults learn to repair garbage disposals.

In reviewing the data in Table 7, we can see that students who required the least assistance in conducting the simulated repair of a garbage disposal were the ones who had the greatest pictorial, diagrammatic, and process knowledge after studying the linguistic and visual information related to the procedure. These, of course, were Students 1 to 4 and 12. On the other hand, students who required the most assistance in conducting the simulated repair of a garbage disposal were also those who had the lowest pictorial, diagrammatic, and process knowledge after studying the procedure. These included Students 10, 11, and 13 to 18. Finally, the students who needed a moderate level of assistance were also those who reflected a moderate amount of pictorial, diagrammatic, and process knowledge. These included Students 5 to 9.

Implications

Perhaps if Frederick Taylor were alive today, his interest in effectiveness and efficiency would be less tied to shoveling and more tied to designing instructional multimedia systems to enhance procedural learning as the new frontier of learning "how to do." Ideally, in considering such systems, Taylor would again recognize the importance of designing them using an underlying, universally generalizable framework. This would avoid the problem of having to reinvent new frameworks to teach new procedures each time.

To the extent that knowledge of states, processes, and procedures can all be represented by the same underlying knowledge models, I would like to conclude by arguing that knowledge modeling itself is an optimal framework for designing multimedia systems of the future (Mosenthal & Cavallo, 1998). Using knowledge modeling, the first step in designing a multimedia system would be to analyze the information content to be taught in terms of its basic pictorial, diagrammatic, process, and procedural knowledge contents. For instance, in designing such a system for garbage disposal repair, this might include an interface screen with the choices: Pictorial, Diagrammatic, Process, and Procedural. Should learners click on "Pictorial," they would be presented with a picture of the most prototypical type of garbage disposal (including one picture with the garbage disposal attached to the sink, one picture representing the outside of the disposal, and one picture representing a cutaway of the inside). Associated with these pictures would be information organized as a knowledge model that would provide a general definition of the garbage disposal as it related to the knowledge model's reference points of parts, attributes, functions, and general structural relations. At this point, learners would have the opportunity to click on "types of disposals," such that a picture list of the different types and varieties of disposals would appear. In clicking on "definitions," this would reveal pictorial knowledge models associated with each of the pictured types and varieties. Because each knowledge model would be structured the same, this would enable learners to quickly compare the models in terms of their respective parts to ascertain similarities and differences.

In choosing the interface category "Diagrammatic," learners would find the various parts of the prototypical garbage disposal (both outside and inside views) labeled. Similarly, in the selection of "types," learners would find each of the various types and varieties of garbage disposal parts also labeled. In clicking on any of these parts, a diagram of that part would be presented along with a knowledge model defining and describing that part's parts and their respective attributes, functions, and structural relations.

In choosing the interface category "Process," learners would be presented with a cutaway diagram of a garbage disposal along with knowledge model outlining each of the stages of how it would work. Learners could highlight one or more of the stages in the knowledge model. This, in turn, would present video information showing the selected process stage as it related to the diagram and its revealed parts. As each stage was played, the processes in relation to the parts would be narrated by the system. Again, this same general procedure would be followed such that learners could select "types and varieties" to see how the processes of disposing food in one garbage disposal were similar or different from those in other disposals.

Finally, in choosing the interface category "Procedural," learners would be presented with a list of common problems (e.g., "disposal does not run," "disposal leaks at sink flange," "disposal leaks from weep hole," and "excessive noise or vibration"). In selecting a problem, a video would play displaying where the breakdown likely occurred in the disposal's operations. In selecting the option "Solution," learners would be presented with a knowledge model of the procedures for fixing the problems. In clicking on one or more of the stages of these procedures, learners could see how the problem could be fixed for any one of the types and varieties of disposals available. In addition, the learner would have the option of calling up a diagram to illustrate the key parts related to one or more procedures identified in the knowledge matrix.

While such a system would provide multimedia instructional designers with a common framework for designing instruction, it would also provide teachers with efficiencies as well. By building assessment into such a system where learners had to identify parts, attributes, functions, processes, and procedures, instructional designers could build into such systems means for profiling the knowledge states of individual learners. Using knowledge modeling principles, teachers could pinpoint where learners' problems appeared; in turn, they could address the problems via a menu structure (much like the menu for fixing the garbage disposal). In this way, the framework for instructing the teacher would be the same in general format as the framework the learner was using to acquire knowledge of a new applied domain and the same for the instructional designer creating the system. Such optimal efficiency would no doubt please Frederick Taylor.

REFERENCES

Anderson, J. R. (1983). *The architecture of cognition*. Cambridge, MA: Harvard University Press.

Boorstin, D. (1972). The Americans: the democratic experience. New York: Random House.

Bovair, S., & Kieras, D. E. (1991). Toward a model of acquiring procedures from text. In R. Barr, M. L. Kamil, P. B. Mosenthal, & P. D. Pearson (Eds.), *Handbook of reading research* (Vol. 2, pp. 206–229). White Plains, NY: Longman.

Guthrie, J. T., & Greaney, V. (1991). Literacy acts. In R. Barr, M. L. Kamil, P. B. Mosenthal, & P. D. Pearson (Eds.), *Handbook of reading research* (Vol. 2, pp. 68–96). White Plains, NY: Longman.

Guthrie, J. T., Seifert, M., & Kirsch, I. S. (1986). Effects of education, occupation, and setting on reading practices. *American Educational Research Journal, 23*, 151–160.

362   PETER B. MOSENTHAL

Kirsch, I. S., & Jungeblut, A. (1992). *Profiling the literacy proficiencies of JTPA and ES/UI populations: Final report to the Department of Labor* (Contract No. 99-8-3458-75-052-01). Princeton, NJ: Educational Testing Service.

Kirsch, I. S., Jungeblut, A., & Campbell, A. (1992). *Beyond the school doors: The literacy needs of job seekers served by the U. S. Department of Labor*. Princeton, NJ: Educational Testing Service.

Kirsch I. S., & Mosenthal, P. B. (1990a). Mimetic documents: Pictures. *Journal of Reading, 34*, 216–230.

Kirsch, I. S., & Mosenthal, P. B. (1990b). Mimetic documents: Diagrams. *Journal of Reading, 34*, 290–294.

Kirsch, I. S., & Mosenthal, P. B. (1991a). Understanding mimetic documents through "knowledge modeling." *Journal of Reading, 34*, 552–558.

Kirsch, I. S., & Mosenthal, P. B. (1991b). Understanding definitions, descriptions, and comparison/contrasts. *Journal of Reading, 35*, 156–160.

Kirsch, I. S., & Mosenthal, P. B. (1992). Understanding process knowledge models. *Journal of Reading, 35*, 490–497.

Mikulecky, L., & Drew, R. (1991). Basic literacy skills in the workplace. In R. Barr, M. L. Kamil, P. B. Mosenthal, & P. D. Pearson (Eds.), *Handbook of reading research* (Vol. 2, pp. 669–689). White Plains, NY: Longman.

Mosenthal, P. (March, 1988). One size fits all: Computer conforming instruction. *The Reading Teacher, 41*, 692–695.

Mosenthal, P. B., & Cavallo, A. M. (1998). Profiling changing states of conceptual knowledge: With designs toward developing a universal knowledge interface system for the 21st century. *Peabody Journal of Education, 73* (3 & 4), 145–177.

Mosenthal, P. B., & Kirsch, I. S. (1989). Designing effective adult literacy programs. *Poetics, 18*, 239–256.

Mosenthal, P. B., & Kirsch, I. S. (1991a). Mimetic documents: Process schematics. *Journal of Reading, 34*, 390–397.

Mosenthal, P. B., & Kirsch, I. S. (1991b). More mimetic documents: Procedural schematics. *Journal of Reading, 34*, 486–490.

Mosenthal, P. B., & Kirsch, I. S. (1991c). Extending prose comprehension through knowledge modeling. *Journal of Reading, 35*, 58–61.

Mosenthal, P. B., & Kirsch, I. S. (1991d). Using knowledge models to understand steady states. *Journal of Reading, 35*, 250–255.

Mosenthal, P. B., & Kirsch, I. S. (1991e). Toward an explanatory model of document literacy. *Discourse Processes, 14*, 147–180.

Mosenthal, P. B., & Kirsch, I. S. (1992a). Understanding knowledge models of simple events. *Journal of Reading, 35*, 408–415.

Mosenthal, P. B., & Kirsch, I. S. (1992b). Understanding knowledge acquisition from a knowledge model perspective. *Journal of Reading Behavior, 35*, 588–596.

Resnick, L. B. (1987). Learning in school and out. *Educational Researcher, 42*, 9–39.

Schumacher, G. M., & Nash, J. G. (1991). Conceptualizing and measuring knowledge change due to writing. *Research in the Teaching of English, 25*, 67–96.

Spiro, R. J., Vispoel, W. L., Schmitz, J. G., Samarapungavan, A., & Boerger, A. E. (1987). Knowledge acquisition for application: Cognitive flexibility and transfer in complex content domains. In B. K. Britton & S. M. Glynn (Eds.), *Executive control processes in reading* (pp. 177–199). Hillsdale, NJ: Erlbaum.

Sticht, T. G. (1977). Comprehending reading at work. In M. A. Just & P. A. Carpenter (Eds.), *Cognitive processes in comprehension* (pp. 221–246). Hillsdale, NJ: Erlbaum.

Venezky, R. L. (1982). The origins of the present-day chasm between adult literacy needs and school literacy instruction. *Visible Language, 16*, 113–127.

Vosniadou, S., & Brewer, W. F. (1987). Theories of knowledge restructuring in development. *Review of Educational Research, 57*, 51–67.

THE CHALLENGE OF MULTIMEDIA LITERACY

Richard E. Mayer

The purpose of this chapter is to offer an expanded conceptualization of literacy appropriate for the new age of multimedia—a conceptualization which I call multimedia literacy. In this chapter, I offer a definition of literacy that goes beyond the ability to read and write words, I provide examples of situations that require multimedia literacy, I examine techniques for learning how to make sense of multimedia messages created by others, I examine techniques for learning how to create multimedia messages that make sense to others, I propose a research agenda, and I offer some closing thoughts.

RECONCEPTUALIZING LITERACY

What does it mean to be a literate person? In its most classic sense, literacy means knowing how to read and write. Literacy entails knowledge that is so fundamental to education that being literate is often equated with being educated. Interestingly, literacy refers to knowing how to gain knowledge rather than specific content knowledge itself. In short, to be literate is to possess the fundamental skills needed

Advances in Reading/Language Research, Volume 7, pages 363–376.
Copyright © 2000 by JAI Press Inc.
All rights of reproduction in any form reserved.
ISBN: 0-7623-0264-X

to be able to learn, but literacy does not necessarily include the specific knowledge that results from learning.

The thesis of this chapter is that the classical definition of literacy is limited in two important ways—by focusing on the content of literacy too narrowly as dealing solely with verbal material (i.e., being literate means being able to read and write words) and by focusing on the process of literacy too narrowly as acquiring and dispensing pieces of information (i.e., being literate means being able to learn and reproduce pieces of information).

These limitations have been well-recognized in the field of literacy (Flood, Heath, & Lapp, 1997; Moore & Dwyer, 1994; Semali & Watts Pailliotet, 1999). Concerning the first limitation, literacy researchers have noted the need for a definition of literacy that goes beyond verbal literacy. For example, Flood and Lapp (1995, p. 1) call for a "broader conceptualization in which literacy is defined as the ability to function competently in the communication arts—which include the language arts as well as the visual arts of drama, art, film, video, and television." Concerning the second limitation, literacy researchers have recognized the need for a definition of literacy that goes beyond traditional views of teaching and learning. For example, Hobbs (1997, p. 7) notes that "this view of literacy posits the student as being actively engaged in the process of analyzing and creating messages."

The information age—with its ability to provide a seemingly endless supply of symbols, graphics, and sounds—requires a reconceptualization of literacy. This point has been a theme in the literacy literature. For example, Semali and Watts Pailliotet (1999, p. 5) argue that "the rise of mass media and technology in society and schools has led to new understandings of what literacy and learning entail." In a similar way, Reinking (1995, p. 17) observes that "evolving forms of electronic reading and writing point to fundamental changes in the way we communicate and disseminate information, the way we approach the task of reading of writing, and the way we think about helping people become literate."

In its reconceptualized sense, literacy means knowing how to make sense out of multimedia messages created by others and how to create multimedia messages that make sense to others. As summarized in Figure 1, this reconceptualization involves two important changes that broaden the definition of literacy—changes in the way we conceptualize the content and the process of literacy.

First, the content of literacy is reformulated from text to multimedia message— that is, from being able to read and write in words to being able to read and write in words, graphics, sounds, and other formats. Multimedia messages may include various combinations of text, graphics, sounds, and other representations. Thus, the classic definition assumes that literacy involves text whereas the reformulated definition assumes that literacy involves a variety of formats including text, graphics, and sounds. For example, current interest in visual literacy reflects a reconceptualized view of literacy that goes beyond the traditional focus solely on verbal literacy (Braden, 1996; Moore & Dwyer, 1994).

	Classic literacy	Multimedia literacy
Content of literacy:	*Written prose*: words	*Instructional messages*: words, images, sounds, actions, etc.
Process of literacy:	*Reading*: ability to read written prose	*Sense making*: ability to make sense of messages
	Writing: ability to produce written prose	*Making sense*: ability to create messages that make sense to others

Figure 1. Comparing Classic and Multimedia Literacy

Second, the process of literacy is reformulated from reading and writing to sense making and enabling sense making—that is, from being able to read and write to being able to make sense and help others make sense. Thus, the classic definition allows that literacy is embodied in the act of reading and writing whereas the reformulated definition allows literacy to involve any act of personal understanding or fostering understanding in others. For example, current interest in how people build and convey mental models reflects a reconceptualized view of literacy that goes beyond the traditional focus solely on piecemeal translation on a word-by-word or sentence-by-sentence basis (Halford, 1993; Johnson-Laird, 1983). This reconceptualized view of literacy is consistent with constructivist theories of learning in which learners are viewed as sense makers who strive to construct their own knowledge (Lambert & McCombs, 1998).

I refer to this reconceptualization as multimedia literacy because of its focus on building coherent mental representations from multiple sources (such as words, graphics, and sounds). The new age of multimedia has broken the suffocating dominance of verbal presentation as the only acceptable mode of academic communication—enabling, for example, the incorporation of graphics into textbooks (Laspina, 1998) and computer-based presentations (Jonassen, 1996). Advances in multimedia technology also enable educational environments that are more consistent with constructivist theories of learning (Petraglia, 1998), including the presentation of material using multiple representations. Computer-based technology is increasingly involved in communications involving multiple representations, such as visual and verbal representations that complement each other (van Someren, Reimann, Boshuizen, & de Jong, 1998).

SOME EXAMPLES OF MULTIMEDIA LITERACY

In this section I provide examples of situations involving multimedia literacy. First, I describe how reading a textbook graph exemplifies the need to make sense of multimedia messages and to design multimedia messages that make sense to others. Second, I describe how viewing a computer-based animation exemplifies the same two aspects of multimedia literacy.

Reading a Textbook Graph

Consider the following scenario. A student is reading a chapter about events leading to the American Civil War in a middle school textbook on U.S. history. As part of the chapter, the student views the graph shown in Figure 2. The author's intention is to show that in the years leading to the Civil War, the northern states were becoming increasingly more urban whereas the southern states remained largely rural. The implication is that the difference between the perspectives from urban and rural cultures could be a contributing factor to the war. The author attempts to make the case visually by presenting all the needed information in the context of the graph.

Unfortunately, the student fails to interpret the graph as the author intended. When asked to summarize the graph, the student focuses on the most salient visual

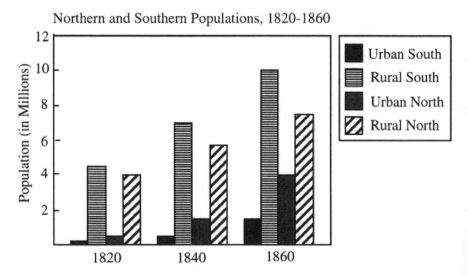

Figure 2. A Graph Depicting Changes in the Proportion of Urban Population in the Northern And Southern States in Three Time Periods Leading to the U.S. Civil War

pattern in the graph by saying: "Rural is greater than urban." When asked to try again, the student reads the graph by listing the number corresponding to each bar: "In 1820, the urban south population is .4 million, the rural south population is 4.5 million, the urban north population is .5 million, the rural north is 4.4 million...." The student has not engaged in any serious sense-making, and has not attempted to relate the graph to the theme of the chapter.

There are two ways of viewing and rectifying this problem: learner-based and designer-based. According to the learner-based interpretation, the student lacks appropriate knowledge of how to make sense of textbook graphics. The solution involves helping the student learn how to select, organize, and integrate relevant information from the graph. Helping students learn how to interpret graphs corresponds to the "reading" side of literacy.

According to the designer-based interpretation, the author has failed to create textbook graphics that make sense to others. The solution involves helping the graph's designer to learn how to construct a graph that primes meaningful cognitive processing in the learner. Helping designers learn how to create graphs that promote sense-making corresponds to the "writing" side of literacy.

Viewing a Computer-Based Animation

As another example, consider the following situation. A student is seated at a computer monitor, using a multimedia encyclopedia. She clicks on the entry for "brakes" and views an annotated animation depicting the operation of a car's braking system. Selected frames are shown in Figure 3. The purpose of the presentation is to help students understand how brakes work as a cause-and-effect system, that is, how a change in one part causes a change in another part and so on. The author attempts to provide a visual and verbal explanation using animation and on-screen text.

Unfortunately, the student fails to understand how the braking system works. She takes a transfer test in which she must use the information from the presentation to solve new problems. For example, when asked how to make the brakes more reliable, she says to "have them serviced regularly" and when asked what might cause brakes to fail she says, "the brakes are broken." These vague answers suggest that the student has not developed a deep understanding of how brakes work. She has not engaged in any serious sense-making, and has not attempted to integrate the actions in the animation with the corresponding text descriptions.

As with the textbook graph scenario, this problem can be attributed to either the learner or the designer. According to the learner-based interpretation, the student lacks skill in how to make sense of animated explanations, including how to pay attention to relevant images and words, how to build cause-and-effect connections between steps in the process, and how to integrate visual and verbal explanations. Fostering multimedia comprehension skills corresponds to the "reading" side of the definition of literacy.

According to the designer-based interpretation, the multimedia presentation is not designed to prompt meaningful learning in students. For example, combining on-screen text with animation may result in cognitive overload that hinders the learner's sense-making activities. Even though all relevant information is presented, it is not presented in a way that meshes with the human information processing system. Redesigning the presentation to foster meaningful processing corresponds to the "writing" side of the definition of literacy.

Overall, these scenarios demonstrate the important role of multimedia literacy in tasks that require going beyond reading and writing of printed words—including knowing how to make sense of multimedia messages and knowing how to create multimedia messages that make sense to others. These two issues are addressed in the next two sections, respectively.

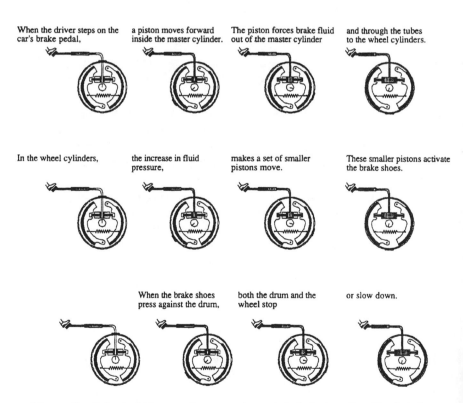

Figure 3.   Selected Frames from an Annotated Animation Explaining
How a Car's Braking System Works

MULTIMEDIA LITERACY: KNOWING HOW TO MAKE SENSE OF MULTIMEDIA MESSAGES

The first aspect of multimedia literacy is that learners must be able to make sense of a variety of printed symbols, visual images, and sounds, that is, learners must possess and know how to use cognitive processes appropriate for understanding multimedia. Figure 4 presents a framework for describing the cognitive processes involved in multimedia learning, in which the boxes refer to representations and the arrows refer to cognitive processes (Mayer, 1997; Mayer, Steinhoff, Bower, & Mars, 1995). Following Paivio's (1986) dual coding theory, the framework assumes that there are multiple information processing systems—such as one system for verbal material and one for visual material. Following Baddeley's (1992) working memory theory, the framework assumes that the processing capacity of each system is limited. Following Mayer's (1987) and Wittrock's (1989) generative theory of learning, the framework assumes that learning involves active cognitive processing.

For example, in one multimedia learning scenario, an animation may be presented along with corresponding narration. The first cognitive process is SELECTING WORDS in which the learner pays attention to relevant words in the narration and uses them to build a mental representation—called a text base—in working memory. Similarly, the second cognitive process is SELECTING IMAGES in which the learner pays attention to relevant images in the animation and uses them to build a mental representation—called an image base—in working memory. Thus, the two SELECTING processes involve paying attention to relevant aspects of the incoming verbal and visual information.

The third process is ORGANIZING WORDS in which the learner builds a coherent verbally based mental model from the text base, such as organizing the events described in the narration into a cause-and-effect chain. Similarly, the fourth cognitive process is ORGANIZING IMAGES in which the learner builds a coherent visually based mental model from the image base, such as organizing the events depicted in the animation into a cause-and-effect chain. Thus, the two ORGANIZING processes involve building coherent mental models from the selected verbal information and from the selected visual information.

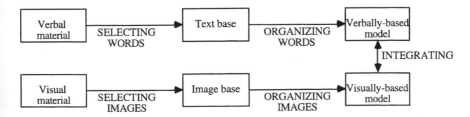

Figure 4. A Cognitive Model of Multimedia Learning

The final process is INTEGRATING the verbal and visual mental representations with one another and with prior knowledge. This process includes making one-to-one mappings between names and images of key objects, as well as making one-to-one mappings between verbal descriptions of key events or states and corresponding visual depictions. It also involves making connections between the newly constructed mental representations and relevant prior knowledge.

Overall, this analysis suggests guidelines for instruction in multimedia literacy. In particular, when multimedia messages consist of words and graphics, students need skill in five basic cognitive processes: selecting relevant words, selecting relevant images, organizing words into a coherent representation, organizing images into a coherent representation, and integrating verbally based and visually based representations with one another and with prior knowledge. Current programs aimed at promoting reading comprehension include techniques for selecting words and organizing words, such as asking students to summarize or outline a passage (Pressley & Woloshyn, 1995). Corresponding techniques are needed to help students develop skill in selecting images and organizing images, such as practice in circling the most important aspects of a graphic and in placing a set of graphics in chronological order, respectively. Finally, students need practice in integrating visual and verbal representations such as describing graphics in words.

In the graph example (in Figure 2), students need skill in each of the following cognitive processes: selecting words, such as underlining the key points in the corresponding text; organizing words, such as writing a summary or outline of the corresponding text; selecting images, such as circling the key points in the graph; organizing images, such as drawing lines connecting the key points in the graph; and integrating text and images, such as writing appropriate text next to connected points on the graph, that is, summarizing the graph using words.

In the animation example (in Figure 3), students need skill in each of the following cognitive processes: selecting words, such as listing the main parts of the braking system and listing the main changes that occur; organizing words, such as creating a flowchart representing the cause-and-effect chain; selecting images, such as circling the main parts of the braking system and circling the major changes that occur in the system (using a collection of still frames from the animation); organizing images, such as placing still frames in chronological order; and integrating visual and verbal representations such as writing a verbal summary for each of several key frames of the animation.

Importantly, multimedia literacy requires more than cognitive skill in being able to use each of these five kinds of cognitive processes; it also requires metacognitive skill in being able to know how and when to use them to accomplish a goal. Given the domain-specific nature of learning, the specific cognitive skills needed for multimedia learning may differ depending on the subject matter of the material, such that skills required for comprehending line graphs may be different from the skills required for understanding animations depicting how a device works.

MULTIMEDIA LITERACY: KNOWING HOW TO
CREATE MULTIMEDIA MESSAGES
THAT MAKE SENSE

The second aspect of multimedia literacy is that students must be able to use a variety of printed symbols, visual images, and sounds to communicate with others—that is, students must know how to create multimedia messages that other people can understand. To accomplish this goal, students need to be able to design multimedia presentations that foster each of the five cognitive processes summarized in Figure 4.

For example, students have difficulty making sense out of the graph shown in Figure 2. How could the graph be redesigned so that it is more likely to foster understanding? One problem concerns the process of selecting relevant images: Student attention is drawn to the bars showing the greatest and least absolute levels of population, whereas the author's intention is for students to focus on the relation between urban and rural population. A second problem concerns the process of organizing images: Student attention is drawn to each of three clusters of four bars each—that is, the four bars for the first time period, the four bars for the second time period, and the four bars for the third time period—whereas the author's intention is for students to focus on across-year comparisons. Students tend to make within-year comparisons among the bars because of the way they are clustered— that is, students may compare urban and rural bars within the first time period, the second time period, and the third time period. A third problem concerns the process of integrating images and words: Students may not know how the data represented in the graph relate to the thesis stated in the text.

Figure 5 presents a revised version of the graph that overcomes these problems and is more likely to prime constructive cognitive processing in the viewer. In this graph, the dependent measure is now the percentage of urban population, and attention is thus focused on the relative amount of urban to rural population rather than the absolute. In this graph, the data are now clustered as two lines each connecting three dots, so the viewer is more likely to mentally organize the data as two across-year comparisons—the one for the south staying steady and the one for

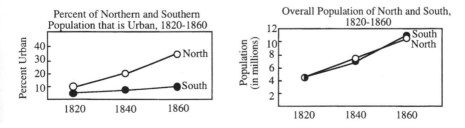

Figure 5. A Revised Version of Figure 2

the north increasing. Finally, to assist viewers in the process of integrating words and pictures, a caption can be added to the graph which summarizes the main point in words. The revised graph encourages viewers to engage in the processes of selecting, organizing, and integrating that lead to understanding of the graph (Shah, Mayer, & Hegarty, 1997).

Similarly, students have difficulty making sense out of the annotated animation summarized in Figure 3, as is indicated by their difficulty in answering transfer questions. What can be done to improve the understandability of the multimedia presentation? The annotated animation summarized in Figure 3 is inconsiderate to the viewer because it places an unreasonable demand on the viewer's visual information processing system. Although both a visual and a verbal explanation are presented, they are presented visually. Thus, the viewer must pay attention to the animation and at the same time pay attention to the on-screen text.

One problem concerns the process of selecting relevant words and images: The viewer is unable to select the words and images because visual information processing resources are overloaded. A second problem concerns the processes of organizing words into a coherent representation and organizing images into a coherent representation: The viewer is less able to actively organize the material because visual working memory is overloaded. A third problem concerns the process of integrating words and images: The viewer is less able to build connections because so much of the material has been lost due to cognitive overload.

To overcome this problem, the on-screen text can be converted into corresponding narration. When the verbal material is presented as speech, it can be processed in the verbal information processing system—allowing adequate capacity for selecting and organizing images. Eliminating on-screen text frees capacity in the visual information processing system that can be applied to selecting and organizing relevant images. Mayer and Moreno (1998) have found that this kind of redesigned multimedia message results in much higher levels of understanding than does the original multimedia message. Simply by changing from on-screen text to narration, the multimedia message becomes more learner friendly.

In recent reviews, I have suggested the following research-based principles of multimedia design (Mayer, 1997, 1999):

- *Multimedia principle*: present an explanation using words and pictures rather than solely in words (e.g., present a series of illustration frames depicting the main steps in operation of automobile brakes with corresponding text describing the process in words, or present an animation depicting the operation of brakes along with a narration describing the process in words).
- *Spatial contiguity principle*: present corresponding text and pictures near each other on the page or screen rather than far from each other (e.g., present each frame of an illustration next to its corresponding text description).

- *Temporal continguity principle*: present corresponding speech and pictures at the same time rather than at different times (e.g., present each portion of an animation simultaneously with its corresponding narration).
- *Modality principle*: accompany an animation with concurrent narration rather than on-screen text (e.g., when presenting an animation depicting the steps in how brakes work, present the verbal description of each step as concurrent narration rather than as concurrent on-screen text).
- *Coherence principle*: minimize extraneous words, pictures, and sounds when giving a multimedia explanation (e.g., do not add interesting but irrelevant sentences and pictures about the history of brakes, or do not add background music or mechanical sound effects to a narrated animation about how brakes work).

Research-based principles such as these can form the basis for instruction in multimedia literacy, that is, instruction in how to create understandable messages.

Overall, all multimedia messages are not equally understandable, even when they convey identical information. Part of multimedia literacy involves being able to create multimedia messages that are consistent with the way that humans learn. Just as writing requires empathy for the audience (Kellogg, 1994), designing multimedia messages requires presenting material in ways that foster meaningful cognitive processing. As research-based principles of multimedia design continue to emerge (Mayer, 1993, 1999), they can form the basis for instruction in multimedia literacy.

AN AGENDA FOR MULTIMEDIA RESEARCH

It is clear that much work needs to be done in order to build a research and theory base to address the challenge of multimedia literacy. The research agenda should include examining how students learn to be better multimedia communicators, including how to foster skills in understanding and creating multimedia messages. How can educators help students to develop multimedia literacy, including the ability to make sense of multimedia messages and to produce multimedia messages that make sense to others? This is the most fundamental question facing researchers of multimedia literacy.

In addition to building a base of scientifically sound research findings, literacy researchers must ultimately develop an educationally relevant theory of multimedia learning. An educationally relevant theory of multimedia learning must account for how people process incoming visual and verbal material, including how they select relevant material, build visually based and verbally based mental representations, and make connections between visual and verbal representations. It must also clarify the nature of the differences between verbal and visual information processing channels and the nature of capacity limitations in working memory. How do people integrate visual and verbal material, and which cognitive processes and which information-processing channels are involved? Answering these kinds of questions will allow educators to derive useful principles for the teaching of multimedia literacy.

In this chapter, I have taken a cognitive approach to multimedia literacy, focusing on the cognitive processes and human information-processing channels related to understanding and designing multimedia messages. A cognitive analysis of multimedia literacy—while a crucial task—is limited. Additional work is needed to deal with the other aspects of multimedia literacy including the affective and motivational, the social and cultural, and the biological and developmental.

CONCLUSION

In the multimedia age, literacy must mean more than the ability to read and write using words. People need to be able to make sense of and to create a wide array of multimedia messages that include some combination of text, symbols, tables, pictures, graphics, animation, movies, speech, music, and sounds. Although verbal aspects of literacy form the core of a traditional education, the multimedia age requires increased attention to other aspects of literacy, including visual and auditory aspects of literacy. Whereas the longstanding technology of print media has tended to emphasize verbal (i.e., text) forms of presentation, recent advances in computer and telecommunication technology have produced an increase in the use of visual (e.g., pictures, graphics, movies, animations) and auditory (e.g., music, sounds, speech) forms of presentation.

Recent advances in computer technology have reactivated the illusive goal of using technology as a means of promoting human cognition (Landauer, 1997). One of the greatest accomplishments of human cognition is the ability to build mental models, that is, to make sense of one's experience. Recent research encourages the idea that multimedia presentations hold potential for greatly increasing this sense-making process (Mayer, 1997). For example, presenting a verbal description of a demographic trend in a textbook is not as effective in promoting understanding as presenting a verbal description along with a corresponding graph; similarly, presenting a narration describing how a braking system works is not as effective in promoting understanding as combining an animation along with verbal narration (Mayer, 1997).

In some ways, it might seem paradoxical to suggest that technology could serve as an aid to this sense-making process, because current implementations of computer and telecommunications technology seem poised to drown humankind in a virtual sea of information. The cognitive danger of the multimedia age rests in a computer-based technology that enables the presentation of large amounts of specific information to humans who are not designed to process it. Humans are not copy machines that carefully record every detail of presented information but rather are sense-makers who focus on a limited portion of presented material and construct a coherent representation (Mayer, 1987).

From an educational standpoint, the challenge of multimedia literacy is to help students develop skill in making sense of multimedia messages and to help students learn to design multimedia messages that make sense to others. In summary, students need to be able to take advantage of multimedia aids for sense making— such as how to learn productively from graphics combined with words or animations combined with prose—and multimedia messages need to become more sense-maker friendly—so they enable rather than preclude cognitive processes leading to understanding. Coming to grips with the challenge of multimedia literacy represents one of the major instructional tasks facing education in the 21st century.

REFERENCES

Baddeley, A. (1992). Working memory. *Science, 255*, 556–559.

Braden, R. A. (1996). Visual literacy. In D. H. Jonassen (Ed.), *Handbook of educational communications and technology* (pp. 491–520). New York: Macmillan.

Flood, J., Heath, S. B., & Lapp, D. (Eds.). (1997). *Handbook of research on teaching the communication and visual arts*. New York: Macmillan.

Flood, J., & Lapp, D. (1995). Broadening the lens: Toward an expanded conceptualization of literacy. In K. A. Hinchman, D. J. Leu, & C. K. Kinzer (Eds.), *Perspectives on literacy research and practice: Forty-fourth yearbook of the National Reading Conference* (pp. 1–16). Chicago: National Reading Conference.

Halford, G. S. (1993). *Children's understanding: The development of mental models*. Mahwah, NJ: Erlbaum.

Hobbs, R. (1997). Literacy for the information age. In J. Flood, S. B. Heath, & D. Lapp (Eds.), *Handbook of research on teaching the communication and visual arts* (pp. 7–14). New York: Macmillan.

Johnson-Laird, P. N. (1983). *Mental models*. Cambridge, MA: Harvard University Press.

Jonassen, D. H. (Ed.). (1996). *Handbook of educational communications and technology*. New York: Macmillan.

Kellogg, R. T. (1994). *The psychology of writing*. London: Oxford University Press.

Lambert, N. M., & McCombs, B. L. (Eds.). (1998). *How students learn: Reforming schools through learner-centered education*. Washington, DC: American Psychological Association.

Landauer, T. (1997). *The trouble with computers*. Cambridge, MA: MIT Press.

Laspina, J. A. (1998). *The visual turn and the transformation of the textbook*. Mahwah, NJ: Erlbaum.

Mayer, R. E. (1987). *Educational psychology: A cognitive approach*. New York: Harper Collins.

Mayer, R. E. (1993). Problem-solving principles. In M. Fleming & W. H. Levie (Eds.), *Instructional message design: Principles from the behavioral and cognitive sciences* (2nd ed., pp. 253–282). Englewood Cliffs, NJ: Educational Technology Publications.

Mayer, R. E. (1997). Multimedia learning: Are we asking the right questions? *Educational Psychologist, 32*, 1–20.

Mayer, R. E. (1999). Instructional technology. In F. Durso (Ed.), *Handbook of applied cognition* (pp. 551–570). New York: Wiley.

Mayer, R. E., & Moreno, R. (1998). A split-attention effect in multimedia learning: Evidence for dual processing systems in working memory. *Journal of Educational Psychology, 90*, 312–320.

Mayer, R. E., Steinhoff, K., Bower, G., & Mars, R. (1995). A generative theory of textbook design: Using annotated illustrations to foster meaningful learning of science text. *Educational Technology Research and Development, 43*, 31–43.

Moore, D. M., & Dwyer, F. M. (Eds.). (1994). *Visual literacy*. Englewood Cliffs, NJ: Educational Technology Press.

Paivio, A. (1986). *Mental representations: A dual coding approach*. London: Oxford University Press.

Petraglia, J. (1998). *Reality by design: The rhetoric and technology of authenticity on education.* Mahwah, NJ: Erlbaum.

Pressley, M., & Woloshyn, V. (1995). *Cognitive strategy instruction that really improves children's academic performance* (2nd ed). Cambridge, MA: Brookline.

Reinking, D. (1995). Reading and writing with computers: Literacy research in a post-typographic world. In K. A. Hinchman, D. J. Leu, & C. K. Kinzer (Eds.), *Perspectives on literacy research and practice: Forty-fourth yearbook of the National Reading Conference* (pp. 17–33). Chicago: National Reading Conference.

Semali, L. M., & Watts Pailliotet, A. (Eds.). (1999). *Intermediality: A teachers' handbook of critical media literacy.* Boulder, CO: Westview.

Shah, P., Mayer, R. E., & Hegarty, M. (1997, April). *Which graphs are better? Textbook graphs as aids to knowledge construction.* Paper presented at the annual meeting of the American Educational Research Association, San Diego.

van Someren, M. W., Reimann, P., Boshuizen, P. A., & de Jong, T. (Eds.). (1998). *Learning with multiple representations.* Elmsford, NY: Pergamon.

Wittrock, M. C. (1989). Generative processes in comprehension. *Educational Psychologist, 24,* 345–376.

A TAXONOMY OF VISUAL LITERACY

Robert Maribe Branch

VISUAL LITERACY: THE CONCEPT

The purpose of this discourse is to consider the meaning of pictures as a form of literacy. This is an attempt to provide an empirically supported, theoretical framework on which skills, constructs, rationale for implementation, and supplemental research about visual messages can be constructed. The concept of visual thinking is mature, but a common taxonomy for identifying the stages of development in visual literacy remains absent. The theories and applications set forth in this chapter are intended to be the beginning of an established rubric for operationalizing the grammar of visual literacy. The assumptions are that images communicate meaning and that literacy means being able to read and compose. Read is defined here as to receive or take in the sense of letters or symbols, especially by sight or touch. Compose means to form by putting together in order to create by mental or artistic labor (Merriam-Webster, 1991). The language of visual imagery is located between communicating perception through visual cues and artistic expression. Both visual cues and artistic expression represent near ends of a continuum of symbols and, therefore, become the foundation for a visual language formed by symbol systems.

Pictures are continually used in instructional contexts in a variety of formats, although research about how individuals process and use pictorial information

Advances in Reading/Language Research, Volume 7, pages 377–402.
Copyright © 2000 by JAI Press Inc.
All rights of reproduction in any form reserved.
ISBN: 0-7623-0264-X

remains unknown. Communication with pictures began with the cave dwellers as they depicted events from their daily life in drawings on the cave walls. Comenius first used pictures in a formal instructional mode in his text, *Orbis Sensualium Pictus,* printed in the 17th century (King, 1975). Basic to all pictorial interpretation is the understanding that drawings can represent three-dimensional objects, and that they can be arranged in such a way as to convey a message (Goldsmith, 1984). Significant improvements in printing processes through the 20th century have made the printed word and picture available to practically everyone at a reasonable cost. Other advanced forms of communication transmission have provided access to multiple channel sources that instantaneously connect everyone to the ever-changing world.

Because of recent advances in computer software and hardware that have made it easy for people with little or no skill in message design to create diagrams, charts, and graphs, graphics have found inclusion in all manner of applications. However, the development of a theory of how people learn from graphics leading to a prescriptive theory for their design is urgently required (Winn, 1990). The word *graphics* means different things to different people. Winn believed such a theory must consist of a thorough description of the symbol system of graphics and of an account of how the symbolic elements of graphics influence preattentive and attentive perceptual and cognitive processes that lead to their interpretation. Winn refers to graphics as "charts, graphs and diagrams, not to pictures, nor to text, though graphics often contain pictures and texts. Charts, graphs and diagrams have an important common characteristic which justifies their study as one family of illustration. They all convey information through the way in which their components are related by spatial layout and not through their resemblance to any physical referent" (p. 553). Winn contends that attempts to develop grammars for graphics modeled after language grammars (Goldsmith, 1984, 1987; Kosslyn, Simcox, Pinker, & Parkin, 1983; Winn, 1989) have likewise failed to provide the needed theoretical foundation. Winn (1990) founded a theoretical framework anchored in the symbol systems of graphics, graphics and perceptual organization, and learning from graphics, particularly as each relates to computer interfaces. Winn notwithstanding, there remains a need for an even broader conceptual framework for determining why visual messages function as a grammar.

Before continuing with a presumption that a need exists for a taxonomy of visual literacy, it is important to first identify the current status of visual learning development. Moore and Dwyer (1994) edited a book entitled *Visual Literacy: A Spectrum of Visual Learning* that has compiled information about visuals which is broad, comprehensive, and represents a variety of disciplines, interests, and functions. Because visuals transmit data, information, knowledge, and emotion that is inclusive of many domains, Moore and Dwyer have appropriately included scholars representing education, medicine, advertising, business, industry, and art. The result is a cross section of topics that provides the reader with a sense scope about learning from visual messages. Moore and Dwyer also promote the goals of the International

Visual Literacy Association (IVLA) which recently celebrated its 31st year as a professional organization dedicated to visual communication and learning. *Visual Literacy* continues the tradition of Debes (1968), Arnheim (1969), and Dondis (1973). Moore and Dwyer (1994) have indeed advanced the legitimacy of visual messaging as a bona fide language, and have begun to answer many of the questions about visual literacy concepts; however, there remains a need to establish a common grammar for visual messages.

The introduction of affordable multimedia computers with digital video capacity, videocassette recorders, and connections to the Internet and the World Wide Web have expanded opportunities to help society develop visual literacy. University courses on visual literacy have been added to college curricula (Robinson & Koos, 1996) as a response to the need for developing visual literacy skills. People throughout the ages have relied on different forms of visualization in an attempt to improve communication. Consequently, it is not surprising that many educators employ visual media in an attempt to improve the teaching–learning process. Visualizing instruction as a continued practice has led to increased interest and research into the impact of visual stimuli on learners. Since the early 1960s, considerable research literature has been devoted to the perceived effectiveness of pictorial materials. Through these more than 35 years of study, research has brought us closer to an understanding of the factors that influence human processing of pictorial materials. Research on the interactive effects of pictorial components and time factors on various types of learning and memory may provide the basis for establishing guidelines for the design of instructional materials.

A visual language should be based on existing knowledge about visual learning, proven concepts for attaining literacy, and innovative paradigms for universal communication. This chapter is an initial attempt to construct an appropriate conceptual framework for attaining a common grammar that will characterize visual literacy. While there are several apparent steps needed to accomplish a visual grammar, the contention here is that a taxonomy of visual literacy is the immediate next step.

Mass media analysts, cultural and critical theorists, sociologists, artists, authors, and illustrators; literacy practitioners and theorists; teachers and teacher educators, media specialists, and instructional designers will be able to build on the conceptual foundation on which a literacy of visual communication can be constructed. Visual literacy research should be undertaken with the intent to ascertain the best ways for people to become visually literate. Research on the concept of visual literacy should follow as a way to provide the empirical support for recognizing a pictorial communication as a language form. Many have tried to define the concept of visual literacy, but so far there is no consensus (Avgerinou & Ericson, 1997). There is a need for reviews of the literature to develop a definition of visual literacy. Avgerinou and Ericson reviewed the literature, explored the parameters of visual literacy, including the history of the visual literacy movement and its aims, its educational significance, and the potential benefits of teaching visual literacy. Hood and Lapp

(1997–1998) suggest the conceptualization of literacy must be broadened from reading and writing skills to a definition that recognizes the layering of information and one inclusive of all forms of the communicative arts. Cassidy and Knowlton (1983) proposed a reconceptualization of the inherent assumptions and visual literacy implications. Braden (1996) contends "there are two major impediments to research on visual literacy. The first is the lack of a widely accepted definition of the term *visual literacy* itself. The second, perhaps a consequence of the first, is a lack of cohesive theory" (p. 491). However, Braden concludes that, "visual literacy research is needed to:

1. Identify the learnable visual literacy skills
2. Identify the teachable visual literacy skills
3. Develop implementation of visual literacy constructs
4. Validate implementation of visual literacy constructs
5. Provide a rationale for visual literacy implementation in our society
6. Provide a rationale for visual literacy implementation in our educational system
7. Supplement research conducted in other fields, including psychology, education, learning, visual perception and eye moment studies, and print literacy." (pp. 510–511)

Rezabek (1999) purports visual literacy is the ability to both accurately interpret and create messages that are transmitted through the sense of sight, with an emphasis on using communication systems that do not rely primarily on traditional text-based alphabetic or numeric codes. Rezabek's perspective is that the principles of visual literacy can be learned, and as we become more visually literate, we enhance our understanding and use of visuals including body language, mass media, fine arts, computer graphics, and other means of communication using the sense of sight. Lacy (1987) identified six visual literacy goals for students of all ages:

1. Students will become more creative and critical thinkers by identifying, analyzing, interpreting, and evaluating what they see.
2. Students will become visual makers themselves, demonstrating the ability to create mental images and to communicate visually to others.
3. Students will be more perceptive individuals by recognizing and appreciating aesthetics of visual imagery and by understanding, accepting, and valuing personal, cultural, and historical differences in image creation.
4. Students will become more responsible citizens by being aware of the roles visuals play in reflecting and influencing a society.
5. Students will become more discriminating consumers, understanding the motives, methods, and emotional appeal of advertising visuals in a modern society.

6. Students will become lifelong learners, with a positive attitude about learning how to learn about visual images.

According to Rezabek (1999), when Lacy's (1987) final three goals for visually literate students are achieved, our students and subsequent generations of students will be able to demonstrate attributes of responsible citizens, discriminating consumers, and lifelong learners. Lacy suggests that developing visual literacy in students will support rational, wise, open-minded citizens of the future.

Visual literacy as a concept illustrates that the many dimensions of visual literacy can be learned, used, and integrated simultaneously into a message. Hood and Lapp (1997–1998) describe 2 hours in the life of an 8-year-old so as to demonstrate that children acquire information and develop language skills from multiple sources. Hood and Lapp suggest the conceptualization of literacy be broadened from reading and writing skills to a definition that recognizes the layering of information and a literacy definition that includes all forms of communicative and visual arts.

Visual messages are fundamental to complex mental processing because they provide information and opportunities for analysis that text alone cannot provide. Learners in complex societies around the world take in information visually, imitating the actions and attitudes they see. Visual information sources, from cave paintings forward, have supplemented (not replaced) oral communication (Katz, 1997). Visual messaging is necessary for increasing human capacity of complex mental processing, although, operational definitions for what it means to be visually literate do not yet enjoy consensus among the communities that promote visual literacy. Therefore, a definition of visual literacy is being put forth here based on what is known about the role of perception, symbol systems, and languages, in order that we may better communicate through images.

VISUAL LITERACY: THE DEFINITION

Visual literacy is defined here as a language of imagery bound by the explicit juxtaposition of symbols in time and space. A recent attempt to explain the parameters of visual literacy, the visual literacy movement and its aims, and the educational significance of the visual literacy concept, was presented by Avgerinou and Ericson (1997) in their review of the concept of visual literacy. According to Avgerinou and Ericson, "the term *visual literacy* was first coined in 1969 by John Debes, one of the most important figures in the history in visual literacy" (p. 280). Debes (1969) offered the following:

> Visual Literacy refers to a group of vision-competencies a human being can develop by seeing and at the same time having and integrating other sensory experiences. The development of these competencies is fundamental to normal human learning. When developed, they enable a visually

literate person to discriminate and interpret the visible actions, objects, and symbols, natural or man-made, that he encounters in his environment. Through the creative use of these competencies, he is able to communicate with others. Through the appreciative use of these competencies, he is able to comprehend and enjoy the masterworks of visual communication. (p. 27)

Levie (1978) claimed Debes's (1969) definition should have described the stimuli of interest in terms of a symbolic modality rather than in terms of a sensory modality. Bieman (1984) claimed Debes's definition should inform us about what visual literacy is, as well as what a visually literate person can do. Horton (1983) defined visual literacy as "the ability to understand (read) and use (write) images and to think and learn in terms of images, i.e., to think visually" (p. 99). There are others who have offered definitions of visual literacy (Ausburn & Ausburn, 1978; Curtiss, 1987; Sinatra, 1986; Sucy, 1985); however, each is symptomatic of one of the two common criticisms of visual literacy definitions:

1. Individuals have defined visual literacy from the perspective of one's own background and professional concerns (Boca & Braden, 1990).
2. Many definitions adhere to the verbal literacy analogy which is restrictive (Sucy, 1985).

Consequently, Avgerinou and Ericson (1997) believe "arguments in favour of taking visual literacy more seriously are probably even more compelling now than thirty years ago" (p. 290).

Robinson's (1984) sentiments about developing visual literacy through film remain one of the best denotations of visual literacy:

Literacy is certainly a familiar concept, and many find the term visual literacy confusing, since for most of us it takes vision to read anything. Visual literacy has been coined as a simple expression of some fairly complicated media appreciation or film criticism concepts. Basically, visual literacy is the ability to process the elements of and to interpret visual messages, the ability to understand and appreciate the content and purpose of any image, as well as its structural and aesthetic composition. A visually literate person can perceive, understand, and interpret visual messages, and can actively analyze and evaluate the visual communications they observe. Visual literacy involves the interpretation of images, movement, design, color, and pattern in media messages of many kinds, from company symbols and street signs to television commercials and *MTV*. (pp. 267–268)

Robinson has been particularly instrumental in outlining ideas for library activities that could help adults and other students develop visual skills, highlighting materials, hardware, software, and programs in the form of films, kits, books, and other teacher resources. Heidorn and Sandore (1997) note that recent technological advances in computing and digital imaging technology have had immediate and permanent consequences for visual resource collections. Libraries are involved in organizing and managing large visual resource collections. The central challenges in working with digital image collections mirror those that libraries have sought to address for centuries: how to organize, provide access to, store, and protect the collections to meet user needs at a reasonable cost.

Pettersson (1988) focused on the visual component of verbo-visual literacy, as a communications concept involving the production, transmission, and perception of verbal and visual images. Pettersson identified four current problem areas in verbal–visual research:

1. Communication (communication models, media consumption, new media, the information society, and screen communication)
2. Perception, learning, and memory (our senses, listening and looking, and learning and memory)
3. Literacy (language, verbal languages, characteristics of verbal languages, visual languages, and current research)
4. Designing visuals for information (content, execution, context, and format)

Definition: Visual literacy is the understanding of messages communicated through frames of space that utilize objects, images, and time, and their juxtaposition. The principles, rules, and form that characterize a visual grammar are based on communicating perception and the ecology of symbol systems.

Communicating Perception

Work in philosophy and psychology has argued for a dissociation between perceptually based similarity and higher-level rules in conceptual thought. Although such a dissociation may be justified at times, our goal is to illustrate ways in which conceptual processing is grounded in perception, both for perceptual similarity and abstract rules. Goldstone and Barsalou (1998) discuss the advantages, power, and influences of perceptually based representations. Goldstone and Barsalou suggest, first, many of the properties associated with modal symbol systems can be achieved with perceptually based systems as well, such as productivity. Second, relatively raw perceptual representations are powerful because they can implicitly represent properties in an analog fashion. Third, perception naturally provides impressions of overall similarity, exactly the type of similarity useful for establishing many common categories. Fourth, perceptual similarity is not static, but becomes tuned over time to conceptual demands. Fifth, the original motivation or basis for sophisticated cognition is often less sophisticated perceptual similarity. Sixth, perceptual simulation occurs even in conceptual tasks that have no explicit perceptual demands. Parallels between perceptual and conceptual processes suggest that many mechanisms typically associated with abstract thought are also present in perception, and that perceptual processes provide useful mechanisms that may be coopted by abstract thought.

Visual organizers reflect patterns of thinking about content knowledge. Clarke (1991) advanced the concept of visual organizers as graphic representations of different kinds of thinking processes, particularly graphic frames. Graphic frames have been used most prominently to organize student processing of text, in both reading and writing. They can also be used to organize student listening (during class lectures or presentations) and speaking (during class discussions). As support for thinking during classroom teaching, teachers can use visual organizers to clarify and strengthen the purpose of improved thinking in the subject areas (Clarke, 1991, p. 526). Using graphic organizers to teach involves developing a visual form that allows students to represent what they know, add new information, and practice critical thinking. Clarke presents four questions as a guide for using visuals to focus on thinking:

1. As I look at this content, what central facts, ideas, arguments, processes, or procedure do I want to understand?
2. What pattern or organization holds the material together and makes it meaningful?
3. What kind of visual organizer will facilitate a way to think through the content?
4. What problems or challenges can be posed that encourage a way to work through the steps of a thinking process?

(adapted and modified from Clarke, 1991, p. 527). Thinking can take many forms and visual organizers support different ways to thinking about a subject, but visual organizers should not be mistaken for thinking itself (Clarke, 1990).

Graphic representations are visual illustrations of verbal statements. Many graphic representations are familiar to most adults, such as flow diagrams, pie charts, and web maps. A good graphic representation can show, at a glance, the key parts of a whole and their relations, thereby allowing a holistic understanding that those words alone cannot convey (Jones, Pierce, & Hunter, 1989). Graphic representations are important because they help the learner to comprehend, summarize, and synthesize complex ideas in ways that tend to surpass verbal statements (Van Patten, Chao, & Reigeluth, 1986). According to Jones et al., "reading with an appropriate graphic structure in mind can help students select important ideas and details as well as detect missing information and unexplained relations. Moreover, constructing and analyzing a graphic helps students become actively involved in processing a text. Graphics foster nonlinear thinking, unlike prose summaries and linear outlines" (p. 21). Graphic representations can be read in practically infinite patterns. They also make very effective organizers to focus thinking.

Deregowski (1968, in Goldsmith, 1984) identifies three levels of image perception: *detection,* acknowledgment of the existence of an image; *recognition,* an ability to match the image with an object; and *identification,* the naming of an image by the subject. The results of an experiment which Deregowski carried out in a remote rural area of Zambia suggest that little difficulty is likely to be experienced at the lowest level of pictorial perception, even by people previously unacquainted with pictures.

Branch (1997) and Branch, Rezabek, and Cochenour (1998) conducted studies that solicited perceptions of three varieties of a flow diagram conveying similar content. Perceptions and interpretations were influenced by the designers' choice of visual elements, which should help show the relationships among elements. Diagrams were the connection between an idea and the formation of a message. Designs depicting processes such as flow diagrams are usually sequential and involve a directional element. Lines are one of the basic design elements found in visual communication. The interpretations of each element represented a micro perspective that influenced the understanding of the entire diagram. Graphic elements that elicit viewer interpretations consistent with the original intent of the entire diagram, improve the communicativeness of the diagram. The implications for introducing models of instructional design suggest the effect of graphic element type and their juxtaposition influence the perceptions of people who read the diagram.

All audiences are unique among themselves, and therefore knowledge about the perceptions of the intended audience is important as a way to improve the effectiveness of the communication. The value of Gee's (1994) analysis of first-language acquisition as a guide for theories of learning and pedagogy is that it initiates a serious discussion of learning based on the most effectively studied developmental mastery—language. Meehan, John-Steiner and Kennedy (1995), contend that a developmental mastery approach underestimates the roles of diverse symbol systems and scaffolding. In a culture rich in images, it is possible to be familiar with the appearance of an infinite number of objects without ever having seen the objects themselves. In a pictureless environment it is impossible to recognize any object which is not familiar; this is therefore a prerequisite of identification of images.

Silverstein and Tamir (1993) examined the learning of biology by means of unguided viewing of television using two different television symbol systems: story animation and documentary. The story animation code consists of unusual complex illustrations and the documentary code is made up of scientific symbols—models, schematic drawings, and other drawings used in the teaching of science. Results demonstrate the educational potential of television in out-of-school situations. Viewing television broadcasts presenting biological concepts resulted in a significant improvement in knowledge. Gain, calculated by posttest minus pretest scores, was found in both codes and the students were equally sympathetic to them. Better knowledge gain and more positive attitudes were found toward the story animation code, but the gain was also accompanied by misconceptions. Results support the theory that perception of the visual field does not depend merely on sight-related factors. Even when no similarity exists between the pictorial representation and reality, a series of inferences can still be drawn from the picture by using the information it contains about itself.

Visual accents can create unique communication graphics to increase attending behavior necessary for learning symbol–referent relationships by students with severe vision loss. According to Bailey and Downing (1994), accenting procedures use size, color, contrast, shape, and graphic pattern to enhance the probability that the learner will self-initiate attending to the visual symbol. According to Metallinos (1997), the scientific study of the visual communication media arts must be based on both general theories regarding these media and specific theories developed for each medium. Metallinos reviews the major developments in the evolution of aesthetics of the arts, relates these developments to the creation of distinctive media aesthetic theories, and examines the newly developed holistic theory of television aesthetics, which stems from the threefold study of perception, cognition, and composition of televised images. A number of contemporary media aesthetics theories are emerging from the significant number of literacy sources on media, primarily visual and auditory communication media such as theater, photography, film, radio, and television. The prominent media aesthetics theories arising from the literature of contemporary media include traditional or philosophical; formalist; contextualist; empiricist; and semiotic. Perception, cognition, and composition are each a fundamental axis for the support of aesthetics.

Media's different and often unique symbol systems are looked at as potentially serving as cultivators of mental abilities. Salomon (1980) discusses the use of visual media as symbol systems that gather, package, and convey knowledge. Cues that visually stimulate ideas in a reader will form the basic mental connection between visual elements and cognition. The connection is formed through the ecology of symbol systems.

The Ecology of Symbol Systems

Visual messages rely on the totality or pattern of relations between symbols and their environment: an ecology of symbol systems. Symbols locate ideas within our minds like a silent language screaming through pictures, shapes, and images. Symbol systems are the fundamental construct for composing and reading coherent visual messages. However, symbol systems are socially constructed, and therefore, meaning can be somewhat arbitrary.

Communication is a multifaceted discipline, which has often neglected the study of images as spatial, stylistic experiences in favor of exploring the social impact of their contents. Burke (1997) offers an addition to the traditional emphases of communication by building on the concepts of framing (perspectives on how meaning is created) and depictions of visual space as means of situating the impact and appeal of imagery. Burke explores a spectrum of deeper window to flatter "frame" or "border" presentation modes for several visual media, noting a conceptual heritage in classic film theory and differences from the recent academic focus on semiotic–ideological perspectives. Burke presents a brief history of Western imagery from the Renaissance to the present for painting, photography, cinema, video, multi-image projections, and computer multimedia. Encouragement is given to understand and incorporate into communication study the visual implications of "Classic" and "Special Case" windows and frames. Burke contends that the full range of communication scholars should choose to incorporate the study of visuals throughout the discipline, both in form and in content, and that will help determine the future history and validity of a multifaceted field (such as visual literacy).

A symbol system is constructed by discrete visual elements such as lines, shapes, and the interaction of lines and shapes. Form, or the physical attribute of a symbol group is also a major component of a symbol system; however, the juxtaposition of visual elements often creates the actual meaning composed using a symbol system. Time and space are also important elements in a symbol system. The movement of visual elements, such as animation, and the distance between visual elements, such as messages that exist in three-dimensional space, are examples of ways in which symbol systems allow messages to be composed and read at different levels of sophistication.

Brown and Wheatley (1997) investigated students' use of imagery in their mathematical activities and found that image forming is crucial in doing mathematics. A student who fails to construct an image in a problem-solving situation is severely limited in giving meaning to the situation.

Silverstein and Tamir (1993) claim literature on the psychology of learning points out that intelligent learning is the formation of concept structures communicated and manipulated by means of symbols. Visual literacy encompasses the ability to generate and make use of visual images to develop or clarify ideas, as a tool both for conveying information and for creative expression. The usefulness of visual thinking in study skills, problem solving, and living in an increasingly visual society is stressed (Eriksson, 1988). A symbol system appears to be the root entity for constructing any type of visual language.

Kourilsky and Wittrock (1986) tested the hypothesis that teaching high school economics concepts first in a familiar mode or symbol system and then elaborating on the concepts in a second or less familiar mode facilitates classroom learning. Using an experimental design, 83 high school seniors were randomly and individually assigned to three separate classes, which in turn were randomly assigned three different classroom instructional treatments, each having a duration of 10 hours and taught by the students' regular economics teachers. Kourilsky and Wittrock found that comprehension of economics is facilitated by a teaching strategy that initially presents the concepts in a familiar verbal mode and then presents them in a more abstract way using graphs or other instructional imagery. The results imply that the type and order of presentation of symbol systems influence the learning of concepts in high school economics classes by facilitating or interfering with the generation of relationships between prior knowledge and new information. The findings also imply that presenting economics concepts in two symbol systems rather than one facilitates learning, provided, contrary to customary teaching methods, the teacher uses the familiar verbal presentation first and follows it with an integrative but less familiar graphic presentation.

Loveless (1997) examined how children approached digital imaging technology to produce a visual image and the knowledge and experience student teachers need to develop children's literacy. Loveless found that children developed a range of strategies to assist them with technical skills. Student teachers needed support in analyzing the nature of the children's learning and the different roles adopted by the participants.

Kellner (1988) contends that the increasingly central role of imagery in contemporary society calls for the development of a pedagogy emphasizing critical media literacy. Using examples from print advertisements for cigarettes, supports the need for cognitive competencies to withstand the onslaught of media messages, empowering individuals to become autonomous, active, engaged citizens.

Aspinwall, Shaw and Presmeg (1997) examined the possibility that at times imagery might be a disadvantage in certain tasks, for example, the notion of a persistent image may be so vivid as to actually block other creative thought. Aspinwall et al. describe one calculus student's images supporting high levels of mathematical functioning which occasionally became so powerful as to obscure more than to explain. Mathematical meanings can be developed when individuals construct translations between algebra symbol systems and physical systems that represent one another (Sharp, 1995). Previous research studies indicated (1) few high school students connect whole number manipulations to algebraic manipulations and (2) students who encounter algebraic ideas through manipulating physical models gain conceptual knowledge of algebra. Sharp conducted a study in which five high school algebra classes used algebra tiles to study operations with algebraic expressions. Results suggested no differences between groups who used or did not use manipulatives when tested with traditional chapter tests. Results of diary narrative data indicated that the majority of students stated that the tiles added a mental imagery that made learning "easier." The researchers indicated that students found it easy to think about algebraic manipulations when they visualized the tiles (Sharp, 1995).

Language

Schwartz (1996) says that no one need deny the importance of language to thought and cognition, and there are studies of mind and mental functioning to assume that properties and principles of linguistic, or languagelike, forms of representation must hold of forms of thought and representation in general. Schwartz calls for a consideration of a wider range of symbol systems. Brophy (1994) adopted a semiotic perspective of visual literacy by contending the concepts of semiotics were relevant to visual literacy along two dimensions: active perception and sign systems. The role of active perception in the language of images is important as it relates to an individual being able to build on what he or she already knows about reading from images and composing more sophisticated visual grammar structures as visual acuity develops.

The importance of recognizing diverse sign systems is the essence of understanding the language of images. Sign systems provide the visual grammar necessary for composing and reading visual language. Brophy (1994) contends that an educational program with a semiotic framework would change its focus from content to process, and that a visual literacy component would enhance learning across modalities, fulfilling a political and social responsibility to students. Reynolds (1980) suggested that experience in the visual arts promote students' development of perceptual skills because visual perception relies on identifying, sorting, and organizing images. Aspillaga (1996) discusses six principles of visual perception and their cognitive implications for screen design:

1. Clear perception determines continuity and flow of information.
2. Perceptual grouping establishes screen sequencing.
3. Placement of information aids recall.
4. Distinctiveness increases retention and retrieval.
5. Consistency in the perception of motion facilitates retention.
6. Visual cues facilitate learning.

Fredette (1993) distinguishes several closely interrelated aesthetics terms, establishes criteria for and facets of the aesthetic experience, and examines aesthetic theories, which have guided values systems for imagery of the past and present. These include (1) mimetic theories of art as imitation, (2) instrumental theories of art as teacher, (3) expressive theories of art as feeling, and (4) formal theories of art as form or composition. What needs updating is the list of aesthetic qualities that must be apprehended in order to develop an educated stance toward new technologically based forms of imagery. Children of the future will especially need to be literate with data and images that are in motion, like animation and holography. Fredette suggests a conceptual model for visual literacy development that would begin with the production of art, and then move to aesthetics as philosophic inquiry, or critical reflection and analysis of exemplars.

According to Barnes (1996), some educators fear that computer technology will create a huge gap between the techno-literate and techno-illiterate. Barnes discusses literacy issues raised by the introduction of graphical interfaces and innovative media education; graphical interfaces and traditional literacy, electronic culture versus print culture, visual literacy skills and language, hypertext and multimedia, and techno-literacy. The language of visual literacy is message design.

Message Design

Good message design should focus attention, develop and maintain interest, promote critical thinking, and facilitate navigation of learning space. This occurs when the components of message design are organized into the following five categories:

1. Typography
2. Layout
3. Type elements
4. Graphic elements
5. Color

According to Fleming and Levie (1993), a *message* is a pattern of signs such as words and pictures produced for the purpose of modifying the cognitive, affective, or psychomotor behavior of one or more persons. Fleming and Levie suggest the term *message* does not imply any particular medium or vehicle of communication. *Design* refers to a deliberate process of analysis and synthesis that begins with a communications discrepancy and concludes with a plan for an operational solution. The process of design is separate from the implementation process. Accordingly, *message design* refers to the process of composing a pattern of signs and symbols that communicate abstract notions, concepts, algorithms, heuristics, or visceral meanings.

Rezabek (1999) believes that a discussion and demonstration of the effectiveness of Edgar Dale's (1946, 1969, 1973) cone of experience helps undergraduates see how the use of visuals can help bridge the gap between concrete learning and abstract understanding. Similarly, the application of Wileman's (1993) *typology* provides an opportunity for people to critically review the verbal–visual relationship.

During the past several decades, video and multimedia presentations have played an increasingly important role in communicating ideas to a variety of audiences. Productions such as television news, TV commercials, and multiscreen instructional presentations present a variety of visuals within a very limited time. "Hypermedia" technologies such as compact disk-interactive (CD-I) and digital video-interactive (DV-I) utilize visuals in complex presentation formats and rates, yet the utilization of viewing time and the choice of visual stimuli need further investigation. A media producer tends to choose a visual and sets the viewing time based on equipment availability or environmental constraints based on the assumption that the audience will be able to process the visual information within that amount of time. However, this kind of decision making may create viewing problems for the audience. In some cases, presentation time may not be sufficient for the information to be processed; in others, visuals may be left on the screen for a long period of time when little processing time is needed. Therefore, the results of studies of brief viewing times may enable designers to present visual materials that will be most effective in terms of recognition and most economical in terms of time.

"Visual displays of information encourage a diversity of individual viewer styles and rates editing, personalizing, reasoning, and understanding. Unlike speech, visual displays are simultaneously a wideband channel and a perceiver controllable channel" (Tufte, 1990, p. 31).

Visual language requires literacy taxonomy because of the different levels of sophistication at which visual messages can be constructed. Further, meaning contained in a visual message can be interpreted at different levels and a variety of ways depending on many factors, including individual experience, language development capacity, the medium of communication, and the grammatical structure of the visual message. The contention here is that a visual literacy taxonomy exists for the language of visuals. The visual literacy taxonomy proposed here is:

1. Visualizing the visceral
2. Visualizing heuristics
3. Visualizing algorithms
4. Visualizing procedures
5. Visualizing concepts
6. Visualizing abstract notions

Objects, sequence, grammar, time, and space will characterize each level of the visual literacy taxonomy. A description of each level of the taxonomy and the components that characterize each level of the visual literacy will serve to form the grammar of visual literacy.

CONSTRUCTING A VISUAL LITERACY TAXONOMY

The main idea is that the essence of any taxonomy is its ability to identify its philosophical origin. Suggested here is a locus of motivation by using a hierarchy similar to the following:

Phenomena → Philosophy → Theory → Model → Paradigm

Phenomenology allows message designers to apply symbol systems that identify abstract and observable knowledge, and events. An example of a message design phenomenon is the supposition that the essence of human existence depends on the capacity to communicate. Message design *philosophy* posits arguments that provide logical reasoning for organizing frames of visual messages. An example of a philosophical supposition is that a message can be composed entirely of images. *Theory* is used to organize the principles, suppositions, empirical evidence, and philosophy that form processes dedicated to instructional design. Message design theories are often marked by a common thematic element that represents a range of thought contained within a theory; such as perception theory or communication theory. Message design *models* permit the manifestation of propositions dedicated to representing the many realities encountered in visual messaging and provide opportunities for testing visual literacy theories. *Paradigms* are a coherent set of concepts, principles, assumptions, and basic axioms that have come to be accepted by a sufficiently significant number of researchers in a field (Kuhn, 1962, 1970), and "are sociological phenomena, as well as psychological" (Dills & Romiszowski, 1997, p. 12). A paradigm, such as visual literacy, provides a macro-level frame of reference for constructing visual messages. Figure 1 presents a hierarchy of conscientiousness used to identify the phenomenological development of the message design process. While exploring a conceptual

Construct	Definition	Attributes
Paradigm	A way of knowing: a conceptual pattern or example that verbally or diagrammatically describes recurring features of phenomena.	Basis or referent for action. Illustrates fundamental interrelationships. Allows for variation in the way a concept is modeled. Facilitates replication of the fundamental concept.
Model	A way of doing: an explicit representation of a reality. An example or pattern that prescribes relationships in a normative sense.	Explains or predicts abstract, and observable phenomena. Varies the levels of generality. The greater the fidelity between application and supporting theory, the higher the relative level of generality. The more conditions required for application, the lower the relative level of generality. Manifests a set of propositions.
Theory	An interpretation about a set of organized principles based on empirical evidence; or opinion, thought, observation, and supposition.	Ability to generate hypotheses; and make predictions. Provides conceptual explanations founded by philosophical argument. Explains a phenomenon. Yet to be disproved. Provides the motivation for modeling.
Philosophy	Arguments posited in the search for truth through logical reasoning. Ways in which an individual [or community] rationalizes propositions.	Contains numerous interconnecting theories. Uses precise terminology, analytical statements and narrative examples to illustrate conditions of an argument. Characterized as *Ethical*: System of values governing conduct and expressions of moral approval. *Epistemological*: Belief system conjured from multi-sensory interactions with the universe. *Metaphysical*: System of relating to the reality beyond what is perceptible to the senses.
Phenomenology	Study of the development of human consciousness, and self-awareness.	Based on human perceptions about the universe. Units of life experiences. Motivation for human action. Based on perceived or observable facts and events.

Figure 1.   A Hierarchy of Conscientiousness with Phenomenology as its Origin

hierarchy as a way to think about a taxonomy of visual literacy is important, it is equally important to acknowledge the existing elements that form any visual message. The basic elements of a visual message are line, shape, color, pattern, motion, and their relation.

Visual Elements

Line

Plane geometric shapes, lines, and pointing devices are three graphic elements commonly found in diagrammatic communication of conceptual processes. The designers' choice of graphic elements should help show the relationships among those elements (Hardin, 1996), and it should also be acknowledged that perceptions and interpretations of a process can be influenced by the choice of graphic elements (Buttolph & Branch, 1993). Flow diagrams that are commonly used to present the instructional design (ID) process "may be heavily influenced by the way in which ID models are visually depicted" (Rezabek & Cochenour, 1996, p. 299). Graphic elements, which elicit viewer interpretations that are inconsistent with the original intent of the whole diagram, diminish the fidelity between practice and the conceptual portrayal of that practice. Branch and Bloom (1995) contend instructional design professionals can improve the fidelity of the messages received by readers through better understanding of the use of visual elements in the portrayal of models, flow diagrams, processes, and ideas.

Branch (1997) perceptions about three variations of a flow diagram conveying similar content without any text, such as rectilinear, curvilinear, and nested (see Figure 2). Branch extended the work of Rezabek and Cochenour (1996) regarding the "importance of the visual display of ID models for professionals teaching the instructional design process" (p. 309). The study also extended the work of Branch and Bloom (1995) who contended instructional design professionals can improve the fidelity of the messages received by readers through better understanding of the use of visual elements in the portrayal of models, flow diagrams, processes, and ideas. The foundation of Branch and Bloom's preliminary investigation is based on perceptions of the reader, variation in graphic element type, and accurate interpretations of visualized process models.

Innovative formats in text technology and instructional message designs (Fleming & Levie, 1993) are used herein to explore and explain trends in visual literacy. The purpose of this chapter is to identify ways that basic visual elements can be used to construct simple and complex messages. The fundamental concepts of visual literacy, symbol systems, the anatomy of a visual message, and a visual literacy taxonomy are presented as a way to acknowledge the language of pictures as commensurate with the reading and writing aspects of verbal literacy.

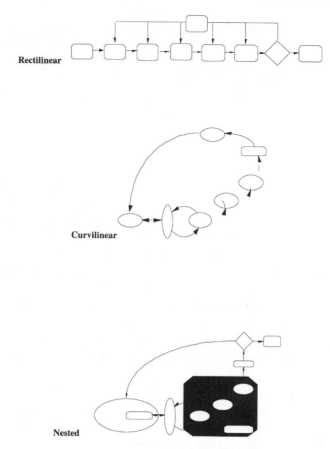

Figure 2. Three Variations of a Flow Diagram

Shape

Shape is important to maintain the consistency of design. Shape allows viewer to focus on changes in information rather than changes in graphical composition. Shape appears in visuals in all types of manifestations.

Color

Color is defined as any combination of colors except standard black background and white foreground. Color can have an impact on the way people view graphics and other visuals. Color can serve aesthetic, motivational, and instructional functions. Baker, Belland, and Cambre (1985) present a study that has implications for designing color graphics that may be used on a monochrome monitor. The most important consideration is related to portraying figure ground separations. The visual may be created in certain colors, but may lose its effectiveness when used on a monochromatic screen. Kennedy and Lacy (1987) investigated how economic factors affected the use of new technology for color and graphics. Because color is mainly used for aesthetic and motivational reasons, it is usually reserved for the front page or advertisements. Readers tend to prefer color, photographs, and informational graphics. Kennedy and Lacy found:

- Large graphics tend to increase story readership.
- Color graphics can also increase impact and may make a complex story easier to understand.

Dwyer and Lamberski (1983) provided evidence of the effect of color cueing and coding on instruction and test materials. Color gained and sustained attention and thus expedited learning. However, for color to be effective, it must be used tactfully in visuals, and the visuals themselves need to be appropriate for the educational objective. Steinberg (1991) discusses the influence of color on learning and the implications for computer-assisted instruction. While color can enhance learning, it is not automatic. Environmental factors also interact with color. At present there is no standardization in the color supported by various computer graphics programs and monitors. Two colors may contrast well on one computer system but not on another. Also, brightly lit or darkened rooms affect the readability of display. Therefore, if possible, the colors should be chosen in the same environment the program will run. Research shows color use should be standardized in a lesson, used consistently and conservatively, for example, the standard colors chosen for instruction may be a blue background and a yellow foreground with directions in white and words that are to be emphasized in green. By using the same color for the same purpose throughout a lesson, the consistency of color is acting as a visual cue. There is no consensus regarding the number of colors that should be used. The general rule is to use no more than four or five colors on a single display. However, there are always exceptions to the rule and sometimes the information being presented may require using more colors. Loosmore (1994) summarizes some guidelines for the use of color (Figure 3).

Motion

Lee (1988) evaluated the effects of blank time (the time between each visual presentation), viewing time, picture type, and context on delayed recognition memory of pictorial materials. Two viewing times (0.5 and 1.0 second) and three blank times (0, 0.5, and 1.0 second) were manipulated to yield six treatment conditions. Ninety undergraduate students were randomly assigned to one of the six treatment conditions. Each group viewed all 60 video images but differed in the amount of blank time and viewing time given. A week after viewing, recognition

Keep It Simple   Use color only when it serves a purpose.

Limit colors to seven for graphic displays.

Limit colors to three or four for text displays.

Keep It Clear   Use color with good contrast of light and dark.
The smaller the graphic element, the more contrast is needed (Rabb, 1990). For example, text in a 12-point font will need higher contrast than the same text in 32 point.
Choose your background color first. Then, choose text colors, which will read well against the background.
Blue is the most preferred background color (Rowell, 1991).
Large area background colors should be quiet or muted (Tufte, 1990).

Be Consistent   Develop color schemes for your presentation and stick to them.
Change your color scheme only when you want to make an effect, e.g., changing topics, indicating importance.
Use color-coding to distinguish between like and unlike items.
Your audience will look for meanings in your color combinations.
Beware of creating unintentional coding.

Do No Harm   When you add colors to your displays, they should not become the focal point of the display. Remember that it is your message that you want to get across.

Figure 3. Guidelines for Effective Color Use in Visual Messages
(Loosmore, 1994)

memory was measured using a two-alternative, forced-choice testing procedure. The video images were presented in the same room and manner as the earlier images except that the test images were presented at a rate of one every 14 seconds. The results indicated: (1) recognition of line drawings and color realistic photos was improved by longer viewing time and by longer blank time, (2) under shorter viewing time and shorter blank time conditions, visuals without contextual elements were recognized more often than were visuals with contextual elements, and (3) adding color and realism to photos did not increase recognition scores.

Thwaites (1993) presents an overview of three-dimensional media technologies (3Dmt). Many of the new 3Dmt are the direct result of interactions of computing, communications, and imaging technologies. Computer graphics are particularly well suited to the creation of 3D images due to the high resolution and programmable nature of the current displays. Computer animation in filmmaking is one example. Research has been undertaken both in conventional television and video display technology and in specialized applications. Auto-stereoscopic or "glassless" 3D television applications are also being developed. Recent advances have been made in real-time computer-generated holography; it demands a high level of involvement and interaction because the virtual information space exists in the mind of the viewer. Three-dimensional film technology has been in use for over 100 years. Widespread public exposure to high-quality 3D films can be found in the Disney theme parks and at many other special venues and international expositions. As interactivity in communication media gained importance, virtual realities became the 3D environment of the user through which they can perform their own acts of creative experience. Research at the 3Dmt Center in Montreal (Canada) has centered on a systemic approach to 3D media from a biocybernetic viewpoint, which concerns how the human sensory system responds to and processes information. A new generation of visually literate users is emerging as use of 3D media technologies becomes more widespread.

Relation

Even though we navigate daily through a perceptual world of three spatial dimensions and reason occasionally about higher dimensional arenas with mathematical ease, the world portrayed on our information displays is caught up in the two dimensionality of the endless flatlands of paper and video screen (Tufte, 1990, p. 12). "Showing complexity is hard work. Detailed micro/macro designs are difficult to produce, imposing substantial costs for data collection, illustration, custom computing, image processing, and fine printing . . . . Still, a single high-density page can replace twenty scattered posterizations, with a possible savings when total expenses are assessed" (Tufte, 1990, p. 50). "Confusion and clutter are failures of design, not attributes of information" (Tufte, 1990, p. 53). Therefore, to reduce visual noise and to enrich content, layer *and* separate as a technique to stratify the various aspects of the data. "Vacant, low density displays . . . over pages and pages, require viewers to rely on visual memory—a weak skill—to make a contrast, a comparison, a choice" (Tufte, 1990, p. 50).

Harris (1997) describes a technique for downloading digital images of a fresh human cadaver from a commercially available CD-ROM and from the Internet. The images can be annotated to illustrate specific anatomic features and display groups of images in a format that is easy to use during lectures and accessible to undergraduate students for study during and after laboratory sessions.

Knupfer, Clark, Mahoney and Kramer (1997) examined the design, aesthetics, and functionality of educational and noneducational Web pages from the perspective of visual literacy. Educational Web pages were subdivided into K–12 and higher education settings, and the noneducation categories included commercial, publications and communications, informational and cultural, and personal Web pages. Research also evaluated print and online materials used by professionals and nonprofessionals to create these Web pages. These "how-to" manuals were evaluated for their discussions of: good screen design; the use of graphics and icons as communication; backgrounds; hypertext; linking; and overall understanding of publishing on the World Wide Web. Two evaluation instruments were developed. One contained 21 questions for evaluating online and printed resource materials; a second contained 57 questions that considered both aesthetics and functionality as embedded in the categories of design, graphics, text, and color. Initial data analysis indicated a wide range of quality among all of the sites. Evaluation of printed and online materials indicated a strong agreement in the use of how to create in hypertext markup language (HTML) and the technical aspects of using specific image formats for World Wide Web publishing. School sites tended to use text rather than images to present information; sometimes overuse of backgrounds interfered with the overall message. In general, the noneducational sites reflected similar quality as the educational sites, with the exception of the professionally developed commercial sites that contained animations and sophisticated graphics. Those met the criteria for evaluation, but tended to target a narrow group of people; some of the Web pages were well designed and met the needs of the general user. The amount of text or graphics used in informational home pages was related to the availability of design resources.

Each element can be used to convey meaning in several ways, each way in turn building on the previous way. First, visual elements are used to visualize abstract notions; second, visualize concepts; third, visualize procedures; fourth, visualize algorithms; fifth, visualize heuristics; and sixth, visualize the visceral. The following taxonomy is constructed:

Visualizing the Visceral
Visualizing Heuristics
Visualizing Algorithms
Visualizing Procedures
Visualizing Concepts
Visualizing Abstract Notions

CONCLUSION

While the purpose of this chapter was to introduce a case for constructing a taxonomy of visual literacy, it is only the first step. The next step is to provide the conceptual, theoretical, and empirical support for the labels that have been associated with a taxonomy of visual literacy. Visual elements, examples, and applications are needed to explain each level of the proposed taxonomy of visual literacy. Then, perhaps we can structure a grammar appropriate for visual communication.

REFERENCES

Arnheim, R. (1969). *Visual thinking.* Berkeley: University of California Press.

Aspillaga, M. (1996). Perceptual foundations in the design of visual displays. *Computers in Human Behavior, 12*(4), 587–600.

Aspinwall, L., Shaw, K. L., & Presmeg, N. C. (1997). Uncontrollable mental imagery: Graphical connections between a function and its derivative. *Educational Studies in Mathematics, 33*(3), 301–317.

Ausburn, L., & Ausburn, F. (1978). Visual literacy: Background, theory and practice. *PLET, 15*(4), 291–297.

Avgerinou, M., & Ericson, J. (1997). A review of the concept of visual literacy. *British Journal of Educational Technology, 28*(4), 280–291.

Bailey, B. R., & Downing, J. (1994). Using visual accents to enhance attending to communication symbols for students with severe multiple disabilities. *REview, 26*(3), 101–118.

Baker, P., Belland, J. C., & Cambre, M. A. (1985). Recognition of computer generated pictures on monochrome monitors. *Journal of Computer-Based Instruction, 12*(4), 104–110.

Barnes, S. B. (1996). Literacy skills in the age of graphical interfaces & new media. *Interpersonal Computing and Technology, 4*(3-4), 7–26.

Bieman, D. J. (1984). Visual literacy in the elementary grades. In K. Everest (Ed.), *AMTEC '84 . . . A kaleidoscope of media* (pp. 5–8). Association for Media and Technology in Education, Ontario, Canada.

Boca, J. C., & Braden, R. A. (1990). The Delphi study: A proposed method for resolving visual literacy uncertainties. In R. A. Braden, D. G. Beauchamp, & J. C. Boca (Eds.), *Perceptions for visual literacy* (pp. 99–106). Selected readings of the International Visual Literacy Association, Conway, AR.

Braden, R. A. (1996). Visual literacy. In D. H. Jonassen (Ed.), *Handbook of research for educational communications and technology* (pp. 491–520). New York: Simon & Schuster Macmillan.

Branch, R. (1997). Perceptions of instructional design process models. In R. E. Griffin, D. G. Beauchamp. J. M. Hunter, & C. B. Schiffman (Eds.), *Selected readings of the 28th annual convention of the International Visual Literacy Association*, Cheyenne, WY.

Branch, R., & Bloom, J. (1995). The role of graphic elements in the accurate portrayal of instructional design. In R. E. Griffin, D. G. Beauchamp. J. M. Hunter, & C. B. Schiffman (Eds.), *Selected readings of the 26th annual meeting of the International Visual Literacy Association* (pp. 166–179). Tempe, AZ.

Branch, R., Rezabek, L., & Cochenour, J. (1998). Perceptions of flow diagram type on the instructional design process. In R. E. Griffin, D. G. Beauchamp. C. B. Schiffman, & W. J. Gibbs (Eds.), *Selected readings of the 29th annual meeting of the International Visual Literacy Association* (pp. 321–328). University Park, PA.

Brophy, J. (1994). Visual literacy in education—a semiotic perspective. *Journal of Visual Literacy, 14*(1), 35–49.

Brown, D. L., & Wheatley, G. H. (1997). Components of imagery and mathematical understanding. *Focus on Learning Problems in Mathematics, 19*(1), 45–70.

Burke, K. (1997, November). *Toward a theory of visual presentation.* Paper presented at the annual meeting of the National Communication Association, Chicago.

Buttolph, D., & Branch, R. (1993). Effect of diagrams and study questions as mathemagenic activities on learner achievement. *Journal of Visual Literacy, 13*(1), 9–34.

Cassidy, M. F., & Knowlton, J. Q. (1983). Visual literacy: A failed metaphor. *Educational Communication and Technology: A Journal of Theory, Research, and Development, 31*(2), 67–90.

Clarke, J. H. (1990). *Patterns of thinking: Integrating learning skills with content teaching.* Boston: Allyn & Bacon.

Clarke, J. H. (1991). Using visual organizers to focus on thinking. *Journal of Reading, 34*(7), 526–534.

Curtiss, D. C. (1978). *Introduction to visual literacy*. Englewood Cliffs, NJ: Prentice–Hall.

Dale, E. (1946). *Audiovisual methods in teaching*. New York: Holt, Rinehart & Winston.

Dale, E. (1969). *Audiovisual methods in teaching* (3rd ed.). New York: Holt, Rinehart & Winston.

Dale, E. (1973). Things to come: The new literacy. In I. K. Tyler & C. M. McWilliams (Eds.), *Educational communication in a revolutionary age* (pp. 84–100). Worthington, OH: Charles A. Jones.

Debes, J. L. (1968). Some foundations for visual literacy. *Audiovisual Instruction, 13,* 961–964.

Debes, J. L. (1969). The loom of visual literacy: An overview. *Audiovisual Instruction, 14*(8), 25–27.

Dills, C. R., & Romiszowski, A. J. (1997). The instructional development paradigm: An introduction. In C. R. Dills & A. J. Romiszowski (Eds.), *Instructional development paradigms* (pp. 5–30). Englewood Cliffs, NJ: Educational Technology Publications.

Dondis, D. A. (1973). *A prima of visual literacy*. Cambridge, MA: MIT Press.

Dwyer, F. M., & Lamberski, R. J. (1983). A review of the research on the effects of the use of color in the teaching–learning process. *International Journal of Instructional Media, 10*(4), 303–317.

Eriksson, G. (1988). Thinking in visual images in the information age: The changing faces of the school. *Gifted Education International, 5*(2), 97–103.

Fleming, M., & Levie, H. W. (1993). *Instructional message design: Principles from the behavioral and cognitive sciences* (2nd ed.) Englewood Cliffs, NJ: Educational Technology Publications.

Fredette, B. W. (1993). Aesthetics for the 21st century: Another challenge for education. In verbo-visual literacy: Understanding and applying new educational communication media technologies. Selected readings from the Symposium of the International Visual Literacy Association, Delphi, Greece.

Gee, J. (1994). First language acquisition: As a guide for theories of learning and pedagogy. *Linguistics and Education, 6,* 331–354.

Goldsmith, E. (1984). *Research into illustration: An approach and a review*. Cambridge: Press Syndicate of the University of Cambridge.

Goldsmith, E. (1987). The analysis of illustration in theory and practice. In H. A. Houghton & D. M. Willows (Eds.), *The psychology of illustration* (Vol. 2, pp. 53–86). Berlin: Springer.

Goldstone, R. L., & Barsalou, L. W. (1998). Reuniting perception and conception. *Cognition, 65*(2-3), 231–262.

Hardin, P. (1996). Arrows: A special case of graphic communication. In R. E. Griffin, D. G. Beauchamp, J. M. Hunter, & C. B. Schiffman (Eds.), *Selected readings of the 26th annual convention of the International Visual Literacy Association* (pp. 299–310). Chicago.

Harris, D. E. (1997). Use of customized digital images for teaching human anatomy. *Journal of College Science Teaching, 27*(2), 127–131.

Heidorn, P. B., & Sandore, B. (Eds.). (1997). *Digital image access & retrieval*. Paper presented at the Annual Clinic on Library Applications of Data Processing, Champaign, IL.

Hood, J., & Lapp, D. (1997–1998). Broadening conceptualizations of literacy: The visual and communicative arts (visual literacy). *Reading Teacher, 51*(4), 342–344.

Horton, J. (1983). Visual literacy and visual thinking. In L. Burbank & D. Pett (Eds.), *Contributions to the study of visual literacy* (pp. 92–106). International Visual Literacy Association.

Jones, B. F., Pierce, J., & Hunter, B. (1989). *Teaching students to construct graphic representations*. Educational Leadership.

Katz, J. (1977, January 19). Old media, new media and a middle way. *The New York Times,* Section 2, p. 1.

Kellner, D. (1988). Reading images critically: Toward a postmodern pedagogy. *Journal of Education, 170*(3), 31–52.

Kennedy, K., & Lacy, S. (1987). Economic forces behind newspapers' use of color and graphics. *Newspaper Research Journal, 8*(3), 33–41.

King, J. M. (1975). *The role of context, imagery and detail in recognition memory for pictorial material*. Unpublished doctoral dissertation, Indiana University, Bloomington.

Knupfer, N. N., Clark, B. I., Mahoney, J. E., & Kramer, K. M. (1997). *Visual aesthetics and functionality of Web pages: Where is the design?* Proceedings of selected research and development presentations at the 18th annual meeting of the Association for Educational Communications and Technology, Albuquerque, NM.

Kosslyn, S. M., Simcox, W. A., Pinker, S., & Parkin, L. P. (1983). *Understanding charts and graphs: A project in applied cognitive psychology.* ERIC Document Reproduction Service No. ED 238 687.

Kourilsky, M., & Wittrock, M. C. (1986). *Verbal and imaginal strategies in the teaching of economics.* California.

Kuhn, T. S. (1962, 1970). *The structure of scientific revolutions.* Chicago: University of Chicago Press.

Lacy, L. (1987). *Visual education: An interdisciplinary approach for students K–12 using visuals of all kinds.* Minneapolis, MN: Minneapolis Public Schools.

Lee, S. (1988). *The effects of blank time, viewing time, picture type, and context on delayed recognition memory of pictorial materials.* Unpublished dissertation, University of Georgia, Athens.

Levie, H. W. (1978). A prospectus for instructional research on visual literacy. *Educational Communications Technology Journal, 26*(1), 25–36.

Loosmore, J. (1994). Color in instructional communication. *Performance and Instruction, 33*(10), 36–38.

Loveless, M. (1997). Visual literacy and new technology in primary schools: The Glebe School project. *Journal of Computing in Childhood Education, 8*(2/3), 97–110.

McAuliff, Christa quote appearing on T-shirt, sold by the Curry School of Education students, University of Virginia, October 3, 1998.

Meehan, T. M., John-Steiner, V., & Kennedy, C. (1995). The implications of "First Language Acquisition As a Guide for Theories of Learning and Pedagogy" in a pluralistic world. *Linguistics and Education, 7*(4), 369–378.

Merriam-Webster. (1991). *Webster's Ninth New Collegiate Dictionary.* Springfield, MA: Author.

Metallinos, N. (1997, May). *Aesthetic theories of the visual communication media arts: Television.* Paper presented at the annual meeting of the International Communication Association, Visual Communication Division, Montreal.

Moore, D. M., & Dwyer, F. M. (Eds.) (1994). *Visual literacy: A spectrum of visual learning.* Englewood Cliffs, NJ: Educational Technology Publications.

Pettersson, R. (1988). *Visuals for information.* Stockholm: Esselte Forlag.

Rabb, M. (ed.). (1990). *The presentation design book: Projecting a good image with your desktop computer.* Chapel Hill, NC: Ventana Press.

Reynolds, N. J. (1980). *Cross-cultural visual-perception: Native American drawings.* Ph.D. dissertation.

Rezabek, L. (1999, February). *Importance of visual literacy.* Paper presented at the annual meeting of the Association for Educational Communications and Technology, Houston.

Rezabek, L., & Cochenour, J. J. (1996). The impact of line on perception of an ID process model. In R. E. Griffin, D. G. Beauchamp, J. M. Hunter, & C. B. Schiffman (Eds.), *Selected readings of the 26th annual convention of the International Visual Literacy Association* (pp. 299–310). Chicago.

Robinson, R. S. (1984). Learning to see: Developing visual literacy through film. *Top of the News, 40*(3), 267–275.

Robinson, R. S., & Koos, M. (1996). *An exploration of the World Wide Web: Art images and visual literacy.* Proceedings of selected research and development presentations at the 18th annual meeting of the Association for Educational Communications and Technology, Indianapolis, IN.

Rowell, J. (1991). *Picture perfect color output for computer graphics.* Beaverton, OR: Tektronix, Inc.

Salomon, G. (1980). The use of visual media in the service of enriching mental thought processes. *Instructional Science, 9*(4), 327–339.

Schwartz, R. (1996). Symbols and thought. *Synthese, 106*(3), 399–407.

Sharp, J. M. (1995, October). *Results of using algebra tiles as meaningful representations of algebra concepts.* Paper presented at the annual meeting of the Mid-Western Education Research Association, Chicago.

Silverstein, O., & Tamir, P. (1993). The role of imagery in learning biology science through television. In verbo-visual literacy: Understanding and applying new educational communication media technologies. Selected readings from the Symposium of the International Visual Literacy Association, Delphi, Greece.

Sinatra, R. (1986). *Visual literacy connections to thinking, reading, and writing.* Springfield, IL: Charles C. Thomas.

Steinberg, E. R. (1991). *Color in computer-assisted instruction.* Illinois University, Urbana. *Computer-Based Education Research Lab.*

Sucy, J. G. (1985). Why do visual literacy projects fail? In N. J. Thayer & S. Clayton-Randolph (Eds.), *Visual literacy: Cruising into the future* (pp. 149–155). Selected readings of the International Visual Literacy Association. Bloomington, IN.

Thwaites, H. (1993). Three-dimensional media technologies: Potentials for study in visual literacy. In verbo-visual literacy: Understanding and applying new educational communication media technologies. Selected readings from the Symposium of the International Visual Literacy Association, Delphi, Greece.

Tufte, E. R. (1987). *The visual display of quantitative information.* Chesire, CT: Graphics Press.

Tufte, E. R. (1989). *Visual design of the user interface.* Prepared for the IBM Design Program. Armonk, NY: IBM Corporation.

Tufte, E. R. (1990). *Envisioning information.* Chesire, CT: Graphics Press.

Van Patten, J. R., Chao, C. I., & Reigeluth, C. M. (1986). A review of strategies for sequencing and synthesizing information. *Review of Educational Research, 56,* 427–472.

Wileman, R. E. (1993). *Visual communicating.* Englewood Cliffs, NJ: Educational Technology Publications.

Winn, W. D. (1989). The role of documents in training documents: Towards an explanatory theory of how they communicate. *IEEE Transactions on Professional Communication, 32,* 300–309.

Winn, W. D. (1990). A theoretical framework for research on learning from graphics. 553–564.

MEDIA LITERACY:
ON-RAMP TO THE LITERACY OF THE 21ST CENTURY OR CUL-DE-SAC ON THE INFORMATION SUPERHIGHWAY?

T. A. Callister, Jr.

Investigations into the study of literacy often resemble a journey through a series of small hostile nation-states. Despite calls for unification (Bolter, 1998; Reinking, 1998; Mosenthal, 1995), each has territory to stake out and maintain, ideological positions to hold, and importantly, professional organizations to nurture and defend. Those who write about literacy often cannot even agree on common definitions for the very thing they study (Hobbs, 1998; Lemke, 1998; Mosenthal, 1995). To enter into such contested and slippery territory is thus fraught with risk and so it is with care that I describe exactly what it is I intend to accomplish in the essay: My purpose is to argue that current mainstream definitions of media literacy are woefully inadequate to meet the policy and political challenges presented by new information technologies. And in keeping with the spirit of this volume, I intend to focus that discussion on the real lives of students and teachers.

Advances in Reading/Language Research, Volume 7, pages 403–420.
Copyright © 2000 by JAI Press Inc.
All rights of reproduction in any form reserved.
ISBN: 0-7623-0264-X

MEDIA LITERACY'S TENTATIVE POSITION

My own background is in the foundations of education and my primary research interests focus on the egalitarian implications, the dangers and the promises, of using new information technologies in educational contexts. From this foundations point of view, from the perspective of someone who admittedly does not regularly study media literacy, and as a former schoolteacher, it does seem to me as if media literacy is often trapped in an uncomfortable irony. On the one hand, media literacy is much about teaching children to fend off the evil influences of what they watch on television—both the programming content and its accompanying mass media advertising. Practicing critical viewing, learning about the deceptive claims and conventions advertisers use to trick a "media illiterate" audience, exposing the many sexist and racist stereotypes presented in the course of creating entertainment to attract large audiences—this seems in large part to be the content of media literacy. Yet all this takes place in an environment that extols the capitalist virtues of free enterprise. "Thank God," we tell children (figuratively and sometimes literally), "you live in a free country where we have the technological resources (television) to educate you about your freedom to choose from 25 different brands of sugar-coated cereals." Even adopting the most simplistic definition of literacy as having to do with the "making of meanings," it should be easy to see the bind here: Children are educated and indoctrinated into a patriotic mindset that blurs the line between democracy and capitalism. We find ourselves in the untenable position of defending the rights of business to prey on children, but then spend precious educational time and resources teaching them techniques to resist what it is we so adamantly advocate has a right to exist. As long ago as the early 1960s, when television was still in its relative infancy, Jules Henry warned us:

> In their relations with children manufacturers and advertising agencies are dedicated surrogates, like any other teacher, for since the central aims of our culture are to sell goods and create customers, they educate children to buy. What should businessmen do, sit in their offices and dream, while millions of product-ignorant children go uninstructed? This would be an abdication of responsibility. Besides, the businessmen might go bankrupt. The argument that advertising campaigns beamed at young children are somehow sickening because such campaigns take advantage of the impulsiveness and uniformed judgement of the child is old-fashioned squeamishness, somehow reminiscent of the fight against vivisection. Time and again we have had to fight off crackpots who do not understand that animals must be sacrificed to human welfare, and that because of anesthetics vivisection is now painless. So it is with the child versus the gross national product: what individual child is more important than the gross national product? And is it not true that TV is an anesthetic? (Henry, 1963, p. 71)

What "meanings" do young people draw from these contradictions of capitalist indoctrination and criticality? Although many have called for teaching to become a more explicitly critical and political act (Freire, 1973; Giroux, 1993; Hall, 1996; Kincheloe, 1993; McLaren, Hammer, Sholle, & Reilly, 1995; Sholle & Denski, 1993), can explicit lessons in resistance, in media literacy, ever begin to overcome the overwhelming implicit lesson that television represents much of what is important about this country: free enterprise, capitalism, abundancy, and the right, if not the duty, to demand consumer choices? This is, of course, less about television than it is about the nature of capitalism, but television is very often the messenger of choice. And even though the movement toward the advocacy of resistance is laudable, media literacy as a field still seems to communicate certain implicit lessons to students. My concern is that studies in media literacy, bereft of the concerns of ideology and policy that I will argue below are a necessary component of any literacy program, too often imply a false neutrality and encourage a glossing over of subject matter instead of raising important issues of public policy and personal accountability. For example, Renee Hobbs, writing in the *Handbook of Research on Teaching and Literacy through the Communicative and Visual Arts*, discusses the need for making "learning more authentic" and how the use of media literacy can facilitate that endeavor:

> . . . in the spring of 1994, teachers collaborated on a district-wide program to help students critically analyze tobacco advertising as part of the health curriculum. Students examined the historical, political, and economic dimensions of tobacco advertising; they reviewed, categorized, and analyzed a huge volume of persuasive materials designed to make smoking look attractive; and they made their own public service messages, targeted at their own community, to persuade them against smoking. More than 2,000 students in grades K–12 participated in the project by designing slogans, writing newspaper editorials, designing billboards, bumper stickers, posters, radio ads and videotape public service announcements. Teachers persuaded the local billboard company to put up one student's billboard design on a major highway of the town, giving thousands of citizens the opportunity to read a child's message, and creating a powerful message for students. *Such examples emphasize the ways in which media literacy activities bring a renewed sense of relevance between the worlds of the classroom and the world of contemporary culture.* (italics added; Hobbs, 1997)

During the 1990s, the percentage of teens smoking in this country has risen (United States Federal Interagency Forum on Child and Family Statistics, 1998) and in 1998 the United States Congress killed an attempt to regulate and control, among other things, the advertising and selling of tobacco to young people. This is not to suggest that somehow the students in the above example did a poor job, but it does suggest the possibility that the field of media literacy is doing a poor job. The activities carried out by the students in this example may certainly have proved instructive for the students—teaching them ways to wage their own media campaigns. But it does seem as if the students were asked to focus on the wrong things. Apparently they studied tobacco *advertising*, but not necessarily the harmful effects of tobacco itself, creating, one can imagine, a situation where ultimately their concentration was focused on persuasion and advertising while the real issues about the subject matter, tobacco, remained neutral. The examination of the role of media in persuading people to smoke or not smoke is different in kind than, for example, an examination of media attempting to convince consumers to buy one brand of automobile over another. Media literacy cannot simply position itself as the neutral examiner of advertising, persuasion, and the construction of meaning found in media. If media literacy is to bring a "renewed sense of relevance between the worlds of the classroom and the world of contemporary culture" it must take into account the moral, ethical, and political aspects of that to which it attends (Considine & Haley, 1992; Giroux & Simon, 1989; Kellner, 1995; McLaren et al., 1995; Semali & Watts Pailliotet, 1999). That is the ideological and political "relevance" students need, not the relevance of some simple sightseeing trip through contemporary culture as seen by a gaggle of media advertisers.

If those involved in media literacy are interested in taking media literacy beyond the simple unidimensional confines of television and print, and I would argue that in a new technologically rich educational environment they must, then I would also argue that those involved with media literacy, including teachers and others responsible for the education of young people, can no longer have it both ways. New information technologies, including the proliferation of the educational use of the Internet and the World Wide Web, bring a new complexity to the notion of literacy. We can no longer ignore the political and ideological dimensions involved in this new literacy.

TECHNOLOGY AND THE NEW LITERACY

It seems reasonably safe to predict that increasingly young people in classrooms will use the Internet to gather information and educational resources, and then communicate the outcomes of those investigations by constructing Web pages and hypermedia documents. This activity will represent a profound change in the way teachers and students conduct their daily work, and it will certainly change conceptions of literacy. The fundamental interactivity of the Web; the nonlinear construction and navigation of hypertext and hypermedia; the evaporating line between reader and writer in cyberspace; the use of graphics, icons, video, and sound; the necessary considerations of the elements of design and composition— these will require a new set of literacy skills and dispositions (Burbules, 1998; Burbules & Callister, 1996, 1997; Kress, 1998). As David Reinking puts it, educators need be concerned about the "transformation of literacy in a post-typographic world" (Reinking, 1998, p. xii). But transformations occur slowly. Roger Desmond, writing in the 1997 *Handbook of Research on Teaching and Literacy through the Communicative and Visual Arts*, focusing primarily on television, defines media literacy as "teaching people to be critical consumers of entertainment and advertising fare" and "teaching them to gain more insight and information from what they watch" (p. 23). Expanding the definition of media literacy to include not just *consumers* of information but also *communicators* of information, Hobbs, also writing in the *Handbook*, urges educators to adopt the following definition:

> Literacy is the ability to access, analyze, evaluate, and communicate messages in a variety of forms. (Hobbs, 1997, p. 8)

The shift from the former definition to the latter seems to be a move in the right direction. Hobbs's definition begins to accommodate an educational practice much more involved with nonlinear, interactive technologies than the more linear, delivery-based technologies of television, video, and print. Literacy, in a more technologically sophisticated, posttypographical educational setting, will have more to do with finding and retrieving information than it will have to do with critiquing and decoding information that is simply "delivered."

The difference between these two educational environments will be as dramatic as the difference between watching a slide presentation of famous art or spending a day at the Art Institute of Chicago. And to be instructive, new ways of teaching, learning, and regarding information will be required. These in turn will demand a rethinking about what it is we regard literacy to be—and since so much of what students will encounter in cyberspace will be presented in varied media, it seems appropriate that new literacies will need, at least in part, to build on notions of media literacy.

My intent, however, is not to formulate a new definition of media literacy, or even attempt to modify an existing one. My concern is to argue for the explicit recognition, in any viable definition of media literacy, that it is necessary to consider the ethical, egalitarian, and ideological dimensions of both the subject matter being investigated and the process of the investigation. Just as new information technologies blur the line between reader and writer, they also blur the line between the process of finding information and the making sense of that information. In cyberspace, the journey cannot be separated from the destination. Students will not only need certain literacy skills to "decode" the information they find in cyberspace, having used new information technologies such as computers, Web browsers, and hypertextual databases, but a new posttypographic notion of literacy will also need to incorporate the skills required to decode the *process* of getting to that information.

Here are some examples: Meanings are often influenced and colored by their position and place in certain schemata and hierarchies. An individual's understanding of abortion, to use a well-worn example, might well be influenced depending on where the information about abortion was found—filed under "Medical Procedures" or filed under "Murder." In a similar fashion, juxtaposition influences meaning. In the nonlinear environment of hypertext, any particular data point may be reachable by numerous other data points. Finding spotted owls via the Oregon Lumberman's Association might give a very different meaning to spotted owls than had they been arrived at via the Sierra Club. The point is, students will need certain skills to not only get to relevant information, they must also be able to judge the ideological impact of the journey on the meaning they assign to that information. As I will discuss below, some of these skills will be traditional, but others will be very new and very important.

FOUR COMPONENTS OF MEDIA LITERACY

In her definition of media literacy for "the information age," Hobbs discusses the "four processes" that make up her "new vision of literacy." They are: access, analyze, evaluate, and communicate (Hobbs, 1997, p. 8)—four perfectly adequate categories. However, I would like to examine these processes for what they include, what they do not include, and what questions or possible courses of action are suggested by their examination in light of the new requirements for literacy that might well be needed for learning in technologically rich environments.

Access

Hobbs (1997) explains the process of access as including "skills related to the locating, organizing and retrieving of information from a variety of sources" (p. 8). Further, she states that "access requires the ability to use the tools of technology." Sometimes termed "information literacy" (whatever that means), access, according to Hobbs, might best be labeled as "driver training for the information superhighway" (p. 8).

It would be hard to argue against driver training—in either the real world or the virtual one—and the organization of information, especially information that exists in different media form, is clearly a crucial skill. But I maintain that there are additional skills and considerations that need to be addressed more explicitly when discussing issues of access. They deal with the conditions of access, the criteria of access, and the reoccurring problems of using "tool" as the generative metaphor in talking about technology.

Conditions of access refer to the circumstances that enable or restrict participation. In this context, conditions of access have to do with whether or not students and their teachers have information technologies available for their use. These conditions can be problematic in two senses: lack of resources and use of resources. On the one hand, there are many schools where a lack of financial resources prevents children from exposure to or benefit from the educational possibilities that new information technologies might provide. As we envision an educational future where information technologies may well play a vital role in the education of young people, the glaring inequalities that exist across schools and populations of children in terms of resources cannot be ignored by educators. It would be unthinkable to hear: "If you can find yourself a book, I'll teach you to read." It should become unthinkable to hear the technological equivalent. New conceptions of literacy need to state explicitly what has only been implicit before—a commitment to literacy must include a commitment to advocate for access to the conditions of literacy. Educators need to stress to parents and administrators and perhaps themselves that new information technologies are bringing about a new form of literacy and that access to these technological resources is just as important as access to traditional print resources—not merely for the information contained therein, but for the purpose of learning the skills of literacy in that particular medium.

Conditions of access are also denied students who suffer not so much from a lack of technological resources, but from a seemingly strange lack of initiative on the part of at least some teachers and administrators to use new technologies. Too often, I've seen perfectly useful computer labs sit idle, or at best underused, while teachers and administrators hem and haw over the construction of policies and procedures, especially as they relate to the use of the Internet. Undoubtedly, some of this has to do with the legitimate apprehension of dealing with technologies they do not understand. But it seems that some of this also has to do with a reluctance of schools to entrust students with the means to facilitate their own learning. Fearful of the very thing they claim they want to teach: questioning, exploration, curiosity, and creativity; schools too often deny to students the conditions of access to a potentially limitless educational resource because of the timidity and provincialism of some teachers and administrators.

Furthermore, as I will discuss below, information technologies, because of the enormous amount of information they can provide, raise the concern of censorship standing in the way of literacy to new and frightening heights. On a practical level, ignorance of the technology by teachers, administrators, parents, and to some extent, even many of us involved in teacher preparation—ignorance that runs from not knowing how to operate the hardware and software to fear of what really is out there on the Internet—blocks for many students the necessary conditions of access to advanced information technologies. We cannot responsibly teach students to become literate in the so-called posttypographic educational environment until we ourselves understand that environment. Students cannot learn without access to that environment.

For those with conditional access, however, a computer with an Internet connection for every student, and every student knowing how to operate the machine still does not necessarily ensure true access. This may satisfy the conditions of access, but it does not address the issues surrounding the criteria of access (Burbules & Callister, 1997). Criteria of access have to do with the dispositions, characteristics, and understandings people need to have in order to take advantage of their conditional access. For example, using the World Wide Web to search for information requires certain criteria of access, one of which may well be the ability to feel comfortable inhabiting complex environments that are constantly changing. The ability to deal with a changing landscape, however, might not be easy for everyone. Working on the Internet often means operating with a great degree of uncertainty; making logical connections as one goes along, and occasionally, getting lost. Dealing with this is not just a matter of learning and experience—cyberspace driver's education—it has much to do with confidence and attitude. Environments that feel exciting and challenging to some users may feel uncomfortably chaotic and frustrating to others. For example, it turns out that the ability to "just mess around," to more or less intuitively "surf," is an important disposition for users in hypertextual and hypermedia environments. But, because of the risk of getting lost, or the uncertainty of where they're going, or just being not very confident in a constantly shifting environment, not everyone is going to find "messing around" easy to do. Yet these kinds of "attitudes" or "dispositions" may well become the necessary criteria for access because without them there may be little opportunity to exercise one's conditional access. I believe that in the near future, we will see some of these issues tied with issues of gender. We seem to socialize young girls into valuing safety, structure, and rule following; yet will increasingly expect them to learn in a chaotic, loose, and unstructured educational environment.

In the case of educational technologies, in thinking about new literacies in terms of driver's education, educators have focused too much on the conditions of access (getting everyone wired and teaching them to how to use the machine) and too little on the criteria of access (teaching them to be comfortable in a hypertextual environment, for example). Too much time is spent on "driver's training" and not enough thought given to the new skills and literacies that need to be taught and developed to exploit new information technologies for positive educational purposes. Beyond the typical appearance over substance problem (better to have an underused computer lab than none at all), this misfocus is primarily caused by continuing to see the technology as simply a tool, as a neutral means to retrieving information—not always understanding that meaning is shaped in great part by the means used to discover it.

Hobbs, like many before her and probably many after, very easily and almost casually invokes the familiar tool metaphor, not realizing, perhaps, how much metaphors matter. Metaphors very much color the way we conceptualize things (Lakoff & Johnson, 1980) and the problem with the tool metaphor, of course, is that it bestows on the computer and other devices and procedures of technology, a neutrality that is just not there (Bowers, 1988). When students and teachers are told they must develop "the ability to use the tools of technology" (Hobbs, 1997, p. 8), they naturally tend to take the tool, the technology, for granted, ignoring the ideological influences of the tool on the process to which it is applied—after all, it's just a tool. Since the information superhighway seems to be such an inexplicably popular metaphor (a web would be certainly a better one), let me use it as an example. If the Internet is a highway, then I suppose that on one level it does make sense to talk in terms of driver training—a matter of learning to "drive" the "car," learning the rules of the road—when talking about the skills needed to move along the highway. But imagine a different metaphor used in some quirky alternate universe: the Internet as the Information Super Appalachian Trail. Now the metaphor is about hiking through the woods and countryside, which raises a very different image than speeding down a superhighway. Certainly driving is quicker, but wouldn't we agree that walking is a richer experience? And when dealing with information, isn't rich preferable to quick? The point is, and this is a point that certainly won't be lost on those who claim to be in the media literacy business: the medium, and the metaphors we use to describe that medium, really does influences the message. To describe technology as a tool, and by implication grant it neutrality, strips away the ideological implications of the search. To declare the technology neutral, turns the primary focus on the conditions of access (getting computers into the hands of students) and focuses too little on the important educational issues of the criteria of access (how to enable students to think independently and responsibly in an almost limitless space of information). If students are to use technology to find answers to their individual educational questions, there needs to be an ex-panded understanding of literacy that allows for the explicit examination of the influence the technology has on the process and product of using the technology.

Serious considerations of the issues of access—conditions, criteria, and neutrality— will require serious considerations of how these issues will play out for real students and teachers in real schools. In a pluralist arena, we need to consider how different populations will approach technical learning environments. Do current technical interfaces and metaphors favor some populations and disfavor others? To what extent are students whose conditional access is denied or delayed ever able to fully acquire the criteria of access, the literacy skills, necessary for learning in techno-logical environments? Although the debate over the degree to which media literacy should foster political and egalitarian ends will certainly not be settled here, how will educators and others involved in media literacy deal with the inherent nonneu-trality of information technologies where the educational line between process and product is blurred? Or asked the other way, how will they respond to the inherent political, social, ideological, and, to paraphrase Bowers's title (Bowers, 1988), cultural dimensions of information technologies?

Analyze

Hobbs' second process of media literacy for the information age is *analyze*:

> . . . the ability to make use of categories, concepts or ideas; determine the genre of a work; make inferences about cause and effect; consider the specific strategies and techniques which are used to construct the work; and identify the author's purpose and point of view. *At the secondary level*, the ability to analyze messages *may* also include a recognition of the historical, political, economic or aesthetic context in which messages are created and consumed. (italics added; Hobbs, 1997, p. 8)

I am puzzled why Hobbs relegates contextual considerations to the secondary level, and then only optionally, but more to the point, I would argue that explicit concern for issues involved with credibility, and not just "author's purpose," or "content in which messages are created and consumed," must be included in any discussion of analysis of materials found using information technologies. The reason for this is that the determination of credibility becomes much more compli-cated and difficult to ascertain in the nonlinear, nonhierarchical constructed realms of cyberspace—a place we might soon expect to find students spending more and more of their educational time. It is one thing to judge the credibility of a printed or linear text or two on a particular topic; it is another matter to sort through and scrutinize the possibly hundreds if not thousands of texts that can be summoned with the simplest of Internet searches.

Determining credibility is clearly an important component of analysis. Students and teachers engaging in an open exchange of ideas must be able to draw on credible sources for the positions they advance and defend—they must have evidence, information, and precedents at their disposal. And in drawing on sources, students must deal with what is credible and what is not—what is true and factual, what is fantasy and opinion. Standard conventions of credibility, of what is believable, valid, and reliable, break down in cyberspace and on the Internet, and new literacies for new technologies will need to construct new conventions of credibility. Traditionally, one solution to the problem of credibility has been to grant credibility by proxy. We chose representatives whom we believe will be credible sources of information about public problems and possible solutions. Ideally, this is how we expect the government to work. Credibility is also granted by credential. Through training or experience, an individual is certified to have some specific knowledge and insight into a specific field or topic. But whether because of representation or credential, one great aid to establishing at least relative credibility is the fact that there are a limited number of voices from which to choose and judge. Choices can be made from among the relatively few voices who have access to the resources through which to express their positions—those with access to the media, authors and writers, teachers, politicians, and those with the specific skills and degrees such as physicians, lawyers, and scientists. Although not entirely democratic, this does represent a certain meritocratic filtering process—only those with something of merit to say are published, or put on the air, or allowed to teach. We expect publishing houses, mass media outlets, and schools to make responsible decisions about who and what is seen and heard.

In cyberspace, however, these kinds of conventions for discerning the credible evaporate. In cyberspace, there are a seemingly endless number of information providers. Everyone gets a turn to talk, and as a result, judging the credibility of what they have to say becomes infinitely more difficult—there are no editors, no filters by way of referees, peer review standards, or professional codes of conduct. In cyberspace, especially in hypertextual environments, even source and authorship, often used as traditional indicators of credibility, become meaningless. For example, it is possible to know where a specific "Web page" resides physically— but that "page" might only be one of many pages in some larger hyperdocument—a document where all of the pages exist at different locations. The discernment of credibility becomes extremely difficult because there is no primary source. Consider too that documents in cyberspace are dynamic. Any page in a hyperdocument may change at any time, or may even vanish from the Net. How can the credibility of dynamic documents be accounted for? In addition, any specific page might also serve as a component page in several hyperdocuments simultaneously—thus raising the issue of having to talk about provisional credibility—credibility depending on context. An individual page may speak the truth in one hyperdocument, but lie in another.

An interesting subset of this problem of determining credibility has to do with the proliferation of images becoming "texts" as the Internet grows as a means of communication and the concern over the manipulation of those images made possible with new digital technologies. Models' navels in print advertisements, for example, may have come and gone at the whim of some ad agency's airbrush, but the digital editing and augmentation of images raises new concerns about the accuracy and credibility of the images we now see. A picture may still be worth a thousand words, but through the process of digital manipulation, those words may tell very different stories.

These changing conceptions of dealing with issues of credibility are a clear example of how technology changes the way we go about doing education and about how current conceptions of what literacy entails will need to be modified. It is no longer sufficient to tell students to simply consider the point of view of the author (there may be no "author"), or to neatly categorize (the nonlinear nature of cyberspace encourages constant recategorization), or to consider a message's "historical, political, economic, or aesthetic context" (information can reside in multiple contexts at once). The very structure of the Internet and the mediating effects of the medium (the technology) have made it much more complicated than that. Students literate in the ways of cyberspace will need to understand the political, social, and ideological challenges to credibility they are likely to encounter: censorship by self-interested parties, the corporate sponsorship of Web pages, the ownership of information, and the idiosyncratic and often repressive policies of schools all serve to prevent a free and open search for information and answers (Callister & Burbules, 1998). They all pose threats to free inquiry and to the discernment of credibility in cyberspace.

How are we to foster understandings of these challenges to credibility? How best to select appropriate texts without censoring pluralistic points of views? One answer seems to argue once again for a more political and ideological agenda for the field of medial literacy. Less restriction, a political and ideological concern, will bring more information, more voices, and more data to digest—and in some ways complicate issues of credibility—the notion of infoglut. On the other hand, more voices provide a greater opportunity for individual students to find answers to their individual questions. And that becomes a matter of evaluation.

Evaluate

Hobbs parses evaluation from analysis by grounding evaluation in the experiences of the reader. This is contrasted with the use of external knowledge that comes into play when analyzing. Evaluation, says Hobbs (1997), is concerned with "judgements about the relevance and value of the meaning of messages for the reader," making use of the student's "existing world view, knowledge, attitudes, and values." On the one hand, the nonlinear, nonhierarchical system of organization in cyberspace makes "judgements about relevance" a very open-ended proposition. On the other hand, the notion that students should search for information based on their individual "existing world view, knowledge, attitudes, and values" makes it all the more important that new conceptions of literacy include the advocacy for the right of students to have open access to all materials.

In cyberspace, the notion of "relevance and meaning" is problematic. The deconstruction of information in cyberspace makes relevance and meaning, well, rather relative. Rather than a student reading through a unidimensional linear narrative, a student on the Internet is more apt to jump from page to page, following links, constructing meaning and determining relevance along the way. In the manner of a hermeneutic circle, where the end influences the beginning, the relevance and meaning of any particular information changes as the student navigates through a (metaphorically) three-dimensional space. In this sense, the judgments that inform the paths a student takes will have less to do with relevance and meaning, because these will most likely change, and more to do with associations—some of which might well border on the intuitive. It is easy to see how one might get lost in such an open-ended environment. It is also easy to see the enormous educational possibilities. Keeping in mind that literacy will have as much to do with the process as with the product, evaluation will no longer be the terminal act in seeking information ("I've found what it is I'm looking for, now I must evaluate it"). Evaluation will become an ongoing process carried out during the seeking process ("I'm at a juncture, which link should I follow?"). Literate students will need the kinds of skills and dispositions (see above) that will allow them not so much to make correct choices (the point is there are no correct choices), but rather to feel comfortable and be productive in such a shifting landscape of information—making judgments on the fly.

It is just because there are no correct paths, because students are looking for their *own* answers based on their *own* worldviews and judgments, that it is critically important that students have no paths closed to them. And it is on this point particularly that posttypographic literacy must concern itself with issues far beyond those of "driver training." If literacy is to include the ability to evaluate material, then students must have a full range of material from which to evaluate. It is the height of hypocrisy for a teacher of literacy (or any teacher, for that matter) to participate in the censoring of materials, yet there is the worry that this may be more common than many suspect. An example is the unfortunate proliferation of filtering software in schools (too often, I worry, with their blessing) and libraries (often, I think, against their will). This kind of software is only slightly less detrimental to the purpose of learning using the resources of the Internet than simply pulling the plug. On second thought, it might be worse—sometimes decisions based on incomplete data may be worse than no decisions at all.

Simply, filtering software works in two ways. In the first, assuming a school setting, an "adult" can block certain sites from being accessed by the Internet browser. This is censorship of the most blatant kind. One individual has the power to determine what many others can read or see or hear. Filtering is not about selection, nor is it about protecting children (more about that below), it is about taking control of information away from those who wish to use it, and placing it in the hands of those who claim to know what is best for others. Filtering is the hypocritical practice of encouraging students to make decisions and to find the answer to their own educational questions (based on their own worldview), but then limiting their arena of investigation to such an extent that they can only arrive at answers to the questions approved by others. Filtering, in the end, is about communicating an antiliteracy message that tells students that they are being taught to discriminate, to evaluate, and to analyze; but at the same time tells them that it is appropriate for "authorities" to preevaluate, prediscriminate, and preanalyze materials, thus preventing some answers and forcing others. It is an old magician's trick made educational: pick a card any card—but unbeknownst to the mark, all of the cards are the two of clubs. Only now the mark is the student: teachers extol free inquiry, but then tell students where they can and cannot look. Worst of all, many people, including teachers and administrators, think this repression of information is quite acceptable, although it remains a mystery how free inquiry can take place in a closed and censored arena.

The second way filtering software works is in a much more subtle and insidious fashion. In this case, the blocking is not determined on a site-by-site basis by some individual, but rather, algorithmically by blocking sites that contain certain keywords deemed objectionable. The folly here is evident—with the possible exception of just a few words, there are countless words that may be objectionable to some in one context but not in another: bull, breast, cock. Although in many cases the results of filtering are unpredictable and often ridiculous (any number of informational sites about women's health issues become virtually inaccessible because the language necessary to communicate the information is objectionable to some, for example), this type of technological censorship is particularly dangerous and offensive to the notion of free and open inquiry because of the way its operation is hidden from the user. It is one thing for a student to know that her cranky teacher has blocked any number of Web sites that the teacher does not approve of—often the software will actually tell the user that access to a site has been blocked. It is like using an encyclopedia, knowing that the authorities have removed many pages. It is an entirely different matter to filter based on words when the user may not even know what those words are, and thus has no idea of what sites might have been blocked. This is like an encyclopedia where certain entries have been removed and the encyclopedia has then been reformatted, erasing any indication that it is not complete. To be prevented from reading or viewing something, as bad as that may be in many educational contexts, is very different from not being allowed to know something exists at all. Students cannot exercise judgment about materials they cannot access or worse, judge the relevance of materials they do not know exists. Educationally, this does not simply lead to a situation of questions not answered; it may well lead to a situation of misanswered questions.

The solution seems surprisingly simple—it's about responsible teaching and teaching responsibility. A critical part of literacy, especially in environments where the amount of information is enormous, is in making good judgments. We educate students to make good judgments by allowing them to actually make judgments—not by making those judgments for them. Certainly students will sometimes fail, but it is often through failure that real learning occurs. Likewise, the best protection for children is by providing them with a good education—one that includes teaching them to make good choices. We do not protect children, and in fact, do them a grave disservice, when we shield them from those areas with which we are uncomfortable. In the real world, students are not stupid—they know for the most part what is appropriate and what is inappropriate. Students are also not all felonious—and as teachers monitor the educational activities of their students, they need to have sufficient trust in their students to know that a student's journey through the Internet looking for certain information may take some strange turns. A Web site that may appear offensive or irrelevant to one student might hold important information for another. If we believe students have an educational and ethical right to explore, question, and come to their own decisions about their own educational concerns, and we should, then by extension, as teachers and promoters of literacy we must defend that right of students to do so in an open and nonrestrictive environment. It seems ironic, but nonetheless important to realize, that in an age where so much information is potentially available, a new literacy must concern itself with teaching students about what is not there, and why.

Communicate

One of the ideas that drives this essay is that students (and teachers) will not only use advanced information technologies, like Internet browsers and the World Wide Web, to gather the materials needed to investigate their own educational questions, they will also use these same technologies to communicate the answers they formulate. It seems that in the past, media literacy has concentrated too much on the decoding of messages, primarily visual and symbolic in nature, and not enough on the communication of what that decoding produced. This may have been caused in part by the traditional boundaries that exist between media literacy and "regular" literacy—one is concerned with text, the other more with nontextual media. Even now, Hobbs, who appropriately incorporates communication as an integral part of a new media literacy for the "information age," continues to focus, too much perhaps, on linear and substantially video-based modes of expression. According to Hobbs, communication skills include:

> the ability to understand the audience with whom one is communicating; the effective use of symbols to convey meaning; the ability to organize a sequence of ideas; and the ability to capture and hold the attention and interest of the message receiver. (Hobbs, 1997, p. 8)

The field of media literacy has much to offer the general literacy required to use advanced technologies—technologies that will be increasingly multimedia based: the Internet, hypertext, and hypermedia. However, the field of media literacy also runs the risk of becoming a rarely traveled cul-de-sac on that information super-highway everyone keeps talking about. It runs the risk of remaining too narrowly defined, too restricted to the concerns of video technologies, and too involved with the process of *viewing* as opposed to the process of *searching* and *communicating* in cyberspace. Television in its present form may be around indefinitely, complete with the advertising and stereotyping we all claim to hate but love to study. Students and teachers will continue to make videos and will need to be concerned with the kinds of skills that Hobbs lists as important for communication: framing, using visual symbolism, and the manipulation of time and space through editing. Televi-sion and video, and certainly print, are not lost technologies, and neither are the skills needed to decode or effectively communicate with them. But if media literacy is to contribute to the promotion of literacy for the "information age" it will need to look ahead, developing and formulating the kinds of skills, abilities, and dispositions that will be educationally important for using newer technologies—skills that in some cases will be nearly opposite the linearly oriented skills needed now.

For example: students will spend increasing amounts of time viewing, manipu-lating, and communicating in hypertextual environments that are "receiver" ori-ented rather "delivery" oriented. To discuss skills like "understanding the audience," and the "effective use of symbols to convey meaning," and "organizing a sequence of ideas," all of which make perfect sense for video, makes much less sense when navigating through cyberspace or constructing hypermedia Web pages. The educational strength of the Internet, of hypertext and hypermedia, is that its nonlinear, nonsequential environment rejects a delivery metaphor where informa-tion (too often disguised as "truth") travels from the expert to the novice. Hyper-media takes advantage of an environment where "readers" *construct* meanings from sources rather than *decode* meanings from information organized, sequenced, and delivered by others to readers *in toto*. In rejecting this conduit model of information exchange, hypermedia also rejects the notion that there is only one answer or only one way to present a given set of information, acknowledging that most issues, most points of information, must be viewed as reflecting the contested perspectives of social, political, and ideological differences (Giroux in Semali & Watts Pailliotet, 1999, p. 15).

At this point in time, it is difficult to predict what specific skills, abilities, and dispositions students will require for the educationally productive exchange of ideas, and the defense and advocacy of positions, in cyberspace. Ideas of literacy will most likely evolve with the technology itself. Some aspects of this literacy will involve practical matters, actually constructing hypermedia-type documents, for example; other aspects, as I have argued above, will need to concern themselves with the ideological issues surrounding new technologies. I have argued that students should not be censored in what they can see, read, or hear in cyberspace. So too they must not be restricted in what they can communicate through a variety of media. But student authors must also learn not to censor themselves—either by holding back information because of repressive environments, or, importantly, by holding back material in order to make a presentation that is less than fair and complete. It is one thing when writing to acknowledge competing points of view, it is another (and necessary) thing to provide links to those competing sources in a comprehensive hypertextual document. Above all, students must understand the ideological influence of the technology they use and the nonneutral, subjective nature of educational discourse and investigation.

CONCLUSION

Most definitions of literacy use a rather simple equation: Literacy equals the ability to do A, B, and C. Literacy for Hobbs, is the ability to "access, analyze, evaluate, communicate." If elementary math serves correctly, the reverse is also true—if you can do these four things (access, analyze, evaluate, communicate), you are literate—media literate in this case. But I want to argue that literacy cannot be explained quite so simply—that it may well be more than the sum of its component abilities. I want to propose this: While it makes sense to say that to be literate you must be able to access information, it also makes sense to say that to access information in some educationally productive manner you must be literate. These are *not* reversals. The former is about the application of certain skills to reach certain ends; the latter is about an understanding of the ideological considerations that must be imbedded in any notion of literacy in order to truly accomplish the process of access, for without this there can be no true literacy regardless of the skills one may possess. The processes of literacy are not some form of neutral intellectual dissection—the finding and picking apart of information. Judgments are made at every juncture—judgments that are political, ideological, and ethical: Smoking *is* unhealthy and spotted owls don't live in politically vacuous forests.

Because of its familiarly with the use of the nontextual, media literacy is well situated to inform an emerging conception of literacy that will build around the educational use of new information technologies. This emerging notion of literacy will require more than simply a new (and as yet, not well defined) set of skills. What will it mean to communicate in cyberspace? What skills, abilities, and dispositions will be necessary for an educationally productive exchange of ideas and defense of positions? Certainly those in media literacy can contribute much with what they do already—addressing the concerns of traditional media literacy discussed previously. But that will not be enough. Media literacy needs to move toward a more critical stance, what Semali & Pailliotet term "intermediality" (Semali & Pailliotet, 1998). What I have tried to demonstrate above is that any new literacy for the "information age" must also explicitly address the ideological confrontations that are brought about by the use of these new technologies and the enormous expansion of potential accessibility. Teachers can no longer simply teach a set of skills and abilities, they must also function as advocates for the conditions and criteria of literacy: the allocation of appropriate resources, the freedom of inquiry and expression without censorship, an education that promotes the dispositions needed for the productive use of hypertechnologies.

REFERENCES

Bolter, J. (1998). Hypertext and the question of visual literacy. In D. Reinking, M. McKenna, L. Labbo, & R. Kieffer (Eds.), *Handbook of literacy and technology: Transformations in a post-typographic world* (pp. 3–13). Mahwah, NJ: Erlbaum.

Bowers, C. A. (1988). *The cultural dimensions of educational computing.* New York: Teachers College.

Burbules, N. C. (1998). Rhetorics of the Web: Hyperreading and critical literacy. In I. Snyder (Ed.), *Page to screen: Taking literacy into the electronic era* (pp. 102–122). London: Routledge.

Burbules, N. C., & Callister, T. A., Jr. (1996). Knowledge at the crossroads: Alternate futures of hypertext environments for learning. *Educational Theory, 46,* 23–50.

Burbules, N. C., & Callister, T. A., Jr. (1997). Who lives here? Access to and credibility within cyberspace. In C. Bigum, C. Lankshear, et al. (Eds.), *Digital rhetorics: Literacies and technologies in education—Current practices and new directions* (pp. 95–108). Brisbane: Queensland University of Technology.

Callister, T. A., Jr., & Burbules, N. C. (1998). Paying the piper: The educational cost of the commercialization of the Internet. *Electronic Journal of Sociology, 3.* http://www.sociology.org/vol003.003/callister.article.1998.html.

Considine, D. M., & Haley, G. E. (1992). *Visual messages: Integrating imagery into instruction.* Englewood, CO: Teacher Ideas Press.

Desmond, R. (1997). TV viewing, reading and media literacy. In J. Flood, S. B. Heath, & D. Lapp (Eds.), *Handbook of research on teaching and literacy through the communicative and visual arts* (p. 23). A project of the International Reading Association. New York: Macmillan.

Freire, P. (1973). *Education for critical consciousness.* Cambridge, MA: Harvard University Press.

Giroux, H. A. (1993). Reclaiming the social: Pedagogy, resistance and politics in celluloid culture. In J. Collins, H. Radner, & A. P. Collins (Eds.), *Film theory goes to the movies* (pp. 37–55). London: Routledge.

Giroux, H., & Simon, R. (1989). *Popular culture, schooling, and everyday life.* New York: Bergin & Garvey.

Hall, S. (1996). *Representation: Cultural representations and their signifying practices.* London: Sage.

Henry, J. (1963). *Culture against man.* New York: Random House.

Hobbs, R. (1997). Literacy for the information age. In J. Flood, S. B. Heath, & D. Lapp (Eds.), *Handbook of research on teaching and literacy through the communicative and visual arts* (p. 8). A project of the International Reading Association. New York: Macmillan.

Hobbs, R. (1998). The seven great debates in the media literacy movement. *Journal of Communication, 48*(1).

Kellner, D. (1995). *Media culture.* London: Routledge.

Kincheloe, J. I. (1993). *Toward a critical politics of teacher thinking: Mapping the postmodern.* New York: Bergin & Garvey.

Kress, G. (1998). Visual and verbal modes of representation in electronically mediated communication: The potentials of new forms of text. In I. Snyder (Ed.), *Page to screen: Taking literacy into the electronic era* (pp. 53–79). London: Routledge.

Lakoff, G., & Johnson, M. (1980). *Metaphors we live by.* Chicago: University of Chicago Press.

Lemke, J. (1998). Metamedia literacy: Transforming meanings and media. In D. Reinking, M. McKenna, L. Labbo, & R. Kieffer (Eds.), *Handbook of literacy and technology: Transformations in a post-typographic world* (pp. 283–301). Mahwah, NJ: Erlbaum.

McLaren, P., Hammer, R., Sholle, D., & Reilly, S. (Eds.). (1995). *Rethinking media literacy: A critical pedagogy of representation*. New York: Peter Lang.

Mosenthal, P. B. (1995). Why there are no dialogues among the divided: The problem of solipsistic agendas in literacy research. *Reading Research Quarterly, 30*(3), 574–577.

Reinking, D. (1998). Introduction: Synthesizing technological transformations of literacy in a post-typographic world. In D. Reinking, M. McKenna, L. Labbo, & R. Kieffer (Eds.), *Handbook of literacy and technology: Transformations in a post-typographic world* (pp. xi–xxx). Mahwah, NJ: Erlbaum.

Semali, L., & Watts Pailliotet, A. (Eds.). (1999). *Intermediality*. Boulder, CO: Westview.

Sholle, D., & Denski, S. (1993). Reading and writing the media: Critical media literacy and postmodernism. In C. Lankshear & P. L. McLaren (Eds.), *Critical literacy: Politics, praxis and the postmodern* (pp. 297–321). Albany: State University of New York Press.

United States Federal Interagency Forum on Child and Family Statistics. (1998). America's Children: Key National Indicators of Child Well-Being. U.S. Government Printing Office: Washington, D.C.

AFTERWORD:
RECOMMENDED PRINT AND ELECTRONIC RESOURCES FOR TEACHING ABOUT MEDIA AND TECHNOLOGY IN THE K–12 CLASSROOM

Kathleen Tyner and Ann Watts Pailliotet

OVERVIEW

The chapters in this book provide many ways for educators, scholars, and researchers to reconceptualize their own media literacy practices, policies, and theories. As an Afterword, we have compiled a list of print and electronic resources that will enable our readers to further extend their understandings and actions. In choosing texts, we employed several criteria: balanced approaches to media rather than protectionist or innoculationist stances; usefulness to media teachers and researchers; inclusion of innovative or seminal theories and practices; and synthesis of varied media theories, texts, methods, and/or formats.

We have summarized content and noted as much information as possible for each selection, adding price information where available. Due to space constraints, we could not possibly include all of the worthy media texts that have been published.

Advances in Reading/Language Research, Volume 7, pages 421–445.
Copyright © 2000 by JAI Press Inc.
All rights of reproduction in any form reserved.
ISBN: 0-7623-0264-X

Our apologies to those authors and organizations we may have inadvertently left out.

Our recommendations are organized according to the following categories: Media Education Texts for Elementary Students; Secondary Students; Production Resources; Research and Reflection on Media Education; Periodicals; Electronic Resources about Media Literacy; Electronic Resources for Teachers; Bookmarks; and Media Education Centers and Organizations.

MEDIA EDUCATION TEXTS FOR *ELEMENTARY STUDENTS*

Andersen, N., Carreiro, P., & Sinclair, D. (1998). *Responding to media violence: Starting points for classroom practice, K–6*. The Metropolitan Toronto School Board, 45 York Mills Road, North York, Ontario M2P 1B6, Canada.

This book takes a balanced approach that does not bash media and popular culture. Instead, the book supports teachers who wish to respond to community concerns from the perspective of research-based, professional practice.

Bazalgette, C. (Ed.). (1989). *Primary media education: A curriculum statement*. London: British Film Institute. BFI Publications, 29 Rathbone St., London W1P 1AG, England. 7.25 (send British pounds).

Ties media education goals and objectives with classroom practices and assessment strategies. Useful for all grade levels.

Bright ideas series: Media education. (1990). Scholastics Inc., P.O. Box 7501, Jefferson City, MO 65102. Order #76296. $14.95.

An excellent text from Scholastics for elementary teachers.

Considine, D., Lacy, L. E., & Haley, G. (1994). *Imagine that: Developing critical thinking and critical viewing through children's literature*. Englewood, CO: Teacher Ideas Press. $27.00.

An analysis of children's literature that encourages visual teaching. Rich with activities for students. The first to link the fields of children's literature and media education.

Leonard, S., & Munde, G. (1994). *At the movies with Bad Dog: Using nontraditional film and video with children*. Fort Atkinson, WI: Highsmith Press.

A handbook for K–6 teachers with activities, plans, resources to improve language and visual arts skills. Highsmith Press has a number of media education titles: 800.558.2110. $55.

Leu, D. J., Jr., & Leu, D. D. (1999). *Teaching with the Internet: Lessons from the classroom* (2nd ed.). Norwood, MA: Christopher Gordon Publishers.

By far the best current source for novice and experienced elementary teachers alike. A plethora of teaching ideas across the curriculum. Up-to-date Net sources and clear directions for their use.

Lloyd-Kolkin, D., & Tyner, K. (1991). *Media & you: An elementary media literacy curriculum*. Englewood Cliffs, NJ: Educational Technology Publications.

Lesson plans, background material, activities for elementary students. Increasingly dated, but still useful. Center for Media Literacy, 800.226.9494. $21.95.

Moline, S. (1995). *I see what you mean: Children at work with visual information*. York, ME: Stenhouse.

A fine initial resource for teachers to begin incorporating visual literacy into their print-based instruction. The varied graphic organizers and activities are applicable to an array of print and media texts.

Ontario Ministry of Education: The common curriculum, Grades 1–9. (1995). Government of Ontario Bookstore Publications, 880 Bay Street, 5th Floor, Toronto, Ontario M7A 1N8, Canada.

Model guidelines for media education in the English, Language Arts, and Reading Curriculum include "viewing/representing" scope and sequence.

Powrie, S., Lewis, K., & Reeves, D. (1997). *Media sense*. Harcourt Brace Canada, 55 Horner Avenue, Toronto, Ontario M8Z 4X6, Canada. 800.387.7278.

A teacher resource book series for Grades 4–6 with background information on media. Over 70 lesson plans and 30 reproducible student activities organized around three media units: Popular Culture, Journalism, and Advertising. There are three books in the series. Each book is specified by grade level (Media Sense 4, Media Sense 5, Media Sense 6). $49.95 each book.

Rosen, E. Y., Quesada, A. P., & Lockwood Summer, S. (1998). *Changing the world through media education: A new media literacy curriculum*. Golden, CO: Fulcrum Resources.

A gem of a book. Clear rationales that stress media education as a means to further democratic values and community action, as well as critical thinking. Varied media activities and ready-to-go materials that empower rather than deskill students, teachers, and families. Sausalito, CA: Just Think Foundation. www.justhink.org or email: think@justhink.org. $17.95. Also available through Center for Media Literacy, Los Angeles, CA.

MEDIA EDUCATION TEXTS FOR *SECONDARY* *STUDENTS*

AML Anthology. (1993). Out of print, but still available. Association for Media Literacy, 40 McArthur, Weston, Ontario M9P 3M7, Canada. 416.394.6990. $70.

Over 300 lesson plans for secondary teachers of media. Written and tested by classroom teachers from the Association of Media Literacy in Canada.

Bowker, J. (Ed.). (1991). *Secondary media education: A curriculum statement*. London: The British Film Institute. BFI Publications, 29 Rathbone St., London W1P 1AG, England. 7.25 (send British pounds).

Created by teachers, this book describes the skills, knowledge, and understanding needed for media education as well as practical classroom activities.

The British Film Institute media education catalog. The British Film Institute. BFI Publications, 29 Rathbone St., London W1P 1AG, England.

Full of numerous teacher-created resources. Order full catalog for up-to-date materials.

The Center for Media Literacy catalog has a comprehensive collection of media literacy workshops. Kits and books. Write for complete catalog. Center for Media Literacy, 4727 Wilshire Blvd., Suite 403, Los Angeles, CA 90010. 213.931.4177. Fax: 213.931.4474. Email: cml@medialit.org. Web site: http://www.medialit.org/

Considine, D., & Haley, G. (1992). *Visual messages: Integrating imagery into instruction*. Libraries Unlimited, POB 3988, Englewood, CO 80155-3988. 333-770-1220. $26.50.

A text designed for a variety of classroom applications. Rich in visual illustration and practical classroom applications, this book is a media education must. A new second edition is forthcoming in 1999.

Costanzo, W. (1992). *Reading the movies: Twelve great films and how to teach them*. National Council of Teachers of English, 1111 Kenyon Ave., Urbana, IL 71801. ISBN 3910-1288. 800.369.NCTE. $14.95.

Language Arts approaches to film with good suggestions and practical activities.

Duncan, B. (1991). *Mass media and popular culture.* Toronto: Harcourt Brace Jovanovich. Theatre Books, 25 Bloor St. West, Toronto, Ontario M4W 1A3, Canada. 412.922.7175. Student textbook, $29.95. Teachers' Guide, $28.95.

Mr. Duncan is a classroom teacher and newspaper columnist who writes widely about media education. This textbook builds activities around essays on popular culture.

The media literacy resource guide: Intermediate and senior divisions. (1989). Government of Ontario Bookstore Publications, 880 Bay St., 5th Floor, Toronto, Ontario M7A 1N8, Canada. Send $7 U.S. currency.

Activities key concepts and ready-to-go lesson units for secondary teachers of media.

O'Reilly, K., & Splaine, J. *Critical viewing: Stimulant to critical thinking.* Midwest Publications, 800.458.4849.

Offers valuable exercises to help Grades 8–12 to think critically about visual material. $12.95. Teacher's Guide, $8.95.

Stewart, C., & Kowaltzke, A. (1998). *Media: New ways and meanings.* The Jacaranda Press, 33 Park Rd., Milton, Queensland 4064, Australia.

An Australian text with a broad range of activities for the classroom about television, the Internet, film, multimedia, and print.

Worsnop, C. M. (1994). *Screening images: Ideas for media education.* Wright Communications, 2400 Dundas St. W., Unit 6 Suite 107, Mississauga, Ontario L5K 2R8, Canada. ISBN 0-9697954-0-8.

Readable theory provides a convincing rationale in the early chapter, but the best part of this text is its abundance of innovative, interdisciplinary media education ideas and useful supporting materials.

PRODUCTION RESOURCES FOR *K–12 STUDENTS*

The Advanced Internet Applications Primer is an online technical document for digital designers. The Primer is loaded with information, tutorials, and links to prepare participants for the Internet Technical Academy, an activity of WestEd, the regional educational research and development laboratory in San Francisco. It is also useful as an orientation for beginning designers. View the primer at <www.wested.org/ita/AIAPrimer.html>.

Black, K. *Kidvid: Fun-damentals of video instruction.* Zephyr Press, 520.322.5090. ISBN Zb13-LA. $19.

A comprehensive guide for use with Grades 4–8 includes many classroom activities.

Educational Video Center. (1996). *YO-TV guide to video production.* EVC, 55 E. 25th St., Ste. 407, New York, NY 10010. 212.725.3534. $15 (special prices for quantity).

This is a great book by teens for teens about how to produce documentary video.

Grlic, R. (1998). *How to make your own movie!* Electronic Vision and Ohio University. www.interactivefilmschool.com. 800.516.9361. $89.95.

A package of three CD-ROMs creates an entire Film School. The interactive software helps students master the concepts and traditional techniques that takes them from an initial story to the final cut. A Production Notebook is included in the package so that students can begin to make their own movie.

Kaplan, D. (1989). *Television in the classroom.* White Plains, NY: Knowledge Industry Publications, Inc. 800.248.5474. $32.95.

Trusty practical guide.

Kyker, K., & Church, C. *Television production for elementary students. A practical guide for grades K–6.* ISBN 1-56308-186-5. Libraries Unlimited, 800.237.6124. $24.

Doable descriptions for teachers and activities that are very age appropriate for elementary students.

Limpus, B. *Lights, camera, action!* 800.998.2208. $19.95.

Offers practical ideas for incorporating video in the classroom.

Newman, B., & Mara, J. (1995). *Reading, writing & tv: A video handbook for teachers.* Fort Atkinson, WI: Highsmith Press. 800.558.2110. ISBN 0-9117846-33-8.

Highly recommended for classroom teachers. Provides thoughtful ideas for integration of video in the classroom.

Roar! The Paper Tiger television guide to media activism. (1993). Paper Tiger Television, 339 Lafayette St., New York, NY 10012.

A book of essays from the Paper Tiger collective that covers everything from camcorder hints to radio piracy. Engaging reading.

Rosenkranz, P. *The classroom video producer's guidebook*. Good production ideas. J. Weston Walch, Publisher. 321 Valley St., P.O. Box 658, Portland, ME 04104-0658.

Covers all the basics, plus good reproducible materials for the classroom.

Schouten, D., & Watling, R. (1998). *Media action projects: A model for integrating video in project-based education, training and community development*. Foreword by Len Masterman. $20 U.S. To order, contact: schoutdi@knoware.nl.

Check out the website <http://utopia.knoware.nl/users/schoutdi> to preview this book.

Valmont, W. J. (1995). *Creating videos for school use*. Boston: Allyn & Bacon.

A comprehensive text that begins with basics like organizing school resources and people, then takes the reader step by step through the production process. Also includes many ready-to-go teaching and assessment materials.

Witfield, J. *Getting kids published*. Prufrock Press.

Prufrock Press offers two resources for hands-on work in the classroom. This is a practical guide for helping young authors see their work in print.

RESEARCH AND REFLECTION ON MEDIA EDUCATION FOR *K-12 TEACHERS , RESEARCHERS, AND TEACHER TRAINERS*

The Aspen Institute's report of the National Leadership Conference on media education. (1993). Aspen Institute Publications, P.O. Box 150, Queenstown, MD 21658.

A landmark report on a gathering of North American media educators. Includes definitions, perspectives, and background for media education in the United States.

Barbour, W. (Ed.). (1994). *Mass media: Opposing viewpoints*. Greenhaven Press, P.O. Box 289009, San Diego, CA 92198-9009. ISBN 1-56510-106-5.

A great little book that presents pro and con essays on such media issues as regulation, bias, influences, politics, and advertising. Excellent beginning for critical discussions and further reflection. Also see Wekesser, C. (Ed.). (1995).

Violence in the media. San Diego: Greenhaven Press, a thorough and readable discussion of media violence.

Brown, J. A. (1991). *Television "critical viewing skills" education: Major media literacy projects in the United States and selected countries*. Hillsdale, NJ: Erlbaum.

A comprehensive historical overview of critical viewing skills projects in the United States and selected other countries. Discusses each program's purposes, participants, materials, methods of evaluation, and conclusions.

Buckingham, D. (1994). *Children talking television: The making of television literacy*. Falmer Press, Rankine Rd., Basingstoke, Hampshire RG24 OPR, England. 15.95 (send British currency).

A definitive study of children's uses and understandings of TV. Original research presented in an engaging style. Also: Buckingham, D. (Ed.). (1992). *Watching media learning: Making sense of media education*, an anthology of the rewards and traumas of media teaching. 10.95. These books may be available from the Center for Media Literacy (see above).

Dines, G., & Humez, J. M. (Eds.). (1995). *Gender, race and class in the media*. Thousand Oaks, CA: Sage.

A hefty volume of media analyses and theories, with chapters authored by many leading critics and educators. Excellent in its scope and the issues it presents. Not a how-to book. The glossary will help novice readers crack the language of "postmodernity."

Dyson, A. H. (1997). *Writing superheroes: Contemporary childhood, popular culture and classroom literacy*. New York: Teachers College Press.

Compelling classroom ethnography that details media influences on children's literacies and how to employ popular culture for sound literacy learning practices.

Fleming, D. (1993). *Media teaching*. Blackwell Publishers, 238 Main St., Ste. 501, Cambridge, MA 02142.

This book is a result of Mr. Fleming's classroom experiences in Ireland and England. Theory, practice, and practical ideas, very well-written and engaging.

Flood, J., Heath, S. B., & Lapp, D. (Eds.). (1997). *Handbook of research on teaching the communicative and visual arts*. New York: Macmillan.

An ambitious, encompassing edited book with varied chapters authored by leading literacy educators that examines varied media and literacy issues, texts, research methods, practices, and policies.

Gee, J.P. (1996). *Social linguistics and literacies: Ideology in discourses*. London: Taylor & Francis.

Foundational concepts for understanding the social construction of media discourses.

Giroux, H., & Simon, R. (1989). *Popular culture, schooling, and everyday life*. New York: Bergin & Garvey.

A classic cultural critique of the media generation and the culture in which they live.

Gitlin, T. (1994). *Imagebusters: The hollow crusade against TV violence. The American Prospect*, Winter (16), 42–49.

Accessible discussion of media violence.

Gorman, P. R. (1996). *Left intellectuals and popular culture in the twentieth century*. The University of North Carolina Press, P.O. Box 2288, Chapel Hill, NC 27515-2288. 919.966.3561. $15.95.

A sweeping historical study of the way that both ends of the political spectrum have come together to critique modern entertainment from comic books to hip-hop.

Graff, H. J. (1995). *The labyrinths of literacy: Reflections on literacy past and present*. Pittsburgh, PA: University of Pittsburgh Press.

Engaging historical overview of literacy understandings, trends, and practices.

Hart, A. (Ed.). (1997). *Teaching the media: International perspectives*. Mahwah, NJ: Erlbaum. 800-9-BOOKS-9 or email: orders@erlbaum.com. $32.00 paperback.

In many ways, the United States lags behind other countries in media education. Great overview.

Hunter, B. (1997). *Learning in an Internet worked world*. "The Internet as paradigm": Annual Review of the Institute for Information Studies, 103–121. Queenstown, MD and Nashville, TN: Nortel North America and the Aspen Institute.

Issues involved in a changing technological environment.

Kellner, D. (1990). *Television and the crisis of democracy*. Boulder, CO: Westview.
  Also, Kellner, D. (1995). *Media culture*. London: Routledge.

Kellner, a cultural critic and philosopher, draws from many disciplines and theories
to discuss politics, education, and critical understandings of society in the media
age. Unlike some cultural studies texts which are laden with jargon and inaccessible
prose, Kellner writes in an accessible and engaging style.

Kerr, S. T. (Ed.). (1996). *Technology and the future of schooling: Ninety-fifth
  yearbook of the National Society for the Study of Education*. Chicago: University
  of Chicago Press.

Varied issues and essays.

Kubey, R. (Ed.). (1997). *Media literacy in the information age: Current perspectives* (Information & Behavior, Vol. 6). New Brunswick, NJ: Transaction Publishers.

Varied theoretical perspectives for understanding media literacy in one volume.

Lester, P. M. (1995). *Visual communication: Images with messages*. Belmont, CA:
  Wadsworth Publishing Company.

This book comes highly recommended because of its great visuals, broad coverage
of many media texts, interdisciplinary applications for teaching and research, as
well as its outstanding combination of historical research, explanation of media
theories, and examples of textual analysis throughout. Also by Lester, P. M. (Ed.).
(1996). *Images that injure: Pictorial stereotypes in the media*. New York: Praeger.
An edited volume that examines racial, age, gender, physical, sexual orientation,
and other stereotypes presented in the media. A great text for media literacy and
cultural studies courses.

Lusted, D. (1991). *The media studies book: A guide for teachers*. London: Routledge.

Excellent rationales for media education, as well as salient chapters on key media
concepts like language, narrative, institution, audience, representation, and the
production process.

Marchand, P. (1989). *Marshall McLuhan: The medium and the messenger*. New
  York: Ticknor & Fields.

An accessible discussion of McLuhan's work and life.

Masterman, L. (1988). *Teaching the media*. London: Comedia Press.

A major academic, theoretical work in the field of media education.

Masterman, L., & Mariet, F. (1994). *Media education in 1990s Europe: A teachers' guide*. The Netherlands: Council of Europe Press and Croton, NY: Manhattan Publishing Co.

Sound curricular international overview of media education.

McLaren, P., Hammer, R., Sholle, D., & Reilly, S. (Eds.). (1995). *Rethinking media literacy: A critical pedagogy of representation*. New York: Peter Lang.

An edited volume where many leading cultural studies and communications scholars lay out issues and theories for a critical pedagogy of media education.

McLuhan, M. (1951). *The mechanical bride: Folklore of industrial man*. Boston: Beacon Press.

McLuhan, M. (1962). *The Gutenberg galaxy: The making of typographic man*. Toronto: University of Toronto Press.

McLuhan, M. (1964). *Understanding media*. New York: McGraw–Hill.

McLuhan, M. (1971). *From cliche to archetype*. New York: Viking Press.

McLuhan, M., & Fiore, Q. (1967). *The medium is the massage*. New York: Random House.

McLuhan, M., & Fiore, Q. (1968). *War and peace in the global village*. New York: Bantam Books.

McLuhan, M,. & Powers, N. (1989). *The global village: Transformations in world life and media in the 21st century*.

McLuhan, who coined such phrases as "the global village" and "the medium is the message," is a foundational and still influential media critic and educator. Although some of his work is cryptic and other volumes are out of print, we have selected a representative list—worth searching used bookstores for.

Messaris, P. (1994). *Visual literacy: Image, mind & reality*. Boulder, CO: Westview.

One of the leading theorists in the field of visual literacy.

Neuman, S. B. (1991). *Literacy in the television age: The myth of the tv effect*. Norwood, NJ: Ablex Publishing Corporation.

Neuman examines a variety of theories about television effects and argues that television, like all popular culture, is a "synergistic" part of modern literacy.

Postman, N. (1992). *Technopoly: The surrender of culture to technology.* New York: Knopf. Also: Postman, N. (1996). *The end of education: Redefining the value of school.* New York: Random House Vintage Books.

Always provocative, Postman, a longtime media educator and critic, discusses relations among education, children, technology, and our society.

Potter, J. W. (1998). *Media literacy.* Thousand Oaks, CA: Sage. Available from Amazon.com for $61.50.

Despite its name, this book has more to do with mass communication study than with media education. Nonetheless, it is a good orientation for postsecondary students of media.

Reinking, D., McKenna, M. C., Labbo, L. D., & Keiffer, R. D. (Eds.). (1998). *Handbook of literacy and technology: Transformations in a post-typographic world.* Mahwah, NJ: Erlbaum.

This edited texts brings together many leading literacy researchers, who examine a variety of issues related to the proliferation of mass media and technology in schools and society. Worth the rather hefty price tag.

Robinson, M. (1997). *Children reading print and television.* London: Falmer.

A wonderful volume that clearly explains how print and media textual processes and elements are interrelated. Drawing from literacy theory, textual criticism, and actual children's talk, this book is a thoughtful and interesting blend of research and practice.

Semali, L., & Watts Pailliotet, A. (Eds.). (1999). *Intermediality: The teachers' handbook of critical media literacy.* Boulder, CO: Westview/Harper Collins.

A text that brings together the why and how of critical media literacy theory and educational practices. Varied research reports by actual classroom practitioners. ISBN 0-8133-3479-9 (hbk) or 0-8133-3480-2 (pap). Also available through the Center for Media Literacy.

Silverblatt, A. (1995). *Media literacy: Keys to interpreting media messages.* Praeger Publishers, 88 Post Road West, Westport, CT 06881. ISBN 0-275-94831-5. 203.226.3571. $19.95.

Useful text with a clear framework for teaching analysis of media from a communication perspective.

Silverblatt, A., & Eliceiri, E. M. E. (1999). *Dictionary of media literacy*. Westport, CT: Greenwood Press.

A very comprehensive volume that enables both technophiles and technophobes to crack the codes of media and technology vocabulary.

Steinberg, S. R., & Kincheloe, J. L. (1997). *Kinderculture: Corporate constructions of childhood*. Boulder, CO: Westview.

Although not just about mass media, worth a read for its sociological explorations of how corporations construct and perpetuate hegemonic images of youth and a widespread consumer culture.

Tyner, K. (1998). *Literacy in a digital world: Teaching and learning in the age of information*. Mahwah, NJ: Erlbaum. 800-9-BOOKS-9 or email: orders@erlbaum.com. $32.50 paperback. Also available through the Center for Media Literacy.

A meaty volume in accessible prose that explores definitions of literacy, historic resistance and acceptance of media technologies, and future directions for media education. Combines clearly written theory with concrete examples of practices and teacher interviews.

PERIODICALS FOR *MEDIA EDUCATORS AND THEIR STUDENTS*

Adbusters! An irreverent quarterly that takes aim at consumer culture. From the Media Foundation, 1243 West 7th Ave., Vancouver, BC V6H 1B7, Canada. 604.736.9401. $40/year.

Clipboard. The media literacy newsletter of the Jesuit Communication Project in Canada. Clipboard has an unparalleled international focus. Write: John Pungente, Editor, Jesuit Communication Project, 47 Ranleigh Ave., #300, Toronto, Ontario M4N 1X2, Canada. 416.488.7280.

Design Science Journal is an online journal. See the editor's interview with media educator Kathleen Tyner. The interview includes an extensive bibliography about literacy (http://www.ignitiondesign.com/journal/).

English Journal. Two issues (November 1992 and January 1998) are completely devoted to media literacy. *English Journal* is available with an annual $40 membership to NCTE. Individual copies can be purchased. NCTE, 1111 Kenyon Ave., Urbana, IL 71801. 217.328.3870.

Journal of Adolescent and Adult Literacy and *The Reading Teacher*, both published by the International Reading Association, have regular columns on media literacy, technology, and Internet practices. For more information, write P.O. Box 8139, 800 Barksdale Rd., Newark, DE 19714-8139, or call 800.336.7323.

Journal of Communication is published by the International Communication Association. The media education issue is Winter 1998; Vol. 48, No. 1. To order: Oxford University Press, Journals Subscriptions Department, 2001 Evans Rd., Cary, NC 27513. Toll-free in the USA and Canada, 1-800-852-7323. Fax, 919-677-1714. Email, jnlorders@oup-usa.org. The price is $15 if delivered to your home or university address.

Journal of Visual Literacy is published four times a year by the International Visual Literacy Association. Issues contain a broad array of media textual analysis and educational practices. For more information, contact Tom Hergert, Editor. Visual Communications, Virginia Tech, Blacksburg, VA 24061-0144. 540.231.8710. Hergert@vt.edu.

Mediacy. The newsletter for the Association of Media Literacy in Canada, the largest media educator organization in North America. The newsletter is a benefit of membership. Mediacy, 25 Marcos Blvd., Scarborough, Ontario M1K 5A7, Canada. $20/year.

Media Matters. The newsletter of the National Council of Teachers of English is a resource for K–12 teachers about teaching media in the language arts curriculum. For a mere $10.00 a year, members receive regular mailings of current media literacy articles and resources, as well as a newsletter. A great deal. Write Robert Happ, Hempstead High School, Dubuque, IA 52002.

Media & Values. Although not currently published, this journal is available through the Center for Media Literacy (address in organization list). Fabulous resource for teachers and researchers. Each edition is thematic in nature, with easy-to-read articles about important topics as media representations of age, masculinity, and gender; the consumer culture; news and ethics; environmentalism; and politics to name a few.

Telemedium. Newsletter of the National Telemedia Council. Free with $30 yearly membership. National Telemedia Council, 120 E. Wilson St., Madison, WI 53703. 608.257.7712.

Video and Learning. A newsletter by and for students and teachers published by Educational Video Center. EVC, 55 E. 25th St., Ste. 407, New York, NY 10010. 212.725.3534.

ELECTRONIC RESOURCES ABOUT *MEDIA LITERACY*

First Light Video Publishing produces and distributes educational videotapes for skill-based work in the media arts: film, video, and music production, audio and radio production, and more. Their new series, The Video Toolbox, is particularly useful for teachers getting started in production. First Light also carries media analysis tapes and some BBC education productions such as "Screening Middle-March" to be taught with the BBC production of George Eliot's book. For a complete catalog, "Master Classes in Media; a Library of Training Videos to Teach Media Skills," call 800.777.1576.

Know TV: Changing What, Why and How You Watch is a kit produced to help secondary teachers teach about documentary. For information: Stephanie Aaronson/The Learning Channel, 7700 Wisconsin Ave., Bethesda, MD 20814-3522. 301.986.0444, ext. 4406. Or Steve Raabe/CTM, 301.656.7900.

L.A. Freewaves: A Catalog of Southern California Youth Media Programs was compiled by media educator, artist, and curator Gina Lamb. The catalog is a rich source of student-produced work at reasonable prices. It also features engaging profiles of students and teachers. Contact: Gina Lamb, 321 E. Beach Ave., Englewood, CA 90302. 310.672.2359.

A National Forum on Television Literacy. Prince Williams County Network produced a distance education series about media literacy issues. Call Stan Woodward, Executive Producer, Prince William County Public Schools, 703.791.7328.

On Television: Teach the Children. Documentary critical of the commercial nature of TV as it addresses research on the effects of television on children. Interviews with Peggy Charren (Action for Children's Television), George Gerbner (Annenberg School of Communication), Dorothy Singer (Yale), and others stress the need for more critical viewing skills training for children. The tape is a useful discussion starter for teachers, parents, and community leaders. Video, $49. California Newsreel, 140 Ninth St./420, San Francisco, CA 94103. 415.621.6196. www.newsreel.org.

Signal to Noise: Life with Television, a series of videos produced for PBS consisting of segments by 21 independent producers, in three hourly programs. Segments are short and creative, but mixed in quality. Some are "preachy" and antimedia; others are brilliant. A fine example, the section on tape two about constructing a news program, provides an excellent basis for student discussion and further media projects. For distribution information contact Mixed Media Projects, 594 Broadway #410, New York, NY 10012. Voice: 212.219.3092. Fax: 212.219.2645. Email: signalcm@aol.com.

Slim Hopes is a powerful and disturbing video about advertising, "the culture of thinness," and how impossible standards of beauty may impact children, particularly young women. Because of its compelling images, it is not appropriate for elementary age children. Media Education Foundation, 26 Center St., Northampton, MA 01060. 800.897.0089 or email at mediated@igc.org.

Taking Charge of Your TV is a family-friendly guide to critical viewing for parents and children. It offers definitions of media literacy, tips on how to use the TV constructively, and family activities. The guide is sponsored by The Family & Community Critical Viewing Project, a partnership of the National PTA, the National Cable TV Association, and Cable in the Classroom. 800.216.2225.

Taming the Tube (VHS) is a humorous and ironic youth-produced instructional video that promotes media literacy. Winner of the Bronze Apple at the National Media Network Festival, the reel is produced through the Community TV Network, a Chicago-based nonprofit media arts organization that has worked for over 20 years to give low-income youth the technical and critical skills to create videos about themselves and their neighborhoods. Community TV Network, 2135 W. Wabansia, Chicago, IL 60647. 312.278.8500. $32.00 each, includes shipping.

Tube Babies.   A documentary by students at EVC about media. This is a fascinating, professionally produced piece of high interest to students. EVC has a complete catalog of student work. Yo-TV/Educational Video Center, 55 East 25th St., Ste. 407, New York, NY 10010. 212.725.3534.

TV Smarts for Kids.   A free video from Girl Scouts USA and the National Cable Television Association. Check out the press release at http://www.ncta.com/tvsmarts.html.

ELECTRONIC RESOURCES FOR TEACHERS: *VIDEO AND MULTIMEDIA FOR THE K–12 CLASSROOM*

The Ad and the Ego.   A comprehensive examination of advertising's influence on culture. The video attempts to make connections between consumerism, environmental degradation, and advertising with mixed success. A favorite of students. California Newsreel, 140 Ninth St./420, San Francisco, CA 94103. 415.621.6196. www.newsreel.org.

AdSmarts is a video and print resource consisting of five kits that explore the techniques of the advertising trade. The kits are designed to teach critical thinking about advertising, tobacco ads, alcohol ads, and to encourage students to create their own messages. Each unit contains a video, black line masters, and a guide that has been carefully keyed to the videos. The Center for Media Literacy, 800.226.9494. $495.00.

Appalshop has a complete catalog of documentaries about Appalachian culture. Write for catalog: 306 Madison St.,Whitesburg, KY 48158. 606.633.0108.

Aristotle Industries offers videotapes of political ads, including every television commercial broadcast by the candidates in the U.S. presidential primaries. Beta or VHS, $75. Aristotle Industries, 800.243.4401.

Buy me that! Home Box Office with Consumer's Union and Action for Children's Television. The three-part documentary covers all aspects of children's television with guides for parents and teachers. Films Inc., 5547 Ravenswood Ave., Reston, VA 22091. 800.327.4222, ext. 43. For supplementary discussion guides: Consumer Reports Television, P.O. Box s2010A, Mt. Vernon, NY 10551. 914.667.9400.

Cannes International Festival of Advertising. Selected Commercials (30-minute VHS) comes with a Media Studies Teacher's Guide, a succinct and clearly written guide of suggested classroom activities for the commercials. Exercises explore PSAs, representation, popular culture allusions, visual narrative, and contemporary issues. ADFILMS LTD., 250 Merton St., Ste. 403, Toronto, Ontario M4S 1B1, Canada. 416.483.3551. $79.95.

Canyon Cinema distributes a comprehensive collection of experimental and avante garde film and video. Their catalog is available for $15. Some films in the catalog may not be suitable for children. Canyon Cinema, 2325 Third St., Ste. 338, San Francisco, CA 94107. 415.626.2255.

Color Adjustment. VHS, 90 minutes. A look at familiar television images with a fresh perspective as it chronicles the history of African Americans on television. California Newsreel, 149 9th St., #420, San Francisco, CA 94103. 415.621.6196. $99.

Consuming Hunger. 3-Part Video Series with Study Guide. Part I: Getting the Story, shows how the Ethiopian tragedy went from "just another famine" to the news story of the 1980s. Part II: Shaping the Image, shows how tragedy moves from news to entertainment through the Live Aid concert. Part III: Selling the Feeling, examines the Madison Avenue treatment for social problems. Rent, $19.95 each part; buy, $50.00 for entire series. MaryKnoll World Productions, Maryknoll, NY 10545. 914.941.7590, ext. 308.

Ephemeral Films. Two 30-minute reels of old educational and industrial films collected by Richard Prelinger Associates. 800.331.6197. $39.95 each. See also,

Our Secret Century, below. Both available from The Voyager Company, 212.431.5999.

Inside Television News (1990, 5-part series, 52 minutes). A behind-the-scenes look at broadcast news. New Dimension Media, 85803 Lorane Highway, Eugene, OR 97495. 800-288-4456. $125.

Magnetic Youth: Teen Powered TV, one of the largest samplings of youth-produced video ever assembled, available for exhibition and rental through LACE, 1804 Industrial St., Los Angeles, CA 90021. Write for catalog. 213-624-5650.

New Ideas for Television: Ads to Make You Think (1991, VHS, 7 minutes). Prosocial, anticonsumerism ads by artists. The Media Foundation, 1234 West 7th Ave., Vancouver, BC V6H 1B7, Canada. $20.

Our Secret Century: From the Dark Side of the American Dream is a 12-part Voyager CD-ROM composed of clips from ads, industrial and educational films from McCarthyism through the Cold War. This dizzying and delightful kaleidoscope of American popular culture was curated and produced by Richard Prelinger. The Voyager Company, 212.431.5999.

Production Notes: Fast Food for Thought.   Jason Simon deconstructs a candy bar ad, complete with comments by the ad executive. Excellent resource to teach about the manufactured nature of media and advertising. 28 minutes. Rent, $50; buy, $200. VHS or 3/4". Preview available, $15 for 1 week. Video Data Bank, The School for the Art Institute of Chicago, 112 South Michigan Ave., Chicago, IL 60603. 312.345.3550. Fax: 312.541.8073.

Scanning Television.   If you only have resource money for one media education resource, this is it! Five videotapes offer a rich database of 40 student-centered video clips and print activities that stimulate students to become active media users in a world awash in information. The creative teacher's guide provides busy teachers with valuable tricks of the trade and classroom-tested activities that fit easily across the regular curriculum and work in tandem with the video. Available from the National Telemedia Council, 120 E. Wilson St., Madison, WI 53703. 608.757.7712. Or from the Center for Media Literacy, 4727 Wilshire Blvd., Ste. 403, Los Angeles, CA 90010. 800.226.9494.

Spin.   Pirated satellite TV feeds reveal U.S. media personalities' behind-the-scenes foibles during the 1996 presidential election. Video Data Bank, The School for the Art Institute of Chicago, 112 South Michigan Ave., Chicago, IL 60603. 312.345.3550. Fax: 312.541.8073. Ask for complete Video Data Bank catalog.

BOOKMARKS: DIGITAL RESOURCES FOR *TEACHING ABOUT MEDIA GENERAL RESOURCES*

Adbusters Culture Jammer's Headquarters
   http://www.adbusters.org/adbusters/main.html

Anticonsumerism, prosocial ads for students to analyze. Provocative ads beg counter readings and encourage student discussion.

American Film Institute
   http://ptd15.afionline.org/CineMedia/welcomes/hello.html

Looking for media resources? The American Film Institute helps you search online for media-related research and resources.

Association for Media, Communication, and Cultural Studies
   http://www.aber.ac.uk/~jmcwww/AMCCS/amccs.html

AMCCS is the English professional association for individual academics across the fields of media, communications, and cultural studies.

CAMEO
   http://interact.uoregon.edu/MediaLit/FE/CAMEOHomePage

The home page of CAMEO, the Canadian Association of Media Education Organizations.

Center for Media Literacy
   http://www.medialit.org/

The Center for Media Literacy in Los Angeles offers a clearinghouse of resources related to media education.

The FCC Home Page
   http://www.fcc.gov/

The Federal Communication Commission site provides information about regulation of media industries.

The Freedom Forum Media Studies Center
   http://www.mediastudies.org/

The Institute for Advanced Interdisciplinary Research
   http://www.systems.org/HTML/lists/topics/dig-age.htm

The Institute for Advanced Interdisciplinary Research talks about living in a digital age.

The Just Think Foundation
  http://www.justthink.org/newindex.asp

The Web Site of Just Think Foundation in California.

Media Awareness Network
  http://www.screen.com/mnet/eng

A great site from Canada. Includes media literacy basics for all grade levels. Good for finding video resources for media teaching.

Media Awareness Network
  http://www.screen.com/mnet/eng/med/class/support/teachtr.htm#distance

The Media Awareness Network offers information about teacher professional development in media education, including a distance education course from the University of Southampton.

The Media History Project
  http://www.mediahistory.com/

The Media History Project offers possibilities for classroom study of media. Bruce Sterling's Dead Media Project is especially interesting.
http://www.mediahistory.com/dead/archive.html

Media Launchpad
  http://www.oise.on.ca/~nandersen/pad.html

MEDIA LAUNCHPAD provides links to Internet sites, documents, and search engines about media education. Developed in Canada by Neil Andersen.

Media Literacy Online Project of the University of Oregon
  http://interact.uoregon.edu/medialit/homepage

This site is the best. Absolutely the most thorough and informative site in the United States. Linked to major media literacy organizations and many resources.

Media Literacy Project in Japan
  http://www.ritsumei.ac.jp/kic/so/seminar/ML/index-e.html

The Media Literacy Project in Japan.

MediaOne
   http://www.mediaone.com/who/index_ourhistory.html

This is a commercial site, but this one page of the site gives some interesting facts on a timeline about the evolution of telecommunications media.

Media3
   http://mediaarts.deakin.edu.au/Media396/Media3main.html

A media education journal from Australia.

Media Workshop
   http://www.mediaworkshop.org/

The Media Workshop New York supports media educators to use new technologies.

Mega Media-Links
   http://www.omni-eye.com/links/

The MEGA MEDIA-LINKS index contains thousands of film, video, radio, television, cinema, and new-media site listings conveniently categorized, subcategorized, and cross-referenced with brief site descriptions.

The Minnesota Center for the Arts
   http://www.mcae.k12.mn.us/

Of special interest to media educators is the Minnesota High School for the Arts Program, listed under the "media" choice on the home page.

MSNBC News
   http://www.msnbc.com/

Point of View's Dissect an Ad
PBS's P.O.V. site on the 1996 campaign ads. Includes a teacher toolkit.

The Professional Cartoonists Index
   http://www.cagle.com

A database of cartoons. See also the teacher's guide at http://cagle.com/teacher

Propaganda Page
   http://carmen.artsci.washinton.edu/propaganda/contents.htm

If you are interested in the propaganda angle, this is your site.

Scottish Screen
   http://www.scottishscreen.demon.co.uk/index.html

A business page of listings for agencies that work in the Scottish film industry.

Southwest Florida Public TV
  http://gator.naples.net/media/wsfp/media.htm

Has an excellent list of media education resources on the Web.

Trendy Interactive Magic
  http://pw2.netcom.com/~sleight/interactivemagic.html

This isn't a media education site per se, but is a lot of fun and showcases interactive technologies.

University of Wales
  http://www.aber.ac.uk/~dgc/media.html

The Media and Communication is a University of Wales, British-based gateway to Web resources useful in the academic study of media and communication.

Visual Literacy Project
  http://www.pomona.edu/visual-lit/intro/intro.html

The Online Visual Literacy Project from Pomona College in California.

Rich Wilson's Communicator Page
  http://www.communicator.com/toppage.html

This is a personal Home Page of Rich Wilson, but includes many interesting media links.

Hands-On Web Resources

Cascadia Moving Images Association
  http://www.stargate.ca/cmia/

The Cascadia Moving Images Association (CMIA) exists to encourage and promote exploration and excellence in film, video, and multimedia production in schools and among independent film and video producers.

Educational Video Center
  http://www.edc.org/FSC/NCIP/EVC_Project.html

The flagship program for hands-on documentary production and school reform in secondary education.

The Media Action Project
  http://utopia.knoware.nl/users/schoutdi/

Many useful essays from the work of the Urban Programm Research Group, University of Nottingham, England. Also previews the book, Schouten, D., & Watling, R. (1998). *Media action projects: A model for integrating video in project-based education, training and community development* (1998).

Video Production Course
http://www.geocities.com/Hollywood/Hills/1902

Teacher Stephanie Rusnak has put her entire nine-week curriculum for video production on the Web. Includes desktop publishing and video. Daily lesson plans and classroom handouts.

VidKids Media Literacy Program
http://cmp1.ucr.edu/exhibitions/cmp_ed_prog.html

Detailed lesson plans for creating media. Samples of student work. Designed for younger children, but adaptable to older kids.

Young Media Partners
http://www.mare.ch/youngmedia/

The site for child and youth media.

Standards and Evaluation Web Resources

Texas Knowledge and Skills, Language Arts Viewing/Representing
http://www.tea.texas.gov/teks/

This is the site for the Texas Knowledge and Skills standards for the state of Texas. Media literacy-related standards are buried deep, but they are there. Here's how you find them: (1) Go to this site and click on the English, Language Arts, and Reading link. (2) Click on any grade level. (3) Media literacy is shown as "viewing/representing. . . ." Use your browser to find all the "viewing/representing" citations. These are the media literacy standards for the state. (4) Go through the scope and sequence and find "viewing/representing" for the grade you want to see. (5) There is also a stand-alone choice for "Media Literacy" as an elective. Also see the related technology standards for the state of Texas on this Web site.

The *media education site for the Center for Children and Technology in New York City* http://www.edc.org/CCT/ccthome/outpost/index.html

Other Web sites that include media literacy educational standards for grades K–12 include:

Massachusetts English Language Arts (adopted February 1997) Media Strand
www.doe.mass.edu/doedocs/frameworks/englishS4.html

Minneapolis Public School District
   www.mpls.k12.mn.us/currstandards.html

North Carolina Technology Standards
   www.dpi.state.nc.us/Curriculum/computer.skills/

Utah Healthy Lifestyles
   www.uen.org/cgi-bin/websql/lessons/c3.hts?core=7&course_num=7150

Washington State
   www.learningspace.org:88/instruct/literacy/esslearnings.html

Articles on the Web Related to Media Education

Atlantic Monthly
   http://www.theatlantic.com/issues/97may/gerbner.htm

An interesting article on the subject of violence in media.

Cable in the Classroom
   http://dpsnet.detpub.k12.mi.us/html/cableclrm.htm

An archive of this magazine for K–12 teachers. CIC and its companion magazine for parents, *Better Viewing*, has a long history of media education articles and activities.

Christian Science Monitor
   http://www.csmonitor.com/durable/1998/02/12/feat/learning.1.html

This is a link to a Christian Science Monitor article on using film study guides in the classroom. "Film Guides May Leave Students in the Dark" by Mark Clayton. The article has a slightly disdainful tone about the use of film guides, but should generate some important discussion.

MEDIA EDUCATION CENTERS AND ORGANIZATIONS FOR *EDUCATORS IN NORTH AMERICA*

Appalshop, 306 Madison St., Whitesburg, KY 48158, 606.633.0108.

Association for Media Literacy, 40 McArthur St., Weston, Ontario M9P 3M7, Canada, 416.394.6992

Center for Media Literacy, 4727 Wilshire Blvd., Ste. 403, Los Angeles, CA 90010, 213.931.4177, Fax: 213.931.4474, Email: cml@medialit.org, www.medialit.org/

Citizens for Media Literacy, 38 1/2 Battery Park Ave., Ste. G, Asheville, NC 28001, 704.255.0182

Educational Video Center, 55 E. 25th St., Ste. 407, New York, NY 10010, 212.725.3534

International Visual Literacy Association, Contact: Dr. Darrell Beauchamp, Director of Learning Resource Center, Navarro College, 3200 W. 7th Ave., Corsicana, TX 75110, 903.874.6501 ext. 320, Internet: dbeau@nav.cc.tx.us

Media Education Foundation, 26 Center St., Northampton, MA 01060, 800.897.0089, mediated@igc.org

The Media Foundation, 1243 West 7th Ave., Vancouver, BC V6H 1B7, Canada, 604.736.9401

Media Workshop New York, 333 W. 17th St., Rm. 324, New York, NY 10011, http://www.mediaworkshop.org/, 212.229.1776

National Telemedia Council, 120 E. Wilson St., Madison, WI 53703, 608.257.7712

Newspaper Association of America, Newspapers in Education Program, Box 17407, Dulles Airport, Washington, DC 20041, 703.648.1051

ABOUT THE EDITORS AND CONTRIBUTORS

Richard Beach is a professor of English education at the University of Minnesota, Twin Cities. He has published ten books, including *A Teacher's Introduction to Reader-Response Theories* and *Teaching Literature in the Secondary School*. His research focuses on response to literature/media, composition, and teacher education. He is a former president of National Conference on Research in Language and Literacy.

Linn Bekins has both industry and academic experience. From 1992 to 1998, she worked as a writer, trainer, project manager, and consultant, in scientific and high-technology environments while pursuing her graduate degrees. She received her Ph.D. from the University of Utah in Educational Studies, emphasizing Rhetoric and Composition. She is an assistant professor in the Department of Rhetoric and Writing Studies at San Diego State University and directs a Certificate Program in Technical and Scientific Writing. Her interests include scientific collaboration, disciplinary rhetoric, and activity theory.

Robert Maribe Branch is an associate professor in the Department of Instructional Technology, College of Education at the University of Georgia. Dr. Branch teaches courses and conducts research in the area of instructional design and message design. His recent publications include *Survey of Instructional Development Models, Instructional Design: A Conceptual Parallel Processor for Navigating Learning Space*, and as senior editor for the last five volumes of the *Educational Media and Technology Yearbook*.

Lynn Briggs is director of the Writers' Center and associate professor of English at Eastern Washington University in Cheney, Washington. Her professional activity involves contributions to the integration of spiritual issues in academe, including an article "Understanding Spirituality in the Writing Center" in the *Writing Center Journal*, a review of *The Spiritual Side of Writing* in *The Journal of Teaching Writing*, and a Conference on College Composition and Communication presentation on Spiritual Work in the Writing Center. Dr. Briggs was Eastern Washington

University's student-selected faculty member of the year in 1998, a past winner of the Conference on College Composition Citation for Outstanding Classroom Practice (with Ann Watts Pailliotet), and runner-up for the CEE Richard Meade Award (with Sharon Kane and Pat Soper) in 1990.

T. A. Callister, Jr., is an associate professor and Garrett Fellow at Whitman College in Walla Walla, Washington, where he teaches educational foundations. His research focuses on the ways new information technologies impact educational practice and policy. He is the author (with Nicholar Burbules) of *Watch IT: The Risky Promises and Promising Risks of New Information Technologies for Education* (Westview, 2000).

David M. Considine is a professor of media studies/instructional technology at Appalachian State University where he coordinates the media studies program. An Australian, he pioneered one of the first media literacy programs in that country before moving to the United States. He is the principal author of *Visual Messages: Integrating Imagery into Instruction* (2nd edition 1999) which has been reviewed as the first comprehensive media literacy textbook in this country.

Barry Duncan is an award-winning teacher, author, consultant, and founder and past president of the Ontario-based Association for Media Literacy. Coauthor of the best-selling textbook, *Mass Media and Popular Culture* (Harcourt-Brace, Canada), he has presented workshops and keynote addresses to over 10,000 teachers in Canada and the United States and at international conferences in the United Kingdom, Brazil, and Spain. In 1990 he received the Jesse McCanse award from the Wisconsin-based National Telemedia and in 1994 was the winner of the Meron Chorney Award from the Canadian Council of Teachers of English for his "outstanding contribution to the teaching of English and Language Arts in Canada." In 1997, he was chosen by his colleagues in the Etobicoke Board of Education as "Teacher of the Year." In May 1998, the association for Media Literacy received an award in Sao Paulo, Brazil, from the World Council on Media Education for AML's role as "the most influential media education organization in North America." His articles have been published in *English Quarterly*, *School Libraries in Canada*, *Mediacy*, *The Australian Journal of Media and Culture*, and *Telemedium*. He has co-authored two language art textbooks for Grades 9 and 10—*Transitions* and *Transformations*.

Jackie K. Giles is the coordinator for Newspapers in Education (NIE) and for the *Leader-Telegram*. She is a former classroom teacher who is very active in promoting literacy in her community. Jackie coordinates and provides inservice programs to reading specialists, undergraduates at the University of Wisconsin-Eau Claire as well as K–12 teachers and students in the region. As a representative to the state NIE, Jackie collaborates with coordinators from across Wisconsin on educational tabloids, organizing summer institutes for educators, as well as preparing and delivering hands-on workshops at regional and state conventions each year. Jackie works closely with the Eau Claire Area Reading Council on the annual 60 Minute Pledge to promote reading each spring. In addition, Jackie serves as a member of the board of directors for the Literacy Volunteers of America of the Chippewa Valley.

Roberta F. Hammett is an assistant professor of education at Memorial University of Newfoundland. She teaches courses in secondary English education, curricular integration of computer technology, and literacies (at the graduate level). Her research interests include the literacy implications and applications of computer technologies, teacher education, and critical media literacy. Her current project is a coedited book about issues in contemporary English language arts education. Her World Wide Web address is http://www.ucs.mun.ca/~hammett/

Lyn Lacy is an elementary media specialist at Keewaydin Community School in Minneapolis Public Schools. She is author of *Art and Design in Children's Picture Books: An Analysis of Caldecott Award-Winning Illustrations* (American Library Association, 1986); *Visual Education: An Interdisciplinary Approach for Students K–12 Using Visuals of All Kinds* (Minneapolis Public Schools, 1987); co-author (with David M. Considine & Gail E. Haley) of *Imagine That: Developing Critical Thinking and Critical Viewing Through Children's Literature* (Teacher Ideas Press, 1994); eight audiovisual biographies for children, and numerous projects in media literacy curriculum development, such as "About TV: What Do You Know About, Think About, Do About TV?" (1995). She served on writing teams for the Media Arts Achievement Standards of the *Minnesota Frameworks for Art Curriculum Strategies*, 1993–1994 and the *Information Media and Technology Content Standards* of Minneapolis Public Schools, 1996–1998. She was granted a Teacher Fellowship by the American Council of Learned Societies in 1992–1993, during which time she piloted an original program in participatory storytelling and began research for a manuscript in progress, *Creative Planning Resource for Holistic Teaching and Learning*.

Sherry L. Macaul is a professor at the University of Wisconsin-Eau Claire. She teaches undergraduate and graduate courses in the area of literacy instruction and assessment in the Department of Curriculum & Instruction. Dr. Macaul is a former classroom teacher, reading teacher, and is a certified Reading Specialist. She is past chair of the Wisconsin State Reading Association's Reading & Technology Committee. She served on the task force for the development of the Wisconsin English/Language Arts Academic Standards. Dr. Macaul presents annually at state and national conferences. Her research interests focus on inquiry, literacy, and the new technologies.

Richard E. Mayer is a professor of psychology at the University of California, Santa Barbara (UCSB), where he has served on the faculty since 1975. His teaching and research interests are in educational psychology, with a focus on cognition and instruction. He is a past president of the Division of Educational Psychology of the American Psychological Association, former chair of the Department of Psychology at UCSB, and recipient of the E. L. Thorndike Award for the year 2000. He is former editor of the *Educational Psychologist* and *Instructional Science*, and currently serves on the editorial boards of 10 journals mainly in educational psychology. He authored more than 200 articles and book chapters mainly in educational psychology, as well as 12 books including *The Promise of Educational Psychology: Learning in the Content Areas*.

Peter B. Mosenthal is a professor in reading education and President of Performance by Design, Inc. He recently received a patent for his work developing a multimedia instructional system called "PDQ" (i.e., a system used to teach prose, document, and quantitative literacy skills to adults). His current work focuses on the development of various assessment instruments that profile children's emergent literacy skills, as well as predict their performance on high-stakes tests at the elementary and secondary levels.

Patricia I. Mulcahy-Ernt is an associate professor in the School of Education and Human Resources at the University of Bridgeport where she teaches graduate courses in the Reading and Language Arts program and directs the Teacher Preparation Programs. Her doctorate is in educational psychology from the University of Minnesota, and she has extensive experience in the fields of teacher education and literacy. Her areas of specialization focus on secondary-level and adult literacy processes and assessment. In 1992 she received the Pauline P. French Outstanding Teacher Award from the Rutgers University Graduate School of Education's Alumni Association.

Ann Watts Pailliotet is an assistant professor of education at Whitman College in Walla Walla, Washington teaches preservice methods, critical reading of children's literature, and media literacy. She is a winner of the National Reading Conference Student Outstanding Research Award, the College Composition and Communication Conference Citation for Outstanding Classroom Practice and the 1999 Whitman College Ball Student Advising Award. Her research involves critical media literacy, preservice education, and values instruction. Her recent publications include numerous book chapters and articles for *National Reading Conference Yearbook, English Education, Journal of Basic Writing, Journal of Literacy Research, Journal of Adolescent and Adult Literacy, International Visual Literacy Yearbook, The Reading Teacher*, and *Teaching & Teacher Education*. She is co-editor (with Ladislaus Semali) of *Intermediality: The Teachers' Handbook of Critical Media Literacy* (Westview, 1999). With Lyn Lacy, she is coauthor of *C.P.R. Creative Planning Resources* (forthcoming, Peter Lang).

Victoria J. Risko is a professor of language and literacy and a research scientist in the Learning Technology Center at Peabody College of Vanderbilt University. Her research interests focus on instructional applications of multimedia, teacher development, diverse learners, and text comprehension. She is a recipient of the 1991–1992 Association of Teacher Education Distinguished Research Award and past president of the College Reading Association. She currently serves as co-chair of the International Reading Association Commission on Diverse Learners and leads its Video and Literacy Special Interest Group.

Rita K. Rodenberg is a certified Reading Specialist and teacher in Grade 4, and Grade 7 and 8 science at Eau Claire Lutheran School. Rita is a teacher with over 25 years of experience in education. During many of her years as an educator, she has worked in multiage classrooms. She has provided leadership to her school in the areas of literacy, assessment, and technology. In addition, Rita has experience in the area of administration having served as principal for her school. Rita possesses an avid interest in new technologies. She promotes the integration of technology and literacy across the curriculum. Rita is an advocate of empowering students to assume control of their learning.

Ladi Semali is an associate professor of education at Pennsylvania State University, where he teaches media literacy to preservice teachers. He authored *Postliteracy in the Age of Democracy* (1995, Austin & Winfield) and is co-editor of *What is Indigenous Knowledge? Voices from the Academy* (1999, Garland) and *Intermediality: The Teachers' Handbook of Critical Media Literacy* (1999, Westview).

Kathleen Tyner is a consultant to international media education and educational technology efforts. She has published numerous articles on media literacy. Her latest book is *Literacy in a Digital World: Teaching and Learning in the Age of Information* (Erlbaum, 1998).

Arnold S. Wolfe is an associate professor of communication at Illinois State University. His teaching and research interests embrace mass media theory and criticism with an emphasis on feminist and semiotic approaches. He has published articles on television and film semiotics in *Critical Studies in Mass Communication*, on theories of mass media audiences in *Popular Music and Society*, and in the *Journal of Media Economics*, on the effects of foreign takeovers on freedom of expression in motion pictorial communication. His "Notes on the Enduring Popularity of a Signature Doors' Song," published in the *Journal of Communication Inquiry* in 1999, attempts to encourage a more media literate grasp of Doors' music. Similarly, his work in this volume attempts to encourage a more media literate grasp of "the information society."